Pro Tools® 8 Power! The Comprehensive Guide

Christopher R. Burns and Colin MacQueen
with Steve Albanese

Course Technology PTR

A part of Cengage Learning

COURSE TECHNOLOGY
CENGAGE Learning

Australia • Brazil • Japan • Korea • Mexico • Singapore • Spain • United Kingdom • United States

COURSE TECHNOLOGY
CENGAGE Learning™

Pro Tools® 8 Power! The Comprehensive Guide
Christopher R. Burns and Colin MacQueen with Steve Albanese

Publisher and General Manager, Course Technology PTR: Stacy L. Hiquet

Associate Director of Marketing: Sarah Panella

Manager of Editorial Services: Heather Talbot

Marketing Manager: Mark Hughes

Executive Editor: Mark Garvey

Project Editor: Kate Shoup

Technical Reviewer: Brian Johnson

Copy Editor: Kate Shoup

Interior Layout Tech: MPS Limited, A Macmillan Company

Cover Designer: Mike Tanamachi

Indexer: Larry Sweazy

Proofreader: Brad Crawford

For product information and technology assistance, contact us at **Cengage Learning Customer & Sales Support, 1-800-354-9706**

For permission to use material from this text or product, submit all requests online at **www.cengage.com/permissions** Further permissions questions can be emailed to **permissionrequest@cengage.com**

Pro Tools 8 is a registered trademark of Avid Technology. All other trademarks are the property of their respective owners.

All images © Cengage Learning unless otherwise noted.

Library of Congress Control Number: 2008941418

ISBN-13: 978-1-59863-898-1

ISBN-10: 1-59863-898-X

Course Technology, a part of Cengage Learning
20 Channel Center Street
Boston, MA 02210
USA

Cengage Learning is a leading provider of customized learning solutions with office locations around the globe, including Singapore, the United Kingdom, Australia, Mexico, Brazil, and Japan. Locate your local office at: **international. cengage.com/region**

Cengage Learning products are represented in Canada by Nelson Education, Ltd.

For your lifelong learning solutions, visit **courseptr.com**

Visit our corporate website at **cengage.com**

Printed in Canada
1 2 3 4 5 6 7 11 10 09

Acknowledgments

Christopher R. Burns Wishes to Thank

My wife Amy, my daughter Miki, my parents, Chris Stubbs, Brian Dorfman, Steve Schmidt, Mike Suarez, Goldcrest Post New York, Mark Garvey, Kate Shoup, Brian Jackson, Marc Schonbrun, Lisa Speegle, Kyle Ritland, Colin MacQueen, Steve Albanese, Mark Williams, Adrian Haselhuber, Marco Alpert, Jordan Stock, Antares, Digidesign, M-Audio, and all the good people I've gotten to know over the years in the music, audio, advertising, and broadcast communities in NYC and Ithaca.

Colin MacQueen Wishes to Thank

My wife Jenny, my mother, the rest of my family; George, Gracie, Lola, and Buddy for canine moral support and occasional comic relief; Kate Shoup, Nikki Smith, Neil MacQueen (Sunday Software), Brian Alexander (SOS Productions), Jenn Agnew (Circa Music), Eric Farnbauch (Upbeat Recordings), Steve Thomas, Adam Castillo, Greg Robles, Claudia Cook, Digidesign, Todd Jensen, Carla Spoon, Michael Tanamachi, Mark Garvey, Robert Guérin, Pep Agulló, Andy Hagerman, Jon Stevens, Jim Kilgore, Marc Ankerman, Luigi Bezzera (thanks for inventing espresso, dude), Camilo Rodríguez (y su salsa combo), Bodegas Muga (viva La Rioja), Steve Albanese, rationality, and the jam side up.

Steve Albanese Wishes to Thank

Digidesign, Colin MacQueen, Ed Grey, Claudio Cook, Benny Sanchez, Mike Freitas, Andy Cook, Scott Wilson, John Whitcore, Dave Froker, Andrew Harris, Chris Hammond, Tom Graham, Dino Virella, Gil Gowing, Jon Ondo, Bobby Lombardi, Mitch Thomas, Paul Bundschuh, Jim Cooper, Larry Berger, Colin McDowell, Chris Borgia, Andy Hildebrand, Marco Albert, Alan Jewitt, Joe Hunt, Joe Schmigaluchi, Lipps Elliot, Dyrk Ashton, Jeff Ciampa, Chris Leatherman, Matt Cooke, Tom Boyer, Chris Fidler, Kris Schultz, Corey Tomasso, Brian Caviness, Dave Egan, Bob Albanese, Steve Thomas, Mark Garvey, Johnson Brothers, Brian Stritenberger, Mom, Dad, my understanding wife Lisa, Luke Isabella, and the man upstairs.

About the Authors

Christopher R. Burns has been an audio engineer in the New York advertising, commercial music, and broadcast community since 1992. Upon entering the industry as an assistant at Russo/Grantham Productions, a music-production company, he moved to audio postproduction at the now-legendary Photomagnetic Sound Studios, working in several capacities on countless national advertising campaigns. After subsequently freelancing as a mixer and sound designer at a number of New York studios, including Sony Music, Chris began his tenure at Sleeveless Productions, where he provided the audio work on the majority of broadcast promotions for the ESPN Classic network. Chris currently is an independent mixer/sound designer in the New York/New Jersey area.

Colin MacQueen is the author of *Pro Tools 7 Power!*; *Digital Audio Dictionary* (Prompt Publications) with the assistance of Steve Albanese; *Pro Tools 6 Power!* (Thomson Course Technology); and *Pro Tools Power!* (Muska & Lipman/Thomson Course Technology). He wrote and created the movie tutorials for various interactive CD-ROMs about audio and MIDI topics, including *Pro Tools 7 CSi Starter* and *Pro Tools 6 CSi Starter*, *Cubase SX2 CSi Starter*, and *Cubase SX CSi Master*. Colin also collaborated with Robert Guérin on *Cubase SX3 CSi Starter*; assisted Dave Egan as co-author of *GarageBand CSi Starter*; and contributed several movie tutorials to *Audio Plug-Ins CSi Master*. A musician, composer, technical writer, sound designer, and virtual audio engineer, he has been involved for years with the music- and video-production industries and live performance, as well as in the distribution of Digidesign products in the USA and Spain. As an educator focusing on digital audio–related topics, he has taught in various broadcast academy and university programs. Colin also created or edited much of the text in the original *Cool School Interactus*, the Cool Breeze CD-ROM series about Pro Tools, general digital audio, and MIDI sequencing topics, as well as serving as technical editor for other *CSi* volumes. Other recent credits include spoken-word projects in numerous languages, as well as original music production and interactive sound design for 15 original CD-ROM titles by Sunday Software. In addition to sound design and audio production, Colin plays a mean guitar, doubles on bass and keys, sings like a bird (albeit some yet unknown species), and quantizes the heck out of a keyboard performance.

Steve Albanese is an interactive media producer, audio engineer, and entrepreneur. Steve is currently president and founder of TutorialFACTORY and TutorialDEPOT, where he specializes in the development and online distribution of *HOW TO* video content for platforms ranging from mobile devices through large-screen HD systems. His years of educational and development experience include his role as media production supervisor at the Recording Workshop, chief instructor at Pro School Midwest, president and founder of Cool Breeze Systems, Inc., and creator of the *Cool School Interactus* training environments. Steve has also worked for years as an audio professional, recording, mixing, and mastering many music projects, as well as posting videos and films, television commercials, radio spots, and interactive media. Steve produces the *HOW TO: Digital Performer* and *HOW TO: Record Drums* podcast series; co-authored the *Digital Audio Dictionary*, previous editions of *Pro Tools Power!*, and *CSi* volumes 1, 2, 3, 5, and 10 (Pro Tools and DAW video training products); and has written the monthly "CoolTip" column for *Electronic Musician* magazine.

Contents

Chapter 3
Your System Configuration   51

Chapter 6
The Edit Window   147

Chapter 7
The Mix Window   207

Chapter 8
Menu Selections: Highlights   239

Chapter 9
Plug-ins, Inserts, and Sends   321

Chapter 10
MIDI   359

Chapter 11
Synchronization   401

Chapter 12
The Pro Tools Groove   419

Chapter 13
A Multitrack Music Session   447

Chapter 16
Bouncing to Disk, Other File Formats   523

Chapter 17
The Score Editor Window   547

Chapter 18
Pro Tools Power: The Next Step   557

Appendix A
Further Study, and Resources on the Web   575

Appendix B
Add-ons, Extensions, and Cool Stuff
for Your Rig   581

Appendix C
Archive and Backup   609

Appendix D
Power Tips and Loopy Ideas   623

Appendix E
Signal Flow in Pro Tools   643

Index   647

Introduction

We've been using Pro Tools since it arrived on the scene, and before that, Sound Tools II, Sound Tools, and the original Sound Designer program. Digidesign has consistently set the standard for reliable, logical systems that respond to real-world needs for audio production. Hats off to 'em!

Pro Tools has basically been an industry standard since it was introduced, and it is used in a variety of industries and applications: multimedia, post and music production, journalism, and broadcast, among others. There are many excellent learning resources for Pro Tools users, including books, support and educational material on the Digidesign Web site, Digidesign/ Avid certified training centers, and university and recording-school programs.

In this book, we've tried to pull together a comprehensive overview of Pro Tools operation, the currently available configurations, the major areas where Pro Tools is commonly used, and the essential technical background necessary to get your Pro Tools rig interacting with the world around it. Our intention is to

- Jump-start new Pro Tools users, both those with a solid audio background and people who are more or less new to hands-on audio production.

- Get more-experienced users much deeper into the program, and into areas that may be more unfamiliar.

- Drop some interesting or thought-provoking tips on the experienced Pro Tools user.

For this reason, we make an effort to communicate on several levels simultaneously: general concepts, step-by-step instructions, technical detail where it helps to clarify concepts, plus suggestions for peripherals and techniques that will save you time. First, we review the currently available Pro Tools configurations (which we revisit in more detail in Chapter 3, "Your System Configuration"), then walk through basic concepts, reviewing the essential functions in the main Pro Tools windows and menus (but not *all* of them—that's what the PDF documentation is for!). Our objective is help you become productive in Pro Tools in as little time as possible. For that reason, we will always try to ground any theoretical aside or description of a Pro Tools function with real-world examples.

How to Use This Book

You can read this book from start to finish, jump directly to certain chapters if you prefer, or graze throughout. We try to use the plainest language possible, but in some of the technical asides, the single simplest way to accurately describe a concept may still be a little dense. (It's the nature of the subject matter!) In these cases, don't sweat technical details upon your first reading. Get the big picture first; you can always review later for further depth.

All users should take a moment to review the basic information in Chapter 2, "Pro Tools Terms and Concepts." These establish bedrock concepts and vocabulary and are essential for understanding how Pro Tools works. If you're new to *all* of this, including audio and MIDI in general, begin with Chapter 1, "About Pro Tools"—we'll give you a jump start.

Who Can Benefit

Aside from covering LE, M-Powered, and HD versions on Mac and Windows, we've challenged ourselves to ensure that this book provides useful information for the following:

- New Pro Tools users

- Experienced users seeking to broaden their knowledge, get up-to-date on recent versions, or branch into other areas of production

- Veteran users (we've been using Pro Tools since it came out, and still found out some interesting tips while researching and writing this book!)

Quick Start for You Impatient Types

You just cranked up Pro Tools, and you're not even sure where to start. Well, the *Pro Tools Reference Guide* (a PDF document included with the program) is definitely worth your time. You might print out some major sections (also a good idea with the *Keyboard Shortcuts* guide) and lug them around with you for the next few weeks; take them to lunch, for instance. Respect where it's due: Digidesign does a good job on its manuals!

If you're a first-timer and anxious to get started with Pro Tools (and have already successfully installed the software and configured the hardware), you might go straight to Chapter 4, "Creating Your First Pro Tools Session." We walk you through creating a session, creating audio tracks and Auxiliary Inputs, recording and editing some audio, inserting effects plug-ins, and performing simple mix automation.

Once you've gotten that out of your system, you can push ahead through the chapters about the Transport, Edit, and Mix windows. Even better, check out Chapter 2 first. We lay down the basic elements and lingo you absolutely must understand to work sensibly with Pro Tools.

Conventions Used in This Book

Besides covering LE, M-Powered, and HD versions of Pro Tools for music, post, and multimedia users at all levels, everything in this book is equally applicable to Windows and Macintosh versions unless noted otherwise.

Keyboard Shortcuts (Macintosh/Windows)

Rather than focusing exclusively on Macintosh or Windows keyboard shortcuts (and making you consult a legend somewhere in the back of the book to find the equivalent for your computer), we've opted to always include both: first the Macintosh keyboard shortcut (since the majority of Pro Tools systems are Mac-based, although not to an overwhelming degree), followed by the Windows equivalent in parentheses.

With several exceptions, for the most part the following Mac/Win key equivalents apply in Pro Tools:

- The Mac Command key is usually the Ctrl key in Windows.

- The Mac Option key is usually the Alt key in Windows.

- The Mac Control key is often the Start key in Windows. (For Mac users who don't have a two-button mouse—highly recommended—Control-click is also sometimes an alternative for right-clicking the mouse.)

Be aware, though, that these Mac/Windows key equivalents don't necessarily apply to other programs!

Pro Tools Versions

This first edition of *Pro Tools 8 Power!* is directed toward all users of Pro Tools 8 in its LE, M-Powered, and HD versions. The previous edition of the *Power!* series for Pro Tools covered version 7.*xx* (ISBN 1-59863-473-9). Another predecessor to this book, *Pro Tools 6 Power!* (ISBN 1-59200-505-5), covered 6.*xx* versions of Pro Tools (and is still available as an appropriate choice for 24 MIX and Digi 001 users, for example, since those hardware configurations don't support Pro Tools 7 or 8).

Digidesign is doing a great job of steadily evolving the Pro Tools platform. It was introduced in 1991 as a four-in, four-out system with a handful of built-in effects—no plug-ins or TDM yet, but with a killer sound and an interface that blew everybody else away! Pro Tools was (and remains) *the* product in the hard-disk recording category that literally revolutionized the recording industry. Since then, top-end configurations have progressed to literally scores of potential I/O channels, a potential depth of signal routing and plug-in processing that's downright scary, and 24-bit audio at sample rates up to 192kHz. Pro Tools systems are used around the world for every conceivable audio application: music, film, television, spoken-word, research, forensics, restoration, sound design, and so on.

There are currently three versions of the Pro Tools 8 software (as detailed in Chapter 3, "Your System Configuration," and elsewhere). Each supports specific audio hardware: Pro Tools LE (Mbox 2 family, Digi 003), Pro Tools M-Powered (purchased separately for use with one of various supported M-Audio interfaces), and Pro Tools HD (Pro Tools|HD hardware).

The now-discontinued Pro Tools|24 MIX, Pro Tools|24, and Pro Tools III systems were based on an earlier TDM plug-in architecture similar to that of the current-generation Pro Tools|HD hardware. Likewise, Digi 001 and ToolBox systems used previous LE versions of Pro Tools. None of these systems are compatible with Pro Tools version 8. Accordingly, in this edition of *Pro Tools 8 Power!* we have deleted various references to this legacy hardware (especially since those configurations are adequately covered in *Pro Tools 6 Power!* and *Pro Tools 7 Power!*).

Where appropriate, we will point out features that are available only in HD systems—or are not available in M-Powered, for example. For the most part, the HD version of Pro Tools includes all software features of the LE and M-Powered versions. Where there are restrictions or changes (for example, recommendations about how to order RTAS and TDM plug-ins in your tracks, or the more full-featured version of Beat Detective that is available in the HD version of Pro Tools), we will let you know.

In addition to the aforementioned configurations, Pro Tools Free 5.01—a limited-feature "legacy" version for Mac OS 9 and Windows 98 operating systems *only*—is available as a free download from Digidesign's Web site.

What's *Not* in This Book

Every effort has been made to make this edition of *Pro Tools 8 Power!* the most comprehensive and multilevel book possible. That said, it should be noted that the Pro Tools program is so powerful, so ubiquitous, that one could go on forever exploring its applications in one specialized field after another. At the same time, we have to assume that the reader has a certain basic level of preparation, and that it's understood that the basic concepts explained here will continue to be valid even as Digidesign continues to release new versions.

Computer Fundamentals

We obviously can't dedicate space here to cover basic computer concepts. If you don't know how to empty your Trash or Recycle Bin, open a menu, or open a Control Panel, or don't know the difference between a folder and a file, you should go to one of the many excellent resources out there to learn about this. Nonetheless, you really *do* need to understand how your computer works as well as how to maintain your operating system, disks and files, and so on to get the most out of your Pro Tools system—there's just no getting around it. Your computer, as the platform for Pro Tools, is one of the tools of your craft. Just as you have to change the strings on your instrument, replace the batteries in stompboxes, clean the heads on your tape recorders (until you've finally gotten rid of them all!), and pick up coffee mugs when clients leave for the day, you have to be able to navigate your computer system; it goes with the territory.

In Chapter 3, "Your System Configuration," we review computer and hard-drive requirements for Pro Tools specifically and the basic peripherals most users need (like MIDI and SMPTE interfaces, mixers and microphone preamps, and a good system for monitoring audio playback).

Older "Legacy" Versions of Pro Tools

Hey, we have a hard enough time keeping up with the *new* versions! Many discontinued Pro Tools systems are just as functional today as when they were new—*very* functional. For example, even though Digi 001 and 24 MIX models were discontinued back in 2004, they deliver excellent performance on an adequate computer system of the same vintage, and will probably continue in production at many facilities for quite some time. (Digi 001 and 24 MIX only support 6.4/6.4.1 versions of the Pro Tools software; they don't work with Pro Tools 6.7 or higher, let alone Pro Tools 8.)

As mentioned previously, the predecessors to this book, *Pro Tools 6 Power!* (ISBN 1-59200-505-5) and *Pro Tools 7 Power!* (ISBN 1-59863-473-9), cover respectively 6.*xx* and 7.*xx* versions of Pro Tools, and will be ideal for users of these systems. In addition to discussing previous version enhancements, those books also distinguish features that are different in the 6.4.*x* and earlier software versions for 24 MIX, Digi 001, and ToolBox systems.

Older-generation Pro Tools III hardware configurations were also TDM systems (with Pro Tools software 5.01 in Mac OS 9 only—this hardware does *not* support any higher versions). However, if you are using any of these older systems, be *very* cautious about upgrading your computer hardware or operating system. By no means should you assume that a newer operating system, even if it *is* compatible with your older computer, is best for your version of Pro Tools. For example, no 5.*xx* version of Pro Tools works under Macintosh OS X, even in Classic mode, and no version prior to 6.9.2 works under the 10.4.*x* versions of the Macintosh operating system. Go to the Support section of Digidesign's Web site for compatibility information on these legacy systems!

Lastly, if your system is limited to one of the 5.*xx* versions of the Pro Tools software (including Pro Tools Free 5.01), consider taking a look at the original *Pro Tools Power!* (ISBN 1-929685-57-2), which specifically covers that generation of the Pro Tools software and hardware.

Future Versions of Pro Tools, TBA Next Week/Month/Year...

We've made an effort to create content that will continue to be meaningful even as new releases of Pro Tools appear. As of this writing, our descriptions are based on currently shipping versions of Pro Tools 8. Minor upgrades are always coming out, usually for bug fixes or to support new hardware options; and farther down the road, more significant upgrades are certain to introduce additional features. Most likely, the actual operational changes will be minor; but compared to these hypothetical future versions, you may note discrepancies in a few of our screenshots. Again, you can expect the basic concepts explained in this book to remain valid well into future versions of Pro Tools.

Computer and digital audio technologies move forward very quickly. As a general rule, if you're using current Pro Tools hardware, you will want the fastest computer out there (although not necessarily the very latest *operating system*), as long as you see that model in the Compatibility listings on Digidesign's Web site. We're always bemused when people berate Digidesign and other digital audio workstation manufacturers for not supporting the latest all-important new operating system from Apple or Microsoft within a matter of weeks. (It's as if you suddenly become a square overnight, just because you don't rush out to get this season's clever haircut, or dumb-looking shoes!) Understand that Pro Tools is a demanding, real-time application. It pushes the capabilities of a computer and its operating system, and it takes *time* to make this program as (relatively) bulletproof as it is!

Again, this book aims to be useful for Pro Tools versions LE (Mbox 2 family, Digi 003 and the now-discontinued Digi 002 family and original Mbox) M-Powered (various M-Audio interfaces) and Pro Tools HD (for Pro Tools|HD hardware configurations). So, if you've got an LE or M-Powered system, for example, please bear with us if we devote time to a number of HD-specific features; at least it will give you an idea what you have to look forward to when all those royalty checks come in!

Other Programs

We do discuss some stereo editing programs for checking, tweaking, or converting bounced files, plus common CD-burning software. But we can't dedicate pages to walking you through step-by-step operations in these audio programs, nor in standard system utilities. There's just not space! However, we will tell you that we find Norton SystemWorks (Norton Utilities) extremely useful for maintaining a Pro Tools rig (especially Disk Doctor and Speed Disk, which we use often—although we *don't* recommend enabling the File Saver feature on Pro Tools systems). Some Macintosh users prefer the Tech Tool or DiskWarrior programs, which also do a great job of keeping your hard disks free of errors that can interfere with Pro Tools' performance.

Also, feature comparisons with other multitrack audio/MIDI programs don't fit our space constraints. Current versions of Logic Pro, Cubase, Nuendo, Digital Performer, SONAR, Reason, ACID, Ableton Live, and others are all fine programs—each, like Pro Tools, with its strengths and weaknesses. Several of them cohabitate with Pro Tools on our own computers! Obviously, many of their features overlap with those of Pro Tools—recording and editing audio and MIDI, applying effects, automation, and bouncing mixes. A few of them can even operate concurrently with Pro Tools, linked together via ReWire. But we can't tell you which is right for your needs; it really depends on your working style and personal preference. Furthermore, sometimes one program is more suited to certain projects than others. But Pro Tools is a powerful production environment; you can do just about anything with it, and the fact that you're holding this book in your hands says a lot already. So, we promise not to go off onto any of those tangents, you know, where we say "one of the things we really like about Pro Audio Munch XXL that we wish Pro Tools had is...." Let's leave that to the online forums!

Thank You!

If you're a new Pro Tools user, you're in for a treat. We can tell you from personal experience that the hands-on, nonlinear audio experience you are undertaking will completely transform your creative process, and for that matter, change your perception of audio in general. If you *already* know your way around the program, we promise to take you much deeper into this powerful production environment. Even if you are already a veteran user, we've made an effort to provide tips and applications that will get you thinking in new directions.

But before all that, let us take the opportunity to say thank you for purchasing this book! We sincerely appreciate your confidence in it, and hope its content serves to energize your learning experience and enrich your creative process.

1 About Pro Tools

If you're just starting in the digital-audio production world, this chapter and the next will help you get a grasp on basic concepts. They introduce Pro Tools, providing a very basic overview of the digital-recording process, digital-audio file formats, and MIDI.

If you're experienced with audio production but completely new to Pro Tools and computer-based recording, prepare yourself for a revelatory experience. In linear methods of working with music and audio (like digital and analog tape recorders, for instance), everything has to be assembled and mixed in real time. You can't change the order of recorded events without creating a new copy or, worse yet, destructively cutting up the tape in order to switch things around! Digital-audio workstations like Pro Tools, on the other hand, allow you to alter the order of audio events on any track, at any time—while still laying down takes or even during the final phases of mixdown. Pro Tools provides microscopic editing precision (down to the sample level—44,100 or 48,000 time slices per second, or even more with Digi 003, Digi 002, Mbox Pro, and Pro Tools|HD systems). This makes it easy to create seamless edits almost anywhere within the recorded audio. And trust us, we've spent enough time meticulously eliminating breaths, lip smacks, chair squeaks, and other noises to assure you that the editing power of Pro Tools is limited only by your perseverance!

Likewise, audio mixing with Pro Tools will completely transform your outlook. Traditionally, mixing down from multiple source tracks to a stereo master was essentially a live performance, often requiring more than one set of hands. Audio engineers would repeat the same song or scene literally dozens of times, each time attempting to repeat and improve upon mixing moves from the previous pass. With Pro Tools, often as not, you will start to build your mix even while still recording tracks. And of course, every aspect of the Pro Tools mix can be automated down to this same microscopic level of precision, so your creative ambitions will increase correspondingly.

Lastly, Pro Tools offers a vast amount of control for shaping and processing your sound. Not only is high-quality signal processing (effects) included with all versions of Pro Tools, but its open architecture accommodates *plug-in* software from third parties—everything from emulations of "vintage" compressors and reverbs to amp and tape simulators and much more. Because the entire virtual signal-processing environment is in the digital domain, the chronic noise-floor problems associated with numerous audio devices and cables in a traditional studio are things of the past. Again, how far you take your audio-effects processing in Pro Tools depends not as much on your system's capabilities (which, budget permitting, can always be upgraded) as on how maniacal, ambitious, or just plain creative *you* want to be!

What Is Pro Tools?

In a nutshell, Pro Tools is computer software for Macintosh and Windows computers used to create audio projects through recording, editing, and automated mixing of hard-disk–based digital audio and MIDI. Current Pro Tools configurations are based on the LE, M-Powered, or HD versions of the software. They include dedicated audio hardware from Digidesign—cards and/or external audio interfaces.

Digidesign develops the Pro Tools software and manufactures cards, external audio interfaces, and other peripheral equipment for your system. Most of Digidesign's own hardware configurations start from a core system including both an audio interface and the Pro Tools software. However, to the M-Powered version of Pro Tools software (which includes a USB-based iLok copy-protection device; more about this later), you must add your choice of one of the supported audio interfaces from M-Audio. To any of these core systems you can add peripherals—MIDI or synchronization interfaces, mixers for monitoring or routing multiple sources, and so on. On HD systems, you can expand the Pro Tools configuration itself to add much more processing power or additional input/output channels.

Here is a brief overview of current hardware configurations and Pro Tools software versions. (Chapter 3, "Your System Configuration," discusses each of these Pro Tools software versions in greater detail. Note that for the sake of completeness, there will be occasional mentions of discontinued systems in this book that are not compatible with Pro Tools 8, such as the Digi 001, 24|Mix, ToolBox/Audiomedia III, and others. (Chapter 18, "Pro Tools Power: The Next Step," also provides more information about expansion options for the various Pro Tools hardware configurations.)

- **Mbox 2.** The successor to the original Mbox, this original product in the Mbox 2 family was introduced by Digidesign in the fall of 2005. This external desktop audio interface includes Pro Tools LE software and is connected to the computer's USB port. In addition to two analog input/output (I/O) channels—each of which has separate input jacks for microphone, line (¼-inch balanced TRS), and instrument levels—the Mbox 2 supports using the S/PDIF digital I/O (with RCA connectors) simultaneously, allowing up to four inputs with a digital mirror of the analog outputs. It also features one MIDI input and one MIDI output. The microphone preamps, designed by Digidesign, offer superior specs compared to the original Mbox.

- **Mbox 2 Mini.** A compact USB audio interface that includes the LE version of Pro Tools, the Mbox 2 Mini has no digital I/O or MIDI connectors. Two channels of analog I/O are provided: Input 1 offers both XLR and unbalanced TS (¼-inch phone, tip-sleeve) jacks, while Input 2 offers an unbalanced ¼-inch TS phone jack that is compatible with line- or instrument-level sources. The two monitor output analog outputs also use ¼-inch jacks. All of these ¼-inch analog audio jacks use unbalanced ¼-inch phone, tip-sleeve (TS) connections.

■ **Mbox 2 Micro.** This extremely compact USB audio interface (it's about the size of a USB drive and could, for example, be attached to your key ring) was added to the Mbox 2 family in the fall of 2007. It includes the LE version of Pro Tools. Unlike all the other audio interfaces mentioned here, the Mbox 2 Micro has no audio inputs whatsoever. The only I/O provided is a single stereo analog output, with a ⅛-inch TRS connector (compatible with either headphone or line output connections) for which a volume dial is provided on the end of the unit.

■ **Mbox 2 Pro.** Currently the top of the line in the Mbox 2 family, this audio interface connects to the host computer via FireWire (IEE 1394). It supports sample rates up to 96 kilohertz (kHz) with Pro Tools LE (as compared to 48kHz maximum with the other two interfaces in this family). Four analog inputs are provided: mic/line inputs 1–2 can be switched between combo jacks (compatible with both XLR and ¼-inch phone) and front-panel DI inputs for guitar, bass, etc., while Aux In line inputs 3–4 can be switched between balanced TRS (¼-inch phone, tip-ring-sleeve) jacks and RCA phono jacks where a turntable can be connected. In addition to the dedicated monitor output pair on the rear panel (for outputs 1–2 from Pro Tools), six analog line outputs are provided: 1–4 are mono with balanced ¼-inch TRS jacks, while 5–6 share a single unbalanced stereo TRS jack. If all the analog and S/PDIF digital I/O is utilized, the Mbox 2 Pro can function as a 6×8 audio interface.

■ **Mbox (discontinued).** This configuration consists of Pro Tools LE software plus an external Mbox audio interface connected to the computer's USB port offering two total channels of audio I/O switchable between analog (with ¼-inch balanced TRS connectors and analog audio inserts) and S/PDIF digital (with RCA connectors). Like its Mbox 2 successors and all the other current Digidesign hardware, the Mbox is capable of 16- or 24-bit operation. While it does support Pro Tools 7 software, the Mbox is now discontinued, having been replaced by the more powerful Mbox 2.

■ **Digi 003/Digi 002.** Both of these configurations consist of Pro Tools LE software (although Pro Tools 8 will *not* work with Digi 002), plus a single external, multichannel audio interface/control surface connected to the computer's FireWire port. Both the Digi 003 and the older Digi 002 (which is now discontinued) support up to 18 channels of audio input/ output (16- or 24-bit recording at sample rates up to 96kHz) between their eight analog, stereo S/PDIF, and eight-channel ADAT Lightpipe digital I/O. Four high-quality XLR microphone preamp inputs with phantom power and individual trim controls are also included on the first four input channels. They provide one MIDI in, two MIDI outs, headphone output (two on the Digi 003), dedicated monitor output for channels 1–2 from

Pro Tools (plus an additional Alternate Monitor output on the Digi 003), and an Aux Input pair (called Alternate Source on the Digi 002) for tape/CD players, etc. These desktop units are not only interfaces for audio I/O, but also a control surface for Pro Tools, including Transport buttons, motorized faders, Solo/Mute buttons, assignable rotary encoders, data displays, and other dedicated buttons for Pro Tools functions. The Digi 002 (now discontinued) can also operate as a standalone digital mixer, with a fixed selection of on-board effects. The Digi 003 offers BNC connectors for word-clock input/output (used for synchronizing the internal sample clock of the audio interface with other devices in your studio configuration).

- **Digi 003 Rack/Digi 002 Rack.** Same as the Digi 003 or discontinued Digi 002 interfaces, but in a rackmountable format without the control surface.

- **M-Powered systems.** These configurations consist of Pro Tools M-Powered software plus one of various supported audio interface options from M-Audio. Some of the M-Audio hardware options are PCI cards with either breakout cables or external interfaces; others are external interfaces connected to the computer's USB or FireWire port. The number and type of audio, MIDI, and word-clock inputs/outputs vary according to the model, and some offer internal mixing capabilities of their own. The Pro Tools M-Powered software can be purchased separately or in a bundled configuration with an M-Audio interface, and includes an iLok USB Smart Key that contains an authorization for the program. This iLok (like the one that many users purchase separately for plug-in authorizations in other versions of Pro Tools) can also be used for authorizing additional plug-ins and programs. Chapter 3 discusses the M-Audio hardware options for Pro Tools M-Powered in more detail. While there *are* some key differences regarding support of external control surfaces and several optional software packages for Pro Tools LE that aren't compatible with Pro Tools M-Powered (DV Toolkit 2 and DigiTranslator, for example), the feature sets of the M-Powered and LE versions of Pro Tools are nearly identical.

- **Factory versions.** The Mbox 2 Pro, Mbox 2, Digi 003, and Digi 003 Rack are offered as factory versions that are bundled with significant packages of additional software. The Digi 003 and Digi 003 Rack factory versions offer the capability of mixing in 7.1 surround configuration. The Digi 003 Rack factory version also includes four more mic preamps and four more instrument DIs than the standard Digi 003 Rack.

- **Pro Tools|HD.** These systems consist of the Pro Tools HD software, one or more PCIe cards (or PCI/PCI-X) installed in the computer, and one or more external audio interfaces. The Digidesign cards incorporate specialized DSP processors to enable the TDM plug-in and signal-routing architecture. HD systems support 16- or 24-bit recording and playback at sample rates of up to 192kHz. The mix engine used in the Pro Tools HD software is also more sophisticated than that of the LE and M-Powered versions, operating at 48-point fixed (as opposed to 32-bit floating point) resolution. Adding more HD cards expands the system's DSP capabilities—to support a more intensive use of plug-ins, for example. While the audio hardware options for LE and M-Powered systems have a fixed number of input/output channels, HD system configurations are expandable. Adding more cards permits attaching more audio interfaces, which increases the available number of audio I/O channels. (Each card supports up to 32 I/O channels—and up to two audio interfaces—with a current maximum of 160 I/O channels on the entire Pro Tools|HD system. An external expansion chassis is used for the largest configurations, since typical computers don't offer enough internal slots for the maximum configuration of seven cards.) HD|2 and HD|3 configurations from Digidesign add one or two HD Accel cards, respectively. Accordingly, you will hear users talking about "HD|4" or "HD|5" systems to describe how many of Digidesign's PCIe (or PCI) cards are in their HD configuration—up to the "HD|7" limit. Pro Tools|HD configurations are discussed in more detail in Chapter 3.

Note: Be sure to see Chapter 3 for more detailed descriptions of the various audio interface options for Pro Tools.

Users often add other hardware devices (from Digidesign and third parties) to complete these configurations. These may include MIDI interfaces, synchronization peripherals for SMPTE time code or video sync, external MIDI controllers, keyboards and modules, digital-audio routers and mixers, microphone preamps, external control surfaces (such as the one shown in Figure 1.1), and interfaces for multitrack digital-audio recorders from Alesis, Tascam, and others. Some of these are discussed in Chapter 3.

Photo courtesy of Digidesign.

Figure 1.1 This Pro Tools rig features Pro Tools|HD hardware, a D-Control work surface, and surround monitors.

Four Generations of Pro Tools (8, 7, 6, and 5)   Interesting as it is, this book *won't* recount the entire Pro Tools history back to 1991, when version 1 hit the street. However, it's useful to understand the general characteristics of the last few major versions of Pro Tools because they're still being used today in both professional and project studio settings.

- **Pro Tools version 8.** Introduced in late 2008, version 8 represents a major overhaul of the graphical user interface as well as the introduction of a multitude of new functions and instruments for music production. Major additions include a new Score Editor, Elastic Pitch, track compositing (by far the favorite of the new features), and quick start when launching Pro Tools. Enhancements include customizable toolbars, a revamped tracks list, a greatly expanded MIDI Editor window, better-resolution waveform displays, and the ability to host multiple audio file formats in the same session. A slew of new plug-ins come bundled with each version of Pro Tools 8, including a number of virtual instruments. One could postulate that this overhaul was brought about by the recent advances and subsequent increased market success of other music sequencers like Apple's Logic Pro, but whatever the reason, Digidesign went a long way in creating a one-stop shop for sequencing and mixing.

- **Pro Tools version 7.** First introduced in the fall of 2005, version 7 boasted a reorganized menu structure and key new features such as region looping, region grouping (even on multiple tracks), real-time (non-destructive) properties for MIDI tracks, sends doubled to 10 per track, enhancements to the Separate Region and Strip Silence functions, REX/Acid file support, Instrument tracks, use of RTAS plug-ins on any track type in HD versions, support for multiprocessor computers and multicore processors, enhanced support for the ICON family of control surfaces, and multiple video file support in the HD version, plus drag-and-drop enhancements from the Regions List and the Workspace window. After version 7.0, key features were added in subsequent upgrades. For example, version 7.3 added continuously resizable track heights, mixer reconfiguration during playback, automation and MIDI enhancements such as diatonic transposition, key signature events, and window configurations. Version 7.4 added Elastic Audio features, including Elastic Audio markers, warp view for tracks, and other features related to time compression/expansion in real time and adjustment of audio events to the session tempo.

- **Pro Tools version 6.** Introduced at the end of 2002, this version marked a major upgrade from previous generations of Pro Tools and was the first version for Macintosh OS X and Windows XP. Along with many other updates to the user interface, the Project and Workspace browsers were new, as were DigiGrooves, Groove Quantize, many features in the MIDI Operations window, the Click plug-in, iLok support for plug-in and software authorizations, and use of core MIDI services on Mac OS X (instead of OMS, used in previous Macintosh versions).

■   **Pro Tools version 5.** Introduced in 2000, this was the first generation of Pro Tools to offer an LE version (host-based plug-in processing, not requiring TDM hardware). All 5.xx versions of Pro Tools required Macintosh OS 9 (although 8.6 was technically supported in some earlier versions, including Pro Tools Free 5.01), Windows 98/ME, or Windows 2000, and Windows NT for TDM systems. The Digi 001 audio interface (now discontinued) was introduced simultaneously with version 5 as the first hardware option for the LE version of Pro Tools. The DigiTranslator program for OMF transfers between Pro Tools and Avid video-editing systems (among others) was introduced with this generation of the Pro Tools software, which also introduced recording/editing MIDI events within Pro Tools, with all the associated features in MIDI tracks. Multiple ruler formats and markers in the Edit window timeline were also introduced, as were marker memory locations and the Trimmer tool's time compression/expansion mode.

How It Works

Pro Tools records both digital-audio and MIDI data and provides software tools for editing both. Let's be very clear about the difference between the two....

Digital Audio Is Data, Representing Audio Waveforms

In digital-audio recording, an input signal from an analog source (a varying voltage from a microphone or other device) arrives at an analog-to-digital (A/D) converter (often abbreviated as ADC). This converter periodically measures the level (amplitude) of the incoming audio signal, and this series of numerical values (samples) is stored in a file or encoded onto a tape. This is the digitizing process, where a continuous, real-world phenomenon is converted into a series of numbers at a fixed rate over time. When audio is recorded digitally, the continuous variations of a natural phenomenon are captured at a fixed resolution, converted into a series of numbers, and then saved within a file.

The goal is to measure these constant voltage fluctuations within the original incoming audio signal often enough (at a high enough sample rate) and precisely enough (at a sufficient bit depth) that when the measurements are played back (converted back into a series of voltage changes on an analog audio output by the digital-to-analog converter, or DAC), they resemble the original source fairly closely. Figure 1.2 provides a signal-flow diagram for the hard-disk–recording process.

MIDI Is Data, Representing Performance Events and Controller Data

MIDI is a data format and communications protocol originally developed for transmitting and receiving (and later recording or playing back) performance events: when a note was triggered

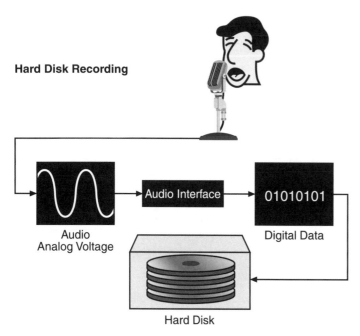

Figure 1.2 Hard-disk–recording: signal flow.

and at what velocity; the movement of pedals, sliders and knobs; and so on. MIDI keyboards, controllers, and sound modules thus speak a common "language" so that they can be connected or so that a performance originally created on one device can be played back on another.

Although Pro Tools also offers many features as a MIDI sequencer and allows MIDI-compatible musical instruments and effects to be incorporated into the same recording/editing environment as audio, MIDI is *not* audio. Sometimes, an external MIDI module is selected as the destination for events sent from each MIDI track, and that's what actually produces sound—in response to the MIDI event messages received. When using external MIDI devices, their audio outputs must be routed back into the Pro Tools audio interface in order for their audio signal to be incorporated into your Pro Tools mix. Typically, this might be done through an Aux Input (or Instrument) track that monitors the physical audio input where they are connected, as shown in Figure 1.3—more about this later.

On the other hand, many users prefer *software*-based instruments—either separate programs or plug-ins that are enabled (instantiated) on Pro Tools tracks. In this case, the virtual instrument is chosen as the destination from one or more MIDI tracks, in much the same way as an external module. Version 7 introduced Instrument tracks, which combine aspects of an Aux In track (as seen in the Mix window) containing an instrument plug-in and a single MIDI track (as seen in the Edit window). Instrument tracks save screen space as well as offering other conveniences, and are covered in more detail in Chapter 6, "The Edit Window," and Chapter 7, "The Mix Window."

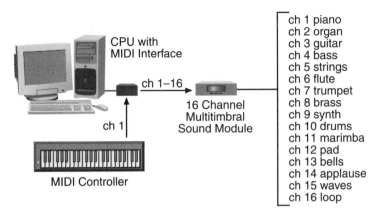

Figure 1.3 A basic MIDI configuration, with an external MIDI keyboard controller and sound module.

More About MIDI The MIDI (short for *Musical Instrument Digital Interface*) standard was developed in the early 1980s by audio and musical-instrument manufacturers to allow synthesizers, drum machines, and similar devices to be interconnected. The MIDI specification describes both a serial communications protocol and a standardized set of data messages that specify the events that these devices generate (or receive). For example, a MIDI message might specify which key was pressed and how quickly, how far the pitch bender or modulation wheel was moved, when the sustain pedal was pressed and released, and so on. MIDI does *not* record or transmit sound; it transmits performance *events* as data.

Very soon after MIDI-compatible synthesizers appeared on the market, dedicated computer programs for recording and reproducing MIDI data, known as MIDI sequencers, became available. Like Pro Tools, these programs capture MIDI events (with the appropriate time references) from an external MIDI keyboard or other controller via a MIDI interface that converts the MIDI protocol into a data format the computer can understand, and provide software-editing tools to modify and play back MIDI events.

Where Audio and MIDI Data Are Stored in Pro Tools   The basic Pro Tools document is called a session file. It contains the mix configuration, references to external audio files and region definitions, automation, track names, and other parameters. The session file also contains all MIDI data you record or create in that session (this includes all the MIDI regions you see in the Regions List, some of which may be currently placed into tracks). In contrast, the audio regions you deal with in Pro Tools are actually pointers (references) to separate audio files on the hard disk.

Multitrack Recording, Mixdown, and Mastering: An Overview

In most audio recordings, numerous channels are separately recorded from multiple microphones, electric instruments, synthesizers, and other sources. These might be recorded onto separate tracks of a tape in a traditional studio or, in the case of Pro Tools, into separate audio files, which you can view within tracks in the Edit window. Having each sound source available on a separately recorded track allows for subsequent manipulation of the sounds, such as changing their relative volumes and apparent locations, plus correcting of any mistakes. You can record additional tracks as you listen to previously recorded material; this process is known as overdubbing.

Mixdown (often called remix in the United Kingdom) is the final stage in the recording process, when multiple sources of audio are combined into a standard playback format—one mono channel, a stereo channel pair, or even more channels in surround mixing. This might be done in real time, as when a stereo mix is recorded to a DAT or other mastering recorder. In the case of Pro Tools, however, often as not the mix is bounced to disk as a new file. During mixdown, the audio engineer (that's you!) balances volume levels, establishes the apparent spatial placement of each sound source, and applies equalization, dynamics processing, and other types of signal processing to alter sounds. Additionally, sounds can be routed to other locations (either external or internal, in the case of Pro Tools), where additional effects processing (such as delay or reverb) might be applied. Obviously, as a performer, Pro Tools offers you unprecedented control over your finished mix. As anyone who has followed commercial music over the past years has observed, creative mixing techniques are often as much a part of the artistic process as the initial performances. For that matter, many musically interesting pieces are being created with Pro Tools that don't directly involve any live performers at all, further obliterating the distinction between performer and engineer.

Mastering is the processing and transferring of finished audio mixes to a medium suitable for duplication. This ranges from simple sequencing of songs and trimming beginnings/endings to applying signal processing to improve uniformity of the material (especially when recorded at different times and places) and sophisticated effects processing (dynamics processing and equalization in particular) that compensates for the characteristics of the final playback medium.

Many of the onscreen objects in Pro Tools resemble traditional elements in this process—the Mix window and the Transport buttons, for example. But although it is convenient to think of Pro Tools as a virtual studio—and certainly, many of the metaphors from traditional audio production do apply—working in this environment does require adjusting to a new mindset; many things simply have no counterpart in a "normal" studio. The reader with old-school audio experience will find all this very refreshing and inspiring! The segmentation of functions and project phases, the linearity, and the relative lack of editing precision that typify tape-based recording (whether analog or digital) disappear with Pro Tools.

Back when digital-audio–workstation technology was still relatively new, we always found ourselves making parallels to traditional recording technology in order to explain the Pro Tools work process (effects racks and patchbays, source/tape switches on mixer channels, gain stages, sync mode, two-track mastering recorders, and so on). As time goes by, though, we meet more users who have never heard of all this stuff! All they've ever known is digital audio—and computer-based implementations at that. The stock metaphors from traditional studios that Pro Tools supposedly emulates are "virtually" losing their meaning for this new generation of audio gearheads; they wouldn't know a splicing block from a wood planer! So if you *are* an audio-production veteran, and this is your first experience with a nonlinear audio production system, be prepared for some pleasant surprises and a new mental geometry for your work process.

Digital-Audio Basics

This section summarizes in a few paragraphs a major subject that typically fills entire books! Obviously, the intent here is simply to set up the context in which Pro Tools exists, not to get you up to speed on the ins and outs of digital audio at large. If all this is brand new to you, you should check out one of the many excellent resources for learning more about sound recording and digital audio. A few are listed in Appendix A, "Further Study, and Resources on the Web."

Introduction: Analog Recording

Electronic audio recording consists of three basic phases: First, there is a sound out there—a disturbance of the air (or other medium) that is an actual mechanical (acoustical) phenomenon. Second, a transducer—a microphone, for instance—converts this acoustical energy to an electrical signal. And lastly, you somehow store these voltage variations produced by the transducer over time so that you can reproduce them afterward.

On traditional (analog) tape recorders, an electromagnet realigns magnetic particles (or domains) on the surface of a moving tape, varying the intensity of its magnetic field in response to variations in the incoming voltage. This is a fairly continuous process—at least as far as the density of the magnetic coating and the speed of the tape permit. When the magnetically stored level variations on the tape are converted back into voltages through an amplifier and speakers, the result is fairly comparable, or analogous, to the original signal. This is analog recording. A real-time chain of physical components directly converts energy from acoustic (mechanical), to electrical, to magnetic form, and then back again.

Sampling Theory Overview

Digital-audio recording proceeds a little differently. Through sampling (capturing a series of data through measurements of the input audio signal at fixed time intervals), each value captured for the incoming audio voltage (called a sample) is converted into a digital word (a binary number with a fixed number of digits) by a logical circuit. This series of numbers is then stored in RAM, on tape, or on a computer disk. In the case of conventional audio CDs, the sample rate is 44,100 times per second (44.1kHz) in stereo. For conventional tape-based video applications, 48,000 times per second (48kHz) is the norm for digital-audio tracks incorporated in videotape formats such as BetaCam, D1, D2, and DVcam (as well as camcorders in Mini DV and DVCAM format). 96kHz is the standard for DVD-Audio discs.

Most Pro Tools configurations enable you to choose between several different sample rates and bit depths, both as the recording format for your session and for any mixdown files you eventually save (bounce) to disk. Both options affect audio quality in very different ways; your best choice for a given situation depends on many factors. You don't *always* want to burden your system's processing capacity or waste disk space by simply choosing the highest possible resolution for each parameter. For now, just keep these two basic principles in mind:

- The more times per second an incoming audio signal is measured, the higher the upper limit for high-frequency information that can be captured. (*Higher Sample Rate = Higher Frequency Range.*) See Figure 1.4.

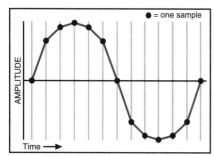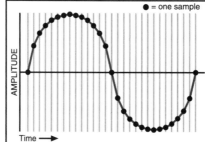

Figure 1.4 Higher sample rates can capture higher frequencies.

- The more binary digits (bits) in the digital word representing each sample (that is, the bigger the number used to represent the sample's relative amplitude), the more intermediate levels of voltage can be used to represent each value before it gets rounded off to the nearest number. Think of it like using graph paper with a more closely spaced grid to represent the finer gradations in signal level. (Higher Bit Depth = Lower Quantization Error, a kind of distortion.) However, don't get the idea that progressively increasing the bit depth of digital recordings will endlessly improve audio quality. For one thing, human hearing has its own limitations for dynamic range—as does any audio playback equipment—and its capacity to distinguish minute level variations in a given frequency range. Many experts will argue that, for practical purposes, a 16-bit audio recording at consistently high levels can sound as "good" as 24-bit recording. All that being said, if your situation involves recording at very low levels (either to allow a lot of headroom, especially when no dynamics processing is applied prior to input, or when the source material to be recorded may have large or unpredictable variations in its dynamic range), recording at 24 bits can be a prudent habit. See Figure 1.5.

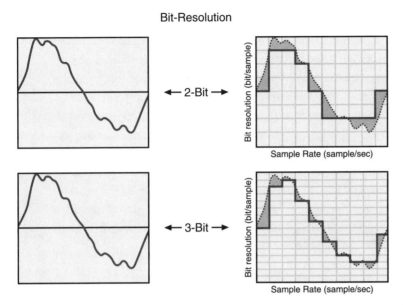

Figure 1.5 Recording at higher bit depths means less rounding in the numerical value for each sample representing an audio signal.

Hard-disk–recording systems like Pro Tools record digital audio and store the sample data on hard disk as audio files. Although one might think it would be great to have an insanely high sample rate and a huge number of bits per audio sample, the resultant audio files will also be proportionately larger. This places more demands on the host computer, requires more disk space, and so on—with no perceptible improvement in audio quality beyond a certain practical limit. (Many also argue that, given the inherent limitations of human hearing, 24-bit resolution is more than sufficient for initial audio recording and the final playback medium. Per this view, improvements in audio quality will center on how digital signals are combined and processed in the software environment—the 48-bit mix engine in Pro Tools|HD versus the 32-bit floating point one in other Pro Tools versions, for example—and the characteristics of ADC and DAC hardware that will always color the sound to some degree.) One of the reasons the audio CD standard was established at 44.1kHz (44,100 cycles per second, or Hertz) was that this sampling rate easily allows maximum fundamental frequencies of up to 20kHz to be captured, roughly corresponding to the upper limit of adult human hearing. At 16 bits per stereo sample, good-sounding streams of audio data could be reliably played back on consumer CD players. For initial recording of audio tracks, however, 24-bit audio is currently the most common practice—regardless of the final resolution of the delivery medium.

Higher Sample Rate = Higher Frequency Range The *Nyquist Frequency* (the highest sine-wave frequency you theoretically can represent when sampling audio) corresponds to half the current sample rate. The *Shannon-Nyquist Theorem* describes how the sample rate (the number of digital measurements per second) must be at least twice that of the highest-frequency sound you want to record so that both negative and positive excursions of a periodic waveform can be captured. If only a portion of a high-frequency waveform were captured, digital artifacts called *aliasing* would be created. Aliasing consists of spurious frequencies present when a digital-audio recording is played back due to partial and erroneous capture of incoming high-frequency information while recording. (In practice, we're talking here about the higher-frequency harmonics of more complex waveforms, not their fundamental pitch.) Therefore, to eliminate the possibility of any incoming frequencies higher than the Nyquist limit hitting the analog-digital audio converters, digital-audio devices incorporate some sort of low-pass filter. In practice, this actually eliminates frequencies substantially below exactly half the sample rate as much due to cost considerations as physical limitations on filter design. That's why the audio CD standard, with a 44.1kHz sampling rate, reaches frequencies up to only 20,000 rather than the theoretical 22,050Hz Nyquist limit (half the sample rate).

Until not too long ago, 44.1kHz and 48kHz were the most common sample rates for professional audio applications, with bit depths of 16, 20, 24, and occasionally 32. (Bit depth refers to the number of binary digits per sample.) The high-end Pro Tools|HD systems pushed the envelope a little further, supporting 24-bit audio at sample rates of 88.2, 96, 176.4, or 192kHz (according to the audio hardware in your Pro Tools|HD configuration), as well as the 44.1kHz and 48kHz sample rates supported on virtually all audio interfaces for Pro Tools. The Digi 003 and Digi 002 families also support sample rates up to 96kHz and 24-bit resolution, as do many of the M-Powered hardware configurations (with some also supporting 192kHz, although not with the Pro Tools M-Powered software itself).

Digital-Audio File Formats   Numerous file formats are used for storing data representing digital-audio waveforms. Here are some of the more common ones that will be relevant to your work in Pro Tools:

- **WAV.** Native to the Microsoft Windows environment and supported by most Macintosh programs, including Pro Tools, the WAV (pronounced "wave") format is similar to the AIF format, described momentarily. Some Windows multimedia programs *only* support audio files in WAV format. Pro Tools 7.4 and below can import and convert WAV files or bounce to disk in WAV format, even while using AIF as the session's recording file format (or SDII format, especially in older Mac versions). Pro Tools 8 can support sessions with mixed file formats, as long as the bit depth and sample rate are the same, WAV files can now live harmoniously with other file formats without the step of conversion.

- **Broadcast WAV Format (BWF).** This is a backward-compatible extension of the WAV format, which you can select in Pro Tools as a new session's recording format.

For recording at any sample rate higher than 48kHz, all versions of Pro Tools require this format on both Macintosh and Windows computers. Broadcast WAV allows ownership information to be embedded in audio files. More importantly, Broadcast WAV files support embedded time-code information, which can be useful for correctly spotting files to their original location—even in other programs that support this format, such as video editors or other digital-audio workstations. Especially when compatibility between Windows and Macintosh versions of Pro Tools is a potential concern, this audio file format is often the best choice. Using Broadcast WAV may also improve compatibility or, at the very least, eliminate a conversion step when sharing audio or OMF files with video-editing systems across platforms. In fact, Broadcast WAV is the audio file format that the Audio Engineering Society (AES) recommends for submission and long-term archival of music projects.

- **Audio Interchange File Format (AIF or AIFF).** A mono/stereo file format originally developed by Apple, AIF has been extensively supported in interactive and electronic media applications for both Macintosh and Windows platforms. However, as with the audio industry, many video editors and interactive content developers are migrating toward Broadcast WAV as the norm for long-term compatibility; be sure to check before starting a project of this type! The AIF format also supports loop points for samplers or sample playback programs (although you have to create these loop points in some program other than Pro Tools). Loop points within an AIF file are also recognized by Macromedia Director and some other interactive applications. The AIF format is supported in Pro Tools for 48kHz and 44.1kHz sessions only; for all higher sampling rates, Broadcast WAV format must be used instead. Note: Director and Flash developers may use markers, or cue points, to tag specific locations within an AIF (or WAV) audio file. Like loop markers, you can't create these directly in Pro Tools, but may be asked to do so using other programs such as Peak (Mac), WaveLab (Windows), or Sound Forge (Windows).

- **Sound Designer II (SDII or SD2).** Earlier Macintosh versions of Pro Tools recorded audio to disk exclusively in Sound Designer II format. Sound Designer was Digidesign's ground-breaking Macintosh audio-editing program, introduced in the 1980s. From its beginnings as a simple mono editing program for samplers (transmitting sample data—slowly—via MIDI), it evolved into a robust stereo hard-disk–recording and editing environment based on Digidesign's Sound Tools II hardware, the precursor to Pro Tools that quickly became the industry standard for editing and mastering stereo audio. SDII files can be mono or stereo, with bit depths of 16, 20, or 24 bits. They include loop points (for samplers) and region definitions (more about this in Chapter 2, "Pro Tools Terms and Concepts"). With current versions of Pro Tools, most users should use AIF or Broadcast WAV format as the file format for their recording sessions because, among other things, these formats are more widely supported by other audio programs, especially on Windows. However, if compatibility with older legacy Pro Tools systems or Pro Tools Free 5.01 for Macintosh is a concern, there may still be rare situations where Mac users will choose this format. SDII files don't support sample rates higher than 48kHz and cannot be used as the audio-recording format for any current Windows version of Pro Tools.

- **QuickTime.** This digital video file format developed by Apple is included in the Mac operating system and is also available as a free download for Windows that includes the QuickTime Player application. Audio-only QuickTime files are essentially AIF files with resources designating QuickTime playback; these will sometimes be requested by interactive developers. The audio tracks within QuickTime movies are also often AIF format. You can import QuickTime movies into Pro Tools sessions as your video master for postproduction and then bounce Pro Tools audio mixes directly back out into a new copy of that QuickTime movie file.

- **MPEG Audio, Layer 3 (MP3).** This compressed audio format uses a lossy compression method in which some amount of the original information is permanently lost in the process. The lower the bit rate (how much data per second, measured in kilobits, is required to play back the audio file), the more noticeable the compromise of audio quality will be. The amount of size reduction in MP3 encoding before drastic degradation is impressive, however—on the order of 5:1 or greater. As the reader is surely aware, the MP3 format is enormously popular for exchanging music files on the Internet. It is also increasingly common in audio files for interactive media because MP3 compression yields much better sounding results than the older method of decreasing file size by reducing sample rate, let alone the drastic measure of converting down to 8-bit resolution. Pro Tools users involved with interactive developers (or bands trying to promote themselves on the Internet) may be asked by these clients to save out mixes as MP3 files.

- **MPEG Audio, Layer 4 (MPEG-4).** Though formalized in 1998, this format did not become an official international standard until 2000. This compression standard builds upon digital-television technology. Apple's QuickTime file format was adapted as the basis for the MPEG-4 file format, and Apple has played an active role in its development. The more advanced audio encoding used in MPEG-4 produces smaller files and better audio quality than MP3.

- **Advanced Audio Coding (AAC).** AAC is implemented in a variant of MPEG-4 that has been popularized by Apple for online purchasing and download of audio files at its iTunes Music Store. It is much more efficient at audio data compression than MP3, producing comparable results at file sizes as much as 30 percent smaller.

- **RealAudio.** Developed by Real Networks, this streaming, compressed audio file format is often used on the Internet. Because RealPlayer is available to any user as a free download (and also supports streaming video files), some companies and media organizations use this technology to deliver audio and video content over the Web, which means you may occasionally be asked to deliver mixes in RealAudio format. Audio can be reduced to various throughputs (with audible compression artifacts at more extreme compression levels) according to requirements. SureStream technology allows several different versions of the audio to be incorporated into a single RealAudio file link, with the appropriate density being selected for playback according to the bandwidth available for each user's Internet connection. Note, however, that many users resist installing RealPlayer on their systems because of the invasive nature of this company's software (changing preferences for media file types, near-impossibility of a complete uninstall on Windows systems, and so on), which can be a major inconvenience—especially for audio and other media-production professionals.

- **ReCycle (REX).** This audio format is optimized for time-sliced loops—that is, audio files that have been analyzed and broken down into their rhythmic components. The format was developed for the ReCycle program by Propellerhead Software, and the current iteration of the file format is actually called REX2. Many loop-oriented programs, such as Reason and Cubase, support using REX2 files in their editing/mixing environment. Loops can then be played at any tempo without pitch changes. Also, having individual rhythmic components automatically sliced up makes it much easier to rearrange them into new rhythmic patterns. You can import REX files into Pro Tools by dragging them from the Workspace browser window or desktop directly into the Regions List. Depending on your audio preferences in Pro Tools, time slices within source REX files can either appear subsequently in the Regions List as "auto-created" region groups or, in versions 7.4 and higher, consolidated for Elastic Audio analysis.

- **ACID.** This is yet another format optimized for time-sliced loops and allowing for transformation to new tempos and keys. It's named for the ACID program by Sony (originally developed by Sonic Foundry). Like REX files, you can bring ACID files into Pro Tools by dragging into the Regions List from the Workspace browser window or desktop, and region groups or Elastic Audio analyses are automatically created for any time-slice information the ACID files contain.

MIDI Basics

As stated earlier, MIDI stands for Musical Instrument Digital Interface. To reiterate: MIDI is a communications protocol (with a standard data structure, cabling, DIN-5 connectors, and interfaces) for transmitting, receiving, and storing performance events. MIDI events are control (and timing) messages—they are *not* audio! The reception of a MIDI event may cause devices to emit audio, such as when a Note On event is transmitted from a Pro Tools MIDI track to a synth module (connected to your computer's MIDI interface) or to a software instrument plug-in. Of course, MIDI also has many other applications. It's used, for example, to change parameters on external effects, to edit internal patches in sound modules, to control lighting, and to automate mixing boards.

When you arm a MIDI (or Instrument) track for recording in Pro Tools, it looks for incoming MIDI event data from the selected MIDI interface/port for that track. When you press a key on your synth keyboard, for example, a Note On message is transmitted to Pro Tools. This Note On event includes two parameters: the number of the note you pressed and the velocity with which the key was struck, as shown in Figure 1.6. Likewise, when you release each key, a Note Off event is sent, specifying the note number and its release velocity. The pitch bend, modulation, aftertouch (channel pressure), and other interpretive moves you perform on the MIDI controller are transmitted in a similar fashion. (Other "interpretive moves," like pouting, booty shaking, and your Serious Artist expression are completely lost on Pro Tools. Sorry!)

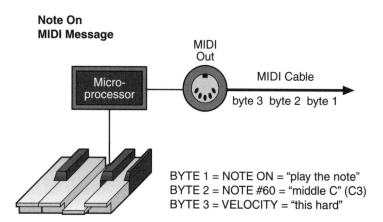

Figure 1.6   MIDI is a language for transmitting performance information (events). Here you see a Note On MIDI event, which is transmitted when you press a key on a MIDI keyboard.

MIDI Connections MIDI is a serial communications protocol. MIDI-compatible devices have 5-pin DIN connectors for MIDI. Your computer requires a MIDI interface to translate between this protocol and its own hardware/software (unless you're using MIDI gear that connects directly to the computer via USB). Fortunately, for Pro Tools, you can start with whatever MIDI interface fits your present needs and budget and then upgrade as required. Digi 003, Digi 002, and Digi 001 interfaces include MIDI ins/outs on the Digidesign interface itself, as do the Mbox 2, Mbox 2 Pro, and many of the M-Audio interfaces that are compatible with the M-Powered version of Pro Tools.

Many consumer-level Windows sound cards already have a built-in MIDI in/out port, which nonetheless usually requires the separate purchase of a short adapter cable that splits out to two 5-pin DIN in/out connectors. Macintosh computers require an external MIDI interface, generally connected to the USB port on recent models. Windows users requiring *multiple* MIDI inputs/outputs or more sophisticated features also use an external MIDI interface. External USB MIDI interfaces are also the norm for Windows users. (Parallel-port MIDI interfaces also existed for older PCs.)

MIDI interfaces range from simple one in, one out models, through 2×2, 4×6, 8×8, 10×10, and more. You can even network certain multiport MIDI interfaces for dozens of MIDI inputs/outputs. Many also provide real-time routing and filtering between their inputs and outputs (handy for larger configurations with multiple MIDI controllers) and synchronization for SMPTE time code. (More about this in Chapter 11, "Synchronization.")

Again, some current musical keyboards, pads, control surfaces, and such use direct USB connections to the host computer. Users of these controllers may not require a MIDI interface at all, especially if their sound sources for MIDI tracks are all software based.

MIDI File Formats

Like MIDI sequencers (Digital Performer, Logic Pro, Cubase, SONAR, and others), Pro Tools records standard MIDI events into its own proprietary file format. Each of these programs offers a wealth of display options for MIDI data (for both musical and mixing applications) and many real-time functions that affect how MIDI events are played back. In the case of Pro Tools, all the MIDI performance data that you record or create is incorporated into the session file itself (as opposed to audio, which is stored into separate files on the disk).

Importing Standard MIDI Files into Pro Tools 8 In Pro Tools 8, the File > Import > MIDI command brings Standard MIDI File–format (SMF-format) files into your session, either to the Regions List only or directly to tracks. An appropriate number of new MIDI regions (and new tracks, if you choose that option in the MIDI Import Options dialog box) is created as required by the contents of the MIDI file. This ability existed in various previous versions of Pro Tools, but in Pro Tools 7 and 8, MIDI files can be managed and imported directly in the Digibase browser windows. You can use the Workspace browser window to navigate to their disk location—and then either drag directly into the Regions List or into the track display area of the Edit window, where an appropriate number of new MIDI tracks will automatically be created. Yet another option is to simply drag an SMF-format file directly into Pro Tools from the Finder (Mac) or Explorer (Windows).

Occasionally, users need to transfer an entire MIDI file (consisting of multiple tracks, with their note events, controller data, program settings, volume, and other data) from one program to another. The Standard MIDI File (SMF) format was defined to facilitate this process. SMF-format files (which typically have the .mid filename extension) are an interchange format, which includes all MIDI events, track names, volume and pan settings, and many other parameters. If you properly prepare before exporting the file, none of the necessary MIDI performance data will be lost or misinterpreted when transferring files between different applications. In Pro Tools, you can also import or export files in SMF format (including tempo map and key signature information in versions 7.3 and higher). This ensures compatibility not only with other MIDI sequencing software, but also with multimedia applications (such as applications on the Web or interactive CDs and DVDs), which can play back these SMF-format files.

Standard MIDI Files and General MIDI   If you are creating SMF-format files for multimedia (which, in Windows, must always have the .mid filename extension in order to be properly recognized), be sure to use General MIDI (GM) program numbers for designating the sounds you want for each track. (Many current synths and modules have a General MIDI bank. GM is also the norm for assigning sounds to MIDI program numbers on current computer sound cards for Windows, as well as QuickTime Musical Instruments for Macintosh computers. However, these may not actually offer unique sounds for each of the 128 program numbers defined in General MIDI. Instead, they may use the same timbre for several different acoustic pianos or drum sets, for example.) By using General MIDI program numbers, if you choose sound #14 for your xylophone part, it will still be a xylophone sound of some type when played back by QuickTime Musical Instruments, Windows Media Player, or standard interactive applications. It may not *sound* quite as good as the xylophone sound you used to compose the piece, but at least it won't be, say, a tuba!

Routing External MIDI Gear into Pro Tools   If you have enough audio inputs on your Pro Tools hardware (for example, with any Digi 003, Digi 002, Mbox 2 Pro, or HD system, as well as some of the M-Audio hardware for Pro Tools M-Powered), you might connect each of your external synthesizer(s) to an input pair on your audio interface and create individual stereo Aux Input tracks to monitor each of them in Pro Tools. Having the synths' audio output routed through the Pro Tools mixing environment, as shown in Figure 1.7, offers many advantages. You can apply automation and real-time plug-in processing to these external sound sources and, of course, incorporate their audio as you bounce your mix to disk as a stereo file, for example. However, in some cases, the number of channels required for all your external modules exceeds the available inputs on the audio hardware—especially considering that while recording, you might want at least an input or two free for your microphones and guitar preamps. Another alternative is to use the M-Audio NRV10 or a small mixer (or even a clean-sounding line mixer) to combine some external sources into a stereo submix prior to the audio inputs on your interface (and then monitor this via a single stereo Aux In track—but we're getting ahead of ourselves).

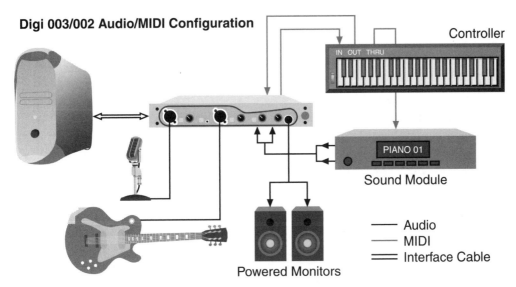

Digi 003/002 Audio/MIDI Configuration

Figure 1.7   A typical configuration with a Digi 003, Digi 002, or one of the M-Audio interfaces with MIDI inputs/outputs. The audio outputs of the external MIDI sound module enter the audio inputs on the interface. MIDI data sent from Pro Tools is passed through the MIDI keyboard to the module.

Software-Based Virtual Instruments for MIDI

We talk much more about this in Chapters 9, "Plug-ins, Inserts, and Sends," and 10, "MIDI," so let's just mention quickly here that, for the Pro Tools composer, software instruments are one of the most exciting technical developments of recent years. In very simple terms, these are either some sort of plug-in (a software construct activated within the host application; Chapters 2 and 9 especially discuss this in more detail) or a separate program whose audio outputs stream into Pro Tools through a software-routing technology called ReWire. You can assign the output from any MIDI track (or Instrument track) to any currently enabled software instruments in the Pro Tools session using MIDI channel assignments and the same MIDI controller messages as with an external MIDI module. Additionally, Instrument tracks (introduced in Pro Tools 7) are similar to a single MIDI track with an associated Aux In that contains an instrument plug-in. Each virtual instrument presents a software interface for altering its parameters and selecting presets according to the kind of sound generator being modeled (sampler, analog, FM or wavetable synthesizer, drum machine, and so on).

Reopening each Pro Tools session can instantly recall myriad settings, effects, and signal-routing configurations for each of its active software instruments. (Of course, if you're using an additional program slaved to Pro Tools via ReWire, its configuration for a given Pro Tools session must be saved and recalled separately, in that program's own format.) If you've ever managed a complex MIDI configuration with multiple external modules, you know what we're talking about—it's practically a full-time job just documenting the setup for each song. Even then, exactly reproducing a given configuration and gain structure months later is often nearly impossible. Better yet, because all the routing is internal within the computer software instead of via multiple cables and outputs from external gadgets…no noise!

Summary

This chapter provides a broad overview of what Pro Tools is and the kinds of system configurations that are possible (although these are reviewed in more detail in Chapter 3), a basic introduction to core digital-audio and MIDI concepts, and a general look at the recording process. As mentioned, any one of these subjects alone often fills entire books (some of which are mentioned in Appendix A), so the intent of this review is to provide you with some context and a basic vocabulary for understanding how things work in digital workstations such as Pro Tools.

The next chapter covers more fundamental concepts—especially the key terms that all users must understand in order to effectively use Pro Tools. For more basic information about MIDI and its applications within Pro Tools, see Chapter 10.

2 Pro Tools Terms and Concepts

Whether you're new to Pro Tools or you have an extensive audio background, take a moment to explore the review of basic concepts in this chapter. These are the conceptual building blocks for your understanding of the Pro Tools program, and will provide a good grounding for your exploration of nonlinear audio and the virtual studio. Some of these terms have specific meanings in the Pro Tools environment (for example, tracks versus channels), so even experienced audio users will benefit from taking a moment to review this chapter. If this is your first time around with digital-audio workstations, and with Pro Tools in particular, this chapter should help you get things sorted out more quickly.

Pro Tools Data and Files

Each Pro Tools session actually consists of multiple files and folders. So in order to manage your Pro Tools configuration, you need to know where Pro Tools puts things! Let's take a look at the master session document where you store your work, the audio files that Pro Tools creates, and how you actually view and edit these within the Pro Tools software.

Session

The session file is the basic document of Pro Tools. After you open the Pro Tools program and select File > New Session, a dialog box new to Pro Tools version 8 asks you whether you want to create a blank session with no prearranged tracks, or whether you want to create a session based on one of several templates that Pro Tools offers. These templates provide a prearranged selection of plug-ins, aux routings, and even MIDI files to jump-start your progress on a session, all of which can be added to or altered. You are also asked to select the sample rate and bit rate of the session you want to create, as well as the audio-file type you want to use within the session. Then you are prompted to choose a location on your hard drive to create and save the session files and folders, as well as to name the session. A new folder of the same name is created in the disk/folder location you specify, within which this document resides (see Figure 2.1). The session file includes information about the name and appearance of any tracks you create, all mix settings and the appearance of the onscreen mixer, routing of audio between tracks, sends, inserts, plug-in effects, audio inputs/outputs, and other parameters. Any MIDI data recorded or created in Pro Tools is stored within the session document. In contrast, the audio regions that you record and edit from within the session are actually pointers to areas within audio files that

Figure 2.1 A Pro Tools session document (inside its folder of the same name), with the Audio Files folder, the Fade Files folder, and other folders that it creates.

reside separately on your hard disk. As soon as you record or import any audio in a new Pro Tools session document, a subfolder named Audio Files is automatically created within that session's folder. The session document is essentially where you work—recording audio and MIDI, creating a signal-routing and effects-processing structure, editing your audio, creating a mix, automating the movement of faders, and so on. Session files are relatively small because they don't actually contain any audio. They *refer* to much larger audio files, portions of which are used within the Pro Tools session. These audio files appear as regions within Pro Tools (discussed momentarily), whose audio waveforms can be viewed where they have been placed within Pro Tools audio tracks.

Audio File

The digital-audio data you record to disk from each audio track in a Pro Tools session is stored in a file (within that session's Audio Files subfolder that Pro Tools creates for this purpose—see Figure 2.2). Each filename inherits the name of the track where it was recorded, so it's a very good idea to give your audio tracks meaningful names as you prepare to record in them. (Of course, you can always change the names of audio files later, by right-clicking or double-clicking that whole-file audio region in the Regions List and choosing the Name Region and Disk File option.) Pro Tools can also import existing audio files (and convert their format or sample rate, if necessary) into the current session. A single audio file may even be used in several different Pro Tools sessions—for example, frequently used items like test tones, station IDs, drum sounds, stock sound effects, and so on. Typically, as you record in Pro Tools, you end up creating a large number of audio files, especially because by default, audio recording is non-destructive—*all* the takes are retained on every track. Because multiple digital-audio files can potentially take up a lot of hard-disk space, file management is an important issue in Pro Tools. It's important to selectively eliminate unneeded audio as your project progresses; the sheer size of these audio files already introduces some pretty hefty data-storage issues without wasting any more space than necessary. (More about this in Appendix C, "Archive and Backup.")

Audio File

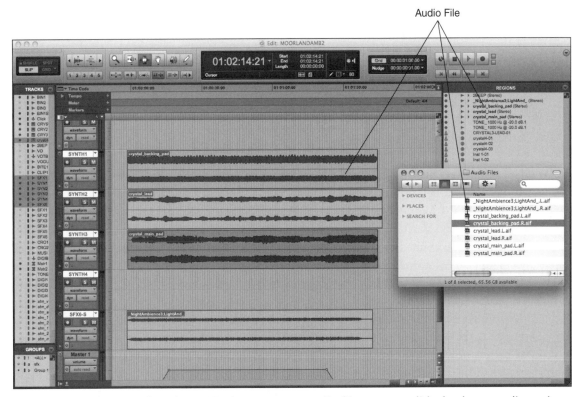

Figure 2.2 Audio recordings in Pro Tools create new audio files on your disks (and new audio regions in your Pro Tools session). Regions that correspond to entire audio files (rather than portions within them) appear in bold type in the Regions List.

Region

An audio region is a segment of audio data of any length—a guitar riff, a four-bar drum phrase, a sound effect, or a phrase of dialog within a longer audio file that is always external to the Pro Tools session document itself. In contrast, the data in all MIDI regions is included within the session document, whether the data is recorded or created within Pro Tools or imported from some existing file. New regions are created automatically when you record to any track. If you are recording to an audio track, audio files are also created on your hard disk. Both audio and MIDI regions appear in a single Regions List, with distinctive icons for each. Entire audio files—whether they are recorded in Pro Tools or are existing files you have imported from their original disk locations—appear in the Regions List, along with other audio regions that represent only specific portions within their parent sound files. (Whole-file audio regions are identified by boldface type in the Regions List.) Once you place existing audio or MIDI files and regions in Pro Tools tracks, you can capture or separate additional region definitions for any selected range within them via commands in the Edit menu. Many of the edits you perform on the regions in tracks (for example, eliminating the middle portion of a longer region) create new, additional region definitions, as do various processing operations in the Pro Tools menus.

Because audio regions are only pointers to external files (or portions within them), you can string regions together in any order by dragging, cutting, pasting, or duplicating within tracks. Pro Tools handles the seamless, nonlinear playback of all these segments within many separate audio files via the Digidesign Audio Engine's (DAE) read-ahead buffer. This is the essential nonlinear (and usually non-destructive) nature of digital-audio workstations like Pro Tools—no matter how much you chop up and reorder the regions in your tracks, the original audio files are not altered.

Creation of additional audio-region definitions occupies only a negligible amount of extra disk space. Multiple region definitions within the same audio file or MIDI region can overlap or coincide in any manner that is convenient. For example, you could define 16 bars of the recorded bass track as a region named Verse2 and substitute it for the bass in Verse3, where the bass player made some mistake. Or, you could select a smoothly looping eight-bar section of a short drum recording, separate a region called DrumGroove, and loop or duplicate this region as many times as necessary to build up your layered dance track. (Separating and capturing a new region name involve very similar commands. Both add a new region definition to the Regions List, but Edit > Separate Region actually replaces the current track selection with the new region definition, while Region > Capture adds the new region definition to the Regions List without replacing the current selection.) No matter how many times you repeat the drum loop, its audio data only occupies those eight bars worth of space within its source audio file on the hard disk.

Regions that are duplicated or copied and pasted in an Edit window track playlist can also keep associated automation information, which includes volume, mute, solo, pan, sends, and plug-in parameter changes. So, for example, if you love the timing of a quick boost in volume automation that is associated with a region that you want to use elsewhere in the session, you do have the option of copying that volume automation move along with the region's audio data.

Figure 2.3 shows how audio regions appear in the Edit window, both as rectangular graphics within audio tracks and in the Regions List (the bin at the right side of the Edit window). During playback, Pro Tools takes care of retrieving all the appropriate sections of audio in multiple files. All regions in a track will play back at the correct time—even if they point to sections within audio files that reside on physically separate sections of the disk(s).

Track

An audio or MIDI track is where regions are recorded or strung together. Each horizontal strip in the Edit window (into which you record or drag audio and MIDI regions) represents one of these virtual tracks. The Mix window displays the same audio and MIDI tracks as the Edit window, but as vertical mixer strips. (Instrument tracks are a sort of hybrid; while they are similar to Aux Inputs as seen in the Mix window, in the Edit window, MIDI regions can be recorded and edited in an Instrument track.) Each audio, MIDI, or Instrument track has its own playlist of regions (see the next section), plus an automation playlist for volume faders,

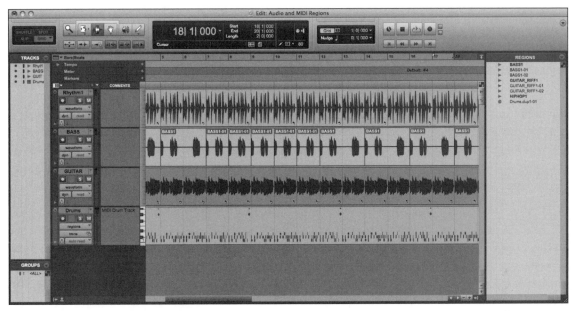

Figure 2.3 Regions are segments of audio or MIDI data; audio regions can represent entire files or portions within files. Some region definitions are created automatically by Pro Tools in the course of editing.

pan, sends, and plug-in parameters. Tracks can be assigned any convenient name and dragged into any convenient order as you work. (On HD systems, when tracks are manually assigned to voices rather than assigned using the default dynamic voice allocation mode, track positions also affect playback priority. Left-most tracks in the Mix window, which are also top-most in the Edit window, always have priority access to their manually assigned voice.) Each track can be muted, soloed, assigned to any audio input/output available on the system, or routed to another destination through Pro Tools' internal mixing busses. Two other classes of tracks that do not contain regions also offer many similar features to audio tracks: Aux Input tracks and Master Fader tracks (see definitions of these terms later in this chapter). Lastly, if you import Quick-Time movies or digital video file types as references for a postproduction project, a Video track is created. Chapter 7, "The Mix Window," explores the various classes of tracks in Pro Tools.

Playlist

In general terms, an edit playlist is a list of audio (or MIDI) regions strung together in a specific order on a Pro Tools virtual track. Recorded audio used by an audio track is stored within files on the hard disk; a playlist is a list of regions (pointers to portions of the audio data within those audio files) indicating which are to be read for playback, at what time, and in what order.

In some programs, you can order the playback of audio regions or files through a single, text-based list—for example, Steinberg's WaveLab and Sony/Sonic Foundry's Sound Forge, not to mention Digidesign's long-discontinued Sound Designer II and MasterList CD programs (and most CD-burning software, for that matter). In Pro Tools, however, each track you see in the Edit window is actually a graphic playlist. Regions can be viewed as blocks within each track or, when the Waveform view is selected for an audio track, visual representations of the actual audio waveforms are displayed within these region blocks.

For example, say you import a few dozen sound effects from a CD library and then drag them out onto an audio track in the Pro Tools Edit window. You trim their beginnings and ends and perhaps create a few fades (which are actually separate files; see the section "Fade, Crossfade," later in this chapter) and resize them in other ways. When you click Play, Pro Tools understands that you want to hear a specific section of one file with a seamless fade on the end followed by another section from a completely different file. Pro Tools follows every audio track's playlist, making sure to pre-load all appropriate audio data from disk into the DAE playback buffer for timely playback.

In the controls for each audio, MIDI, or Instrument track, a pop-up Playlist selector (to the right of each track name in the Edit window) switches between alternate playlists for that track (as shown in Figure 2.4). This is useful for experimentation; you duplicate the current version of the

Figure 2.4 Each audio or MIDI track in Pro Tools graphically represents a playlist that indicates which regions of audio or MIDI data should be played, and when. You can switch between multiple playlists for each track, using the pop-up Playlist selector shown here.

track's region order as a playlist so that you can always go back to it! (Users familiar with video-editing systems will note that the playlist for each Pro Tools track is comparable to an edit decision list, or EDL for short.) Unlike audio tape, playback order is not restricted to the original physical order of your source material on the recording medium.

Track Automation Versus Playlists of Regions There is only one automation playlist for each Pro Tools audio track, regardless of which edit playlist (region order) is selected. This is extremely important to keep in mind—for example, if you want to experiment with cutting and pasting audio regions within alternate playlists in the same audio track. By default, any automation data (for example, volume, pan, or effects parameters) overlapping the regions you select will also be copied. Sometimes, however, these resulting automation shapes may not be appropriate when you use the track's Playlist selector to switch to a different edit playlist. If you need to experiment not only with audio-region order but also with automation within a track, it may be better to create a new duplicate of the audio track rather than using multiple playlists in the source track for this purpose. Worth noting is that other types of tracks, such as Master Fader, VCA, Instrument, and Auxiliary tracks, will also have only a single automation playlist associated with them.

MIDI tracks also allow you to view and edit automation, of course. The appearance of MIDI volume, pan, and other automation data in MIDI tracks is similar to audio, but it is handled quite differently by Pro Tools. Automation shapes in MIDI tracks actually represent MIDI controller messages for parameters that will be transmitted along with the note events on the track's MIDI channel (damper pedal, mod wheel, breath controller data, or MIDI volume and pan, for example). The only automation-playlist data types that are part of the MIDI track itself are mute/unmute events (which, like audio automation, are part of the track itself). All other MIDI automation—for volume, pan, pedals, modulation, aftertouch, and so on—is actually contained within the MIDI regions themselves as MIDI controller information. So except for mute/unmute automation events (which affect anything in that MIDI track, no matter which edit playlist is selected), in MIDI tracks you can freely edit the volume, pan, and other MIDI controller data types in each alternate playlist without worrying about this affecting any of the other playlists in the same track. In fact, when you duplicate an edit playlist in a MIDI track, Pro Tools automatically creates duplicate MIDI regions to reflect any edits you make to these parameters.

How Pro Tools Handles Audio

Using conventional mixing boards and tape recorders, it's fairly easy to see where your audio enters and exits individual channels, auxiliary inputs or outputs, and so on. For the sake of convenience, Pro Tools uses mixer strips and tracks as familiar metaphors, but in fact it's much more flexible than that. If you look at alternative configurations in Pro Tools with a traditional tape-based mindset, you might think, for example, that for equivalent functionality to a 24-track recorder, you need 24 channels of input/output (I/O) on your Pro Tools audio interfaces. It ain't necessarily so! *Especially* if you're coming to this program from a traditional MIDI or audio background, you need to readjust your thinking about voices, tracks, and, in particular, channels to truly understand the power of Pro Tools.

Voice, Track Priority

The number of voices in a digital-audio workstation determines the number of separate audio tracks it can play at any given moment. Voices in Pro Tools are like a pool of digital-audio converters, which audio tracks must use to play back the audio regions they contain. By default, Pro Tools dynamically assigns voices to tracks (via the dyn setting in the Voice Assignment selector for each track) to avoid conflicts. In LE and M-Powered versions of Pro Tools (using Digi 003, Digi 002, Mbox 2, or M-Audio hardware, for example), this is the only option for managing voice allocation—other than setting a track's voice assignment to "off" so that it doesn't play at all, as shown in Figure 2.5. The optional Music Production Toolkit 2 (for either LE or M-Powered) or the DV Toolkit 2 (for Pro Tools LE only) increases the capabilities of these systems to 64 audio tracks, either mono or stereo, when the sampling rate of the session is 44.1kHz or 48kHz. And the LE-only Complete Production Toolkit allows for the editing and mixing of a whopping 128 audio tracks simultaneously at a 44.1kHz or 48kHz sampling rate.

Figure 2.5   A track's voice selector in the Edit window from an LE system. Note that the two choices are Dynamic where Pro Tools automatically handles voice allocation, and Off, which silences the track.

On HD systems (like their TDM predecessors), however, you can *manually* assign a voice number to each Pro Tools track. Whenever two tracks want to use the same manually assigned voice at the same moment, the one with the highest playback priority will win. The scheme for managing voice allocation is very simple: Whichever track is higher in the Edit window—or further left in the Mix window—is the higher priority. Wherever the higher-priority track contains an audio region, it will play, even if that means cutting off a region already sounding in another lower-priority track assigned to the same voice number. If you drag tracks into a different order, you also change their priority. Multiple tracks can be assigned to the same voice as long as their regions don't overlap at any point in time. Each can play back all required audio. This effectively gives you much more polyphony out of whatever fixed number of voices your Pro Tools system provides. Each track maintains its own completely independent routing, effects, automation, and so on, which is unaffected by that of any other tracks assigned to the same voice.

Bear in mind that multichannel tracks (stereo and surround) utilize a corresponding number of voices. This is why high-end configurations such as Pro Tools|HD support such high voice counts. For complex soundtrack mixes with many surround submixes, stereo tracks, and so on, the number of voices required for playback can get large very quickly. Also, on HD systems (but not LE/M-Powered versions), each active ReWire channel in your Pro Tools session uses one of your available voices. See "ReWire (and the DigiReWire Plug-in)" later in this chapter for more information. As explained in Chapter 7, in Pro Tools HD, the first instance of an RTAS plug-in on a track doubles its voice usage—for example, two voices for a mono track or four for a stereo track.

Back in the early days of Pro Tools, voice assignment was quite an art form. (Systems with four or eight channels and four or eight voices were the norm, whereas today anywhere from 32 to 192 voices are supported.) On current Pro Tools|HD systems, though, most users leave the default dyn (dynamic) setting for track voice assignments, letting the software automatically handle this. Therefore, unless you inadvertently assign two tracks to the same voice manually (*and* their audio regions coincide at some point), voice assignment won't necessarily be a daily issue for you. One exception would be when you're specifically using this voice-stealing feature to assemble a composite (comp) track or to bleep out certain words in a voice recording or lyric. In the latter case, you would place the bleep sounds into a higher-priority track that's assigned to the same voice as the track you want to bleep.

Channel

Although the mixer strips in the Pro Tools Mix window are sometimes called mixer channels, this term is really more of a holdover from traditional analog mixing boards, where each channel actually does correspond to an audio input. In the Digidesign realm, we prefer to reserve the term channel strictly for describing the I/O capabilities of the audio hardware itself. For example, Digidesign's 96 I/O audio interface for HD systems simultaneously offers up to 16 channels of input and output using various combinations of its eight analog inputs/outputs, eight-channel ADAT Lightpipe input/output, and AES/EBU and S/PDIF digital inputs/outputs. The Mbox 2 Mini is a two-channel system: two inputs (one of which can be switched between microphone and line/instrument jacks on the rear of the interface) and two line-level outputs. The Mbox 2 can operate as a 4×2 system if you use the two channels of analog I/O and the S/PDIF digital I/O simultaneously. The Mbox 2 Pro, if you use all available analog/digital I/O, supports up to six input channels and four output channels (plus dedicated monitor output jacks that mirror the signal on outputs 1–2). The Mbox 2 Micro offers stereo output only. If you're using M-Audio's FireWire Solo or Audiophile interface with the M-Powered version of Pro Tools, four inputs and six outputs are available (including their digital I/O in S/PDIF format). Nevertheless, in the Digidesign manuals (and for that matter, several places in this book) you will occasionally see colloquial references to the channels or channel strips in the Mix window. Indeed, an audio track *is* a virtual signal path whose input(s) and output(s) can be configured to any physical input/output or internal mixing bus within the software mixing environment.

In Pro Tools, the number of audio tracks playing back simultaneously can be significantly greater than the number of audio channels that the hardware interface provides, as shown in Figure 2.6. The number of output channels on the interface determines your options for the main mix output assignment, for additional sends to external effects or headphone mixes, for looping audio through external audio devices, and so on. Obviously, the number of input channels on your audio hardware determines the number of discrete external audio sources that can be recorded simultaneously (and the return capabilities from external effects devices, whether these are monitored via Aux Inputs or used as hardware I/O inserts).

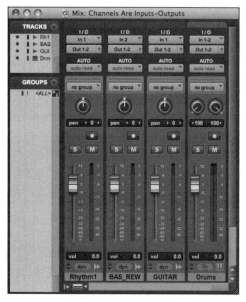

Figure 2.6   In the Pro Tools environment, channel refers to an audio input or output (analog and/or digital) on the audio interface. The number of input channels on this hardware determines how many audio sources you can record simultaneously, even though a much larger number of tracks may play back audio.

Digidesign Audio Interfaces—Past and Present   In the past, model numbers given to Digidesign's external audio interfaces for Pro Tools described their input/output capabilities (going back to the original four-channel interface for Pro Tools, later known as the 442 I/O). For example, 882 I/O interfaces had eight analog inputs, eight analog outputs, and two channels of digital I/O (one S/PDIF); the 1622 I/O had 16 analog inputs, two analog outputs, and two digital channels (one S/PDIF); the 888 I/O interfaces had eight analog inputs, eight analog outputs, and eight channels of digital I/O (four AES/EBU). At a certain point, however, this handy (albeit unexciting) nomenclature was abandoned.

The Digi 001 (now discontinued), for example, had eight analog inputs, eight analog outputs, plus up to eight channels of ADAT Lightpipe digital I/O and two channels of digital I/O (two RCA connectors for S/PDIF in and out). Plus, it provided a headphone output, MIDI in/out, and two microphone preamplifiers. So they called it the Digi 001—because it was a catchy name!

The Digi 002 (now discontinued) and Digi 003 families were the next steps up in hardware for Pro Tools LE (hence the names). Like their Digi 001 predecessor, they include eight analog inputs/outputs plus ADAT Lightpipe and S/PDIF digital I/O. Four higher-quality mic preamps are provided. These interfaces also offer a dedicated monitor output, a second MIDI output, and a footswitch jack for controlling playback or hands-free punch-in of recordings. The full Digi 002/Digi 003 audio interface is also a desktop control surface with motorized faders, while the 002R/003R versions consist of only a rack-mountable unit with the same connections. The 003 Rack + Factory offers eight mic inputs, eight line outputs, eight line/DI inputs, and two aux inputs, plus ADAT Lightpipe and S/PDIF digital I/O.

The original Mbox interface connects to your computer's USB port, offering two channels of audio I/O with inputs switchable between analog jacks and S/PDIF digital connectors. (It was called the Mbox because "222" would have been too too too boring!) The Mbox 2 model also connects to the host computer via USB, adding the capability to use both the analog and digital I/O simultaneously for 4×2 operation. It also features a MIDI input and output (as does the Mbox 2 Pro, which connects via FireWire and offers expanded I/O capabilities). The Mbox 2 Mini provides analog stereo I/O via a USB connection, while the Mbox 2 Micro provides stereo analog output *only*.

The names of external audio interfaces introduced with Pro Tools|HD highlight their most notable characteristic: the capacity for very high-resolution audio. The 96 I/O and 96i I/O offer 24-bit conversion at sample rates up to 96kHz. The 192 I/O is also 24-bit, supporting sample rates up to 192kHz, while the 192 Digital I/O is a digital-only version without the analog input or output sections. Most of these interfaces also incorporate AES/EBU and S/PDIF digital connections, plus simultaneous ADAT Lightpipe (eight Lightpipe channels on the 96 I/O, 16 on the 192 I/O, plus eight additional channels of Tascam TDIF on the 192 I/O) for interconnection with digital multitrack recorders from Alesis or Tascam and any other device compatible with these multichannel optical connection standards. In contrast, the 96i I/O has no Lightpipe or TDIF connectors, but offers 16 channels of analog input and stereo analog output, plus a single stereo S/PDIF digital I/O. You can use various combinations of the available connections on these HD interfaces for a maximum of 16 channels of I/O on any individual interface (and up to two interfaces connected to each HD card installed in the host computer). Chapter 18, "Pro Tools Power: The Next Step," provides more detailed information about hardware options for Pro Tools|HD systems.

Virtual Tracks Versus Physical Tracks

On a traditional multitrack tape recorder (analog *or* digital), audio information is recorded physically onto the tape, at a location directly corresponding to its playback time. During recording, audio data entering a Pro Tools audio track is written to a hard disk; a playlist then controls the triggering of audio playback at the appropriate time. The audio tracks in Pro Tools are virtual tracks. Instead of being recorded to any specific physical location, the source audio files for the audio regions you record and play back can sometimes actually reside at widely scattered locations on your computer's hard disk(s). At any moment, you can move audio events from one location or audio track to another regardless of where they were originally recorded or the disk location where they currently reside in order to experiment with different arrangements.

On most multitrack tape recorders, the assignment of outputs or playback voices to tape tracks is fixed. Its physical audio inputs and outputs 1–8 correspond to tape tracks 1–8, and that's it. In Pro Tools, however, the inputs and outputs on the audio interface are available to many different tracks for diverse purposes during all the phases of a project. One or more voices may handle playback for several of the audio tracks that you edit onscreen, but each of these can be independently assigned to different inputs and outputs (any physical input or output or an internal mixing bus). Simply put, voices act as a pool of audio converters enabling tracks to play. Each voice is available to play back a single channel of any audio tracks assigned to it, but it can only service one channel (for example, mono track, or one of the channels in a stereo track) at any given moment.

The basic LE and M-Powered versions of Pro Tools offer a maximum of 96 voices as they can play 48 stereo audio tracks simultaneously, and voice allocation is dynamically handled by Pro Tools to avoid conflicts. (The Music Production Toolkit option expands this capacity to 64 mono/stereo tracks on these systems, as does the DV Toolkit 2 for Pro Tools LE when a session is at a sample rate of 44.1kHz or 48kHz.) With the use of the Complete Production Toolkit at those sampling rates, you can play 128 mono or 64 stereo tracks at the same time! In HD versions, voice allocation can be dynamic or assigned manually, and the total number of tracks can exceed the number of voices. Figure 2.7 provides a simple representation of this concept. Many tracks are assigned to share the same voice, but as long as no two regions of audio within these tracks ever coincide, each can play all its required audio. Where they do overlap, whichever track is higher in the Edit window or further left in the Mix window has higher priority to play the regions it contains, even cutting in on another previously sounding track if necessary and stealing the voice.

It's as if you had many more channels of audio available than the number of voices (or audio polyphony) on your system might otherwise imply. That's where the concept of virtual tracks arises in the Digidesign realm—unlike a multitrack tape recorder, the number of available, mixable tracks actually exceeds the number of physical output channels. Again, the selected input and output of each track—and its routing, plug-ins, automation, and other parameters—are completely independent of any other tracks assigned to the same voice.

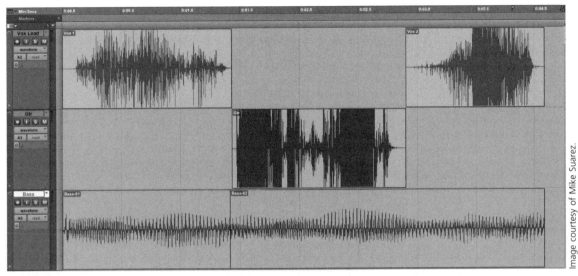

Figure 2.7 The virtual audio tracks in Pro Tools are graphic representations of playlists that determine when audio regions should be played. In HD systems, for an audio region to be heard, the voice assigned to the track must be available at that moment. The rest of the time, that voice is available to any other tracks assigned to it.

Destructive Versus Non-destructive Editing

Destructive editing is what happens when you cut and splice audio tape. In this scenario, the editing process permanently alters the actual recording medium in order to make changes. Recording on traditional multitrack tape recorders (even digital) is likewise destructive; if you record a new take of a solo or voice-over, the audio previously recorded on that same tape track is gone forever.

In contrast, the non-linear access provided by Pro Tools and other digital-audio workstations permits playing back regions (segments) of audio in any order, without altering the original recorded data. Therefore, hard-disk editing is non-destructive by nature. No matter how many regions and fades you create or how much you alter their playback order, the original recorded take is still intact on the disk. Even process-based effects (like the AudioSuite version of pitch shifting, for example) are non-destructive by default. They create new audio files to contain the result of the audio processing you apply.

As you record a solo or voice-over in Pro Tools, unless you specifically enable Destructive Recording mode (by choosing Options > Destructive Recording), each take is separately recorded to disk. Sequential numbers are automatically assigned to each region name so you can tell which takes are most recent. You can even composite together an ideal version using sections of various takes, all recorded on the same Pro Tools track (perhaps in Loop Record mode, in which case all your loop-recorded takes are actually regions within a single audio file).

Fade, Crossfade

A fade gradually increases the audio volume from zero at the beginning of an audio region or decreases it to zero at the end. Pro Tools offers a variety of shapes that determine how audio will fade from or to silence at the beginning or end of an audio region. These include a variety of Equal Power and Equal Gain curves, linear fades, S-curves, and so on. A crossfade occurs when the fade in and fade out for two adjacent regions in the same track overlap across the immediate boundary between them.

To create a fade, highlight a portion of audio at the beginning or end of an audio region in a track and select Edit > Fades > Create. The Fades dialog box (shown in Figure 2.8) allows you to audition and select various fade-in or fade-out shapes. (Actually, a new audio file is created in the Fade Files folder and appended to the beginning or end of the region for playback at the appropriate moment. Fades are therefore non-destructive—they don't alter the original audio file and can be revised as many times as necessary.) When two regions adjoin each other on the same track and your selection creates a fade across the boundary between them, the resultant crossfade overlaps each region, using material in each parent audio file beyond the current regions' current boundaries in the track. (Sometimes there is insufficient additional material available because one of the fades you're trying to create would extend beyond the beginning or end of its parent audio file. In these cases, Pro Tools will inform you.) Crossfades are very useful for overlapped effects. They can also minimize the audibility of edits—for example,

Figure 2.8 When you create a crossfade at the boundary between two adjacent audio regions, additional portions of the audio within their parent audio files are played before and after the transition. This figure shows the Fades dialog box, where fade-in and fade-out shapes are displayed.

where the decay of a cymbal needs to overlap the beginning of the next drum region in order to sound natural, when you're duplicating a shorter section of background ambience to fill a given amount of time and don't want the splices to be obvious, or when you're slicing up a stereo mix to create a new arrangement.

Mixing Concepts

Chapter 7, "The Mix Window," and Chapter 9, "Plug-ins, Inserts, and Sends," go into depth about mixing and signal routing in Pro Tools. This chapter limits its discussion of these topics to mentioning just a few key terms that acquire more expanded meanings in the Pro Tools environment (versus traditional analog mixers).

Grouping Tracks

In Pro Tools, a group is formed when multiple tracks are linked; in this way, their volume faders (as well as any volume automation you create while the group is active) are ganged together. Also, selections made in one track are mirrored in the other tracks in that group. For example, after selecting four backing vocal, drum, or sound-effects tracks, you could use the Track > Group command to create a Mix group and/or Edit group so that all four tracks can be treated as a unit. (Each group you create can be active in both the Mix and Edit windows, or in just one of these.) When a group is active, all changes made to volume, selections, and display format on one track in the group will apply to the others as well (as will the action of their Solo and Mute buttons and possibly the levels and mute status of their sends, if these items are enabled for that particular group in the Create Group or Modify Groups dialog boxes).

As you drag the volume for any one of the tracks in an active group, *all* their faders move up and down together. However, the relative volume levels of each individual fader, from when the group was created, are maintained. Output assignment and panning for each of the tracks in a group remain independent, as do voice-assignment and plug-in settings. By default, the mute status and level of any sends from individual tracks in a group are also independent. However, for each group, you can also link mutes and send-level adjustments by enabling these checkboxes when creating the group or in the Modify Groups dialog box (to access this dialog box, right-click or click and hold that group's name in the Groups List).

As shown in Figure 2.9, a track can belong to more than one group. Grouping tracks in Pro Tools can also make it easier to manage sessions; for example, you can select all tracks belonging to that group by clicking the group ID indicator of one of its member tracks in the Mix window and selecting from the pop-up menu that appears or by clicking next to that group's name in the Groups List panel. Pro Tools provides a Groups List in both the Mix and Edit windows for enabling, modifying, deleting, and renaming groups. You can also assign custom colors to each group to make it quicker and easier to identify its member tracks. While previous versions of Pro Tools were limited to 32 group IDs, versions 7.3 and higher support up to 104 group IDs, arranged in four banks of 26 each.

Figure 2.9 Grouping tracks can simplify mixing and editing. In this figure, the Group ID pop-up shows that the SFX2 audio track is included in the (a)sfx1 Mix group

---

Grouping Regions Version 7 of Pro Tools introduced the possibility of grouping regions in the Edit window (via the Region > Group command). For example, you might select several regions on a single track (segments of a guitar solo you've just edited together, for example), and then group them so that you can manipulate them as a single unit. A small icon appears in the lower-left corner to indicate that this object contains multiple source regions. You can even create groups across multiple tracks. (More about this in Chapter 6, "The Edit Window"; behavior and appearance of multitrack region groups depends on whether they were created with Time Grabber or Object Grabber selections.) In either case, you can also create fades on these region groups, even if they span source region boundaries or consist of multiple tracks. And of course, you can always ungroup regions later for further editing. Cool stuff!

Busses

A bus is an audio pipeline (or virtual audio cable) used to route signals within Pro Tools and can be used for many different purposes. You can use them individually, in stereo pairs, or in multi-channel groups. You can set the input or output of any audio, Aux Input, or Instrument track to one of the many busses that Pro Tools provides, and you can assign each of its sends to a bus. You can use busses in mono, as stereo pairs, or as multichannel paths in surround mixing. Busses are frequently used to group signals from multiple sources. For example, you could assign the main outputs from multiple tracks to a common stereo bus pair where they are combined, and then create an Aux Input track (covered later in this chapter) assigned to monitor that bus pair as its selected input source. This Aux Input's level fader now provides a single volume control for all tracks assigned to this bus. In turn, its own inserts (see the section "Inserts," later in this chapter) and sends also allow you to use effects that will affect this entire submix. (In conventional mixing boards, this is also sometimes known as a subgroup; this book, however, always uses the term submix to avoid any potential confusion with Edit and Mix groups in Pro Tools, described in the previous section. Also, the input and output paths for the physical audio ports on your audio interface, as defined in the I/O Setup dialog box, are also busses in their more general sense. To avoid confusion, however, this book will only use the term bus in reference to these internal pathways within the Pro Tools software itself.)

It's also common to use a bus in Pro Tools as the destination for sends from multiple tracks, combining their signals on their way to an Aux Input track with a reverb or delay insert, for example (something like the main Aux Send outputs on a live mixing console). Pro Tools|HD provides 128 internal mixing busses. Pro Tools LE and M-Powered support 32 busses (versus 16 busses prior to version 7).

Sends

Also known as an auxiliary send (or aux send) on traditional mixers, a send is a secondary audio signal pathway in a mixing console (or from tracks in the Pro Tools mixing environment). In Pro Tools, sends are used to additionally route signal from any audio, Aux Input, or Instrument track to another destination, independently from this track's main output assignment. You can route the 10 send points on each mixer strip either to a physical output on the audio hardware (the signal source for a performer's cue mix or an external effects processor, for example) or to any one of Pro Tool's internal mixing busses. Sends are frequently used from various tracks to a single destination—for instance, to apply a reverb or delay effect by selecting that internal mixing bus as the audio input source for an Aux Input track where one of these plug-in effects has been inserted. Unlike inserts, where a track's entire signal passes through the processor (a typical way to, for example, use a compressor or EQ plug-in), sends are *additional* destinations for a track's signal and have no effect on its main output. So if you've sent some of your vocal track to an Aux Input track where a reverb plug-in was inserted, both the dry (unprocessed) signal from the track itself and the reverb's wet output from the Aux Input track can be present in the main mix from Pro Tools. Sends can be mono, stereo, or multichannel. Of course, the level, pan, and muting of each send can be automated.

Aux Input Tracks

Aux Input tracks have a similar appearance to audio tracks in the Pro Tools mixing environment, but they cannot contain audio regions. They can be mono, stereo, or multichannel. The input selector on each Aux Input track allows you to select its audio source: actual, physical audio inputs on the hardware interface—as defined by the Input paths in the I/O Setup dialog box—or one of the internal mixing busses in Pro Tools. Alternatively, you could instantiate a virtual instrument plug-in on an Aux Input track, and that would be the source of the audio you hear at its output. Like audio tracks, you can also insert plug-in effects on Aux Inputs, create sends to other destinations, and automate their volume, pan, sends, or plug-in parameters. The output of each Aux Input can be assigned to any internal mixing bus or to an output path for one or more physical outputs on the audio hardware. Common uses of Aux Input tracks include the following:

- **Effects busses.** You might insert a reverb or delay plug-in on a stereo Aux Input and set its input source to stereo bus 1–2. You would then route stereo sends from various audio tracks to bus 1–2 so that you can feed some of their signal into the reverb or delay effect.

- **Subgroups.** You could assign the outputs of your seven drum tracks to bus 3–4 and then create a stereo Aux Input track with that bus pair selected as its input. Not only does this provide a single volume fader for the entire stereo drum submix, it also makes it convenient to, say, insert a single stereo compressor or other effect on it.

- **Monitoring external sources.** As mentioned previously, if you have an external synthesizer or module that is the sound source for MIDI tracks transmitted from Pro Tools, you will want to bring that device's audio output up in the Pro Tools mixer if possible. This allows you to incorporate that device's audio output when you bounce your mix to disk as a new file. (However, since you will sometimes want to permanently incorporate the audio output from these external sound sources into your Pro Tools, it is often preferable to record the device's output onto an audio track for this same purpose.) Of course, you can also insert effects (for example, reverb, compression, and EQ) on the Aux Input or audio track where an external source is being monitored. You could also use Aux Inputs to monitor (and process) audio channels from a multitrack tape recorder within the Pro Tools mixing environment.

- **Click track.** The Click plug-in, used to provide a metronome for your Pro Tools session, is usually instantiated on a mono Aux Input track. (This will be the case if you use the Track > Create Click Track command or set your preferences so that a click track is automatically created in all new sessions.)

- **Virtual instrument plug-ins.** Aux Input tracks were traditionally used for instantiating software instrument plug-ins in Pro Tools. Although these instrument plug-ins can still be used in this way in Pro Tools 8, Instrument tracks (see the next section) provide another option.

- **ReWire.** When you use this virtual signal-routing technology—see the section "ReWire (and the DigiReWire Plug-in)" later in this chapter—to stream audio channels from virtual-synthesizer or sampler programs into Pro Tools, their outputs can also be monitored via Aux Input tracks (or on audio tracks in HD versions of Pro Tools).

Instrument Tracks

Instrument tracks were introduced in version 7 of Pro Tools. An Instrument track can be roughly described as an Aux Input with a single incorporated MIDI track. As seen in the Mix window, an Instrument track is very similar to an Aux Input track, with an additional Instrument section that can be displayed at the top of its channel strips. In the Edit window, however, an Instrument track looks and acts more like a MIDI track. It contains MIDI notes and regions and provides breakpoint editing for automating volume, pan, and other MIDI controllers. (Details about MIDI track elements are provided in Chapters 6 and 7.) It is still possible to instantiate virtual-instrument plug-ins on an Aux Input or audio track, as in previous versions of Pro Tools. In fact, for multitimbral plug-ins (that respond to incoming MIDI data on more than one channel simultaneously, producing different sounds for each), this may still be your preferred method. However, when a single MIDI track is used for a monotimbral instrument, managing these directly as a single, combined Instrument track is easier, reducing onscreen clutter. Instrument tracks have their own distinctive icon in the Mix window, making it easier to distinguish them at a glance from Aux Inputs being used for other purposes—especially in larger sessions.

Master Fader Tracks

Master Fader tracks act as the last stage before audio signals are sent to the physical outputs. When a Master Fader is created and assigned one or more physical outputs, all audio signals ultimately routed to the same physical outputs can be boosted or attenuated by the Master Fader. Like audio and Aux Input tracks, Master Fader tracks enable you to insert plug-in effects into the signal chain for any of the output paths or internal mixing busses in your Pro Tools session and automate volume and plug-in parameters if desired. On Master Fader tracks, however, the Inserts section is post-fader only, as opposed to pre-fader on audio, Aux Input, and Instrument tracks. Master Fader tracks appear in the Edit and Mix windows alongside audio, Aux Input, MIDI, and Instrument tracks and have a similar appearance and behavior except that, like Aux Input tracks, they cannot contain regions. Master Fader tracks can be mono, stereo, or multichannel. They have no Record, Solo, or Mute buttons, no pan controls, and no input source selector (because, by definition, Master Fader tracks represent *only* the output stage of the selected physical output path or bus).

Adding Master Fader tracks has a negligible impact on system performance because in the Pro Tools software mixing environment, this object *already exists* in the signal path for all busses and output paths. Making this stage visible by creating a Master Fader track allows you to apply gain control, plug-in processing, automation, and so on to the selected mono, stereo, or multi-channel signal path.

A very typical use of a Master Fader track is to provide a final monitoring and control stage for your main mix output. For example, you might use outputs 1 and 2 on your audio interface for this. Creating a Master Fader track for that output pair provides a level meter, so you can confirm that your mix output isn't overloading. Even when you're bouncing a mixdown file to disk—described later in this chapter and also in Chapter 16, "Bouncing to Disk, Other File Formats"—rather than recording to some external device, clipping can still be a problem. You might also apply final EQ, dynamics processing (or dithering, when bouncing from 24-bit audio resolution down to 16-bit, for example), and other finishing effects (again, as post-fader effects) at this last output stage of your mix.

Master Fader tracks have many other uses, however. Many users create Master Fader tracks for the busses they're using for send effects—using its volume fader or dynamics plug-ins to avoid clipping due to signals being combined from many source tracks, for example. Others find Master Fader tracks extremely useful for the sole fact that their Inserts section is post-fader, meaning that the audio signal reaches the inserts after it passes through the fader stage, and is possibly boosted or attenuated by the fader. Depending on the sound you're after and how you want the effect to interact with any volume-fader automation prior to it in the signal chain, this can also be a powerful technique.

To make a very broad recommendation: Before starting work on a stereo project, you should always create a Master Fader track—at the very least so that you can see what's going on with your output levels. (As you will learn in Chapter 7, if you open an Output window for your main output's Master Fader track, it can always be visible even when you're working in the Edit window—*very* handy.) Other potential uses are limited only by your imagination and the degree of cleverness your projects demand!

Unity Gain When you create a new Master Fader track to monitor and/or control the path to an audio output or mixing bus in Pro Tools, its volume fader defaults to 0dB. This setting for a volume fader doesn't apply any gain change to audio signals passing through it. (That is, their volume isn't increased or decreased.) In professional audio, this is also known as unity gain.

Plug-ins

Like some other audio-, video-, and image-editing software, the Pro Tools software architecture is flexible and fairly open, allowing you to enhance your software mixing environment with additional processing modules according to your needs. One of the significant innovations Digidesign introduced in the digital-audio–editing field was the ability to incorporate additional effects-processing plug-ins into virtual insert points in the Pro Tools mixing/signal-routing environment. Most commonly, plug-ins are used for applying real-time effects to audio signals (something like using an insert point on an analog mixing board to patch in a compressor, for example). There are also process-based plug-ins (that is, instead of working in real time, they create a new audio file to store the transformed results of the selected effect settings). In Pro Tools, non–real-time effects are accessed via the AudioSuite menu.

Generally speaking, a plug-in is an algorithm or auxiliary software program that functions as an add-in module within another program; it cannot work by itself. Plug-ins add functionality to the host application and may be provided by the manufacturer or by third parties.

Third-Party Plug-Ins When Digidesign introduced the plug-in concept in Pro Tools' stereo predecessor, Sound Tools II, the company made the then-revolutionary choice to make the programming code available so that third parties could develop their own compatible plug-ins and market them to Digidesign users. Today, scores of companies offer plug-in software modules that are compatible with Pro Tools, some of which are virtual musical instruments, in addition to a wealth of sophisticated effects processors. Not only does this increase the variety of special-purpose effects available, it also allows plug-in developers to tailor sound quality and interfaces to suit every taste.

Many plug-in software modules are included with Pro Tools (in AudioSuite, RTAS, and/or TDM format, depending on the system you're using), including ones for equalization, dynamics processing, reverb, modulation, harmonic processing, and delays. Naturally, the more effects-processing plug-ins you use simultaneously, the more demands are made on your system's audio-signal–processing capabilities.

One of the great advantages of using plug-in software processing is that because the virtual signal-routing environment is completely software based, signal-degradation problems associated with a traditional analog studio setup (due to each device in a lengthy processing chain having its own input/output stages, digital converters, and other self-generated noise) are a thing of the past. Also, from a user's perspective, having the parameter editing for many different effects accessible from a reasonably consistent interface within a single program means that you spend a lot less time wading through manuals, proprietary operating systems, and jargon. Adding effects processing via plug-ins tends to be less expensive in the long run, too, because you aren't buying stacks of redundant boxes, each with its own inputs/outputs, displays, and so on. The ability to automate plug-ins' parameters opens up a whole new world of creative possibilities. Furthermore, a single plug-in can be used simultaneously at several locations in the same mix, so you're getting several effects for the price of one! Figure 2.10 represents the signal flow in an audio track, showing the location of the Inserts section where plug-in effects are instantiated.

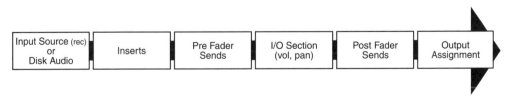

Figure 2.10 Signal flow of an audio track. During recording, an audio track's volume fader has no effect on the recorded level from the input. However, you can apply up to 12dB of additional gain to the monitoring level.

Instantiate   Just what does it mean to instantiate? The standard dictionary definition of the word goes something like this: "To represent an abstraction by a tangible or concrete example." So when you select a plug-in on an insert slot, you're creating an "instance" of this software process at that point within the host program's virtual signal-routing environment—a software object called EQ III, for example—that now demands some portion of your system's available processing power. You might instantiate numerous EQ, compressor, and other types of plug-ins on individual tracks.

Inserts

An insert, also known as an insert point, is a feature found in mixing consoles (and in the Pro Tools mix environment). Simply put, an insert is a break in the signal chain—an access point allowing a track's audio to be routed through an external device or, even more typically, to an analogous plug-in. Each audio track, Aux Input track, Instrument track, or Master Fader track in Pro Tools offers an Inserts section, with five slots where plug-ins can be instantiated. The pop-up menus for each slot in the Inserts section of a track are used to select and "patch in" a software plug-in—in which case the audio signal passes completely through that plug-in before proceeding through the rest of the track's plug-in slots and eventually to the track's volume/pan controls and output assignment. In Pro Tools, insert points are all pre-fader except on Master Fader tracks, where they are always post-fader.

Hardware I/O inserts can also be created at these same insert points. You can use them to send the audio signal out to an external device and back from an insert point via real physical audio inputs/outputs—either analog or digital—on your audio interface. This is how you might incorporate some specialized external effects processor into the Pro Tools mixing environment, for example. However, if you're using a 2×2 system like the Mbox 2 Mini (or an M-Audio interface such as the Fast Track USB, M-Audio Transit, Ozone, or Black Box), this isn't a practical option because your main outputs are already in use for your stereo mix.

Bouncing to Disk

When you issue the File > Bounce to > Disk command, a new audio file is created in real time, incorporating the sum of all the editing and automation information in the current session document that's passing though the output pair you select. Exactly what you're hearing during the bounce process (muted/unmuted tracks, automation, and everything else currently affecting the mix) is reflected in the resultant audio file. Bouncing to disk is comparable to the traditional studio practice of mixing down multitrack recordings to a stereo master recorder, except that it's a completely digital process, of course; no audible noise is introduced, as is the case when recording to an analog master tape. If you make any selection within the timeline of your Pro Tools session, only that portion will be included in the bounced file; otherwise, it includes the entire session from beginning to end. To burn an audio CD from your Pro Tools mix or save out a stereo file when collaborating with a video editor or multimedia author, you use this File > Bounce to > Disk command.

Also, if you've run out of playback voices or your computer's performance has begun to suffer from too many tracks and plug-ins in the current session, you might bounce down a stereo submix of multiple backing tracks (with effects) so that those voices are again available for record/playback of additional tracks. Of course, you can always retrieve the original backing tracks and revise that submix; like so many things in Pro Tools, it's a non-destructive process.

If you have external MIDI modules being triggered by MIDI tracks in your Pro Tools session, their audio output will need to be routed into Pro Tools in order to be incorporated into your bounced mix, usually through Aux Inputs.

Using Audio from Pro Tools in Other Programs The File > Bounce to > Disk command is one way to export selections of audio for use with other audio-capable programs. As noted, you might bounce out stereo files in order to create an audio CD with Mac programs such as Roxio's Jam or Toast or Apple's iTunes, or with Windows programs such as Steinberg's WaveLab, Roxio's Easy Media Creator, Sony/Sonic Foundry's CD Architect or Sound Forge, and so on. Converting regions or bounced mixes to AIF, WAV, or MP3 files at various resolutions is also a frequent intermediate step when producing audio for interactive media (CD-ROM, Internet, interactive DVD, and so on) with programs such as Macromedia's Director, Flash, or AuthorWare; Adobe's Premiere; Microsoft's PowerPoint or Visual Basic; ToolBook; 3D Game Studio; and others.

The Bounce to Disk dialog box allows you to choose an audio file format, including AIF, SD2, Broadcast WAV, QuickTime audio, MP3, and others. You can also choose the number of channels, bit-depth (16, 24, and in some cases 8 bits per sample), and sample rate for the bounced file. You may be able to select between 8-, 16-, and 24-bit resolution in the bounced file—but why would you ever want to bounce to a lesser resolution than the original recording? One extreme example would be in order to produce 8-bit files for interactive media (multimedia CD-ROMs and such) in situations where limitations on disk space or system throughput don't permit playback of full CD-quality 16-bit, 44kHz stereo audio. (By all means, though, try reducing the sample rate or compressing the audio data before resorting to 8-bit audio if possible!) For music production, you might bounce from a 96kHz, 24-bit session down to 44.1kHz, 16-bit files because that's what you'll need to burn an audio CD for demo or evaluation purposes. For in-depth information about this process, see Chapter 16.

Digidesign Technology

Following are several key technical terms that are constantly referenced in Digidesign's manuals and other documentation. More than simply marketing constructs, these terms refer to important technical innovations by Digidesign and are enabling technologies for Pro Tools in general.

DAE (Digidesign Audio Engine)

An operating-system extension for real-time digital-audio processing, DAE automatically operates in the background when you launch Pro Tools. It mediates access between the Pro Tools software and the audio hardware. It also handles the pre-loading of digital-audio data from disk into the DAE playback buffer for smooth playback at the proper time. You may occasionally need to change the size of this playback buffer, depending on your hardware configuration and how fragmented or slow your hard disks are.

Occasionally, if something about your system is producing a performance error in Pro Tools, an alert box may appear with a numerical reference to a "DAE error." If you type this number into the Digidesign Answerbase, found in the Support area of the company's Web site (http://www. digidesign.com), you will often find useful information about possible causes of and solutions to your problem.

TDM (Time-Division Multiplexing)

TDM is a multichannel signal-routing matrix implemented within the Pro Tools software environment (HD version only, not the LE version used with Digi 003, Digi 002, and Mbox 2/Mbox configurations or the M-Powered version used with M-Audio interfaces). TDM operates at a much higher multiple of the audio sample rate so that more than one stream of audio can be routed and processed within a single data bus. TDM requires specific Digidesign hardware configurations, all of which feature dedicated digital signal processing (DSP) chips on PCI cards in the host computer and sometimes an expansion chassis for additional PCI cards in larger system configurations.

TDM is also a plug-in architecture that requires a TDM-capable hardware configuration. TDM plug-ins can often be much more robust (in other words, processing intensive) than host-based effects (the RTAS processing and routing architecture supported by Pro Tools LE and M-Powered) because they can rely on dedicated DSP chips on the Digidesign cards rather than sharing the host CPU's processing power with the operating system and Pro Tools itself. TDM is the plug-in architecture used in Digidesign's high-end Pro Tools configurations (although these also support RTAS and AudioSuite plug-in formats), including all the Pro Tools|HD systems. (Their predecessors—24|Mix, Pro Tools|24, and Pro Tools III—were also TDM systems, but don't support current versions of the Pro Tools software.)

TDM II is the revamped version of Digidesign's TDM bus architecture that was introduced with the Pro Tools|HD hardware and is used in versions 7.0 and higher of Pro Tools HD software. TDM II doubles the number of time slots in previous TDM systems (from 256 to 512), which is essential for handling the higher sampling rates supported by HD hardware. Its redesigned architecture also makes much more efficient use of the available TDM resources. However, for simplicity's sake, this book will often simply refer to TDM systems when discussing HD systems (as well as the older, TDM-based 24|Mix systems, which don't support Pro Tools software higher than 6.4.1) using the HD version of the Pro Tools software.

More about Signal Processing and Routing in Pro Tools   For more information about how Pro Tools routes audio within its virtual mixing and processing environment, see Chapter 9, which discusses TDM and RTAS plug-ins, ReWire, and other features of the totally integrated virtual studio provided by Pro Tools.

ReWire (and the DigiReWire Plug-in)

ReWire is a technology developed by Propellerhead Software (developers of the Reason program) for routing digital audio, MIDI, tempo, and transport commands between multiple programs running on the same computer. A ReWire application (such as Reason or Ableton Live, for example) is slaved to Pro Tools. Any sequences, loops, or drum patterns in the slaved ReWire program will start and stop under the control of the Pro Tools Transport and tempo. Likewise, you can assign the output from any Pro Tools MIDI track to one of the active MIDI-compatible modules within the slave program.

After enabling, say, Reason on a track in Pro Tools, you can then choose which of the virtual output audio channels from that program you want to appear in that particular track. Because these programs have their own mixing capabilities, the channel(s) from the slaved ReWire program that you enable for routing into Pro Tools may represent a single instrument module or a submix that sums many of these together. This is enabled by the DigiReWire plug-in (see Figure 2.11), which must be active within your Plug-Ins folder in order for you to use ReWire.

Figure 2.11   Examples of mono (left) and stereo (right) DigiReWire plug-ins.

Elastic Audio (Versions 7.4 and Higher)

Elastic Audio is Digidesign's term for a set of audio-processing features introduced in version 7.4 of Pro Tools. Elastic Audio combines beat and tempo analysis, transient detection, and sophisticated, non-destructive algorithms for real-time time compression and expansion of audio regions in Pro Tools tracks. Among other things, because the "native" tempo and transient events (such as the attack of a note or chord, or a drum hit) within the audio region are detected, it is possible to reposition ("quantize") these audio events to a given rhythmic value—$1/8$ notes, for example. Event markers identify the transients and other audio events, whether automatically detected by the selected Elastic Audio algorithm (whose sensitivity to transients can be adjusted, using the Elastic Properties window) or manually placed by the user. Warp markers can then be used to drag an audio event to a given position in the Pro Tools timeline, with the immediately surrounding audio stretched or squeezed to accommodate this shift. An important part of Elastic Audio, which is explained in more detail in Chapter 12, "The Pro Tools Groove," is that when drum loops and other audio files that have been pre-analyzed are previewed in the DigiBase browser windows, they can play back at the current session tempo. In Figure 2.11, normal waveform view is seen in the lower track, while the Elastic Audio analysis view reveals Event markers detected by the Elastic Audio algorithm as vertical bars superimposed over the audio. You can add, move, or remove Event markers as necessary.

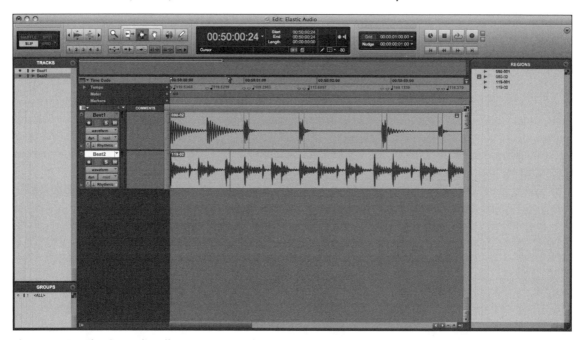

Figure 2.12 Elastic Audio allows events within audio regions to be adjusted to the session tempo or quantized via the same grid and groove options that have been available for MIDI events in previous versions of Pro Tools.

Introduced in Pro Tools version 8 is Elastic Pitch, which allows real-time pitch transposition over a two-octave range. On tracks with Elastic Audio enabled, pitch changes can be applied to whole regions. If a user needs to affect only a portion of a region—for example, a single word in a vocal track—then that portion needs to be made into a region of its own before Elastic Pitch is applied.

Summary

While you've hopefully found this overview of the fundamentals useful, these ideas will become clearer as you work through practical examples in the rest of this book. It's essential to have a good handle on basic concepts and to know the proper names for things in order to organize your thoughts, solve problems, and effectively use this software. The *Pro Tools Reference Guide* also provides an excellent overview of these concepts, and should be thoroughly explored by all users. It is a PDF document that you can access in the Digidesign > Documentation > Pro Tools folder or directly from the Help menu within Pro Tools. As stated elsewhere, this book is *not* intended to be a substitute for the *Reference Guide*! At about 700 pages, when combined with the *Keyboard Shortcuts* (30+ pages) and *DigiRack Plug-ins Guide* (120+ pages), this is the most comprehensive and detailed reference available for Pro Tools. *Pro Tools 8 Power!* distills this wealth of information into the strategic essentials, offers real-world examples and recommendations, explores how Pro Tools interacts with other studio gear, provides practical tips for both new and experienced users, offers primers for specific applications (like postproduction, music, and interactive media), and gets you up and running as soon as possible. Appendix A of this book, "Further Study, and Resources on the Web," guides you to other learning resources for Pro Tools and digital audio in general. Chapter 3, "Your System Configuration," provides guidelines for a working computer and audio hardware configuration for Pro Tools, and Chapter 4, "Creating Your First Pro Tools Session," dives right into creating a session in Pro Tools. If you're already a Pro Tools user, you may want to skip ahead to Chapter 5, "The Transport Window," Chapter 6, "The Edit Window," and Chapter 7, "The Mix Window," which, you guessed it, break down the elements in the Transport, Edit, and Mix windows. Some of this information may be review, but you're guaranteed to find some useful tidbits there as well.

3 Your System Configuration

It can be hard to separate marketing and hype from reality when dealing with computers—or pro audio in general, for that matter. And of course, just as computers evolve from year to year, Pro Tools software and hardware are constantly improved and upgraded, which in turn can increase the system requirements needed to run them. There are some fundamental ideas to keep in mind, though, plus some peculiar requirements for multichannel digital audio and hard-disk recording that are definitely worth reviewing here. You also need to understand the basic peripheral devices required to successfully interconnect Pro Tools with other devices in your studio.

Basic Components

Let's consider the basic hardware components—computer and peripheral gear—you need in order to run any version of Pro Tools.

Computer

Exact system requirements vary widely according to your Pro Tools configuration—audio interfaces, Pro Tools software version, and optional hardware and software (including virtual instruments and other processing-intensive plug-ins). But even for currently shipping LE and M-Powered versions of Pro Tools, the central processing unit (CPU) of your Macintosh computer needs to be at least a G5 or faster G4. (More recent Intel-based Macs are preferable, including dual-core, quad-core, and 8-core models. This is especially true for HD configurations and situations where higher sampling rates and larger numbers of tracks are required.) Absolute minimum Windows configurations start with Pentium 4, Xeon, or some AMD Athlon XP and Opteron CPUs, with dual processors recommended for many applications. As you can imagine, requirements for an expanded Pro Tools|HD system are even more demanding, including specific chipsets on the motherboard, CPU models, and voltage capacities in the PCIe (or PCI) slots, to name a few. High-powered computer configurations that may be excellent for other application types (such as graphics or 3D rendering, for instance) can have some characteristics that represent serious drawbacks for high-resolution multitrack audio. If you're purchasing a system as a first-time Pro Tools user, you would be well advised to distrust the advice of any computer "expert" friends unless they are actually Pro Tools users!

The system requirements for Pro Tools evolve over time as newer versions of the program are released and available Digidesign hardware changes. For this reason, before purchasing *any* computer for Pro Tools use, be sure to check the Compatibility section of the Digidesign Web site's (http://www.digidesign.com) Support area for current system requirements and detailed compatibility documents. You will also find links there for companies that provide audio-optimized Windows systems for Pro Tools such as Terra Digital Audio, Sweetwater, Guitar Center, PC Audio Labs, Rain Recording, and others. Such a system can be an excellent investment for a serious production rig. Although the Digidesign Web site is always your best source for up-to-date information, you might also take a look at the DUC (Digidesign Users Conference) site at http://duc.digidesign.com for test results, advice, and recommendations from other Pro Tools users. Windows users in particular will want to note the ongoing "sticky" threads (which always stay at the top of the list) in the forums for Windows LE and M-Powered versions, where users share their experiences with different CPUs and system components.

Given the unusual demands that digital audio makes on the computer, only very specific operating system versions are supported or recommended for a given release of Pro Tools software. Don't upgrade your operating system until you've confirmed that it works properly with the version of Pro Tools you're using. Here are some general guidelines about Windows/Macintosh operating systems and Pro Tools:

- **Windows.** Windows XP with Service Pack 2 is the absolute minimum requirement for current Windows versions of Pro Tools. While most Pro Tools configurations are compatible with either the Home or Professional versions of Windows XP, the latter may be required with certain Avid network and video peripherals. Service Pack 3 is approved as well with no known compatibility differences between SP2 and SP3. Windows Vista (32-bit) Ultimate and Business versions with Service Pack 1 are approved by Digidesign for running Pro Tools 8.

- **Macintosh.** Mac OS X version 10.5.5 (a.k.a. "Leopard") or higher is required for the Macintosh version of Pro Tools 8.

OS Requirements for Older Versions of Pro Tools Older versions of Pro Tools require the following:

- **Macintosh.** For Pro Tools 7.x, OS 10.4.x (a.k.a. "Tiger") was required, with Pro Tools 7.1.3 being the first version to be adapted for use on Intel chip-based Macintoshes. OS X was required for all Pro Tools 6.xx versions (Mac OS 10 or higher, with some version of 10.3.x usually preferred, depending on your software/hardware combination). Pro Tools Free 5.01 and some legacy Pro Tools software/hardware may work on older computer platforms, including some faster models among the pre-G3 PowerMac series. Mac OS 8.6 is the minimum for most 5.xx versions of Pro Tools (including Pro Tools Free 5.01), with Mac OS 9 highly recommended. None of the legacy Pro Tools software versions 5.31 and lower are supported under Mac OS X, even in Classic mode!

- **Windows.** Pro Tools 7.4 was the first version to run on Windows Vista. For Windows XP Home and Professional users who installed Service Pack 2, Pro Tools 7.0 to 7.4 was available. Windows XP with Service Pack 1 is required for 6.xx versions of Pro Tools. Note, however, that legacy Pro Tools software versions 5.3 and lower do not support Windows XP, and Pro Tools Free 5.01 works with Windows 98 SE or ME only.

As with most other software, you may find both minimum and recommended amounts of memory (RAM) listed among the system requirements on Digidesign's Web site. Count on needing the recommended amount in order to truly work comfortably.

By the way, you will want to run a lean machine because, as you can probably imagine, multitrack digital audio is fairly taxing on the computer's resources. Don't clutter up your operating system with a lot of background processes that may interfere (for example, screen savers, file and printer sharing, disk indexers, MP3 and Internet time servers, Norton's File Saver, and so on).

Caution: If It Ain't Broke... Users of processing-intensive, real-time applications like Pro Tools should never automatically download operating-system updates before confirming through the Digidesign Web site that the updates are compatible with their current software version. Admittedly, Digidesign is very cautious and can be somewhat slow to "bless" a given OS update. After seeing a couple dozen users report no problems on the Digidesign User Conference, you may decide to assume a certain amount of risk, installing a minor but not-yet-qualified update. (For Macintosh Pro Tools users it is always preferable to download the Combo Update from the Apple Web site rather than allowing the Software Update utility to install any upgrade of the Mac OS itself.) However, when the update is a full decimal number on the Mac OS or a Service Pack update on Windows, make *sure* you have thought out an exit strategy (including a full system backup) before potentially debilitating your production system with an incompatible update.

Monitor(s)

For all versions of Pro Tools, the monitor needs to be set at 1024×768 resolution or higher. Although a 15-inch monitor is definitely workable, you will be much more comfortable with a 17-inch or larger model. Most high-end Pro Tools users prefer to use *two* large monitors—for example, opening the Pro Tools Mix window on one and the Edit window on the other. Guitar and bass players using Pro Tools in their project studios should opt for an LCD flat-panel display because traditional CRT monitors create buzzing through their magnetic instrument pickups unless the instrument is moved a meter or two away from the monitor while recording—not terribly convenient if you're the sole operator! Most users also find that LCD monitors cause less eyestrain. They also produce less heat, which is always a concern in small project studios.

Hard Drive(s)

You need a very large, fast hard drive for recording and playing back multiple tracks of digital audio. We suggest several dozen gigabytes at the very least, especially because larger hard drives routinely also offer better performance. As a general rule, count on using a 7,200 RPM or faster hard drive for recording audio. If you are an HD user recording at higher sample rates, 10,000 RPM drives are definitely worth a look. As with the basic computer model itself, sustained throughput and other performance requirements for drives used on digital-audio workstations such as Pro Tools are different from non–real-time applications such as graphics-processing and network servers. For high performance, it is worthwhile to investigate disk-drive offerings from companies that specialize in products for audio recording such as Glyph and Avid. Be sure to consult with your Digidesign dealer or experienced Pro Tools users before making any sizable investment in disks for audio recording. Although it is possible to use them on LE and M-Powered systems, Universal serial bus (USB) hard drives do not offer optimal performance for recording audio.

Currently, the most common disk configuration among Pro Tools users consists of one or more Digidesign-certified hard drives connected to the computer's FireWire (IEEE 1394) port. This is very cost-effective for Mac users especially, because all recent models include built-in FireWire ports. The drive mechanism *must* be based on the Oxford 911 chipset to work properly with Pro Tools, however. All current LE and M-Powered systems can achieve their maximum track counts using multiple FireWire drives, an increasingly affordable option to help get the most out of your setup. SCSI disk subsystems are not obligatory.

In the past, larger Pro Tools configurations used multiple drives on a SCSI connection (which would require an add-in SCSI card in virtually all current computer models). For example, expanded Pro Tools|HD (or 24 MIX) configurations can use SCSI drives attached to one of several ATTO SCSI accelerator cards that Digidesign supports for audio. It's been many years since Mac and Windows computers have incorporated factory SCSI drives. Instead, they have an internal SATA drive where the operating system and programs are loaded. You can either add SCSI drives internally and/or connect external drives. Although these systems can also use FireWire drives, in order to obtain maximum track counts on some configurations, a SCSI card and disks may still be desirable—especially if this helps lighten the load on the CPU itself.

SATA drives are also an excellent option for Windows users, offering very high performance to support large track counts of high-resolution audio. One example is the Raptor 10,000 RPM drive by Western Digital, which, when combined with the Intel ICH-5 controller chipset on the computer's motherboard, can deliver levels of performance comparable to UltraSCSI disks.

Users of Pro Tools hardware in the Mbox 2 family, original Mbox, and even Digi 003 or Digi 002 systems (as well as the now-discontinued Digi 001 or ToolBox configurations) can rely to a certain extent on the high-capacity, high-speed internal ATA hard disks in more powerful current computers. However, it is always preferable to dedicate a separate hard drive for audio data even on these systems, especially to achieve 32 tracks of simultaneous playback. (A dedicated hard drive is obligatory for HD systems.) If this isn't possible, you should at least format your large internal drive into two or more partitions, dedicating the larger one exclusively to Pro Tools session documents and audio files and reserving the other for the operating system and programs. Along with the performance benefits, using separate drives or partitions makes maintenance and disk reorganization much easier and allows for disk optimization of the audio volume(s) while still booted off the system volume. If you're working at 44.1kHz sample rates and your audio-track counts typically don't exceed a dozen or so, you may find that this setup provides acceptable performance for your Pro Tools LE or M-Powered system.

Figure 3.1 shows the Workspace window in Pro Tools, where you can view all the hard disks on your system, their capacity, and available free space. You can also specify which are eligible for audio recording and search for audio files by name anywhere on the system. Once you locate the audio or MIDI files you want on your system's hard disk, you can drag them from the Workspace browser into the Edit window's Regions List or track display area. To provide some perspective on just how much space digital audio requires on your hard drive, Table 3.1 shows the effects of sample rate and bit depth on audio file size.

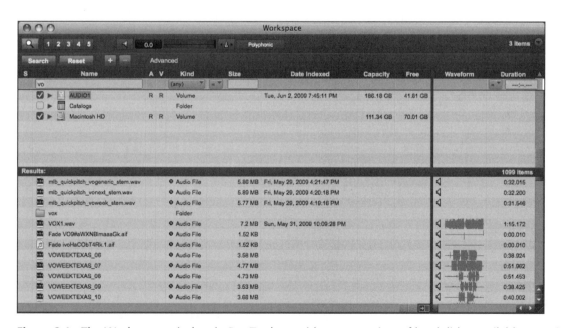

Figure 3.1   The Workspace window in Pro Tools provides an overview of hard disks, available capacity, and which of them can be used for recording or playback (transfer) only. You can also search for files here and drag them into the tracks or Regions List of your current session.

Table 3.1 Big and Bigger: The Effects of Sample Rate and Bit Depth on Audio File Size

Sample Rate	Bit Depth	1 Minute (Mono)	1 Minute (Stereo)
44.1kHz	16 bits/sample	5MB	10MB
44.1kHz	24 bits/sample	7.9MB	15.8MB
48kHz	16 bits/sample	5.7MB	11.4MB
48kHz	24 bits/sample	8.6MB	17.2MB
96kHz	24 bits/sample	17.2MB	34.4MB
192kHz	24 bits/sample	34.4MB	68.8MB

Tech Support Folder The Digidesign Web site (http://www.digidesign.com) offers a downloadable set of utilities and test Pro Tools sessions called the Tech Support Folder. A few useful examples: The PC Wizard program generates a complete listing of what components are installed on your Windows system. The Generate Version List feature creates a text file with the version number of the Pro Tools program, all installed plug-ins, and other optional programs from Digidesign. Lastly, the Delete Preferences and Databases feature lets you eliminate all these in a single step. (On Windows, these files are moved into the Local Settings/Temp folder for your user name, and on Macintosh they are moved directly into the Trash folder.)

Peripheral Equipment

Pro Tools expansion options and additional hardware peripherals are covered in more detail in Chapter 18, "Pro Tools Power: The Next Step." In the meantime, this section takes a look at some of the basic equipment that will complement your Pro Tools configuration in a studio setting.

MIDI Interface

If you will use external MIDI controllers or modules with Pro Tools (for example, to record performances into MIDI tracks, to play back MIDI data being sent from Pro Tools, or to connect certain external control surfaces to Pro Tools), some sort of MIDI interface is required unless these can be connected to the computer directly via USB. MIDI is a serial communications protocol that uses 5-pin DIN connectors. Your computer's MIDI interface acts as an adapter to convert the MIDI protocol to a format usable within the software environment. Various MIDI interfaces can be purchased, depending on your requirements and the connection methods your computer supports for this optional piece of gear. One example is shown in Figure 3.2.

Digidesign audio interfaces in the Mbox 2, Digi 003, and Digi 002 families offer built-in MIDI In and MIDI Out connectors (as did the older Digi 001 interface). So do some of the

Figure 3.2   A multiport MIDI interface. (Shown: the MOTU MIDI Express XT, which connects to the computer via USB.)

Pro Tools–compatible audio interfaces from M-Audio and the Command|8 external USB control surface from Digidesign. Otherwise, your options include the following:

- **Windows.** The cheapest MIDI interface option is to use a standard PC sound card, most of which have a small, built-in port for MIDI. (Be aware, however, that some of these consumer sound cards may present conflicts for Pro Tools applications.) Usually, you must separately purchase a small Y adapter cable, which splits out from a 15-pin D-shaped connector on the card into two 5-pin DIN connectors for MIDI in/out. However, for more serious applications, you will want a more professional, dedicated MIDI interface. For multiple MIDI ports or SMPTE synchronization, an external MIDI interface is generally required, connected via a card installed in the computer's PCI slot, a parallel port device, or, most commonly among current models, an external device connected to the computer's USB port.

- **Macintosh.** External MIDI interfaces are attached to the USB port.

It's easy to upgrade your MIDI interface as requirements change. The Mac version of Pro Tools interacts with the configuration defined in the operating system's Audio MIDI Setup utility, an intermediate software layer that facilitates managing the naming and connecting of MIDI peripherals and negotiates between programs like Pro Tools and the MIDI interface along with any external MIDI devices that are connected to it. After changing to another model of MIDI interface and setting it up in this system utility (found in the Utilities subfolder of the Applications folder on your system volume), the new port configuration will appear the next time you access MIDI output assignments from the MIDI tracks within Pro Tools. Again, the Digi 003, Digi 002, Mbox 2, and Mbox 2 Pro feature MIDI in/out connectors built into the external interface, as do some of the M-Audio interfaces and the Command|8 control surface. If that's sufficient for your needs, no separate MIDI interface may be required for your system.

In Windows, the MIDI Studio Setup window (discussed in Chapter 10, "MIDI," and shown there in Figure 10.4) provides very similar functionality. After configuring an external MIDI instrument on the appropriate port of your MIDI interface, its enabled send/receive channels for MIDI and patchname documents (if available) can be selected from MIDI tracks within Pro Tools.

Digidesign manufactured its own high-end MIDI interface, the MIDI I/O (now discontinued), which connects to Windows or Macintosh computers via USB. Along with 10 MIDI inputs and 10 MIDI outputs, it also supports MIDI timestamping features in Pro Tools. This feature uses a data buffer within the interface itself to maintain proper timing even when very dense streams of MIDI data from multiple tracks are being sent out through the interface. Chapter 10 includes a section about the MIDI I/O, providing more details and a look at the front and back panels of this unit.

Direct USB Connections for MIDI Controllers Some controller keyboards (and sound modules) can connect directly to the computer via its USB port. These range from very simple models to full-featured controllers. In such cases, if you are relying exclusively on software-based instruments for Pro Tools as the sound source for your MIDI tracks—via ReWire, RTAS, or TDM plug-ins—you may not require a MIDI interface at all.

SMPTE Interface

SMPTE time code is used in the video and film industry to synchronize audio devices to a master video deck, and also for synchronizing MIDI and audio software to multitrack audiotape machines. A series of numbers representing hours, minutes, seconds, frames, and subframes is encoded either into an audio signal (linear time code, or LTC) or within the upper lines of the video frame (vertical interval time code, or VITC). An SMPTE interface for digital-audio workstations translates these encoded signals into MIDI time code (MTC), which carries the same information encoded in the MIDI protocol. With SMPTE synchronization, when the Pro Tools transport is in Online mode, it will know what time location is currently playing on the video and correctly play the part of that session's timeline that corresponds to that SMPTE location. (SMPTE stands for Society of Motion Picture and Television Engineers.)

In many cases, multiport MIDI interfaces from manufacturers such as Mark of the Unicorn, M-Audio, and others additionally incorporate audio inputs/outputs for synchronizing to time code in LTC format. Because LTC is a way of encoding SMPTE time code as an audio signal, this is also the most common method for synchronizing Pro Tools with multitrack tape decks (both analog and digital). There are also synchronization peripherals for VITC (time code embedded into each frame of a video signal). More sophisticated units, such as the Sync I/O (now discontinued) by Digidesign (shown in Figure 3.3); its successor, the Sync HD; or Mark of the Unicorn's MIDI Timepiece AV, also allow the internal sample clock of your Digidesign audio hardware to be resolved or slaved to incoming time code or video sync so things stay perfectly locked together over long periods of time. For more information, see Chapter 11, "Synchronization."

Photo courtesy of Digidesign.

Figure 3.3   Sync I/O, an SMPTE synchronizer from Digidesign.

MIDI Instruments/Controllers

Your keyboards, drum modules, MIDI modules, MIDI effects, and other MIDI controllers (guitar, wind, or percussion, for example) usually feature MIDI in/out—and sometimes thru—connectors. Multiple MIDI devices can be daisy-chained on a single MIDI output if your MIDI interface only features one in/out (like the Mbox 2, the discontinued Digi 001 interface, and many of M-Audio's audio interfaces for Pro Tools M-Powered). However, routing tracks from Pro Tools out to several multitimbral modules (which can respond with different sounds to incoming events on multiple MIDI channels) could be a little tricky in this setup because you've only got 16 MIDI channels to work with, and each module may be listening to all of them. With a larger number of independently addressable MIDI out ports (such as on Digi 003 and Digi 002 interfaces or the Command|8 control surface, which have one input and two outputs for MIDI), you could connect each external module to a separate port for 32 outgoing MIDI channels with two ports, 96 channels if your MIDI interface has six MIDI out ports, and so on. Digidesign's own MIDI I/O features 10 MIDI inputs and outputs for a potential total of 160 MIDI channels.

The important thing to remember is that MIDI events going between Pro Tools and your MIDI devices are data, and the MIDI interface connections described here have nothing to do with how all the audio outputs of your MIDI modules get back into the Pro Tools mix (so that these sound sources can be bounced to disk together with your audio tracks and software instruments). If you have enough available inputs on your external audio interface, audio from MIDI modules can enter the Pro Tools mix via various Aux In tracks (or Instrument tracks, which, without instrument plug-ins instantiated on them, behave like Aux In tracks). The input source for those tracks would be set to monitor the physical outputs where those devices are attached to your audio interface. Otherwise, particularly if you're using an audio interface that provides only two analog audio inputs, you might use a good small mixing board. This would allow you to pre-mix all the MIDI modules to stereo before that signal enters the Pro Tools mix—via a single stereo Aux In track set to monitor the stereo inputs on the audio interface where the mixer's outputs are connected. Figure 3.4 shows a typical MIDI configuration for a project studio.

Software Instruments   Software-based virtual synthesizers and samplers represent another increasingly popular class of MIDI instrument. Their virtual audio outputs are routed within audio/MIDI programs such as Pro Tools. Benefits of these virtual instruments over external physical sound sources for MIDI parts include elimination of noise (because there are no analog connections in the signal path) and the fact that you can use many MIDI sound sources—with superior user interfaces—without stacking up a lot of bulky modules in your studio! If you're just starting to build up your Pro Tools/MIDI studio (and if your computer has sufficient processing power to handle running additional software instrument plug-ins or programs simultaneously with Pro Tools), this is a great way to go. It's much simpler, offers total recall and greater control, and takes up less space.

Among the industry-standard software architectures that have emerged in recent years, here are the methods Pro Tools currently supports for using virtual (software-based) instruments:

- Many virtual instruments are available in RTAS format (which can be used in Pro Tools LE, M-Powered, and HD versions). Examples include IK Multimedia's SampleTank 2; Ultimate Sound Bank's PlugSoundPro, Retro Organs, Synths Anthology, and X-Treme FX; MOTU's MX4 (Mac only), MachFive, Ethno Instrument, and Symphonic Instrument; Applied Acoustics' Tassman-4, String Studio, VS-1, Ultra Analog VA-1, and Lounge Lizard EP-3; fxpansion's BFD 2 and Guru; Spectrasonics' Stylus, Trilogy, and Omnisphere; Tascam's GVI; and Native Instruments' B4 Organ II, Acoustik Piano, Elektrik Piano, Battery 3, Absynth 4, Massive, Pro-53, and FM8.

- Virtual instruments in TDM format (not supported on LE or M-Powered systems) include McDSP's Synthesizer One (also available as RTAS), Access Music's Virus Indigo, Digidesign's SoundFuel SOLID, and Duy's SynthSpider.

- HDTM is an older plug-in format that supported virtual instruments on Pro Tools TDM systems using versions 6.*xx* of the software. It is *not* supported under Pro Tools 7 and 8. In most cases, when you open an older session containing HTDM plug-ins, these will automatically convert to RTAS format.

- ReWire is a software architecture that allows audio from other audio programs and virtual instruments to appear in the Pro Tools mix. Examples include Propellerhead's Reason, Celemony Melodyne Studio, and Ableton's Live. Various output channels of virtual audio signals from these separate programs can then be routed into the Pro Tools mix via DigiReWire, an RTAS plug-in.

"Soft synth" offerings by various companies grow exponentially every month, and exciting new developments in plug-in synthesis are regularly unveiled. For more information about software-based instruments, see the section "Virtual Instruments" in Chapter 10.

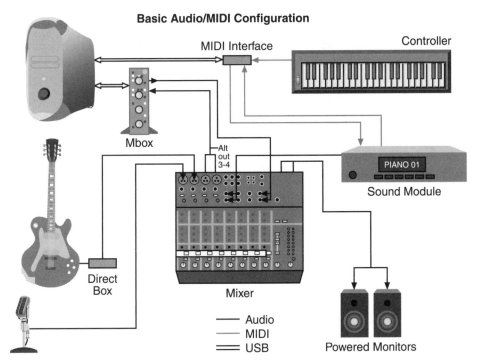

Basic Audio/MIDI Configuration

Figure 3.4 In this example, a separate MIDI interface handles transmission of MIDI data between Pro Tools, an external MIDI controller, and an external MIDI module. For the sound from external MIDI instruments to be incorporated when you bounce out a mix file from Pro Tools, their audio outputs are typically routed into the inputs of your Pro Tools audio hardware and monitored via an Aux In track in Pro Tools.

CD/DVD Recording Drive

A CD- or DVD-recording drive is not officially a system requirement for Pro Tools, but trust us, you need one! First, you're working with audio, so no matter what your area of expertise, you will occasionally need to burn audio CDs from the mixes you bounce out of Pro Tools. And if you're creating audio files for interactive media, you will want to throw all those AIF, MP3, or WAV files onto a CD-ROM or DVD-ROM for delivery to developers. If you're in video production, it can sometimes be simpler and more economical to burn CDs when delivering your OMF or AIF files to Avid, FinalCut Pro, or Media 100 video editors (assuming you don't share a network server for media files) rather than using some other removable media.

More importantly, however, when your Pro Tools session folders (including the Audio Files folders within them) run into hundreds of megabytes, how are you going to back them up for data security or archive them off the system when projects are completed? CD recorders and media have become very inexpensive, and this may be sufficient for many home-studio users. That said, the 700MB capacity of a CD isn't so impressive when you consider the typical size of audio projects, and it can be very confusing to split a large project onto multiple CD-R (CD-recordable) discs in order to get it archived off your system. Mind you, this is only getting worse, as most users record at 24-bit resolution, not to mention the 96kHz and 192kHz sampling rates on some systems! The availability of affordable recordable DVD drives for computer data has been a real boon for digital audio/video users. Several gigabytes fit onto a single recordable DVD, allowing entire projects to be backed up in a single operation. And the easier it is, the more often you'll do it. Even if the size of a Pro Tools project exceeds the space available on a single write-once DVD, burning programs like Roxio's Toast will automatically spread the project's data among multiple blank DVDs, creating a price-effective, long-term backup. In short, all Pro Tools users need a DVD-recording drive on their computer (which can also record data and audio onto CDs, of course). *Whatever your method, you need to back up your data often!*

Audio Mixer or Mic Preamp

Isn't the idea of Pro Tools to be a complete studio in a box? Well, sort of... especially with systems like Digi 003, Digi 002, and many of the M-Audio hardware options, which combine multiple audio inputs/outputs, MIDI in/out, and microphone preamps into a single audio interface. Digidesign's Mbox 2 (a compact USB audio interface) also incorporates MIDI in/out and two mic preamps with 48-volt phantom power for studio condenser microphones. It also supports Hi-Z (high-impedance) input from musical-instrument pickups, which can produce impressive results with a guitar amplifier simulation plug-in like AmpliTube. High-end Pro Tools audio interfaces for HD systems feature only line-level audio inputs (plus at least one digital audio input, naturally). This means that signals from microphone sources must be stepped up to this level in order to record their signal. A good mixer with multiple high-quality microphone preamps can be excellent for this purpose, and very cost effective. You might even use the mixer's insert points to patch in a compressor on a microphone source prior to recording it at the Pro Tools input if you happen to like the coloration that particular compressor adds to your sound or have concerns about unexpected peaks in a live situation. The audio mixer can also be handy for other purposes, such as monitoring different sources in your studio (for example, a CD player, DAT, or turntables) or as a pre-mixer for multiple MIDI devices on their way into Pro Tools. Lastly, for certain users, it can be more expedient to use the mixer itself to combine all the audio outputs from Pro Tools tracks, external effects such as reverb, and multiple MIDI modules in the studio when mixing in real time to DAT or some other stereo recorder—especially if the audio interface on their Pro Tools system doesn't offer a sufficient number of simultaneous inputs for all the external devices.

Other users might opt for one of the extremely high-end microphone preamps available on the market. This can be a very effective choice for project studios in particular. Because single users don't typically require a large number of simultaneous mic inputs (unless a drum set needs to be recorded, for example), a single high-quality microphone preamp can deliver pristine sound on all the microphone sources it records. A given microphone preamp may have specific desirable sonic characteristics or offer its own on-board signal processing. Other users simply prefer the convenience of having everything rack mounted; several eight-channel mic preamps on the market are very good quality and cost effective. Many even offer digital outputs, meaning that after the mic preamp stage itself, the signal need not pass through any additional analog stages before entering Pro Tools. These multiple-channel, rackmountable microphone preamps are also very popular for Pro Tools users who do location recording because a computer and a single small rack represent the entire recording system, making it easy to transport. All you have to do is set up the microphones and you're ready to go. Even Digidesign manufactures its own high-end, eight-channel rack-mounted mic preamp. The Digidesign PRE (shown in Figure 3.5) offers the notable advantage of being completely configurable (via MIDI) from inside the Pro Tools (TDM) software, which means that its previous settings will be recalled the next time you open a session.

Photo courtesy of Digidesign.

Figure 3.5   PRE, Digidesign's eight-channel microphone preamp.

Speakers, Amplification

You need to hear the audio while you work! If you're just setting up your project studio, you should look at some of the small, powered studio monitors that are available. These can be directly connected to the audio outputs you're using for your main stereo mix (on your computer, card, or external audio interface). Here's a special note for you multimedia and video folks: Granted, the cheap speakers that came with your computer are a bonus if you need to start working *today*. But don't kid yourself: All kinds of audio garbage—especially background noise, hiss, and hum—are going to sneak right by you into your final mixes until you acquire a decent set of speakers, and turn 'em up loud! If you have to place the speakers near a CRT computer monitor, make sure the speakers you buy are magnetically shielded so that the magnetic field they produce doesn't interfere with your monitor, distorting the colors of the display or creating interference patterns. A good set of headphones can also be very useful to check the stereo localization (panning) and reverb, and to help you be picky about minor edit noises, clicks, and pops that may not be obvious when listening in a room (especially if you have other noisy gear—or human beings—in your studio).

Turn Down Your Speakers Before Rebooting   If you have your Macintosh built-in audio outputs connected to your main speakers at nice, loud monitoring levels, don't forget to turn down the audio output before you shut down or restart the system. That Macintosh startup sound is loud as heck! This also applies to Windows users who have connected their computer's main audio output to studio monitors. Pops from system startup or launching/closing of certain audio programs can be annoying and even potentially damaging to your speakers. A good rule of thumb when it comes to powering on or off your speakers during your audio gear's boot up or shut down is this: last on, first off.

Pro Tools Hardware Configurations

This section reviews the configurations of Pro Tools that are currently available. (Note that Chapter 18 breaks down hardware configurations and expansions in more detail.) The variety of possible Pro Tools setups means there is a configuration that's right for just about every purpose and budget.

Mbox 2 Family (Pro Tools 8 LE and a Digidesign Audio/MIDI Interface)

The Mbox 2 family—the Mbox 2, Mbox 2 Mini, Mbox 2 Micro, and Mbox 2 Pro—consists of lightweight, portable audio interfaces, each with the LE version of the Pro Tools software. Pro Tools 8 LE software supports 48 tracks of simultaneous audio playback (expandable to 64 mono/stereo tracks via the optional Music Production Toolkit 2 or DV Toolkit 2) and synchronization to SMPTE time code when the Transport's Online button is enabled. In addition to offline AudioSuite processing, Pro Tools LE supports the RTAS plug-in architecture, which uses the computer's processing power for audio effects and software instruments. The DV Toolkit 2 option adds time-code rulers and other postproduction-related features. Audio recording at 16- or 24-bit resolution is supported (except for the Mbox 2 Micro, which has no audio inputs). Sample rates of 44.1 or 48kHz are supported by all interfaces within the Mbox 2 family, while the Mbox 2 Pro supports additional sample rates up to 96kHz. Bandwidth limitations of the USB connection itself—version 1.1, in the case of the Mbox 2—preclude 96kHz and other higher sample rates on USB interfaces for Pro Tools.

Mbox 2 (USB)

The Mbox 2 is an external USB audio/MIDI interface with two simultaneous channels of analog I/O, plus two more channels of digital input (S/PDIF jacks) that can be used simultaneously for 4×2 operation. (Because the S/PDIF output always mirrors analog outputs 1–2, there are only two separately addressable output audio channels on this interface.) It also incorporates one MIDI input and output. The 24-bit analog/digital converters on this USB-powered external interface, which are also capable of 16-bit operation, were also improved over the original Mbox (106dB signal-to-noise ratio versus 102dB, THD+N significantly reduced to 0.0008 percent versus 0.003 percent in the original Mbox). Its analog inputs incorporate microphone preamps designed by Digidesign with 48-volt phantom power that is enabled/disabled for both channels simultaneously via a button on the front of the unit. Except for the ¼-inch headphone output, all audio connections are on the rear panel. Separate XLR, TRS (¼-inch phone, tip-ring-sleeve) balanced, and TS (tip-sleeve) instrument-level (Hi-Z, high impedance, for direct connection from electric guitar or bass) jacks are provided for each of the two analog input channels,

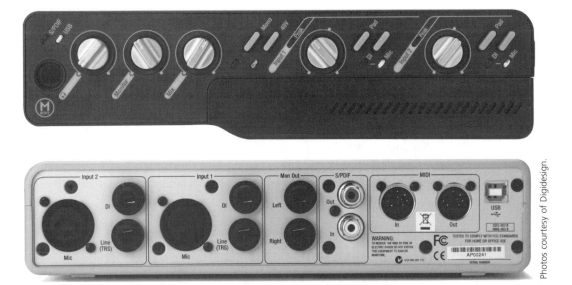

Figure 3.6   Pro Tools Mbox 2 configurations use the Pro Tools LE software plus the Mbox 2 external USB audio/MIDI interface.

reducing the need for recabling when switching sources. On the front panel, buttons for each input channel toggle between these mic, line, and direct inputs. The main studio monitor outputs on the rear panel are also balanced ¼-inch TRS. S/PDIF digital in/out (for channels 3–4) is provided via coaxial RCA jacks. Front-panel gain knobs are provided for the headphone output and main monitor output. Like its Mbox predecessor, the mix knob on the Mbox 2 adjusts the relative levels between the interface's input and playback from Pro Tools (a workaround for monitoring latency during recording). Input gain indicators are provided for each analog input channel, as well as a mono switch, −20dB pad switches, and single-LED peak indicators. Like the original Mbox before it, the unit is exclusively powered by the USB connection itself; no AC power is required.

The Mbox 2 (shown in Figure 3.6) is an excellent choice for location recording with your computer—even an appropriately configured laptop. It is also ideal for any home or project studio configuration where the computer offers a USB port. If you generally are recording only one or two channels at a time (as in a home studio), being limited to two analog channels plus two more digital channels is a relatively minor handicap. The availability of digital I/O on the Mbox interface allows you to transfer DAT recordings into Pro Tools for subsequent editing and mastering. You could also upgrade to a guitar preamp or high-end microphone preamp that has digital output as your front end for recording via this interface's S/PDIF digital input. The Mbox 2 can be appropriate not only for project recording but also for video postproduction (using a digital video file as the master, for instance), voiceover and broadcast audio, multimedia, spoken word, and many other applications. Digidesign also offers the Mbox 2 Factory, which includes bundled software with the hardware interface at a significant discount.

Mbox 2 Mini (USB)

The Mbox 2 Mini (shown in Figure 3.7) is a simpler external USB audio interface, offering only two channels of analog I/O. Input 1 offers both XLR (microphone) and ¼-inch phone jacks, while input 2 offers ¼-inch phone only. The stereo monitor output analog outputs also use ¼-inch jacks. Except for the XLR microphone input, all the audio jacks use unbalanced ¼-inch phone, tip-sleeve (TS) connections. There are no inputs for digital audio or MIDI on this interface. Like the Mbox 2, the Mini doesn't require any additional AC power (being completely powered via the USB connection to the computer), and provides a single ¼-inch headphone output on its front panel. A single output level knob affects both the monitor output and headphone levels (as opposed to the Mbox 2, which has dedicated level knobs for each of these).

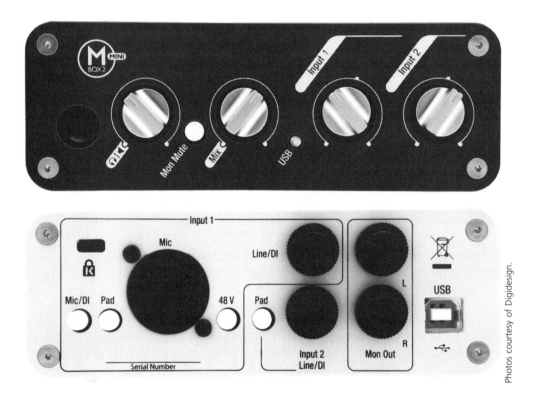

Photos courtesy of Digidesign.

Figure 3.7 The Mbox 2 Mini is a two-channel, analog-only USB interface for Pro Tools LE.

Mbox 2 Micro (USB)

The Mbox 2 Micro (shown in Figure 3.8) is a very small audio interface for Pro Tools LE (at 3.5 inches long and 1.25 inches wide, it's small enough to fit on a key ring), offering only a single stereo output with an ⅛-inch TRS jack. There are no audio inputs on the Mbox 2 Micro. It is powered via the USB (1.1) connection to the computer; an LED on the unit indicates when this

Figure 3.8   The Mbox 2 Micro is a USB interface for Pro Tools LE, with a single, stereo output.

power is active. A volume dial is provided for the analog stereo output jack, which can be used for either headphone or line-out connections. Sample rates of 44.1 and 48kHz are supported at 16- or 24-bit depths. As you can imagine, this is a very handy option for users who would like to edit or perform stereo mixes on a laptop, for example.

Mbox 2 Pro (FireWire)
The Mbox 2 Pro (shown in Figure 3.9) is an external audio/MIDI interface connected to the host computer via a FireWire cable. It can be powered directly via the FireWire connection to the computer or via the included AC power cable. The audio specs of the Mbox 2 Pro are superior to those of the other two interfaces in the Mbox 2 family, and it supports sample rates up to

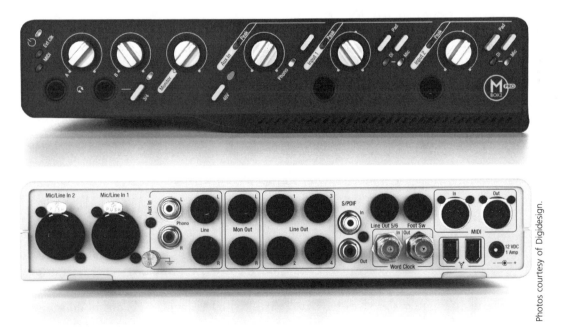

Figure 3.9   The Mbox 2 Pro is a FireWire interface for Pro Tools LE.

96kHz. Four analog inputs are provided on the rear panel: mic/line inputs 1–2 use combo jacks (compatible with both XLR and ¼-inch phone), while Aux In line inputs 3–4 use balanced TRS (¼-inch phone, tip-ring-sleeve) jacks. Among all the current Digidesign audio interfaces for Pro Tools, only the Mbox 2 Pro includes a built-in phono preamp with RCA jacks for connecting a turntable. (A front-panel switch selects this input source for Aux In inputs 3–4.) In addition to these inputs, two front-panel DI inputs for channels 1–2 with ¼-inch phone jacks (tip-sleeve) are included for direct connection of electric guitars, basses, and similar instruments. Front-panel buttons permit switching channels 1–2 between their mic, line, and DI inputs. The Mbox 2 Pro and the Digi 003 are also the only Digidesign interfaces for the LE version of Pro Tools that provide BNC connectors for word-clock input/output (external clock rates up to 96kHz are supported) to facilitate hardware-level synchronization of the unit's internal sample clock with other audio and video equipment. The Mbox 2 Pro features two front-panel headphone outputs, each with its own dedicated volume control. Two dedicated monitor outputs on the rear panel correspond to outputs 1–2 from Pro Tools, and use unbalanced ¼-inch TS (tip-sleeve) jacks. In addition to this, line outputs 1–4 provide balanced ¼-inch TRS jacks, and line outputs 5–6 share a single (unbalanced) stereo TRS jack. S/PDIF digital I/O is provided via coaxial RCA jacks. If you use all the available analog and digital connections, the Mbox 2 Pro can function as a six-in, eight-out interface. The Mbox 2 Pro is also offered as a factory package with bundled software.

Digi 003 and Digi 003 Rack (Pro Tools LE and an External FireWire Audio/MIDI Interface)

There are two versions of the Digi 003 hardware:

- The Digi 003 (shown in Figure 3.10) is an external audio interface for the LE version of Pro Tools that connects to the computer via a FireWire connection. It incorporates a control surface for Pro Tools, offering motorized faders, transport controls, and many other dedicated functions for the Pro Tools software.

- The Digi 003 Rack (Digi 003R) version offers all the same connections and audio specifications, but without the control surface.

These audio interfaces offer eight analog inputs. Individual mic/DI switches on the front panel allow the selecting of the source for inputs 1–4 to be either their balanced ¼-inch TRS jacks for line levels or XLR connectors for their built-in microphone preamps. (Note that these microphone preamps also have switchable 48-volt phantom power, as well as a front-panel switch for a 75Hz high-pass filter for reducing low-frequency rumble or noise.) Inputs 5–8 offer balanced ¼-inch TRS jacks for line-level sources and offer enough gain to accommodate instrument-level sources. There are also eight analog outputs, each with balanced, ¼-inch TRS jacks. Additionally, the main and alternate monitor outputs are controlled by a single level control and mirror outputs 1–2 from Pro Tools. These output pairs also provide balanced, ¼-inch TRS jacks for each channel.

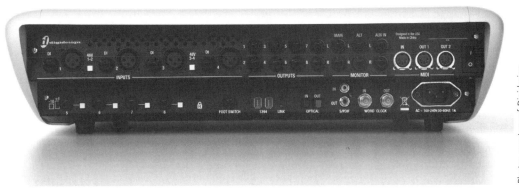

Figure 3.10   The Digi 003 interface incorporates a virtual control surface for Pro Tools.

Toslink connectors are provided for ADAT Lightpipe digital I/O (up to eight more channels of audio, alternatively configurable as stereo optical S/PDIF). However, it should be noted that ADAT Lightpipe audio is limited to 48kHz. RCA jacks support stereo coaxial S/PDIF digital I/O at up to 48kHz in consumer mode (IEC60958-3), and up to 96kHz in professional mode (IEC60958-4). Bear in mind that it is always important to use proper 75-ohm coaxial cable with *all* S/PDIF digital connections, especially at cable lengths over three feet. BNC connectors are provided for word-clock connections in order to synchronize the unit's internal sample clock with other digital devices in your studio configuration.

Like its predecessor, the Digi 002, the Digi 003 provides one MIDI input, two MIDI outputs, and a footswitch connector for controlling playback or punching in and out of recording mode using the QuickPunch feature of the Pro Tools software. Two stereo headphone outputs on the front panel have separate level controls. Headphone 1 mirrors the output of main outputs 1–2, while a front-panel switch allows monitor outputs 3–4 to be selected as the signal source for the headphone 2 output.

The Digi 003 Control Surface

As mentioned previously, while the Digi003R is a rackmountable version, the full Digi 003 version includes all the same audio/MIDI capabilities plus a control surface for Pro Tools. It offers a two-row LCD display strip across the top of the panel for displaying track information or edit parameters during operation. Each of its main mixer strips offers a 100mm motorized touch-sensitive fader, a rotary encoder, dedicated solo and mute buttons, plus a Channel Select button. (You use the Channel Select button to select a channel as the target for various functions, such as modifying its plug-ins, inserts, or sends using the rotary encoders in the upper Console/ Channel view section of the control surface.) A global flip switch allows you to globally swap the functions of the faders and rotary encoders on all mixer strips. There is a dedicated section of buttons for automation modes and modifier keys such as Shift and Command/Option/Control (Ctrl/Alt/Start in Windows versions). There are also various dedicated buttons for frequently accessed functions such as Save, Undo, and Enter, as well as for toggling between the Mix, Edit, and Plug-in windows. The Transport section offers dedicated buttons, plus dual-concentric jog/shuttle wheels. Lastly, the Digi 003 control surface can be used to control applications other than Pro Tools, either directly (with iTunes or Ableton Live, for example) or via MIDI. With the appropriate ASIO (Windows) or CoreAudio (Macintosh) drivers, it can be used to record and play back audio with a variety of other programs.

Offered are the Digi 003 Factory Complete and the Digi 003 Rack Factory Complete, which bundles the Complete Production Toolkit with the 003 hardware, enabling the setup to be configured for 7.1 surround mixing if desired. It also ups the track count to 128 mono and 64 stereo tracks at a sample rate of 48kHz, or 96 mono and 48 stereo tracks at a sample rate of 96kHz. Another package for the Rack version of the 003 is the Factory, which bundles a huge amount of plug-ins as well as the necessary iLok USB Smart Key that will store the authorizations of all these plug-ins. That's a lot of toys to play with!

The Digi 003 Rack + Factory

Unlike the Mbox Factory versions, which are standard Mbox hardware interfaces bundled with software packages, the Digi 003 Rack + Factory (see Figure 3.11) is an expanded hardware version of the 003 Rack, again with a bundle of additional software. Hardware differences from the original 003 include eight mic preamps, all with 48-volt phantom power and one MIDI I/O.

Photos courtesy of Digidesign.

Figure 3.11   The Digi 003 Rack interface offers the same audio capabilities as the Digi 003, but without the control surface.

M-Powered (Pro Tools M-Powered and an M-Audio Interface)

Various audio hardware options from M-Audio (which has been a subsidiary of Avid, Inc., Digidesign's parent company, since 2004) can be used with the M-Powered version of the Pro Tools software, which is purchased separately. You can also use M-Audio hardware with many other audio-MIDI programs—for example, via the ASIO2 or DirectX protocols.

The capabilities of the Pro Tools M-Powered software are nearly identical to the LE version, with the following exceptions:

■ An iLok copy protection device (USB dongle) provided with the Pro Tools M-Powered software is required to run the program.

- The third-party programs and plug-ins bundled with Pro Tools M-Powered are different from those that come with Pro Tools LE. Additionally, most M-Audio interfaces include other bundled software of their own. In either case, the manufacturers vary the exact contents of these bundles from time to time.

- While the Digidesign Dither plug-in *is* included with M-Powered, Pow-R Dither is available only in the LE version.

- Pro Tools M-Powered doesn't support Digidesign's Control24 control surface.

- The optional DV Toolkit 2 software is not compatible with M-Powered. (This software bundle increases the maximum track count from 32 to 48. It also includes DigiTranslator and DINR LE noise reduction, allows Pro Tools LE users to work with SMPTE time code or Feet+Frames in the Edit window timeline, and supports pull-up or pull-down sample rates for film-video conversions.)

In this book, therefore, unless specified otherwise, comments about Pro Tools LE will also apply to the M-Powered version.

For detailed specifications on M-Audio's hardware offerings, go to M-Audio's Web site at http://www.m-audio.com (you can also reach this site via the M-Powered page on Digidesign's own Web site). There you will find more information about signal-to-noise ratios, frequency response, software drivers, and so on. What follows are functional descriptions to help you sort out the general characteristics of the M-Audio hardware that is currently compatible with Pro Tools M-Powered.

FireWire-Based Systems

The following M-Audio hardware systems are all external audio interfaces, connected to the host computer via its FireWire port. They are all capable of either 16- or 24-bit resolution for digital audio. While FireWire has been standard on Macintosh computers for a number of years, some Windows computers may require an optional FireWire card. Also, Macintosh OS X or Windows XP with Service Pack 2 is the minimum requirement for using *any* of M-Audio's FireWire-based audio interfaces with Pro Tools M-Powered. Mac users are encouraged to check both the Digidesign and M-Audio Web sites for compatibility between Mac OS versions and the various M-Audio interfaces, especially for older products.

FireWire Solo. The FireWire Solo (shown in Figure 3.12) features two inputs with gain controls on the front panel: one dedicated to microphone sources (and providing 48-volt phantom power) and the other to guitar or bass (also known as Hi-Z, high-impedance) sources. There is also a headphone output on the front panel. The rear panel offers two additional channels of analog input with TS (¼-inch phone, tip-sleeve, unbalanced) jacks, analog output with TRS (¼-inch phone, tip-ring-sleeve, balanced) jacks, as well as stereo coaxial S/PDIF digital I/O with RCA jacks. A switch on the front panel of the unit allows you to select between front (mic/instrument) and rear (line-level) inputs. If you simultaneously use both analog and S/PDIF digital

Photos courtesy of M-Audio.

Figure 3.12 M-Audio's FireWire Solo interface is compatible with the M-Powered version of Pro Tools as well as with other audio/MIDI programs.

I/O, you can use up to four input channels and four output channels on the FireWire Solo at the same time. The FireWire Solo supports 24-bit audio at sample rates up to 96kHz, and can be powered either directly from the FireWire bus or the included 12-volt DC power supply.

ProFire 2626. As the name denotes, the ProFire 2626, shown in Figure 3.13, features 26×26 simultaneous analog/digital I/O, including eight preamps made with M-Audio's Octane technology. A user-assignable master volume control knob allows one to choose any or all of the eight analog output pairs for control, effectively creating the possibility for a user to configure a 7.1 surround output uniformly attenuated by one volume control. The interface can work with sample rates up to 192kHz (96kHz with Pro Tools M-Powered software). In setups with multiple pieces of gear that would need a single clock source, the ProFire 2626 can act either as the clock master or a slave. A flexible onboard DSP mixer offers the option to send any of the 52 audio streams to any of the hardware outputs and lets the user create internally up to eight stereo mixes. It is fully compatible with Pro Tools M-Powered version 8. Inputs include eight ¼-inch TRS balanced line inputs, eight XLR mic inputs with phantom power, and two ½-inch TS instrument inputs. Digital connections include 2×2 optical S/PDIF or 16×16 ADAT I/O, as well as a 2×2 coaxial S/PDIF connection. Outputs include eight ¼-inch TRS balanced line outputs and two ¼-inch TRS headphone outputs. A 1×1 MIDI I/O and word-clock I/O are also featured.

Photos courtesy of M-Audio.

Figure 3.13 The M-Audio ProFire 2626 features eight preamps, an onboard digital mixer and the ability to create eight stereo mixes.

ProFire 610. A travel-friendly interface, the ProFire 610, shown in Figure 3.14, features 6×10 simultaneous analog/digital I/O including two preamps, again with M-Audio's Octane technology. Like the 2626, it features a user-assignable master volume knob that can be configured to control any or all of the four analog output pairs. Also echoing the 2626 is a DSP mixer coupled with a software control panel that enables the user to configure several stereo mixes, perfect for sending cue feeds of audio to the talent being recorded. When used with Pro Tools M-Powered version 8, it can work with sample rates up to 96kHz, but like the 2626 can work with audio at 196kHz when used as a standalone piece of hardware. Inputs on the 610 include two XLR/TS combo jacks for instrument-level or mic-level inputs, two ¼-inch TRS balanced line inputs, and a stereo S/PDIF in. Outputs include eight ¼-inch TRS balanced line outputs and a stereo S/PDIF out. Also included are a 1×1 MIDI interface, two ¼-inch TRS headphone outputs, and two FireWire ports.

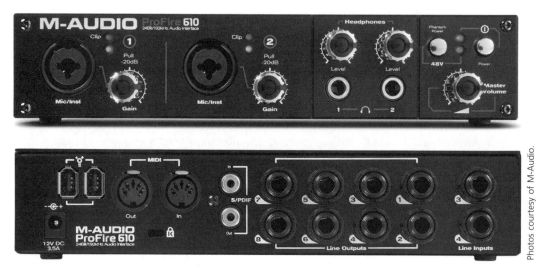

Figure 3.14   The M-Audio ProFire 610, a portable interface featuring 6×10 analog/digital I/O.

Photos courtesy of M-Audio.

ProjectMix I/O. The ProjectMix I/O (shown in Figure 3.15) combines a FireWire-based 18×14 audio interface with a control surface. As an audio interface, it is directly supported by Pro Tools M-Powered 7 and 8 (as well as several other audio programs). If offers eight analog inputs, each with an input gain knob and a mic/line switch for selecting between its separate XLR (with phantom power) and TRS jacks (plus a selectable instrument-level input on the front panel, for channel 1). Four TRS analog outputs are also provided. Additionally, the ProjectMix I/O has digital input/output in S/PDIF and ADAT Lightpipe formats, two headphone outputs on the front of the unit with independent level controls, MIDI input/output, and word-clock input/output with BNC connectors. As a control surface, it offers transport buttons and a jog wheel, plus motorized faders for eight channel strips (each with an assignable rotary encoder plus dedicated

Photos courtesy of M-Audio.

Figure 3.15 M-Audio's ProjectMix I/O combines a FireWire audio interface and control surface.

record-enable, channel select, solo, and mute buttons) and the master level. A flip button allows you to use the 100mm faders for writing more precise automation moves instead of the rotary encoders. The ProjectMix I/O features a two-line LCD display across the top of the control surface. Various other dedicated buttons are provided for functions such as nudging, looping, and so on; a footswitch input is also available. The ProjectMix I/O can be used with many other programs, as it supports Mackie Control, HUI, and Logic Control emulation modes.

ProFire Lightbridge. The ProFire Lightbridge interface (shown in Figure 3.16) offers up to 34 digital input and 34 digital output channels: four ADAT Lightpipe inputs/outputs that support eight digital audio channels on each of the Toslink connectors, plus stereo S/PDIF digital I/O with RCA coaxial connectors. (Current Pro Tools M-Powered versions only support 18 channels of simultaneous I/O on all hardware, however.) It also provides two additional analog output channels with ¼-inch TRS line-level jacks and a headphone output that all carry the same signal but have their own volume control. In addition to normal Lightpipe mode at up to 48kHz, the ProFire Lightbridge also supports 16-channel Lightpipe operation at 88.2 and 96kHz sample rates via the S/MUX protocol (which requires two Toslink connections for each eight-channel

Figure 3.16   M-Audio's ProFire Lightbridge.

group in order to support higher sample rates). The ProFire Lightbridge is configured via the included control panel software.

NRV10. The NRV10 (shown in Figure 3.17) combines an 8×2 analog mixer with an audio interface that connects to the host computer via FireWire. Mixer channels 1–4 can be switched between separate XLR microphone (with globally switchable phantom power) and line-level inputs with TRS jacks, and provide analog inserts. The next mixer channel is switchable between a mono microphone input 5 or balanced stereo line inputs 5–6, while balanced inputs 7–8 are on a single stereo mixer channel. All channels have 45mm faders. Three-band EQ is provided on each channel, along with a pre-fader Aux 1 mono send and a post-fader Aux 2 mono send that feeds both the mixer's Aux 2 analog output and the mixer's DFX internal effects unit (which can be used to feed reverb to the headphone mix while recording, for example). Channel source buttons above each of the NRV10's six faders can switch their signal sources between their analog inputs (Channel) and up to 10 digital-audio streams (FW) coming from Pro Tools during playback and recording. The master section of the mixer provides separate volume controls for the headphone and control-room outputs as well as two stereo returns. The main mix level fader affects the main stereo analog outputs on the rear of the interface, which offer both XLR and balanced ¼-inch TRS jacks. (There are also analog insert connections on the main output bus.) Next to this in the master section is a control room fader, which affects a separate set of outputs, also with balanced TRS jacks. The FW 9/10 to phones button allows routing of FireWire digital audio streams 9–10 from the host application (Pro Tools, in this case) out through the head-phone output of this analog mixer. Another button in the master section, pre-EQ/post-EQ, affects all the analog mixer's input channels and determines whether the signal source entering

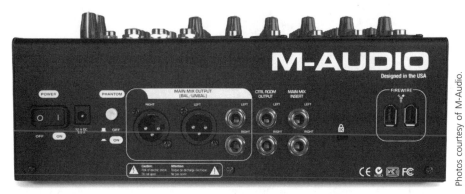

Figure 3.17   M-Audio's NRV10 combines an analog mixer and a FireWire interface.

Pro Tools comes from a point before or after their 3-band EQ section (but after their gain stage and analog insert points). The included control-panel software displays input/output levels on the device's 10 FireWire audio busses. The NRV10 supports 24-bit audio at sample rates up to 96kHz. As a FireWire audio interface for Pro Tools, its inputs support recording up to 10 channels simultaneously.

Good Audio Cables Are a Sound Investment Be sure to always use proper 75-ohm "digital" coaxial cable with all S/PDIF digital connections, especially at cable lengths over three feet.

USB-Based Systems

All these M-Audio interfaces connect to the host computer via USB. With the exception of the Ozone and Black Box, most are also powered via this connection; no AC adapter is required.

MobilePre USB. The MobilePre USB (shown in Figure 3.18) is a stereo audio interface that exclusively supports 16-bit audio at a 48kHz sample rate. This interface has two TS (¼-inch unbalanced) outputs on the rear panel, which are mirrored by an additional ¹/₈-inch stereo output. Gain knobs are provided on the front panel for channels 1 and 2. Two TRS (¼-inch phone, tip-ring-sleeve, balanced) jacks support instrument- or line-level sources—one on the front panel, the other on the back. Alternatively, the rear panel of the interface offers balanced XLR inputs for mic/line sources and a ¹/₈-inch stereo microphone input (with no phantom power available). The MobilePre USB does not feature any digital I/O.

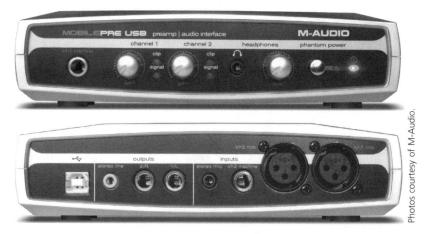

Figure 3.18 M-Audio's MobilePre USB interface.

FastTrack USB. The FastTrack USB (shown in Figure 3.19) is a compact stereo audio interface that supports 16- or 24-bit audio at sample rates of 44.1 or 48kHz. The stereo outputs use RCA (unbalanced) jacks. One TRS (¼-inch phone, tip-ring-sleeve, balanced) input can be switched

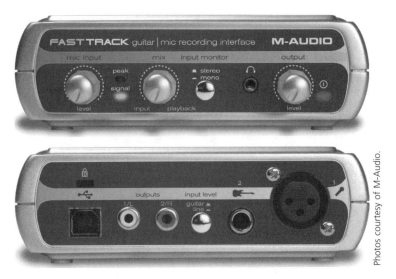

Photos courtesy of M-Audio.

Figure 3.19   M-Audio's FastTrack USB interface.

between line and instrument levels. A second XLR input supports microphone sources, with an associated front-panel gain control for its mic preamp. No phantom power is provided for this microphone input. No digital I/O is available on this interface. The FastTrack USB features a front-panel mix knob (similar to that found on Digidesign's Mbox 2 and original Mbox) for balancing direct input levels (in mono or stereo) and playback from the host audio program as a way to circumvent monitoring latency issues.

FastTrack Pro. The FastTrack Pro (shown in Figure 3.20) is another USB audio interface that supports 16- or 24-bit audio at sample rates of 44.1 or 48kHz. It features two front-panel analog audio inputs with combo XLR/TRS connectors (for microphone or balanced line-level sources), S/PDIF digital I/O with RCA jacks, and four unbalanced analog outputs with RCA jacks. Front-panel buttons provide for switching the ¼-inch TS input between line and instrument levels, as well as enabling a −20dB pad on the input signal. A headphone output is provided on the front panel, which mirrors the audio signal at the main outputs 1–2. A front-panel mix knob allows for the adjustment of the balance between the input signal and audio being passed back from Pro Tools as a workaround for monitoring latency while recording. There is a single headphone output on the front panel. The FastTrack Pro also incorporates one MIDI input and one MIDI output, and can be powered via either USB or the included 12-volt power adapter.

FastTrack Ultra. The FastTrack Ultra (see Figure 3.21) is a USB 2.0-connecting audio/MIDI interface that features the ability to mix eight hardware inputs and eight software returns to eight hardware outputs, allowing the user to record on eight channels simultaneously. With built-in effects processing for the headphone outputs, the unit can save some DSP processing that the computer host would otherwise handle. The FastTrack Ultra also allows the user to

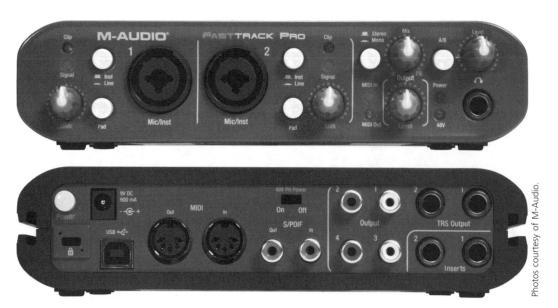

Photos courtesy of M-Audio.

Figure 3.20 M-Audio's FastTrack Pro interface.

Photos courtesy of M-Audio.

Figure 3.21 The M-Audio USB2 interface FastTrackUltra, featuring eight hardware inputs and outputs, and the ability to record on eight tracks simultaneously.

connect outboard gear and synthesizers to the hardware inputs, mixing those sources with a possible eight audio sources from the computer host to create a 16-input/eight-output configuration. Inputs offered include six channels of ¼-inch-jack analog ins and two-channel RCA-jack S/PDIF input. There are also four preamps with 48-volt phantom power included for use with the XLR microphone inputs. Outputs include six analog ¼-inch jack outs and two-channel

RCA-jack S/PDIF digital output. Also included are two analog ¼-inch jack inserts, allowing the user to send the first two channels to outboard gear and return those channels' audio signals before the unit's analog-to-digital conversion stage. In addition, there is the capacity to create two separate headphone mixes for cue feeds, corresponding to the two physical headphone outputs included on the unit. M-Audio also offers the FastTrack Ultra 8R, which adds an additional four preamps to the four included on the original Ultra.

Transit. The Transit (shown in Figure 3.22) is another compact stereo audio interface. It has a stereo mini ⅛-inch connector that doubles as line/headphone output, a Toslink connector for S/PDIF optical output, plus a single input that doubles as a ⅛-inch stereo mini line/mic input or optical input (via a provided adapter). Ostensibly, 16- or 24-bit audio is supported at sample rates up to 96kHz; however, due to the limitations of the USB 1.1 connection used by these units, this highest frequency would be possible only if you were using the inputs or outputs *only*—not a practical option with Pro Tools.

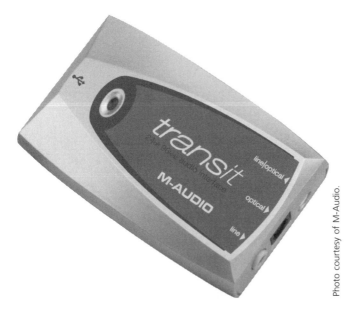

Figure 3.22 M-Audio's Transit interface.

PCI Card–Based Systems

The following M-Audio hardware systems use a PCI card installed in the host computer. In some cases, a breakout cable provides some or all of the actual audio connections, while in others an external box is connected directly to the PCI card. All of these PCI-based systems include M-Audio's Delta Control Panel software, which allows for level adjustments and signal routing between inputs and outputs on the hardware itself (for direct monitoring, for example). As before, all of these interfaces are capable of either 24- or 16-bit operation.

Audiophile 2496. The Audiophile 2496 audio card (shown in Figure 3.23) features two analog audio inputs and outputs with RCA jacks on the rear of the PCI card itself. Alternatively, stereo coaxial S/PDIF digital I/O with RCA jacks is available via a breakout cable that attaches to a 15-pin D-sub connector on the rear of the card, which also provides one MIDI input and output. As the name implies, the card supports 24-bit audio at sampling rates up to 96kHz. The coaxial digital outputs are Dolby Digital 5.1 surround-sound capable (for sending out to an external decoder).

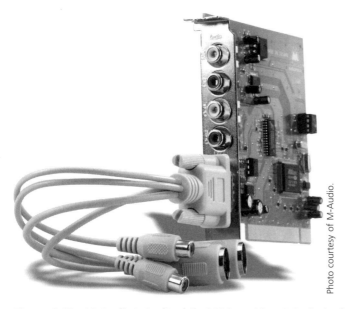

Photo courtesy of M-Audio.

Figure 3.23   M-Audio's Audiophile 2496 card has RCA jacks for analog I/O on the card, plus S/PDIF and MIDI I/O via a breakout cable.

Audiophile 192. The Audiophile 192 audio card (shown in Figure 3.24) features stereo coaxial S/PDIF digital I/O with RCA jacks on the rear of the PCI card itself. A breakout cable attaches to a 25-pin D-sub connector on the rear of the card. This cable provides TRS (¼-inch phone, tip-ring-sleeve) jacks for analog audio I/O: two analog audio inputs, two main outputs, plus two dedicated monitor outputs. The monitor outputs can mirror the main output from Pro Tools (or another DAW program) and/or pass through signals from the inputs on the Audiophile 192 itself, whose levels are controlled by a software mixer in the included Delta Control Panel software. One MIDI input and output is also provided on the breakout cable. The Audiophile 192 supports 24-bit audio at sampling rates up to 192kHz (although this highest sample rate is not currently supported by the Pro Tools M-Powered software). The coaxial digital outputs are Dolby Digital 5.1 surround-sound capable (for sending out an external decoder) and offer a "professional" setting for running the AES/EBU protocol over the S/PDIF connection.

Delta 44. The Delta 44 PCI card (shown in Figure 3.25) connects to an external audio interface called the Delta series breakout box, which provides all its audio and MIDI connections via a

Figure 3.24   M-Audio's Audiophile 192 card supports 4×4 operation if all analog and digital I/O is used.

Figure 3.25   M-Audio's Delta 44 card includes analog I/O only.

cable with 15-pin D-sub connectors. Four analog inputs and outputs use TRS (¼-inch phone, tip-ring-sleeve) jacks, and can be switched between −10dBV and + 4dBu nominal levels via the included Delta Control Panel software. As with the other M-Audio interfaces listed here, the software allows for the routing of input audio signals directly to outputs on the interface as a workaround for latency issues when monitoring audio sources being recorded through the host program. No digital I/O is included with the Delta 44. It supports 24-bit audio at sampling rates up to 96kHz.

Delta 66. The Delta 66 (shown in Figure 3.26) uses the same external breakout box and cable as the Delta 44 but expands I/O capability to six channels if the RCA jacks on the rear of the Delta 66 PCI card itself are used for stereo coaxial S/PDIF digital I/O (in other words, four channels of analog I/O plus two digital). Other characteristics are similar to the Delta 44.

Figure 3.26 M-Audio's Delta 66 card adds S/PDIF digital I/O to the capabilities of the Delta 44.

Delta 1010. The Delta 1010 (shown in Figure 3.27) consists of a PCI card that connects to an external, rackmountable audio interface. This external rack-mount converter unit provides all the analog audio, MIDI, and word-clock connections, while stereo coaxial S/PDIF digital I/O is

Photo courtesy of M-Audio.

Figure 3.27   M-Audio's Delta 1010 card with external interface.

available via RCA jacks on the rear of the PCI card itself. The external audio interface provides eight channels of audio input via TRS (¼-inch phone, tip-ring-sleeve) jacks, with individual switches for choosing −10dBV or + 4dBu nominal levels independently on each input and output channel. Word-clock input and output on the rear of the interface provide for synchronizing the sample rate of the Delta 1010 with external systems using 75-ohm coaxial cables with BNC connectors. One MIDI input and one MIDI output are provided on the front panel of the external audio interface. The Delta 1010 supports 24-bit audio at sampling rates up to 96kHz.

The optional Delta 1010-AI (a separate interface module; not pictured here) adds ADAT Light-pipe digital I/O capabilities to the Delta 1010 (up to eight channels of audio on this optical connection). However, the maximum of 10 I/O channels does not change. Instead, the Delta 1010-AI allows you to globally switch between all eight of your analog input channels or all eight Lightpipe channels as the input source. Alternatively, you could route these eight Lightpipe channels directly to the analog or Lightpipe outputs on the interface itself. The Delta 1010-AI is connected between the Delta 1010 external interface and PCI card. ADAT Lightpipe I/O is limited to 48kHz and 44.1kHz sample rates.

Delta 1010LT. The Delta 1010LT (shown in Figure 3.28) consists of a PCI card with two breakout cables. The "analog" breakout cable attaches to a 25-pin D-sub connector and provides eight analog outputs with RCA jacks plus eight analog inputs. Six of the inputs have RCA jacks, while female XLR jacks on channels 1 and 2 can be switched between microphone or line levels via a jumper on the PCI card itself (not accessible from outside the computer). The "digital" breakout cable attaches to a 15-pin D-sub connector and provides stereo coaxial S/PDIF digital I/O with RCA jacks, one MIDI input and output, plus a word-clock input and output (for synchronizing sample rates between the Delta 1010LT and external systems, using 75-ohm coaxial cables with BNC connectors). Using the eight analog and two digital channels simultaneously, a maximum of 10 channels of I/O is available on the Delta 1010LT.

Photo courtesy of M-Audio.

Figure 3.28 M-Audio's Delta 1010LT card with its breakout cables.

A Comparison of M-Audio Interfaces for Pro Tools M-Powered

With so many choices for compatible audio interfaces for Pro Tools M-Powered, you can see why it is worth the time to investigate all their technical characteristics on the M-Audio Web site. Table 3.2 summarizes how these interfaces connect to the host computer, and the number and type of audio inputs/outputs each of them provides.

Pro Tools|HD (External Audio Interfaces)

Presently, the most powerful generation of Pro Tools, Pro Tools|HD systems support recording of 24-bit audio (with 16-bit operation also supported, as with all 24-bit interfaces) at sample rates up to 96kHz or 192kHz, depending on the HD audio interface(s) from Digidesign that you purchase separately to complete your system. For example, the 192 I/O allows you to select sample rates of 44.1, 48, 88.2, 96, 176.4, or 192kHz. Pro Tools HD 1, the basic Pro Tools|HD system, consists of one Digidesign card in the host computer (either an HD Core card for computers with PCI slots or an Accel Core card for computers with PCIe slots), cabled to an external audio interface; it supports up to 32 channels of I/O (with the appropriate audio interfaces). Pro Tools HD 2 Accel systems add the HD Accel card (available in both PCIe and PCI versions) for more mixing and processing power. Adding this second Digidesign card supports up to 64 channels of I/O when using a sufficient number of audio interfaces, because each HD Accel card also supports 32 channels of I/O. Pro Tools HD 3 Accel systems have two HD Accel cards (potentially up to 96 channels of I/O). You can expand the processing power and I/O capacity on your Pro Tools|HD system by adding more HD Accel cards. For example, a total of five or more Digidesign cards, which requires an expansion chassis attached to the host computer, would support Pro Tools|HD's maximum capacity of 160 audio I/O channels.

Table 3.2 M-Audio Interfaces for Pro Tools M-Powered: I/O Channels

Model	Connection	Input Channels Analog / S/PDIF / ADAT	Output Channels Analog / S/PDIF / ADAT
FireWire Solo	FireWire	4/2/–	2/2/–
ProFire 2626	FireWire	8/2/16	8/2/16
ProFire610	FireWire	4/2/–	8/2/–
ProjectMix I/O	FireWire	8/2/8	4/2/8
ProFire Lightbridge	FireWire	–/2/32*	2/2/32*
NRV10	FireWire	8/–/–	2/–/–
MobilePre USB	USB	2/–/–	2/–/–
FastTrack USB	USB	2/–/–	2/–/–
FastTrack Pro	USB	2/2/–	4/2/–
FastTrack Ultra 8R	USB	8/2/–	8/2/–
Transit	USB	2/2/–	2/2/–
Audiophile 2496	PCI	2/2/–	2/2/–
Audiophile 192	PCI	2/2/–	4/2/–
Delta 44	PCI	4/–/–	4/–/–
Delta 66	PCI	4/2/–	4/2/–
Delta 1010	PCI	8/2/–	8/2/–
Delta 1010LT	PCI	8/2/–	8/2/–

* Limited to 18 channels when used with Pro Tools M-Powered.

Pro Tools HD Software Prior to version 7, versions of the Pro Tools program that supported TDM hardware and plug-ins were known as Pro Tools TDM. This term was used for the first Pro Tools|HD systems with Pro Tools 6.xx software, as well as 24 MIX and various other predecessors that supported the TDM plug-in architecture. Now the software itself is called Pro Tools HD (and the hardware configurations are called Pro Tools|HD). The plug-in architecture is still called TDM, however, and currently shipping versions of TDM plug-ins operate in Pro Tools HD software. (This software also supports RTAS plug-ins, as do the LE and M-Powered versions. RTAS plug-ins rely on the CPU's processing power rather than on the DSP chips available on the HD cards.)

PCIe Cards for Pro Tools|HD Systems   Digidesign offers PCIe card configurations for Pro Tools|HD on current computers with PCI-Express (PCI-X) slots—the Macintosh G5 Quad and all Intel-based Mac Pro models, for example. PCI/PCI-X cards for Pro Tools|HD are not directly compatible with this newer slot format. However, they could be used via an expansion chassis, which would be connected to the host computer via a single PCIe card. For HD configurations of three or fewer cards on computers using PCI/PCI-X slots, however, you can purchase the HD Core and HD Accel cards (instead of the Accel Core and PCI version of the HD Accel cards).

Multiple audio interfaces can be added to expand these systems, including the 192 I/O, 192 Digital I/O, 96i I/O, and 96 I/O. Several interfaces from the 24 MIX hardware family can optionally be connected to the legacy port of the HD audio interfaces for additional channels of audio I/O.

Pro Tools|HD systems use DigiLink cabling, allowing audio interfaces to be separated from the Digidesign cards in the host computer by as much as 100 feet (for operation at sample rates up to 96kHz; 50-foot cable lengths are the limit for 192kHz operation). The TDM II signal-routing bus and processing architecture used in HD systems offers more efficiency and doubles the number of time slots available in the original TDM architecture used on the discontinued Pro Tools| 24 MIX system and its predecessor, Pro Tools III. (Note that if you upgrade to Pro Tools|HD from an older 24|Mix system, upgrades will be required for your third-party TDM plug-ins.)

Obviously, Pro Tools|HD lends itself to the most demanding audio applications, like music and film or video. Among other things, HD systems support the software-based Delay Compensation feature, which automatically adjusts for processing delay due to plug-ins and signal routing in order to maintain extremely precise time alignment in your mixes. User-configurable amounts of delay compensation can also be applied to hardware I/O inserts to adjust for the latency of external devices and the inputs/outputs on the Pro Tools audio interface itself. The high-resolution audio-recording formats used by Pro Tools|HD provide forward compatibility with the latest standards—for example, in DVD-Audio.

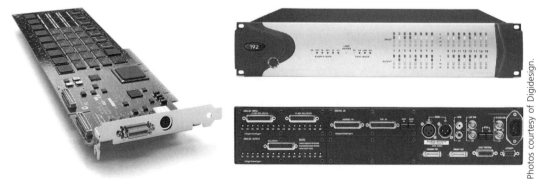

Photos courtesy of Digidesign.

Figure 3.29   Pro Tools|HD systems consist of the Pro Tools HD software and PCIe or PCI cards in the host computer, plus separately purchased multichannel audio interfaces attached to those cards.

Chapter 18 explores some of the expansion options for Pro Tools|HD and Digi 003/002 configurations and provides more specific details about the currently available audio interfaces for Pro Tools|HD systems. Figure 3.29 shows a basic Pro Tools|HD configuration.

Pro Tools|HD Cards: Then and Now   In the original Pro Tools|HD hardware, in addition to the single HD Core card in the HD 1, HD Process cards were included in HD 2 and HD 3 configurations. The HD Process card was quickly superseded by the PCI version of the current-generation HD Accel card, however. Using more powerful 321 chips for digital signal processing, HD Accel delivers twice the power of the older HD Process card (and quadruple that of the Mix Farm cards used in the older-generation 24 MIX systems). Among other things, this increased the practical limit for voice counts by up to 50 percent at a given session sample rate compared to the original Pro Tools|HD configurations. For computers with PCIe slots, typical current Pro Tools|HD configurations start with a single Accel Core card to which HD Accel cards (PCIe version) can be added to expand the configuration.

Older PT Configurations

The Digi 002 and Mbox interfaces (discontinued in 2006 and 2005, respectively) are still compatible with current LE versions of Pro Tools 8. Be sure to check compatibility on http://www.digidesign.com, though. And once your hardware/software configuration is working, do not upgrade to new a CPU or operating system before confirming that this will work with your older Pro Tools hardware!

Some previous incarnations of the Pro Tools hardware (especially 24 MIX and Digi 001 at the time of this writing) continue to be viable options for many users, even though they don't support versions 7 and 8 of the Pro Tools software. Some of these legacy hardware configurations offer excellent audio specs and certainly are as functional today as when they enabled Digidesign to become the foremost manufacturer of digital-audio workstations. For instance, repurposing this legacy hardware may be an excellent way to use an older Macintosh model that would otherwise be considered out of date. For recording voice-overs, beat mixing in your project studio, and other simple tasks, this can be an extremely cost-effective way to get into the game or have a second workstation in your facility. Be aware, however, that third-party plug-ins for this older generation of the Pro Tools software may be no longer be available or supported by the manufacturer.

Used Pro Tools systems can be found for sale on eBay and in Digidesign user forums. You can license your used Pro Tools system with Digidesign so that you are a registered user when the time comes for updates and upgrades. (Again, these upgrades to the Pro Tools software may not be compatible with your older hardware or host computer!) The Transfer of Ownership form is available as a downloadable PDF file in the Tech Support area of Digidesign's Web site, and must be signed by both you *and* the seller. (If the used Pro Tools version you are buying uses an authorization diskette to enable software installation, be sure to confirm with the seller that all authorizations have been restored to that diskette.)

Digi 002 Family (Pro Tools LE and External Audio Interface/Control Surface)

Pro Tools Digi 002 configurations consist of the Pro Tools LE software plus an external audio interface/control surface connected to the host computer via its FireWire port. It is compatible with Pro Tools version 8. The Digi 002 hardware (shown in Figure 3.30) features eight analog inputs and outputs, ADAT Lightpipe digital I/O (up to eight more channels of audio, also configurable as stereo optical S/PDIF), plus stereo coaxial S/PDIF digital I/O with RCA jacks. XLR jacks and microphone preamps with individual gain controls, 75Hz hi-pass filters, and 48-volt phantom power (switchable by channel pairs) are provided for the first four input channels, as well as balanced TRS jacks for line/instrument-level inputs. Front-panel switches for these channels allow you to select between the inputs. The TRS inputs for channels 5–8 can be switched (by pairs) between −10dBV and + 4dBu level. The Digi 002 offers one MIDI input and two MIDI outputs. There is a front-panel headphone jack, a dedicated monitor output with TRS jacks, and a dedicated volume control (which mirrors outputs 1–2 and is switchable to mono), plus a fixed-level output (with RCA jacks at −10dBV level). The Digi 002 interface also has a −10dBV dedicated alternate source input, which can be routed to inputs 7–8 or directly through to the monitor output. This is typically used to monitor playback from CDs, computers, video decks, DATs, and other audio devices in the studio. It supports 16-bit or 24-bit recording at sample

Photo courtesy of Digidesign.

Figure 3.30 The Digi 002 (discontinued) is connected directly to the host computer via FireWire.

rates up to 96kHz. (Eight-channel ADAT Lightpipe I/O is limited to a 48kHz sample rate. If this Toslink connector is used as stereo optical S/PDIF instead, sample rates up to 96kHz are supported over that connection.)

The Digi 002 external audio interface is also a dedicated control surface for Pro Tools (as is the current Digi 003 model). It includes eight channel strips with motorized 100mm faders and solo/mute buttons; eight soft rotary encoders (for controlling panning, sends, and plug-in parameters, among other things); LED-based scribble strips, which can selectively display various track and plug-in parameters; Transport controls for Pro Tools; and trim controls for the four microphone preamps. There are also a number of other dedicated buttons for Pro Tools functions (for instance, buttons for the Mix, Edit, and current Plug-in windows; F-keys; and a button for activating QuickPunch mode).

Digi 002 can be used without any computer (or Pro Tools) at all as a standalone 8×4×2 digital mixer complete with EQ, dynamics, delay, and reverb effects, plus the ability to store and recall mix snapshots from its built-in memory.

More Faders for the Digi 002   When used in conjunction with the Digi 002, the eight faders on Digidesign's Command|8 control surface can act as an expansion to the Digi 002 itself, as faders 9–16.

The Digi 002 Rack (shown in Figure 3.31) offers the same features as the Digi 002, but without the control surface and in a two-unit-high rackmountable chassis. It's useful for mobile recording racks or for users who generally prefer to create mix automation graphically or by moving onscreen controls in Pro Tools with the mouse. If desired, the Command|8 control surface can also be added to this configuration.

Photos courtesy of Digidesign.

Figure 3.31   Digi 002 Rack (discontinued).

Mbox (Pro Tools LE and External USB Audio Interface)

This predecessor to the Mbox 2 was discontinued in the fall of 2005 but remains compatible with current LE versions of Pro Tools 7 and 8. The original Mbox (shown in Figure 3.32) is an external USB audio interface with up to two simultaneous channels of analog or digital I/O. The 24-bit analog/digital converters are provided on this USB-powered external interface, and its analog inputs incorporate Focusrite microphone preamps with 48-volt phantom power and balanced I/O using combo connectors (compatible with both XLR and ¼-inch phone) from Neutrik. Unlike the subsequent Mbox 2 model, TRS (¼-inch phone, tip-ring-sleeve) analog insert jacks were provided on the original Mbox—for example, for patching in a compressor/limiter prior to the Pro Tools recording input. S/PDIF digital in/out is supported via coaxial RCA jacks. (The digital output always mirrors analog outputs 1–2, while input for channels 1–2 can be switched between analog and digital sources within the Hardware Setup dialog box of the Pro Tools software. In any case, the original Mbox is always a 2×2 interface.) Buttons on the front panel toggle either channel among mic, line, and instrument level (Hi-Z, high impedance, for direct connection from electric guitar or bass). The Mbox includes front and rear headphone jacks, plus a mono switch. Front-panel knobs allow adjustment of input gain, adjustment of the balance between input and playback to ameliorate monitoring latency while recording, and control of the output level for the headphone jacks. Mbox users can record at 16- or 24-bit resolution, and at 44.1 or 48kHz sample rates.

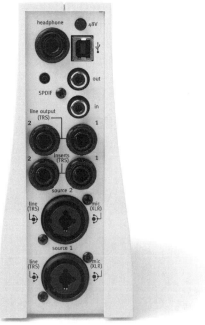

Photos courtesy of Digidesign.

Figure 3.32 The Digidesign Mbox (discontinued) is a two-channel USB audio interface.

Caution: Use the USB Cable That Came with Your Mbox! The USB cable supplied with the Mbox incorporates a cylindrical ferrite *choke* to eliminate RF interference. If you substitute some other USB cable (regardless of whether it has a choke or is advertised as very high quality, shielded, and so on), you will probably hear a high-pitched whining from the Mbox's outputs (not unlike the sound of SMPTE time code, but higher pitched). The same thing will occur if you try to use a USB extender cable to increase the distance between the Mbox and the host computer. Although this noise is strictly on the outputs and doesn't end up in any mix files you bounce to disk, it can be quite annoying, especially in headphones.

Pro Tools|24 MIX, Pro Tools|24 MIXplus, Pro Tools|24 MIX³ (TDM)

This is one of Digidesign's legacy (discontinued) high-end systems for more professional applications. MIX hardware does not support any version of the Pro Tools software higher than 6.4.1, and is therefore not usable with Pro Tools 8. As shown in Figure 3.33, the basic Pro Tools|24 MIX system consists of the Pro Tools TDM software, a Mix Core PCI card, a selection of external audio interfaces (sold separately), plus the cables to connect the audio interfaces to the PCI card and each other. MIX systems support multiple audio interfaces (up to 16 channels of I/O per Mix Core or Mix Farm card). A MIXplus configuration adds a second Mix Farm card with additional DSP chips for more powerful signal routing and processing within the Pro Tools TDM architecture. Each additional Mix Farm card supports additional audio interfaces for up to 16 more channels of I/O per card, and increases simultaneous playback voices from 32 to 64. MIX³ is a bundled configuration with two Mix Farm cards for even more DSP capabilities and another 16 channels of I/O (maximum of 72, versus 160 potential I/O channels in current HD configurations using Pro Tools 8). The TDM version of the Pro Tools software (5.*xx* through 6.*xx* versions) was included with Pro Tools|24 MIX systems, supporting AudioSuite, RTAS, and TDM plug-in architectures, as well as HTDM plug-ins. The older HTDM plug-in format is no

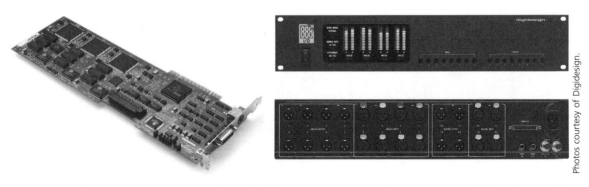

Photos courtesy of Digidesign.

Figure 3.33 Now discontinued, Pro Tools|24 MIX systems consist of the Pro Tools TDM software, PCI cards in the host computer, plus separately purchased external multichannel audio interfaces.

longer supported in Pro Tools 7 and 8; where possible, these are converted to RTAS plug-ins when an older TDM session is opened in the Pro Tools HD software.

Although no longer manufactured, the Pro Tools|24 MIX product line is still used in many professional music and postproduction facilities. Like the current Pro Tools|HD hardware, one could start from a single-card, single-interface configuration and then, as dictated by requirements and budget, expand by adding cards and/or additional hardware interfaces. Be aware, however, that the PCI audio cards used in MIX systems are incompatible with subsequent G5 and Intel-based Macintosh models.

Again, Pro Tools TDM 6.4.1 is the highest software version supported by Pro Tools|24 MIX systems. These hardware configurations are *not* supported for version 7 or 8. Automatic Delay Compensation for plug-in processing and routing latency is not supported by 24 MIX systems, nor are the D-Control (a large-format external control surface for HD systems) and D-Command control surfaces. Also, availability and support for third-party plug-ins that are compatible with this older generation of the Pro Tools software and hardware is extremely limited.

G5 Compatibility (Macintosh Versions) Due to changes in how card voltages are supported by the PCI bus in these models, many of the discontinued Pro Tools hardware systems—including 24 MIX (the Mix I/O, Mix Farm, and DSP Farm cards), Digi 001, Tool-Box (Audiomedia III card), and d24 card used by Pro Tools|24 systems—are incompatible with Macintosh G5 computers and their Intel-based successors. None of these older Digidesign hardware options are compatible with Pro Tools 7 or 8 either, of course.

Digi 001 (Pro Tools LE and Digi 001 Card, External Audio Interface)
The now-discontinued Pro Tools Digi 001 configuration (see Figure 3.34) included the Pro Tools LE software, the Digi 001 PCI card and cable, plus the Digi 001 I/O, a rack-mountable external audio interface. It is *not* compatible with Pro Tools 8 (or any other Pro Tools version higher than 6.4.1) and cannot be installed in any G5 or Intel-based Macintosh computer. The Digi 001 I/O has eight analog inputs and outputs, ADAT Lightpipe digital I/O (up to eight more channels and

Photos courtesy of Digidesign.

Figure 3.34 Pro Tools Digi 001 (now discontinued) consists of the Pro Tools LE software, a single PCI card in the host computer, plus a single external, multichannel audio interface.

also configurable as stereo optical S/PDIF), stereo S/PDIF coaxial digital I/O (with RCA jacks), two microphone preamps with 48-volt phantom power that can be selected as inputs for channels 1 and 2, one MIDI input and one MIDI output, plus a headphone output. It's possible to use all these inputs/outputs simultaneously, for 18 channels of I/O.

Digi 001 was a revolutionary product, offering good specs at a very economical price. For recording a band or for multiple microphones in live theatre, Digi 001 provided a reasonable number of simultaneous recording channels (especially if the ADAT Lightpipe and S/PDIF digital inputs were also used). It could still be a very practical companion for editing ADAT tracks that have been digitally transferred into Pro Tools, for example. As an excellent all-in-one solution, the Digi 001 broke important ground in the evolution of digital-audio workstations, combining the audio I/O, MIDI interface, and two moderate-quality microphone preamplifiers into a single rack-mounted interface. Combined with a high-quality mic preamp (especially when this can be connected to the 001 interface digitally, via the S/PDIF or ADAT Lightpipe output, and when using a high-quality clock source), the Digi 001 could produce very good-sounding results! (Note that Pro Tools LE 6.4 is the highest software version supported by Digi 001 systems—and again, the Digi 001 is *not* supported for Pro Tools version 8.)

iLok USB Smart Key

The iLok USB Smart Key (see Figure 3.35) is a USB hardware device used for authorizing various programs and plug-ins on both Windows and Macintosh computers, including many of the plug-ins used with Pro Tools. It's manufactured by PACE Anti-Piracy, which also developed the authorization diskette copy-protection mechanism used by many previous versions of Pro Tools and other audio/MIDI programs. An iLok is also included with the M-Powered version of Pro Tools and must be attached to the host computer in order for that program to run. Although many audio and MIDI programs require some sort of hardware dongle (a hardware authorization device that is specific to a single program) to be attached to the computer (usually via USB in most current versions) in order to operate, the iLok's important innovation was that it could store the authorizations for multiple programs and plug-ins, even from different developers.

Figure 3.35   A single iLok USB Smart Key stores authorizations for multiple programs and plug-ins.

iLok owners need to register for a free account at http://www.ilok.com to download any new licenses. With an active iLok account, you can purchase plug-ins online, and if the iLok is attached, it can be automatically authorized for the plug-in as part of the purchase process. More typically, the plug-in vendor will deposit the license to your iLok account; from there, you download it into your iLok. Digidesign Customer Service also uses this site for processing upgrades from plug-ins that relied on the older authorization-diskette method to the iLok system. Incidentally, authorizations can be obtained by connecting the iLok to any computer that has access to the Internet and has the iLok Client Software installed, whether it has Pro Tools hardware attached or not.

Alternatively, a license card may come with some plug-in software you've purchased. The working part of this is actually a smaller GSM plastic chip—a cutout that you remove from the larger protective card. It uses smart card technology, which is also used on GSM cell phones and some credit cards. During the process of authorizing a plug-in or program, you insert the license card into a slot in the end of the iLok USB Smart Key.

Sometimes, a plug-in vendor will provide you a downloadable license for your iLok that permits you to use a fully functional version of their product for a limited period in demo mode. For many plug-ins, however, this is also a possibility even if you *don't* have an iLok.

The drivers that iLok requires are automatically installed with current LE, M-Powered, or Pro Tools HD software. These drivers are updated periodically, and updaters will sometimes be included when you purchase a plug-in. Whenever plug-ins are found that haven't been authorized yet, upon launch, a Pro Tools dialog box will prompt you to click the Authorization button in order to begin the process.

So, what's the advantage of all this, you might ask? First, plug-in developers have a right to protect their intellectual property, ensuring that only users who have paid for their product can use it; that's a given. However, if you're a new user and have never lived through the drawbacks of diskette-based software authorizations, here's a brief glimpse of the bad old days. First, you would install the software (from a CD or, in the *really* olden days, from many, many diskettes). Upon launching the software, you would be prompted to insert a separate authorization diskette. The authorization routine would install invisible key files somewhere on your hard disk that enabled the program to run, and then would write onto the diskette, decreasing its available authorization count from, say, two to one. Later, if you needed to install the software on a new disk or machine, you would de-authorize the program on the original machine, which removed the invisible key files and again wrote to the original key diskette to restore the authorization count. If your hard disk crashed—or you reformatted without remembering to de-authorize all the necessary programs and/or plug-ins—you lost that authorization forever. Rewriting authorizations to the diskette also increased the probability that it would eventually fail, despite your potentially spending hours on the authorization process, depending on how much software you were dealing with. In any case, diskette drives are now a rarity on current computers!

Conventional dongles—hardware authorization devices that are specific to a single program— also work pretty well. Like the iLok, they let you reformat and restore the contents of your hard disk without worrying about invisible key files or authorizations, move up to a new machine by simply transferring the dongle to the new software installation, and so on. Obviously, losing or breaking your dongle could be a real crisis—but this is equally a concern with the iLok system. The Zero Downtime coverage offered on iLok.com for a moderate yearly charge provides immediate replacement of your licenses should your iLok get damaged, lost, or stolen. This is highly recommended for all professional applications.

Traditionally, one of the problems with dongles has been that dongles from certain programs can be incompatible with others—this was especially true back in the days of SCSI and parallel port dongles. But with the iLok, the same shared programmable device stores licenses for up to 100 different programs and plug-ins. You can back up your software and do a low-level reformat on your system disks, reload the programs, and then simply reattach the iLok to get back to work with your previously authorized plug-ins. That's the attraction of the iLok system, which has been overwhelmingly accepted by plug-in developers in the Pro Tools arena.

Note: It should be noted that some other audio programs, as well as certain plug-ins for Pro Tools, are protected by a Syncrosoft USB dongle, which also stores downloadable licenses.

The M-Powered version of Pro Tools comes with an iLok that has been pre-authorized for the program—no separate license card is required. This iLok must be attached to the computer's USB port in order to run Pro Tools M-Powered and can also be used to store authorizations for other programs or plug-ins.

Digidesign Control Surfaces for Pro Tools

Many users find that a mouse or trackball and keyboard are all they need to work with Pro Tools. Nevertheless, a physical control surface has its advantages. Among other things, having dedicated faders and buttons that you can actually feel under your fingers can be a productivity enhancement when you're interacting with musicians in the studio or mixing long sequences for film and video. Also, it's obvious that being able to move multiple faders simultaneously is a must for intuitive, seat-of-your-pants mixing. It all comes down to your personal preference and the kind of work you do. Appendix B, "Add-ons, Extensions, and Cool Stuff for Your Rig," revisits the subject of external control surfaces, including these and other options from Mackie, CM Labs, and other third parties. The following, then, briefly summarizes the current offerings from Digidesign.

Command|8

Command|8 connects to the host computer via USB. Transport controls, eight motorized faders, and eight rotary encoders with LED rings around them indicate current parameter values or metering. These can be assigned to Pro Tools channels in groups of eight. A back-lit LCD display (two rows of 55 characters) shows track information and parameter values. Command|8 incorporates a 1-in, 2-out MIDI interface and a footswitch jack for hands-free punching in/out of recording. Its monitoring section, designed by Focusrite, includes a main Pro Tools audio input, an external source input (for CD players and other audio devices around your studio), and dedicated control room/headphones outputs.

The Command|8 (seen in Figure 3.36) can be used with HD, LE, and M-Powered versions of Pro Tools, as well as with Avid Media Compose. It can be used as a fader expander for other legacy tactile control surfaces from Digidesign such as the Pro Control, Control|24, or the Digi 002. The Command|8 offers a standalone MIDI controller mode for use with other MIDI applications.

Photo courtesy of Digidesign.

Figure 3.36 The Command|8 control surface is compatible with HD or LE versions of Pro Tools and other MIDI programs.

Control|24 (Discontinued)

This control surface, shown in Figure 3.37, connects to the host computer via Ethernet (10BaseT, RJ-45 connectors). It features Transport controls with a scrub/shuttle wheel; a built-in talkback microphone; an 8×2 analog line submixer; 24 motorized faders with dedicated level meters; mute, solo, record-enable, channel select, automation mode, EQ, and dynamics buttons on each channel; as well as 16 class A mic/line preamps by Focusrite, with 48-volt phantom power. The Control|24 also includes an LED display for Transport locations, plus 26 illuminated scribble strips for names and parameter values. Dedicated modifier keys for use when pressing other buttons include Command, Option, and Control (equivalent to Ctrl, Alt, and

Figure 3.37   The Control|24 control surface is compatible with HD and LE versions of Pro Tools (but not with M-Powered).

Start on Windows). Control|24 is compatible with HD or LE versions of Pro Tools, but *not* with M-Powered.

C|24

This control surface (shown in Figure 3.38) was introduced in fall of 2007. The C|24 is compatible with HD and LE versions of Pro Tools, but *not* M-Powered. It includes many of the features listed for the Command|24 (and is also connected to the computer via Ethernet), in a format redesigned by Digidesign. The faders are arranged in three banks of eight each, and the LED scribble strips have two lines of six characters each. The mic input section uses mic preamps based on Digidesign's own Digi 003 design, with high-pass filters and −20dB pads on each channel. The 8×2 mixer section can be routed directly to the monitoring section. The C|24 also includes an updated 5.1 analog monitoring section whose outputs can be individually trimmed in .5dB increments for calibration. Soft keys are also provided for controlling certain functions, and a Window Configuration button directly accesses the Window Configuration feature available in Pro Tools versions 7.3 and higher.

ProControl (Discontinued)

The ProControl also connects to the host computer via Ethernet (10BaseT, RJ-45 connectors). It features Transport controls with a weighted scrub/shuttle wheel, eight motorized 100mm faders, and eight rotary encoders with LED rings around them to indicate current parameter values or

Photo courtesy of Digidesign.

Figure 3.38 The C|24 control surface is compatible with HD and LE versions of Pro Tools (but not with M-Powered).

metering. An analog monitoring section supports analog I/O via DB-25 connectors. The control surface also features a built-in talkback microphone and input for a listenback microphone; a dedicated control-room section with its own level controls, source selectors, and mute/dim, stereo/surround, and mono switches; a numeric keypad; and Edit/Assign scribble strips that show five insert slots on the selected channel or parameters for the effect currently being edited. A dedicated Send section is usable on any currently selected channel. The base ProControl unit (shown in Figure 3.39) is expandable via the Edit Pack option (featuring a machine control section; eight 40-segment level meters; Start, End, and Length LED displays; two joystick panners; a trackball; and a built-in color-coded keyboard with Pro Tools function labels), or additional fader expansion packs (eight faders each, up to a maximum of 48 channels). While the newer D-Command control surface supplants much of its functionality, ProControl units continue to operate at many professional studios not only with current Pro Tools|HD systems but especially with the previous-generation 24 MIX hardware.

D-Control

The ICON family of hardware from Digidesign is based around the D-Control, D-Control ES, D-Command, and D-Command ES work surfaces, the rack-mounted XMON monitoring and communications module, and a Pro Tools|HD system. The D-Control is currently Digidesign's most sophisticated external control surface for use with Pro Tools|HD systems in a studio environment. The D-Control ES variation, introduced in fall of 2007, features a darker color scheme; updated, higher-contrast text and graphics; and a new LED color layout for switches. Core D-Control tactile worksurfaces for Pro Tools|HD systems consist of a master module plus a single 16-channel fader module, which can be mounted to either side. From there, additional

Photo courtesy of Digidesign.

Figure 3.39   The ProControl control surface is for use with TDM systems (including HD and 24 MIX) only.

fader modules can be added, up to 80 channels/faders total. Each channel strip has six rotary encoders, with LED rings around them to indicate current parameter values or metering. LED metering is provided for each channel, plus eight channels of metering for the master section. Twenty-nine illuminated pushbuttons per channel strip are provided for switching channel modes and attributes. LED displays indicate channel names or the currently selected editing parameter for each, and there are dedicated LED displays for the main/sub time indicators and for the Start, End, and Length fields in the Pro Tools software. A Focus channel strip in the center master module can be used for editing any selected channel without leaving the center of the console. In addition, the D-Control has dedicated EQ and Dynamics panels, usable on any selected channel. Its Transport section includes separate Pro Tools Transport and Machine Transport switches, a scrub/shuttle wheel, a master record enable switch, dedicated buttons for selecting the various Pro Tools recording modes, pre/post-roll, and zoom/navigation controls. There's a built-in alphanumeric keyboard, a two-button trackball, and a swinging arm for mounting a flat-panel display of the user's choosing. The D-Control connects to the core Pro Tools|HD Accel system via Ethernet.

An optional surround panner is also available for installation in the D-Control. In addition to hardware and software buttons, it incorporates a color LCD touchscreen as well as two touch-sensitive joysticks and two rotary encoders with LED rings, any of which can be used for surround panning in the X-Y axis or for controlling plug-in parameters and other mix features that are unrelated to panning.

Completing any ICON system (whether based on the D-Control or D-Command work surface) is a rack-mounted XMON monitor system. In addition to supporting surround mixing, it provides dedicated outputs for three separate stereo cue mixes, talkback, listenback, studio monitors, and headphones.

The D-Control (shown in Figure 3.40) is for use with HD systems only, and does not support M-Powered or LE versions of Pro Tools.

Photo courtesy of Digidesign.

Figure 3.40   The basic D-Control consists of a master module plus a 16-channel fader module. This can be expanded to up to 80 channels/faders.

D-Command

The D-Command worksurface offers a more compact alternative to the D-Control. In its basic eight-fader configuration, D-Command is about 32 inches/82cm wide by 29 inches/74cm deep versus 55 inches/166cm wide and 42 inches/107cm deep for a basic 16-fader D-Control console.

The D-Command main unit features a central control section with monitoring and communications controls and eight touch-sensitive motorized channel faders. It communicates with the host Pro Tools computer system via Ethernet. (A separate Ethernet hub is required, to which all these devices are attached.) Each channel strip has two rotary encoders, with LED rings to show either the current parameter setting or metering. The D-Command is expandable up to 24 faders via a single 16-channel fader module (connected to yet another port on the Ethernet hub). On each channel, one six-channel LCD displays information about the current parameter selected for the rotary encoder, while another serves as a scribble strip. Each of these channels can function independently, in a different mode from the others. There are illuminated pushbuttons and bar-graph meters on each channel, plus eight more bar-graph meters in the master section. The center section has dedicated control panels for editing EQ (with 12 rotary controls) and dynamics plug-ins (with six rotary controls). The D-Command includes the same XMON remote, rack-mounted analog I/O audio monitoring and communications module (two rack-units high) as the D-Control, to which it is connected via a proprietary 15-pin cable. The monitoring section on the D-Command itself provides control for up to two 5.1 surround inputs, three stereo inputs, and two cue sends.

Like the D-Control, the D-Command (shown in Figure 3.41) is for HD systems only, and does not support M-Powered or LE versions of Pro Tools. Also, the ES version features a darker color aesthetic, as well as a center section with panels dedicated to EQ and dynamics plug-in editing.

Photo courtesy of Digidesign.

Figure 3.41   This basic eight-fader configuration for the D-Command worksurface has been expanded with a 16-fader fader module.

Venue

Venue is Digidesign's live digital mixing console. It consists of the D-Show mixing console shown in Figure 3.42 (the main unit plus one sidecar fader module) and its FOH rack (which contains the computer for its mix engine and the expandable audio and MIDI I/O), an expandable stage rack I/O unit with remote-controlled preamps and recallable settings, plus multichannel digital snakes with BNC connectors that each support up to 48 bidirectional signals over distances of up to 500 feet. A fully expanded Venue system (including two additional sidecar modules with 16 faders each) supports up to 96 microphone inputs and routing to 27 audio busses. We won't go into all the Venue features here—snapshot automation; the Personal Q option, which enables performers to control their own monitor mixes; real-time use of plug-in effects during live mixing/recording with dynamics processing on every input channel; four plug-in inserts and one hardware insert on every input channel and output bus; and many others—that's a subject that would fill another book! Venue is mentioned here because, in addition to its capabilities as a live mixer, it can simultaneously act as the front-end for Pro Tools recording in live situations. With the optional FWx card, multichannel recording and playback with Pro Tools LE systems is supported. After you record the live event, the native Pro Tools LE session that results can subsequently be edited and mixed on any Pro Tools system. The optional TDM Record card will support direct connection via DigiLink cables to HD Core and HD Accel cards on a Pro Tools|HD system, without any external audio interfaces required on that system in order to record. A native Pro Tools HD session is produced that can subsequently be edited and mixed in the studio. Various plug-in manufactures, including Drawmer, Waves, and others, have introduced plug-ins that are specifically designed for live applications with Venue systems. In addition to the D-Show system, Digi offers Venue Profile, Mix Rack, and SC48 systems, which provide entries into Venue technology with compactness and budget in mind. Full details can be found at http://www.digidesign.com.

Photo courtesy of Digidesign.

Figure 3.42   Venue is a live mixing solution that also offers options for direct recording to Pro Tools. Shown here: the D-Show console.

Summary

As stated at the beginning of Chapter 1, "About Pro Tools," Pro Tools consists of a program that runs on a computer plus specialized audio cards and/or interfaces. So aside from being an audio expert, you need to be on top of the computer game. For example, you *must* back up and archive your data on a regular basis (unless you don't mind losing it)! Also, try to use some common sense about installing other programs on the same computer (especially older games, background-operation utilities, and operating-system upgrades).

Pro Tools makes your hard disks work very hard, so they need to offer good performance levels and be properly maintained. Additionally, Pro Tools needs much more RAM than, say, your typical spreadsheet program. If you need to connect external MIDI devices or synchronize to SMPTE time code or video, additional hardware is generally required; it's not incorporated into all Pro Tools hardware because user requirements vary so widely. (Various interfaces in the Mbox 2, Digi 003, and Digi 002 families, as well as the now-discontinued Digi 001, have built-in MIDI inputs/outputs. So do many M-Audio interfaces and the Command|8 control surface.) In short, you're probably going to need a more robust computer setup than most of your non-audio friends (with the obvious exception of video editors, 3D designers, and obsessive gamers). But then again, you're going to have a *lot* more fun!

A final reminder: When you are excitedly preparing to load Pro Tools or connect a new interface onto your computer, take the time to read the documentation that is bundled with your product. Digi recommends various tweaks for both Macintosh and Windows-based systems for better performance, and there is a specific order to when interfaces and consoles are connected to the computer during the loading procedure that will save headaches if followed correctly. In addition, consulting the Digidesign Web site's Support section for the specific product before loading can prevent mind-numbing troubleshooting. Closely read the documentation associated with your product concerning the computer platform you are using, paying special attention to Digi-approved boards, chips, and hard drives, as well as approved versions of common software like QuickTime. Lastly, it doesn't hurt to peruse the Digidesign User Conference support forum to see if other users are reporting issues. In short, the Digidesign Web site could be your best friend if used judiciously, possibly preventing hours of hair-pulling frustration when starting the loading and setup process with a new system, thus allowing you to create audio magic (or havoc) all the sooner.

4 Creating Your First Pro Tools Session

S o you've installed the Pro Tools program and completed the appropriate installations and configurations for your MIDI interface and any external MIDI modules, opened the program, checked your settings in the Pro Tools Hardware Setup and Playback Engine dialog boxes, and now you're ready to rock. Let's walk through a new session, look at some of the most important features, and get a feel for how you start on a Pro Tools project.

This chapter provides a quick tour of the basic Pro Tools working style for the impatient new user. If you're somewhat familiar with Pro Tools already, you may wish to skip ahead to Chapters 5, "The Transport Window," 6, "The Edit Window," and 7, "The Mix Window," to explore those subjects in much more detail. Note that this chapter assumes that all default preferences for a new installation of the Pro Tools program have been left unchanged.

For the sake of simplicity, in this chapter, you're going to record and edit only audio, not MIDI. We assume that you have *some* audio source that can be recorded from the channel 1 input of your audio hardware—a microphone (perhaps via a mixer or preamplifier, unless your Digidesign hardware provides this), a guitar preamp, your kid brother's portable CD player, whatever. We also assume that you have some 16-bit, 44kHz audio files somewhere on your audio disks—for example, in AIF or WAV format. You can also use Pro Tools to import entire audio CD tracks by dragging them into the Regions List from the Workspace browser window. Otherwise, you could import a small section of audio from within a CD track (for now, it's not important exactly what) using QuickTime Pro (Mac), Peak (Mac), Sound Forge or WaveLab (Windows), Audacity (Mac/Win), or whatever your favorite CD audio-extraction program is (MusicMatch Jukebox, CD Spin Doctor, and so on).

You May See Things Differently! As we've explained in previous chapters, not only are there several versions of the Pro Tools software (associated with various hardware configurations), but this program is also being updated fairly regularly by Digidesign. We've been careful to make the examples in this chapter equally applicable for all current versions of the software. For the record, though, most of the screenshots throughout this book were created in Macintosh version 8 of the Pro Tools software (HD, M-Powered, and LE versions).

Your First Session

First, you're going to open Pro Tools from the Macintosh Dock (or Windows Start menu) or by double-clicking its icon on the desktop or a window and set up a new Pro Tools session document. Notice that you select the audio file format (including sample rate and bit depth) for a new Pro Tools session *before* recording any audio! There are two ways of getting audio into your Pro Tools session: using an audio track's Record Enable button in the Mix (or Edit) window and the Record button in the Transport window to record an audio source, or by importing existing audio files from other disk locations.

Setting Up a New Session

As explained in Chapter 2, "Pro Tools Terms and Concepts," when you create a new session document, this file resides within a folder of the same name, which Pro Tools automatically creates on your hard disk. An Audio Files subfolder is automatically created within this folder to store any audio files created by recording or processing in this session. With the advent of Pro Tools 8, the user now has the choice of using a template as the basis of a new session or using the traditional blank session to start fresh. These choices are presented, along with Open Session and Open Recent Session options, in the Quick Start dialog box that appears when Pro Tools 8 is opened. (Note that you can choose to *not* have the Quick Start dialog box appear when you start the program if you desire; simply uncheck Show Quick Start in the lower-left corner of the dialog box.)

The templates that come with Pro Tools 8 are designed to allow users to get working quickly and to provide users with some creative elements to jump-start music making. For instance, the Ballad Guitar template comes with a pre-programmed MIDI drum track with the Xpand2 plug-in as a sound source. It also has tracks with pre-assigned plug-ins and routings for bass, synth pad, rhythm guitar, lead guitar, and any sound source like a microphone for vocals. For new Pro Tools users, these templates can save time as well as provide good examples of signal routing within the program. Other users, however, might prefer to use a blank template to custom-design their signal routings and plug-in assignments.

In addition to using the Quick Start dialog box's Create Blank Session option, users can start a new session in Pro Tools the reliable old-school way:

1. After opening Pro Tools, choose File > New Session. In the New Session dialog box (shown in Figure 4.1), name the new session document anything you like, but be sure to create it on the disk drive you will be using for audio recording. The name you specify applies not only to the Pro Tools session document, but also to a new folder containing this document. For this test session, let's choose either WAV (BWV) or AIF file format, 44.1kHz as the sample rate, and a bit depth of 24 bits.

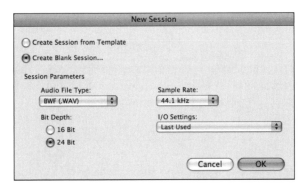

Figure 4.1   The New Session dialog box is where you name the new session file and configure its audio parameters. Some options (like sample rates) in this dialog box vary according to which version of Pro Tools you're using.

Note: Unless there's some specific reason *not* to do so, we recommend 24-bit resolution for all Pro Tools sessions where you plan to record new audio. Working at this higher bit depth allows you to be less concerned about always trying to record at relatively high input levels, especially when source levels may be unpredictable and/or you don't apply any dynamics processing prior to the inputs of your audio interface. There's also less quantization noise in proportion to very low-level signals or reverb decays on recorded tracks. Lesser bit depths could theoretically come back to haunt you if you ever needed to dramatically boost the level of an extremely low-level recording later on. At recording levels, you also leave more margin for unexpected volume peaks in the source signal you're recording. This is especially handy because, unlike most analog recording situations, many Pro Tools users don't use compression or any other dynamic processing prior to the inputs of their audio hardware. On the other hand, in music production, many people will apply compression, limiting, and so on prior to the input of Pro Tools precisely because of how it colors the sound.

2.   There are three main windows in Pro Tools: the Transport (which looks like the controls of a tape recorder and always floats on top of the other two windows), the Mix window (which displays Pro Tools tracks in a similar fashion to traditional audio mixers), and the Edit window (which displays the contents of individual tracks along a horizontal time scale, and can also display duplicates of the Transport's buttons). In a newly created session, there are no tracks to display yet (in Pro Tools, you create tracks as needed). A toolbar with various indicators and buttons is always visible at the top of the Edit window, while the Mix window is completely blank until you start creating

tracks to work in. For the purpose of this quick tour, we want the Edit window to be visible. Choose Track > New.

Tip: You can toggle, or alternate, between the Mix and Edit windows by pressing Command+= (Mac) or Ctrl+= (Windows). That is, hold down the Command key or Ctrl key while pressing the equal-sign key. Remember that!

---

3. In the dialog box that appears (shown in Figure 4.2), type 4 in the Audio field to create four new audio tracks, and then click the Create button.

Figure 4.2   The New Tracks dialog box is where you create new audio or MIDI tracks, Aux Input tracks, Instrument tracks, and Master Fader tracks in Pro Tools. In this dialog box, you can hold down the Command key (Ctrl key in Windows) and use the up/down arrows on your computer keyboard to cycle through the various track class options. As shown here, you can create multiple classes of tracks simultaneously.

4. Four new audio tracks appear in the Edit window, named Audio 1, Audio 2, Audio 3, and Audio 4. These names aren't terribly descriptive, so let's rename them. Double-click the name of the first track (Audio 1, at the left side of the window) and rename it MyStuff. Click the Next button without leaving this dialog box and name the second track Drums, the third track FX1, and the fourth track More FX2. (By the way, there's a keyboard shortcut for using the Next button to move from one track to another within this track naming dialog box: Command+Return [Ctrl+Enter in Windows] on the alphanumeric keyboard—a very good one to know!) Click OK or simply press Return (Enter in Windows) on the alphanumeric keyboard when you're finished naming tracks.

5. Choose File > Save. (Be sure to also check out Chapter 8, "Menu Selections: Highlights," for information about the Auto Backup function in Pro Tools, which is

configured in the Operation tab of the Preferences dialog box.) It's important to save as you work! In fact, getting to know the shortcut for saving (Command+S for Macintosh, and Ctrl+S for Windows) as a second-nature action after any change in the session could be the best tidbit you learn about Pro Tools early on.

6. Use the Track > New command again (notice the keyboard shortcut indicated next to this menu selection). This time, though, change the right-most pop-up selector within the New Tracks dialog box to create an Aux Input track (mono) instead of an audio track. After clicking the Create button to close this dialog box, double-click this Aux Input track's name as before and change its name from Aux 1 to Delay.

7. Press Shift+Command+N (Shift+Ctrl+N in Windows) to open the New Tracks dialog box one last time. Create a Master Fader track (stereo), keeping the default name, Master 1. (Actually, you could have used the New Tracks dialog box to create all these tracks in a single operation, as shown in Figure 4.2. Hey, *now* we tell you!)

8. Now, select View > Mix Window. The Mix window is now the top-most window in Pro Tools, although the Edit window is still open behind it. These windows present two different views of the tracks you've created.

Renaming Tracks in Pro Tools 7.3 to 8 There are several ways to rename a track in Pro Tools. You can double-click its name in the Mix or Edit window as described in the preceding steps. Alternatively, in versions 7.3 and higher, you can right-click any track name (even inside the Tracks List if it's displayed at the left side of these windows) to open a pop-up menu. Along with offering the Rename command, this menu also lets you duplicate or delete tracks, as well as hide them, make them inactive, export MIDI data, and several other common operations.

Your First Recording

Each time you record audio in a Pro Tools session, new digital audio files are created. Pro Tools automatically creates an Audio Files subfolder within the session's main folder on your hard disk to contain them. For our purposes, it's not terribly important exactly *what* you record—and 30 or 60 seconds worth of material will be sufficient. Our goal is simply to familiarize you with how to enable individual tracks for recording in Pro Tools. (On the other hand, if you just happen to record a masterpiece your first time out, go ahead and take it all the way!) To record, do the following:

1. Click the R (record enable) button on the MyStuff track to arm (enable) this track for recording. If you have your sound source properly connected, you should see some activity on the track's level meter. (In the Mix window, a pop-up Input selector for each audio track allows you to select any bus or physical input on the audio hardware that's

the source for recording. Again, we're assuming here that Analog Input 1/Left appears as the default selection for your first audio track, and that your audio source is connected there.) Test your levels; if the red clipping indicator on this track comes on, click it once to reset it, reduce the volume of your input source (or the source gain control for this audio input, if your audio interface offers one), and test again.

Audio Record Levels Are Adjusted at the Source (Not Via the Track's Fader) Unlike conventional mixing boards and tape recorders, volume faders on audio tracks have *no effect* on the level actually being recorded to disk. You can therefore adjust these to whatever level is convenient for listening purposes. If you see the track's red clipping indicators light up when the track is record-enabled, you must reduce the level either at the source device or on the audio interface itself if this feature is provided (for example, using gain controls on the Mbox 2 family, original Mbox, and some of the M-Audio interfaces; gain controls for microphone inputs on the Digi 003, Digi 002, and Digi 001 interfaces; or the gain adjustments in the Hardware Setup dialog box for the 96i I/O interface).

---

2. In the Transport window, click to arm the Record button and then click Play. (As mentioned earlier, Transport window controls are similar to those of a tape recorder. Chapter 5 explains the features of the Transport window in much more detail.) If for any reason the Transport window isn't visible, you can always open it via the Window > Transport command or by holding down the Command key (Ctrl key in Windows) as you press 1 on your computer's numeric keypad.

3. Make whatever noises you like using your microphone or guitar/bass preamp. If the Edit window is still visible, you'll notice that a red rectangle within the track gradually increases in length as you record, reflecting the duration of the audio region being created (shown in Figure 4.3).

4. Click Stop in the Transport window. If you wish, you can now arm other tracks for recording and repeat these steps in order to create additional parts.

Importing Audio into Pro Tools

In some Pro Tools sessions, you want to use existing audio files from some other disk location on your computer. These may be standard elements used in many projects (station identifications, tones, recurring sound effects, and so on) or elements from other Pro Tools sessions being used to create a remix or submix. The File > Import > Audio command is typically used for this. In the Import Audio dialog box, you can probably guess that the Convert button appears when audio files to be imported are not directly compatible with the current session—for example, if their audio file format, sample rate, or bit depth is different from what you have selected for this session. If you use the Convert or Copy buttons in this dialog box, new copies of any imported files are created within the current session's Audio Files folder.

Clipping
Indicator

Record-Enable
Button

Level
Meter

Figure 4.3 An audio track during recording in the Edit window. The top segment of the level meter is a clipping indicator. It lights up in red if levels are too high, which would cause digital distortion in the recorded audio. Digital clipping is not pretty—avoid it!

Chapter 6 provides more detailed information about importing existing audio files into Pro Tools (which is somewhat different in versions prior to 7.3), but here's the basic procedure:

1. If necessary, press Command+= (Ctrl+= in Windows) to switch back to the Edit window.

2. Select the File > Import Audio command. (You'll notice that the Regions List at the right side of the Edit window contains only the single audio region you've recorded so far.)

3. In the Import Audio dialog box (shown in Figure 4.4), navigate through your disks and folders to the audio file you've chosen to import. Double-click the file to copy it into the list of audio to be imported (and converted, if necessary, to match the current session's audio format), and then click the Done button.

4. The Audio Import Options dialog box appears, as shown in Figure 4.5. For the moment, you will just click the Regions List button so that the new audio regions appear there. (See the sidebar in this section for information about the New Track option in this dialog box.)

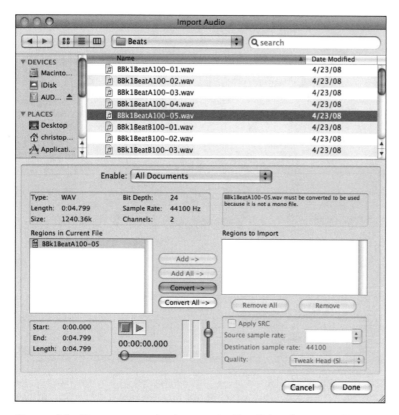

Figure 4.4 You can use the Import Audio dialog box to add existing audio files (or specific regions within them) to the current Pro Tools session's Regions List. Pro Tools references these files in their original disk locations unless you click the Copy button or unless conversions are required to create new copies that match the audio file format, sample rate, or bit depth of the current session.

Figure 4.5 In the Audio Import Options dialog box, you can choose to create new audio tracks for each mono audio file (or stereo pair) that you're importing.

5.   The audio files you just imported now appear in the Regions List for this session. Note that if any file you imported was stereo, it will have been split into two new mono files with the suffixes .L and .R because Pro Tools doesn't directly support stereo

interleaved files for use within tracks. However, it will appear as a single stereo audio region unless you click its triangular icon to reveal the left/right subregions. If you chose to place the imported files directly into tracks in the previous step, the imported audio regions will also appear at the locations you specified.

Creating New Tracks While Importing Audio When you use the File menu's Import > Audio command, a dialog box lets you choose whether to simply leave the audio you're importing in the Regions List or to place those files directly into one or more new tracks. (In Pro Tools versions prior to 7.3, there were separate commands for Import > Audio and Import > Audio to Track.) If you select New Track, for each mono file or stereo pair that you import, Pro Tools automatically creates a new audio track with a region corresponding to that audio file already placed at the location you specified in the dialog box (Session Start, Song Start, at the start of the current selection or cursor location, or to a position you will specify in the Spot dialog box). The newly created track inherits the name of the source file. This can be a real time-saver. An alternative method is to drag an audio file either from the Workspace browser window, the Macintosh Finder or the Windows Explorer directly into the Tracks List (assuming that this pane at the left side of the Edit window is currently visible); in a similar fashion, a new audio track will be automatically created and named after the source file.

Editing and Effects

In this section, you'll perform some basic edit operations on the audio you recorded and imported, and then apply some plug-in effects to alter the sound.

Editing

Now you're ready to start editing your audio—where the real fun starts! Unlike tape-based audio systems, where you actually have to cut up your original recording (a risky, destructive process), Pro Tools enables you to freely move segments of audio around, adjust their length, and so on—without altering the original recordings in any way. So feel free to experiment! To get started, do the following:

1. Click the Grabber tool's button to select the tool. It's the button that looks like a hand in the toolbar at the top of the Edit window, shown in Figure 4.6.

Figure 4.6 Use the Grabber tool to select and drag regions around within tracks (and also to move MIDI notes within MIDI tracks in Notes display format or to edit automation data.) Shift-click with the Grabber to select additional regions. If you hold down the Option key (Alt key in Windows) as you drag a selected region with the Grabber, it is copied rather than moved.

2. Locate the audio region you just imported into the Regions List and drag it out into the track display area, releasing the mouse button to drop it anywhere near the beginning of the Drums track. Notice that as soon as you drag this region out onto the track display area, an outline of the region appears, reflecting its duration.

3. Again using the Grabber, click and drag the region, pulling it down into the FX1 track. Audio regions can reside in any Pro Tools audio track with a matching number of channels (mono, stereo, or various multichannel formats in the Pro Tools HD software), regardless of where they were originally recorded.

4. Click the Trimmer tool's button. It's also in the toolbar at the top of the Edit window, and looks like part of a rectangle with left/right arrows, as shown in Figure 4.7.

Figure 4.7 Use the Trimmer tool to alter the length of existing regions within a track, change the duration of fades, lengthen/shorten MIDI notes, scale automation or MIDI controller data, and (in versions 7.3 and higher) create or change the length of looped regions.

5. Click and drag with the Trimmer tool at a point somewhere near the end of the region you recorded in the MyStuff track. Notice that as you drag back and forth without releasing the mouse button, the region gets shorter or longer (but cannot be stretched any longer than its original length, of course). Because you can see the audio waveform, you can trim the region to a shorter duration to make it end right at the point where you actually stopped playing (or singing or speaking, or whatever noise you made). After you release the mouse button, a new region definition is created, with –01 added to the end of the original region's name. Both this new region name (created as the result of an edit) and the original whole-file region it came from now appear in the Regions List. Most editing in Pro Tools is non-destructive, meaning that the original audio is unaltered. This gives you a great deal of flexibility for experimentation.

6. Click the Selector tool's button; it's between the Trimmer and Grabber tool buttons and looks like an audio waveform with a selection in its middle portion, as shown in Figure 4.8. Click and drag the Selector tool's I-beam cursor to highlight a portion in the *center* of the region now residing in the FX1 track (the file you imported from disk).

7. Now delete that selection either by pressing the Delete/Backspace key or by using the Edit > Clear command. Notice that new region names were created for the two remaining pieces at the beginning and end, with –01 and –02 appended to the original region name. No matter how many times you delete, cut, or resize audio regions with tools in the Edit window, the process is always non-destructive—the original audio regions and files remain intact in the Regions List and the complete audio file on disk is unaffected by any resizing or deletion in the Edit window.

Figure 4.8 Use the Selector tool to make selections within a region or to make larger selections encompassing multiple regions or tracks. To adjust the boundaries of a currently highlighted selection, hold down the Shift key as you click or drag. Shift-clicking in additional tracks adds them to the current timeline selection. Pressing Shift+Tab extends the selection to the end of the current region. Pressing Option+Shift+Tab (Alt+Shift+Tab in Windows) extends the selection to the region's beginning.

The Regions List The Regions List is a sort of "bin" where all the audio, MIDI, and video referenced by the current Pro Tools session appears. You can drag audio regions directly from here onto an audio track (but not onto an Aux Input or Master Fader track, because these track classes cannot contain audio regions.) You can also drag MIDI regions onto MIDI or Instrument tracks and video files onto video tracks. As you just saw in step 7, some region definitions are automatically created by Pro Tools as a result of editing operations (although an option in the Show submenu of the local menu for the Regions List allows you to suppress display of these auto-created regions, if preferred). Other chapters explain instances where you create your own new region definitions—for example, via commands in the Edit and AudioSuite menus. *Whole-file* audio regions (as opposed to others that represent only smaller portions within their parent audio files) always appear in bold type in the Regions List. (One exception to this is when whole file audio regions are imported from an OMF, or Open Media Framework, file. OMFs are discussed in Chapter 14, "Postproduction and Soundtracks.")

---

8. Click the Zoomer tool button; it features a magnifying glass, as shown in Figure 4.9. The Zoomer is used for changing the magnification on your horizontal (time) view of the contents of Pro Tools tracks. This enables you to be extremely precise when cutting/copying audio data within regions or trimming their length. Click and drag to highlight a very small area of the waveform within any visible audio region. Repeat. Now double-click the Zoomer to zoom out to a level of magnification where the entire session's duration fits in the Edit window.

Figure 4.9 With the Zoomer tool, click anywhere in a track to zoom in. Option-click (Alt-click in Windows) to zoom outward instead of inward. Click and drag to magnify a specific horizontal area within a track. Double-clicking the Zoomer button zooms out so that the entire session's duration fits within the Edit window.

9. Be sure you've trimmed the boundaries of the audio region you recorded into the MyStuff track (with the Trimmer tool) so that it doesn't include any silences at the beginning or end. Now select this region by clicking it once with the Grabber tool.

10. Choose Options > Loop Playback to enable this feature, and then press the spacebar to start playback. Your current *selection* will be looped rather than the session's entire timeline. If for some reason the portion of the timeline being played doesn't change no matter *what* you select, confirm that the Options > Link Timeline and Edit and Selections option is enabled. (As you will discover, there will be times during editing when you don't want the play selection to be altered by the current edit selection.) Also, deselect the Timeline Insertion Follows Playback button right under the Pencil tool in the Edit window. This prevents you from losing your selection when playback stops. Press the spacebar again to stop playback, but for the moment, leave the current region highlighted.

Inserting Plug-in Effects

Digital signal processing (DSP) allows you to shape the sound of your recorded audio in Pro Tools. On conventional mixing boards, effects-processing elements are generally of fixed types and at fixed locations. For instance, each source audio channel may have several equalization stages, while submasters or groups have none, and any external effects (for example, reverbs, delays, and so on) must be connected to the mixer's auxiliary sends and returns or to the insert point of individual channels. Worse, if each song in a project requires a different effects-processing setup, you not only have to change parameters on every external effects unit, but you may also need to reconfigure your whole cabling setup. Even if a patchbay provides flexible access to all the inputs and outputs of these devices (both multiple external effects processors and the mixing board itself), this is a laborious process.

In contrast, within Pro Tools, each virtual signal processor is actually a modular software construct called a *plug-in*. These can be inserted into the signal chain of *any* audio-related track type, including audio, Aux Input, Instrument, or Master Fader tracks (but not MIDI tracks). The entire processing and signal-routing setup within each Pro Tools session document is recalled when it is reopened. Obviously, with software-based processes, additional noise is not an issue (unlike when using external effects units). The complexity of any effects treatments that you create is limited only by the available processing power of your system and/or your imagination! Here, you'll take a look at two typical locations for plug-in effects processors in Pro Tools: in the signal chain of an individual audio track and on an Aux Input track. (One of the most frequent uses of Aux Input tracks is as a common destination for signals sent from multiple tracks.)

1. If necessary, press Command+= (or Ctrl+= in Windows) to switch from the Edit window to the Mix window. Press the spacebar to start looped playback again.

2. The mixer strip for the MyStuff track includes a volume fader, a pan knob (a stereo track would have two), and a mute button. Take a moment to experiment with these; you probably won't find them very mysterious!

3. Now you want to create (instantiate) an insert effect on this track. In the top section of the track's mixer strip, you'll notice five small rectangles with sideways arrows in them. Click and hold on any one of these inserts to open its pop-up menu, and then choose Plug-in > EQ > EQ 3 7-Band (mono), as shown in Figure 4.10. The Parameters window for the DigiRack 7-band equalizer will open. (DigiRack is Digidesign's name for the standard plug-ins included with the Pro Tools software.)

4. Press the spacebar to start looped playback again, and experiment. Drag the gain and frequency sliders around in the various bands of the EQ until you find some settings that amuse you, and then press the spacebar to stop playback. As you do this, keep in mind that if you Option-click (Alt-click in Windows) any of these sliders, they return to their default values. You will find that *many* controls in Pro Tools work the same way.

5. Now instantiate a compressor plug-in (which you will find under the Dynamics submenu of the Insert Selection pop-up menu) on one of this track's other insert points. Go back to the beginning of the song, start playback, and experiment with the threshold slider (which determines the level at which gain reduction starts to be applied, per the selected input/output ratio).

6. Now let's go over to the Aux Input track you've created (named Delay) and instantiate a plug-in effect on one of its inserts, just as you did for the audio track. Let's choose the Medium Delay effect for this Aux Input track (choose Plug-in > Delay > Medium Delay II).

7. Click and hold on the Input selector for the Delay Aux Input track and select Stereo Bus Pair > Bus 1–2 as its input source. The Input selector is at the top of this track's I/O section, just below the Sends section, as shown in Figure 4.11.

8. Option-click (Alt-click in Windows) on the Aux Input track's main volume fader to set it to 0dB. (This is also known as unity gain, because no gain change is being applied between the fader's input and output.)

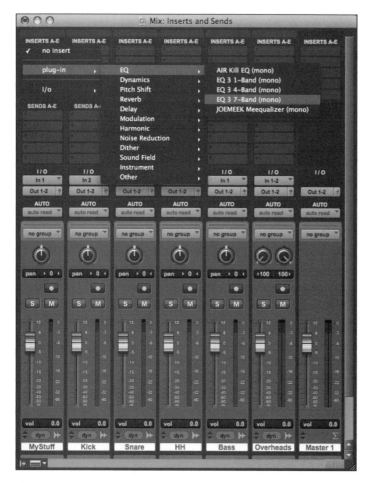

Figure 4.10 Each audio track, Aux Input, Instrument track, or Master Fader in Pro Tools has 10 insert locations. A pop-up menu allows you to route the track's entire signal through a software effect called a plug-in or loop it out through physical audio connectors on your hardware. The sends on audio tracks, Aux Input tracks, and Instrument tracks allow you to additionally route some of that track's signal to a secondary destination, like a physical audio output or one of Pro Tools' internal mixing busses. Sends can be mono, stereo, or multichannel (if you've created multichannel paths for surround mixing, cue mixes, or broadcast feeds, for example).

9. If you were to click Play now, you wouldn't hear anything passing through the delay because you haven't yet routed anything to this Aux Input track. Let's do that now. Click and hold on any one of the 10 sends for the MyStuff audio track (in two groups of five, located underneath the Inserts section of the Mix window) to open its pop-up menu, and select Bus > Bus 1–2 (Stereo).

10. An Output window opens for the mono send you just created. Option-click (Alt-click in Windows) on the level (volume) slider to set it directly to 0dB (instead of −[infinity]).

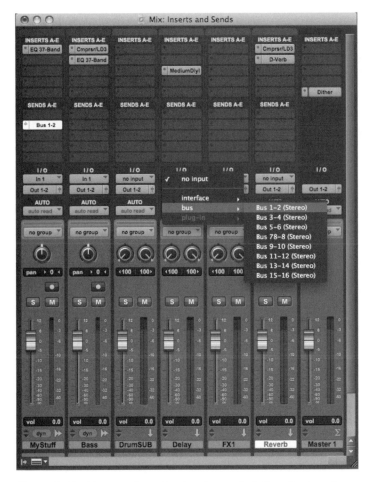

Figure 4.11   Here, we're selecting bus pair 1–2 as the input source for the Aux Input track where we've inserted the delay effect.

11.   Start playback. You should now also hear the sound of the audio in the MyStuff track being delayed. Reduce the level slider of your track's send to suit your taste.

12.   If necessary, click the Medium Delay insert button in this Aux Input track to reopen the delay's plug-in parameters window. Experiment with the feedback parameter, which determines how much of the delay's output is routed back into its input. This is how you produce multiple repeats.

Mixdown

Okay, you're ready to consider the basics of mixing your audio to stereo and saving it. Granted, this may not be the most impressive recording of your career, but don't let that stop you!

Mixing

As we've said elsewhere, mixdown is the process by which a larger number of source audio tracks are combined into a standard playback format (for example, two tracks for stereo or six tracks for 5.1 surround). For each track, you can adjust volume, apparent spatial placement and ambience, frequency content, and so on to create the desired audio perspective. In a Pro Tools mix, most parameters can change dynamically over time; you can automate the movement of faders, sliders, plug-in parameters, and so on to create an ideal mix or to create special effects. Here you'll explore the two ways you can create mix automation in Pro Tools: by recording changes you make to mixing controls in real time or by using the mouse to directly create graphic shapes for the automation data within each track.

1. If you wish, take some time in the Edit window to drag or duplicate (choose Edit > Duplicate) some of your existing regions so that you have a longer mix to deal with than what you've been listening to so far.

2. Click the Return to Zero button in the Transport window (to the left of the Rewind button) to make sure the playback cursor is at the beginning of the session's timeline.

3. The Automation Mode indicator for the MyStuff audio track now displays Auto Read. Using its pop-up selector, change it to Auto Touch so that any mix changes you make to this track during playback—on any controls that you actually touch—will be recorded as automation. (Pro Tools also has an Automation Enable window, which allows you to globally enable/disable different types of automation. We're assuming here that all automation types are currently enabled, which is the program's default.)

4. Start playback and move the volume fader and pan control for this track a few times. Then stop playback.

5. Start playback again, and you'll see that Pro Tools repeats the volume and pan moves you just created.

6. Switch back to the Edit window.

7. A Display Format selector is available among the track controls at the left of each track in the Edit window. Right now, for the MyStuff track, it shows Waveform. Use this pop-selector to switch to displaying volume automation for this track. The volume moves you just recorded appear graphically, as a line with breakpoints.

8. Experiment with using the Grabber tool to drag these breakpoints around. This is one of the most common ways to edit automation data. You can also click anywhere on this line to create a new breakpoint. For many users, rather than recording automation in real time, it's just as easy to draw automation directly in the Edit window—which is exactly what you're going to do next.

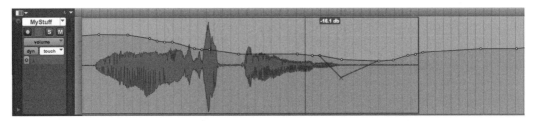

Figure 4.12   By changing the display format on the MyStuff audio track to Volume, you can view and graphically edit breakpoint automation data for that parameter. You can also do this for the track's pan control; the level, pan, and mute for any active sends on the track; and parameters on the track's plug-ins.

9.   Change the display format for this track from volume to pan (see Figure 4.12). The vertical ruler at the left edge of the track now shows L and R. With the Grabber, click at several places along the line (near the beginning of the track) to create some new breakpoints and drag them to several extreme left/right positions.

10.   Now switch back to the Mix window. Click the Return to Zero button in the Transport window again, and then click Play. You will now see the pan knob moving back and forth according to the automation contours you created.

Automation Breakpoints   The automation for volume, pan, and many other mix or plug-in parameters can be displayed and edited graphically within Pro Tools tracks. When viewing a track in Volume, Pan, or any other mix-automation format, lines represent the changing values for that automation parameter (superimposed over a dimmed version of the audio waveform on audio tracks). The breakpoints on these lines (also known as envelope points or automation event points in some other audio programs) are the handles you use to create automation shapes. Many of these are created automatically when you create automation by moving an onscreen control or by using one of the Pencil tool's drawing modes (like the Line or Free Hand mode, for example). Whether they've been created this way or with the Grabber tool as in steps 8 and 9 of this example, you can always drag breakpoints with the Grabber, select a range of them with the Selector, and copy, delete, or scale their values up or down with the Trimmer.

- To delete a breakpoint, Option-click it (Alt-click in Windows).
- For finer control, hold down the Command key (Ctrl key in Windows) while adjusting (or trimming) breakpoint values.
- To restrict movement of breakpoints to the vertical direction while dragging (so that their horizontal position in the timeline is unaffected), hold down the Shift key.

■ The Nudge value is described in more detail in Chapter 6. To nudge a selected
range of automation breakpoints right or left in the timeline (without affecting
any audio underneath them in audio tracks), use the + and − (plus/minus) keys
on the numeric keypad.

Bounce to Disk

In traditional audio studios, the mixdown would be performed in real time and the mix output
would be recorded to another audio device (for example, a two-track master recorder). In fact, this
is sometimes done with Pro Tools, especially when laying off a mix to a DAT or video tape. More
commonly, though, you will bounce the results of your Pro Tools mix into a brand-new file, which
can then be used to create an audio CD or given to a computer-based video editor, interactive or
DVD author, and so on. In Pro Tools, this is a real-time process, so you also have the option of
incorporating external audio sources, such as MIDI modules, multitrack tape recorders, or effects
processors, into the resultant file. To bounce your mix to a new audio file, do the following:

1. Select File > Bounce to > Disk. In the Bounce dialog box (shown in Figure 4.13),
    change the Format setting to Stereo Interleaved, and accept the default values for the
    other options.

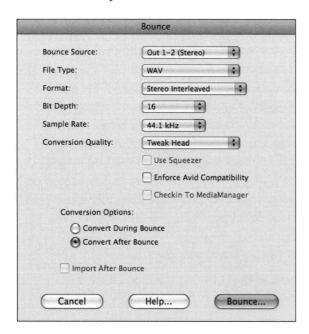

Figure 4.13 The Bounce dialog box creates new audio files based on your current mix. You name the
resultant file and select the Pro Tools output that will be the source for the bounced file, its audio file
format and resolution, and so on.

2. Click the Bounce button. In the dialog box that appears, type a name for the bounced mix and choose the location on your computer setup where the resulting file will be saved and click OK. As you hear your session play back in real time, a small window opens that shows a countdown of the time remaining until the bounce is completed. (If you enable the Import After Bounce option—which is available only when bouncing mono or split mono audio files to the same file format as the session itself—the resultant audio file/region appears in the Regions List afterwards. This would be useful, for example, when bouncing out a submix in order to free up tracks or CPU power.)

What's Included in Your Bounced Mixdown File When nothing is selected in the Edit window, the entire session—from the beginning of the timeline to the end of the last region in any track—is included in the resultant file. If you make an edit selection in any track, however (assuming that Options > Link Timeline and Edit Selections is enabled, meaning that edit selections also change Timeline selections as indicated by the start and end times in the Transport window), only that selected range will be included in your bounced file. Beware: Reverbs, echoes, and so on might need a few seconds to tail out beyond the actual end of the last region. When bouncing to disk, be sure to lengthen your selection enough for these to decay completely to silence before its end!

Summary

Obviously, you would carry the recording, editing, and automation process to much more useful extremes than what's been described here. Hopefully, however, the rudimentary exercises in this chapter have given you a basic idea of what Pro Tools is about. We'll get into all the details in the rest of this book; you'll especially want to check out the next three chapters about the Transport, Edit, and Mix windows, and review the basic concepts laid out in Chapter 2. Read on!

5 The Transport Window

This chapter and the next two provide specifics about most (but not all!) elements of the Transport, Edit, and Mix windows of Pro Tools. These key windows are where you will spend most of your time. If you get a handle on them, you'll be ready to tackle serious Pro Tools projects. We will highlight the most essential features and techniques you must know in order to be an all-around competent Pro Tools user. For that reason, please note that we don't comment on every selection in every menu—that's what the Pro Tools documentation is for. Two documents, the *Pro Tools Reference Guide* and the *Menu Guide*, provided in PDF format with Pro Tools and also purchasable in printed form, are excellent sources for more detailed information.

Other chapters in this book provide additional practical examples for many of the features briefly described here. Although we clarify some concepts and point out many useful tips and shortcuts along the way, much of the material in this chapter, as well as in Chapters 6, "The Edit Window," and 7, "The Mix Window," may be review for readers with significant Pro Tools experience. If that's your case, feel free to browse!

The Transport window (shown in Figure 5.1) includes basic tape-type controls for controlling playback and recording, with numeric displays for the current selection, pre-/post-roll settings, and MIDI controls. This chapter reviews each of the elements in the Transport, which is a floating window that can overlap either the Mix or Edit window in Pro Tools, staying in place even as you switch from one to the other. (Unlike most other windows in Pro Tools, it doesn't have a title bar or scrollbars.)

Pro Tools Documentation Be sure to check out the PDF (Acrobat Reader) documents that Digidesign provides in the Documentation folder (Digidesign > Documentation > Pro Tools). These documents (along with the book currently in your hands, of course) will be a great help getting you up to speed. Even more convenient, you can open these documents directly from the Help menu inside Pro Tools.

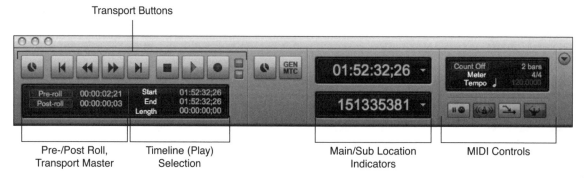

Figure 5.1 The Transport window.

Keyboard Shortcuts   Like any complex program, Pro Tools offers many keyboard short-cuts, especially for frequently used features. In this book, we always start from the visible menu command or onscreen control, but will emphasize keyboard shortcuts that we find most important for basic operations (that is to say, worth the effort to memorize). That being said, you should absolutely print out and study the *Keyboard Shortcuts* PDF document included with Pro Tools. In particular, because the Transport is so essential to the operation of Pro Tools, we recommend that you learn all its keyboard equivalents—it will save you time!

Also, for this chapter, we're assuming that in the Operation tab of the Preferences dialog box (Preferences > Operation), Numeric Keypad Mode is set to Transport (more about this later in this chapter) so that keys on the numeric keypad can be used to control the Transport functions discussed here. We're also assuming that in the View > Transport dialog box, all four options—Counters, MIDI Controls, Synchronization, and Expanded—are enabled.

Another reminder: Unlike with many Mac and Windows programs, the Return key on the alphanumeric keyboard (a.k.a. the Enter key in Windows) and the Enter key on the numeric keypad are usually *not* equivalent! The Enter key on the numeric keypad is often used for different purposes in Pro Tools—for example, for creating memory locations.

Transport Buttons

Obviously, some of these buttons (shown in Figure 5.2) behave like their equivalent controls on a video, CD, DVD, or tape deck. They are used to control playback and recording. As indicated in the descriptions provided here, keyboard shortcuts are available for all the button functions,

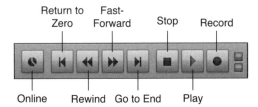

Figure 5.2   The Transport window buttons resemble a tape recorder's controls.

which are summarized in Table 5.1 at the end of this chapter. If you're just starting with Pro Tools, these should be among the very first keyboard shortcuts you memorize.

Play/Stop

When you click the Play button in the Transport, playback starts at the current position noted by the Main and Sub location indicators seen in the right side of the Transport. (You can link these to the Main/Sub counters at the top of the Edit window via the Options > Link Timeline and Edit Selections command; more about this in Chapter 6.) When the Transport's start and end values are identical (and the length is therefore zero), playback continues indefinitely until you click Stop. Otherwise, playback begins at the start location, and stops when the end value is reached (or loops back around if you've enabled the Options > Loop Playback option). If you prefer using your computer keyboard to issue commands, pressing the spacebar or pressing 0 on the numeric keypad is the same as clicking the Play button; press the same key again to stop playback. Later in this chapter, we discuss Dynamic Transport mode (available only in versions 7.3 and higher), which allows you much more flexible control over exactly what portion of the timeline will play back when you press the spacebar or 0 on the numeric keypad or click the Transport windows' Play button.

Half-Speed Play/Record in Pro Tools Using Pro Tools, you can record things at half speed and play them back at double speed. Don't worry, we won't tell your friends you can't really sing that high—hey, Alvin—or shred like Eddie on too much caffeine. To record at half speed, hold down the Shift and Command keys (Shift and Ctrl keys in Windows) as you press the spacebar. For half-speed playback, hold down the Shift key as you press the spacebar.

Rewind/Fast Forward

Like the Play/Stop buttons, the Rewind/Fast Forward buttons are similar to the equivalent controls on a tape deck. You can also repeatedly click either of these to jump forward or backward through the session timeline in increments determined by the units currently being displayed in the Transport window's Main location indicator—entire seconds or entire bars, for example. (If you're in the Edit window, however, it may be just as easy to click with the Selector tool anywhere within the timeline ruler or track to reset the current play position—as long as the Options > Link Timeline and Edit Selections option is enabled.) You can also click and hold on these buttons to shuttle through the Pro Tools timeline. Keyboard equivalents for the Rewind/ Fast Forward buttons are 1 and 2 on the computer's numeric keypad, respectively.

Audio During Rewind/Fast Forward To hear the audio you are passing over while using the Rewind and Fast Forward functions (either via the buttons in the Transport or Edit windows or the keyboard shortcuts mentioned previously), enable the Audio During Fast Forward/Rewind option in the Operations tab of the Preferences dialog box. While you hold down either of these buttons, playback skips forward or backward through the timeline in a similar fashion as when the scan buttons on a CD player are used. This makes it easy to locate or replay a range within your audio material, and we recommend enabling this option for all users.

During rewind/fast forward in Pro Tools, audio doesn't play back at fast speed or in reverse as on analog tape, and MIDI tracks don't play at all. However, some TDM users opt to change their numeric keypad Preferences to Shuttle, as opposed to the more conventional Transport mode generally assumed throughout this book. In that mode, audio does play back at accelerated speed while shuttling forward or backward through the timeline. Use either technique—whatever helps you find your way!

Return to Zero/Go to End

Clicking the Return to Zero button sets the playback position (and the timeline selection) to the beginning of the Pro Tools timeline. Return to Zero sets the current playback position to the left edge of the timeline, regardless of what timeline units are in use or what actual bar number or session start time this corresponds to. Clicking the Go to End button resets the current playback position to the end of the last region in the session (its right edge). If you had anything selected in the Edit window (for example, a region you've been looping as you made adjustments), clicking Return to Zero or Go to End also deselects it. The keyboard equivalent for Return to Zero is Return (Enter in Windows) on the alphanumeric keyboard; the equivalent for Go to End is Option+Return (Ctrl+Enter in Windows) on the alphanumeric keyboard.

Online

Clicking the Online button puts the Transport in Online mode, where playback/recording starts and stops according to SMPTE time code received. (SMPTE time code is explained in Chapter 11, "Synchronization.") In the Session Setup window (opened via the Setup menu), you can set the start time for the current session. This determines what incoming SMPTE time-code value will correspond to the left edge of the Edit window (the beginning of your session's timeline).

When you enable Online mode, if the incoming SMPTE time-code values (for example, from a multitrack audio recorder or a video master) correspond to a location *prior* to the session start time for the current session, Pro Tools waits until that position is reached and then starts playback. (Playback stops after you press Stop on the master device sending time code and the flow of SMPTE time-code values into Pro Tools ends.) If the incoming SMPTE time-code values correspond to a location *later* than the session start time, Pro Tools jumps to the corresponding position and commences playback (even if this position is actually beyond the last region of audio in your session). The Command+J keyboard shortcut (Ctrl+J in Windows) toggles Online mode on/off.

Synchronizing Pro Tools to Video and Multitrack Recorders As mentioned, in Online mode, Pro Tools' playback is triggered at a position determined by incoming time-code values (and the Start Time value specified in the Session Setup window). An external SMPTE synchronizer is required to convert the incoming SMPTE (encoded into an audio or video signal) to MIDI time code (MTC). This, in turn, is communicated to Pro Tools via the optional MIDI/SMPTE interface in your configuration. For more details about SMPTE time code, MTC, and synchronization in general, see Chapter 11.

Record

Clicking the Record button arms Pro Tools for recording mode. (At least one audio or MIDI track must first be record-enabled before Pro Tools will allow you to start recording.) After you click the Record button, it flashes; recording then commences when you click the Play button. If the Pre-Roll option is enabled (discussed later in this chapter, under "Transport Window Fields"), playback begins before actual recording starts by the indicated time interval. If the Post-Roll option is enabled, playback continues after recording ends by the indicated time interval. If Timeline and Edit window selections are linked, selections in the Edit window (or directly changing the Start, End, or Length values in the Transport window) can be used to specify where recording will punch in and punch out. Remember that unless you've deliberately enabled Destructive Record mode (in the Options menu), every record pass is saved. A new file/region is created for each take and automatically assigned a name derived from the track name where it was recorded. (This is why it's good practice to assign meaningful names to your tracks *before* recording—it saves time later!)

Pro Tools offers various recording modes: Normal, Destructive, Loop Record, QuickPunch (and TrackPunch in Pro Tools HD). The mode that is currently selected affects the appearance of the Record button itself, as shown in Figure 5.3. You can cycle through these recording modes by right-clicking the Record button (and/or Control-clicking the button on a Macintosh). Each of these recording modes is discussed in further detail in the "Options Menu" section of Chapter 8, "Menu Selections: Highlights." If you prefer, you can use your choice of several keyboard shortcuts to start recording: Command+Spacebar (Ctrl+Spacebar in Windows), the 3 key on the computer's numeric keypad, or the F12 key. (Mac users: See the upcoming sidebar about reassigning the shortcut key for Dashboard.)

Figure 5.3 The appearance of the Record button indicates the current recording mode: Normal (non-destructive), Destructive, Loop, QuickPunch (and TrackPunch, in Pro Tools HD). You can cycle through these modes by Control-clicking the Record button (Mac) or by right-clicking the Record button (Windows).

Macintosh, Pro Tools, and Using Function Keys F9–F12 Traditionally, in Pro Tools, the F9 function key selects the Scrubber tool, F10 selects the Pencil tool, and (if this option is enabled in Preferences) F11 toggles the Wait for Note function of the Transport on and off. In Macintosh operating system versions 10.3 (a.k.a. Panther) or higher, however, these F-key shortcuts in Pro Tools won't work properly. Starting with Mac OS 10.3, Apple introduced an immensely useful feature called Exposé, which enables you to hold down certain function keys from within any program to can temporarily view all open windows simultaneously including folder views, application windows only, or the desktop. While in these temporary views, you can click within another document or application window to switch, or even double-click to navigate through disks and folders in the Finder without leaving your original program at all. However, inconveniently for Macintosh Pro Tools users, the default F keys for toggling to these three views are F9, F10, and F11! Moreover, in OS 10.4 (a.k.a. Tiger) and 10.5 (a.k.a. Leopard—required for Pro Tools 8), a Dashboard feature is integrated for popping open utilities called Widgets. While this can be done from the Dock, there's also a default keyboard shortcut: F12, which is also used in Pro Tools to initiate recording.

Fortunately, both of these conflicts are very easy to fix:

1. Open the Apple menu and choose System Preferences.
2. In the Personal section, click Dashboard & Exposé.
3. You will see the F keys currently assigned to the three Exposé options for temporarily switching the view. Use the pop-up menus to reassign them to something else. For example, on our systems, to make them easy to remember, we've simply added the Shift key to the default shortcuts. If you'd like to do the same, simply hold down the Shift key while opening the pop-up menu for each Exposé option in order to reassign these to Shift+F9, Shift+F10, and Shift+F11. Then do the same for the fourth pop-up menu, reassigning the Dashboard shortcut to Shift+F12.

About Numeric Keypad Modes (Preferences) In the Preferences dialog box, you can switch the mode of numeric-keypad operation in Pro Tools. In Transport mode, the numeric-keypad equivalents shown in Table 5.1 are enabled. We consider Transport to be the most generally useful mode, and throughout this book, always refer to numeric-keypad shortcuts based on this recommendation, but users are encouraged to try out the other modes to see what is to their liking. Classic mode emulates how the numeric keypad worked in Pro Tools versions prior to 5.0. On HD (and older TDM) systems, a third mode called Shuttle allows these keys to control Pro Tools playback at extra-slow or extra-fast speeds, stopping once you release the key; many users also find this handy.

Transport Window Fields

This section discusses additional fields that can be displayed in the Transport window if the View > Transport > Expanded option is enabled. Not only can you directly enter numeric values into these fields (which can be seen in Figure 5.4), but several of them can be directly affected by your actions in the Transport and Edit windows, serving as data displays for your current timeline selection, play position, and so on.

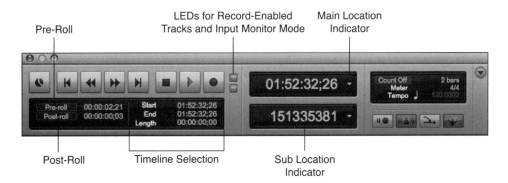

Figure 5.4 Various Transport window fields provide information about your current selection, playback position, pre/post-roll times, and whether the Pro Tools Transport window is master or slave to other devices in your studio.

Main/Sub Indicators for Current Location

The Main and Sub location indicators are counters that display the current play position. They are static while stopped, continually change during play/record, and can be set to different time units. When the Options > Link Timeline and Edit Selections option is enabled, making a selection in the Edit window also resets the Transport's timeline selection—the current play position corresponds to the beginning of that selection. (The Main and Sub counters at the top of the Edit window represent the Edit selection, which, when convenient, can be unlinked from the actual timeline selection that will play back when you press the spacebar.) A pop-up menu to the right of each counter lets you change the time units of each indicator. For example, you might choose to display musical bars and beats in the Main counter and minutes and seconds in the Sub counter.

You can change the location value in the Main counter in several ways:

■ Using the Transport buttons—Rewind/Fast Forward, Return to Zero/Go to End, and so on

■ By making a new selection or clicking anywhere in the Edit window's main time ruler—assuming the Options > Link Timeline and Edit Selections option is enabled

■ Recalling a user-defined memory location (more about these in Chapter 6)

■ Clicking in the field and typing a new value (see the upcoming sidebar)

Quick Entry of New Locations in the Main Location Indicator Pressing the asterisk (*) key on the numeric keypad selects the Main location indicator for data entry, pressing the period (.) key switches between columns, pressing the up/down arrows let you increment/decrement the selected value, and pressing the Return key on the alphanumeric keyboard (Enter in Windows) confirms your entry into this numeric field. So if you're using Minutes:Seconds as the time unit in the Main location indicator, to go to 1 minute, 30 seconds, you would press the following sequence on the numeric keypad: *1.30 (Return/Enter). If you were in Bars:Beats mode and wanted to set the playback cursor directly to bar 15, beat 3, you would press the following sequence on the numeric keypad: *15.3 (Return/Enter). Alternatively, if you're working on a musical piece using Bars:Beats mode, you could press the asterisk (*) key, press the up arrow four times, and then press Return (Enter on Windows) on the alphanumeric keyboard to move the play position four bars later.

Play Selection: Start/End/Length Fields

Assuming that the Options > Link Timeline and Edit Selections option is enabled, if you simply click somewhere in the Edit window with the Selector tool, the values in the Start and End fields of the Transport window will be identical. (This is also the case if you use the Rewind, Fast Forward, Go to Zero, or Go to End buttons to change the playback location or if you recall a Marker memory location. These are discussed in Chapter 8.) The Start value is the position where playback will begin when you click Play.

On the other hand, if you make a selection, either by clicking and dragging with the Selector or highlighting an existing region with the Grabber, the beginning, end, and duration of the current selection are indicated in the Start, End, and Length fields (again, unless you've disabled the Link Timeline and Edit Selections option in the Options menu). You can also click in any of these three fields to manually enter new values. Time units displayed in the Transport's Start, End, and Length fields always match those of the Main location indicator.

The Start and End fields determine where recording stops and starts in Record mode. In both recording and playback, these start and end points may be preceded or followed by the specified pre-roll and post-roll intervals, if that option is enabled—see the following section in this chapter for more details. When loop playback (or recording) is enabled, Pro Tools will continuously cycle the material between the start and end values until you stop playback.

Quick Entry into the Transport Window's Start/End/Length Fields Hold down the Option key (Alt key in Windows) and press the forward slash key (/) on the numeric keypad to directly select the Start field in the Transport window. Each subsequent press of the / key cycles through the Start, End, and Length fields for numeric entry, as well as the Pre-Roll and Post-Roll fields. As with other time-value fields in Pro Tools, you can use the period key (.) or left/right arrow keys to switch columns as you enter values, type numeric values (or use the up/down arrow keys), and then hit Return or Enter to confirm your entry or the Esc key to exit without changing the field.

Pre-Roll/Post-Roll

If the Pre-Roll button is enabled, when you click Play, playback actually starts before the current value in the Start field or the current selection in the Edit window by the time interval you enter in the Pre-Roll field. Time units in this field always match those of the Main location indicator display (Bars:Beats, Minutes:Seconds, Samples, SMPTE time code, and so on). The Post-Roll button and field work in a similar fashion; playback continues past the current value in the End field or the end of the current Edit window selection by the specified amount. In Record mode, however, recording (on record-enabled tracks) will always punch in and punch out exactly at the values in the Start and End fields. Having Pre-Roll enabled therefore facilitates making inserts or drop-ins on previously recorded takes because you can monitor the surrounding audio material as you record the new segment.

Besides double-clicking to manually enter new time values into the Pre-/Post-Roll fields, you can use the Pre-Roll and Post-Roll flags in the Edit window's main time ruler, as shown in Figure 5.5. (They're white if inactive, yellow if enabled.) To change pre-/post-roll intervals, simply drag the corresponding flag to the left and right of the current Start/End indicators. The Command+K keyboard shortcut (Ctrl+K in Windows) toggles both the Pre- and Post-Roll buttons on and off.

Dynamic Transport Mode (Versions 7.3 and Higher Only) The first time you enable Dynamic Transport mode (via its command in the Options menu) pre- and post-roll are automatically disabled, the Link Edit and Timeline Selection option is disabled, and Loop

Playback is automatically enabled. In Dynamic Transport mode, an additional Play Marker strip appears below the main timeline ruler. The position of the Play Start marker (shown in Figure 5.6) determines where playback will start, and you can click or drag in the strip to reposition this marker to new time locations—even during playback. You also can make different timeline selections within your tracks without affecting the position of the Play Start marker. (If you want the position of the Play Start marker to follow the current timeline selection, this can be enabled in the Operation tab of the Preferences dialog box in conjunction with the Options > Link Timeline and Edit Selection command.) While Loop Playback is enabled—which happens automatically the first time you enable Dynamic Transport mode—playback can start from the current position of the Play Start marker; afterward, the current play selection (as shown in the Transport window) will loop.

When you enable the Timeline Insertion/Playback Marker Follow Playback option in the Operation tab of the Preferences dialog box or by selecting the button under the Pencil tool in the Edit window, the Play Start marker and edit cursor both advance to the point where you last stopped playback. We have found this especially useful for long spoken-word projects, for example.

Lastly, make note of these essential keyboard shortcuts that are available in Dynamic Transport mode:

- To move the Play Start marker to the start of the current edit selection indicated in the Edit window (per its Start field), press the period (.) on the numeric keypad and then the down arrow.
- To move the Play Start marker to the start or end of the current timeline (Play) selection shown in the Transport window, press the period (.) on the numeric keypad and then the left or right arrow key.
- To nudge the current position of the Play Start marker earlier or later according to the current Nudge value, press 1 or 2 on the numeric keypad.

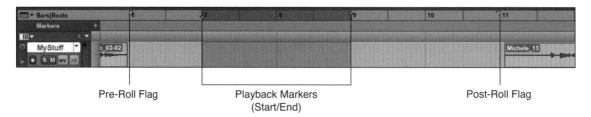

Pre-Roll Flag   Playback Markers   Post-Roll Flag
                        (Start/End)

Figure 5.5 The Edit window's main time ruler, shown here in Bars:Beats format. Start and end points for recording are currently at bars 7 and 9, with two bars of pre-roll and one bar of post-roll.

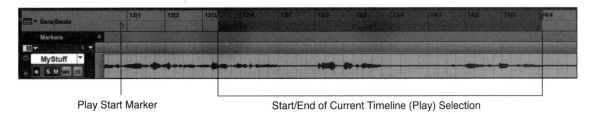

Play Start Marker   Start/End of Current Timeline (Play) Selection

Figure 5.6 When Dynamic Transport mode is enabled (in versions 7.3 and higher), the Play Start marker can be repositioned underneath the main timeline ruler—even during playback.

Transport Master

Most users will leave the Transport Master set to control Pro Tools, the default option. However, if you want some other machine to directly control Transport functions in Pro Tools (which requires appropriate hardware/software, like the synchronization peripherals discussed in Chapter 11, and optional MachineControl software from Digidesign), you would make that selection in the Transport Master field, selecting Machine Control, MMC (MIDI Machine Control), or ADAT. When MMC is selected, the playback position of Pro Tools is controlled by the position values transmitted from an external device via MIDI.

Record Enable Status/Input Status

These small indicators to the right of the Record button look like LEDs. The top red indicator is lit whenever any track is record-enabled (that is, the R button in its track controls is red). The lower green indicator is lit when you enable Track >Input Only Monitoring so that all tracks monitor their selected input (regardless of whether any regions already reside on the track).

External Control Surfaces and the Pro Tools Transport Transport functions can be remote-controlled from external control surfaces. Options include Digidesign's D-Control, D-Command, ProControl, Command|8, C|24, and Control|24; the Mackie HUI; the J.L. Cooper CS-102; and others. (See Appendix B, "Add-ons, Extensions, and Cool Stuff for Your Rig," for more information.)

MIDI Transport Controls

The Transport controls discussed in this section are related to tempos, time signature (meter), metronome settings, countoff settings, recording modes, and other features that are useful for music production, and especially for using MIDI tracks and instruments in Pro Tools. If you don't have any MIDI devices in your studio setup (and don't use meter/tempo changes with the Event > Identify Beat command), you may save screen space by choosing not to view

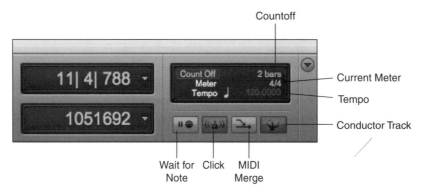

Figure 5.7   The MIDI controls portion of the Transport window.

these MIDI Transport controls. By default, they appear at the right end of the Transport window (see Figure 5.7). To hide the MIDI Transport controls, choose View > Transport > MIDI Controls or de-select MIDI Controls from the pop-up menu in the upper right-hand corner of the Transport window.

Wait for Note

When the Wait for Note button is enabled during Record mode, recording on any record-enabled audio/MIDI tracks will not commence until a MIDI event is received from your controller. This option is really handy if you need time to hustle across the room to your keyboard! Naturally, if the Pre-Roll option is enabled, Pro Tools will still begin playback from some earlier point, with actual recording not punching in until the value in the Start field is reached. The keyboard shortcut for enabling/disabling the Wait for Note option is F11. (Mac users should see the sidebar at the beginning of this chapter about changing the default F-key shortcuts for Exposé in System Preferences.)

Remote-Starting Record in Pro Tools via MIDI The Wait for Note function can also be handy while recording audio tracks, likewise giving you time to get across the room to a microphone or instrument without recording a lot of dead air after clicking the Record button. Even if you don't record any MIDI tracks at all, if you have an inexpensive MIDI keyboard and a MIDI interface on your computer, you could stretch a MIDI cable all the way over to the keyboard inside your isolation booth. Click Record in Pro Tools (with Wait for Note enabled). Then, when you're in position and ready to sing or play, pressing any note on the MIDI keyboard will start recording (after the designated Pre-Roll interval, if enabled). You could even use the sustain pedal on this keyboard to activate recording so that your hands stay free!

Metronome Click

Clicking the Metronome Click button, located to the right of the Wait for Note button, turns the metronome click on and off. Double-click the button to open the Click/Countoff Options dialog box (see Figure 5.9 in the next section), where you can specify whether this metronome sound should occur only while in Record mode, in Record and Play modes, or only during the countoff bars (see the next section).

The Click plug-in (shown in Figure 5.8) is used as an insert on an Aux In track. The Click plug-in automatically responds to the Pro Tools tempo when the Transport's Metronome Click button is enabled; no routing to it is necessary from the Click/Countoff Options dialog box. (Volume levels for accented and unaccented beats are set directly within the plug-in itself.) Alternatively, some external MIDI device (or software-based instrument) can be used to produce an audible click sound in response to Note On MIDI events transmitted from Pro Tools. If you do this, you can configure the MIDI note and velocities, output, and channel in this dialog box. To toggle the Metronome Click button on and off, you can also press the 7 key on the computer's numeric keypad.

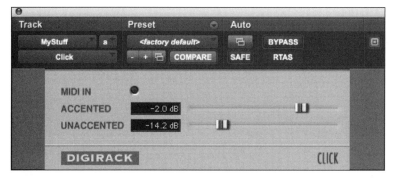

Figure 5.8   The Click plug-in can be used on a mono Aux In track and produces a variety of metronome sounds according to the current Pro Tools tempo.

Creating Instances of the Click Plug-In in Versions 7.3 and Higher In the MIDI tab of the Preferences dialog box, you can elect to have an Aux In track with an instance of the Click plug-in created automatically when you create each new Pro Tools session. Additionally, in versions 7.3 and higher of Pro Tools, the Track > Create Click Track command was added for adding an Aux In track with an instance of the Click plug-in to existing sessions.

Countoff

When the Countoff button is enabled, Pro Tools plays the metronome click sound for the specified number of measures (according to the current tempo and time signature) before playback or recording begins. The countoff click sound will play even if the Click button is turned off, in which case the click sound stops once Play or Record mode begins. Double-clicking the display of the amount currently chosen for the countoff opens the Click/Countoff Options dialog box (shown in Figure 5.9), where you can specify how many bars of countoff you want. (Notice that if you wish, countoff can occur only when you're in Record mode.) To toggle the Countoff button on and off, you can also press the 8 key on your computer's numeric keypad.

Figure 5.9 Open the Click/Countoff Options dialog box by double-clicking the Click or Countoff button in the Transport window.

MIDI Merge

With the MIDI Merge button enabled, when you record MIDI into a track already containing MIDI regions, the newly recorded MIDI data is combined into the existing material instead of replacing it as a new MIDI region. For example, to build up a drum track while looping a couple bars, make your timeline selection, ensure that Pro Tools is not in Destructive Recording mode, and enable the Options > Loop Playback option. Then enable the MIDI Merge button. The notes you play in each repetition of the looped selection are *added* to the previous MIDI data instead of replacing it. (In Loop Recording mode, the MIDI Merge button is dimmed because it has no effect. Instead, for every cycle of loop recording where you input new MIDI data, a new separate take/MIDI region is always created.) To toggle MIDI Merge on and off, assuming as always that the numeric keypad mode is set to Transport in the Preferences dialog box, press the 9 key on the computer's numeric keypad.

Conductor Track

Clicking the Conductor Track button (which has a "conductor" icon) enables the tempo map. If the tempo ruler in the Edit window contains tempo-change events, enabling this button makes these active. (To make the tempo ruler visible, choose View > Ruler > Tempo.) When the Tempo Ruler Enable button is *not* enabled, the current manual beats per minute (bpm) setting in the Transport's Tempo field applies to the entire session; it can be edited numerically or via the tempo slider. Conversely, Pro Tools will *not* allow you to make manual changes to the Transport's Tempo field while this button is enabled.

Current Meter

The Current Meter indicator displays the musical meter (time signatures of 4/4, 5/4, 6/8, and so on) at the current play position. Of course, different bars can have different meter settings in Pro Tools! You can use the Time Operations/Meter Change window, shown in Figure 5.10, to create time signature events in Pro Tools.

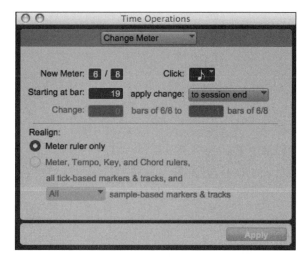

Figure 5.10   You can create changes of time signature (meter) in the Time Operations window.

Alternatively, double-clicking the Transport window's Current Meter indicator (or clicking the + sign in the Edit window's Meter ruler) opens the Meter Change window, shown in Figure 5.11. The initial location for meter changes can be edited but defaults to the current Start position. Be sure to place it at the beginning of bar 1 (and select To Session End, if using the Time Operations window) if you want this new time signature to apply to the entire session!

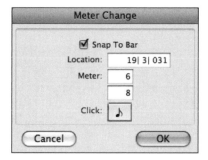

Figure 5.11   You can open the Meter Change window by double-clicking the Meter button in the Transport window.

Tempo

In this field, tempo settings appear in bpm (beats per minute). When the Conductor Track button is not enabled, the reference note value for the tempo (¼ note, ⅛ note, and so on) appears in the pop-up Tempo Resolution selector at the left of the Tempo field. When the Conductor Track button is *not* enabled, there are two main ways to manually change the musical tempo setting in the Transport window:

- Click in the Tempo field and type tempo values directly. As in many numeric fields in Pro Tools, you can also click and drag with the mouse to scroll these values upward or downward.

- Select the Tempo field and tap in the tempo in real time from your MIDI controller or the T key on your computer keyboard—if this option is enabled in the MIDI tab of the Preferences dialog box. Pro Tools computes the average tempo based on your last eight taps. As pointed out in Chapter 13, "A Multitrack Music Session," this is by far the best method for setting up a click-track tempo when working with live performers. Just have them play through the song naturally and tap along to set your correct tempo *before* feeding any click track into their cue mix. With bands that are inexperienced in the studio, you should also consider tapping in the tempo based on a cassette of a rehearsal or performance (audio quality is irrelevant), since their sense of appropriate tempo may be unreliable in this unfamiliar context.

Alternatively, the Identify Beat command can be used to create a tempo setting based on an audio selection. To use this feature, you must first enable the Conductor Track button (which disables the field for manual tempo settings in the Transport window). As with meter events, if you use the Tempo Operations window shown in Figure 5.12 to create tempo-change events, select Bar 1, Beat 1 (1|1|000) and To Session End if you want these to apply to the entire session.

Another method for creating tempo-change events is to click the plus sign (+) in the Edit window's tempo ruler. Remember, though, that whenever the Conductor button is enabled (so that events in the tempo and meter rulers are in effect), you cannot manually make changes to the Tempo setting. You can also *graphically* edit tempo changes in the Edit window using an editing pane that opens from the tempo ruler. To learn more sophisticated techniques for managing tempo settings in Pro Tools, see Chapter 8.

Traditionally, tempo changes always affected the position of events within MIDI tracks in Pro Tools. (That is, they were always tick-based, and event positions were relative to bars and beats.) However, version 7 introduced the option to change the timebase of any MIDI track to Samples so that the positions of the MIDI events within it will not be affected by subsequent tempo or meter changes. Users of MIDI-based sound effects for soundtrack work will find this especially useful.

Aux Input and Master Fader tracks can also be set to Ticks (relative) timebase instead of the conventional Samples (absolute) timebase (as can Aux Input and Master Fader tracks). For all

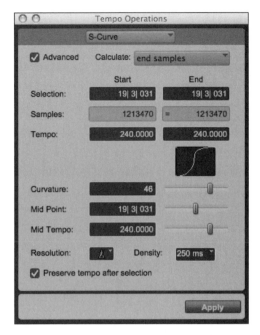

Figure 5.12 Tempo Operations window.

track types assigned to the Ticks timebase, positions of all events within them are relative to the session's tempo and will shift when you create or edit tempo changes (manually or in the Conductor track).

Punching Recordings In/Out Within Previously Recorded Material Do you need to automate the replacement of one line of lyrics or dialog within an existing recording or one portion of an instrumental part? Here's a quick how-to. First, in the Edit window, use the Selector tool to precisely highlight the section of the track you want to replace. (We're assuming here that the Options > Link Timeline and Edit Selections option is enabled.) By the way, we recommend that you *don't* use Destructive Recording mode while doing this! Then enable the Pre-/Post-Roll buttons and set appropriate times in the Pre-/Post-Roll fields so that the performer can match the levels and sound of the material before and after the newly inserted recording. Click on that track's Rec button to record-enable it, click the Record button in the Transport, and then click Play. Repeat as necessary!

Although this technique is useful when you know exactly when recording needs to begin and end, QuickPunch and TrackPunch recording modes allow you to punch in and out of recording mode on the fly. For more details, see the descriptions of these functions—which can be controlled via a footswitch with the Digi 003 and Digi 002 interfaces—in Chapter 8.

Table 5.1 lists just a few of the Transport-related keyboard shortcuts in Pro Tools. However, there are many more. Among the PDF documents included with the program is one entitled *Keyboard Shortcuts*, which we mentioned previously. Print it out and keep it handy. In fact, consider using card stock or even having it laminated. Learning keyboard shortcuts early in the process is one of the most important things you can do to increase your productivity with Pro Tools.

Table 5.1 Essential Keyboard Shortcuts for Transport Functions

Function	Macintosh	Windows
Play start/stop	Spacebar	Spacebar
	0 on numeric keypad	0 on numeric keypad
Loop Playback On/Off	4 on numeric keypad	4 on numeric keypad
	Right-click Play button	Right-click Play button
	Control-click Play button	
Rewind/Fast Forward	1 and 2 on numeric keypad	1 and 2 on numeric keypad
Return to Zero	Return on alpha keyboard	Enter on alpha keyboard
Go to End	Option+Return on alpha keyboard	Alt+Enter on alpha keyboard
Record start	Command+spacebar F12	Ctrl+spacebar F12
	3 on numeric keypad	3 on numeric keypad
Record stop	Spacebar	Spacebar
Record stop and discard take	Command+. (period)	Ctrl+. (period) Esc key
Loop Record On/Off	5 on numeric keypad	5 on numeric keypad
Toggle through Record modes	Control-click on Record button	Right-click on Record button
	Right-click on Record button	
Pre-/Post-Roll On/Off	Command+K	Ctrl+K
Show/Hide Transport	Command+1 on numeric keypad	Ctrl+1 on numeric keypad
Online mode On/Off	Command+J	Ctrl+J
	Option+spacebar	Alt+spacebar

Table 5.1   Continued

Function	Macintosh	Windows
Online Record On/Off	Command+Option +spacebar	Ctrl+Alt+spacebar
Wait for Note (MIDI)	F11	F11
Click On/Off (MIDI)	7 on numeric keypad	7 on numeric keypad
Countoff On/Off (MIDI)	8 on numeric keypad	8 on numeric keypad
MIDI Merge On/Off (MIDI)	9 on numeric keypad	9 on numeric keypad
Select & cycle through time fields for numerical entry	Option+/ on numeric keypad	Alt+/ on numeric keypad
Select Main Counter for numerical entry	* (asterisk) on numeric keypad	* (asterisk) on numeric keypad
Move between columns during numeric entry in time fields	Period or arrow keys	Period or arrow keys

Summary

The Transport functions are the most frequently used features in Pro Tools, so make an effort to learn these keyboard shortcuts early; they work whether the Transport window itself is currently visible or not. (Once again, throughout this book we're assuming you're using the default Transport mode for the numeric keypad, specified in the Preferences dialog box.) The next chapter explores the most important elements in the Edit window.

6 The Edit Window

The Edit window (see Figure 6.1) is the heart of Pro Tools. This is where you view the contents of your tracks, edit audio and MIDI regions, edit MIDI notes, create fades and crossfades, and draw automation changes for volume, panning, and plug-in parameters. In many respects, however, the Edit and Mix windows present two views of the same thing. Some items appear in both windows, including track names and the Mute, Solo, and Record Enable buttons. Furthermore, some users choose to have the sends, inserts, and I/O sections (which appear by default in the Mix window) or the instrument section appear in the Edit window. In any case, the Edit window is where you will likely spend most of your time in Pro Tools. The fact that this chapter is among the longest in this book should give you an idea how essential the features in this window are for mastering Pro Tools!

The basic idea of the Edit window is simple enough. Underneath the toolbar and numerical display area at the top of the screen are the tracks in your session, stretching along a timeline from left to right. There are seven types of tracks in Pro Tools: Audio, Aux Input, Master Fader, Instrument, MIDI, and Video, plus VCA Master tracks in Pro Tools HD only. The Regions List is a "bin" that can be displayed or hidden at the right side of the Edit window. Regions (segments) of audio or MIDI you've recorded or imported into Pro Tools appear here, including region names automatically created by Pro Tools as a result of editing or processing—whether or not they're currently placed into a track. You can drag regions directly from the Regions List out onto tracks (audio, MIDI, or Instrument, as appropriate). You can also preview audio regions right inside the Regions List, and rename, export, or delete regions using either the pop-up menu at the top of the list or, in versions 7.3 and higher, the local menu that appears when you right-click one or more selected regions.

You can change the display format of each track in the Edit window. For example, you can graphically edit changes to each track's volume or panning, viewing this automation as lines and breakpoints. On audio or MIDI tracks, this breakpoint automation is superimposed over a dimmed-out version of the audio waveforms (or MIDI notes) within the regions that the track contains.

The four basic edit modes in the Edit window are Slip, Shuffle, Grid, and Spot. These determine how regions behave as they are moved within tracks, how automation and MIDI data can be

Figure 6.1 The Edit window, showing various track types and display formats.

moved, and how editing tools behave. Briefly, the Slip mode allows free movement; Shuffle mode makes regions snap to each other like magnets; Grid mode adjusts movement to certain increments like the snap-to-grid mode in drawing programs; while Spot mode allows new locations to be entered numerically. By the way, you can use the ~ (tilde) key to toggle between the four edit modes, or you can select a mode using the F1, F2, F3, and F4 keys, respectively. Later in this chapter, you will find more specifics on the edit modes and how they affect the behavior of various tools.

Before getting into these specifics, however, this chapter elaborates on edit tools, edit modes, and track types, and reviews automation and other important elements in the Edit window.

Edit Tools: The Zoomer, Trimmer, Selector, Grabber, Smart Tool, Scrubber, and Pencil

The editing tools, shown in Figure 6.2, provide a multitude of ways to manipulate regions, automation, and MIDI events within Pro Tools tracks. (You can also use many of these in the graphic Tempo editor.)

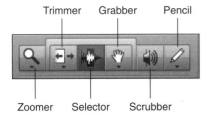

Figure 6.2 Editing tools: Zoomer, Trimmer, Selector, Grabber, Scrubber, Pencil, and the Smart Tool.

Zoomer

When you select the Zoomer tool, the cursor turns into a miniature magnifying glass, as shown in Figure 6.3. Click anywhere in a track to zoom in. Hold down the Option key (Alt key in Windows) to switch from zooming *in* to zooming *out* (the plus sign in the zoom cursor changes to a minus sign). Click and drag over a specific area within a track to magnify it horizontally to fill the current width of the Edit window's track display area. Hold down the Command key for Mac or Ctrl key for Windows while performing this action, and the area will be magnified vertically and horizontally. The Zoomer tool has a drop-down selector for two modes: Normal Zoom and Single Zoom. Single Zoom deselects the Zoomer tool after one zoom, returning to whatever editing tool was previously selected—a good feature to remember! Later in this chapter, you will find a section about zoom controls and preset buttons, keyboard shortcuts, and the Zoom Toggle icon. Use the F5 keyboard shortcut to select this tool and to toggle between the two Zoomer modes.

Figure 6.3 The Zoomer's magnifying glass cursor.

Trimmer

The Trimmer tool can be used to shorten or lengthen regions and MIDI notes and to scale automation shapes up or down. Depending on the current cursor location within the note or region, the tool automatically determines whether you are trimming the beginning or end. For example, the cursor changes from a left trim to a right trim as you move across a region's midpoint, as can be seen in Figure 6.4. To force the Trimmer to flip to the opposite direction, hold down the Option key (Alt key in Windows). In Grid edit mode, the Trimmer snaps to each time increment on the editing grid as you drag, therefore adjusting your region's end or beginning to these grid

Figure 6.4   The Trimmer cursor is a left or right bracket at the beginning/end of regions and MIDI notes, or a horizontal bracket when scaling automation or MIDI controller data up or down.

subdivisions (per the current Grid value). Think of a region as a window into an audio or MIDI recording, which you can make wider or narrower with the Trimmer. (Obviously, you can't lengthen a region beyond the actual beginning or end of its parent audio file.)

The Trimmer can also be used to scale automation shapes (such as volume, pan, send parameters, and some MIDI controller types) up or down within a track—for example, if you're satisfied with the overall volume changes you've created but want to trim them downward a few decibels. (Abbreviated dB, *decibels* is a measurement unit for power levels.) Switch the track's display format to Volume (using the pop-up selector, described later in this chapter), select the entire track (or any portion), and then use the Trimmer to pull the entire volume shape downward. As you drag volume or send levels with the Trimmer, the *delta*, or amount of change, is indicated in dB.

The Trimmer tool has a drop-down selector for different modes: Standard, Scrub, and Time Compression/Expansion, or TC/E. (In the Trimmer mode, the audio within the current selection is stretched or squeezed to match the time range you've trimmed.) In addition, in Pro Tools versions 7.3 and higher, a Loop Trimmer mode allows you to loop audio regions or adjust of the length of looping regions. Place the Loop Trim cursor over the upper half of a looped audio or MIDI region to trim either its beginning or end.

You can also use the TC/E on MIDI regions, scaling the MIDI data they contain. While the Tempo Operations window offers more practical ways to adjust tempos to specific durations or start/end points, users who compose or arrange music in Pro Tools may appreciate this function's usefulness for creating half-time or double-time versions of selected regions. For example, in Grid edit mode, you could select a four-bar region and then select the Trimmer Tool's TC/E mode (the Time Trimmer) to compress it to a two-bar duration. Use the F6 keyboard shortcut to select the Trimmer and to switch between its modes.

Selector

When you use this tool, the mouse cursor changes to an I-beam, as shown in Figure 6.5. Click and drag within a track to select any horizontal range in the timeline within a track (regardless of whether that selection includes or overlaps any regions). Hold down the Shift key and click or drag to adjust the current selection's duration. Shift-click in additional tracks to select the same

Figure 6.5 Use the Selector tool to select a horizontal range in the timeline within a track.

range in multiple tracks. Whatever range you select is reflected in the Start, End, and Length indicators of the Transport window, and you'll hear it when you press Play (unless you've disabled Link Timeline and Edit Selections). Be aware that the currently selected edit mode also affects the behavior of the Selector (see the next section in this chapter) as you click and drag. For example, in Grid edit mode, the beginning and end of your selections are snapped to the nearest time increment. The keyboard shortcut for the Selector is F7.

Fine-Tuning Your Selections Let's say you've selected four bars within a drum or rhythm track and you're going to use that selection to establish a tempo setting in Pro Tools (via the Event > Identify Beat command) and then loop the phrase to start building up a groove. It's extremely important that this selection be precise and that it loops smoothly back onto itself. We will go more deeply into beat-mixing techniques in Chapter 12, "The Pro Tools Groove," but here's a selection method that is also handy for many other situations:

1. After selecting Slip edit mode, click with the Selector tool to place the playback cursor exactly at the beginning of the four-bar phrase. (Zoom into the sample level, make absolutely sure your cursor is *precisely* at the zero crossing where the downbeat begins, and then zoom back out.) Now, hold down Control+Shift (Start+Shift in Windows) to *temporarily* select the Scrubber tool. Click and drag the Scrubber rightward until you locate the downbeat of the bar following the end of your four-bar phrase, then release the mouse button (and the modifier keys). Your selection should now *roughly* correspond to the four bars and the Selector tool should still be active. (You can also create a selection on the fly during playback: Press the down arrow at the beginning and the up arrow at the end of the desired selection.)

2. Enable Options > Loop Playback and press the spacebar to play the selection. You'll probably notice a hiccup in your looping phrase, meaning you need to refine your selection. Pressing the spacebar again stops playback. Let's assume for a

moment that the beginning point is correct; your only problem is adjusting the end point of the selection to create a smooth loop.

3. Underneath the Main Counter and Sub Counter in the Edit window is a numerical field labeled "Nudge." This sets the increments by which nudging is applied. Open the pop-up menu to the right of the Nudge field, select Minutes:Seconds as the reference time units, and then select 1 millisecond as your initial nudge amount.

4. As you hold down Command+Shift (Ctrl+Shift in Windows) and press the + and − (plus and minus) keys on the numeric keypad, the end point of the current selection moves forward or backward by the 1-millisecond nudge increment. To adjust the start point, use the same technique, but instead hold down Option+Shift (Alt+Shift in Windows.) Note that even while in Loop Playback mode, the selection to be looped will *not* be adjusted on the fly each time you nudge the selection end with the + and − keys. You must stop and then restart playback after making each adjustment to the looped selection's duration.

5. At some point, you will be so close that one millisecond is too large a nudge increment. Select Samples as the Nudge value and work your way down through 10-, 2-, or 1-sample nudge increments as necessary until the loop is completely smooth. Alternatively, a more advanced method is to enable the Tab to Transient button. Then, after placing your edit cursor roughly at the start of the section to be looped, press Tab. Press Play and, when you reach the end of the phrase, press the up arrow. If necessary, press Shift+Tab to extend the resultant selection to the next transient.

6. Go ahead and separate this selection as a new region (using the Edit > Separate Region > At Selection command). Name it "4 bars."

7. If you're ambitious, with this exact four-bar region still selected, try out the Event > Identify Beat command. Then switch to the Grid edit mode. Use the Region menu's Loop command (Option+Command+L on Macintosh, Alt+Command+L in Windows) to create any number of loop aliases. Have fun!

Grabber

When the Grabber tool is selected, the mouse cursor turns into a hand shape, as shown in Figure 6.6. The Grabber can be used to click and drag regions to new locations within tracks, drag and create/ delete breakpoints in a track's automation, drag notes within MIDI tracks, drag tracks up and down by their name fields to change their order, and drag markers in the timeline ruler, among other things. The currently selected edit mode (see the section "Edit Modes: Slip, Shuffle, Grid, and Spot" later in this chapter) determines how regions will behave when you use the Grabber to

Figure 6.6 You can use the Grabber's hand cursor to drag regions, MIDI notes, and automation breakpoints.

move them around within tracks. For example, in Shuffle mode, a region will always snap to the beginning or end of another existing region (or to the beginning of the track). When you are in Grid mode, the movement of regions (and automation breakpoints) is snapped to the nearest time increment, according to the current Grid value.

Several important modifier keys alter how the Grabber tool operates:

- When viewing automation, clicking with the Grabber creates a new breakpoint. Option-click (Alt-click in Windows) on existing automation breakpoints with the Grabber cursor to delete them. For finer adjustment of breakpoint levels (for example, volume increments), hold down the Command (Mac) or Ctrl (Windows) key as you drag the breakpoint with the Grabber. You can also obtain fine adjustment of *many* fader and slider values in Pro Tools by holding down this same modifier key as you drag.

- Option-drag (Alt-drag in Windows) audio/MIDI regions or MIDI notes with the Grabber tool to *copy* instead of move them.

- When dragging or copying a region from one track to another, hold down the Control key (Start key in Windows) to constrain its movement to the vertical direction—meaning that the region will maintain its original timeline location regardless of the current edit mode.

The Grabber tool has three modes:

- **Time Grabber.** The Time Grabber mode is the standard mode for the Grabber tool. You can use this mode to drag entire regions within tracks.

- **Separation Grabber.** Once you've made any selection with the Selector tool, the Separation Grabber mode of the Grabber tool automatically splits the selection into a new region as you either drag to move or Option-drag (Alt-drag in Windows) to copy. If your initial selection was across multiple tracks and regions within them, several new regions are created in each track.

- **Object Grabber.** The Object Grabber mode allows selection of non-contiguous regions, even on different tracks. This means that as you Shift-click to select additional regions within a track, for example, the range in the timeline between them is not also selected, as is the case with the Time Grabber mode.

The F8 keyboard shortcut selects the Grabber, and switches between the various Grabber tool modes.

Enhanced Grabber Features in Pro Tools 7.3 and Higher In newer versions of Pro Tools, if you right-click a region and there are other regions before or after it in the same track, the pop-up menu will offer the Snap to Next and Snap to Previous commands. These move the affected region to be adjacent to the boundary of the next or previous region, respectively, without requiring you to switch to Shuffle mode in order to accomplish the same thing.

Smart Tool

If you highlight the bar above the other tools, you activate the Smart Tool. This tool enables you to alternate between the Trimmer, Selector, and Grabber without having to click the tool buttons to select them. The Smart Tool guesses which tool you want to use based on the position of the cursor over regions or MIDI notes (see Figure 6.7). To switch to the Smart Tool with a keyboard shortcut, press F6 and F7 simultaneously (or F7 and F8) on both Macintosh and Windows setups.

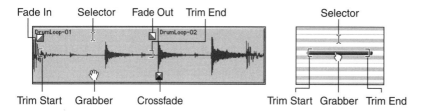

Figure 6.7 When you use Smart Tool mode, Pro Tools selects the appropriate tool according to the cursor's position within a track or region; the cursor shape changes accordingly. Shown here are cursors and edit operations within an audio track (Waveform view) and a MIDI track (Notes view).

Here's how the Smart Tool knows what you want:

- When the cursor is over the middle of any region—in Waveform (audio), Regions (MIDI), or Blocks track display format—and in the lower half of the region graphic, the Grabber tool is active. In the upper half, the Selector tool is enabled.

- When the cursor is near the beginning or end of any region in these same views and in the region's lower half, the Trimmer tool is enabled.

- When the cursor is near the beginning or end of an audio region and in the region's upper half, Pro Tools creates a fade in/out instead of trimming the region's duration when you click and drag. (Fades are not applicable to MIDI regions.) If your cursor is near the boundary between two adjacent audio regions and in the lower half of either region graphic, you can drag with the Smart Tool to create a crossfade between them (assuming there is enough additional audio available within their parent audio files to do so).

- On MIDI tracks in Notes view, the cursor changes to the Selector tool whenever you are not directly over any MIDI notes, to the Grabber tool when it's directly over the middle of any MIDI notes, and to the Trimmer when it's over the beginning or end of a MIDI note.

- When you view automation on a track (and certain MIDI controller parameters, such as volume, pan, pitch bend, mod wheel, mute, aftertouch, velocity, and so on), the cursor changes from the Selector to the Trimmer when you're in the upper portion of the track. Also, when you view the velocity stalks for MIDI note events, the cursor changes to the Grabber when directly over the head of each stalk.

Using Modifier Keys with the Smart Tool Pro Tools provides several options for temporarily switching to other editing tools while the Smart Tool is still selected:

- On audio tracks, switch to scrubbing mode while using the Smart Tool in Waveform view (for example, to locate an audio event by ear) by holding down the Control key (Start key in Windows) and dragging.

- On MIDI tracks, make the cursor change to the Pencil while using the Smart Tool in MIDI Notes view (for example, to insert a note event) by holding down the Control key (Start key in Windows).

- To make the cursor change to the Grabber while using the Smart Tool in Automation view (for example, to insert or drag breakpoints), hold down the Command key (Ctrl key in Windows). For finer control, keep this modifier key pressed down as you as you drag the breakpoint; otherwise, release the key for coarser adjustments.

Note that when you select the Smart Tool, the selection you had for the Trimmer tool (e.g., TC/E, Scrub, etc.) will be in effect. This also applies to the selection you have for the Grabber tool previous to using the Smart Tool, with the exception of the Object Grabber, which will revert to the Time Grabber when the Smart Tool is selected.

Scrubber

When you click and drag on an audio region with the Scrubber tool (see Figure 6.8), you hear the audio playing backward or forward depending on which direction you drag. This is handy for

Figure 6.8 The Scrubber's speaker cursor.

locating audio events. The farther and faster you drag away from the initial click point, the faster the playback. Note that you *cannot* scrub MIDI tracks.

So why is it called *scrubbing*? On professional analog tape decks, you can engage the playback head and rock the tape back and forth across the head. The audio on the tape is heard as you drag (or *scrub*) the tape across the engaged playback heads—for example, to locate the beginning of a song before cutting the tape. This was the standard method for locating the boundaries of audio events on magnetic tape prior to physically cutting the tape in order to make edits.

Note that the Trimmer tool has an additional Scrub Trimmer mode, which scrubs audio in a similar fashion as you click and drag to lengthen or shorten audio regions. To select the Scrubber tool from the keyboard, press F9.

Scrubber Operation Modes: Using Modifier Keys If you hold down the Shift key as you scrub audio playback and then release the mouse button, a range within the track is selected from the previous playback position to the point where you released the Scrubber tool. This makes it easier to find where specific sounds begin or end as you're selecting them for edits.

For finer control and slower playback while using the Scrubber, hold down the Command+Control keys as you click and drag (Ctrl+Start in Windows). You can also combine these modifier keys with the Shift-scrubbing technique described in the preceding paragraph. Hold down the Option (Mac) or Alt (Windows) key as you scrub for extra-fast scrubbing (Shuttle mode).

You can also temporarily switch from the Selector tool (or Smart Tool) to the Scrubber by holding down the Control key (Start key in Windows) as you click and drag.

Pencil

When you are zoomed in far enough on the Waveform view of audio tracks, you can actually *destructively* (in other words, permanently) draw changes to the waveform with the Pencil tool (see Figure 6.9)—for example, to eliminate clicks. In MIDI tracks, you can draw in note events with the Pencil (and then drag them around with the Grabber, of course). If you draw a series of

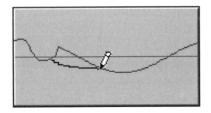

Figure 6.9 You can use the Pencil tool to draw MIDI controller events or even correct small clicks in audio waveforms (once you are zoomed into sample level).

notes with the Pencil tool, their spacing reflects the current Grid value, but you can also set a custom duration if you wish (for instance, to draw notes with $\frac{1}{8}$-note duration and 1/2-note spacing between them). You can also use the Pencil tool's Line shape to draw new velocity contours for existing MIDI notes (in Velocity display format). When displaying automation on audio and MIDI tracks (such as volume, pan, send levels, or other parameters), you can also draw new shapes with the Pencil, although the Grabber tool is often more convenient for this purpose. The Pencil tool has a drop-down selector for its various drawing shapes: Free Hand, Line, Triangle, Square, Random, Parabolic, and S-Curve. Use the F10 keyboard shortcut to select the Pencil and toggle through its modes.

Table 6.1 includes the keyboard shortcuts for the various editing tools.

For the Zoomer, Trimmer, Grabber, and Pencil tools, you can also repeat their function key shortcuts to toggle through their operation modes. (Mac users should see the sidebar in Chapter 5, "The Transport Window," about reassigning function keys F9, F10, F11, and F12 for Exposé and Dashboard.)

Table 6.1 Keyboard Shortcuts for Editing Tools

Keyboard Shortcut	Tool
F5	Zoomer
F6	Trimmer
F7	Selector
F8	Grabber
F6+F7 or F7+F8	Smart Tool
F9	Scrubber
F10	Pencil

To cycle through the editing tools, press the Esc key or click the center mouse button (Windows only).

Oops! If you make a mistake, don't panic! Pro Tools supports up to 32 levels of undo. (The exact number is set in the Editing tab of the Preferences dialog box; users with slower computers can improve system performance slightly by choosing a smaller number.) As a general rule, Pro Tools clearly warns you when a critical action cannot be undone. The Undo History window displays a list of undoable actions (optionally including their creation times), allowing you to return to one of these previous states—even if you've saved the session to disk several times since then.

Edit Modes: Slip, Shuffle, Grid, and Spot

The four edit-mode buttons in the upper-left area of the Edit window (see Figure 6.10) affect the behavior of the editing tools: how regions and MIDI notes respond when moved or placed within tracks (or lengthened/shorted by the Trimmer tool), how selections can be made, and how markers and breakpoints (for automation and tempo events) can be placed or moved around in the timeline. During the course of a project, you will often find yourself switching between edit modes for specific tasks; we suggest you immediately get used to using function keys F1–F4 for this.

Figure 6.10 Edit modes affect selection, movement, and trimming of automation, audio, and MIDI regions/notes.

Slip

In Slip edit mode, no restrictions are applied. You can freely drag regions and MIDI notes to any position within tracks, and the exact ranges you highlight with the Selector and Scrubber tools are not adjusted in any way (as is the case in Grid mode, explained later in this section). When using the Grabber, you can even place regions so that they overlap existing regions in the track. (If, in the View menu, you choose to display an overlap icon, these are added to indicate wherever a region boundary overlaps another underlying region.) Slip mode allows extremely accurate selection, positioning, and trimming, all the way down to the level of individual audio samples on audio tracks that are set to this format, with no restrictions. The keyboard shortcut for Slip mode is F3.

Shuffle

In Shuffle mode, regions move more or less like magnets. If you use the Grabber to drag a region from the Regions List onto an empty track, it snaps to the beginning of the track. If you drag it into a track already containing a region, the region you're dragging snaps to the beginning or end point of the nearest region already on the track, depending on where you release the mouse button. All regions (and empty spaces between them) following the newly inserted region in the track are then pushed later in time (or *shuffled* to the right) by the new region's exact duration. When you use the Trimmer tool in Shuffle mode, as you lengthen or shorten regions in a track, adjacent regions are moved as necessary so that they remain adjacent. When you have regions lined up in a track (for example, sections of a musical arrangement or drum variations) and use the Grabber to change their order in Shuffle mode, they remain stuck together, with no gaps between them, as you move them around. The keyboard shortcut for Shuffle mode is F1.

Shuffle Lock Mode and Individual Region-Locking Commands To avoid accidentally enabling Shuffle mode, in which the positions of later events will change if you cut, paste, or trim earlier events, Command-click the Shuffle button (Ctrl-click in Windows). Also, you can edit-lock or time-lock regions while in Shuffle mode. The Edit-Lock Regions command (referred to as the Lock Regions command in earlier versions of Pro Tools) prevents any editing or timeline movement from occurring to the selected regions. The Time-Lock Regions command locks the selected regions to their current location in the timeline but allows certain editing functions to be applied to the region. Both the Edit-Lock Regions and Time-Lock Regions commands are found in the Region menu.

Grid

Grid mode works like the snap-to-grid function in many drawing programs. All selections, trimming, and dragging of regions (as well as drawing of breakpoint automation) is adjusted, or rounded, to the nearest time increment on the grid. You can use the Grid Value indicator and its pop-up menu, to the right of the Event Edit window, to adjust the time units and spacing of this grid. The keyboard shortcut for Grid mode is F4.

All Pro Tools versions support Minutes:Seconds, Samples, and Bars:Beats formats for grid increments. As shown in the "Grid Value Display" section later in this chapter, time units in the Grid Value selector can either follow the time scale of the Main Counter or can be set independently. On LE systems equipped with the DV Toolkit option (which is not compatible with M-Powered versions of the Pro Tools software), the SMPTE time-code format is also available for grid units, as is the Feet+Frames format used for film work.

Following are some key points for understanding how the edit tools interact with Grid mode:

- When you enable the Conductor track (or tempo map), if you set the Edit window's Main Counter to Bars:Beats and the Grid value to ¼ or ⅛ notes, your selections within audio and

MIDI regions are automatically corrected to these musical values. If you'd like to use the Grabber to drop a snare sample on the second and fourth beats of each bar, for example, adjust the Grid value to ¼ notes, and you won't have to squint!

■ Grid mode can be very handy when you're dragging (Grabber) or drawing (Pencil) MIDI notes. You might say that Grid edit mode quantizes their movement. As you drag an existing region on a track to a new location, its left boundary (or sync point, if it contains one—these are described further in Chapter 8, "Menu Selections: Highlights," in the "Identify Sync Point/Remove Sync Point" section) is adjusted to the nearest grid increment, snapping from one to another as you drag left or right. Likewise, as you click (or click and drag) with the Pencil tool to create MIDI notes, their beginnings and ends snap to the nearest grid increment. To temporarily suspend Grid mode so that you can freely reposition any event, hold down the Command key (Ctrl key in Windows).

■ Grid mode is convenient for snapping the automation breakpoints you create for volume or panning to exact beats and bar lines.

■ Regions and MIDI notes resized with the Trimmer tool are snapped to the nearest grid increment while in Grid mode.

■ Pro Tools users working on video and film projects will appreciate Grid mode for precisely adjusting the boundaries of audio events to whole seconds or frames. For sound designers, when you know that each button sound or background you bounce out must be exactly 2 seconds, 500 milliseconds, or some other round number, trimming regions or selecting time ranges to bounce to disk in Grid mode can save time.

■ If you activate the Regions/Markers option in the Grid Value pop-up menu (shown in the "Grid Value Display" section later in this chapter), your selections, resizing, and movement of regions and MIDI notes will not only snap to the nearest grid increment, but also to marker locations and the boundaries of any region in any track (or sync points within audio regions). Be sure to explore this feature; it's overlooked even by many experienced Pro Tools users!

A new feature in Pro Tools 8 is the ability to temporarily enable a version of Grid mode, called Snap To Grid, while in any of the other edit modes. This blends some aspects of Grid mode with features of the other primary mode. For instance, enabling Snap To Grid while in Shuffle mode enables you to make a precise grid-based selection of regions, move them elsewhere in the session, and have the regions that precede the edit selection in the track shuffle to the right.

Spot

Spot mode is convenient for placing regions at precise numerical locations—for example, when placing (*spotting*) sound effects during a film or video project. In this edit mode, the Spot dialog box (shown in Figure 6.11) appears as soon as you click a region with the Grabber, drag it out

Figure 6.11 You can use the Spot dialog box to specify positions (and selections) numerically. This can be especially powerful when Pro Tools is slaved to an external device via SMPTE time code.

onto a track from the Regions List, or click it with the Trimmer. In this dialog box's fields, you specify time values *numerically* for the start and/or end, duration, or sync point (Grabber only) of the selected region.

Spot mode is especially handy for audio editors in video facilities. Using a video master tape with a time-code window burned into the video image, you can jog the video tape exactly to the frame where an audio hit needs to be placed, click an audio region or drag it onto a track, and then simply type the correct time into the Spot dialog box. Even easier, as time code is received into Pro Tools, if the Spot dialog box is open—and the master video transport is in Play mode using LTC (longitudinal time code, which is embedded in an audio signal) or even paused or stopped using VITC (vertical interval time code, which is embedded into each video frame)—you can press the = (equals sign) key on your computer keyboard to automatically enter the current SMPTE position into its numeric fields. For more information about using SMPTE time code in postproduction, see Chapter 14, "Postproduction and Soundtracks." The keyboard shortcut for Spot edit mode is F2.

Quick Entry in the Spot Dialog Box with the Plus/Minus Keys Here's a quick way to add or subtract a given number of video frames to any of the time value fields in the Spot dialog box when using SMPTE time code as your time scale (available on HD systems, or LE systems equipped with the DV Toolkit option):

1. Make sure the pop-up Time Scale selector in the dialog box is set to SMPTE time code.

2. Click in the last segment of the number to select the frames column.

3. Press + or − (plus or minus) on the numeric keypad.

4. Enter the number of frames.

5. Press Return (Enter in Windows) on the alphanumeric keyboard.

Even on M-Powered and LE systems without DV Toolkit, you can do this in the Seconds column when using Minutes:Seconds as your time scale in the Spot dialog box—as well as *any* column of the Bars:Beats or Samples time scales.

   As with other time value fields in Pro Tools, you can use the up- and down-arrow keys on your computer to nudge numerical values in the Spot dialog box, and pressing the period or right- and left-arrow keys lets you move from one column to another. You can also press Tab or Shift+Tab to toggle forward or backward from one field to another and use the Esc and Enter keys as shortcuts for the Cancel and OK buttons, as in many dialog boxes.

Zoom Controls and Zoom Preset Buttons

The zoom controls and zoom preset buttons, shown in Figure 6.12, change your view magnification for the contents of tracks in the Edit window either horizontally for the time scale or vertically for audio amplitude or MIDI pitches. You can store and recall your own zoom presets—an important time-saving habit, which you should acquire as early as possible! Note that if you don't see the zoom controls in the Edit window toolbar, look for the triangle icon in the upper-right corner that drops down choices for displaying features in the toolbar. Simply select the Zoom Controls option, and they will appear to the right of the Edit Mode selectors.

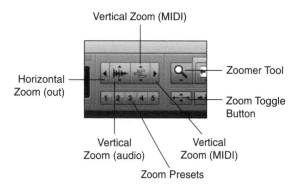

Figure 6.12 Zoom controls in the Edit window toolbar.

New to Pro Tools 8 are Edit window zoom buttons, found in the lower-right corner of the Edit window (see Figure 6.13). The vertical Edit window zoom buttons raise or lower the waveform heights, and the horizontal Edit window zoom buttons zoom the timeline in or out, similar to the zoom buttons in the toolbar.

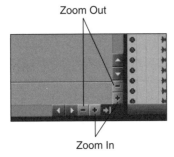

Figure 6.13 Vertical and horizontal zoom buttons in the Edit window.

In addition, Pro Tools 8 has audio and MIDI zoom buttons, located in the upper-right corner of the Edit window (see Figure 6.14). As with the audio and MIDI zoom controls in the toolbar, you click the top of the button to zoom in and the bottom of the button to zoom out.

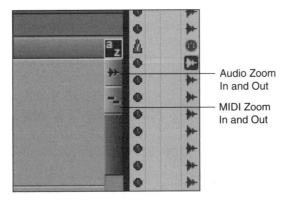

Figure 6.14 Audio and MIDI zoom buttons in the Edit window.

You will spend a lot of time zooming in and out as you edit data in your tracks. After reading the following descriptions for each zoom control, be sure to check out the sidebar that follows about keyboard shortcuts for zooming. Along with the basic Transport functions, zooming shortcuts should be among the first ones you memorize in Pro Tools!

- **Horizontal Zoom In/Out.** Clicking these buttons expands or contracts your current view along the (horizontal) time scale of the Edit window. The further you zoom in, the more detail is available while editing (although a shorter duration will fit in the Edit window).

- **Vertical Zoom In/Out (Audio).** These buttons affect the displayed range on the amplitude (vertical) axis of audio waveforms within audio tracks only. They have no effect on the view of other track types.

- **Vertical Zoom In/Out (MIDI).** These buttons zoom the vertical axis (pitch, or note number) on all MIDI and Instrument tracks only. They have no effect on your view of MIDI *controller* data in these tracks, and don't affect other track types.

- **Zoom Presets.** These buttons (1–5) are used to store horizontal (time scale) zoom presets for the current session document. Command-click (Ctrl-click in Windows) on any of these buttons to store the current horizontal zoom settings there, and then later click any Zoom Preset button to recall its stored zoom settings. Take some time to learn how to use the Zoom Preset buttons; it's surprising how many otherwise competent Pro Tools users repeatedly click the zoom buttons to go back and forth between the same two magnifications!

Zoom! Faster!—Zooming Shortcuts Getting around quickly in your project is essential, not only for building up creative momentum but also to avoid making your clients impatient! Here are some shortcuts to make navigation a bit easier:

- Hold down the Command key (Ctrl key in Windows) and press the square bracket keys ([or]) to zoom in and out horizontally in the Edit window.

- Hold down the Command+Option keys (Ctrl+Alt in Windows) and use the square brackets ([or]) to zoom in and out vertically on all audio tracks.

- Hold down the Command+Shift keys (Ctrl+Shift in Windows) and use the square brackets ([or]) to zoom in and out vertically on all MIDI tracks.

- Hold down the Command key (Ctrl key in Windows) while highlighting an area of an audio waveform with the Zoomer tool to simultaneously zoom in horizontally and vertically.

- Double-click the Zoomer to zoom completely out so that the entire session fits into the Edit window.

- Option-click (Alt-click in Windows) the Zoomer tool to horizontally zoom your current track selection to fill the current width of the Edit window.

- Use the zoom arrow buttons (or the Vertical Zoom buttons) to recall the *previous* horizontal zoom setting. Let's say, for example, that you're viewing tracks at a comfortable horizontal zoom level, but just to confirm where you are within the entire session, you double-click the Zoomer tool so that the entire session's duration fits into the Edit window. Option-clicking (Alt-clicking in Windows) on either of the Zoom In/Out buttons returns you to the previous zoom level.

- Learn how to use the Single Zoom mode of the Zoomer tool (which reselects the previous editing tool after zooming once). This is a real time-saver, and all too easy to overlook.

■   Memory locations can store zoom settings as an attribute of any marker or selection. (See the "Timeline Display: Timebase Rulers and Marker Memory Locations" section later in this chapter.)

Zoom Toggle Icon

This icon appears beneath the Zoomer tool. It allows you to store certain parameters of an Edit window view, to which you can switch at any time by clicking this icon. The parameters affected by stored Zoom Toggle settings are track height, display mode, horizontal and vertical (audio/MIDI) zoom, and Grid value. Here's how you use it: Click the Zoom Toggle icon to enable it, and then manually set up your zoom levels, track heights, and Grid value. Click it again to disable. After you've changed view parameters, you can simply click again on the Zoom Toggle icon as you work to return to the stored zoom toggle settings. To alter these settings, just change these view parameters while the Zoom Toggle icon is enabled (lit).

Be sure to check out the Zoom Toggle preferences provided in versions 7.3 and higher of Pro Tools. For example, you can choose whether zoom toggling inward corresponds to the current timeline selection or to the last zoom toggle state that has been stored. You can also choose to have zoom toggling inward automatically switch to waveform audio tracks and notes display format on MIDI/Instrument tracks. Everyone's working style is different, but we find the Selection setting for vertical and horizontal zoom especially useful for editing audio. In this mode, the current selection automatically zooms to fill the current track height and the width of the Edit window.

More Vertical Zooming Features for Audio Pro Tools versions 7.4 and higher offer a couple more handy tricks for zooming the height of audio waveforms in your tracks:

■   To zoom the amplitude scale on a single audio track in relation to others in the same session, hold down the Control key (Start key in Windows) as you drag up and down within the track.

■   To zoom amplitudes on all tracks simultaneously, add the Shift key to the previous combination.

Event Edit Area (Selection/Position Indicators)

How can you edit your audio if you don't know where you *are*? The indicators in the Event Edit area, shown in Figure 6.15, let you know where you are in the session's timeline, the time values for your current selection, and where your cursor is as you move it around within Pro Tools tracks. You will find these very useful when making edit selections, when selecting audio material for bouncing out mix files to disk, and for controlling playback in Pro Tools.

Figure 6.15 The Event Edit area provides information about the current selection and playback location.

Edit Selection Indicators (Start/End/Length)

The Start, End, and Length numerical fields display information about the current Edit window selection in the Main Counter's current time units. As you use the Selector and Grabber tools to make selections within tracks, these will be indicated in the Start, End, and Length fields. When using the Trimmer to lengthen or shorten regions, the values here also change in real time as you drag the Trimmer cursor.

You can enter values directly into these fields to modify or create a selection and/or change the current playback cursor location if Options > Link Timeline and Edit Selections is enabled. Here are a few shortcuts for quick entry into these fields:

- Use the / (forward slash) key to toggle between the Start, End, and Length indicators.

- Use the . (period) key or right and left arrows to switch from one column to another within these fields.

- Use the up- and down-arrow keys to incrementally increase or decrease the selected value.

- As with the Spot dialog box, you can also select a column, press the + or − (plus or minus) key, type a number, and then press Return (Enter in Windows) to increase or decrease its value by a specific amount.

Main/Sub Counters

During playback or recording, the Main and Sub Counters display the current play position. If the Sub Counter is not displayed, click the triangle drop-down menu next to the Main Counter and choose Show Sub Counter. If Options > Link Timeline and Edit Selections is enabled (a function that can also be enabled via a button underneath the Edit window's toolbar), the Start and End fields in the Transport window are also adjusted to match your current timeline selection in the Edit window. If not, the Transport's timeline (play) selection and Main Location indicator (the playback cursor position) are not altered by making a new edit selection. This can be useful while editing; for example, the same four-bar selection would always play when you press the spacebar, even as you edit and drag around regions within that range.

A pop-up menu to the right of the Main Counter and Sub Counter allows you to select different time units. The time units you select for the Main Counter will affect the time units displayed in the Edit window's main active ruler (and vice versa). The units currently selected for the Main Counter are also reflected in the Cursor Location indicator and in the Start, End, and Length indicators for edit selections.

Main Counter To directly highlight the Edit window's Main Counter, press the = (equals sign) key on the numeric keypad. Like other time value fields in Pro Tools, there are several methods for directly entering values here: direct numerical entry, up and down arrows, or plus and minus keys, for example. Press Return or Enter to confirm your entry, moving the playback cursor to the new position. Remember that you can use the period key or right and left arrows to navigate between columns in any time indicator that has multiple segments (for example, minutes, seconds, or milliseconds). Lastly, if you open the Big Counter (via that command in the Window menu), the Main Counter's values are displayed large enough for you see them from across the room while recording takes; you can also type values directly into this oversized view.

MIDI Note Attributes

When a single MIDI note is selected in a MIDI or Instrument track in Notes or Velocity track view, the editable value fields shown in Figure 6.16 display the note's pitch, attack velocity, and release velocity. The keyboard techniques described for the Main Counter and Sub Counter also work in these fields—once you click within them to enable them for editing values. Additionally, you can enter new values for each of these MIDI note attributes by striking keys on your external MIDI keyboard or other controller. This saves time because if you record-enable the track while performing this data entry, you hear the result of the new values in real time as you repeatedly strike the key.

Figure 6.16 Additional fields appear in the Event Edit area when MIDI notes are selected.

When *multiple* MIDI notes are selected, each of these fields initially appears with a zero value and a delta symbol (for the amount of change). As you drag the group of selected notes to a new pitch, the corresponding amount of transposition (in semitones) is displayed in the Pitch field. Alternatively, you can select the Pitch field and enter the amount of transposition you want on all the selected notes—for example, +7 semitones to raise them by a perfect fifth or +12 for an octave. Typing numbers or clicking and dragging also works for altering Attack and Release Velocity values of multiple notes, except that in this case, the amount of change (the *delta*) is displayed here (compared to whatever the original velocity value was for each note in the selection). As always with MIDI, there are upper and lower limits for both pitch and velocity; values can't exceed these, no matter how much change you apply.

Edit Window Transport Buttons

The Transport buttons in the Edit window (see Figure 6.17) duplicate the buttons in the Transport window for more convenience while working in the Edit window. Even when the Transport window isn't visible, all the same keyboard shortcuts apply; for example, you can press the spacebar to start and stop playback, press Return (Enter in Windows) on the alphanumeric keyboard to return to the beginning of the session timeline, press Command+spacebar (Ctrl+spacebar in Windows) to start recording, and so on.

Figure 6.17   For convenience, the Transport buttons are duplicated at the upper-right corner of the Edit window.

Get a Scroll-Wheel Mouse for Your Older Mac! Dual-button mice with scroll wheels have long been commonplace on Windows computers, but until the 2007 introduction of Apple's Mighty Mouse, with its scroll ball and touch-sensitive shell for left- and right-click capability, wheel-less mice had always been the factory-supplied option for Macintosh.

Like most Internet browsers, word processors, and other programs, Pro Tools supports use of the scroll wheel. Trust us, your productivity in Pro Tools will be greatly improved if you upgrade your older Macintosh mouse to a newer mouse or trackball with two buttons and a scroll wheel (or the Mighty Mouse). This is even more so in versions 7.3 and higher, which introduce additional scroll-wheel techniques to improve your editing workflow. These include the following:

- You can roll the mouse wheel to scroll vertically in any active window or area in which a scroll bar is currently visible—for example, the Mix and Edit windows, Memory Locations, the Regions List, or the MIDI Event List—whenever their entire contents don't fit into the current window.

- In Pro Tools 7.3 and higher, to scroll your view horizontally in the Edit or Mix windows, you can hold down the Shift key as you use the mouse's scroll wheel.

- To zoom your view horizontally in the Edit window, hold down the Option key (Alt key in Windows) as you roll the wheel up or down.

- In Pro Tools 7.3 and higher, to continuously zoom audio waveform display heights in the Edit window (as with its vertical zoom buttons for audio), hold down the Option+Shift keys (Alt+Shift keys in Windows) as you scroll.

- To continuously zoom the vertical scale for MIDI notes in the Edit window, hold down the Control+Option keys (Alt+Start keys in Windows) as you scroll up or down.

- To scroll the Notes display of a specific MIDI or Instrument track up or down, hold down Command+Control+Option keys (Alt+Start+Ctrl in Windows) as you scroll up or down.

Other Edit Window Fields

Other useful fields and indicators appear between the edit tool selectors and the track display area below them. Several of these are shown in Figure 6.18.

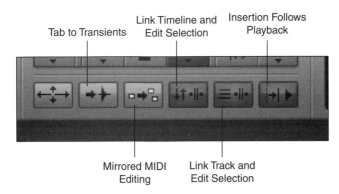

Figure 6.18   Additional fields above the track display area of the Edit window.

Tab to Transients

When this button is enabled, pressing the Tab key within an audio track automatically moves the cursor to a location immediately before the next transient peak in the track or to the next audio region boundary (beginning or end). This can be an important time saver when editing a long voice-over. Within a vocal or guitar overdub, for example, you could also highlight audio waveform data all the way from the current location or selection to the beginning of the next phrase by holding down the Shift key as you tab. (As when selecting regions within tracks, pressing Option+Tab moves backward, and you can combine it with the Shift key to make selections.) Tab to Transient also works when multiple tracks are selected, moving the playback location (or extending the selection, if you're holding down the Shift key) to the next transient found in *any* of these tracks. This is especially convenient when editing multiple drum or backing vocal tracks! When using Tab to Transients within MIDI tracks, you can tab to the start of subsequent or previous MIDI notes in the same manner as you do transients in audio tracks.

Tab to Transients in Versions 7.4 and Higher In version 7.4 of Pro Tools, a more sophisticated transient-detection algorithm called Enhanced Resolution was introduced for the Beat Detective features. This algorithm is now also used with the Tab to Transients feature, making it more reliable on a wider variety of audio material.

Link Timeline and Edit Selection

When the Link Timeline and Edit Selection button is enabled, the selections you make within tracks or rulers or by simply repositioning the playback cursor will not only reset the values of the Start and End indicators at the top of the Edit window (the edit selection), but also in the Transport (the play selection, which determines where playback starts and stops when you press Play). In the event you wish to unlink the two, simply deselect this button (refer to Figure 6.18). For example, you might want to select and edit individual notes and regions while a longer four-bar selection loops or edit a different part of the session without losing your current timeline selection for playback. Toggling this button on and off is the same thing as using the Options > Link Timeline and Edit Selection menu selection.

Note: In Pro Tools versions 7.3 and higher, activating Dynamic Transport mode, via the Options > Dynamic Transport command, automatically enables loop playback and disables Link Timeline and Edit Selection.

Link Track and Edit Selection

When this option is enabled, via the Edit window button or the corresponding command in the Options menu, selecting any material for editing within the track also automatically selects the track itself, highlighting its track name. This is a convenient way to select one or more tracks for track-level operations—for example, grouping them, making them inactive, or dragging them to a new position in the Tracks List. If you hold down Option+Shift (Alt+Shift in Windows) as you change a track parameter, this change is applied to all currently *selected* tracks. In contrast, if you hold down the Option key (Alt key in Windows) without the additional Shift key modifier, the change applies to *all* tracks, whether selected or not. Used in conjunction with the Link

Track and Edit Selection feature, this Option+Shift (Alt+Shift) technique is a convenient way to change the track height, view format, Record/Solo/Mute button states, automation mode, time-base format, and other track attributes based on your current selections within multiple tracks.

Mirrored MIDI Editing

When you use this feature, any changes you make to a MIDI region are also applied to all other MIDI regions with the same name. For instance, suppose you start with a very simple four-bar drum figure—say, a MIDI region called Drum4—to build your arrangement and you want to edit velocities or otherwise embellish this basic pattern after adding a few more instrumental parts. With Mirrored MIDI Editing enabled, as you make each edit in a single instance of this MIDI region, this button blinks red once, reminding you that the same change is being applied to all other MIDI regions called Drum4.

Insertion Follows Playback

When selected, this feature relocates the edit cursor to the point on the timeline where playback stops. So if you instigate playback for two bars, the edit cursor and playback cursor are relocated to the end of the second bar. This feature will be helpful in most Pro Tools workflows. If not selected, the playback cursor returns to the point on the timeline where playback started. Also, if you have made a selection in the timeline you want to keep, but would like to playback a portion of the timeline, make sure to deselect Insertion Follows Playback to prevent loss of your selection start and end points upon stopping playback.

Grid Display and Grid Value Display

The Grid Display button controls whether a grid can be seen in the Edit window. When the button is green, the grid is displayed. The Grid Value setting reflects the current time increments that govern the selection and movement of regions, trimming, and automation when Grid edit mode is enabled. As shown in Figure 6.19, the pop-up Grid Units Selector menu to the right of

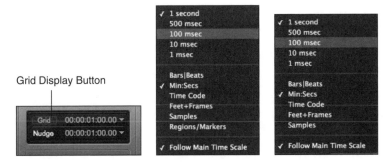

Figure 6.19 The Grid Value display, along with the Nudge Value display (discussed next), incorporates pop-up menus for selecting Grid/Nudge increments. This shows an LE system with the DV Toolkit installed, which, like HD systems, also supports SMPTE time code and Feet+Frames as grid or nudge time units.

this indicator lets you change this value. Its time units default to those of the currently active ruler, but you can also set time units for the Grid Value field separately. When Grid edit mode is selected, movement and trimming (resizing) of regions and MIDI notes in the Edit window (as well as the location of automation breakpoints) is snapped (quantized) to the nearest increment on this time grid. When you drag with the Selector tool, the beginning and end values of the selected time range are also snapped to the nearest grid increment. (Refer to the "Grid" section under "Edit Modes: Slip, Shuffle, Grid, and Spot," earlier in this chapter.)

Nudge Value Display

This field's pop-up selector (also shown in Figure 6.19) sets the time increment to be used when you nudge regions and events with the + and − (plus and minus) keys on the numeric keypad (as discussed previously). As with the Grid value, the units for nudging can reflect those of the currently active ruler or you can set them separately. For example, if you select an audio or MIDI region and use the pop-up display to the right of the Nudge Value indicator to select a 1-millisecond nudge increment (or one SMPTE frame, or one $\frac{1}{8}$ note), each time you press the + or − key, the region is moved forward or backward from its present position by that amount of time. This lets you make fine adjustments to timing without zooming all the way in to drag regions around. Nudging also works on MIDI note selections within MIDI tracks as well as selected breakpoints for MIDI controller data, such as mod wheel, pitch bend, aftertouch, and others. Besides the preset Nudge values, you can also type in any other amount. This can be useful if, for example, you are nudging sound effects and you find that 100 milliseconds is too large while 10 milliseconds is too small.

Here are some other useful techniques for nudging:

- To nudge the start and end points of the selection forward or backward by the current Nudge value without altering the selected audio or MIDI data, use the + and − (plus and minus) keys on the numeric keypad. This works when you use the Selector tool to highlight a selection either within an audio or MIDI region or across multiple regions.

- To nudge only the end of the selection, hold down the Command key (Ctrl key in Windows) as you nudge with the + and − (plus and minus) keys on the numeric keypad.

- To nudge only the beginning of the selection, hold down the Option key (Alt key in Windows) as you nudge with the + and − (plus and minus) keys on the numeric keypad.

- To nudge the waveform contents of an audio region without affecting the region's current start and end points in the track, hold down the Control key (Start key in Windows) as you nudge with the + and − (plus and minus) keys on the numeric keypad. (Additional audio must be available within the region's parent audio file for this to work.) This is handy if, for example, you have some excess silence at the beginning of a region containing a cymbal sound, which you've already placed exactly on the ¼ note. You can nudge this region's definition further back in the parent audio file so that it doesn't include the silence prior to the cymbal attack. The result is that the cymbal attack ends up at the beginning of the region, right on the ¼ note.

■ When Commands Keyboard Focus mode is enabled (the AZ button in the upper-right corner of the Edit window's tracks area), you can nudge selections—regions, notes, and ranges of automation, for example—using your computer keyboard. (This is in addition to many other time-saving shortcuts; be sure to read about Commands Keyboard Focus mode in the *Keyboard Shortcuts* PDF document!) The . (period) and , (comma) keys move the selected events forward or back by the current Nudge value. To nudge forward or backward by the next-largest Nudge value (e.g., ¼ notes if your current setting is ⅛ notes), use the / (forward slash) and M keys. In fact, as with many other Commands Keyboard Focus shortcuts, you don't necessarily have to enable this mode at all—just hold down the Control key (Start key in Windows) as you use these same keyboard shortcuts for nudging.

Cursor Location/Cursor Value

The Cursor Location display reflects the (horizontal) time location as you move the cursor within the Edit window (in whatever units the Main Counter is using). The Cursor Value display reflects the current vertical position of the cursor within a track. For example, while moving your cursor vertically over a MIDI track in Notes view, the Cursor Value display shows note numbers to indicate its current position. But if the display mode of a track is set to Volume, the value shown for the current cursor position is decibels (dB) for audio or 0–127 for MIDI track volumes. Both of these fields are shown in Figure 6.20. They're not editable fields, but instead provide feedback about the current position as you move the cursor—for example, while dragging automation breakpoints up and down or resizing notes and regions.

Figure 6.20 These fields indicate that the cursor is currently within a MIDI track, at SMPTE time code 1 hour, 59 minutes, 20 seconds and 8 frames, with a vertical position corresponding to MIDI volume 82.

Ruler View Selector

This pop-up selector, shown in Figure 6.21, enables/disables the different ruler types in the Edit window and duplicates options in the View > Rulers submenu.

Edit Window View Selector

Use this pop-up selector, also shown in Figure 6.21, to display the Comments, I/O, Inserts, Sends, Instrument, Real-Time Properties, and track color sections at the left side of the Edit window's tracks. You can also use it to toggle display of the Edit window's transport buttons. This selector duplicates options also available in the View > Edit Window submenu.

Ruler View Selector

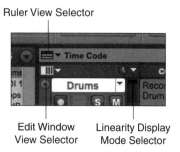

Edit Window   Linearity Display
View Selector   Mode Selector

Figure 6.21   The Ruler View Selector, the Edit Window Selector, and the Linearity Display Mode Selector.

Linearity Display Mode Selector

You can use this display timebase selector, also shown in Figure 6.21, to switch the horizontal scale for displaying all track events in the Edit window between Linear Sample Display (absolute time) and Linear Ticks Display (relative to the current tempo settings). In Linear Sample Display format, the display corresponds to actual audio samples at the current sample rate, so if you increase the musical tempo, each bar (in the Bars:Beats ruler, for example) occupies less space. Conversely, in Linear Ticks Display format, all bars of 4/4 occupy the same amount of horizontal space in the Edit window, even if tempo changes actually mean that each bar corresponds to a different amount of absolute time (as measured in samples).

Commands Focus

In all versions of Pro Tools, AZ Commands Keyboard Focus buttons are available in the upper-right corner of the Regions List and the Groups List. Another Commands Keyboard Focus button is in the upper-right corner of the Edit window tracks area, providing key-focus shortcuts for commands (see Figure 6.22). When one of these buttons is highlighted, its keyboard-focus commands (single-key shortcuts from the alphanumeric keyboard) are active. For example, when the Keyboard Focus button for the Regions List is enabled, you can select regions in that list by typing the first few letters of a name. When Keyboard Focus is active for the Groups List, you can toggle Edit and Mix groups on and off by typing the group ID letter. When Commands Keyboard Focus is active, you can access many editing and play commands via single keystrokes on the alphanumeric keyboard.

Figure 6.22   The Commands Keyboard Focus button, available for the Regions List, the Groups List, and the Edit window tracks area.

Regions List

This "bin" at the right edge of the Edit window, shown in Figure 6.23, lists all the MIDI and audio region names referenced within the session—whether they have been placed into tracks or not—as well as region group names.

Figure 6.23 The Regions List shows audio regions, MIDI regions, and region groups.

When you create a new session, of course, the Regions List is empty. As soon as you record into any audio, MIDI, or Instrument track, a new region name is created based on the name of the track in which it was recorded. You can also import external audio files directly into the Regions List (or directly into a track) by dragging from the Workspace browser window or Finder (Desktop or Explorer in Windows) or by using the File > Import > Audio command. Imported audio files and regions appear with their original names in the Regions List; to change a region's name, double-click it and type the new name in the Name dialog box that appears.

Renaming Regions As mentioned, you can double-click to rename any region in the Regions List. In addition to this, you can use the Grabber to double-click regions directly within tracks; this opens the renaming dialog box. Alternatively, in Pro Tools versions 7.3 and higher, you can right-click any region—either in the Regions List or within a track—to display a pop-up menu that enables you to rename that region. Remember that as you record into audio and MIDI tracks, region names are created based on the track name in which they were recorded. Take a moment to name your tracks as you prepare to record; it will save time and confusion later!

Note: Many region names represent portions within longer "parent" audio files. Other region names represent entire audio files, in which case their names appear in bold type inside the Regions List. When you rename any of these whole-file audio regions, an additional option appears in the dialog box, enabling you to specify whether you want to also rename the source disk file or only the region name as it appears within the current Pro Tools session.

Many of your edits in Pro Tools will cause additional regions to be created. For example, if you cut the middle out of an existing audio region, there will now be three region definitions, all referring to different selections with the same parent audio file: the original region, plus two additional region definitions for the portions before and after the cut. An option in the local menu of the Regions List allows you to choose whether these auto-created regions should be shown.

As elsewhere, you can Shift-click to select multiple adjacent items in the Regions List and/or Command-click (Ctrl-click in Windows) to make non-contiguous selections. If you wish, you can also choose to display the source file names, full directory paths, and/or disk locations in the Regions List, although doing so will make the displayed region names much longer.

Previewing Audio and MIDI Regions in the Regions List   Option-click (Alt-click in Windows) and hold on any audio or MIDI region in the Regions List to listen to it without having to drag it out onto a track. MIDI regions will be previewed via the default Thru instrument defined in the MIDI tab of the Preferences dialog box; this can be configured to always follow the MIDI output assignment of the first selected MIDI/Instrument track. Of course, you can also preview audio and MIDI regions in the Project and Workspace browser windows, even before importing them into the current Pro Tools session.

How Pro Tools Creates Region Names as You Record and Edit   As mentioned previously, when you record the first audio (or MIDI) region into a track, a new region name is created based on that track's name. For example, say you create a new Pro Tools session, then create some new audio tracks (using the Track > New command). Here's what happens:

1.   In the Edit window, double-click the name field of the Audio 1 track and rename it something else (such as Cornet). Click this track's Rec button to arm it for recording.

2.   Click Record, and then click Play in the Transport window. Let Pro Tools roll in record mode for a few seconds (you'll see your recording in progress as a red rectangle within this track).

3.   Now click Stop. The region name "Cornet_01" appears in the Regions List, and a similarly named file is created inside your session's Audio Files folder. (We're assuming you're seeing Pro Tools' default options for region display here—that is, you haven't opted to also display the lengthier file names, disk names, or directory paths within the Regions List.)

4.   Click Play and Record again, and let it run a couple of seconds longer. A second region, Cornet_02, appears in the list, and replaces the previously recorded region in the Cornet audio track. Are you getting it so far? The first part of the numerical suffix automatically numbers successive recordings.

5.   Use the Selector tool to highlight a portion anywhere in the middle of the second region you just recorded and press the Delete key on your keyboard. Pro Tools automatically assigns two new region names to the segments remaining before and after the cut (assuming that this default option is enabled in the Editing tab of the Preferences dialog box), appending -01 and -02 to the original region's name—in this case, Cornet_02-01 and Cornet_02-02. Pro Tools will often create new region definitions as a result of editing operations, using these numerical suffixes to identify them.

If you get confused about what regions are used where, select any region name within the Regions List and it will also be highlighted every place it occurs within a track and vice versa. (This assumes that these default options are enabled in Preferences > Editing; some users prefer to have Regions List and Edit selections be independent of each other.) Even better, start double-clicking (or right-clicking in versions 7.3 and higher) to rename your regions—call the flute solo Flute Solo, and so on!

Using the Regions List's Local Menu

Audio files are very large. No matter what your system's disk capacity is, it is still important to limit your audio projects to a reasonable amount of disk space. For one thing, this will make the backing up and archiving of your project data more efficient.

Many of the commands in the Regions List's local menu (shown in Figure 6.24) are self-explanatory, but here we list a few that are especially useful for making sure your projects don't needlessly occupy disk space for unused audio data. As you will be reminded many times in this book, it is extremely important to assign meaningful names to regions as you work in Pro Tools. (Always naming tracks *before* recording into them is a good start, by the way.) If you're sorting through a hundred or more regions from dozens of tracks (and takes) in order to delete unused files

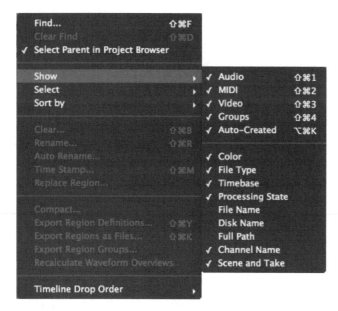

Find...	⇧⌘F
Clear Find	⇧⌘D
✓ Select Parent in Project Browser	

Show	▶		✓ Audio	⇧⌘1
Select	▶		✓ MIDI	⇧⌘2
Sort by	▶		✓ Video	⇧⌘3
			✓ Groups	⇧⌘4
Clear...	⇧⌘B		✓ Auto-Created	⌥⌘K
Rename...	⇧⌘R			
Auto Rename...			✓ Color	
Time Stamp...	⇧⌘M		✓ File Type	
Replace Region...			✓ Timebase	
			✓ Processing State	
Compact...			File Name	
Export Region Definitions...	⇧⌘Y		Disk Name	
Export Regions as Files...	⇧⌘K		Full Path	
Export Region Groups...			✓ Channel Name	
Recalculate Waveform Overviews			✓ Scene and Take	
Timeline Drop Order	▶			

Figure 6.24 The Regions List's pop-up local menu helps manage regions (and region groups) as well as MIDI and audio files in Pro Tools projects.

and reduce the amount of disk space utilized by your session folder, think how much easier this will be if the region for your tenor sax solo is actually named TenorSax_12 rather than, say, Audio 17_12!

Select (Unused Regions, Unused Regions Except Whole Files, Offline)

The Select Unused Regions and Select Unused Regions Except Whole Files commands highlight all regions in the list that are not currently placed on any audio tracks in this session. Audio regions that represent entire audio files appear in bold type within the Regions List. (These may have been created by new recordings, by importing audio files into the session, as a result of menu commands such as Consolidate Selection, or by applying any function in the AudioSuite menu with the Create Continuous File or Create Individual Files option enabled.) It's common to exclude whole-file regions (via the Select > Unused Regions Except Whole Files option) if you're going to use the Clear Selected command. That way, the whole-file regions that represent the parent audio files for other smaller regions that actually reside in your tracks will remain in the Regions List. This makes it easier to compact these later on to recover disk space; see the section "Compact Selected" in this chapter for more information. The Select Offline Regions command removes from the Regions List any files or regions that correspond with audio files that Pro Tools could not locate when the project session was launched. The names of offline files are italicized and dimmed in the Regions List.

Clear Selected

When the selected audio regions represent portions within larger parent audio files, the Clear Selected command simply removes this reference from the current Pro Tools session document. For whole-file regions that correspond to entire sound files (and therefore appear in bold type within the Regions List), you have the option to either simply remove the session's reference to the file (leaving it intact on your disk) or to delete the file from the disk entirely. Obviously, the second option is potentially dangerous, especially if you've forgotten that you also use this audio file in a different session. (Be sure to pay attention to what you're doing!) After using the Select Unused Regions command, you can always Shift-click to deselect several of them before executing the Clear Selected command.

Compact Selected

Applying the Compact Selected command to selected regions in the Regions List eliminates any portions within the selected audio file that are not actually being used in any region definitions in the current session document. Suppose you press Record at the beginning of a song for some backing vocal harmonies that the singers want to put down. Out of the four minutes you record, they only sing two lines at the bridge, plus another few lines at the closing refrain. No problem; use the Edit window tools to cut and trim, leaving only the regions in the track where vocal lines are actually sung. At this point, however, your original four-minute recording is still taking up many megabytes of disk space! After eliminating all the unused region names created as a result of your editing (with the Select Unused Regions Except Whole Files and Clear Selected commands), select the whole-file region that corresponds to that complete four-minute file for the backing vocal take (whole-file regions appear in bold type within the list) and then execute the Compact Selected command.

The Padding setting in the Compact dialog box determines how close to the actual boundaries of currently used regions the Compact function will eliminate excess audio. It's nice to have a little extra in case you inadvertently trim the attack or release of a region too much and later need to lengthen it by a few fractions of second. The other advantage of compacting your audio files is that because your overall project size is reduced, it's somewhat quicker to back up and archive your audio data. One drawback is that compacting often frees many small increments on many files, which will increase disk fragmentation over time. (Of course, since you'll be defragmenting and optimizing your disks on a routine basis, that won't be a problem.)

As with the Delete option in the Clear Selected dialog box, keep in mind that the Compact Selected command only looks at usage of this audio file in the current session. Beware if you are also using the same audio file in other sessions; applying the Compact Selected command in the current session could eliminate portions of audio in those files that you actually still need in other sessions!

Right-Click Menu in the Regions List (Pro Tools 7.3 and Higher) Among other right-click functionalities available in Pro Tools versions 7.3 and higher, you can right-click directly on a selected region to access a pop-up menu with common operations such as clearing and renaming. For audio regions, you can also compact, edit their time stamp, export, recalculate waveform overviews, select the region in the Edit window, or select their parent audio file in the Workspace window.

Export Region Definitions

The Export Region Definitions command incorporates the selected region definitions used in this session into their parent audio files. This is necessary if you want the option to view and import those regions into a completely different Pro Tools session. For example, you might find this useful after chopping up a drum loop into useful segments or if you've taken the time to define regions for specific events within a much longer sound-effects file. (The Bias Peak Pro program and several others also recognize region definitions exported into their parent AIF audio files from Pro Tools as well as the older Sound Designer II format. There is also a very useful Windows utility, Region Synch from Rail Jon Rogut, that converts these Pro Tools region definitions exported into parent audio files to Sound Forge regions, which are recognized by CD Architect, WaveLab, Vegas, Adobe Audition, and other audio programs.)

Export Regions as Files

The Export Regions as Files command batch-exports the currently selected audio regions to external files. (Shift-click to select multiple regions in the list.) In the Export Selected dialog box, you can select the destination directory, file formats, number of channels, sample rate, bit depth, and other attributes. However, the results of this operation will not reflect any automation or plug-in effects processing applied on the Pro Tools track in which these regions reside. For that, you might consider soloing the track (and any send destinations to which it may be routed) and bouncing to disk in real time instead.

Importing Audio Files and Regions Besides recording audio directly into Pro Tools, you may often import existing audio files into a Pro Tools session—for example, sound effects (or drum grooves) that you've created yourself or copied from a CD library to your hard disk. Or you might want to use an audio file that resides within another Pro Tools session's Audio Files folder. Current versions of Pro Tools can directly import the following audio file formats:

- AIFF (.AIF)

- WAV, including Broadcast WAV

- Acid WAV files

- REX (Recycle)

- Sound Designer I and II (.SD2)

- QuickTime (audio only)

- Sound Resource (Mac versions only)

- WMA, Windows Media (Windows versions only)

- CD-DA (audio tracks on standard, "red book" audio CDs)

- MP3

- AAC (a variant of MPEG-4)

- MXF (Material eXchange Format)

If you need to import a 44.1kHz file into a session set to a 48kHz sample rate or vice versa, the Import Audio dialog box will alert you that conversion is required and enable the Convert/Convert All buttons instead of Add/Add All. The same will apply if the bit depth doesn't match that of the current session. By default, Pro Tools stores converted files in the current session's Audio Files folder (although this is not mandatory). New to Pro Tools 8 is the ability for WAV, AIFF, and SDII (Mac only) audio files to co-exist in the same session, as long as the sample rate and bit rate of the files are the same.

If no conversion is required, files (or regions within them, which can also be imported instead of the entire parent audio file) that you import into Pro Tools can remain in their original disk locations. If you want to be absolutely certain that a duplicate copy of the file is added to your session's Audio Files folder even if conversion is not otherwise required, click the Copy or Copy All button in the Import Audio dialog box instead of clicking Add or Add All.

Pro Tools must convert any imported stereo files into two new, separate mono files in your session's Audio Files folder. In this case, Pro Tools not only shows you a stereo region group in the Regions List, but also two subregions underneath it with the suffixes .L and .R added to the original file name.

If you already know that multiple files on your hard disk need to be imported into the currently open Pro Tools session, you can batch-import them by selecting one or more files from the desktop or the Workspace browser window and then dragging them into the Regions List, onto an existing track, or directly into the Tracks List so that the appropriate number of new tracks will be created. Pro Tools will automatically handle any necessary conversions for the session's audio format. Repeat as necessary!

Lastly, when the Automatically Copy Files on Import option is enabled in the Processing tab of the Preferences dialog box, new copies are made in your session's Audio Files folder for *all* imported audio files, whether conversion is required or not. This is one way of ensuring that all audio files a session requires reside within its own folder and reduces the possibility of accidentally deleting or altering source files if they happen to also be used in a different session.

Importing Audio from CDs   There are handy utilities out there for extracting audio tracks from audio CDs into various hard-disk file formats. These are especially useful when you only want a specific portion within a given CD track. For Macintosh, you can open the CD icon on your desktop and drag entire tracks to any disk location, or use iTunes or the QuickTime Player itself (if you upgrade to QuickTime Pro). For Windows, other programs including Roxio's CD Spin Doctor, the MusicMatch Jukebox, and the Windows freeware program CDex can extract CD tracks onto the hard disk as WAV files. (Be aware that MP3 or AAC formats are undesirable if you intend to import these files into Pro Tools because they compress the audio data in a lossy manner.) Many audio-editing programs, such as Bias' Peak (Mac), Audacity (Mac/Windows/Linux), Steinberg's WaveLab (Windows), and Sony/Sonic Foundry's Sound Forge (Windows) can also extract audio directly from CDs.

You can also use the File menu's Import > Audio command to import from audio CDs—keeping in mind any applicable copyrights, of course—using the same preview and selection options as with audio files residing on your computer's hard disks. There's a much easier way to accomplish this in Pro Tools, however—especially if you want to bring the entire track into your session. Simply place the audio CD in your computer's drive, open it either in the Workspace browser window or in the operating system itself, open the CD's icon to view the tracks it contains, and then drag any of these into the Edit window—into the Regions List or directly onto an existing stereo audio track. You can also drop them into the Tracks List (a panel at the left side of the Edit window) if you want new audio tracks automatically created in the process. The CD track's audio data will be converted to the current session's audio file format, bit depth, and sample rate, and stored in its Audio Files folder.

Edit Groups List

Chapter 2, "Pro Tools Terms and Concepts," discussed groups. You can use the pop-up local menu in the Edit Groups List (shown in Figure 6.25) to choose whether edit or mix groups are displayed in the list area below it, delete or create new groups, or suspend all groups. (See Chapter 7, "The Mix Window," for further details about the Mix Groups selector.) By default, edit and mix groups are linked, but you can change this in Preferences > Mixing > Link Mix/Edit Group Enables.

Figure 6.25 Local menu for the Edit Groups List.

You can also use the Color Palette window to assign colors to selected edit and mix groups. If it helps you keep track of your material while editing, an option in the Display tab of the Preferences dialog box allows you to automatically reassign the colors of audio and MIDI regions in the Edit window according to the group assignments of the tracks where they currently reside.

In Pro Tools versions 7.3 and higher, the features for grouping tracks are more powerful than in previous versions. In the Groups List pop-up menu, the Modify Groups command allows you to quickly add or remove tracks from existing groups. When you create new groups (either via the Groups List pop-up menu, the Track menu, or the Command+G shortcut, which is Ctrl+G in Windows), the Create Groups dialog box lets you choose whether the new group should be for the Edit window, Mix window, or both. In addition to linking the main volume faders of the grouped tracks (which, of course, can maintain the same relative levels as when they were grouped), you can also choose whether Mute buttons, Solo buttons, send mutes, or send levels should also be linked within the group. Figure 6.26 shows the Create Groups dialog box. You can also right-click a track name in the Groups List to access a pop-up menu that lets you select all tracks within that group, hide or display only those tracks, or show *all* tracks. Lastly, while previous versions offered 26 possible groups (assigned group IDs from a–z), in versions 7.3 and higher there are four banks of 26 group IDs each, for a total of 104 possible groups in each session.

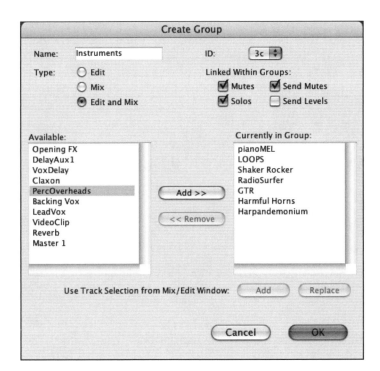

Figure 6.26 In the Create Group dialog box, in addition to linking the main track faders, you can also link additional controls.

Tracks List

The Tracks List panel can be displayed at the left edge of the Edit and Mix windows. To conserve screen space, you can enable/disable display of individual tracks by highlighting them in the Tracks List. Hidden tracks will still play (unless they're muted, of course). The pop-up menu at the top of the Tracks List offers other options for controlling the display of tracks. The Show Only Selected Tracks command in this selector's local menu is especially handy when you briefly need to focus on only a small number of tracks (perhaps increasing their height for detailed editing) or when you're running out of room to display all tracks at their current sizes. Another especially useful feature here is to hide or show all audio tracks, MIDI tracks, Aux Input tracks, Instrument tracks, or Master Faders.

Another Way to Create New Tracks If you drag and drop an audio or MIDI region from the Regions List into the Tracks List at the left edge of the Edit window, a new track is automatically created with a similar name (minus any audio file-name extensions).

Track View Selector for Track Data

The Track View selector for each track enables you to change how its contents appear in the Edit window. This selector opens a pop-up menu, as shown in Figure 6.27. Available display format options for the data contained in a track depend on its type (audio, Aux Input, Master Fader, Instrument, or MIDI).

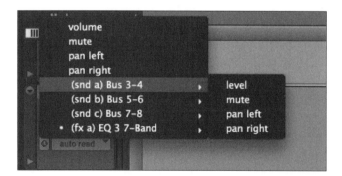

Figure 6.27 Display options for an audio track (with three active sends and one plug-in insert).

Audio

The Track View pop-up menu for audio tracks offers the following options:

- **Waveform.** In this default view for audio tracks, audio regions appear as rectangles (containing the region name, if View > Region > Name is enabled), with a graphic representation of the audio waveforms they contain. If a sync point has been defined within any region, this also appears as a small inverted triangle at the bottom of the rectangular region graphic.

Region Layers You can layer regions to overlap within a track (although only the top-most visible region plays at any given point), and then change their order via the Region > Send to Back/Bring to Front commands. A dog-ear graphic on the corner of a region rectangle indicates that its boundary overlaps another region in the same track (if the View > Region > Overlap option is enabled).

- **Blocks.** This is similar to the Waveform track view, but the waveform is not displayed inside the region rectangles. This option is mainly useful for users on underpowered systems who find that screen redraws for audio waveforms are slowing the operation of Pro Tools.

- **Volume.** This track view format represents volume graphically. Lines and moveable *breakpoints* represent how values for the volume parameter on the track (corresponding to its main volume fader) change over time. You can draw volume changes directly with the editing tools or record volume automation in real time using onscreen faders or an external control surface. Either kind of volume automation can be edited graphically afterward. For example, you can use the Grabber tool to insert, delete, or drag existing breakpoints, while you can use different modes of the Pencil tool to create automation for a track's volume. You can highlight automation events with the Selector tool and cut, paste, and so on without affecting the audio waveforms shown underneath. You can also use the Trimmer tool to scale existing automation events up or down.

- **Pan.** Pan view also shows lines and moveable breakpoints for creating or editing this kind of automation data, which affects the audio track's position in the sound field. A single Pan control is provided for mono tracks; the Left Pan and Right Pan controls are separate for stereo tracks. (Note that even if your source audio region is mono, inserting a stereo plug-in on a track makes its output and panning controls stereo.) On multichannel surround channels, the number of pan options available for display and editing depends on the surround format in use. For example, on a 5.1 track, separately editable pan automation includes Front Position, Rear Position, Front/Rear Position, Front Divergence, Rear Divergence, Front/Rear Divergence, and Center.

- **Mute.** This view shows the mute/unmute status of a track, Not Muted and Muted being the only possible values.

- **Sends (Level/Mute/Pan).** For each of the sends currently enabled on an audio, Aux Input, or Instrument track, you can record and graphically edit automation for the send's level, mute, and pan parameters in a similar fashion to the volume, mute, and pan parameters for the track's main output described previously. For each of the track's active sends, a submenu lets you select which of these send parameters will be displayed as breakpoint automation within this track.

■ **Plug-in parameters.** Many parameters can be automated. The Plug-in window for each plug-in has an Auto button, which opens a dialog box where you can individually enable its parameters for automation. Each enabled plug-in automation parameter then appears as a Track View option in the pop-up selector for the track where you enabled that plug-in. For example, if you instantiate the 7-band EQ 3 plug-in as insert effect "a" on a track and then enable the gain parameter of its high-band filter for automation, an option labeled "(fx a) 7-Band EQ 3 > Hi Band Gain" appears among that track's view options.

■ **Volume Trim (Pro Tools HD only).** When you record volume automation on HD systems in Trim automation mode (a subsequent editable automation pass that applies a *relative* change to volume and send levels within existing breakpoint automation), breakpoints for that automation type can be displayed within the track.

■ **Analysis (versions 7.4 and higher).** This view is used in conjunction with the Elastic Audio features introduced in Pro Tools version 7.4. When any Elastic Audio mode is enabled on an audio track via its pop-up selector, an audio analysis is automatically performed on any regions it contains as well as any subsequent regions that are placed or recorded onto the track. This analysis identifies audio events according to the transients detected by the selected Elastic Audio detection algorithm for that track. In Analysis view, you can add, delete, or move event markers to a more appropriate location for transients within the audio waveform.

■ **Warp (versions 7.4 and higher).** Warp view is also related to Elastic Audio, and allows you to display up to three types of Elastic Audio markers. Event markers appear as vertical gray lines and indicate where audio events have been detected. You can drag event markers to new positions, which will stretch or squeeze the surrounding audio in the affected regions. Warp markers are used to anchor a point in the audio waveform to a specific position in the timeline so that its location won't be altered even as surrounding event markers in the region are dragged around. Tempo event–generated warp markers are not editable, but appear on tick-based tracks to show where Elastic Audio processing has conformed the audio to the session tempo(s) at that location.

■ **Playlist (version 8).** By using the Playlist view, any track with alternate playlists can be set to display all simultaneously. Keeping the primary playlist as the main track display and expanding the alternate playlists as lanes underneath the primary one, the Playlist view creates a convenient, easy way to move or copy parts from the track's playlists onto the primary master playlist, an action called *compositing*.

Aux Input

The Track View pop-up menu for Aux Input tracks features the same options as the pop-up for audio tracks, minus the Block, Playlist, and Waveform options (because Aux Input tracks contain no regions).

VCA Master (Pro Tools HD Only)

Only three view options are available for VCA master tracks, which pass no audio but can be used to "slave" the controls of multiple tracks in a mix group: Volume, Volume Trim, and Mute.

Master Fader

By default, the only view for a Master Fader track is Volume (plus Volume Trim on Pro Tools HD systems only). If any of the plug-ins inserted on a Master Fader track have parameters currently enabled for automation, however, those parameters appear as additional view options, as with audio plug-ins on audio, Aux Input, and Instrument tracks. There are no pan controls or sends on Master Faders.

MIDI and Instrument Tracks

As mentioned, MIDI tracks and the regions within them contain MIDI *events* (note events, data for pedals, modulation, pitch bend, and other types of MIDI controllers) rather than audio data. This is also true of Instrument tracks (although they behave more like Aux Input tracks in the Mix window; see Chapter 7 for more information). Accordingly, the display format options shown in Figure 6.28 for MIDI and Instrument tracks are rather different from those offered

Figure 6.28 View options for an Instrument track. Except for the three audio-related options in the lower panel, the options for MIDI tracks are identical.

for audio, Aux Input, and Master Fader tracks. In fact, on MIDI tracks, the only data type that *is* the same kind of track-based automation as on these other track types is Mute/Unmute. The volume and pan shapes you view and edit as breakpoint automation on MIDI tracks actually represent a type of MIDI controller data that is stored as part of the MIDI regions themselves. In contrast, while Instrument tracks offer all the same Track View options as MIDI tracks, you can additionally view and edit audio volume and panning automation on their output as well as plug-in parameters for instrument or other audio plug-ins that you have instantiated on the track and enabled for automation. You might say they're like an Aux Input track with a MIDI track on the front end. Both MIDI and Instrument tracks offer the following display-format options:

- **Regions.** In this display format, MIDI regions appear as rectangles, with the region name and bars representing MIDI note events within each. The Grabber and Trimmer tools work on the region boundaries, but when viewing a track's contents as MIDI regions, you cannot edit individual MIDI notes.

- **Notes.** This display format enables you to edit MIDI notes with the Grabber (to move or copy a note) and Trimmer (to change a note's length). You will often find it useful to switch your main time ruler to Bars:Beats format and enable the Grid edit mode. You can then change the grid increments to different note values as necessary to facilitate accurate positioning of notes and breakpoints for controller data. You can also draw notes with the Pencil tool while in Notes view; click once to create notes whose duration corresponds to the current Grid value (whether or not Grid mode is currently active) or click and drag to extend the note you're creating to some longer duration.

- **Blocks.** Blocks display format is the same as Regions format, but without MIDI note events shown within each rectangular region graphic.

- **Velocity.** If you use MIDI and Instrument tracks in Pro Tools, you will find yourself using Velocity display format often (as well as the Notes view). Velocity stalks appear for each MIDI note event. You can scale them with the Trimmer or drag up and down with the Grabber. When you click any MIDI note, its velocity stalk will also be highlighted. You can also use the Pencil tool to draw across multiple velocities—for example, using its Line drawing mode to create a decrescendo at the end of a phrase.

- **Volume, Mute, Pan.** These views of mix parameters work pretty much the same way as described for audio regions, but with one important difference: Volume and pan data are sent out as MIDI *controller* messages to the external MIDI device (or software synthesizer) rather than being audio mixing events. MIDI volume and pan data are part of the contents of each MIDI region rather than pertaining to the MIDI track itself. On MIDI tracks, Mute/ Unmute are the only automation events that are actually part of the MIDI track itself, as opposed to MIDI controller messages contained within the regions. (In contrast, since Instrument tracks are like an Aux Input tracks with an associated MIDI track, they also include all the audio-related Track View options that you would find in an Aux Input.) You should be aware that some MIDI devices (or patches) don't respond to incoming volume and pan messages. For example, most drum patches don't respond to MIDI panning because the elements of a drum set are already spread across the stereo field as part of the patch's design.

■ **Other (Pitch Bend, Aftertouch, Mod Wheel, Program Change, and so on).** You can view additional MIDI controllers as breakpoint automation in the Edit window and edit them with the same tools. Pro Tools automatically detects when any MIDI controller type is recorded that doesn't already appear in the pop-up list by default and adds it accordingly.

About Instrument Tracks As mentioned in the previous section, all MIDI-related options in the Track View pop-up menu for Instrument tracks are identical to MIDI tracks. However, an Instrument track combines the functionality of an Aux Input (especially as seen in the Mix window) with a MIDI track in the Edit window. Accordingly, in addition to MIDI parameters, it offers the same display options as an Aux Input track for volume (and volume trim, on Pro Tools HD systems), pan, and any plug-in parameters that you enabled for automation.

Track Height Selector

The Track Height selector is fairly self-explanatory: It's a pop-up menu that allows you to change the height of each track (see Figure 6.29). In Pro Tools versions 7.3 and higher, the basic options are Micro, Mini, Small, Medium, Large, Jumbo, Extreme, and Fit to Window, and you can also continuously resize any track vertically by dragging its lower border. As

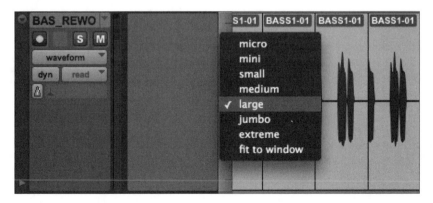

Figure 6.29 Click an audio track's Track Height Selector button or anywhere in its amplitude ruler to open this pop-up menu. In Pro Tools 7.3 and higher, you can also continuously resize any track by dragging its lower border.

your sessions get larger, you will tend to minimize the size of the tracks you're not currently editing in order to save screen space. (Options in the Tracks List are also useful when you start running out of space in the Edit window.) On MIDI tracks, you have the additional option of displaying only a single note (the MIDI note value D1 for all snare hits, for example). Hold down the Option key (Alt key in Windows) as you change any track's height to simultaneously change the height of *all* tracks.

Simultaneously Changing a Parameter on All Tracks With many track parameters in Pro Tools, if you hold down the Option key (Alt key in Windows) as you make a change on the current track, the new value is applied to *all* tracks. For example, to set the display view for all tracks to Volume, hold down this modifier key as you change this option for any individual track. This also works with the Mute and Solo buttons, Input and Output selectors, track heights, and other items.

Playlist Selector (Audio and MIDI Tracks)

As explained in Chapter 2, a *playlist* is a list of the regions to be played back by each audio or MIDI track. This pop-up selector, immediately to the right of the track name (see Figure 6.30), enables you to create and duplicate any edit playlists for the track and to quickly change from one playlist to the other. If you want to experiment with different arrangements, edits, and so on, but still be able to quickly change back to the original version, it's important to master this feature. The automation (for example, volume, panning, or send levels) on audio tracks is global for the track, so a single automation playlist applies no matter which edit playlist (arrangement of audio regions and their fades on a track) is currently active. MIDI volume and panning events actually comprise part of the data within MIDI regions, so these can be different in each edit playlist on a MIDI or Instrument track. (Mute events in these tracks are the only exception; these *are* Pro Tools automation events, so they apply no matter what edit playlist is selected for the MIDI/Instrument track.) Feel free to experiment; playlists are non-destructive and don't occupy

Figure 6.30 The Playlist selector opens a pop-up menu, where you can select between alternate playlists for each audio or MIDI track, create new playlists, and duplicate or rename existing ones.

significant disk space! In fact, if you change the notes and other events within a MIDI region that Pro Tools knows is used in another playlist, it automatically creates a new MIDI region name for the altered version. Lastly, the Note Chasing parameter affects what happens when you initiate playback at any point between the Note On and Note Off messages for MIDI note events on a given track. For example, if a chord played with a string sound is supposed to sustain from bars 9 through 16, you will probably want to hear those notes sound even if you happen to start playback at bar 13. The only exception to this would be when MIDI note events are triggering rhythm loops that play on a sampling instrument (either external or a similar instrument plug-in). If Note Chasing were enabled on that track, playback of the loop would get triggered at whatever point you start playback—and not necessarily in time with the music!

Pitched MIDI and Instrument Tracks (Pro Tools Versions 7.3 and Higher) When the Pitched option is enabled in the pop-up selector for MIDI and Instrument tracks, the pitches of MIDI note events on that track will be affected when you create key-signature events in the session timeline. The notes will be transposed and/or diatonically constrained to the new scale.

Samples/Ticks Timebase Selector

The pop-up Samples/Ticks Timebase selector, shown in Figure 6.31, enables you to choose whether the time references for location of events on this track are to be treated as *absolute* (samples) or *relative* (ticks—subdivisions of the musical beat, in thousandths). When these are absolute, changing Pro Tools tempos, whether via events in the Tempo ruler or manual settings in the Transport window's Tempo field, will not affect the location of events already placed into this track. On the other hand, if a track's timebase is relative (ticks), when you make tempo adjustments, events move to a new position in order to maintain the same bar/beat location relative to the new tempo.

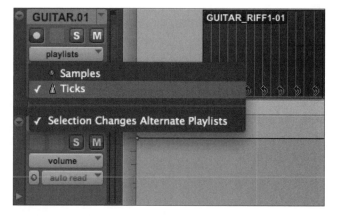

Figure 6.31 The timebase for event locations in audio, MIDI, and Instrument tracks can be absolute (samples) or relative (ticks).

When Ticks timebase is chosen for an audio track, the regions it contains will shift if you apply a tempo change afterward either manually, via the Tempo Operations window, or by using the graphical Tempo Editor that you can open beneath the Tempo ruler. Any crossfades between audio regions on the affected tracks will be re-rendered if their positions are altered as a result of tempo changes, but durations of fade ins and fade outs will be unaffected.

Existing automation data on tick-based tracks will also be remapped to reflect subsequent tempo changes. With this capability, for example, any shots from a send to a reverb or delay effect, or the Master Fader's volume fade at the end of a song, will automatically have their locations adjusted for the new tempo so that they still occur at the same bar and beat relative to the new tempo.

Prior to Pro Tools version 7, MIDI tracks could *only* be tick-based. In all current versions, however, MIDI and Instrument tracks can also be set to the Samples timebase. This is useful not only for sound-effects design based on external or software MIDI instruments but also when recording free-form MIDI performances.

Track Color Indicators

Display of this color strip to the left of all tracks in the Edit window (also visible in Figure 6.31) is toggled using the View > Edit Window Views > Track Color option. You can then use the Color Palette window to reassign colors for selected tracks to conveniently flag groups of tracks that are related. For example, you might assign one color to all percussion tracks, whether MIDI or audio, or use different colors for basic tracks versus instrumental overdubs—whatever helps you keep track of things in a complex session. Additionally, you can display Track Color indicators at the top and bottom of the Mix window, as discussed in Chapter 7. Some users prefer *not* to display Track Color indicators in the Edit window in order to conserve horizontal screen space for displaying track data, however.

Timeline Display: Timebase Rulers and Marker Memory Locations

You can display various timebase rulers along the top of the Edit window: Time (Minutes:Seconds, Bars:Beats, Samples, SMPTE Time Code, or Feet+Frames), Tempo, Meter, Key Signature (in Pro Tools versions 7.3 and higher), Chord Symbols, and Markers. Enable these rulers either via the View > Rulers submenu or the Ruler Options pop-up menu beneath the zoom buttons in the Edit window. The available rulers are shown in Figure 6.32. The display units for the main Time ruler reflect those of the Main Counter at the top of the Edit window. Conversely, you can click the title area at the left end of any Time ruler to switch the Main Counter to that ruler's time units and display its Grid Line increments in the Edit window (if this preference is enabled). This main, active ruler is always indicated by the blue background behind its title (versus the gray background on other visible rulers), and determines the default time units that will appear

Figure 6.32 You can display multiple timeline rulers at once: Bars:Beats, Minutes:Seconds, Samples, SMPTE Time Code, and Feet+Frames. Additional rulers display markers, tempo events, meter events, and (in versions 7.3 and higher) key-signature events.

in the selectors for Grid and Nudge values. Click and drag rulers by their titles to change their vertical order in the Edit window.

Note: The Feet+Frames ruler is only available on HD systems, and on LE systems the DV Toolkit 2 option—which is not compatible with M-Powered versions—must be installed for the Time Code ruler to be available.

No matter which editing tool is currently selected, the cursor changes to the Selector tool's I-beam shape when the pointer is over any of the rulers in the Edit window (except when Dynamic Transport is enabled in Pro Tools 7.3 and higher, in which case the cursor becomes the Grabber tool). Click and drag here to highlight a timeline range in all tracks.

In all Pro Tools versions 7.3 and higher, if Options > Dynamic Transport is enabled, an additional lane for the moveable Play Start maker appears underneath the main timeline ruler. On LE systems 7.3 and higher with the DV Toolkit Option 2 installed, a secondary time-code ruler called Time Code 2 is also available; it can be configured to display a different SMPTE frame rate from the main timebase ruler.

Markers Ruler

The Markers ruler displays all Marker memory locations (but not Selection memory locations) created in your session. Markers identify single points in time. Among other things, you can use markers to identify parts of a song, scenes, punch in/out points that you expect to use again, or any other location that you might want to quickly find later. Click the button at the left end of the Markers ruler or simply press the Enter key on the numeric keypad to create a new memory location (Marker or Selection) based on the current playback cursor position or selection. (Incidentally, you can do this even while in Play or Record mode! Many users drop markers into the Pro Tools timeline while recording a performer to identify song sections or spots where punch-ins may be necessary.)

A Marker memory location specifies a single time value (and appears in the Markers ruler with the name you've defined), while a Selection memory location represents a *range* of time. Typical selections might include the verse of a song, a portion within a longer session that you may bounce to disk more than once, or a section that you will repeat numerous times (perhaps in Loop Recording mode) while overdubbing a solo. Selection memory locations not only recall the timeline range but also *which* tracks were highlighted. Both markers and selections can be displayed and recalled in the Memory Locations window (see Figure 6.33). Because the stored attributes of any memory location can optionally include zoom settings, pre- or post-roll times, group enables, track show/hide, and other track-display options (including window configurations in versions 7.3 and higher), some users create memory locations with no time reference at all for the specific purpose of storing and recalling these customized views.

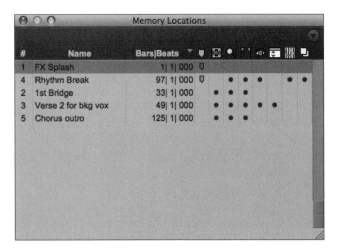

Figure 6.33 The Memory Locations window displays markers and selections, including their absolute or relative position. The icons indicate additional view properties stored with each memory location.

Markers and selections can reference either an absolute position in the session's timeline or a relative position in Bars:Beats:Ticks whose absolute time position is affected by tempo changes in the session. In the New Memory Location dialog box, the default reference type reflects the time units currently displayed in the Main Counter.

Colors can be manually or automatically assigned to each marker using the Color Palette window. We strongly recommend that you enable the Always Display Marker Colors option in the Display tab of the Preferences dialog box. Fill colors in the Markers ruler will reflect each marker's assigned color until the next one is encountered; from that point on, the Markers ruler switches to that marker's color. This is useful, for instance, for keeping track of what section of the song or soundtrack you're currently seeing, even while editing track data at a very high zoom level.

You can drag markers to new positions within the Markers ruler; their movement will be affected by Grid mode (if enabled). You can also use markers to make timeline selections in the Edit window. Shift-clicking a marker highlights the range between the current Main Counter location and that marker. To delete a marker in this ruler, Option-click it (Alt-click in Windows). Double-click any marker to edit its properties—for example, to change its time reference or to restore the current pre- and post-roll times every time this marker is recalled. To redefine an existing Selection memory location, highlight a different range, open the Memory Locations window, and Control-click (or right-click in Windows *or* Macintosh) on that selection's name. This technique also works on Marker memory locations; the current Start value replaces the marker's original time reference. See the "Memory Locations" section of Chapter 8 for more details. They're often an underused feature of Pro Tools; take some time to learn how to use them!

Recalling Memory Locations from the Keyboard   When the numeric keypad is in Transport Mode, you can recall memory locations (both Marker and Selection) from your computer's numeric keypad. Press the period key on the numeric keypad, then the desired memory location number, followed by another period.

Pro Tools Gives You Ticks!   Memory locations can be absolute (time) or relative (Bars: Beats). An *absolute* time reference is a specific number of minutes, seconds, and samples from the session's start, and is unaffected by tempo settings. In contrast, the actual time location of a *relative* Bars:Beats reference depends on musical tempo. If the tempo is set to 60 beats per minute (bpm), each beat lasts one second; therefore, the ninth beat (the downbeat of the third bar in 4/4 time) occurs precisely eight seconds into the session's absolute timeline. But if you double the tempo setting to 120 bpm, the downbeat of that third bar is now only four seconds into the session timeline.

In the Bars:Beats time scale, Pro Tools subdivides each ¼ note into 960 pulses, or *ticks*. The actual time represented by each tick depends on the tempo. So a full ¼ note has a duration of 960 ticks (one second at 60 bpm, but only 500 milliseconds at 120 bpm), an $^1/_8$ note is 480 ticks, a $^1/_{16}$ note 240 ticks, and so on.

If you need to tie the markers or selections that you create to musical events and the Pro Tools tempo, use the pop-up selector in the New Memory Location dialog box to make their positions relative (Bars:Beats). When you change the tempo settings, the memory location's absolute time position will also be altered such that it stays in the proper musical location.

Tempo and Meter Rulers

In Pro Tools, changes of tempo and meter (how fast the beat is, and how many beats per bar) are represented by tempo and meter events. Clicking the plus-sign buttons next to the Tempo and Meter rulers creates a new tempo/meter event at the current position. Another triangle button to the left of the Tempo ruler opens the Tempo Editor, where you can use the editing tools to graphically edit a series of tempo events, as discussed in the section "Tempo Editor" later in this chapter. Click and drag to change the position of any event in these rulers or double-click to alter its properties. To delete any event in the Tempo or Meter ruler, Option-click the event (Alt-click in Windows) or simply drag it up or down to remove it from the ruler.

Song Start Marker

By default, in new sessions, the Song Start marker appears at the beginning of the timeline within the Tempo ruler. Double-click this marker to enter a new bar number or time signature in the Edit Bar|Beat Marker dialog box. If you want bar 1 of the song to begin at some other point in the timeline (for example, at exactly seven seconds), drag the Song Start marker to that location within the Tempo ruler. Its movement will be affected by Grid mode, if enabled. By default, the location of events (regions, automation, and so on) within any track set to Ticks timebase will be also be displaced to maintain their previous positions relative to the Song Start marker's new location. However, you can hold down Control+Shift while dragging (Start+Shift in Windows) if you don't want the position of events in tick-based tracks to be affected by moving the Song Start marker. (MIDI and Instrument tracks can optionally be set to samples timebase, in which case the locations of MIDI events within them are unaffected by changes to the tempo and location of the Song Start marker.)

The Move Song Start page of the Time Operations window provides a more precise method for changing the location of the Song Start marker in the Tempo ruler. For example, you can specify its new position numerically using any timeline units available in your version of Pro Tools regardless of which main ruler is currently active in the Edit window. At the same time, you can assign a new bar number to the Song Start marker's new location. The Time Operations and Tempo Operations windows are discussed further in Chapter 8.

Key Signature Ruler

The Key Signature ruler was introduced with Pro Tools version 7.3. You add a new key-signature event either via the Event > Add Key Change command or by clicking the plus sign at the left end of the Key Signature ruler. As can be seen in Figure 6.34, all the standard major and minor key signatures can be selected in the Key Change dialog box. These are useful when MIDI data will be exported from Pro Tools to the Sibelius music notation program. However, the most important use of key signatures within Pro Tools is for diatonic transposition. In versions 7.3 and higher, the Transpose page of the Event Operations window offers a Transpose in Key option for shifting MIDI pitches by a specified number of scale steps (rather than semitones, as with conventional transposition). So, if the key signature in effect for the currently selected

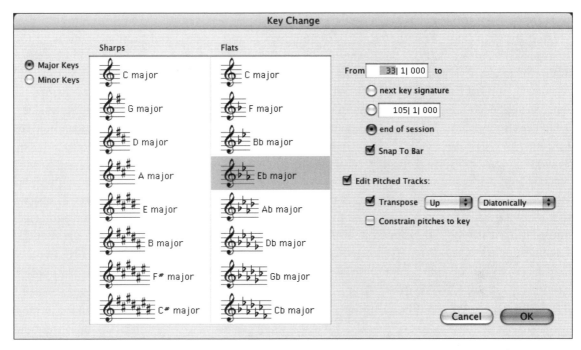

Figure 6.34   When you create key-signature events in Pro Tools versions 7.3 and higher, the Key Change dialog box appears. Existing MIDI notes in pitched tracks can be transposed and/or have their accidentals (sharps/flats) adjusted to match the new key signature.

MIDI events is F major (one flat), shifting the note sequence F-G-A-B♭ upward diatonically by one scale step would change this to G-A-B♭-C, whereas a simple transposition upward by two semitones would have produced the sequence G-A-B-C. (The Real-Time Properties windows for tracks and regions also offer an In Key option for diatonic transposition.)

A related feature introduced along with key-signature events is the Pitched option for MIDI and Instrument tracks (enabled via the pop-up Playlist selector menu for each track). When this option is enabled, the pitches of MIDI note events in this track will be adjusted automatically if you introduce key-signature events in the ruler that affect the portion of the timeline where those MIDI note events reside. Appendix D, "Power Tips and Loopy Ideas," includes an example of using this feature to create a repeating ostinato figure on a pitched MIDI track whose notes will shift diatonically (according to key-signature events in the timeline) to match a chord progression.

Managing Multiple Takes

When you've recorded multiple takes with the same start and end time within a track—perhaps by using Loop Record mode, or because you've used a timeline selection and pre-/post-roll fields to automatically punch in a series of recordings at the exact same place—Pro Tools offers several features to help you keep track. As mentioned elsewhere, new region names are automatically created for each take (Trackname_01, Trackname_02, and so on), and these all appear in the Regions List. Additionally, though, there's a really quick way to review and select among these alternate takes: Using the Selector tool, Command-click (Ctrl-click in Windows) within the region. A pop-up Takes List appears (see Figure 6.35), allowing you to choose what criteria will be applied in choosing alternate takes via the Match Criteria menu. The Alternates List, which is also available in the pop-up menu that appears if you right-click a region, also includes options to expand alternates to either new playlists or new tracks and the list of alternate takes. The Matching Criteria options for refining the Alternates List are Track ID for all audio files recorded on a specific track, Track Name for all audio files sharing the same root name, and Region Rating (see the next section, "Assembling a Comp Track"). In addition, you can choose to narrow down the alternates to those that share the region start, share the region start and end, and that are entirely within the edit selection. Upon choosing your Matching Criteria settings, Command-click (Ctrl-click in Windows) the region and look at the alternate audio files that are listed. As you do this, take some time to edit these region names to organize your thoughts (for example, "Gtr fill OK," "Gtr fill bad," "Gtr fill best," and so on). Don't just leave the default numeric suffixes; big sessions get confusing enough as it is!

Figure 6.35 Here we've used the Selector tool to Command-click (Ctrl-click in Windows) the top-most region of several that were just recorded in Loop Record mode. The Takes List pop-up menu allows you to select between multiple takes recorded in this mode.

Assembling a Comp Track

Comping multiple takes together (that is, assembling a composite take using segments of each) is very easy to do in Pro Tools. There are many possible approaches, but Pro Tools 8 has introduced a greatly improved workflow for creating comps. Using the example of a session containing a loop record of several passes, choose the Selector tool and Command-click (Ctrl-click in Windows) the record track's audio region, which is the last take recorded. Choose the Expand Alternates to New Playlists option to display all the takes created from the loop record below the main track display, including a track that represents all the recorded audio from the looped session displayed as one long audio region (see Figure 6.36). Using the Solo buttons on the various playlist lanes, play the individual takes back and choose your desired region. Alternatively, with the Selector tool, choose segments of regions that you want to use in the "master" playlist. Then, move your first selection by clicking the Copy Selection to Main Playlist button on the playlist lane or choosing Edit > Copy Selection To > Main Playlist). Do this until your master playlist is complete, with all your selections included.

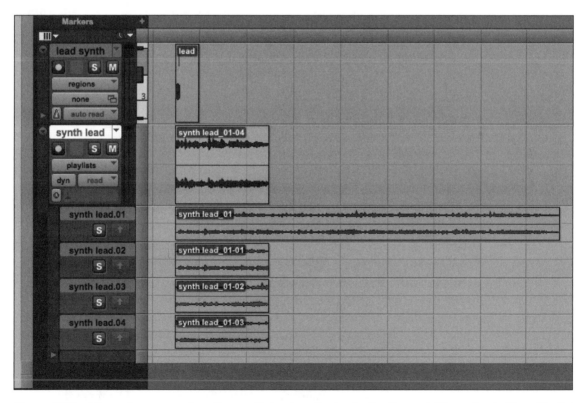

Figure 6.36 After a loop record on the synth lead audio track, the Expand Alternates to New Playlists command creates playlists of all the takes, including the full uninterrupted record that was displayed on the first lane. Notice that the main track displays the last take recorded.

A new feature to aid with comping in Pro Tools 8 is Region Rating. This enables you to assign numbers from 1 to 5 to identify a region's worth in creating a comp for better organization when there are several playlists from which to choose. To assign a number to a region, choose Region > Rating or right-click on the region to display the pop-up menu and choose Rate. Then choose a number from 1, the worst, to 5, the best. Make sure that View > Region > Rating is selected in order to see the rating number in the region.

Real-Time MIDI Properties on MIDI/Instrument Tracks

This feature is immensely useful for anyone who composes and edits MIDI performances. Real-time MIDI properties are non-destructive, real-time versions of many of the MIDI processes already available via the MIDI menu in previous versions of Pro Tools. Without altering the original contents of the MIDI regions on the track, you can apply quantization (including the same parameters available in the "destructive" version, such as swing and groove quantize), duration and velocity changes, delay offset, and transposition (including diatonic transposition within the current key signature in Pro Tools versions 7.3 and higher). You also have the option of permanently incorporating the result of the current real-time MIDI properties into the affected region or track using the Write to Region/Write to Track button in the Real-Time Properties window. You can display these parameters in the Edit window (see Figure 6.37) via the View > Edit Window > Real-Time Properties command. Using real-time properties on MIDI and Instrument tracks is discussed further in Chapter 10, "MIDI." That chapter also discusses how you can apply real-time properties to individual *regions* on MIDI and Instrument tracks, as well as apply real-time properties to the track itself that will affect all MIDI data played back through it (including regions that already have their *own* real-time properties).

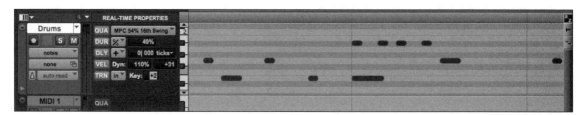

Figure 6.37 The Real-Time Properties column for MIDI and Instrument tracks in the Edit window.

More About Automation in Pro Tools

As mentioned previously, there are two ways to create mix automation in Pro Tools:

- Record your automation moves in real time using either the mouse and the onscreen controls in the Pro Tools software, the control surface built into the Digi 003 or Digi 002, or an external control surface such as Digidesign's D-Control, D-Command, Command|8, ProControl, Control|24, CM Labs' MotorMix, the HUI, or Mackie Control Universal.

- Draw breakpoint automation directly in the Edit window using the Grabber or Pencil tool.

Of course, you can use any combination of these two techniques during a project. Many new Pro Tools users with a background in old-school mixing consoles and tape tend to place a lot of priority on the real-time automation recording capabilities, but with time, they find that in many cases it's faster to draw in volume, panning, and other automatable parameters by hand using the Grabber tool (or the Pencil and Trimmer tools). Nevertheless, there will always be times when you prefer to record (or revise) automation by ear, in real time—with the mouse or, even better, with an external control surface.

Automation Modes

Mix automation is so essential to Pro Tools that, by default, the Automation Mode selector for each track appears in both the Edit and the Mix windows. It is a pop-up menu with these options:

- **Off.** This mode disables all automation in the track.

- **Read.** This mode plays all enabled automation types in the track.

- **Touch.** This mode records automation only while any of the faders or other controls for the track are touched, moved with the mouse, or moved via a touch-sensitive fader or control on an external control surface. When you release the control, it returns to its position according to the previous automation values for this track (per the current settings for Touch Timeout and AutoMatch Time in Preferences > Mixing). Touch mode is handy for punching in a section within the track's existing automation data.

- **Latch.** Like Touch mode, automation recording in Latch mode doesn't start until a fader is moved. However, when you release the fader in Latch mode, it *stays* at its current level, recording new automation data for that fader until playback is stopped. This mode is especially handy for automating plug-in parameters, for example, or other situations where you want to overwrite existing automation data from a certain point forward.

- **Write.** This mode records automation for a track from when playback is started until it's stopped, regardless of whether you move any faders. In the Preferences, you can choose whether tracks automatically switch to Touch or Latch mode when you stop playback after an automation pass in Write mode. This reduces the danger of accidentally overwriting the data you just recorded when you press Play again!

- **Trim (HD/TDM systems only).** This mode applies to volume and send-level automation only. Trim mode works in conjunction with other automation modes—but the fader changes you make in Trim mode apply *relative*, rather than *absolute*, value changes to the existing automation data in the track. While recording automation in Trim mode, onscreen faders show the delta value (the amount of increase or decrease to their level) rather than the usual absolute value.

Trimming Automation Data You can use the Trimmer tool to scale existing automation data up or down within Pro Tools tracks, as shown in Figure 6.38. For example, to reduce

Figure 6.38 You can use the Trimmer tool to scale selected automation data up or down.

the overall level of a send from an audio track that you've routed to an Aux Input where a delay effect has been inserted, first change the display format of the track to show the level for the send you want to edit. Next, use the Selector tool to highlight the portion of this send's level automation you want to alter. Then, drag it upward or downward with the Trimmer; you'll notice that as you do so, the amount of change being applied (that is, the *delta*) is indicated in decibels (dB). The contour of your send-level changes will be retained, but the overall level will be louder or softer.

Automation Window

The Automation window, opened via the Windows menu, and shown in Figure 6.39, enables you to suspend playback of *all* animation in a Pro Tools session or to individually enable or disable entire categories of automation data for recording (volume, pan, and mute for track outputs; any enabled plug-in parameters; or level, pan, and mute for sends).

Figure 6.39 The Automation window globally affects how automation is recorded/played back in the entire Pro Tools session. (The LE/M-Powered version is shown here; TDM offers additional options.) If recording or playback of automation on your tracks doesn't seem to be working, check here to make sure automation isn't suspended!

Basic Rules for Cutting and Pasting Automation Data Editing automation is somewhat different from editing audio/MIDI regions. Knowing how any region editing you do interacts with existing automation data in the same area of the track will help you unlock the power of editing tracks to further shape your projects. Here are some of the most basic rules to keep in mind:

- If Options > Automation Follows Edit is enabled, when you cut, copy, paste, or drag audio waveform selections/regions (in Waveform or Blocks view for audio tracks) or MIDI data (in Regions, Blocks, Notes, or Velocity views), their automation data accompanies them to the new location. You can disable this if you don't want these operations to affect the concurrent automation data in your tracks.

■ Trimming audio regions to change their length does *not* affect any overlapping automation data.

■ When an audio track's display format is set to any of the automation types, you can select, cut, copy, and paste automation data without affecting the audio regions visible underneath it.

■ You can't paste automation from an audio track into a MIDI track or vice versa.

Automatically Enabling Automation on New Plug-ins In Pro Tools versions 7.3 and higher, a setting in the Mixing tab of the Preferences window lets you choose to automatically enable all available parameters of each plug-in as it is instantiated in your Pro Tools session.

Automation and Controller Lanes

New to Pro Tools 8 is the addition of Automation and Controller lanes, which enable you to look at a single track's multiple displays of automation and controller data all at the same time. As shown in Figure 6.40, the lower corner of the color strip of each track in the Edit window features a triangle button; clicking it reveals a lane of automation or controller data. The user can change the type of automation or controller data displayed by the same method used in the primary tracks: via the Automation Type Selector. You can add lanes to display data by clicking the plus button in the previous lane's color strip. Similarly, you can remove (not delete) an automation/controller lane by clicking that lane's minus button. The size of the lanes can also be changed by the same method as the primary tracks: by clicking the left edge of the track's waveform display area to access a pop-up menu.

Tempo Editor

Clicking the button to the left of the Tempo ruler opens a resizable, horizontal pane beneath it called the Tempo Editor. In a manner similar to automation, you can use the edit tools to create (Pencil), select (Grabber and Selector), or scale (Trimmer) tempos graphically. As you can see in Figure 6.41, each tempo change in Pro Tools is a discrete event that stays in effect until another tempo-change event is encountered. Even if they are drawn with the Pencil tool, the end result of graphically editing tempos is a series of separate tempo events, which are visible in the Tempo ruler even after this graphic editor is closed.

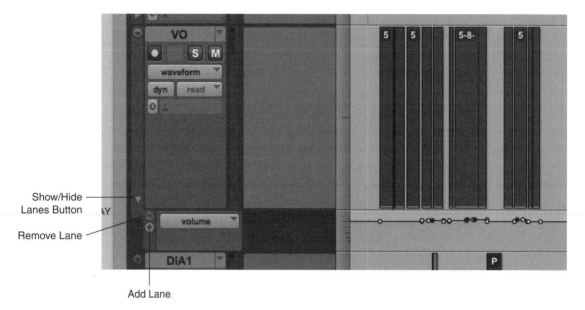

Show/Hide
Lanes Button

Remove Lane

Add Lane

Figure 6.40 Clicking the triangle button on the lower end of a track's color strip reveals an Automation/Controller lane, which includes buttons to choose the type of data displayed and to display or remove additional lanes of data.

Figure 6.41 The Tempo Editor allows you to graphically edit the tempo track. (You can also use the Tempo Operations window.)

Use the Grabber tool to drag a tempo event vertically to a new bpm (beats per minute) setting or horizontally to a new position in the timeline. If enabled, Grid edit mode snaps the horizontal movement of tempo events to the nearest grid increment as you drag them. As with automation breakpoints within tracks, you can delete existing tempo events in this editor by Option-clicking (Alt-clicking in Windows) with the Grabber. While dragging or trimming tempo events in the Tempo Editor, you will notice that the units in the Cursor Location Display switch to bpm.

You can use the Trimmer tool to scale multiple tempo events up or down—either within a previously highlighted range or with the entire session timeline when no range was previously highlighted.

You can use the Pencil tool to create a series of tempo events in this editor using the Freehand, Line, or Curve drawing modes (you cannot use the Triangle, Square, or Random drawing modes in the Tempo Editor). The pop-up Density menu gives you control over the spacing of these newly created tempo events, specified in either note-value or millisecond time units. The pop-up Resolution menu determines the note value that will be the basis for all beats-per-minute settings created when you draw tempo curves with the Pencil tool. When you have just created a tempo curve using the Pencil tool, blue adjustment handles appear; these allow you to adjust its beginning and end points (and also the midpoint, if you used the S-curve drawing mode). You can only do this immediately after creating the curve, however; as soon as you apply any other editing command, select another editing tool, or switch the drawing mode of the Pencil tool, these adjustment handles are no longer available.

If you move the Song Start marker (either by dragging in the Tempo ruler or using the Time Operations window), the locations of existing tempo events usually shift accordingly. (This is not obligatory, though; in the "Time Operations" section of Chapter 10, you will find more techniques and applications for moving the Song Start marker, renumbering bars, and so on.) To extend the currently selected range in the Tempo Editor to the next tempo event in the timeline, press Shift+Tab. To instead extend the current tempo selection to the previous tempo event, press Option+Shift+Tab (Ctrl+Shift+Tab in Windows).

You can use the Tempo Editor instead of, or in conjunction with, the Tempo Operations window (discussed in the "MIDI Menu" section of Chapter 10). However, in some situations, using the Tempo Operations window may allow you finer control—especially when adjusting tempos to match musical events with absolute time references in minutes, seconds, and frames while scoring video or film, for example.

You can switch the main timebase for the Edit window between Linear Samples (absolute) and Linear Ticks (relative). This will affect how tempo events are displayed in the Tempo Editor. For example, in Linear Sample format, tempo events at bars 3 and 5 would appear more closely spaced after increasing tempo settings because the absolute time difference between their positions has been reduced.

You can set the timebase that controls references to positions of regions and/or automation events in each track to Samples or Ticks. Here's a brief summary of how these are affected by tempo changes in Pro Tools:

- If your session is set to Linear Sample Display (absolute), as you trim or otherwise alter tempos in this editor, you will see bar numbers shifting in the Bars:Beats ruler if it's visible. Events inside any tracks whose timebase selector is set to Ticks will shift in relation to this absolute (samples) timeline. This means that if you use individual audio samples in conjunction with tick-based MIDI or Instrument tracks (for example, individual drum hits or cymbal crashes), you would set their timebase to Ticks so that individual region locations will be automatically adjusted to the same relative musical position if you ever change the Pro Tools tempo.

■ If your session is set to Linear Tick Display (relative; there are 960 ticks per ¼ note), you will instead see the markings for units in the rulers for absolute time formats (like Minutes: Seconds, Samples, SMPTE, or Feet+Frames) shifting around as you alter tempo events, while the horizontal size of each MIDI bar stays fixed throughout all tempo variations.

■ Events in individual tracks set to the Ticks timebase format won't slide around onscreen as you alter tempos, but tracks set to Samples timebase format *will*.

■ Even though they cannot contain regions, you can set Aux Input and Master Fader tracks to either Ticks or Sample timebase. As with other track types, when using Ticks timebase, any existing automation breakpoints will be automatically adjusted to the same relative musical location as you alter tempos. The best display format for the Edit window depends on where your editing focus is, and you can change the display at any time.

■ Previous versions of Pro Tools only supported Ticks timebase for MIDI tracks. Pro Tools versions 7 and higher, however, support setting MIDI and Instrument tracks to Sample (linear) timebase as well.

Summary

Because the Edit window is where you will probably spend much of your time, this chapter has covered a lot of ground. It is only an introduction, however. You will find many other Edit window operations covered in other chapters. Be sure to consult your *Pro Tools Reference Guide* (a PDF document included with the program) for further details. There are many more time-saving shortcuts and tips to find there. Also, print out *Keyboard Shortcuts*, another PDF document provided with the program, and keep it handy!

7 The Mix Window

To a certain extent, the Mix window is an alternative view of the same material found in the Edit window. In fact, you can view many track parameters in both the Mix window and the Edit window, including comments, track I/O, inserts, sends, and other options via the View > Edit/Mix Window submenus. However, it's usually more convenient to deal with audio and MIDI mixing via the familiar metaphor of a conventional mixing board. Therefore, in the Mix window, the same tracks whose contents appear as horizontal strips in the Edit window are shown as vertical mixer strips, with the familiar volume faders, level meters, pan controls, effects sections, and sends.

This "virtual mixer" metaphor is especially relevant for those who prefer to use physical control surfaces, such as those included on the Digi 003 and Digi 002 interfaces, or other control surfaces such as the Command|8, C|24, Control|24, ProControl, D-Control, D-Command, and so on. Other users find that using a mouse or trackball—combined with Edit window automation—is quite sufficient for their needs. But most users alternate between real-time and graphical control of their mixes, frequently switching back and forth between the Mix and Edit windows.

Tip: Having two monitors on the computer you use for Pro Tools is a huge productivity boost, especially because you can leave the Mix window open on the second monitor (and perhaps an output window or two, as discussed later in this chapter) as you work in the Edit window.

Chapter 9, "Plug-ins, Inserts, and Sends," goes into more detail about the use of inserts, sends, signal routing, and plug-in architectures; this chapter mainly focuses on the elements of the Mix window's user interface. If any of the basic Pro Tools terminology you see here is unfamiliar, refer to Chapter 2, "Pro Tools Terms and Concepts."

Mixer Strip Elements

Every track you create in Pro Tools appears in the Mix window as a vertical mixer strip. These are also called *channel strips* in Digidesign's documentation. Although this isn't strictly incorrect, we prefer to reserve the term *channel* for actual input/output channels on the audio hardware, and call these *mixer strips* to avoid confusion. Again, each mixer strip in the Mix window corresponds to a horizontal track in the Edit window—they're two different views of the same thing (although Instrument tracks have somewhat of a dual personality, as discussed later in this chapter). The controls available for each track in the Mix window depend on its type: audio, MIDI, Aux Input, Instrument, VCA Master, or Master Fader. Let's start by reviewing the track classes in Pro Tools and the elements that can appear in the mixer strip for each track type.

Audio Tracks

Audio tracks contain *playlists* that designate which audio regions should be played and when. Like Aux Inputs, Instrument tracks, VCA Masters, and Master Faders, audio tracks also contain automation data. Mixer strips for audio tracks in the Mix window are shown in Figure 7.1. The main output from an audio track can be routed either to any physical audio output path on the

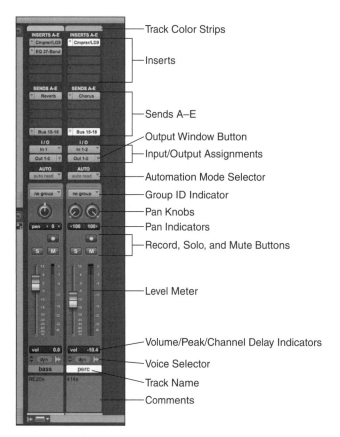

Figure 7.1 Mixer strips for mono and stereo audio tracks in the Mix window (on an LE or M-Powered system), showing the Inserts, Sends, I/O, Track Controls, Comments, and Color Strip sections.

system or to one of Pro Tools' internal mixing busses. Audio tracks can be mono, stereo, or multichannel. An audio track can record from any physical audio input path (that is, mono, stereo, or multiple channels on your audio interface, according to the track's channel format) or from any one of Pro Tools' internal mixing busses. In Pro Tools, only audio tracks can record audio and contain audio regions.

Track Name and Comments

Double-click the Track Name field to enter a meaningful name for your audio tracks. Not only is this useful for keeping tracks in your session properly labeled, but it is important because new regions and audio files created by recording into each track are automatically assigned names derived from the track's current name. This is also true of regions created as a result of the Edit > Consolidate command, as well as any AudioSuite plug-in processes that create new regions. Because you can change track names at any time, some users take advantage of this feature so that each set of new recordings into the same track creates a group of similarly named regions in the Regions List. For instance, if you record scratch lead vocals during the basic tracks session before recording keeper versions in the same track, you might change the track name from "ScratchVox" to "VoxGood." Region and file names created by subsequent recordings will begin with the text "VoxGood," and can appear grouped together in alphabetical order within the Edit window's Regions List.

The Comments area (beneath each Track Name field) is for your own reminders, recording notes, and so on, and has no effect on audio recording or playback. Use this scribble strip however you like; it's the equivalent of that strip of tape that people use for writing on conventional mixing boards. For example, you might make note of which microphones were used and how they were positioned; settings or patches on a source guitar amplifier, MIDI device, or effects unit; settings and other information about additional programs being used with Pro Tools via ReWire; or items on that track that need to be fixed before mixdown. It's also a great idea to type the names of the performers you're recording into the Comments area for each track. This provides some historical data in the archived session document (if you ever want to contact that talent again, for example, having a phone number or e-mail address here might be handy). More importantly, anyone who has ever recorded bands has probably experienced that awkward moment when you need to address the bass player, for example, and can't remember his name! Besides the technical information, wouldn't it be convenient if you had also typed "Larry" or "Curly" (because Moe is the drummer) into the Comments area when introductions were made during setup?

Right-Click Options for Track Management In Pro Tools versions 7.3 and higher, right-clicking any track name in the Mix or Edit window opens a local menu for common operations such as renaming, deleting, and duplicating the track, as well as hiding it or making it inactive.

Track and Channel Color Strips

You can toggle display of these color strips above and below all tracks in the Mix window using the View > Mix Window > Track Color option. Use the Color Palette window to assign new colors to selected tracks so that you can immediately identify groups of tracks that are somehow related. For example, to help keep track of a complex session, you might assign distinct colors to all vocal tracks, guitar tracks, drum and percussion tracks, or sound effects. To reassign a track's color, double-click its color strip to open the Color Palette window. New to Pro Tools 8 is the ability to apply a lighter shade of the chosen track color strip to the channel with the Apply to Channel Strip button.

Volume Fader and Level Meter

The volume fader adjusts the output level of this audio track on whatever output path(s) you've assigned to it. The output selection can be a path to one or more physical audio outputs (as configured in the I/O Setup dialog box) or to any internal Pro Tools mixing bus. The track's level meter appears to the right of its volume fader. If the top-most red segment (the clipping indicator) lights up while you record, your input level to this track is too high and you need to adjust it to avoid distortion. The clip indicator may also light up during playback due to gain changes applied in one of the track's inserts or its main volume fader setting (assuming that the Options > Pre-Fader Metering option is not enabled—this option *should* always be enabled while recording, however). Click to clear a track's clipping indicator or Option-click it (Alt-click in Windows) to clear the same indicator on *all* tracks. (There's also a handy keyboard shortcut for clearing all clip indicators: Option+C on Mac or Alt+C in Windows versions.) Volume faders can boost the track's level by as much as +12dB. For finer adjustment of any volume fader (as with many other onscreen controls), hold down the Command key (Ctrl key in Windows) as you drag the control. To return a track's volume fader to its default setting of 0dB (Unity), Option-click (Alt-click in Windows) the fader. If the sends on this track are set to post-fader, their level will also affected by the track's main volume fader level (see "Sends," later in this section, for more information).

In the Mix window, each track's class is indicated by a distinctive icon (audio, MIDI, Aux Input, Instrument, or Master Fader) just below its main level meter. You can hold down Command+Control (or Ctrl+Start in Windows) as you click on this icon to make a track inactive, which conserves CPU power. (This duplicates a function in the Track menu and is not available for MIDI tracks.) Repeat the same action to make a track active again. The Group ID indicator, which is above the pan knob, opens a pop-up menu for track-group management. While this pop-up menu was a simply informational in previous versions, in Pro Tools versions 7.3 and higher you can use it to delete or duplicate groups, modify their attributes (such as whether mute, solo, and send controls are also affected in a given group), select, show, or hide all tracks that belong to the same group, and other useful functions.

Setting Input Recording Levels Volume faders on audio tracks affect only the track's output, *not* the input recording level! On most Pro Tools hardware configurations, if you want to change the input signal level to a Pro Tools audio channel, either to avoid clipping or to increase its level to take full advantage of the dynamic range offered by your audio hardware and selected recording resolution, you must do this *prior* to its input—for example, in your mic preamp, mixer, or guitar preamp that's connected to the selected audio input on your interface, and/or some Aux Input track you're using as the front end for an audio track while recording. Exceptions to this include the Mbox 2 family and many of the M-Audio interfaces, which have knobs for input gain on their front panels. The Digi 003 and Digi 002 families have gain controls on their four microphone preamps, as does the 96i I/O interface for HD systems. Unlike analog tape recorders, on digital audio recording systems, when input recording levels go into the red and the track's clip indicator lights up while recording, the results are decidedly *not* warm or pleasant sounding! While recording on an audio track, feel free to change its main volume fader level—whatever's convenient for your listening requirements. This has no effect on the actual audio level being recorded to disk. It's highly recommended, however, to always enable the Options > Pre-Fader Metering option while recording into audio tracks. That way, you see what the levels are at the selected input for each track, regardless of its current fader setting or the effect any of its insert effects may have on the track's final output level.

Pan

In a stereo mix, a *panner* determines the left-right position of each track's audio output. Mono tracks have a single left-right pan knob. If the track is stereo or you inserted a stereo plug-in on a mono track that converts its output to stereo—for example, a mono-to-stereo delay—the track will have two separate pan knobs for the track's left and right channels. In surround mixing, on tracks whose outputs are assigned to multichannel paths (more about this in Chapter 14, "Post-production and Soundtracks"), you can use an XY panner to move the track left/right and front/rear in the surround field. You can always Option-click the pan controls (Alt-click in Windows) to return the track's position to center.

Setting Each Audio Track to a Separate Output Sometimes it's convenient to set the output from each audio track in Pro Tools to a separate mono path—for example, the individual physical outputs on your audio interface. This might be useful when transferring all your individual Pro Tools tracks to the inputs of a multitrack tape recorder in real time. You *could* set the output assignments one by one, but there's a quicker way: After using the I/O Setup dialog box to create individual mono paths for each output on your audio interface, hold down the Command and Option keys (Ctrl and Alt keys in Windows) as you set the Output selector of the first track (left-most in the Mix window) to Output #1. The remainder of the audio tracks will be automatically assigned to consecutive output paths.

Track Controls: Solo, Mute, Record Enable, Voice Selector, Track Input Enable

While the basic functionality of the Solo, Mute, and Record Enable buttons is familiar to anyone who has used a multitrack tape recorder, Pro Tools offers a few enhancements for these. The Track Input Enable button is roughly similar to the selector on traditional recording consoles that switches a channel strip to its mic/line inputs instead of the tape input, while the Voice selector represents a digital audio workstation–only concept.

- **Solo button.** Enables playback for this track only, muting all others (although you can always solo additional tracks, because more than one track can be soloed at the same time). Command-click (Ctrl-click in Windows) any track's Solo button to put it in Solo Safe mode; its Solo button will be dimmed. Tracks that are in Solo Safe mode will not be muted even if other tracks are soloed.

- **Mute button.** Disables audio output from this track on its main output assignment. This also mutes any *post*-fader sends (the default send type; a track's *pre*-fader sends are not affected by muting the track, however). You can mute more than one track at the same time. Option-click (Alt-click in Windows) any track's Mute button to mute/unmute all tracks at once.

- **Record Enable (Rec) button.** Enables the track for recording and, when an audio track is in the default Track > Auto Input Monitor mode, switches the track to monitoring audio signals at its selected input source—either a physical input path or a bus that you are using to route audio from other tracks within Pro Tools. When you press the Record and Play buttons in the Transport window, all record-enabled tracks start recording their selected sources. Only audio, MIDI, Instrument and VCA Master tracks have Record Enable buttons.

- **Voice Selector.** Determines which of Pro Tools' floating pool of voices this audio track will use to play back its audio regions. Ordinarily, you leave this set to dynamic (dyn) so that Pro Tools will automatically make a voice assignment according to your system configuration. (On LE or M-Powered versions of Pro Tools, that and "off" are the *only* available voice assignment modes.) Dynamic voice allocation is usually the most convenient choice, even if you have an HD system providing a relatively large number of voices—unless you are deliberately using *voice stealing* so that regions in one track interrupt playback in another (when bleeping dialog, for example). Alternatively, in the HD software (as on previous TDM systems), you can manually assign voice numbers to each track. At any particular point where two tracks attempt to use the same voice for playback, the track with higher priority (because its current position is farther left in the Mix window or higher in the Edit window) always "wins"—even if this means cutting off the previously playing audio in the other track. In Pro Tools HD, the Voice Selector pop-up menu displays voices that are already in use by other tracks in bold type.

- **Track Input Enable (HD systems only).** Switches an individual audio track to monitoring its input, whether record enabled or not, and regardless of whether the Track > Input Only Monitor setting is enabled.

Record-Safe Your Tracks Record Safe mode disables recording on an audio, MIDI, or Instrument track. Especially when working with large sessions and/or viewing tracks at small sizes, this simple technique can help you avoid mistakes as you record new takes into additional tracks. When you are finished making new recordings in a track, Command-click (Ctrl-click in Windows) its Rec button to put it in Record Safe mode (the button will be dimmed; see Figure 7.2). Repeat this if you ever need to re-enable recording on the track.

Figure 7.2 Dimmed Rec buttons in several of these tracks indicate they are in Record Safe mode. The dimmed Solo button in the Aux 1 track indicates it is in Solo Safe mode (so it won't be muted when other tracks are soloed).

Don't... Stop... In Pro Tools versions 7.3 and higher, many aspects of the mixer configuration can be changed during playback (although not during recording). You can create, delete, or move tracks, inserts, sends, and track I/O assignments on the fly.

Automation Mode Selector

A track's Automation Mode pop-up selector determines how its mix automation will be recorded and played back. Options are Off, Read, Touch, Latch, and Write, plus Trim mode on HD systems only. For more details about these automation modes, refer to Chapter 6, "The Edit Window." Remember that you can also use the Automation Enable window (again, discussed in Chapter 6) to *globally* enable or disable recording and playback of entire classes of automation for the current Pro Tools session.

Input/Output Section: Output Selector, Input Selector, Pan Indicator, Volume/Peak/Channel Delay Indicators

As you can imagine, the I/O section of each track's mixer strip provides selectors that determine where its audio is coming from... and where it's going! The numerical value displays in this section are also essential for keeping an eye on the level and position (for example, left-right panning in a stereo perspective) of each track in your mix.

- **Input selector.** Determines what physical input or internal bus will be monitored when this track is record enabled (and recorded to disk when you click Record and Play on the Transport) or when the Track > Input Only Monitor option is enabled. Software instrument plug-ins can have extra, auxiliary outputs enabled, if available. If this is the case, these will appear among the options in the Input selector for audio and Aux Input tracks.

- **Output selector.** Determines the main destination where a track's audio will be routed within the Pro Tools mix environment. You can choose any of the available physical audio output paths on your system or any of Pro Tools' internal mixing busses. The output paths available in this pop-up selector—and especially the grouping of their mono subpaths—depend on the track's channel format (mono, stereo, or multichannel) and the currently active configuration in the I/O Setup dialog box (which determines the naming conventions and grouping for physical audio outputs on your audio hardware and the internal mixing busses within Pro Tools).

Routing a Track's Output to Multiple Destinations In addition to using sends for routing a track's audio to another destination, as discussed in the next section of this chapter, the main output from each Pro Tools track (except VCA Masters and Master Faders) can be assigned to *multiple* destinations. After you've made the main output assignment, hold down the Control key (Start key in Windows) as you open the track's output selector again to choose additional paths. When you assign a track to multiple output destinations, a plus sign appears in front of the main output assignment displayed within the Output selector.

- **Pan indicators.** Numerical display for the current positions of the pan knobs (either a single value for mono tracks or dual values for stereo tracks). Displayed values change in real time as you make adjustments and, during playback, continuously reflect the changing values for any pan automation on this track.

- **Volume/Peak/Channel Delay indicators.** These fields are actually located at the bottom of the mixer strip, just above the Track Name field. They display current values for the track's volume fader, peak level, or channel delay, as well as automatic delay compensation on HD systems. (See the following sidebar for more information.)

Volume/Peak/Channel Delay Indicator Modes The Volume/Peak/Channel Delay indicator for any Pro Tools track has three modes (except MIDI tracks, which display only MIDI volume). Click on the indicator while holding down the Command key (Ctrl key in Windows) to toggle between these modes.

- **Volume (the default).** Reflects the current level of the track's main volume fader. Values displayed here change in real time as you move the fader or display volume fader automation values during playback.

- **Peak.** Displays the most recent peak playback or input level in the track. In other words, if the audio on this track reaches a maximum level of −3dB during playback, that value is displayed. Click it to reset it. This setting is useful for managing your session's gain structure and lets you know exactly how much headroom is left on the track— especially since its output level may be affected by level changes made in its plug-ins or hardware inserts. For both the Peak/Hold and Clipping Indicator functions, you can choose whether you want these to hold their values infinitely (for instance, the most recent peak level during playback, even after you hit Stop), for three seconds, or not at all in the Display tab of the Preferences dialog box. You can clear the red clip indicators on *all* tracks simultaneously by Option-clicking any one of them (Alt-click in Windows) or via the Option+C keyboard shortcut (Alt+C in Windows). Experienced mixers will also find the metering options in the Signal Tools plug-in extremely useful—this is included in Pro Tools versions 7.3 and higher.

- **Channel Delay.** This setting indicates the processing delay introduced on this track as a result of whatever plug-ins you've added, in samples. Obviously, the absolute amount of delay time this represents is proportionate to your session's sample rate. A given number of samples is a progressively smaller amount of time at higher rates. Note that on LE and M-Powered systems, this indicator may display a delay of zero samples on certain third-party plug-ins—even when that's audibly not true! For most RTAS DigiRack plug-ins supplied with LE and M-Powered systems, however, the effective latency added by these plug-ins is indeed very small and correctly displays as almost, but not quite, zero. At any rate, for fine adjustment of time alignment on tracks in LE and M-Powered systems, the Time Adjuster plug-in is very useful. On Pro Tools|HD systems, you can adjust the Automatic Delay Compensation feature to eliminate delays caused by processing latency in the plug-ins on your tracks.

In addition to their default appearance in the Mix window, you can also display the Volume/Peak/Channel Delay indicators for each track in the Edit window, where an additional button in the I/O panel can be used to directly open an output window for the track. On HD systems, you can expand these indicators to additionally display the current amount of automatic delay compensation (if any) being applied to each track. There is also an editable field where you can manually enter a negative or positive offset value for each track if you feel that any additional adjustment for time alignment is necessary. To show this expanded view, choose View > Mix Window > Delay Compensation View.

Sends A–E, F–J

As explained in Chapter 2, *sends* are access points in a track's signal chain from which you can additionally route its audio signal to other destinations independently from the track's main output assignment. In a traditional mixing console, this is how you route part of a vocal track's signal to an external reverb—for instance, using a knob on each channel strip that feeds an audio output labeled "Aux Send" or something similar. In Pro Tools, you can enable up to ten sends. In the Mix window, these are grouped into two sections (labeled "A–E" and "F–J") from each audio, Aux Input, or Instrument track. Like the Inserts section of the Mix window, discussed in the next section of this chapter, display of the two sends sections can be toggled on and off to conserve screen space. Sends are not available on MIDI, VCA Master, or Master Fader tracks. Each send can be either mono or stereo (or multichannel on HD systems), as shown in Figure 7.3. You can assign the destination of each send to any of the physical outputs available on your system—connected to an external effects device or a performer's headphone mix out in the studio, for example. For most Pro Tools users, it's even more frequent to route sends to one of Pro Tools' internal mixing busses. When you create sends, they default to post-fader, but you can switch them to pre-fader if required. Controls in the output window for each send include Output Assignment, Pre/Post selector, Level, Pan (stereo and multichannel surround sends only), Mute, and FMP (Follow Main Pan, which links the pan setting of the send to the main pan control of the track itself).

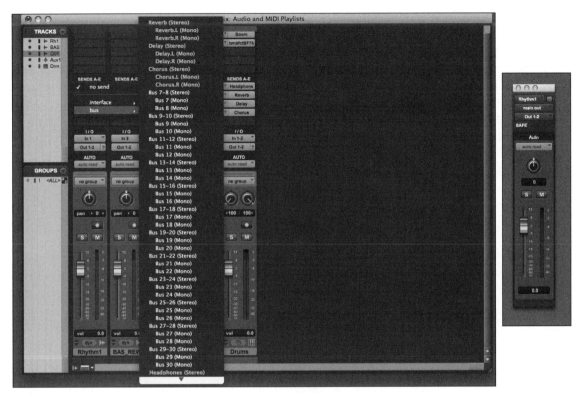

Figure 7.3 You can enable up to 10 sends from each audio, Aux Input, and Instrument track. If you disable (dim) the Target button in a send's output window, it remains open even as you select other tracks or sends.

Whether you choose the pre- or post-fader position for each send depends on how it's being used, and this varies a lot from one session (and Pro Tools user) to another. Here are two typical examples:

- *Post-fader sends* are often used for sends to effects. Prior to the level setting of the send itself, the amount of signal entering the send (and consequently arriving to its assigned destination) also varies in proportion to the track's main volume fader. When you mute a track, all its post-fader sends are also muted.

- In contrast, a *pre-fader send* routes audio from the track to the specified destination, strictly according to the send's own level (volume) setting. The level reaching the destination of a pre-fader send is unaffected by the track's main volume fader and Mute buttons since its signal originates from a prior point in the track's audio signal path. Pre-fader sends can be very useful—for example, for creating an independent headphone mix for performers out in the studio. Even if you change volumes or mute tracks while you're monitoring the recording session in the control room, this won't affect what they hear in the headphone mix.

Send Compatibility with Older Pro Tools Versions Versions prior to Pro Tools 7 support only five sends per track. If compatibility with older versions is a concern (for example, when using the File > Save Copy In command to create a 6.*xx* version of your session for a Digi 001 or 24|Mix user), be aware that sends F–J and their associated automation data will be dropped in the process of converting to the older PTS session format.

Example: Creating an Aux Send to a Reverb Effect. If you'd like to send audio from multiple tracks to a stereo reverb, do the following:

1. Create a stereo, post-fader send on each track, assigned to bus pair 1–2.

2. Create a stereo Aux Input track whose input is set to bus pair 1–2.

3. Insert the D-Verb plug-in on this stereo Aux Input (checking to make sure its Mix parameter is set to 100 percent wet, meaning that that no direct, unprocessed signal passes through it).

Now you can use the send levels on each source audio track (each track's send level and pan can of course be automated) to determine when and how much of that track's signal will be sent to the reverb.

Don't Be Afraid to Name Names! The I/O Setup dialog box, which you can open via the Setup > I/O command, allows you to assign names to your inputs, outputs, inserts, and busses. Although you *can* set the name assignments you create as a default for all other new sessions, it's also useful to create name assignments specifically for the current session (and we're amazed at how few users actually do so!). For instance, in the preceding example, a stereo Pro Tools bus is the send destination and an Aux Input whose input is assigned to monitor that bus contains a reverb plug-in. So why not go into I/O Setup and change the name of bus pair 1–2 to Reverb? This allows you to see at a glance where the sends from each track are going instead of having to remember a lot of bus numbers. Afterward, when you open any output assignment pop-up to select a bus, it appears by name instead of a number. Simple, right? So why don't more people do it?

The I/O Setup dialog box is also where multichannel paths for inputs, outputs, busses, and sends are managed. This enables surround mixing, of course; templates for this are provided with Pro Tools HD. Speaking of templates, as you get more adept at using the I/O Setup dialog box, be sure to learn how to import and export its settings so that you can reuse them in other sessions. (The default I/O Settings subfolder of the Pro Tools program folder is a good place to store your collection. You might split this up even further if things get unwieldy.) In the long run, your life will be *much* simpler if you use a consistent set of configurations for the I/O Setup dialog box in all your sessions, especially if, for example, you use distinct names and path groupings during record and mix phases of your projects.

Inserts

As explained in Chapter 2, a track's entire audio signal passes through each of the insert points in series. Using the insert selectors A through J that Pro Tools provides, you can patch in a plug-in (a software-based effects processor) at any insert point. Alternatively, you can loop the track's signal through external outputs and inputs on your Pro Tools hardware via a hardware I/O insert before it continues out through the main output assignment for the track. For example, you might use such a hardware insert to route the track through some favorite high-end compressor or signal-processing device in your studio.

These 10 insert points, which are not applicable to MIDI tracks, are always *pre*-fader on audio tracks, Aux Inputs, and Instrument tracks, but always *post*-fader on Master Faders. Bear in mind that a track's audio passes through each insert in series, from A through J. The order in which you place effects in these inserts makes a difference in the resultant sound. For example, placing the EQ (equalization) after the compressor (a dynamics processor) will generally sound different from doing it the other way around. To move the insert effects on a track into a different order, drag their buttons in the Mix window; any existing automation for these inserts is adjusted accordingly. Alternatively, Option-drag (Alt-drag in Windows) the plug-in buttons to copy them instead of moving them to the new location—either on the same track or any other track that has a matching number of audio channels.

Right-Click Tricks for Managing Sends and Inserts In Pro Tools versions 7.3 and higher, you can right-click any send or insert button in the Mix (or Edit) window to access a pop-up menu. From this menu, sends can be renamed, muted, or made inactive; inserts can be bypassed, made inactive, or put into automation-safe mode to avoid overwriting existing data; or a dialog box for enabling automation parameters can be opened.

Using RTAS Plug-Ins in HD Versions of Pro Tools. Unlike older versions, in Pro Tools 7, you can place RTAS and TDM plug-ins on any track type (except MIDI tracks and VCA Master tracks). However, here are some points to keep in mind about usage of playback voices:

■ The first instance of an RTAS plug-in on an Aux Input or Master Fader track takes up two additional voices per channel (for example, two voices for input/output on a mono Aux Input track or four voices for stereo).

■ On *any* track type, wherever an RTAS plug-in follows a TDM plug-in in the same track's signal chain, it also takes up two additional voices per channel.

- When RTAS plug-ins are used on any track, any use of sidechaining (on a dynamics plug-in, for example) or multiple output assignments for the track also uses additional voices.

- Given these limitations, and especially if running out of playback voices is already an issue on your system, try to use TDM equivalents on Aux Inputs and Master Faders when they are available. Place RTAS plug-ins *prior* to TDM plug-ins on all track types if practical.

- There may be one exception to this: When an audio track is record-enabled (or switched to Input Monitor mode), any RTAS plug-ins that precede other TDM plug-ins in the track's signal chain are bypassed. If you really need to hear these as you record on that track, you might want to place these *after* the TDM plug-ins, despite the voice-usage considerations.

Selecting Favorite Plug-Ins In the pop-up selector menu used to configure each insert on a Pro Tools track, the available plug-ins are grouped within hierarchical submenus by default. Users with large collections of plug-ins might change settings in the Display tab of the Preferences dialog box so that the plug-ins are grouped by manufacturer. In either case, you can also select some favorite plug-ins to always appear at the top of the plug-in submenus, *before* any additional categorized submenus. Just Command-click (Ctrl-click in Windows) any insert button in any track and, while still holding down this modifier key, select the plug-in you want to add as a favorite. Repeat this procedure to add more or to remove existing favorites. (Stereo favorites won't appear on mono tracks, and vice versa.) In versions 7.3 and higher, the Mixing tab of the Preferences dialog box lets you designate default plug-ins for EQ and dynamics. These will at the top-most level of the insert pop-up menu, *prior* to either the plug-in or I/O insert submenus for insert selection. Most users will find it very convenient to enable this preference.

Aux Inputs

Aux Inputs behave much like audio tracks, although they cannot record or contain audio regions. Aux Inputs act in real time upon incoming audio in their selected audio input(s)—either a physical input path on your system or one of Pro Tools' internal mixing busses. You can automate the controls on Aux Inputs and place hardware and software inserts into their signal paths. You can also route a portion of their signals to one of the sends they provide. Like audio tracks and Master Faders, Aux Inputs can be mono, stereo, or multichannel, and you can assign the output of each Aux Input track to any physical audio output path or internal mixing bus. Figure 7.4 shows how Aux Input tracks appear in the Mix window.

Typical uses of Aux Inputs include the following:

- **Global send effects.** An effects plug-in, like a reverb or delay, is placed as an insert on the Aux Input. The selected input for the Aux Input is a bus (mono, stereo, or multichannel), which is used as the destination for sends from various source audio tracks.

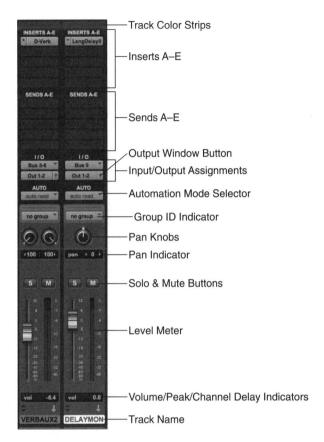

Figure 7.4 Aux Inputs (mono and stereo) in the Mix window (in a stereo mix).

■ **Subgroups/submasters.** The main outputs from multiple source audio tracks are assigned to a common bus, which is selected as the input source for an Aux Input. A single volume fader on the Aux Input thereby controls the entire submix—for example, multiple drum microphones, a wind section, multiple backing vocals, or a complex sound-effects background. Also, you can conveniently apply plug-ins to the entire submix by placing them on this Aux Input. This not only makes more efficient use of available DSP resources but may also produce more appropriate-sounding results—for example, applying a single stereo compressor plug-in to a submix of backing vocals instead of many individual compressors on their mono source tracks. Some people route the same source audio simultaneously through multiple subgroups (generally called *mults* when used in this fashion) so that they can apply radically different effects treatments to each. During mixdown, you can blend them together, making sure to check whether manual delay compensation is required to maintain proper time alignment between them if using Pro Tools LE or M-Powered software, or drop them in and out at strategic points in the arrangement. This is a popular technique for processed drum loops, for example.

- **Monitoring external sources.** You can use Aux Inputs to monitor the input from external MIDI instruments, tracks from a multitrack audio recorder, and so on. You can even use Aux Inputs to premix multiple external input sources during the recording process (the outputs from multiple Aux Inputs would be assigned to a single bus, which is then selected as the input for recording into an audio track).

- **Software instruments.** You can instantiate software instruments, including the Click plug-in, which functions in a somewhat similar manner, as inserts on Aux Input tracks (as well as on Instrument and audio tracks).

- **Monitoring audio from ReWire sources.** If you're running a ReWire application concurrently with Pro Tools with the ReWired application in slave mode so that its transport and tempo are controlled by Pro Tools, you can instantiate a plug-in that allows you to monitor that program's output through an Aux Input (or Instrument track).

Subsequent sections review the available controls and indicators for Aux Inputs. For some individual elements, we make no comment—in these cases, you should assume that the element behaves exactly as already described for audio tracks.

Don't Overload the Bus When you route sends or main output assignments from multiple tracks to the same bus and Aux Input destination, beware of exceeding the maximum input level of that bus! If the clipping indicator lights up on the Aux Input track (assuming that Options > Pre-Fader Metering is enabled), you may need to slightly reduce levels being sent to it from all these tracks in order to avoid unpleasant digital distortion. One strategy is to enable the display of a Master Fader for that bus by creating a mono or stereo Master Fader track, as appropriate, in order to display what kind of levels are being produced as the audio sent from all its audio sources is combined into the same bus. Master Faders have virtually no impact on system resources, so don't hesitate to create them for such purposes!

Pan

Pan controls on Aux Inputs behave the same as on audio tracks. Bear in mind that when individual sends or main outputs from other tracks are routed to a stereo or multichannel Aux Input, their original pan positions also predetermine how they are affected by the pan control on the Aux Input itself.

Aux Input Track Controls: Solo, Mute

These buttons on Aux Inputs behave the same as on audio tracks. Remember, however, that when you *solo* an Aux Input—containing your delay effect, for example—other tracks will be muted. This might include sends from other tracks (and/or their main outputs) that are routed to the selected input bus for this Aux Input!

Solo-Safe Your Aux Input Tracks In Solo Safe mode, a track cannot be muted even if you click the Solo button on other tracks. Command-click (Ctrl-click in Windows) any track's Solo button to put it in Solo Safe mode (the button will be dimmed). This is *especially* useful for Aux Inputs. Whether you're using the Aux Input as a send destination with an effect plug-in or as a stereo subgroup to which various audio tracks' output assignments have been routed, you probably *won't* want the Aux Input to be muted just because you momentarily solo some other track.

Input/Output Section: Volume/Peak/Channel Delay and Pan Indicators, Output Assignment, Input Selector

You can set the Input selector on an Aux Input to any appropriate physical audio input path or internal mixing bus available on your configuration. Aux Inputs can be mono, stereo, or multichannel, and this pop-up Input selector will only display input paths that match the format of the Aux Input itself. For mono Aux Inputs, you select single audio inputs or mixing busses; for stereo Aux Inputs, you select stereo pairs of physical inputs or busses; and for multichannel Aux Inputs, you select matching multichannel inputs or bus paths. This is all configured within the I/O Setup dialog box, which is discussed in more detail in Chapter 8, "Menu Selections: Highlights." If any software instrument plug-ins have auxiliary outputs enabled, these will also appear among the input options for an Aux Input track.

You can also assign the output of an Aux Input track to any physical audio output path (often the main mix output, but it could be an output pair feeding a cue mix to your performers' headphones, for example) or internal mixing bus. Again, the available selections depend on your system configuration; whether the Aux Input is mono, stereo, or multichannel; and how you have set up your output paths in the I/O Setup dialog box.

Sends

Sends on Aux Inputs behave the same as on audio tracks. As with audio tracks, sends from Aux Inputs can be either *post*-fader or *pre*-fader.

Inserts

Inserts on Aux Inputs behave the same as on audio tracks. As with audio tracks, the Inserts section on Aux Inputs is always *pre*-fader.

Pro Tools, the Ultimate Digital Mixer You can use Pro Tools configurations with multichannel audio hardware as an automated digital mixer, even if you don't record any tracks to hard disk. For example, the Digi 003 and Digi 002 family, 96 I/O, 192 I/O, and 192 Digital I/O audio interfaces, as well as the M-Audio 1814 for Pro Tools M-Powered, feature not only analog audio inputs but also an eight-channel Lightpipe connector compatible with ADAT multitrack digital recorders. (Lightpipe is an eight-channel digital audio connection standard, using optical cables that terminate in a Toslink connector.) M-Audio's ProFire Lightbridge offers up to 18 simultaneous channels of Lightpipe I/O when used with current versions of Pro Tools M-Powered.

Connect the Lightpipe output from the ADAT (or compatible device) to the Lightpipe input on your audio interface. Create eight mono Aux Inputs in your Pro Tools session and set each of their inputs to a separate ADAT Lightpipe channel. Alternatively, you can group some of these as pairs on stereo tracks if appropriate. Option-click the volume fader for each Aux Input to set its level to 0dB (also known as *unity gain*, because no gain change is being applied). The tracks recorded on the ADAT are now digitally routed into the Pro Tools mixing environment. (Hey, you could also use *analog* audio inputs to bring multiple tracks into Pro Tools—for instance, on an audio interface such as 96i I/O or 1622 I/O. Just between us, it will still sound great!)

You can insert plug-in effects onto these Aux Inputs in order to apply signal processing to their incoming audio and use sends to route part of their signal to other effects (such as reverb and delay) within the Pro Tools mixer. Then, either bounce it all to a disk file or mix in real time to a DAT recorder to create your stereo "master." (Obviously, the simple method we're describing here doesn't address synchronizing Pro Tools to the tape source, so you wouldn't be able create real-time automation without purchasing one of several synchronization peripherals that are available for this purpose.)

Master Faders

Like Aux Inputs, Master Fader tracks cannot contain regions. Master Faders can be mono, stereo, or multichannel. Figure 7.5 shows mono and stereo Master Faders as they appear in the Mix window. They can act as a master gain stage and control for the audio signal going through an output bus for a physical output path on your audio hardware (mono, stereo, or multichannel) *or* through any of Pro Tools' internal mixing busses. To name the most typical example, Master Faders are very useful as a final level control over the output bus being used for the stereo (or surround) mix or for the output pair that is the source for mix files bounced to disk. Not only does this provide a volume fader, but more importantly, the Master Fader's level meter facilitates final adjustment of your session's gain structure, always making sure the Master Fader's clipping indicator is not being lit. Using a Master Fader for your main mix output also provides post-fader insert points, where you could apply compression, limiting, EQ, or other effects to an entire mix—especially dithering, which is useful when bouncing down to a lower resolution or recording digitally to a lower-resolution device. You should never bounce a mix to disk (or record to an external device, for that matter) without first creating a Master Fader where you can monitor and optimize the levels on your main mix output!

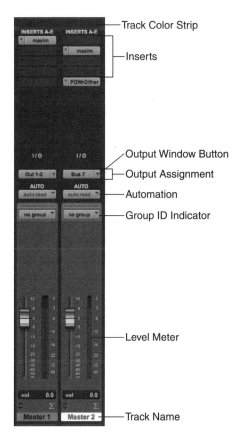

Track Color Strip

Inserts

Output Window Button

Output Assignment

Automation

Group ID Indicator

Level Meter

Track Name

Figure 7.5   Master Faders (mono and stereo) in the Mix window. (These can also be multichannel on HD systems.) Master Faders have no sends or pan controls, and their inserts are post-fader.

Although you can place inserts (both hardware inserts and software plug-ins) into a Master Fader's signal path, sends are *not* available from Master Faders. Also, keep in mind that, unlike audio tracks and Aux Inputs, the inserts on Master Fader tracks are always *post*-fader. You can automate volume on Master Fader tracks as well as the parameters for any plug-ins inserted into their signal paths. As before, if we make no particular comment about an element in the following sections, it behaves in the same way as described previously for audio tracks.

Input/Output Section: Volume/Peak/Channel Delay Indicator, Output Selector

Unlike audio tracks and Aux Inputs, Master Faders have no Input selector—only a selector for choosing the output path (or internal mixing bus) whose signal path you want to control with that particular Master Fader track. Master Fader tracks also have no pan controls.

Sends

Master Faders do *not* have sends!

Inserts

Inserts behave the same way here as they do in audio tracks, except that, as mentioned earlier, the inserts on Master Faders are always *post*-fader. In other words, the input level to their Inserts section *is* affected by the Master Fader track's main volume fader—unlike audio tracks, Aux Inputs, and Instrument tracks, where inserts are always *pre*-fader.

Wide Meters View You can change the width of all the track level meters if this helps you keep a better eye on what's going on in your mix. To switch to a wide meters view, hold down the Command, Option, and Control keys (Start, Alt, and Ctrl in Windows) as you click on the level meter for any track. Repeat the same operation to switch back to the normal meter width.

MIDI Tracks

MIDI tracks contain MIDI regions (see Figure 7.6). The output assignment for each MIDI track determines where the MIDI data contained in its regions will be transmitted—to one of the MIDI destinations available on your system (as determined by your current MIDI setup for external MIDI connections and the software instruments that are active in the current session) and on a specific MIDI channel. Remember that MIDI is data, not audio! If you want to route the *audio* outputs of your external MIDI devices into Pro Tools, you must connect them to physical audio inputs on your Pro Tools audio hardware and monitor their audio via audio tracks (or Aux Inputs). Prior to bouncing your final mix, and especially before archiving the finished project, you will want to record their output to audio tracks anyway. Years down to the road, even if the same source instruments are available, it may be difficult to re-create patch settings or output levels. If the sound sources used by your MIDI tracks are synthesizer and sampler plug-ins or external programs via ReWire, these are generally also instantiated on and/or monitored through Aux Inputs (or Instrument tracks, especially in the case of monophonic software instruments).

Track Name and Comments

As on audio tracks, the MIDI regions created as a result of recording into MIDI tracks inherit the current track name. So again, it's much better to assign meaningful track names as you record (for example, "bass," "drums," or "strings"); it will prevent confusion later. On *all* track types, take advantage of the Comments field to make notes to yourself—for instance, any manual settings that must be restored on one of your external MIDI devices the next time you open this session.

MIDI Volume and Velocity Level Meters

The volume fader on MIDI tracks sends out values for MIDI Controller #7, Main Volume, which range from 0 to 127, on the MIDI channel selected for each track. The level meter on

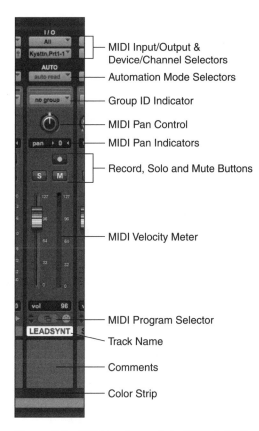

MIDI Input/Output &
Device/Channel Selectors

Automation Mode Selectors

Group ID Indicator

MIDI Pan Control

MIDI Pan Indicators

Record, Solo and Mute Buttons

MIDI Velocity Meter

MIDI Program Selector

Track Name

Comments

Color Strip

Figure 7.6   MIDI tracks contain MIDI data. Each track is assigned to a MIDI channel, program number, and output (either a physical port on the MIDI interface, a direct USB connection, or a virtual instrument).

MIDI tracks displays Note On velocities of the MIDI note events being played back—*not* the output audio volume of whatever instrument (physical or software-based) is playing back the MIDI events being sent from this track!

MIDI Volume and Panning Are Controller Data   Volume and panning (and other MIDI controller events) work differently in MIDI tracks and the MIDI component of Instrument tracks than in other Pro Tools track types—especially in relation to automation and alternate playlists on the same track. On MIDI tracks, both volume and pan are numerical MIDI values from 0 to 127, transmitted like any other MIDI controller type. It is actually your MIDI device or software instrument that responds, changing the volume on some sound that's configured for the same MIDI channel where this MIDI controller information is being received.

When you record fader automation or draw volume changes into a MIDI track, these become part of the data actually contained in each affected MIDI region. Even if you record or draw automation outside the track's existing regions, their boundaries will be extended to include the new automation/controller data events. In audio tracks, there's only one automation playlist for the track. Therefore, when you choose between alternate edit playlists (the list of audio regions and fades to play), the same automation data for that track still applies (for example, breakpoint automation you've created for volume or pan). Also, if cutting and pasting audio regions in one playlist on an audio track causes overlapping automation events to be moved, this underlying automation affects *all* of that track's playlists. In contrast, because on MIDI tracks the controller data for volume, pan, and other types of MIDI controller data are part of the MIDI regions themselves, the automation data for these can be completely different in each playlist on the same track. If you alter the MIDI data within MIDI regions after switching to an alternate track playlist for a MIDI track, a new MIDI region is automatically created and the existing MIDI regions in the previous playlist are unaffected.

MIDI Pan

The pan knob on MIDI tracks sends out values for MIDI Controller #10, Pan, on the track's selected MIDI output channel(s). Values range from 0 to 127, with 0 equaling hard left, 127 equaling hard right, and 64 equaling centered.

Who's the (MIDI) Boss? If you assign two MIDI or Instrument tracks to the same MIDI output and MIDI channel, that external MIDI device or software instrument will respond to MIDI volume, pan, and other controller messages arriving on either channel. This can get confusing, especially if you're using automation for MIDI controllers! If you ever *do* need to assign multiple MIDI tracks to an identical output and channel (for example, to create and edit left- and right-hand keyboard parts separately or to use separate tracks for the individual elements for the drum kit in your software instrument), it's better to choose beforehand which track to use for controlling volume and pan—and for all MIDI controller automation—and stick to it. Otherwise, things can get very confusing!

MIDI Track Controls: Solo, Mute, Record Enable, MIDI Program Selector

On MIDI tracks, the Solo, Mute, and Record Enable buttons work in a comparable way to audio tracks. The MIDI Program selector (below and to the left of the track's main volume fader) opens a dialog box displaying patch numbers from 1–127 The program number you choose (for example, an electric piano sound, program #005 on your synthesizer) is sent as a MIDI program change message on the MIDI channel number currently selected for the track. However, once you have the patch name file for your synthesizer properly configured with the Audio MIDI Setup utility provided with the OS X operating system, you can use the Change button shown in Figure 7.7 to load a MIDNAM file. (This feature is also available in Windows

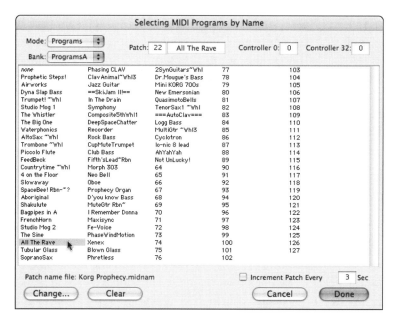

Figure 7.7 Loading a MIDNAM file for the external synth used by this track allows selection of sounds by name rather than by MIDI program numbers.

versions, working in conjunction with the MIDI Studio Setup window of Pro Tools rather than a separate operating system utility.) This is a list of program names and numbers that, when active, allow you to select sounds on that particular synth (a device that was previously defined, attached to a specific port on your computer's MIDI interface) *by name* rather than program number in this dialog box. Once you import a patch name file for an instrument that's available in your MIDI setup, it is also available in any other Pro Tools session.

Automation Mode Selector

The Automation Mode selector for MIDI tracks behaves more or less like the one for audio tracks, as described earlier in this chapter; you select between Off, Read, Touch, Latch, and Write (and on HD systems, Trim for volume and pan). However, this automation on MIDI tracks—with the exception of mute/unmute events—is recorded into the current MIDI regions as MIDI controller events instead of controlling an aspect of audio signal flow or processing within the Pro Tools mixer. The destination MIDI module or software instrument then responds to incoming data for volume, pan, or other MIDI controller types on the relevant MIDI channel.

Input/Output Section: MIDI Volume/Pan Indicators, Device/Channel Selectors for MIDI Input/Output

Again, remember that changes in MIDI volume and pan are actually MIDI *controller* messages, sent on that track's currently assigned MIDI channel! They also get stored as contents of the MIDI regions on that track.

You can change the MIDI device (and output path) and channel for each MIDI track's input and output via a pop-up selector. Available choices depend on your configuration, per the Audio MIDI Setup utility for Mac users or the MIDI Studio Setup window in Windows—and, of course, the active software instruments, MIDI interface, and devices on your system. For editing convenience, you may occasionally assign more than one track to the same MIDI destination (device and MIDI channel, or software instrument). Bear in mind, however, that volume, pan, and program changes arriving at the same destination from multiple MIDI tracks can cause confusion.

You can also assign a single source MIDI track to *multiple* devices/channels or software instrument destinations. Once you've made the main assignment, hold down the Control key (Start key in Windows) before you click to open the track's MIDI Device/Channel selector again to choose additional destinations. This could be a down-and-dirty way to double the current part you've created within a MIDI track, using some completely different MIDI device or channel with a distinct timbre. You could also simply duplicate the current MIDI track (using the Track > Duplicate command) and assign that duplicate track to its own output destination. In fact, in many cases, you will eventually do so anyway to have separate control over its real-time properties—for example, volume and panning. The Automatic Delay Compensation feature available on HD hardware also extends to MIDI tracks that are routed to software instrument plug-ins.

Instrument Tracks

You might say that Instrument tracks are like Aux Inputs with a MIDI track on the front end. When you create a new Instrument track in the Mix window, except for the distinctive keyboard icon at the bottom of the mixer strip, for all intents and purposes it *is* an Aux Input (except that it has a Record button for MIDI events and a MIDI patch selector). However, when you view the same Instrument track in the Edit window, it generally looks and acts like a MIDI track.

Unlike Aux Inputs, Instrument tracks can contain MIDI regions and record MIDI. Once you instantiate a software instrument in one of the insert points on an Instrument track, this can be selected as the MIDI output destination that will respond to MIDI events recorded or placed on this Instrument track. As with software instruments residing on ordinary Aux Inputs, however, you can select software plug-ins on Instrument tracks as the output assignment from any other MIDI or Instrument track. (As with MIDI tracks, you could also route the MIDI output of an Instrument track to some other destination, for that matter.) Instrument tracks save screen space—especially when using monotimbral instrument plug-ins, which can only respond to events on one incoming MIDI channel at a time.

In the Mix window, if you enable display of the top-most Instrument panel (shown in Figure 7.8), it shows MIDI input/output selections for each Instrument track, plus MIDI volume, pan, and a Mute button (the main I/O selection, down by the main volume fader, is identical to an Aux Input track and affects this track's *audio* signal path). In the Edit window, the Track View selector for an

MIDI Input Selector

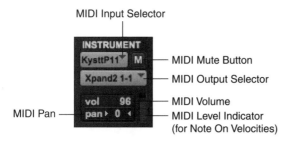

MIDI Mute Button

MIDI Output Selector

MIDI Volume

MIDI Pan

MIDI Level Indicator
(for Note On Velocities)

Figure 7.8   On Instrument tracks, the Instrument panel in the upper portion of the Mix window offers controls for input/output, volume, pan, and mute.

Instrument track shows the usual options for MIDI tracks (including MIDI volume and pan and other controllers, which are really part of the controller data contained in the MIDI regions on that track), plus volume, pan, and mute automation data (identical to the ones on Aux Input tracks) that affect the audio output of the Instrument track itself. If you enable any audio plug-in parameters for automation in that track—for example, one of the sound parameters on the Structure software instrument—these will also appear in the Track View selector.

Volume Fader and Level Meter
These elements behave the same way on Instrument tracks as they do in audio tracks and Aux Inputs, described earlier in the chapter. Bear in mind, though, that volume settings and levels here are related to the *audio* output of the Instrument track (following the output of its software instrument plug-in, if applicable), not to the MIDI data being sent from that track to its own instrument plug-in or other destination.

Pan
Pan behaves the same way on Instrument tracks as it does in audio tracks and Aux Inputs, but again, this affects the *audio* output of the track (and doesn't send MIDI pan data like the pan control on MIDI tracks does).

Instrument Track Controls: Solo, Mute, Record Enable
The Solo and Mute buttons on Instrument tracks work as on Aux Input tracks, affecting their audio output only. These buttons don't affect playback of any MIDI data the Instrument track contains. In fact, if the MIDI output of the track is assigned to some MIDI destination other than the track's own instrument plug-in, that MIDI data still sounds even when the main Mute button for the track's main audio output is engaged. In contrast, the Record Enable button on an Instrument track (which is *not* available on Aux Inputs) arms the track for MIDI recording, just as on MIDI tracks.

Input/Output Section: Input Selector, Output Selector, Pan Indicators, Volume/Peak/Channel Delay

These elements behave the same way on Instrument tracks as they do on audio tracks and Aux Inputs. Note that certain software instrument plug-ins may require that *something* be selected as the audio input for the Instrument track on which they reside—even if they don't use that incoming signal in any way! Unlike MIDI tracks, there is no MIDI output selector in this section of Instrument tracks. Instead, the Instrument section at the top of the Mix window is used for this. You can toggle display of the Instrument panel in the Mix window either via the View > Mix Window submenu or, more conveniently, by using the Mix Window View selector in the bottom-left corner of the Mix window itself.

Inserts

Inserts behave the same way on Instrument tracks as on audio tracks and Aux Inputs, described earlier in this chapter. Remember, however, that most software instrument plug-ins don't use the track's input signal. In those cases, it doesn't make any sense to place plug-ins in insert slots prior to the instrument plug-in itself. Only effects plug-ins that you place *after* the instrument plug-in in the track's signal chain will affect that instrument's audio output.

Instrument Section

This area at the top of the Mixer window is blank on every track type except Instrument tracks. When virtual instruments have been instantiated on an Instrument track (but not audio or Aux Input tracks, for example, even if they *do* have software instruments on their inserts), parameters including MIDI volume, MIDI pan, and MIDI input and output assignments are displayed here. This is discussed further in the section "Instrument Tracks" in this chapter, as well as in Chapter 10, "MIDI."

Mix Window View Selector

This pop-up selector, in the lower-left corner of the Mix window (see Figure 7.9), provides the same options as the View > Mix Window submenu, allowing you to enable/disable display of the following sections for each channel strip: Instrument, Inserts, Sends A–E, Sends F–J (none of which are applicable for MIDI tracks), Track Color Strips, and Comments.

Figure 7.9 The Mix Window View selector offers the same options as the View > Mix Window submenu.

Reconfiguring the Pro Tools Mixer During Playback/Recording In Pro Tools versions 7.3 and higher, you can change which sections of the Mix and Edit windows are visible during either playback or recording. Tracks, sends, and inserts can be created or moved during playback, but not during recording.

Output Windows

Just above the pan knob or knobs for each track (except MIDI tracks) is an icon that opens the track's output window (see Figure 7.10). This is a floating window that stays open and in place even as you switch between the Mix, Edit, and other windows. An output window provides a secondary set of controls for the track's volume fader, pan controls (including surround panners, if appropriate), and Mute, Solo, and Automation Mode selectors. Output windows also feature

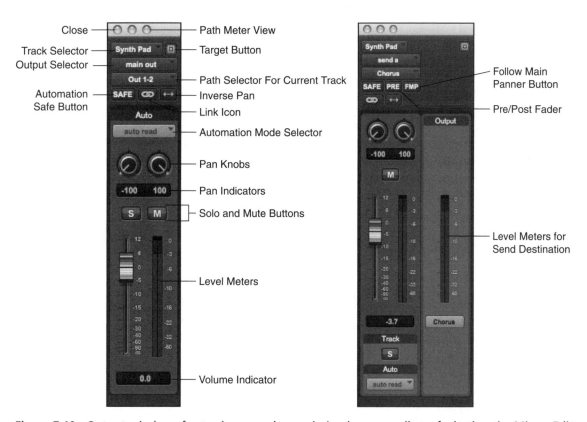

Figure 7.10 Output windows for tracks or sends remain in place regardless of whether the Mix or Edit window is currently visible. You can toggle them between a track's main output (shown on the left) and any of its send assignments (shown on the right). In the right half of this figure, the Path Meter view has been opened to simultaneously view levels for both the reverb send from the track itself and the Verb-Bus mixing bus being used as the input for that reverb.

an automation Safe button, which prevents writing of automation data on the track in question. Additionally, for stereo audio tracks, Aux Inputs, and Instrument tracks, Link and Inverse buttons are provided; they are discussed later in this section.

Clicking on any send button in the Sends section of the Mix window (or Edit window, if displayed there) also opens an output window. Output windows for sends have an additional Pre button for selecting whether the currently viewed send should be pre- or post-fader. In Pro Tools versions 7.3 and higher, sends also have an FMP button (Follow Main Panner), which links the pan control for the send control to that of the main pan control for the track itself. A Path Meter View button in the upper bar of the output window, next to its Close button, is of particular interest when viewing sends. It opens a side panel showing a level meter for the send's destination (a bus used to route audio to a reverb or delay effect, for example). This expanded view of an output window can be seen in the right half of Figure 7.10. As a matter of fact, without leaving the output window, you can switch between displaying the track's main output section to displaying any of its 10 sends using the pop-up Output selector in the upper panel of the output window.

You can leave output windows open to provide quick access—regardless of whether the Mix window or even the track itself is currently visible. By default, the target icon is lit in an output window, which means that clicking the Output icon for a different audio track (or send) in the Mix window replaces the contents of the current output window. However, if you click on the current output window's target icon to disable (dim) it, the window stays open; clicking other sends or the Output icon for another track will open an *additional* output window. (Be aware that the new window might appear right over the previous one, giving the impression that the first output window has been replaced. It hasn't—just click and drag the new window to its own location.)

Using Output Windows By default, the target icon in the first output window you open is enabled. As you click on other sends or track output window buttons, their contents are swapped into the output window that is already open. As mentioned, disabling (dimming) the target icon lets the current output window stay open, even as you open others. Especially for large sessions, keeping several output windows open can make your life *much* simpler, with frequently accessed controls always immediately available even as you scroll through huge numbers of individual source tracks in the Mix or Edit windows. Here are a few applications where you might want to keep an output window open:

- Reverb sends from key vocal and soloist tracks. (Don't forget to open the Path Meter view so that you can also avoid overloading by monitoring levels on the send bus!)

- Aux Inputs that are used as mixer subgroups for multiple source tracks routed through a common bus—for instance, the entire rhythm section, a drum set, a bed of backing vocals or guitars, a set of choir microphones within a larger ensemble, or submixes of dialog, effects, or music for postproduction.

■ The Master Fader for the main mix output. Having this visible in an output window makes it easier to keep an eye on your levels because in very large sessions, this Master Fader track might not always be visible as you scroll back and forth in the Mix window.

Safe Button for Automation

When enabled, the automation Safe button prevents writing of automation data on the track currently displayed in this output window. This can save a lot of hassle. Especially if you might record subsequent real-time automation passes on other tracks, get in the habit of using the automation Safe button to avoid accidentally overwriting your mix automation.

Linked Panners (Multichannel and Stereo Tracks Only)

When the Link icon is enabled in an output window, both pan knobs in the output window move left and right in sync, with identical values. If you additionally activate the Inverse buttons, the two pan knobs are linked, but move in opposite directions. This is useful for adjusting the width of a stereo track, for example.

Inverse Pan (Multichannel and Stereo Tracks Only)

The Inverse Pan button is used on stereo or multichannel tracks in conjunction with the Link icon. In Inverse mode, the panners mirror each other in opposite directions. As you move the one pan control toward the middle (using either the knobs in the output window or the pan knobs in the Mix window itself, whose operation is also affected by this inverse linking function), the other one automatically moves inward by a corresponding amount. For a stereo track, for instance, enabling Panner Linking and Inverse mode provides a convenient way to reduce the stereo width.

As counterintuitive as it may seem, sometimes it's desirable to *narrow* the stereo image of a track— for example, reducing clutter by having a stereo drum loop not extend as far out to the edges of the mix as other loops and percussion tracks that are layered over it. However, in surround mixing, inverse linking of panners acquires a whole other dimension—literally—because you can link the two front channels, the two rear channels, or front and back.

Tracks List

The Tracks List (shown in Figure 7.11) is a pane that can be displayed at the left edge of both the Mix and Edit windows for monitoring the state of a session's tracks as well as controlling what tracks are visible in the Edit and/or Mix window. Each track is represented by a small black toggle button that controls whether it is visible for editing, a mini strip to show the track's color coding, an icon denoting what type of track it is, and the track name. Track listings that are

Figure 7.11   The Tracks List and its pop-up menu.

highlighted gray are currently selected. The pop-up menu at the right-top of the Tracks List offers commands for showing, hiding, and sorting tracks in various configurations.

Here's a typical scenario for hiding tracks: You're posting a video project and have assembled a fairly complex mix for the background ambience and sound effects in a scene, requiring many tracks. You're ready to work on several tracks of dialog, but your Mix and Edit windows now contain such a huge number of tracks that it makes your work cumbersome. The solution: Change the output assignment of each sound-effects track to one of Pro Tools' internal bus pairs and create a stereo Aux Input that monitors that same bus as its input. Now you can hide all these sound-effects tracks (by using their Track Show/Hide toggle button in the Tracks List pane) and use this Aux Input's track's fader to control their overall level.

Slimming Down Your Mix Window When the number of tracks in your Mix window exceeds what will fit in the current screen, you have several options:

- Scroll back and forth—and live with not being able to see all the tracks at once.

- Use the Tracks List to view only certain tracks or track types.

- Enable the View > Narrow Mix option, which squeezes each vertical mixer strip into a smaller space.

- Purchase a *much* larger monitor, which is always nice!

Lastly, in the Tracks List, you can also drag tracks around to change their order. This has the same effect as dragging tracks around by their names, either horizontally in the Mix window or vertically in the Edit window.

Mix Groups List

This area displays any mix groups you've created with the Track > Group command. However, the group name "All" always exists. When a group's name is highlighted in the Mix Groups List, it's active. Volume changes on any track belonging to the group will be mirrored in the others (maintaining their original *relative* levels, of course). As discussed in Chapter 6, in the Create Groups and Modify Groups dialog boxes, you can choose whether Mute and Solo buttons, send levels, and send mutes of tracks in the group should also be linked (as well as various other track controls in Pro Tools HD versions, which can also store and recall group attribute presets). In Pro Tools LE and M-Powered versions, settings for record-enable, panning, and output assignments remain independent for grouped tracks.

When you deselect a group name, it is inactive; you can make changes on any of its tracks without affecting the others in the group. By default, Pro Tools creates groups that are active in both the Mix and Edit windows. In that case, enabling of groups in either window affects the other. However, if you need to deal with Mix and edit groups separately, click the Edit or Mix button (instead of clicking the Edit *and* Mix buttons) in the dialog box as you create or modify each group and deselect the Preferences > Mixing > Link Mix/Edit Group Enables option.

Color-Coding Mix Groups You can use the Color Palette window to assign colors to selected mix or edit groups (independently of color assignments for the tracks that pertain to them and/or the colors assigned to audio and MIDI regions *within* those tracks). Not only will these colors appear in the Mix Groups List shown in Figure 7.12, they will also in the pop-up Mix Groups button for each track in the Mix window.

Double-click the Group symbol to the left of any group in this list to change its name and properties (for example, to convert a mix and edit group into a mix-only group). Click on any group's letter in this list to select all tracks belonging to it. The pop-up menu at the top of the Mix Groups List (see Figure 7.12) also allows you to delete any group or *suspend* all groups. Remember that underneath each track's level meter, a pop-up menu allows you to confirm the active mix group(s) to which that track is assigned and what other tracks share that same group assignment (as well as duplicate, delete, and modify existing groups).

Figure 7.12 Mix groups allow you to select or mute/solo multiple tracks with a single operation and change their volumes simultaneously.

Adjusting Individual Volumes on Grouped Tracks   When tracks are grouped in the Mix window, moving any one of their volume faders changes the levels of the other tracks in the group by a corresponding amount. Their *relative* levels are maintained, however, from when they were first grouped. In this way, for example, you could drag the faders for all drum tracks up and down together without altering the relative balances. However, you can always make independent volume adjustments on individual tracks within a mix group; it's not strictly necessary to suspend the group. Just hold down the Control key (Start key in Windows) as you drag the fader for any grouped track; other tracks in the same mix group won't be affected. Alternatively, in versions 7.3 and higher, you can independently adjust a grouped track's volume by holding down the right mouse button as you drag its fader. As always, if you hold down the Command key (Ctrl key in Windows) as you drag *any* onscreen control, its value changes in smaller increments, allowing for fine adjustments. You can use both these modifier keys simultaneously.

Summary

Whether you control (and automate) your mixes in Pro Tools mainly through graphic breakpoints in the Edit window or using the controls in the Mix window depends on the nature of your work and on personal preference. This chapter focused on the onscreen elements of the Mix window and how they behave; the issue of signal routing within Pro Tools is explored in more detail in Chapter 9. For a more schematic view of Pro Tools' signal-routing architecture, see the illustrations in Appendix E, "Signal Flow in Pro Tools."

8 Menu Selections: Highlights

This chapter does *not* review every selection in every menu. Most of the functions are well documented in the *Pro Tools Reference Guide*, and especially in the *Menus Guide* (PDF files provided with Pro Tools, located inside the Digidesign > Documentation > Pro Tools folder). Instead, the intent of this chapter is to highlight those menu items that are key to Pro Tools' operation, have specific characteristics in the Pro Tools environment, are new, or simply are ignored by too many Pro Tools users.

File Menu

Some commands in the File menu concern creating new session files, opening existing ones, or saving the current session under a different name. Others enable you to import audio or MIDI files *into* your Pro Tools session (although this is often more efficiently accomplished via the Workspace browser window) or to bounce mixes out to disk as new audio files. You can also import data from other Pro Tools session documents, send items via DigiDelivery (if you have an account on a DigiDelivery server), and export MIDI data for the Sibelius music-notation program (in all versions 7.3 and higher). Remember that by nature, most Pro Tools projects consist of multiple files; the audio files that you use and create are not actually part of the Pro Tools session document itself. Again, here we will mention only some of the items under this menu.

Save, Save As, Save Copy In, Revert to Saved

These commands concern saving the currently open session document to disk, either under the present name or with a different name and location.

Save

The File > Save command writes the current session document to disk—including all edits, settings, and MIDI recordings up this point—under the existing file name. Remember: You must save *often* as you work; get used to using the Command+S (Ctrl+S in Windows) keyboard shortcut as soon as possible!

Oh No! My Computer Crashed Before I Saved My Session! If the unthinkable should happen as you record audio—that is, your computer hangs before you can save the session—don't despair! All MIDI recording, automation, parameter changes, and region edits you've performed since the last save will be lost, but you won't necessarily lose all the recorded audio takes. And although the recording that was in progress when the computer got hung up may not be retrievable, other completed audio recordings will probably be usable. That's because in Pro Tools, each time you click the Stop button on the Transport after recording, the resultant audio files are stored within your session's Audio Files folder—*whether you save the session file or not.*

So even though you will have to start over from the last saved version of the session document—which won't have these new recordings placed into their audio tracks—you can do the following:

1. Re-create the audio tracks if necessary, and then use the File > Import > Audio command to import these audio files from this session's Audio Files folder into the Regions List. (Aren't you glad you always give your tracks meaningful names so you can easily identify files and regions, and that Pro Tools automatically numbers your takes?)

2. Drag these regions out onto the appropriate tracks. For example, drop the whole-file region named GtrSolo_03, the third take of the guitar solo overdub, into the track named GtrSolo. Don't worry about the exact position for now—the cool part is coming next.

3. Switch to Spot edit mode and click one of the regions you just dragged onto the tracks. The Spot dialog box opens. In the lower half of this dialog box, click the button next to the Original Time Stamp value. That value is automatically entered into the Start field. Click OK. Your region is spotted to the exact time location where it was originally recorded! This is possible because Pro Tools automatically time-stamps regions as they are created by recording.

Even so, you still may have lost a good amount of work done since the last time you saved the session—because automation, MIDI recordings, region edits, plug-in or software instrument settings, assignment of sends, enabling of hardware or plug-in inserts, and so on are all stored within the session document itself. That's why you must be sure to save your session often (Command+S on Mac, Ctrl+S in Windows) as you work!

Save As

This command saves the current session document under a new file name. From that point on, you're working on (and saving to) that new session name. (That said, the same Audio Files and Fade Files folders are being used by this new copy as under the previous session name.

All additional audio recordings or fade files you create in the new copy will continue to be stored inside these same folders.) The File > Save As command is useful for saving different versions of a session—for example, if you want to try some extended experimentation but maintain the possibility of returning to a previously saved session document.

Saving Iterations of Your Pro Tools Session In addition to using the Auto Backup feature (discussed in the "Preferences" section later in this chapter), many experienced operators use the Save As command as a backup strategy in case the current session document should become corrupted for any reason. They append the date, time, or version number to successive versions of the same session (for example, MySession_01, MySession_02, or MySession_Sept20, MySession_Sept21). This not only protects you against file damage (although you need to be saving incremental backups of your important work files anyway) but also gives you a specific "go back" state for your project, in case you make any mistakes or bad decisions … or clients change their minds!

For users with extremely limited tracks or DSP power on their systems, it can be practical to bounce out submixes from a session, create a new copy using Save Session As, import the submix, eliminate source tracks bounced to disk in the submix (or merely disable them using the Track > Make Inactive command), and then start recording more overdubs. Because you created the session using the Save Session As command, both the previously existing and new audio files reside together in a single Audio Files folder.

Save Copy In

This command saves a snapshot of the current session document (even in a completely different location) without leaving the session document that's currently open or changing its name. If you close the current session and then open this other copy, any subsequent audio recordings or fade files will be stored within that session's own Audio Files and Fade Files folders. (When using Save Copy In, always be sure to create a new folder for that session copy to reside in, to keep things orderly.) You could also use the Save Copy In command simply as a method for saving snapshots of the work in progress without changing the main session file name you're still using (as would be the case with the Save As command). This is also the command you will use for saving Pro Tools 8 sessions (with the .ptf extension on the session file name) to earlier formats, such as for Pro Tools 6 (with the .pts extension) or Pro Tools 5 (with the .pt5 extension).

The Save Session Copy dialog box (shown in Figure 8.1), which opens when you choose the Save Copy In command, also provides several other important options. For example, you can choose to save audio files for the session copy in 24-bit or 16-bit format or choose a different sample rate. When saving back to Pro Tools format 5.1–6.9, enabling the Enforce Mac/PC

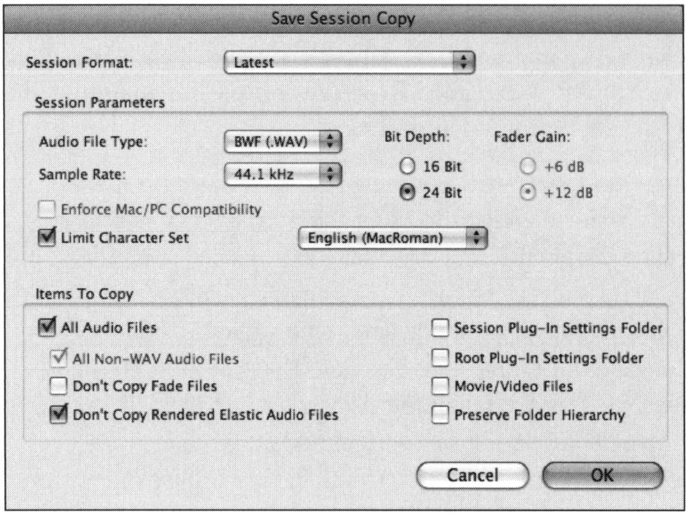

Figure 8.1 The Save Session Copy dialog box.

Compatibility option facilitates opening this session from either Mac or Windows, especially in versions prior to 6.7. You can choose whether the maximum gain boost permitted by track volume faders in the new session copy is +12dB or +6dB. (This is necessary only if session compatibility with versions prior to 6.4 is a concern. However, be aware that any existing fader settings over +12dB will automatically be reduced to +6dB.) Sessions can even be saved back to Pro Tools version 5.0 or 4 (and 3.2 on Mac versions). In this case, the total track count in your session may change, since these older versions don't support stereo or multi-channel tracks.

The Items to Copy section at the bottom of this dialog box provides further options:

■ **All Audio Files.** Selecting this option duplicates the Audio Files folder *and its entire contents* to the folder where you save the session copy. If you choose a different sample rate or bit depth from the current session, this option is automatically enabled because the new session copy will require all audio files it references to be at the same resolution. The new session file copy will reference the new Audio Files folder created by this operation—that is, all audio regions in the new session's audio tracks and Regions List refer to the new file copies rather than to the originals. But whether or not you enable this option to copy the audio files, in the new session created by the Save Copy In command, all subsequently created audio files or fades will be stored into their own Audio Files and Fade Files folders. There is also a Don't Copy Fade Files option (these can be regenerated or relinked when you open that session copy); in Pro Tools versions 7.4 and higher, a Don't Copy Rendered Elastic Audio Files option is also available.

Tip: When copying all audio files from a source session, it can save time and disk space if you take a moment beforehand to identify unused files/regions and apply the Clear Selected command in the local menu of the Regions List, as well as apply its Compact command on some of the remaining whole-file regions.

- **Session Plug-In Settings Folder.** Selecting this option copies plug-in settings from the current session to a new folder, which will be referenced in the new copy. This ensures that the plug-in presets for that session continue to appear by name (and are available for assignment to additional instances of those plug-in types) when you open this session on another system supporting the same plug-in architecture.

- **Root Plug-In Settings Folder.** Selecting this option copies the main Plug-In Settings folder into a subfolder of the disk/folder location where you create your session copy, named Plug-in Settings Folder. This is also useful when moving sessions from one Pro Tools system to another because all saved plug-in settings (for example, a favorite compressor or EQ setting that you generally use for the same voice) can then be recalled by name on the new system, whether used in the current session or not. (The same plug-in and plug-in architecture must be available on that system. TDM plug-ins, for example, are omitted when an HD or TDM session is opened on a system that only supports RTAS plug-ins, such as Pro Tools LE or M-Powered.)

- **Movie/Video Files.** If you have imported a digital video file into your Pro Tools session, this option copies it into the new session's folder (and the new session will point to this new copy of the video). Otherwise, the new session copies continue to reference video files in their original locations.

- **Limit Character Set.** This is automatically enabled when saving to older session formats; it is especially relevant when saving sessions to or from Japanese, Chinese, or Korean character sets.

It should be noted that when opening a Pro Tools 8 session with any 7.*xx* version of the software, the newly introduced features will not be available. Thus, certain displays of data or altered audio files will not be accessible. This includes Elastic Pitch, Region Ratings, the Chords Ruler, MIDI and Score Editor windows, Playlist views used for compositing, edit and timelock settings, and inserts F–J.

Saving Pro Tools 8 Sessions to Older Formats The session compatibility between Pro Tools 8 and 7.4*xx* is close enough that the Save Session Copy dialog box does not give you a choice to resave to version 7.4*xx*, only to 6.*xx* and earlier. Obviously, you can't retain many of the features introduced in Pro Tools 8 when you save a session back to 6.*xx* format, much less 5.*xx* or earlier. When you use the Save Copy In command to save a session back to 5.1–6.9 formats, the following occurs:

- Pro Tools 8 enables you to use file names with as many characters as your operating system supports. For previous versions, however, those file names are shortened to 31 characters, including the file-name extension. This affects the session file name; more importantly, any source audio file names that exceed this limit are truncated and placed into a new folder called Converted Audio Files.

- Sends F–J are dropped, along with any associated automation for them (versions 6.9 and earlier only support five sends per track).

- In LE and M-Powered sessions, busses 17–32 are omitted, since only 16 busses were supported in previous versions (versus 128 in the HD version of Pro Tools).

- Region groups are omitted, as are region loop aliases.

- Markers/memory locations 201–999 are dropped (only 200 are supported in 6.9 and earlier).

- Sample-based MIDI regions and tracks are dropped. Both the sample-based MIDI track and the regions it contains are completely deleted from the session.

- Instrument tracks are split into separate Aux Input and MIDI tracks.

- VCA Master tracks are deleted after their results are automatically coalesced into the affected tracks.

- Regions on audio tracks that have been warped using Elastic Audio will revert to their original timings, playing back unwarped.

- While versions 7.4 and higher support all Unicode characters, when saving back to older session formats in Japanese, Chinese, and Korean, you should enable the Limit Character Set checkbox and choose the appropriate language.

Revert to Saved

This command reverts the session to its previous state as saved on disk, undoing all changes since the last time you saved it. However, as Pro Tools will warn you, you cannot undo some operations. For example, if, while using the Regions List menu's Clear Selection command, you opt to delete a selected audio file completely from disk, you can't use the Revert to Saved command to get it back!

The Open Recent Command (Versions 7.3 and Higher) Command+O (Alt+O in Windows) accesses the Open file dialog box, where you can choose any Pro Tools session. However, if you add Shift to this keyboard shortcut, the most recent session in the Open Recent submenu is opened directly. Learn this shortcut!

Bounce to > Disk

The most typical use of this command is to create a single new audio mix file (or multiple mono files) of the entire Pro Tools session (or the current timeline selection, as shown in the Transport window's Start and End fields) in real time—including all plug-in processing, automation, auxiliary inputs, and other factors that affect the mix you're currently hearing through the main mix output. You choose the desired audio output path to use as the source for your bounced mix, and you can specify a variety of file formats and resolutions for the resultant audio file. (See Chapter 16, "Bouncing to Disk, Other File Formats," for more detailed information.) You will often use Bounce to Disk to save out stereo files for CD mastering, stereo or mono mix files for video editors, interactive authors, and so on.

If you've chosen a multichannel audio output path as the source for your bounce (for example, a surround mix), in addition to stereo and mono, the pop-up Format selector in the Bounce dialog box has a multiple mono option. One audio file is created for each mono subpath in your surround mix. When you select a stereo bus or output pair as the source for the bounce, you can also create split stereo files (pairs of mono files, with .L or .R inserted into their file names) using the multiple mono option. This is the best choice if you're planning to enable the Import After Bounce checkbox to automatically re-import bounced files into your current session (for instance, if you're bouncing in order to submix tracks, freeing up voices or DSP resources). Interleaved stereo files must be split into separate left and right mono file copies to be usable from within a Pro Tools session.

You can also use the Bounce to Disk function to "print" tracks to disk (after soloing them, or muting other unwanted tracks), incorporating all their current effects processing and automation. In very large or complex sessions, you might max out the digital signal processing (DSP) capacity your CPU and/or Pro Tools HD hardware provides. Bouncing one or more tracks to disk (or submixing multiple tracks) and then re-importing the bounced files into your session is one way to free up DSP resources for additional tasks on a slower system, and is also a convenient method for loop creation.

Yet another option is to choose any active bus (mono, stereo, or multichannel) in your Pro Tools session as the source for your bounce. If you enable display of the Master Fader for that bus, its (post-fader) effects will be included in the bounced mix.

Loud Is Good, Louder Is Better? Careful use of gain-optimization plug-ins like Digidesign's Maxim, and L1, L2, or L3 from Waves, can ensure that your mixes are peaking at the maximum possible output level without digital *clipping* (signal overload, which distorts the audio waveforms by cutting off their peaks). Nevertheless, for burning one-off CDs or turning mix files over to a video editor (as well as preparing a final music mix for mastering), it *can* sometimes be convenient and prudent to normalize bounced mixes.

Peak-mode normalization (as opposed to RMS mode) is very straightforward: It finds the peak level within the audio file and adjusts that to whatever level you designate. (If 100% is "full code," or 0dB, then 94.4% is equivalent to −.5dB. For bouncing out music mixes, it's recommended to normalize somewhere between this and a more conservative −2dB, which is just under 71% on an absolute scale, in order to prevent clipping during sample-rate conversion. This is also good advice for avoiding potential distortion on some older CD players!) As a result of the normalization process, the level in the rest of the audio file changes proportionally … including any previously inaudible background noise if the normalization parameters you specify dramatically increase the file's level (beware!). Still, if you're trying to get gigs, local airplay, or 30 seconds of attention from an agent or record-company rep, it's always a good thing if your CDs aren't dramatically softer than everyone else's!

Contrary to what you might hear, however, normalizing does *not* "decrease your dynamic range" or make everything slam up against maximum level all the time (which *can* definitely be the case when gain optimization, maximizer plug-ins, or even conventional limiters are abused!). As a matter of fact, as pointed out in Chapter 15, "Sound Design for Interactive Media," normalization is frequently used to make the peak levels of entire batches of files more consistent, often effectively *reducing* their original level—for example, when creating large collections of button sounds or background effects that should be uniformly lower in volume than accompanying voice-overs in a multimedia project. Again, Chapter 16 goes into much more detail about bouncing files to disk in other formats and the use of normalization.

It is always best to optimize your mix output levels in the 32-bit mixing environment (48-bit if working on an HD system) of Pro Tools itself by adjusting track and Master Fader levels prior to bouncing to disk (as opposed to normalizing a mix file that has already been reduced to 16 bits). If someone else will be doing the final mastering on your mix, mastering engineers *always* prefer that you do not normalize or apply your own aggressive dynamics processing to the supplied mixes (including plug-ins on the Master Fader for the mix output) because this severely limits their options!

You can even normalize a bounced mix without leaving Pro Tools:

1.   Select Multiple Mono as the file format and enable the Import After Bounce checkbox in the Bounce dialog box. (The audio file type, bit-depth resolution, and

sample rate must match that of the source session for this option to be enabled.) Click to highlight the new stereo file pair that appears in the Regions List after the bounced mix is re-imported. Select AudioSuite > Other > Normalize. In the Normalize dialog box, select Regions List (instead of Playlist), and the Overwrite Files option (instead of Create Individual Files). As mentioned, it's safer to choose a peak level of 94.4% (−.5dB) or even less to leave a little bit of headroom and possibly avoid distortion on older CD players. Finally, click the Process button.

2. If the audio CD recording program you're using doesn't support split mono source files, you still have to convert these two mono files into a stereo file. With the .L and .R split audio files for your normalized stereo mix still selected in the Regions List, select Export Regions as Files in the Regions List's local menu. Choose AIFF or WAV as the file type, stereo format, 44,100 (44.1kHz) sample rate, and 16-bit resolution (unless you're using one of the more sophisticated CD-creation programs that include their own options for sample-rate and bit-depth conversion, in which case you would bounce at the native resolution of your source session).

For those who prefer to use a separate program to normalize or perform final trimming on stereo or mono bounced mixes, here are some common options (which also offer many other processing and conversion features):

■ **Mac:** Peak Pro (Bias), Soundbooth CS3 (Adobe), Cleaner (Autodesk), Audacity (open source freeware), and Cacophony (shareware, by Richard F. Bannister)

■ **Windows:** Sound Forge (Sony; formerly Sonic Foundry), WaveLab (Steinberg), Nero Ultra (Nero AG), Soundbooth CS3 (Adobe), Audition 3 (Adobe), Cleaner XL (Autodesk), and Audacity (freeware originally developed by Dominic Mazzoni, with subsequent contributions from many others)

Bounce to > QuickTime Movie

In a similar fashion to the Bounce to > Disk command, this command bounces the session's audio mix (or currently selected range) directly into a new copy of the QuickTime video file currently in use in this session. 48kHz is the most common sample rate for professional video applications. For multimedia applications, some interactive authors (especially those whose applications don't support more current codecs such as MP4 or good data-compression codecs for audio inside their video files) may request a lower sample rate for the audio in their Quick-Time movies (like 22,050Hz or even 11,025Hz) in order to keep file size and throughput requirements to a minimum. See Chapter 15 for more information.

Import Submenu

This menu offers options for importing audio files and regions, MIDI files, video files (and audio soundtracks from within them), as well as region groups. You can also import track data from other Pro Tools sessions.

Import > Session Data

Use this command, which opens the Import Session Data dialog box (see Figure 8.2), for importing tracks and other data from other Pro Tools sessions into the current one. You can reference the source audio and video files for tracks you're importing from the other session at their original location (via the Refer to Source Media selection in the pop-up selectors for Audio and Video Media Options) or copy those files into the current session's Audio Files folder (via the Copy from Source Media option). The Consolidate from Source Media selection, seen in the figure, has an effect similar to the Compact command in the local menu for the Regions List.

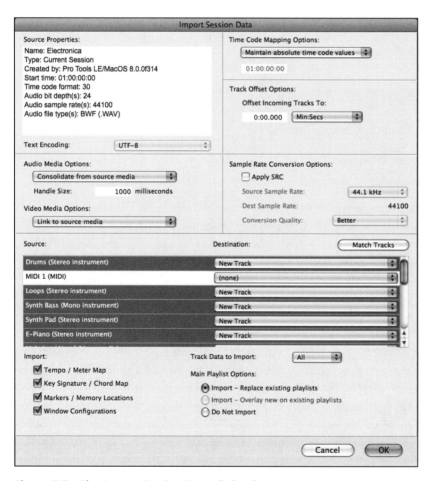

Figure 8.2 The Import Session Data dialog box.

It copies only the utilized portions of the imported track's audio files, with the "handle" size providing a padding factor in case you need to slightly lengthen any of its regions afterward. If necessary, you can convert the file type, sample rate, and bit depth of source audio files to those of the current session.

Location of regions and events in the newly imported tracks can be identical to the absolute time references in their original session, adjusted relative to those of the current session, or offset by a given amount. For music and soundtrack work, you can even import the tempo/meter map and markers from the source session, as well as key-signature events and window configurations (in versions 7.3 and higher). Tempo events, markers, and key-signature events could be handy, for example, when you bring various work sessions for musical segments into the final master session for a film or video soundtrack.

Saving Session Templates In Appendix D, "Power Tips and Loopy Ideas," you will find instructions for saving session templates. Both this and importing session data from other "boilerplate" Pro Tools sessions are important time-saving techniques that you will want to incorporate into your working style.

Import > Audio, Import > MIDI

These File menu commands are used for importing audio files and standard MIDI files. In all Pro Tools versions 7.3 and higher, after you select one or more source audio or MIDI files and then click the Done button in the dialog box shown in Figure 8.3 (and after specifying the destination audio files folder, if applicable), a second dialog box will appear. In this Audio (or MIDI) Import Options dialog box, if you click the Regions List button, new regions simply appear there without being placed onto any track—just as with the Import Audio command in older versions of Pro Tools. These new region names will be based on the source file name and, in the case of a standard MIDI file, the MIDI track names within it. If you choose New Track instead, a new audio track is created for each imported audio file, or a new MIDI track for each MIDI channel within the Standard MIDI File (SMF) file you import. The audio or MIDI regions are automatically placed into these new tracks; likewise, the new track names reflect the names of the source files.

The Location pop-up selector in the Audio Import Options dialog box (shown in Figure 8.4) determines where these new regions will appear within your newly created tracks:

- Session Start is similar to the behavior in all previous versions of Pro Tools in that it places the imported file at the earliest existing point in the timeline.

- Song Start corresponds to the current position of the Song Start marker (which typically might indicate where bar 1 occurs after some pickup bars or some other sort of intro).

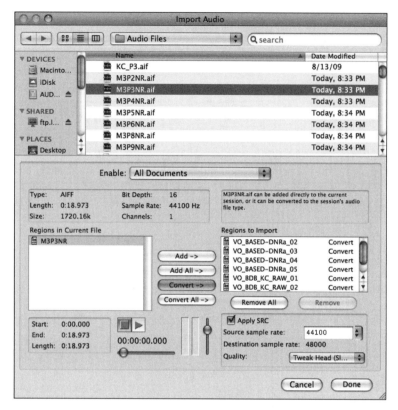

Figure 8.3 The Import Audio dialog box enables you to import entire audio files or regions within them. You can also preview audio files here.

- Selection places the newly imported regions at the current location of the edit cursor or the beginning of the current selection.

- Spot opens the Spot dialog box, where you can specify the new location numerically or capture it from incoming time code.

For importing and previewing larger numbers of files, be sure to learn how to use the Workspace browser window; it enables you to browse the contents of disks on your system, dragging audio and MIDI files directly into the Regions List or Tracks List.

MIDI Import Options. In versions 7.3 and higher of Pro Tools, the MIDI Import Options dialog box offers some additional flexibility for bringing Standard MIDI File (SMF) files into the current Pro Tools session. When the Regions List button is selected here, a separate region will be added to the Regions List for each MIDI channel that actually contains data—just as in previous versions of Pro Tools. However, additional MIDI import options (shown in Figure 8.4) give you more control. If you import the Tempo map from the incoming MIDI file, any tempo and meter

Figure 8.4 In versions 7.3 and higher of Pro Tools, these dialog boxes for Audio and MIDI Import Options offer flexibility when importing audio or standard MIDI files into the current session.

events already existing in your session will be overwritten. The same applies if you choose to import key-signature information (if any exists) in the MIDI file. Other checkboxes (as shown in Figure 8.4) allow for deletion of existing Instrument tracks, MIDI tracks, or regions, when appropriate.

Import > Video

Use this command to import digital video files in QuickTime, AVI, MPEG, and other formats into your Pro Tools session. The Video window displays this video during Pro Tools' playback and freezes the movie's current frame wherever you stop the Transport. A Video track is also created in the Edit window, where the movie can be seen as a region block or as individual video frames. (Be aware that the system overhead for redrawing all these thumbnails—called *picons*, or picture icons by Digidesign—as you zoom in and out can slow your pace in the Edit window. You can improve the speed of screen operations by setting the Video track to Blocks display format most of the time, except when you specifically want to use these thumbnails for spotting events.) Many professionals prefer to dedicate a separate video card/monitor and hard drive for video playback.

The imported digital video files will play back in the Video window, in sync with the Pro Tools Transport functions. Users who create video soundtracks and interactive sound designers who create audio for video files will definitely appreciate these nonlinear video-playback features. You can jump around in the session's timeline, with the Video window and Video track (whose default view option displays small thumbnails of individual video frames) serving as a frame-accurate reference for *spotting* audio events to specific locations.

As you can guess, using an onscreen digital video file as your master can be extremely useful when collaborating with video editors (for example, users of Avid Media Composer, Media 100, Adobe Premiere, or FinalCut Pro). This is all discussed in more detail in Chapter 14, "Postproduction and Soundtracks," and in Chapter 15. Here's a brief overview of a typical work process (when *not* using one of the Avid hardware options for video with Pro Tools):

1. The editor exports a low-resolution video for you to use in Pro Tools. This should be full frame rate, but with the image compressed to a much smaller size and data rate (generally, 320×240 pixels or less is fine). This is so that video playback doesn't clobber Pro Tools' performance . Obviously, you want the video editor to provide full-resolution, uncompressed *audio* inside this video file. If you're a newcomer to audio for video, don't overlook the fact that audio soundtracks in video-editing systems (and PCM audio tracks in professional video-tape formats) typically use a 48kHz sampling rate! Generally, your Pro Tools session also should be set to this rate.

2. Bring this digital video file into your session via the File > Import > Video command. In the Video Import Options dialog box, you can choose to import the audio soundtrack of that video file, if it contains one. A Video track is created automatically, and the Video window opens. (In Pro Tools versions prior to 7.3, a second step was required to import the soundtrack from the video file, via the File > Import > Audio from Current Movie command.)

3. You can now do a complete audio postproduction on their project—music, sound effects, and dialog or voice-over—without requiring a video deck in your setup at all. Furthermore, because of the frame-accurate display in the Video track, extremely precise placement of sound effects and other audio events is easy.

4. After you finish the soundtrack, there are several options for returning this finished mix to the video editor. You could simply use the File > Bounce to > Disk command to give the video editor stereo, 48kHz files for the entire soundtrack (in AIF or Broadcast WAV audio file format, for example). If you have the optional DigiTranslator program (which is not compatible with Pro Tools M-Powered), you might instead export an OMFi file if the video-editing system supports this interchange format. A third option is to bounce your audio mix into a new copy of the original video file using the File > Bounce to > QuickTime Movie command, also discussed in this section.

Import > Region Groups

Region groups were introduced with version 7 of Pro Tools. Once you create a region group from currently selected regions (via the Region > Group command), you can treat it as a single object while editing. Region groups can span multiple tracks, even if they are not in contiguous order in the Edit window. Other commands in the Region menu allow ungrouping and regrouping regions. As soon as you create any region groups, a Region Groups subfolder is created for the current session. You can use a command in the local menu of the Regions List to export region groups as separate files, which you can then import into other sessions via the Import > Region Groups command.

Edit Menu

Obviously, you're going to find the Cut, Copy, Paste, and Clear commands here, plus Select All and your best friend in the whole world: the Undo command! The Edit menu also includes many of the key functions you will use for editing regions. Here we will review only recently changed or most essential selections.

Cut/Copy/Paste/Clear Special

The "special" versions of these basic editing commands enable you to apply them only to automation in the Edit window or, even more specifically, only to pan or plug-in automation. The Repeat to Fill Selection command enables you to automatically paste the required number of repetitions of the audio or MIDI data currently in the clipboard to fill the current track selection. When MIDI data is in the clipboard, another Paste > Special command enables you to merge it into the existing MIDI data at the destination (instead of replacing it as with the normal Edit > Paste command).

Selection Submenu

Especially if you occasionally unlink the edit and timeline selections while editing your Pro Tools tracks, you will want to learn the keyboard shortcuts for two important commands in this submenu:

- **Play Edit.** Play Edit plays back the current edit selection (the range between the Start and End fields at the top of the Edit window, which updates automatically to reflect what's currently selected in your tracks). Its keyboard shortcut is Command+[(left bracket), or Ctrl+[in Windows.

- **Play Timeline.** Play Timeline plays back the current timeline selection (the range between the Start and End fields in the Transport window). Its keyboard shortcut is Command+] (right bracket), or Ctrl+] in Windows.

Other commands here enable you to change the timeline selection to match the edit selection, and vice versa.

Duplicate, Repeat

Too many users overlook these commands. Duplicate makes one copy of the current selection immediately following its current position, even if the selection is on multiple tracks. Repeat does the same thing, but lets you specify how many copies you want—for example, 15 more copies of a four-bar drum loop you've just dropped into the track. If the currently highlighted selection in any track is only some portion within a longer region, a new region definition is created in the process. In contrast, if an entire region is selected, these commands simply create additional instances of the same region within their tracks. Naturally, if you're in Shuffle edit mode, any material that follows the current selection within the track(s) will be pushed back later in the track by a corresponding amount.

That said, for repeating ambient or musical loops, the Region > Loop command (discussed later in this chapter) offers a much more effective method. If you're new to Pro Tools or to version 7 or higher, be sure to learn how to use this feature.

Shift

Shift is another underused command. It opens a dialog box for moving the current selection (even on multiple tracks) earlier or later in the track. You can specify the amount of displacement for the selection in Bars:Beats, Minutes:Seconds, or Samples time-scale format (as well as SMPTE time code or Feet.Frames, if these time-scale formats are available in your version of Pro Tools). If your selection is within an existing region or if its new location will overlap existing regions in the track, new region definitions are created as necessary.

Tip: Although you *can* use the Shift function on all the tracks in your session simultaneously, the Insert Time tab of the Time Operations dialog box offers a much more effective and flexible way of achieving this.

Trim Region Submenu

The Trim to Selection command (whose keyboard shortcut is Command+T, or Ctrl+T in Windows) replaces the current region with a new region definition based on the currently highlighted portion within it. This is another of the most-overlooked commands in Pro Tools! After you have selected the Trimmer tool and dragged both the beginning and end inward on about 10,000 regions, you might want to think about finally incorporating this shortcut into your routine. On MIDI tracks in Notes display format, you can also use Trim to Selection to crop beginnings or ends of MIDI notes to the boundaries of the current selection.

The Trim Start/End to Insertion commands are fairly simple: The left or right boundaries of one or more currently selected regions are trimmed (cropped) to the current location of the Selector tool's insertion cursor. You can use the Trim Start/End to Fill Selection commands when multiple regions are selected in the same track(s). Each region's start/end is extended to adjoin the boundary of the previous/next region in the track. Alternatively, highlight an additional range of time before or after a single region, and the Trim Start/End to Fill Selection command extends the boundary of the region definition up to that point.

Separate Region Submenu/Heal Separation

After making a selection within an existing audio or MIDI region, you can give that selection a name (create a new region definition) using the Separate Region > At Selection command.

A new region name is inserted within the existing region on the track. (As required, additional region names are created for portions of the existing region before and after the newly separated region name.) This command is handy when you're planning to drag the new region elsewhere. You will also notice two variations on the basic Separate Region command in this submenu: On Grid splits the new regions at the nearest grid value increment, while At Transients creates the split at the nearest transient peak in an audio region.

Note: The Capture Region command in the Region menu serves a similar function. The only difference is that while the Separate Region commands insert the new region definition into the track, Capture Region merely adds it to the Regions List.

Another Way to Create Region Definitions from the Current Selection Copying any track selection within an existing region also automatically creates a new region definition in the Regions List, even if you *don't* paste that selection afterward. This can be a very quick way to create a series of new region definitions, using the Command+C shortcut, or Ctrl+C in Windows.

Heal Separation restores an audio selection that was split using the Separate Region command—as long as its segments are still in their original, adjacent locations and haven't been moved. Separate Region operations are non-destructive; the original region name still exists and resides in the Regions List. Region definitions are merely pointers (references) to sections of audio within the parent sound files.

Strip Silence

The basic Strip Silence mode breaks up currently selected audio regions into smaller ones, omitting sections where the audio level falls below the specified Audio Threshold value. (This threshold is typically *not* complete silence; there may be low-level background noise, bleed from other microphones, and so on.) In the Strip Silence window (shown in Figure 8.5), the Min Strip Duration setting establishes the minimum size, in milliseconds, of the regions to create when the Strip Silence function is applied to the selection (because an excessive number of extremely short regions would be cumbersome). The Region Start Pad and Region End Pad leave that specified amount of silence appended to the boundaries of the resultant regions, providing a cushion to ensure that you don't drastically cut off soft attacks, low-level breath intakes, finger noise, decays, or other low-level sounds that might otherwise get completely eliminated at the specified threshold audio level for the Strip Silence function. As you adjust all these parameters, you'll see a preview of the results in the Edit window. Because Strip Silence is a non-destructive process (it merely creates new region definitions—the original, longer region is still intact in the Regions List), you can always make adjustments afterward by trimming or editing the new regions it has created on the track.

Figure 8.5 The Strip Silence window. The basic function breaks longer regions into a greater number of smaller ones by eliminating sections where the audio level falls beneath the specified threshold.

While the Strip and Rename buttons were present in older versions, the Extract and Separate modes were introduced in Pro Tools version 7. Extract is the inverse of the ordinary Strip Silence mode: Only those portions of audio that *aren't* above the threshold (and within the minimum duration or padding amounts) are left in the track. As the *Pro Tools Reference Guide* points out, this can be useful for extracting room tone, amp buzz, or background noise for some other use. The Separate mode leaves everything intact in the track but applies a variant of the Separate Region command so that the "keeper" and "stripped" portions are split into separate, adjacent regions.

Consolidate

The Consolidate command is very useful: It creates a new region (and a new audio file, on audio tracks) based on the current track selection (containing multiple regions) and substitutes it for the original selection. If multiple tracks are selected, Consolidate creates new regions in each. Because the new region also contains any silence that was between regions or preceded them, Consolidate also can be handy for creating new region definitions that begin (or end) right on a bar line or ¼ note, even if they contain silence at the beginning. This simplifies dragging regions around in Grid edit mode, for example, or using the Edit menu's Duplicate and Repeat commands if their duration corresponds to an even number of bars or beats.

You should bear in mind that any fade-ins or fade-outs (but not automation) on the selected regions will be permanently incorporated into new regions created by the Consolidate command. If you're dealing with an audio event that consists of numerous short regions strung together in a track (maybe a four-bar drum phrase cobbled together out of various sections, or a sound-effect sequence) and will be used at various other locations in the session, it can be a hassle to select and drag around so many small pieces. Instead, you could select the whole event and then consolidate it into a single region using the Consolidate command. (However, the Region > Group command offers a more efficient alternative for this scenario.)

Mute/Unmute

Muting and unmuting individual regions within a track (rather than the entire track) enables you to experiment without making the commitment of removing these regions from their original track locations. In the Edit window, muted regions appear dimmed (grayed out). You can use the keyboard shortcut Command+M (Ctrl+M in Windows) to mute/unmute selected regions.

Fades

Creating fade-ins, fade-outs, and crossfades on audio regions is discussed in many places in this book. New Pro Tools users very quickly learn to select the first or last portion of audio regions and then use the Command+F (Ctrl+F in Windows) keyboard shortcut to create fades using the dialog box shown in Figure 8.6. (Fades are actually separate audio files; each session has a sub-folder where these are stored. If the contents of this folder are ever missing or damaged, the next time you open that session, a dialog box offers you the option to re-create the missing fades.) Later, of course, fades can be lengthened or shortened with the Trimmer tool, double-clicked with the Grabber tool to edit their fade curves, and so on.

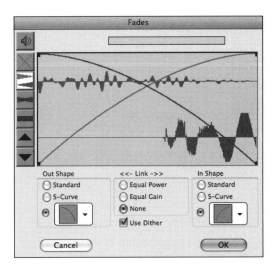

Figure 8.6   The Fades dialog box. Shown here, a crossfade between two adjacent audio regions.

Creating fade-ins, fade-outs, and crossfades for audio regions is a fundamental technique for working in Pro Tools. However, even many experienced users overlook the other commands in the Edit > Fades submenu—especially their keyboard equivalents. Although the submenu itself is a good way to start, you will save a lot of time by assimilating the following shortcuts:

■ When a portion of an audio region that includes its beginning or end is selected, Command+F (Ctrl+F in Windows) opens the Fades dialog box with a single fade-in or fade-out shape.

- When the selection crosses the boundary between two contiguous (adjoining) regions in the same track, this same keyboard shortcut also opens the Fades dialog box, but with both the fade-in and fade-out shapes (and the ability to link the two shapes so that changes in one are reflected in the other). You can use this for creating crossfades between those regions.

- After clicking with the Selector tool's I-beam cursor anywhere within an audio region, the Fade to Start command creates a fade from the region's beginning up to that point, using the default fade-in shape (which you can edit anytime afterward by double-clicking with the Grabber tool). The keyboard shortcut for Fade to Start is Option+D (Alt+D in Windows).

- The Fade to End command does the opposite, creating a fade from the insertion point to the *end* of the region using the default fade-out shape. The keyboard shortcut for Fade to End is Option+G (Alt+G in Windows).

- Default in, out, and crossfade shapes for fades can be changed in the Editing tab of the Preferences dialog box. Be sure to alter these preferences if the current default shapes aren't what you use most frequently!

View Menu

Options in the View menu enable you to optimize your screen display during each phase of a project. You can select items to be viewed in the Mix, Edit, and Transport windows; how sends are displayed; which Timebase rulers are visible; and what time units are used for the Main counter and main Timebase ruler. You can also choose whether you want names and/or various time values to be displayed within the regions on your Pro Tools tracks. All this merely serves to help you work more comfortably and efficiently and to manage the content of your sessions with ease. Some of the options are fairly self-explanatory or only need to be tried once for their purpose to be clear. For that reason, like other sections in this chapter, this section discusses only the key items in this menu.

Narrow Mix Window

This option makes all the mixer strips in the Mix window narrower, allowing more tracks to fit on the screen.

Mix Window/Edit Window Submenus

These options affect what items are visible in these windows. You may change this often, during different phases of your work on a project. Like other items in the View and Options menus, the most recently selected options here will also be initially enabled by default in sessions that are created with the File > New Session command (as opposed to opening a template document, for example). For instance, if the last saved session displayed the MIDI section of the Transport window, Transport buttons in the Edit window, and comments in the Mix window, the next new session you create will also have these options enabled.

By default, the Instrument section, located in the upper part of the Mix window, is not displayed. When you use Instrument tracks, the Mix Window > Instrument option enables display of these track controls (which include MIDI volume, pan, solo, and mute, and affect playback of MIDI data on that Instrument track).

In addition to (or instead of) their default location in the Mix window, some items can optionally be displayed in the Edit window: the Instrument, Inserts, Sends, Comments, I/O, and Real-Time Properties sections for each track. For example, if you rely mainly on *drawing* automation shapes for creating your mixes, displaying these track elements in the Edit window may enable you to spend almost all your time there—as long as your monitor is large enough that the added width this requires won't cramp your style. Otherwise, use the options in these submenus to optimize your use of screen space during each phase of a project.

You can also toggle display of track color strips (in the Mix and/or Edit window) in this submenu. On HD systems, you can enable Delay Compensation View here to display—and adjust for—the total amount of plug-in delay on each track.

Rulers Submenu

You use this submenu to select which Timebase ruler types are visible in the Edit window in addition to the main Timebase ruler: Bars:Beats, Minutes:Seconds, Samples, SMPTE Time Code (HD and DV-equipped LE systems only), and Feet.Frames (again, HD and DV-equipped LE systems only). Pro Tools LE systems equipped with the DV Toolkit 2 option can also display a secondary time-code ruler called Time Code 2. Remember that the format indicator at the left end of the ruler that represents the main time scale is always gray. By default, its units always correspond to the Main counter—changing units for the main ruler affects the Main counter, and vice versa. (Time units for the Sub counter can always be set separately, however.) When multiple rulers are enabled, just click in any one of their name plates to make it the main ruler. This also changes the default units for the Grid value and Nudge value, among other things. Alternatively, you can use the Main Time Scale pop-up selector to the right of the Main counter.

Other available rulers include Markers, Tempo, Meter, Chords, and Key Signature. The Tempo Editor (a pane underneath the Tempo ruler, where you can graphically edit tempo events) can be opened from this View > Rulers submenu, although it's quicker to just click the triangular Expand/Collapse button at the left side of the Tempo ruler's name plate. The Key Signature Staff can be opened beneath the main Key Signature ruler (available in versions 7.3 and higher) in a similar fashion.

Region Submenu

Here, you can choose what information is displayed within the regions in your Pro Tools tracks: the sync point symbol, warp indicator, processing state, region name, "dog-ear" overlap icon, current time, and original/user time stamp. Display of metadata from field recorders, such as Channel Name and Scene and Take, can also be enabled here (versions 7.3 and higher). New to Pro Tools 8 is also the ability to display rating numbers assigned from the Rating submenu in the Regions menu.

Sync Point

When this option is enabled, a small triangle indicates the location of sync points within regions in the Edit window. If a region has a sync point at a location other than at its beginning, this is the "hook" that will be adjusted to the nearest time increment in Grid edit mode (or to a specified time location in Spot mode) rather than the default sync-point location at the left boundary of the region itself.

Warp Indicator (Versions 7.4 and Higher)

The warp icon appears for audio regions upon which Elastic Audio processing has been performed by Pro Tools. For example, this icon appears for regions where you have edited Event or Warp markers while in Warp view mode or applied quantization, or on regions that have been automatically warped to conform to a tempo change. (Display of the warp icon can also be toggled on/off for audio regions in the Regions List.)

Overlap

Enabling this option displays a "dog-ear" edge (i.e., the corner is cut) on each region graphic that overlaps a single boundary of another region. Even though the edges of regions can overlap each other in the same track, only one of them can sound at a time. Two Region menu commands, Send to Back and Send to Front, are used in conjunction with this feature. The top-most region at any point is the one that is heard; when it ends, any underlying region that extends beyond that point will be again be audible. (It is worth noting here, however, that this applies only to cases where one edge of a region overlaps another. In contrast, when a longer region is placed so that it completely covers a short one already in the track, the previous region is removed from the track. Likewise, placing a shorter region completely within the boundaries of a longer region splits that long region into two new regions; it will remain that way even after you remove that shorter region from within its boundaries.)

Track Number

Pro Tools assigns numbers to tracks in ascending order from the top of the Edit window (or from the left of the Mix window, which amounts to the same thing). If you drag tracks into a different order in either window, numbers are reassigned automatically. Making track numbers visible is convenient when using the Track > Scroll to Track command.

Transport Submenu

The Transport submenu enables/disables display of three sections aside from the basic Transport buttons: counters (Main and Sub location indicators), MIDI controls (Metronome, Wait for Note, Countoff, Tempo, Meter, and others), Synchronization, and Expanded (if disabled, the lower section, with Pre/Post-Roll, Start, End, and Length fields, as well as the Sub counter and some MIDI controls, is not displayed). The range of time between the Transport window's Start and End fields determines what will be heard when you click Play or press the spacebar to initiate playback, and also what will be included in audio files created by the File > Bounce to Disk command.

Main Counter Submenu

These last selections in the View menu change the format of the main time ruler for the session: Bars:Beats, Minutes:Seconds, Samples, and, in Pro Tools HD, Time Code or Feet+Frames. (LE systems equipped with DV Toolkit 2 can also use Time Code units and Feet+Frames in the rulers.) If the desired ruler for one of these time formats is already visible in the Edit window, you can make it the main time ruler by clicking its format indicator; the name of the ruler that represents the main time scale is highlighted in grey.

Track Menu

Options here have to do with creating, duplicating, and grouping tracks, as well as deleting them or making them inactive. There are also options for splitting stereo tracks into mono, changing their input monitoring mode, and so on.

New (Tracks)

The New command (Shift+Command+N, or Shift+Ctrl+N in Windows; learn this keyboard shortcut!) opens the New Tracks dialog box (shown in Figure 8.7). The timebase for events in any track can be either *absolute* (Samples) or *relative* to musical bars and beats (Ticks). On tick-based tracks, events will be shifted to maintain their relative musical position if you alter the tempo of the Pro Tools session. You can change the timebase of tracks in the Edit window at any time, as well as the timebase for display of events for the session in general. However, a selector in the New Tracks dialog box assigns an initial timebase for each track as it's created.

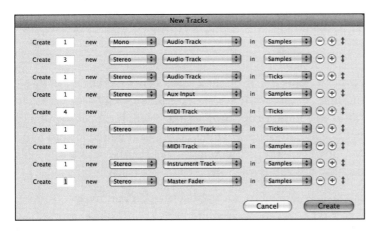

Figure 8.7 The New Tracks dialog box enables you to create multiple track types simultaneously.

The New Tracks dialog box enables you create many different types of tracks *simultaneously*— for example, multiple mono/stereo audio tracks, Aux Input tracks, Instrument tracks, Master Faders, and MIDI tracks. Just click the button with the plus sign (+), and a new row of fields appears for creating additional tracks of a different type. Some very useful keyboard shortcuts within this dialog box are explained in the "Editing Tips" section of Appendix D.

Note also that newly created tracks in your session are initially in the same order that they appeared in the New Tracks dialog box. Within the dialog box, you can use the button on the right end of each row to drag the rows into your preferred order before clicking the Create button. Keep this in mind; it may save you some time dragging your tracks around into the proper order afterward.

Group (Tracks)

When you group two or more selected tracks, their faders move together in the Mix window. Changes in track view and track selections in one track of the group can also be made in the others (as well as solo, mute, and other track controls, depending on which of these you have enabled for that group; eligible track controls for grouped operation differ between the HD and LE/M-Powered versions of Pro Tools). Any group-enabled automation type that you draw within a grouped track is also reflected in the others. Groups can be active in the Mix or Edit window only, or both (the default), and are managed in the Groups List at the left edge of the Mix and Edit windows. (This command, whose keyboard shortcut is Command+G, or Ctrl+G in Windows, also appears in the local menu of the Groups List.) Be sure to give your track groups meaningful names!

Split into Mono

Sometimes you need to separate a stereo track into two separate mono tracks. For example, even though you may have recorded a source into a single track with a stereo pair of microphones (a piano or acoustic guitar, for instance), there may be occasions when you would like to apply different plug-in processing to each side. The Track > Split Into Mono command creates the two new mono tracks, but leaves the original stereo track intact until you disable or delete it.

Make Inactive/Active

Even if you mute a track in Pro Tools, its audio/automation data—especially its sends and insert plug-ins—still consumes the same amount of your system's processing capacity for audio. In other words, a muted track still requires the same proportion of the available DSP, or digital signal processing, of your CPU and/or TDM audio cards. If you use the Make Inactive command to make the track completely inactive, however, the processing power for the selected track's plug-ins, sends, and audio playback is now available for other Pro Tools tracks.

If your system is underpowered for the task you need to accomplish (hey, it can happen to anyone sooner or later), you might find the Make Inactive command very useful. For example, say you're near the end of a complex project and have just decided that layering 10–12 additional backing vocal parts is just the ticket (or thicket, if you prefer!). But with all the existing tracks and effects already active in the session, after laying down just a few vocal parts, you may start to hear audio glitching and choppy playback if your system can't keep up with the demand. Of course, the first thing to check is your hardware buffer size in the Setup > Playback Engine dialog box, especially if you're an LE or M-Powered user. You may find, however, that this buffer size is already at the maximum, or that increasing it induces a delay for input monitoring that is unacceptable for the singers, who hear themselves back through the Pro Tools mixer. (This might be the case on LE and M-Powered systems where low-latency monitoring or the mix knob on the Mbox 2 family and some M-Audio interfaces isn't available, or where direct input monitoring through an external mixer, mic preamp, or the interface itself isn't a practical option.) In that case, take a look at which of your tracks are using the most processing-intensive plug-ins. Reverbs are obvious candidates, especially some of those gorgeous-sounding, CPU-hungry ones from third parties. You could try making the Aux Input tracks where these reverbs are instantiated inactive while tracking the backing vocals. Or perhaps you have a complex chain on some instrumental part, such as a third-party amp simulator, compressor, EQ, and then flanger on a lead guitar part. If you can do without hearing that part while tracking these voices, deactivating that track might free up enough of your DSP capacity.

After you finish, bounce your backing vocals to disk as a split stereo file (checking the Import After Bounce selection so that this mix file will be brought right back into this session on its own stereo track). Then select all those source backing vocal tracks and apply the Make Inactive command. If you ever change your mind about the balance in this vocal submix, you can simply use the Make Active command on those tracks again, and repeat the process.

> **Shortcuts for Making Tracks Inactive/Active** At the bottom of each mixer strip in the Mix window, each track type has a distinctive color icon just below its Mix Groups selector. Click this icon (Ctrl-click in Windows) to toggle any track to its active/inactive state. In the Edit window, the pop-up menu that appears when you Control-click (Start-click in Windows) on the track name (also accessible by right-clicking in versions 7.3 and higher) also allows for making one or more selected tracks active/inactive.

Delete

This command deletes the currently selected track(s) and any playlists (audio, MIDI, or automation) that they contain. However, after using the Delete (track) command, any audio or MIDI regions residing on the affected tracks will remain in the Regions List.

Write MIDI Real-Time Properties

This command permanently alters the MIDI data within regions on the affected track, applying the net results of the track's current real-time property settings to the MIDI events themselves. On MIDI and Instrument tracks, *track*-level real-time properties apply non-destructive changes to all MIDI played back through the track—for example, quantization, transposition, changes to velocity and duration, and so on.

> **Note:** There are also *region*-level real-time properties, which are applied prior to any real-time properties assigned to the MIDI or Instrument track itself. When you open the Real-Time Properties window for a selected MIDI region via the Event menu, a Write to Region

button enables you to permanently alter the contents of any currently selected regions, incorporating the results of the their current real-time properties settings. The Apply To selector in this window lets you toggle back and forth between region- and track-level properties. Its Write to Region changes to Write to Track if that's what you have selected in the Apply To field, and has the same effect as this Track menu command.

Input Only/Auto Input Monitoring

As the name implies, when Input Only monitoring is enabled, *only* input signal will be heard on any record-enabled tracks—regardless of whether a punch-in point exists and whether Record mode is engaged. In the "normal" Auto Input monitoring mode, when playback is *stopped*, you hear the input signal on any record-enabled audio tracks. Likewise, if you simply start recording without making any selection for punch in/out, you hear that record-enabled track's audio input. However, when recording a punch-in in Auto Input monitoring mode, you hear the pre-existing audio in the track before and after the punch-in point (which helps you match its level and timbre), and then the input source during the punched-in segment. Note that in the HD version of Pro Tools, each audio track has a TrackInput button, which toggles the track itself between Input Only (with the button enabled) and Auto Input (button disabled) modes. In Pro Tools HD, the effect of the TrackInput button is not affected by which mode you choose here in the Track menu.

Scroll to Track

Each track is assigned a number reflecting its current position: ascending from left to right in the Mix window, or top to bottom in the Edit window. To display these numbers, enable that option in the View menu. The Scroll to Track Number command scrolls the Edit or Mix window as necessary, so that the specified track is visible. This helps you get around in large sessions. Of course, in Pro Tools, you can drag tracks into any order, at any time, which changes their track numbers! The keyboard shortcut for the Scroll to Track Number command is Command+Option+F (Ctrl+Alt+F in Windows).

Clear All Clip Indicators

As mentioned in Chapter 7, "The Mix Window," and elsewhere, when the red clipping indicator lights up in the level meter for any track or plug-in window, it indicates that excess signal level may have overloaded and distorted the audio passing through it, clipping off the top of its wave-form at that channel's maximum level. You can click clip indicators to clear them, and Option-click (Alt-click in Windows) any clip indicator to clear *all* of them simultaneously. The Track > Clear All Clip Indicators menu command can also be used. Even more convenient (and worth memorizing!) is its keyboard equivalent: Option+C (Alt+C in Windows). These menu commands and keyboard shortcuts don't affect the clip indicators within plug-in windows, however; these must be clicked individually to be cleared.

Don't forget that, aside from the track output level determined by the main volume fader itself, the settings for each active plug-in on a track affect the level entering the next plug-in in the track's signal-processing chain. Additionally, the audio signal entering all sends (both pre- and post-fader) is subsequent to the entire Inserts section in a track's signal chain. Also, be sure to watch for clipping at your send destinations if your insert effects end up applying a significant amount of gain increase—for example, if you radically boost some frequency range with an EQ plug-in. To do this, either enable the Path Meter View panel in the send's Output window or, even better, create a Master Fader track for the bus path you're using for sends from multiple tracks.

Create Click Track

This command (available in all versions 7.3 and higher) automatically creates a mono Aux Input track with the Click plug-in enabled. If almost all of your sessions are music-related, an option in the MIDI tab of the Preferences dialog box allows automatic creation of a click track in each new session.

Region Menu

Region menu options affect both audio and MIDI regions currently placed in Edit window tracks. Learn their keyboard shortcuts early; you will probably be using some of these commands quite often.

Edit Lock/Unlock

When a region is locked, a small padlock graphic appears in its lower-left corner. You can't drag, trim, or delete edit-locked regions. Also, edit-locked regions won't be pushed aside as a result of moving other regions in Shuffle edit mode. You can still edit the automation that overlaps a locked region, though, or record over it (so always be especially careful when recording in Destructive Recording mode). As you can guess, edit locking a region protects you from yourself, and is definitely a feature you want to be familiar with. You can use the keyboard shortcut Command+L (Ctrl+L in Windows) to edit lock/unlock selected regions.

Time Lock/Unlock

The Time Lock command is similar to the Edit Lock command in that a region cannot be moved from its location. Time lock differs from edit lock in that it allows a region to be edited in any way that does not shift the region to another time, such as trimming and separating. In addition, unlike edit lock, a time-locked region can be deleted. Time-locked regions will not be displaced in Shuffle mode by any activity. The shortcut is Control+Option+L (Command+Alt+L in Windows).

Send to Back/Bring to Front

Pro Tools allows regions to be layered within a track (although only one audio region can play at a given time within a single track). With the View > Region > Overlap option enabled, a dog-ear icon on the upper corner of regions indicates where their boundaries overlap a single boundary of some other region underneath them in the same track. The top-most region always has priority; they can't both sound at once. The keyboard shortcuts for sending regions to the back/front are Option+Shift+B and Option+Shift+F (Alt+Shift+B and Alt+Shift+F in Windows), respectively.

Group/Ungroup/Ungroup All/Regroup

When you group multiple regions together, a new region group graphic is created, with a waveform representation of the regions it contains. This enables you to move a more complex group of audio events around as a single unit. By the way, it isn't even necessary for grouped regions to reside on adjacent tracks. As you can see in Figure 8.8, a rectangular region group graphic helps to distinguish region groups from individual regions on a track. When creating region groups, be sure to name them something meaningful for your project. They appear in the Regions List; from there, they can be dragged out into tracks and exported to disk for use in other sessions.

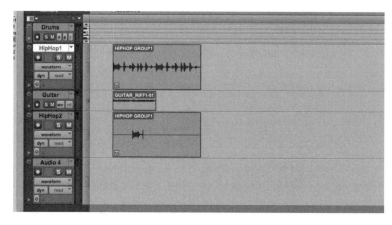

Figure 8.8 The "broken" region group graphics here indicate that the members of the GtrFX region group are on non-adjacent tracks. The looped arrows indicate that the region in the last track was looped via the Region menu command.

Loop/Unloop

You can use this command on audio regions, MIDI regions, and region groups. A specified number of loop *aliases* are created that mirror the original source region. In the Region Looping dialog box (see Figure 8.9), you can specify a duration and shape for crossfades between loop repetitions; this is especially useful for ambient, sustained, and background loops. Note that unlike the Duplicate and Repeat commands (when the Options > Automation Follows Edit option is enabled), the automation coinciding with the source loop is *not* copied along with the loop aliases. In contrast, selecting the Unloop command presents you with a dialog box in which you can choose to simply revert to a single instance of the source loop (Remove) or to flatten the loop (Flatten), which creates individual regions for each loop alias.

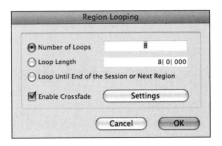

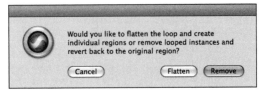

Figure 8.9 Options in the Region Looping dialog box enable you to control how many times the region or region group will repeat. When you unloop regions, you can either revert to the original or retain each repetition as a separate region copy.

Capture

This command creates a new region definition based on the current track selection. Unlike the Edit > Separate Region command, however, the new region(s) created by the Region > Capture command don't take the place of the current selection and split existing regions. Like Separate Region, you can use this command on mono, stereo, or multichannel tracks, as well as on multiple tracks simultaneously.

Identify Sync Point/Remove Sync Point

A *sync point* is a precise location within a region that will be used as the positional reference whenever that region is snapped to the nearest time increment in Grid mode (rather than the beginning of the region, which is the ordinary mode of operation). Likewise, in Spot mode, it's the sync point that's moved to the specified position (an SMPTE time-code location, for example), along with the rest of the region surrounding it.

You might think of the sync point as the hook used for positioning that region at specific timeline positions in Grid or Spot mode. By default, the sync point is always at the region's beginning. Identifying a new sync point within a region moves this hook to a new location.

In the Edit window, sync points within regions appear as small inverted triangles at the bottom of each rectangular region graphic. You can drag sync points with the Grabber tool to alter their locations within the region. You can also use the Scrubber tool to drag a sync point, providing audible feedback as you drag it within the audio waveform for audio regions.

Sync points are relevant both for music and during postproduction. Say you've got a spunky little backward-reverb snare sound you'd like to drop on the occasional backbeat. (Of course, it needs to actually begin *before* the backbeat, and fade up to it.) Position the Selector tool precisely at the peak of the backward sound (somewhere near the end), and then select the Region > Identify Sync Point command. You now see a small triangle at the bottom of the region, which indicates the location of the sync point within it. Now switch to Grid mode and select ¼ notes as the Grid value. When you drag this region to a specific ¼ note, the sync point, rather than the beginning of the region, is snapped into position. The backward snare ramps up to its loudest point right on the ¼ note, regardless of how much sooner this region's sound actually begins to fade in.

With regard to postproduction, one classic sync-point example is a train (or plane) passing through the video frame. You should hear it coming *before* the SMPTE time-code location where it actually enters the frame. However, as you position this sound effect, the point inside the audio region that interests you is that loudest moment, where the Doppler effect changes pitch. You want *that* point to coincide with where the train enters the picture. Again, use the Selector to position the cursor right at that loudest spot in the region and create a sync point. Based on your video master's time-code location (visible in its Transport or time-code window), use Spot mode to enter the exact reference where the train enters the frame. The sync point itself will be spotted to that time-code position, although the audio region for the oncoming train sound actually begins sooner.

Sync Points in the Edit Window The View > Region > Sync Point option enables you to choose whether sync points are visible within regions in the Edit window. You can drag sync points with the Grabber or the Scrubber tool. Their movement will be affected by Grid edit mode, if enabled.

Quantize to Grid

This menu command moves the beginning of all currently selected regions (audio or MIDI) to the nearest grid increment, according to the current grid value. However, for any region that contains a sync point, the sync point itself is moved to the nearest grid increment instead of the region's actual beginning (left boundary). The Quantize to Grid command does not alter region durations; it simply moves the regions. When used on MIDI regions, the command does not apply any quantization to notes contained within the MIDI region; they just get repositioned along with the region itself, maintaining their relative locations within its boundaries. (The Event Operations > Quantize command is used for adjusting individual note positions within MIDI regions and tracks!)

Elastic Properties (Versions 7.4 and Higher)

This menu command opens the Elastic Properties window for one or more selected audio regions (see Figure 8.10). You can open this window via a pop-up menu, accessible by right-clicking the region. Generally, you will only alter the Source Length and Source Tempo fields if you find that they have been calculated incorrectly by the Elastic Audio analysis when the audio file was imported. However, this analysis always assumes that all files are in 4/4 meter, so you will definitely want to change this if you know that a loop is in 3/4, 5/4, 7/8, or what have you. The Time Compression/Expansion field is for display only when viewing properties of regions on tick-based tracks, but can be changed manually on sample-based tracks. By reducing the

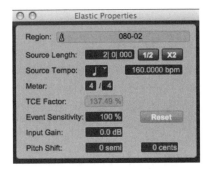

Figure 8.10 The Elastic Properties window for an audio region.

Event Sensitivity value, you can reduce the number of false transients detected by the elastic audio analysis. Lastly, especially if levels in your source regions are close to full-code (0dB), time compression can sometimes produce clipping; in that case, reducing the Input Gain value will resolve the problem.

Conform to Tempo (Versions 7.4 and Higher)

The Conform to Tempo command relates to Elastic Audio features, and can also be executed via the right-click pop-up menu for any audio region on a track with one of the Elastic Audio analysis modes enabled. For audio regions that were not automatically conformed to the session tempo upon import (for instance, if no Elastic Audio algorithm was enabled on that track when it was recorded, or the Pro Tools session was originally created in a version prior to 7.4), this command performs the Elastic Audio analysis, as confirmed by the Elastic Audio icon that appears afterward for the region both within tracks and in the Regions List.

Event Menu

This is where you will find the commands related to time and tempo operations, setting tempos according to track selections, creating time slices and groove templates for quantization, plus most of the MIDI-related operations in Pro Tools.

Time Operations Submenu: Change Meter, Insert Time, Cut Time, Move Song Start

All four of these operations open the Time Operations window, within which you can switch directly from one page to another. These features may be useful when the song you're going to record has multiple time signatures, you need more room in the timeline for an intro, or you need to move a music cue to a different time location while scoring a video or film. Because these are explained in more detail in Chapter 10, "MIDI," the following descriptions are relatively brief.

Change Meter

Use this command to insert a meter change into the Meter ruler. You can choose to have meter settings stay in effect through the end of the session, during the current selected range in the Pro

Tools timeline only, or only until the next bar. The Change Meter page of the Time Operations window also provides a pop-up selector to change the note value for the metronome click in the new meter. For example, the click could change from ¼ notes in a 4/4 time signature to ⅛ notes during a section in 6/8 time, and then revert back to ¼ notes for the remainder of the song. If a range of time is selected when you open the Change Meter page of the Time Operations window, you can also use this dialog box to change a given number of bars at one time signature to a different number of bars at another. Depending on what combination of bar numbers and time signatures you enter in these fields, some bars in the timeline may be added or deleted as a result. See the "Time Operations" section in Chapter 10 for more information.

Another Way to Insert Meter Changes in Pro Tools You can also insert meter changes using the Meter Change dialog box, which you can open by clicking the plus sign (+) in the Meter ruler or double-clicking the Meter field in the Transport window. As in the Change Meter page of the Time Operations window, you can either accept the current Start value as the location for the new meter change event or type some other location, and also change the note value for the metronome click.

Insert Time, Cut Time

The units for inserting or cutting time in these two pages of the Time Operations window always reflect those of the main Timebase ruler. You can choose whether the time shift is applied to tick-based (relative) and/or sample-based (absolute) tracks.

Move Song Start

This feature is especially handy for film and video scoring. For instance, suppose you've created an entire musical arrangement starting at the left edge of the Pro Tools timeline. In this window, you can quickly move the song beginning to a specific location—perhaps the Minute:Second or SMPTE time-code reference where this musical cue needs to begin in relation to the picture. Events in the Meter and Tempo rulers will shift accordingly. The Move Song Start page of the Time Operations window (shown in Figure 8.11) also enables you to specify that any bar number be assigned to the new location of the Song Start marker. This is useful if you worked out a musical arrangement but later decide you need to insert some pickup bars (or a full intro) before the beginning of the song proper, which should be identified as bar 1, beat 1.

If the timebase is set to Bars, you additionally have the option to move the Song Start marker without affecting the positions of any events in your tracks. Also, note the pop-up selector that lets you choose whether the positions of sample-based (absolute) markers and events in sample-based tracks should also be affected by the Move Song Start operation.

The Move Song Start function is described in more detail in the "Time Operations" section of Chapter 10. As described there, you can alternatively drag the Song Start marker to a new

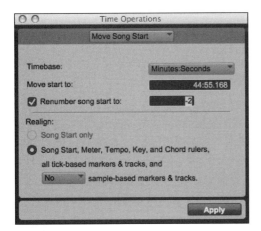

Figure 8.11   The Move Song Start page of the Time Operations window.

location in the Tempo ruler. Its movement will be affected by Grid edit mode, if enabled. When you change the Song Start setting by dragging this marker, any events in all MIDI, audio, Aux Input, Instrument, or Master Fader tracks whose timebase is set to Ticks will be adjusted to new positions in the timeline in order to maintain their previous relative position to the Song Start marker. (The previously mentioned option to move only the Song Start setting without affecting tick-based events is only available via the Move Song Start page of the Time Operations window shown in Figure 8.11.) Any markers whose reference is set to Bars:Beats (relative) rather than absolute will also change positions accordingly.

Additional Information about Time and Tempo Operations More details about changing meter and tempos, renumbering bars, and other music-related options are provided in Chapter 10.

Tempo Operations Submenu

The options in this submenu open the Tempo Operations window. (We discuss it only briefly here; more details are provided in the "Tempo Operations" section of Chapter 10.) You can use the Tempo Operations window to create a single tempo event or to apply a constant tempo over the currently highlighted range in the Edit window's timeline. Alternatively, you can apply a variety of curve shapes (line, parabola, S-curve, and so on) for increasing or decreasing the tempo over a range of time, in which case the result is a series of tempo events at the density specified in this window (see Figure 8.12). You can use the Scale page of the Tempo Operations window to increase or decrease an existing series of tempo events by percentage. The end point in minutes and seconds (or other ruler time units available on your system) are automatically calculated. As you can imagine, this can be very useful for soundtrack or jingle work!

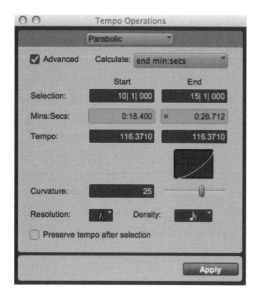

Figure 8.12 In the Tempo Operations window, you can create a variety of shapes to increase or decrease musical tempo over time.

The Stretch page of the Tempo Operations window can also affect an entire tempo map (a series of tempo events) within the currently selected portion of the session's timeline, adjusting all these relative tempos so that this selection's start or end point coincides with a desired time location. This is how you might adjust a complex underscore, with multiple tempo and time signature changes, so that it ends at precisely the close of a scene, minutes later. Remember that the location of events (including automation) in all MIDI, audio, Aux Input, Instrument, or Master Fader tracks whose timebase is set to Ticks is affected by tempo changes, as are any memory locations whose Reference attribute for Time Properties is set to Bars:Beats (rather than Absolute).

Event Operations Submenu

Obviously, many of the functions here, along with several other commands in the Event menu, are of most interest to people who use MIDI instruments (either external or software-based) with their Pro Tools configuration. All these menu selections open the Event Operations window. A pop-up field enables you to switch directly from one function's page to another. This window doesn't close after you apply each function—or successive iterations of the same function, like some percentage of quantization, for instance. Except for Quantize, which is equally applicable to audio regions and the events that have been detected within them by Elastic Audio analysis, the other commands act only upon MIDI data, within MIDI regions. Because there is an entire section dedicated to these MIDI functions in Chapter 10, we include just a few brief descriptions here.

Quantize (on MIDI Events)

This command snaps all notes within the current MIDI data selection to a specified rhythmic value. Make special note of the Strength parameter; if you set it to less than 100%, notes are not moved all the way to the specified quantization grid increment. This preserves some of the natural feel of your performance (assuming that's a good thing). The Swing parameter is also very useful for making your MIDI performances sound in time but not completely mechanical. For a subtle effect, start at about 10% and work from there.

Being able to add a swing factor to a straight quantization is great ($1/16$ notes, for instance), but for some music, you really need a more complex sort of grid for adjusting timing in order to accomplish specific feels. Various preset DigiGrooves are included in the pop-up Quantize Grid selector, along with the more conventional straight, dotted, and triplet note values. With Beat Detective, you can extract DigiGroove templates from audio selections, saving these either to the Groove Clipboard or as a DigiGroove template. Groove information can also be extracted from MIDI selections and applied to audio material (and vice versa).

To Learn More About Quantization and MIDI... More details about the Quantize feature and other options in the Event Operations menu that affect MIDI events are provided in Chapter 10.

Quantize (on Audio Regions)

One of the interesting aspects of the Elastic Audio features introduced in Pro Tools 7.4 is that after an audio region has been analyzed, in addition to the manual warping possibilities, the detected transient events within it can also be quantized in similar ways to MIDI note events. This includes not only even divisions of the beat as shown in Figure 8.13, but also swing factors and DigiGrooves that have previously been extracted from other MIDI or audio selections using Beat Detective. Just as when conforming audio files to various Pro Tools tempos, a large number of very short time compression/expansion operations are applied to ensure smooth playback after the timing of audio events within the region is adjusted.

Change Velocity and Change Duration

These transformations of MIDI notes are frequently used, especially the Add, Subtract, and Scale By methods.

Transpose

MIDI users will use this feature often. For example, you might select a group of notes or an entire region and select Transpose to transpose it up or down an octave (plus or minus 12 semitones) either because you're doubling another part at the octave or because you've changed to another sound on the MIDI module or software instrument plug-in playing this track's data and it's pitched in a different octave. For applying transposition to entire tracks or regions, however,

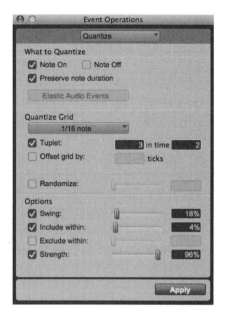

Figure 8.13   In versions 7.4 and higher of Pro Tools, Elastic Audio features permit events within audio regions to be quantized in a manner similar to MIDI notes.

the Real-Time Properties feature will usually be the better choice. When used in conjunction with Mirrored MIDI editing mode, if you change note events or controllers within the original MIDI region, these will be reflected immediately in other identically named copies of the same region, each with their own region-level transposition (and/or other real-time properties). In all versions 7.3 and higher, in conjunction with key-signature events, you can alternatively apply diatonic transposition—by a certain number of scale degree within the currently applicable key signature—in addition to the more traditional transposition by a fixed number of semitones.

Select/Split Notes

The Select Notes and Split Notes functions are combined into a single dialog box, shown in Figure 8.14. Select Notes enables you to select only notes within a given pitch range or the top/bottom notes of each chord. After making this selection, you can drag the selected notes, copy them, apply velocity or duration changes, and so on. You might be able to accomplish the same thing by drawing a rectangle around many different notes with the Grabber tool (holding down the Shift key to select/deselect additional notes), but it would be awfully cumbersome! The Split Notes feature is also useful for composing and arranging. The options for Split Notes are identical to Select Notes, except for the additional options in the lower half for cutting or copying notes that meet the pitch criterion. This places those note events onto the Clipboard so you can paste them elsewhere: directly into a new track or split onto multiple new tracks by pitch (useful for splitting drum parts onto separate drum tracks, for example).

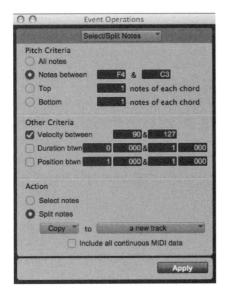

Figure 8.14   The Select/Split Notes page of the Event Operations window applies only to MIDI note events.

Input Quantize

This feature, also known as Auto Quantize on many MIDI sequencers, applies quantization upon input. The options in the Input Quantize page of the MIDI Operations window are identical to those in the Quantize page, except for an additional checkbox that enables or disables this feature. In truth, however, you may never use this, because it's just as easy—and a *lot* more flexible—to experiment with quantization after the fact (especially through the non-destructive method of using real-time properties on the region or track) instead of discarding the original timing in your performance during the recording process. (That said, Input Quantize can be undone with the Restore Performance command.)

Step Input

The Step Input feature will be familiar to users of other popular MIDI sequencers. In this step-entry mode, you can enter MIDI notes or chords one by one, with the input cursor advancing by the specified increment each time you enter something. Not only can this non–real-time entry of note events be just the thing for creating "impossible" rapid-fire arpeggios and so on, it can also be useful for entering certain types of drum parts.

The "Step Input" section of Chapter 10 goes into the details of Step Input mode for MIDI notes, but here's the basic idea behind the Step Input page of the Event Operations window (shown in Figure 8.15): First, you select which MIDI track in your current Pro Tools session to use as the destination for the note events created in this mode. You can then choose the step increment (the rhythmic spacing between the notes that will be created), a percentage of that note value to use

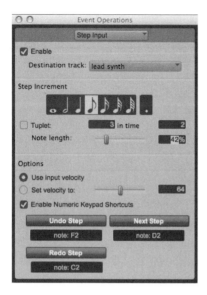

Figure 8.15 The Step Input page of the Event Operations window, for non–real-time creation of MIDI events.

as the duration for notes created in each step, and whether the velocities for these note events should be a fixed value or represent how you actually struck the keys during step input. Finally, Undo Step and Next Step buttons (which, if desired, you can assign to keys on your MIDI keyboard) enable you to back up and redo a step or skip a step entirely in order to create rests for syncopated rhythms. You can change all of these parameters while you continue to create notes, and you can even switch from one target MIDI track to another within this window.

Restore Performance

This command restores the selected MIDI region to its original recorded form (or to the most recent flattened version; see the next paragraph) with respect to timing, duration, velocity, and/ or pitch. It can also be used to undo the effects of the Input Quantize feature.

Flatten Performance

Flattening a selected MIDI region freezes it at its current state. This is the state to which the region will return the next time you apply the Restore Performance command. You can select timing, duration, velocity, and/or or pitch parameters for flattening. In Chapter 10, you will find a practical example of the Flatten and Restore Performance commands.

MIDI Event List

The MIDI Event List window (shown in Figure 8.16) displays MIDI events in a track as numerical data in a table format, as opposed to the standard graphical representation within MIDI tracks in the Edit window. Some MIDI editing operations are easier to perform in this list view.

99| 1| 689	△ 1	14		mod wheel	
99| 1| 701	△ 1	10		mod wheel	
99| 1| 712	△ 1	6		mod wheel	
99| 1| 724	△ 1	2		mod wheel	
99| 1| 750	△ 1	0		mod wheel	
99| 2| 079	♩ F3	81	64	0| 0| 720	T
99| 2| 563	♩ E3	72	64	0| 0| 513	T
99| 3| 041	♩ D3	66	64	0| 0| 865	T
99| 3| 451	♩ E3	66	64	0| 0| 513	T
99| 3| 902	♩ F3	39	64	0| 0| 472	T
99| 4| 365	♩ E3	63	64	0| 1| 473	T
100| 1| 223	∿ 264			Pitch Bend	
100| 1| 236	∿ 1849			Pitch Bend	
100| 1| 249	∿ 3434			Pitch Bend	
100| 1| 264	∿ 5020			Pitch Bend	
100| 1| 277	∿ 7134			Pitch Bend	
100| 1| 291	∿ 8191			Pitch Bend	
100| 1| 475	∿ 6605			Pitch Bend	
100| 1| 487	∿ 5020			Pitch Bend	
100| 1| 501	∿ 2906			Pitch Bend	
100| 1| 516	∿ 1321			Pitch Bend	
100| 1| 529	∿ 0			Pitch Bend	
100| 1| 959	♩ D3	82	64	0| 0| 193	T

Figure 8.16   The MIDI Event List window displays the actual data that selected MIDI parts contain and transmit out to their selected destination.

In a sense, this is the most accurate view of what is recorded and played back in your MIDI performances—even though it may not be especially intuitive, musically speaking! The MIDI Event List window is also the only place where you can view and edit polyphonic key pressure data (sometimes called *polyphonic aftertouch*, as in Pro Tools—MIDI data for the pressure applied to each individual key, as opposed to the more common *monophonic* aftertouch data sent from most keyboards, which is more properly known as *channel pressure*). When you enable real-time MIDI properties on the regions or tracks containing the selected MIDI data, the display in the MIDI Event List window will reflect this. An R indicates events that are affected by region-based properties, while a T indicates those affected by track-based properties.

MIDI Track Offsets

Some MIDI devices (especially older ones) have an appreciable latency time before they respond to incoming MIDI events, but this is not the most common reason for using MIDI track offsets. A more typical scenario is when you are using Aux Inputs (and audio inputs on your hardware) to monitor audio coming from your external MIDI devices; these must be digitized and brought into the Pro Tools mixing environment. On any Pro Tools LE or M-Powered system, there is a certain latency factor involved—a processing delay due to the analog-to-digital conversion process, the current size of the hardware buffer, and the overhead of the operating system itself—in addition to the amount of time it takes the external MIDI modules themselves to respond to incoming MIDI note events. The MIDI Track Offsets window enables you to individually specify a negative offset, in samples or milliseconds, for each MIDI track in your Pro Tools session. You can also set a global MIDI offset (also accessible via the MIDI tab of the Preferences dialog box), which is probably all you need if there is only one external MIDI synth in your configuration. Bear in mind that the offset for each MIDI track is a playback parameter only; it doesn't affect where MIDI events are displayed within Pro Tools tracks. The following sidebar provides a fairly simple technique that will get you in the ballpark for calculating your system's overall MIDI-to-audio latency factor. In Pro Tools HD software, however, the Automatic Delay Compensation feature also applies to MIDI tracks; especially when using software instrument plug-ins as the sound source for MIDI tracks, this sort of manual adjustment may not be required.

Calculating Monitoring Latency for MIDI Track Offsets To calculate the latency caused by MIDI transmission and the response times of your external MIDI modules, do the following:

1. Create a MIDI track with a cow bell or wood block sound playing ¼ notes, and then record the output of that synth into an audio track.

2. Switch your main time scale to samples (activating that Timebase ruler), and select one of these MIDI notes.

3. Take note of the precise sample number shown in the Edit window's Start field.

4. Zoom in on the corresponding attack in the audio track you just recorded.

5. Click the Selector tool precisely at the initial attack of the audio waveform and note the (higher) sample number now shown.

The difference between the sample numbers approximates the total amount of monitoring latency (between MIDI transmission of the note event from Pro Tools, the MIDI device's response time, and then the redigitization into Pro Tools via whatever Aux Input or audio track is monitoring this external MIDI device). This time setting would be the ideal negative offset amount (in samples) for MIDI tracks played through this particular device.

Here's a typical situation in which a negative MIDI track offset is definitely required: Say you're doubling a MIDI snare sound with a snare sample in a Pro Tools audio track whose attack is *precisely* on the ¼ notes. If you hear a flam effect (closely spaced double attacks), you could empirically adjust the MIDI snare part's negative offset until you hear the two attacks converge.

MIDI Real-Time Properties

Real-time properties apply non-destructive changes to the contents of MIDI regions or tracks—for example, quantization, transposition, changes to velocity and duration, and so on. They can be track-based (affecting all MIDI events on the track) and/or region-based (affecting only the currently selected instance of that region). The Real-Time Properties window has a pop-up

Apply To selector that defaults to region based if one or more MIDI regions are selected when you launch this command or to track based if a MIDI or Instrument track is selected but not any regions within it. However, you can use the Apply To selector to switch between these two modes without leaving this window. (By the way, a third choice in this selector, Default Track Properties, is a handy way to toggle the entire set of real-time properties off and on for the affected track or region.) There is also a Real-Time Properties column that can be displayed in the Edit window, for track-based properties only. Real-time properties assigned to a selected region take effect prior to any real-time properties that may be assigned to the track on which it resides. You will probably use both types, in various combinations. In the Real-Time Properties window for a selected MIDI region, you can also permanently incorporate the effect of these parameters into the actual MIDI data that region contains. (For example, note locations would be changed according to the quantization settings, velocities and durations would be altered, and transposition applied.) Figure 8.17 shows the Real-Time Properties window for a selected MIDI region.

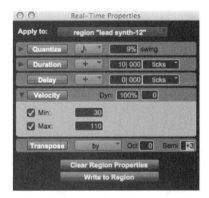

Figure 8.17   Real-time MIDI properties are applied to individual MIDI regions. The Apply To selector also lets you choose to apply track-based real-time properties to currently selected MIDI or Instrument tracks.

Remove Duplicate Notes
Especially when loop recording a MIDI part, it is all too easy to create duplicate notes at a given location. This can also occur as a result of quantization. The Remove Duplicate Notes command takes care of the problem.

Add Key Change
The Key Change dialog box is discussed in Chapter 6, "The Edit Window," in the section about the Key Signature ruler. This command enables you to create a key-signature event at the current location. Key-signature events affect pitched MIDI and Instrument tracks, and are also used by the diatonic transposition options in the Event Operations and Real-Time MIDI Operations windows.

Beat Detective

This feature conforms an audio region to the session's tempo by breaking it up into multiple regions and aligning these to the beats—or conversely, generates a tempo map based on transients contained within the selected audio (by creating a *beat trigger* map). You can also use Beat Detective to extract DigiGroove templates from audio and MIDI selections. You can use these templates with the Groove Quantize function for MIDI parts, for example, effectively applying the feel extracted from an audio selection in the Beat Detective window to a MIDI performance. The Analysis button in the Beat Detective window enables you to specify whether low or high frequencies should have more weight for the beat-detection process in the source audio selection— for example, whether the kick drum or the hi-hat may be a more reliable tempo indicator. Collection mode, for analyzing multiple tracks simultaneously, is included with Pro Tools HD and can be added to LE or M-Powered versions (which already have the basic Beat Detective LE feature) via the Music Production Toolkit option or, for LE users, the Complete Production Toolkit option. (Music Production Toolkit also provides LE/M-Powered users of Pro Tools versions 7.4 and higher the Enhanced Resolution analysis option in Beat Detective—otherwise only available to HD users—which offers more flexible and reliable results.) The Beat Detective window (shown in Figure 8.18) is a fairly complex subject; Chapter 12, "The Pro Tools Groove," provides more discussion of its basic modes.

Figure 8.18 The Beat Detective window is immensely useful for beat mixing and dance production, allowing you to utilize source audio with differing tempos to deconstruct beats and build entirely new arrangements.

Identify Beat

Use the Identify Beat command to indicate what the current position (or selection) should be in musical bars and beats. This creates a tempo/meter event in the Tempo ruler based on the bar number(s) and meter you indicate. For dance mixing (or something similar), the Identify Beat function can be very important—be sure to check out Chapter 12 for more information! (The Pro Tools tempo map must be active in order for the Identify Beat command to be available; click to enable the Conductor button in the MIDI section of the Transport window.) You can also use Identify Beat to (rather painstakingly) create a tempo/meter map for music that was not recorded with a click, or even at a strict tempo.

Let's say you've imported an interesting drum figure or a musical phrase under which you will build a rhythm groove in Pro Tools. Select *exactly* four bars of the phrase. If necessary, enable Options > Loop Playback, and then press Play. If the four bars don't loop around smoothly, you could zoom in and adjust the selection length (while holding down the Shift key) with the Selector tool. Alternatively, you could nudge your selection by holding down the Command key (Ctrl in Windows) as you press the + and − (plus/minus) keys to adjust the end point of the current selection until you get a sample-accurate, smooth loop. (In Pro Tools, every time you adjust or nudge the boundaries of a selection, you must click Stop and then Play again to reset the timeline selection for looped playback.)

After you've created an *extremely accurate* four-bar selection that loops in correct rhythm (take the time to get this right!), select Event > Identify Beat. In the Add Bar|Beat Markers dialog box shown in Figure 8.19, enter the correct meter (4/4, for example) and bar numbers for the beginning and end of the selection. For example, if the beginning of a four-bar phrase is 1|1|00, the end is 5|1|00, right? Make sure your main time ruler is set to Bars:Beats, set the Grid value to ¼ notes or ⅛ notes, and activate Grid edit mode. You're then ready to start chopping up the longer musical piece (assuming it was recorded at a steady tempo in the first place). Because you're in Grid mode, selections within regions or adjustments to their lengths will be snapped to the nearest note value. As you start dropping drum sounds or recording and quantizing additional MIDI or Instrument tracks, everything can be snapped to the tempo grid you created based on that first phrase (which is why it was so important to be so precise before using the Identify Beat command). See Chapter 12 for more examples and a few more tips about how Elastic Audio features (available in versions 7.4 and higher) fit into this process.

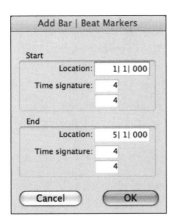

Figure 8.19   You can use Identify Beat to create Pro Tools tempos based on timeline selections corresponding to a precise number of bars and beats (such as audio files containing drum loops or phrases within musical arrangements).

Renumber Bars

This command assigns a new number to the first bar of your session; all subsequent bars are renumbered accordingly. Negative numbers are supported in case you prefer bar one to be somewhere farther into the session's timeline because that better reflects the song structure.

All MIDI Notes Off: The Panic Button!

Use the All MIDI Notes Off command if you ever need to turn off stuck MIDI notes on your MIDI instruments. The keyboard shortcut for the All MIDI Notes Off command is Shift+Command+period (Shift+Ctrl+period in Windows). If you're a MIDI user, memorize this now!

AudioSuite Menu

AudioSuite plug-ins appear in this menu, grouped into categories (although you can change your preferences to group them first by manufacturer and then category). By default, the following plug-in categories appear: EQ, Dynamics, Pitch Shift, Reverb, Delay, Modulation, and Other. Additional categories may also appear if other optional plug-ins are installed on your system. AudioSuite effects are strictly file based. In other words, they create new audio files (or *destructively* overwrite the current selection within audio files, if you wish) and don't operate in real time.

In addition to the AudioSuite plug-ins supplied with Pro Tools, you can purchase third-party plug-ins in the RTAS format (and/or TDM/HD format, of course) separately. Some RTAS plug-ins also function as AudioSuite plug-ins, while others, like software instruments and the Click plug-in, can only be used as real-time effects on tracks—in which case they won't appear among these AudioSuite menu selections.

Favorite Plug-ins If you designate a plug-in as a favorite, it always appears at the top of the plug-in submenu when you are selecting inserts for a track. Just hold down the Command key (Ctrl key in Windows) as you open the pop-up menu for selecting plug-ins in the AudioSuite menu (or the pop-up selector for real-time inserts on tracks) and select the item you want to add to your favorites. Repeat this procedure to remove a plug-in from your favorites. This is a very useful feature; creating your own hot half-dozen plug-in favorites will save you a lot of time!

The precise contents of the parameters window differ for each AudioSuite effect, but a Process button is always available. Clicking that button creates new regions, which are placed into the affected track instead of the current selection (unless you select Overwrite Files, in which case the data in the source file itself is destructively overwritten). AudioSuite plug-in windows frequently also include a Preview button and a Bypass button so that you can toggle the preview between the processed and unprocessed version. The Use In Playlist button, if enabled, substitutes the processed result for the selected original in the track. Most importantly, a pop-up menu enables you to copy and save settings for each plug-in—or import them from another session's plug-in settings folder. Additionally, if any part of the current selection includes multiple audio regions within a single track, you can choose whether the result of the AudioSuite processing creates a single new region for that entire track selection or individual regions/files corresponding to each original region in the track.

Free Up Your DSP Resources   For users with limited DSP capacity, a point may come in your project where Pro Tools tells you that you are low on DSP resources and won't, for example, enable you to add any more plug-ins, Aux Input tracks, Instrument tracks, or sends. At that point, it may be practical to commit some of your real-time effects to new regions to free up that signal-processing power for the rest of your mix. Fortunately, most real-time DigiRack RTAS insert effects are also available as process-based functions in the AudioSuite menu. You can copy settings from the effect's insert version (via a pop-up menu in its plug-in window), disable or remove the plug-in from the audio track, select all audio in the audio track, and then paste these settings into the corresponding file-based (non–real-time) AudioSuite effect before clicking the Process button. For real-time plug-in effects, or to print (that is, permanently incorporate) several effects to a new file in a single operation (also often required if your Pro Tools sessions will later be used by someone who doesn't have all the same plug-ins), you can alternatively use the Bounce to > Disk command, muting all tracks but the one(s) you want incorporated into the bounced file. (The Bounce dialog box's Import into Session after Bounce option is also very useful in these cases.)

Options Menu

The selections in the Options menu affect the operating modes of Pro Tools: recording modes, monitoring modes, synchronization status, pre/post-roll, and looped playback—how edit selections affect play selections, for example. Here, we concentrate on the options in this menu that we consider essential for *any* Pro Tools user. For information about other commands not discussed here, see the *Pro Tools Menus Guide*, provided in PDF format with the program; it describes every selection in every menu of Pro Tools, including those in the Options menu.

Destructive Record

In Destructive Recording mode, any new audio recorded into an existing region *replaces* and *erases* the previously recorded audio data in the same location. Ordinarily, recording in Pro Tools is *non-destructive*. Even if you record right over a region already in the track, replacing it with a new region, the previous region is still intact and can be dragged out from the Regions List (and returned to its original timestamp location via the Spot dialog box). Saving every take of audio uses more disk space (until you delete unwanted audio regions/files, of course), so users who are obliged to be extremely conservative about disk space will occasionally use the Destructive Record command to switch over to Destructive Recording mode. Recording books on tape might be a typical situation for using Destructive Recording mode, especially if your disk capacity is relatively limited. Otherwise, using the Regions List's local menu to eliminate unused regions and compact existing audio files is the customary and effective way to keep the disk space used by your sessions under control.

Loop Record

Hey, musicians! This cool feature is of special interest to you! When this recording option is enabled, you can keep looping the same timeline selection (between the Start and End locations, as indicated in the Transport window) as you record multiple takes. Every take you record for a track is saved within a single audio file, containing all the takes. While still in Loop Recording mode, you can discard all takes since you last began loop-recording by pressing Command+period (Ctrl+period in Windows). Each take recorded in Loop Recording mode appears in the Regions List after you stop recording and is numbered sequentially. You can also choose to have Pro Tools make each looped recording a new playlist by selecting Automatically Create New Playlists When Loop Recording within Setup > Preferences (choose the Operations tab).

After recording multiple takes, you may want to listen to each one to decide which is the keeper. Click with the Grabber to highlight the most recent take currently appearing within the track, and then switch to the Selector tool and Command-click and hold (Ctrl-click and hold in Windows) on that region. A pop-up Takes List appears, where you can toggle between all the takes (alternate regions) matching that edit selection. (Note that several selections in Preferences > Editing affect behavior of the Takes List.) Yet another method for selecting among alternate takes, available in versions 7.3 and higher, is to right-click the region; a pop-up menu provides a Matches submenu, where you can also select among alternate takes. (If you ever wanted region definitions corresponding to the multiple takes within a loop-recorded audio file to be visible in other Pro Tools sessions, it would be necessary to apply the Regions List's Export Region Definitions command beforehand.) Also, if the Automatically Create New Playlists When Loop Recording preference was selected before recording, you can display the looped records as individual playlists and use the solo buttons in each lane while playing back to audition each take. Incidentally, the Options > Loop Record option only affects how audio plays while in Record mode; the Options > Loop Playback option is used to enable looping during normal playback.

QuickPunch

This menu command toggles on and off the QuickPunch recording mode for audio. When QuickPunch mode is enabled, you can manually click the Record button during playback to punch recording in and out on any record-enabled audio tracks. Owners of Digi 003 and Digi 002 systems can connect a footswitch for this function in QuickPunch mode.

Using QuickPunch What do you do when the performer hasn't given you a clue about when you will need to punch in recording? (Maybe he or she doesn't have a clue yet either!) The QuickPunch feature enables you to avoid recording a lot of empty space on the timeline before you get the high sign, letting you turn the Record button on and off during playback to activate recording into any record-enabled tracks. Here's how you do it:

1. Choose Options > QuickPunch. (In Pro Tools 7.3 and higher, this can also be enabled via a pop-up menu that appears when you right-click the Record button.)

2. Record-enable any tracks on which you want to record by clicking their Rec (Record Enable) button. Notice that the Record button in the Transport (and in the Edit window) now has a P in it and starts flashing when you click Play.

3. When your helpful performer gives you the signal that he or she is about to do something great (hopefully), click the Record button. Pro Tools starts recording in all record-enabled tracks.

4. Once the greatness is over, click Record again to exit Record mode. Pro Tools continues playback; you can click the Record button again to punch in at a different section (backing vocals in the second verse of the song, for example). Alternatively, click Stop or press the spacebar when the performer has finished.

The Command+spacebar (Ctrl+spacebar in Windows) keyboard shortcut also works for dropping in and out of QuickPunch mode, as does the F12 key—although Mac users must be careful to not assign this Exposé shortcut key to something else. (Again, on Digi 003 and Digi 002 systems, you can connect a footswitch to the appropriate jack on your audio interface to achieve the same effect as pressing the Record button in the Transport window—nice!) Only those portions of time when the Transport's Record button was enabled will have created new audio regions in your record-enabled tracks.

Be aware that while using QuickPunch mode on Pro Tools LE and M-Powered systems, the total number of tracks and available DSP power is reduced. Although the number of tracks on which you can simultaneously record in QuickPunch mode is determined by the current number of free voices, on LE and M-Powered versions you are limited to punching in a maximum of 16 audio tracks in QuickPunch mode (with the exception of LE with DV Toolkit, which enables punching in 32 tracks simultaneously at 48kHz, and 24 tracks at 96kHz). Also be aware that in QuickPunch mode, as long as a track is armed, Pro Tools records audio to disk once playback begins regardless of whether you are punched in and can see the resulting recording on the timeline. This can result in sizeable audio files. If you plan to use QuickPunch, make sure you have a good amount of open space on the audio drive or drives.

QuickPunch is *not* required on MIDI tracks! Any record-enabled MIDI tracks go in and out of Record mode when you toggle the Record button during playback, even during *normal* Play mode. QuickPunch is only required for audio tracks.

Note: On HD systems, you should disable the Options > Use Delay Compensation option while recording in either QuickPunch or TrackPunch mode.

TrackPunch (HD Systems Only)

This menu command toggles the TrackPunch recording mode for audio on/off. TrackPunch lets you independently use Record Enable buttons in multiple tracks, punching each one in and out of Record mode in real time during playback. As with QuickPunch mode, crossfades are automatically generated at the punch-in/punch-out points; their duration is determined in the Editing tab of the Preferences dialog box.

Using TrackPunch Imagine for a moment that you're recording a jazz session in which multiple soloists will each take a few choruses, but it's not clear exactly when. You have individual microphones on each solo instrument and you want to avoid recording multiple takes of the entire song on six tracks simultaneously. With TrackPunch recording mode, you have the option to drop in and out of Record Enable mode on the fly on individual tracks—enabling microphones for each player at the opportune moment. (You might also use this technique for a Foley artist, expansive percussion setups with numerous microphones, conference recordings, and so on.)

1.   Activate TrackPunch mode by selecting Options > TrackPunch. In Pro Tools versions 7.3 and higher, TrackPunch (as well as QuickPunch, Loop, Destructive, and Normal) recording mode can also be enabled via a pop-up menu that appears when you right-click the Record button.

2.   Control-click (Start-click in Windows) the Record Enable buttons on all the individual tracks that may be required to make them active for recording in TrackPunch mode. Up to 16 tracks can be in TrackPunch mode simultaneously. These Record Enable buttons turn blue, as does the Record button in the Transport window itself. (This button now displays a T, for TrackPunch.)

3.   Press the spacebar to start playback.

4.   When you're ready to punch in recording on any TrackPunch-enabled track, click its Record Enable button. The Transport button turns solid red while recording is in progress.

5. Click the track's Record Enable button again to punch it out of Record mode. The Transport button turns blue again.

6. Repeat as many times (and on as many tracks) as necessary.

To punch in simultaneously on *all* TrackPunch-enabled tracks, hold down the Option key (Alt key in Windows) as you click any of their Record Enable buttons, or click the Record button in the Transport window.

Video Track Online

When this option is enabled, contents of the movie window scroll according to cursor position and selections (and as you drag regions back and forth in the timeline, to spot them to video events). When disabled, playback of the video is frozen at its current point. If you find that playback in the Movie window is significantly affecting performance on your system configuration, you might occasionally take the movie offline to free up system overhead for metering and other display tasks or while editing a sequence when you don't need the video as a reference.

Video Out FireWire (Mac Only)

If you have a DV-compatible video deck, camera, or monitor with a FireWire input (officially known as IEEE 1394, and also called i.Link by Sony), enabling this command sends playback of the current video file in your Pro Tools session out that port on your computer.

Scrub In Video Window

This enables the user to choose the Scrub function on the session's Video track or tracks. Simply choose the Scrub tool, click in the Video track, and drag the scrubber back and forth.

Loop Playback

This command loops the current Timeline selection (displayed in the Start/End/Length fields of the Transport window) until you press Stop or the spacebar. This is really handy for repeating a section while you make mix and effects adjustments. You can also loop playback while refining a musical phrase selection so that it loops exactly at a precise number of bars or beats, either to capture/separate a new region definition or to establish a precise selection as the basis for the Identify Beat command. The keyboard shortcut to enable looped playback is Shift+Command+L (or Shift+Ctrl+L in Windows). In versions 7.3 and higher it can also be enabled via the pop-up menu that appears when you right-click the Play button.

Link Timeline and Edit Selection

When this option is enabled (the default), selections you make in the Edit window immediately change not only the values in the Edit window's Start, End, and Length indicators (the Edit Selection), but also those of the Transport window (the Timeline Selection). The Timeline Selection in the Transport window (whether currently visible or not) determines what happens when you click Play, what loops in Loop Playback mode, and punch-in/out points for recording, for instance. In other words, when Options > Link Timeline and Edit Selections is enabled, values in the Transport's Start, End, and Length fields are always slaved to the current Edit selection (identically named fields, up in the Event Edit area at the top of the Edit window), and will change as you select regions and MIDI notes or highlight any area of the timeline within the tracks or Timebase rulers.

Sometimes, however, you don't want track selections in the Edit window to alter the Transport window's Start, End, and Length values. For example, you might want the same portion of the timeline to keep looping around, even as you select, drag, or trim regions and notes within the Edit window. In this case, you would temporarily disable the Link Timeline and Edit Selections mode. In addition to this Options menu selection, you can use the Link Selection button located just underneath the Grabber tool in the Edit window, or its keyboard shortcut, Shift+/ (forward slash).

Playing the Edit Selection Versus the Timeline Selection The Edit > Selection > Play Edit command plays back the Edit Selection only, with no pre-roll, even when the edit and play selections are linked. The keyboard shortcut for Play Edit Selection is Option+[(left bracket) (Alt+[in Windows).

Link Track and Edit Selection

When enabled, this option automatically selects the track whenever you make any selection within it, highlighting its name in the Edit/Mix windows. This feature facilitates applying track-based commands as you edit. For example, with this option enabled, you might group the tracks that get selected as a result. Also, if you hold down the Option+Shift key combination (Alt+Shift in Windows) when changing a track parameter (track view, automation mode, or track timebase, for instance), the same change will be applied to all currently selected tracks. Even better, when Commands Keyboard Focus mode is enabled (via the AZ button, in the upper-right corner of the Tracks pane in the Edit window—learning the shortcuts in Commands Keyboard Focus mode is *well* worth your effort!), pressing the minus (−) key on your alphanumeric keyboard (the main QWERTY keyboard, *not* the numeric keypad) toggles any currently selected tracks between two predefined track views: Waveform (regions) and Volume on audio tracks, or Regions and Notes on MIDI and Instrument tracks.

Changing Track Heights for the Current Selection To change track heights on tracks with highlighted selections or where a blinking edit cursor appears, press Control+Up/Down arrow key (or Start+Up/Down arrow key in Windows).

Mirror MIDI Editing

When Mirrored MIDI editing is enabled, edits you perform on a MIDI region (changing notes or drawing new MIDI controller automation, for example) are automatically applied to all MIDI regions of the same name, in any track. Say you've created a very basic four-bar drum pattern named Groove, which you've copied to various places in a MIDI or Instrument track in order to start laying down parts. Once you have a couple more instrumental parts working, with Mirror MIDI Editing enabled you can tweak any instance of this Groove MIDI region (altering the hi-hat, for instance, or adding a kick drum accent), and that change is immediately reflected in its other instances. Being able to mirror MIDI regions is important not only in this linear sense, but also for simultaneously doubling parts in separate tracks (where different output assignments and real-time MIDI properties could be applied to each).

Automation Follows Edit

When this option is enabled, the effect of editing operations on Pro Tools data is exactly the same as in all versions prior to Pro Tools 8: Dragging or pasting regions to a new location also moves or copies all their overlapping automation data. For example, you may have created automation for the send level to the delay effect in a track, so that a single note in a lead vocal or guitar line spikes the delay. In the default Automation Follows Edit mode, if you copy or drag this region to a new location, it still has that automation event at the same relative location within the region. However, for certain editing tasks, you may choose to disable Automation Follows Edit. In that case, the automation on a track stays in place, even as you drag, cut, copy, and paste regions to different locations within it.

Click/Countoff

This menu command simply turns the metronome click on or off—which can also be done by clicking the Metronome Click button in the Transport window. To set up what kind of click sound you want and how it will behave, open the Click/Countoff Options dialog box (shown later, in Figure 8.26) by double-clicking the Metronome Click button or the Countoff display in the MIDI controls section of the Transport window, or by selecting Setup > Click/Countoff.

MIDI Thru

Generally, the MIDI Thru option should be enabled. Here's a typical setup: You turn local mode *off* on the external keyboard (or MIDI guitar, wind, or percussion controller, of course) that you're using for the MIDI performance. This cuts the internal connection between the keyboard and its own internal sounds. Otherwise, every note you play would be doubled, because your synth would not only play a note in response to its *own* keyboard, but also when that same note event comes echoing back from the record-enabled track in Pro Tools (perhaps on a different channel, and with a different sound). On record-enabled MIDI tracks, the MIDI data received from your keyboard (usually via one of the MIDI inputs on your MIDI interface, unless you're using a keyboard with a direct USB connection) is echoed back out through the MIDI interface or USB connection— redirected to the MIDI port, channel, and MIDI program number assigned to this track.

So why use MIDI Thru? Without changing anything on your keyboard, you can quickly switch between its own MIDI channels and program settings and those of a software instrument (either a Pro Tools plug-in or some other ReWired application) or some completely different external MIDI module connected to another port on your MIDI interface as shown in Figure 8.20. Changes to volume, pan, and other parameters are done on the Pro Tools track rather than on the controller itself.

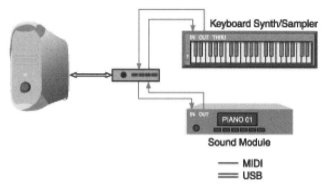

Figure 8.20 A simple MIDI setup for a Pro Tools system: one keyboard synth/sampler, one multitimbral MIDI module, and a multiport external MIDI interface connected to the computer's USB port. Some MIDI keyboard controllers and sound modules can also be connected directly to the computer's USB port.

Pre-Fader Metering

When the Pre-Fader Metering option is enabled, level meters for each track in the Edit or Mix window display the level prior to its main volume fader (which of course can apply gain changes of its own). Pre-fader levels are unaffected by the volume fader's current position, and more accurately reflect the levels for whatever audio source is feeding the track (disk-based audio data, a hardware input path, a bus, or the output from a software instrument). However, because pre-fader metering derives from a point in the track's signal chain immediately after the Inserts section, the pre-fader levels *do* reflect gain changes caused by any plug-ins on the track.

This is actually quite useful. For example, when track meters are displaying *post*-fader levels (in other words, when Options > Pre-Fader Metering is disabled), a low main volume setting on a track's output makes it all too easy to overlook the fact that make-up gain on the compressor and boosted EQ settings are producing clipping (overload) prior to its main output. This book will remind you many times that digital clipping is not pretty; you need to manage the gain structure of your session (that is, the amount of boost or cut at the various stages in the signal chain from track inputs and outputs to the Master Fader track for your final mix output) so that it doesn't occur anywhere. Experienced users will switch between pre- and post-fader metering many times at different stages of the work process (generally using pre-fader metering while recording into tracks, for example).

Auto-Spot Regions

Available in HD systems and LE systems with DV Toolkit, this feature is especially useful when using VITC or the MachineControl option (or with LTC while the transport of the master device is in Play mode). When Options > Auto-Spot Regions is enabled, clicking any region with the Grabber *spots* its beginning (or the sync point within it) to the current time-code location. With MachineControl or VITC synchronization, you can jog or shuttle the master video transport itself in order to spot a selected region to the desired location.

Low-Latency Monitoring (Digi 002 Systems Only)

On these Pro Tools systems, this Options menu item can be very useful while laying down tracks. Instead of a relatively long monitoring delay (latency) between the input signal and when it is heard back through the Pro Tools mixer (especially noticeable when larger hardware buffer sizes are selected in the Playback Engine dialog box), this feature reduces latency to a minimum—on tracks whose output is assigned to outputs 1–2 only. When Options > Low-Latency Monitoring is enabled, however, all plug-ins and sends are automatically bypassed on all record-enabled tracks assigned to outputs 1–2. (Other audio interfaces for Pro Tools offer alternative workaround for monitoring latency. For example, the Mbox 2, Mbox 2 Mini, and original Mbox offer a front-panel mix knob to adjust the balance between incoming analog signals and audio playback from Pro Tools. Various M-Audio interfaces feature internal mixing capabilities, controlled by their included control panel software, that allow routing incoming signals directly through to their line and headphone outputs.)

Bouncing to Disk on Digi 002 Systems Digi 002 users should not forget to disable the Options > Low-Latency Monitoring option before bouncing to disk! Although this feature is very handy while tracking, if you forget to turn it off, only the output from *audio* tracks will be included in your audio mixdown file and none of the Instrument or Aux Input tracks (where you might have instantiated plug-ins for reverbs, delays, or software instruments, for example).

"Zero-Latency" Monitoring on the Mbox 2 Family   Digidesign documentation and marketing materials often use this somewhat misleading term for a useful feature on several members of the Mbox 2 family of audio interfaces (as well as the original Mbox, which continues to be compatible with current versions of Pro Tools). A Mix knob on their front panel adjusts the balance between the input signal entering the interface's analog inputs and playback (the main stereo output from Pro Tools LE). Because the interface's analog input is heard via a direct signal path to the analog outputs, there's no latency. (This feature is not required on the Mbox 2 Pro— and isn't applicable to the Mbox 2 Micro because that model doesn't have any audio inputs.) When recording a mono source using this

Mix-knob monitoring feature, don't forget to press the Mono button on the front panel of these units so that it comes out both sides of your headphones or speakers.

Use Delay Compensation (HD Systems Only)

In Pro Tools HD software, this Options menu item enables Delay Compensation. This feature adjusts for the processing latency (delay) of each plug-in insert and any audio routing (for example, internal bussing), which consequently improves your mix by maintaining better time alignment between its various tracks. For most DigiRack plug-ins, the delay for each is only on the order of four samples or so. This can accumulate to a noticeable amount, however, when several are used in series and also when a given track's audio passes through its own plug-ins, those of an Aux Input, plus a couple more in the Master Fader prior to the main output, for example. Third-party plug-ins and processing-intensive plug-in types such as reverb or noise reduction can have much greater amounts of inherent latency. Expert operators on LE and M-Powered systems (as well as pre-HD TDM systems) compensate for accumulated latency manually, using the Delay indicators at the bottom of tracks in the Mix window and the Time Adjuster plug-in, for example. Maintaining proper time alignment between all the tracks in your mix keeps it more phase coherent. This is especially important when the same signal is somehow present in several tracks with different routing or processing setups (because it bleeds into two different microphones in a drum set or in live-performance situations, for example). Small time-alignment discrepancies can create phase cancellation in high frequencies, and even very tiny amounts can affect the overall coherency of your mix. You can adjust the parameters for delay compensation in the Setup > Playback Engine dialog box. You can also use the I/O Setup dialog box to manually compute and adjust latency compensation for external hardware connected via hardware I/O inserts.

If you're just getting started with audio recording, we should mention that when recording from multiple simultaneous microphone sources, your first time-alignment concern should be with microphone placement and acoustical isolation of each sound source. To cite a common example, if you have a snare or cymbal crashes bleeding into a vocal microphone 11 feet away, you've already got time-alignment discrepancies (somewhere in the neighborhood of 10 milliseconds in typical studio conditions) and phase-cancellation issues on your tracks—before even using any plug-ins!

Setup Menu

Selections here not only pertain to the hardware on your system, but also enable you to control how available disks on your system are used for recording on each audio track in the current session. It is also here that you establish your preferences and your MIDI setup, as well as inform Pro Tools what sort of external hardware peripherals are attached to your computer (for example, synchronization peripherals, external control surfaces, and devices linked via the Machine-Control protocol). Another extremely important feature accessed via the Setup menu is the

I/O Setup dialog box, where you can define and select audio paths for use within Pro Tools, representing inputs, outputs, inserts, and busses, from simple mono and stereo paths to multi-channel configurations for surround mixing.

Hardware (Setup)

The contents of the Hardware Setup dialog box (shown in Figure 8.21) depend on your Pro Tools hardware configuration. On Pro Tools LE hardware—like the Digi 003 and Mbox 2 Pro, for example—you may be able to set your audio hardware's sample rate and input gain (although not on the Mbox 2, Mbox 2 Mini, or original Mbox, since they have front-panel knobs for this), select between analog or digital input, use sync mode for the digital input, use DAT-compatibility features, and set other options specific to the audio hardware. On M-Powered systems, however, control of all these parameters for your M-Audio interface is turned over to the setup program included with the M-Audio interface; it is launched by a single button in the Hardware Setup dialog box. Additional options for HD systems may include the following:

- Selection of digital or analog connectors for various input channels on the audio interface

- Reference levels for analog connectors (+4dBm or −10dBV, respectively) associated with pro and consumer equipment)

- Clock source for sample rate and external clock output

- Level sensitivity and peak hold characteristics on the audio interface's front-panel display (if applicable)

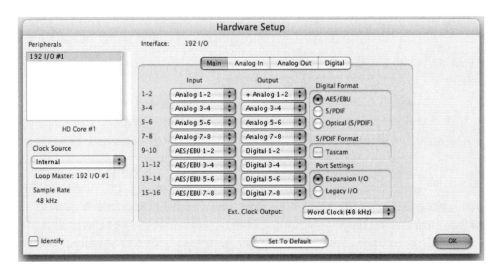

Figure 8.21 The contents of the Hardware Setup dialog box depend on your Pro Tools hardware. Shown here are the options for a Pro Tools|HD system, with a 192 I/O audio interface.

Pro Tools|HD systems offer auto-configuration features, so you don't have to manually select the interface when installing or expanding the hardware configuration. Users of the 96i I/O (but not the 96 I/O) with Pro Tools|HD can also use the Hardware Setup dialog box to adjust gain on the inputs of the audio interface itself.

Playback Engine

As with the Hardware Setup dialog box, the contents of the Playback Engine dialog box (shown in Figure 8.22) depend on your hardware configuration. On HD systems, a Delay Compensation Engine setting in the Playback Engine dialog box lets you specify how much of your DSP resources should be dedicated to this task. Options are None, Short, and Long (which may be required on slower systems or when using relatively high-latency plug-ins).

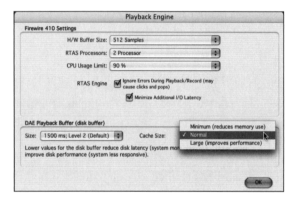
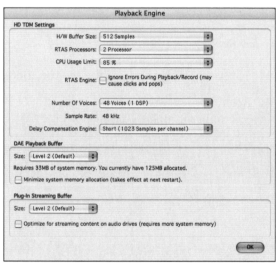

Figure 8.22 Contents of the Playback Engine dialog box depend on your Pro Tools hardware. Shown here are the options for M-Powered (left) and HD software (right).

Pro Tools LE and M-Powered users, however, should be especially aware of three all-important settings in the Playback Engine dialog box (which also affect HD systems):

■ If you hear glitching or choppiness during playback, especially due to intensive use of plug-ins or virtual instruments (even with only a dozen or so tracks, for example), try increasing the H/W Buffer Size value. The larger this value, the more plug-ins are supported; this can be especially beneficial when using more processing-intensive plug-in types like reverbs and software instruments, for instance. Additionally, larger hardware buffer sizes enable you to record a larger number of tracks simultaneously on LE and M-Powered systems. However, larger buffer sizes also increase latency (processing delay) issues when monitoring input signals through the Pro Tools mixer during recording (unless you're circumventing this by enabling the Low-Latency Monitoring option on a Digi 002, the mix knob on one of the Mbox 2 family or the original Mbox, or one of the direct input monitoring options provided by M-Audio hardware). You might therefore start with a lower H/W Buffer Size setting when recording relatively small numbers of tracks, increasing these as necessary if activating lots of plug-ins during mixdown causes your system to hiccup during playback.

- The CPU Usage Limit setting controls how much of the CPU's processing power can be devoted to audio-processing tasks for Pro Tools. Larger settings allow smooth playback of sessions with more numerous or processing-intensive RTAS plug-ins. However, higher percentages of CPU usage take away processing power from screen redraws (including moving faders and real-time displays in track level meters), video playback, and any other program running concurrently with Pro Tools on the same computer, which could consequently seem sluggish. A good initial setting for the CPU Usage Limit option on single-processor systems is 85%, although you can increase this parameter up to 99% on any computer, whether single- or dual-processor. For dual-processor systems, the RTAS Processors parameter lets you choose how much of the computer's CPU to allocate to processing tasks for RTAS plug-ins. Choosing a larger number—and yes, configurations with more than two CPUs are supported —spreads the processing load. Along with the H/W Buffer Size parameter, increasing your CPU Usage Limit setting is another possible strategy if you start to hear choppy playback or other artifacts while using many tracks containing software instruments. The System Usage window (Window > System Usage) provides a graphic display of how heavy the combined load is on *all* the currently enabled processors. In sessions with many processing-intensive RTAS plug-ins (reverbs and software instruments, for example), there will be a notable difference when you switch between one and two RTAS processors. The CPU usage limit and the number of RTAS processors interact, and requirements vary according to the particular session, computer model, and your working style, so it's impossible to make a blanket recommendation for these values. Generally speaking, however, if you're using a lot of RTAS plug-ins and hear glitching or get an alert box from Pro Tools about CPU usage (and increasing the H/W Buffer Size setting doesn't help), try increasing your CPU Usage Limit setting. Conversely, if your onscreen fader movement and Movie window updates seem sluggish during playback, reducing the CPU Usage Limit value might help.

- The DAE Playback Buffer setting affects how much of your computer's RAM is used to manage disk buffers for audio playback. Generally, you should start out with the default setting of 2. If you find that your hard disk can't keep up with playback and recording in complex sessions (with lots of tracks, regions, and automation), try the next-larger size. Of course, also make sure that your disks for audio recording and playback are properly maintained and defragmented in the first place! The tradeoff is that with larger DAE playback buffer sizes, Pro Tools takes a moment longer to start playback or record after you click Play.

Disk Allocation

If you have multiple hard drives available for audio recording on your system, you can use the Disk Allocation dialog box to specify which drives and folders are used to record new audio for each individual track. This helps to spread out the load on your disks (although it could make manual backup of a session's audio data more confusing if you don't have a Pro Tools–savvy backup program like Mezzo). Alternatively, in some sessions you may choose to record all tracks onto a single drive while using a different drive for other sessions, clients, or users. (For convenience, you can highlight multiple tracks in this dialog box and simultaneously assign them to the same destination.) The Disk Allocation dialog box offers a pop-up Disk Destination selector for each audio track, where you can even choose specific *folders* for new recordings from each track. Another option is round-robin allocation: For each new track you create, a different audio-recording drive on your system is selected in rotation.

Make Your System Volume/Partition Transfer-Only If you can avoid it, try not to include your startup system volume (the drive with the operating system and programs such as Pro Tools) among the eligible disks for audio recording. If you must use a single drive in your computer for both the operating system and audio recording, at the very least create two separate logical partitions (for example, using Apple's Disk Utility, Computer Management > Disk Management in the Administrative Tools control panel of Windows XP, or Manage > Storage > Disk Management in Windows Vista and Windows 7). Of course, you will need to reload your operating system and programs after doing this! For one thing, this permits running disk optimization or simple defragmentation on the audio volume (partition) while still booting from the system volume. It also makes your disk-management routines a little simpler in general. In Pro Tools' Workspace browser window (discussed later in this chapter), you can designate each drive (or partition on a physical drive, which will appear as a disk volume) on your system as Playback and/or Record, or Transfer Only. Volumes set to Transfer Only won't appear in the Disk Allocation window at all, and will never be used during round-robin allocation for new tracks.

Peripherals

The Peripherals dialog box (shown in Figure 8.23) includes choices for SMPTE time-code source (port and device type, such as Digidesign's USD or Sync I/O), MIDI MachineControl (MMC) settings, and MachineControl (the MachineControl software option is required for use of 9-pin controller connections with video decks, DATs, and other compatible devices). External MIDI controllers for Pro Tools are also configured here, such as the Mackie Control Universal or its predecessor, the HUI (which is also emulated by several other controllers including the wireless TranzPort); the CM Labs MotorMix; or one of the J.L. Cooper controllers. Also configured here are Digidesign's Command|8 USB controller for Pro Tools and the company's Ethernet-based

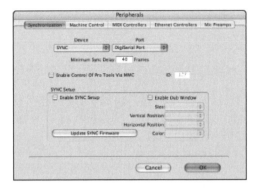

Figure 8.23 The Peripherals dialog box, where you identify external sources for SMPTE time code, MIDI MachineControl, and external controllers for Pro Tools functions. (Options for an HD system with a Sync I/O are shown here.)

controllers: the D-Control/D-Control ES, D-Command, ProControl (now discontinued), C|24, and Control|24. Also included is a tab for Satellites (which displays selections for software options), Video Satellite, Video Satellite for LE, and Satellite Link.

I/O

The I/O Setup dialog box (shown in Figure 8.24) is where you manage signal paths (also known as *paths*) for inputs, outputs, inserts, and busses (plus inputs on Digidesign's optional PRE microphone preamplifier for HD systems, as well as delay-compensation adjustments for external devices on hardware I/O inserts), assigning them meaningful names to match how you're actually using them. On larger system configurations and for surround mixing, this can be a fairly complex subject—in the *Pro Tools Reference Guide* PDF document included with the

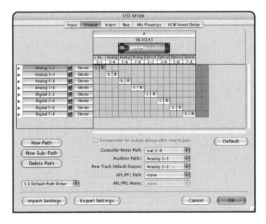
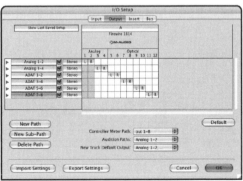

Figure 8.24 The I/O Setup dialog box lets you define named paths for inputs, outputs, inserts, and internal mixing busses. (Shown here: an HD system with a single 96 I/O, and an M-Powered system using the ADAT Lightpipe outputs on a FireWire 1814 interface.)

program, an entire chapter is dedicated to I/O setup—so only a brief overview and some general recommendations are provided here.

The I/O Setup dialog box is organized into various tabs (Inputs, Outputs, Inserts, and Busses, plus Mic Preamps and Hardware Insert Delay on HD systems), each of which contains a channel grid that varies according to the audio interface(s) available in your configuration. A *path* is essentially a label for one of these audio pathways, which can be either mono, stereo pairs, or multichannel. The available choices for Input and Output selectors on audio, Aux Input, or Instrument tracks, Output selectors on Master Fader tracks, send assignments, and Hardware I/O inserts are all determined by the paths that have been defined in the I/O Setup dialog box. Stereo and multichannel *main paths* are logical groupings of multiple mono *subpaths*; use the dialog box's Channel grid to specify exactly which physical inputs and outputs correspond to each of these mono subpaths. (Templates are provided for the common surround formats, and of course, you can create your own configurations. Chapter 14 provides more information about surround mixing in Pro Tools.) Note that you can use the checkboxes in front of each main path in the Channel grid to toggle their active/inactive status. This can reduce clutter in pop-up menus, when selecting inputs, outputs, and send destinations.

Especially if your audio hardware has multiple inputs and outputs, it's a good idea to assign meaningful names to the inputs, outputs, hardware I/O inserts, and busses on your Pro Tools system. For example, you might have your Focusrite microphone preamp more or less permanently connected to inputs 1–2 of the audio interface and a Korg Triton synth connected to inputs 7–8. Why not create two stereo input paths named Focusrite and Triton, each consisting of two mono subpaths for the corresponding physical inputs so that these names always appear when you pop open the Input selector on audio tracks or Auxiliary Inputs? Likewise, if you have an external reverb more or less permanently looped into outputs 5–6 so that it can be used as a stereo I/O insert from Pro Tools tracks, go ahead and assign this insert path a default name. On Pro Tools|HD systems, you can also manually set a latency amount for each hardware I/O insert. This delay time (representing how long it takes for audio to get out through that external device and back into the Pro Tools mixing environment) is compensated for when the Automation Delay Compensation engine is enabled on Pro Tools|HD systems. If outputs 3–4 on the audio interface are always connected to an audio tie line or studio feed, go ahead and set a default name for this stereo output path that will always be obvious.

Alternatively, you may use the I/O Setup dialog box to assign names that are pertinent only to the *current* session simply to make a complex routing scenario easier to manage. When you use internal mixing busses to route multiple sends to a stereo Aux Input with an effect, it can make life simpler, for example, if you name that bus pair Delay. The bus pair will appear by this name in the Output selectors for each stereo send and also the Input selector for the Aux Input track where you've instantiated this effect—a heck of a lot easier to remember than, say, bus 7–8, right?

Another good habit is to create default names for a couple of your busses (or stereo bus pairs)—perhaps Verb Send or Delay Send. As already mentioned, when you select busses with descriptive names as the source for send or output destinations and inputs on Aux Input tracks with effects, it's much easier to see at a glance what's going on in your session. Consistent naming conventions and regular habits like these save you time later and become *extremely* important when more than one operator has a hand in the same session document! (In all versions 7.3 and higher, you can change the names of input/output paths and internal mixing busses at any time. You do so in the Mix or Edit window by right-clicking the audio input/output or send selectors on any audio-related track and selecting Rename in the pop-up menu. The contents of the I/O Setup dialog box will be updated accordingly.)

Click the Default button in the I/O Setup dialog box to reset the channel grid for the path type (Input, Output, Insert, or Bus; plus Mic Preamps and HW Insert Delays on HD systems) being displayed in the current tab to a factory-defined default configuration. In this default configuration, all possible main stereo paths are created for your audio hardware, plus two mono subpaths for each.

Use as Many (Or as Few) Paths as You Require If you're using an M-Audio audio interface with ADAT Lightpipe I/O, you may be surprised to discover that, by default, these inputs and outputs don't appear in the I/O Setup dialog box. If you don't have Lightpipe devices in your studio configuration, that's appropriate. Otherwise, these unnecessary selections would appear every time you select track inputs and outputs. If you *do* want to use this type of I/O on your interface, however, two steps are usually required. First, in the device's own setup application, be sure to activate the ADAT input/output. Then, in Pro Tools' I/O Setup dialog box, click the Default button in both the Input and Output tabs to automatically create all possible stereo paths (with mono subpaths) for ADAT input/output on this interface.

After configuring I/O Setup to your taste, click the Export Settings button (seen in Figure 8.24) so that you can recall this setup at any time. Experienced users will have many different I/O configurations stored this way as presets for various tasks. It is also a great idea to periodically back up the contents of the IO Settings subfolder of the main Pro Tools program folder, especially before installing any new version of the Pro Tools software.

Session

Some of the parameters displayed in the Session Setup window (see Figure 8.25) are fixed when you first create the current Pro Tools session—audio file format, sample rate, and bit depth, for example. The Session Start Time setting, however, is important when synchronizing to incoming SMPTE time code (converted to MIDI time code by your SMPTE synchronization peripheral)

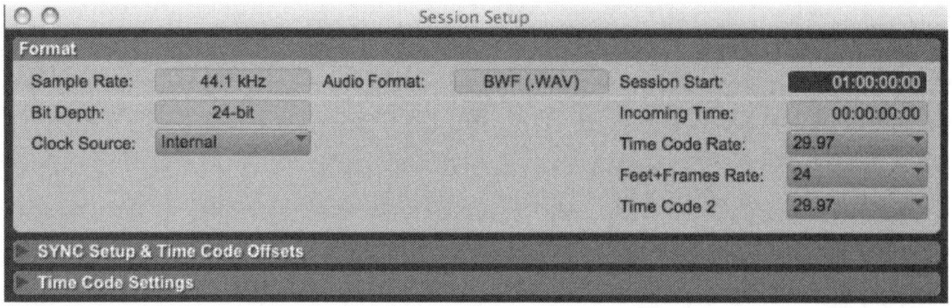

Figure 8.25 Use the Session Setup window to specify a session's frame rate and other options for SMPTE time code. (The LE version is shown here; options vary in HD and M-Powered versions.)

because this is how Pro Tools knows what time-code position corresponds to the beginning of the session's timeline. The frame rate (number of frames per second) you specify for your Pro Tools session must match that of the incoming time code in order for Pro Tools to synchronize properly to the video (or audio) master. Pro Tools can also *generate* time code with certain peripherals, as well as MIDI time code. (See Chapter 11, "Synchronization," for more detailed information about synchronization.) In the HD version of Pro Tools, you can select the sync I/O or a digital audio input here as the external clock source that controls the sample rate of your audio hardware, as opposed to its internal clock. Clock-source changes here are reflected in the Hardware Setup dialog box and vice versa. However, in the M-Powered version of Pro Tools, you select the clock source in the audio interface's own control panel software.

Reminder: When you record from a digital input (S/PDIF coaxial or optical, AES/EBU, TDIF, or ADAT Lightpipe, according to the audio interface you're using), it's common to switch the clock source from internal to the source digital input. (This will be the case unless you're using a central, high-quality clock source as the master for both Pro Tools and the external device that's your audio source.) This slaves the sample clock of your Pro Tools hardware to that of the specified incoming digital audio signal. Okay—so far, so good. Then, as you continue working, maybe your DAT powers itself off (or perhaps you leave it turned off the next time you open this session). If the clock source is still set to the digital input, your audio hardware tries to synchronize to a non-existent external timing reference, and your playback speed may be very slow and peculiar—or playback may simply non-existent on M-Powered systems! Just switch the clock source back from the digital input to internal clock, and you'll be back to normal. (Don't laugh—it may happen to you!)

In larger studios with multiple digital audio devices, however, it's common to use a highly stable, centralized clock source to which the sample rates of all the devices are slaved in a sort of star configuration. Not only does this improve synchronization as these devices play back together, but the better units can noticeably improve audio quality by reducing jitter and other irregularities in the clock that controls audio sample rates. The "Word Clock and Sync Generators" section of Appendix B, "Add-ons, Extensions, and Cool Stuff for Your Rig," provides a few examples of these master clock devices.

Time Code Formats Around the World We discuss SMPTE time code in greater detail in Chapter 11, but if you're configuring the Session Setup window, here's a quick reference for where the various frame rates are commonly used:

- For audio-only applications, 30 frames per second (fps) non-drop is very common throughout the world (although theoretically, you could use any frame rate for syncing two MIDI or audio-only devices).

- For video in North America, parts of Latin America, most of the Caribbean, as well as South Korea, Taiwan, and Japan, 29.97 fps drop or non-drop is the norm for video work (it makes a difference whether it's drop or non-drop; be sure to ask!) because this frame rate is associated with the NTSC color television format used in these parts of the world.

- 25 fps is used for video projects in Europe, Africa, Brazil, Argentina, Paraguay, Uruguay, Australia, parts of the Middle East, and most of Asia. The 25 fps frame rate corresponds to that the PAL and SECAM television formats common in these regions.

- 24 fps is used for film everywhere.

Setup > MIDI Submenu
These options affect how MIDI data is sent and received from Pro Tools in general.

MIDI Studio Setup (Mac)
Audio MIDI Setup (sometimes referred to as AMS) is a utility included in Mac OS X (that is, any Mac operating system 10 or higher) that manages your MIDI configuration—i.e., what kind of MIDI interface you're using and how many ports/channels it has, which MIDI controllers and modules are available on your system, where they are attached to the interface, and so on. In Mac versions, the Setup > MIDI > MIDI Studio menu selection in Pro Tools launches the operating system's Audio MIDI Setup utility. You indicate where your MIDI keyboards and modules are connected by dragging cables between symbols for input/output ports to those of your MIDI interface. You specify whether each is a controller, is multitimbral, what channel it transmits/receives, and other attributes. You can also assign logical names to each MIDI device, which then appear as you select MIDI destinations for tracks within Pro Tools (and any other MIDI-compatible program under Mac OS X). Lastly, you can subscribe to a patchname document in Pro Tools for your MIDI device so that you can use the MIDI Program Selector button for each MIDI track in the Mix window to select programs for MIDI tracks on the destination device by *name* rather than by program number. Note that if your MIDI device doesn't appear in the pre-configured list included with Audio MIDI Setup or Pro Tools itself, there are user-supported Web sites where you can download patchname documents.

MIDI Studio Setup (Windows)

The MIDI Studio Setup window in Windows versions of Pro Tools serves a similar function to the Audio MIDI Setup utility for Mac, and is discussed further in Chapter 10. Briefly, you can define instruments for each of the external MIDI controllers or modules, also indicating where each is connected to the available ports of your system's MIDI interface. (You can also daisy-chain multiple devices on a single port of the interface, of course, via their In/Out/Thru ports.) You can assign a descriptive name to each port on your MIDI interface.

You can click the MIDI Program Selector button on each MIDI track in the Mix window and assign a MIDI patchname file (.MIDNAM) so that you can select sounds on its destination device by *name* instead of by program number. (The ability to select patchname files is also available in all Mac versions, via the Audio MIDI Setup utility provided in the operating system.) As with the patchname files on Macintosh, these are simple text files containing data in the XML language. You can very easily edit these files' contents in Notepad, WordPad, or any word processor capable of saving back to TXT format. This is highly recommended if you've altered the contents of the user banks on the device, for example.

MIDI Beat Clock

Some external drum machines, sequencers inside keyboard workstations, and arpeggiators can synchronize to Pro Tools using this method. Part of the original MIDI data specification, MIDI Beat Clock doesn't contain any absolute time-code (location) information. Instead, it's tempo related—at 24 pulses per ¼ note (PPQN). In the MIDI Beat Clock dialog box, you simply indicate the MIDI device/output where you want MIDI Clock data to be transmitted. Appendix D contains information about transferring sequences from external MIDI workstations (or drum machines) into Pro Tools.

Input Filter

In this dialog box, you select what types of MIDI data Pro Tools will record and/or pass through. For example, you may choose to disable polyphonic aftertouch received from your MIDI controller if you know that none of the MIDI modules or plug-ins you're using respond to this type of data (especially since polyphonic aftertouch dramatically increases the number of MIDI events recorded on the track). Or, in a scenario where you're recording keyboardists via MIDI during a live performance, you might choose not to record their changes to the master volume control (MIDI controller 7) made for the purpose of onstage monitoring levels.

Input Devices

In larger MIDI configurations, there may be many MIDI devices that you could potentially use as controllers. To minimize the number of selections that appear each time you select the MIDI input source for MIDI and Instrument tracks, you can use this dialog box to disable display of certain devices.

Click/Countoff

To set up what kind of click sound you want and how it will behave, open the Click/Countoff Options dialog box (shown in Figure 8.26), also available by double-clicking the Metronome Click button or Countoff display in the MIDI controls section of the Transport window. When you instantiate the Click plug-in on a mono Aux Input track (although technically it could also be instantiated on audio or Instrument tracks), it produces a metronome click sound per the tempo map or manual tempo setting in Pro Tools. The Click plug-in itself enables you to choose what sound to use for the metronome click and the relative levels of accented and unaccented beats. If you instead prefer to use some external MIDI device as the source for your click sound, you'd select its MIDI output and channel, as well as the MIDI note numbers, velocities, and durations to use for accented and unaccented beats, in the Click/Countoff Options dialog box. It should be noted, however, that some users are more comfortable recording the click sound (whether from this plug-in or some external source) onto an audio track to ensure that there will be absolutely no timing variations in DSP-intensive sessions. As you can see in the figure, you can enable the click always, only during record, or only during countoff bars. You can also set the desired number of countoff bars (during which only the metronome click sounds) in this dialog box.

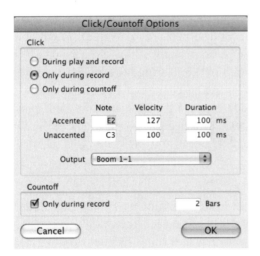

Figure 8.26   You can open the Click/Countoff Options dialog box by double-clicking the Metronome Click button or Countoff display in the Transport window as well as via Setup > Click/Countoff.

Preferences

Many of the items in the Preferences dialog box are self-explanatory, so this section mentions only a few of the most important or poorly understood selections. Note that a few items were located in a different tab of the Preferences dialog box in Pro Tools versions prior to 7.3.

Display Preferences

Options in this tab of the Preferences dialog box affect how track data is displayed and how peak levels and clipping indicators are handled in Pro Tools.

- **Color Coding > Always Display Marker Colors.** We recommend that most users enable this option. In the Markers ruler, the color assigned (automatically or manually) to each marker will fill the ruler until the next marker is reached in the timeline. If you're using markers to identify sections of a song or scenes in a video, this helps you see at a glance where you are in the session. If, however, the colors bother you, or you're using a large number of markers for a different purpose, disable this option.

- **Color Coding > Default Track/Region Color.** These two options determine how colors are assigned to tracks and regions. Color-coding for tracks and especially the regions within them helps you keep track of what's going on in a large session. Tracks and MIDI Channels is perhaps the best initial setting; then, as you experiment with the use of colors to keep track of your session material (such as Mix and Edit groups, MIDI devices, or location of regions between markers in the timeline), you will discover other useful settings for specific editing tasks or project types.

- **Meters > Peak Hold.** A small, horizontal yellow line in the level meters on tracks indicates the highest peak level reached during playback. Three modes can be selected for this feature: 3 Second, Infinite, and None. For most uses, the 3 Second setting is practical, although you can also set this to Infinite. The Peak Hold feature helps you monitor how close your levels are getting to maximum, for example. Another approach to monitoring peak levels on audio, Aux Input, Instrument, or Master Fader tracks is to Command-click (Ctrl-click in Windows) the Volume/Peak/Delay indicator at the bottom of each track in the Mix window to display peak levels. This peak indicator holds the maximum level attained during playback infinitely until you Option-click (Alt-click in Windows) to clear it. Because it provides an actual numerical value, the peak indicator field is usually a more practical tool than the level meter display when you are interested in monitoring peak levels.

- **Meters > Clip Indication.** Level meters on audio, Aux Input, Instrument, and Master Fader tracks feature a top red segment that indicates when 100% is exceeded (which causes clipping, distorting the original audio waveform passing through that track). Some people prefer the 3 Second setting. When set to Infinite, however, the clipping indicator remains lit until you reset it (by clicking it). But remember: You *never* want to see the red clipping indicator light up—on any track (or in any plug-in window)! Be especially sure to check for this before bouncing out any mixes. This digital distortion is undesirable, and you should adjust your gain structure (the audio levels going in and out of each component in the mixing environment) to avoid it.

PhaseScope Plug-in For more detailed information about signal level and phase (either on the Master Fader for your main mix output or any other audio-related track type), you should use the PhaseScope metering plug-in, provided with all Pro Tools versions 7.3 and higher. Metering views include Peak, RMS, Peak+RMS, VU, BBC, DIN, Nordic, and Venue.

Operation Preferences

As you become more adept with Pro Tools, you will find it convenient to change some of the options in the Operation tab of the Preferences dialog box for specific projects, or even for different phases of the same project.

- **Transport > Timeline Insertion/Play Start Marker Follows Playback.** Ordinarily, when you click Stop after recording or playback, the Transport's Start value (and therefore the position in the timeline where playback will next commence) remains the same. When you enable Timeline Insertion/Play Start Marker Follows Playback, the Start value (where playback or the next recording will start) and the location of the Play Start marker (used in Dynamic Transport mode) always update to wherever you last clicked Stop. This is very useful, for example, when recording spoken-word projects like long narrations or books on tape. When recording live speakers and theatrical presentations, you could stop during pauses and then simply click Record again to pick up recording at the exact point in the session's timeline where you left off. Also note the button in the Edit window below the Pencil tool that represents this preference.

- **Transport > Edit Insertion Follows Scrub/Shuttle.** If you frequently use the Scrub tool or a scrub wheel on an external controller to scan through audio regions, there may be situations where you want to enable this item. Similar to the Timeline Insertion Follows Playback option, the time value for the Edit insertion point (indicated by the Main/Sub location indicators of the Edit window) is updated to wherever you stopped scrubbing. When you hold down the Rewind or Fast Forward button (or the 1 or 2 key on the numeric keypad—a very good shortcut to know!), Pro Tools shuttles quickly through the timeline. In a similar manner, when you enable Edit Insertion Follows Scrub/Shuttle in Preferences, the Edit insertion point ends up at whatever point you stopped shuttling.

- **Numeric Keypad Mode.** Although a few users prefer the Classic or Shuttle modes for controlling Transport functions with the numeric keypad, try leaving this set to Transport for now; otherwise, the cool numeric keypad shortcuts given for Transport functions in this book won't work!

- **Record > Link Record and Play Faders.** When enabled, any volume changes you make on a track during recording (remember that these do not affect the actual levels recorded to disk!) are retained in Playback mode. Generally, most users prefer to leave this disabled. That way, you can adjust volumes while recording (for example, to hear a part better, or to *reduce* its level if you're otherwise hearing some of the direct signal during recording anyway) without having to worry about this affecting this fader's level in the mix during playback.

■ **Record > Open Ended Record Allocation.** Unless you are recording extremely long performances (as in live theater, or a symphonic piece) and are not sure how long they may last, it is generally prudent to limit the number of minutes here instead of enabling Use All Available Space. For one thing, Pro Tools jumps into Record mode slightly faster because it doesn't have to pre-allocate *all* the free space available on the hard drive being used for each track (assignable via Setups > Disk Allocation) before starting to record. But there's an additional advantage: If Pro Tools should ever hang catastrophically during recording, an entire audio drive can appear full upon restart (on rare occasions), even though you don't see files to account for all that space. (The recording work files that were in progress when the computer froze up may still have disk space allocated, even though they are invisible to the operating system.) With effort, you can remedy all this, but limiting this hard-drive allocation in the first place may help you get Pro Tools back into Record mode more quickly—before your clients get peevish!

■ **Enable Session File Auto Backup.** When this option is enabled, backup copies of your session files are automatically saved while you work. Here, you specify how often this happens and how many backup copies should be saved. These are stored inside your session folder in the Session File Backups subfolder, which is created automatically. Backup copies are numbered, and .bak is added to your session's file name. If your main session file ever becomes corrupted—or if you completely mess it up yourself—this feature could save a lot of frustration. You can open any auto-saved backup copy of your session with the File > Open Session command. (Pro Tools will add "recovered" to the title bar for this session document to prevent you from confusing it with the original file when/if you save this backup version of the session to disk.) This is a very important feature of Pro Tools that can save the day—and your reputation. Unless you have overpowering reasons not to (such as marginal system performance), it is strongly recommended that you enable Auto Backup!

Editing Preferences

You will change some of the settings in the Editing tab of the Preferences dialog box to suit your working style. As with previous tabs in Preferences, only several of the most critical options are mentioned here; more details for the other selections are available in the *Menus Guide* PDF document supplied with Pro Tools.

■ **Auto-Name Memory Locations While Playing.** Ordinarily, when you use the numeric keyboard's Enter key to create markers during play or record, a dialog box appears. You enter a marker name, specify its properties (absolute or relative, zoom settings, track heights, and other attributes, including comments), and then click OK. If you don't want to go through these steps (for example, because you're creating frequent markers while recording or listening back to a performance and don't want to be distracted), enable this option. Pro Tools automatically assigns new marker names each time you hit the Enter key—Marker 1,

Marker 2, and so on—*without* the dialog box appearing each time. You can always change marker names, properties, and locations afterward.

■ **Default Fade Settings.** This is fairly self-explanatory: Change the default fade shape display format for the fade-in, fade-out, and crossfade types to match the settings you use the most. It's mentioned here only because too many users never seem to get around to changing this preference!

■ **Zoom Toggle.** This feature was significantly upgraded in version 7.3 of Pro Tools. The Edit window's Zoom Toggle button (beneath the Zoomer tool) is used to switch between the current zoom level and some other defined zoom level for the current selection. Here are just a few examples, although as you get adept at Pro Tools editing you will definitely want to explore these functions more. If you set your preference to Selection for vertical and/or horizontal zoom, the current selection will be zoomed in to fill available space when you click the Zoom toggle button. Click it again, and the track selection reverts to the previous zoom level. You can also define a track view (for example, waveform) and a track height that will always be enabled when you click the Zoom toggle button.

■ **Levels of Undo.** The default setting is 32, and this is fine for most users. The Undo History window also greatly facilitates the process of stepping back through many editing operations to a previous state of the session. The number of steps available in the Undo History window is also determined by this Preference setting.

Mixing Preferences

The options in the Mixing tab of the Preferences window are mostly self-explanatory. Among other things, they affect automation behavior, and how external control surfaces interact with the Pro Tools Mix and Edit windows. It's also where you determine whether the level of newly-created sends should default to $-\infty$ (minus infinity).

■ **Set Pans Default to Follow Main Pan.** We generally recommend that this option (introduced in version 7.3) be enabled. On new tracks, by default the FMP (follow main pan) button will be enabled. This means that the send's position in stereo or the surround-sound field will be slaved to that of the track's main panner for its output. When required (for example, when you want panning for a delay or reverb send to be on the opposite side from its main output), you can always disable this button on any track.

■ **Default EQ, Default Dynamics (versions 7.3 and higher).** The EQ and Dynamics plug-ins you choose in these two fields will automatically appear at the top of the pop-up menu for selecting insert plug-ins in your tracks, making it much quicker to access these frequently used effects.

Processing Preferences

Processing preferences affect the operation of AudioSuite plug-ins, time compression and expansion, audio-file import options, and the defaults for Elastic Audio processing.

- **Automatically Copy Files on Import.** If the audio files you import into a session already match its bit depth and sample rate (and don't need to be split into mono pairs), they don't necessarily have to be copied into its Audio Files subfolder unless you deliberately click the Copy button instead of the Add button in the Import Audio dialog box. However, users quickly learn that they can simply double-click source files in this dialog box to add them to the list of regions currently chosen for import. If you generally *do* want to copy files rather than import them from their original locations (especially if they're on a CD-ROM or some other removable media, for example, or in order to avoid potential risk when the same source files are used in multiple sessions), enable this option.

- **Drag and Drop from Desktop Conforms to Session Tempo (versions 7.4 and higher).** This is related to the Elastic Audio features. The default is for only Rex and ACID files (with their inherent support of timeslices) to automatically conform to the session tempo when dragged in from the operating system's desktop. Especially if most of your work involves conforming existing loops to existing tempos in the Pro Tools session, or when you're merely experimenting with a large number of alternatives for this purpose, you might want to enable this automatic conforming option for all audio files.

- **Elastic Audio > Enable Elastic Audio on New Tracks (versions 7.4 and higher).** When enabled, the default Elastic Audio mode (polyphonic, unless you change that in this same section of the preferences) will be enabled on all new audio tracks.

- **TC/E Plug-in.** The default plug in for using the Time Compression/Expansion mode of the Trimmer tool is Time Shift. However, if it's available, you could also choose Digidesign's X-Form or some other third-party time-compression/expansion plug-in if you prefer.

MIDI Preferences

Most users will find the default settings here to be a good starting point—although you may eventually set your own default Note On velocity for when you create notes with the Pencil tool, for instance, or enable Use MIDI to Tap Tempo. Here, we mention several essential options in the MIDI tab of the Preferences dialog box.

- **Use F11 Key for Wait for Note.** As mentioned in Chapter 5, "The Transport Window," when the Wait for MIDI Note function is enabled, after you click Record in the Transport, recording still doesn't begin until the first MIDI event is received (even if you are recording on an audio track). This option enables the F11 key as a shortcut for turning the Wait for Note button on and off. Note that Macintosh users should see the sidebar in Chapter 5 entitled "Macintosh, Pro Tools, and Using Function Keys F9–F12" about reassigning the default function keys for Exposé, which otherwise interfere with the Wait for Note feature in Pro Tools.

- **Default Thru Instrument.** This is where you select the MIDI output and channel that appear by default in new MIDI and Instrument tracks. This is also the destination that is used when you preview MIDI regions. Just as you can Option-click (Alt-Click in Windows) on an audio region to preview it in the Regions List, doing this on a MIDI region will play it through the destination chosen for the Default Thru Instrument setting. Generally speaking, the most useful option in this pop-up menu is Follows First Selected MIDI Track. When this is enabled, you can first select a MIDI or Instrument track whose assigned output has an appropriate-sounding patch so that its sound will be used for previewing MIDI regions in the Regions List.

- **Global MIDI Playback Offset.** Especially when using external MIDI instruments, you may find that there is a more or less fixed amount of delay with respect to the actual start point of the note events on your MIDI and Instrument tracks. It does take some small interval of time for MIDI events to be transmitted from your MIDI interface, plus some degree of analog-to-digital conversion delay that is added when you monitor these external sources through inputs on your audio interface. Much more significant, however, is that, after receiving a Note On event, many MIDI keyboards and modules can take quite a few milliseconds to get around to triggering an actual sound in response. Setting a negative playback offset globally for MIDI tracks here in Preferences can be the easiest way to compensate for this. Nevertheless, remember that the MIDI Track Offsets dialog box (discussed in this chapter, under the Event menu) always enables you to set offsets for each MIDI or Instrument track individually.

- **Automatically Create Click Track in New Sessions (versions 7.3 and higher).** If the majority of your projects are music sessions, you will want to enable this setting. That way, in each new Pro Tool session, a mono Aux Input track is automatically created with the Click plug-in already instantiated.

Window Menu

The selections in this menu are for showing/hiding the various windows of Pro Tools. Many are discussed elsewhere in this book and won't be covered here, but several are worth special mention.

Window Configurations

Window configurations, available in Pro Tools versions 7.3 and higher, enable you to store view sets in Pro Tools. These include the size and location of most Pro Tools windows (including Mix, Edit, and Transport), plug-ins and panners, memory locations, Workspace/Project browsers, time/tempo/event operations, the Video window, and various others. When you create a new window configuration, a checkbox in the New Window Configuration dialog box enables you to choose whether current display settings in the Mix, Edit, and Transport windows should also be stored as part of the window layout. Alternatively, you can store display settings for the Mix, Edit, and Transport windows separately, without including size or location settings that affect

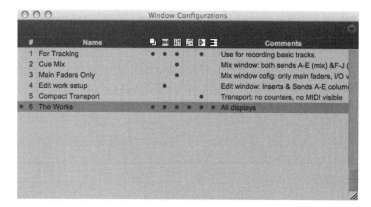

Figure 8.27 Use the Windows Configurations window to store your own presets for the size and locations of the numerous windows in Pro Tools or display settings within the Mix, Edit, and Transport windows.

any other windows. From the Window > Configurations submenu, you can open the Window Configurations window, shown in Figure 8.27. Its keyboard shortcut is Command+Option+J (Ctrl+Alt+J in Windows). In this figure, you can see window configurations that are specific to the Mix, Edit, and Transport windows, plus others that are more general for use during specific phases of a project.

Task Manager Window

Many tasks in Pro Tools occur in the background—for example, fade creation, relinking to files that are missing or were moved since the last time a Pro Tools session was saved, copying source files as you import track data from other Pro Tools session documents, redrawing audio waveforms, and so on. All these have some effect on your system's performance at any given moment, so it's handy to be able to check what's going on. Be sure to check out the options in the pop-up menu in the upper-left corner of the Task Manager window. For one thing, you can cancel, pause, or resume individual tasks.

If a complex project is heavily taxing the capabilities of your system as you edit and play audio, pausing or canceling these background tasks may be a short-term solution. In particular, though, notice the last item in this pop-up menu, Pause During Playback. This global preference prevents background tasks from diverting resources while Pro Tools is in Record or Playback mode. If your system is already underpowered for the kind of projects you work on, be sure to enable this option.

Take time to explore the *DigiBase Guide*, a PDF document provided with Pro Tools. It covers features of both DigiBase (all versions) and DigiBase Pro, which is included with Pro Tools HD and can be added to LE via the DV Toolkit 2 and Complete Production Toolkit options. This document provides much more detailed explanations (over 80 pages' worth) of the Task, Workspace, Project, and Catalog browser windows.

Status Indicators for Timeline and Session in the Edit Window Two indicators, called Timeline and Session, appear below the Edit Selection display in the Edit window. When the Timeline indicator is green, it means that all files used by regions within audio tracks are properly linked and available for playback. Otherwise, this indicator is red, meaning that some files need to be located and relinked (if you check in the Task Manager window, this may already be in progress). When the Session indicator is green, it means that all source files referenced by the session (both audio and video) are properly linked and available for playback, whether they are currently being used within a track or not.

Workspace Browser Window

This window is used with the Project browser window, discussed in the next section. The Workspace and Project browser windows are the two browsers for the DigiBase technology, an audio (and video) file database engine that is an integral part of the Pro Tools platform. (The DigiBase Pro version included with Pro Tools HD and the DV Toolkit 2 or Complete Production Toolkit options for LE systems offers additional features, including a third Catalog browser window.) At the simplest level, the Workspace browser window provides a bird's eye view of all eligible disk volumes for audio playback and recording on your system, their capacity, and how much space is currently available. You can also specify whether each of your disk volumes should be used for playback, recording (and playback), or for transfer only—meaning that you can view and copy files from that disk but not play back audio files from it in real time. In addition, you can unmount disk volumes directly from the Workspace browser by highlighting the drive and choosing Unmount from the pull-down menu in the upper-right corner of the browser. Within this window, you can browse the entire folder/file hierarchy on each disk without leaving Pro Tools, as well as view audio file attributes and audition audio files. You can rename, duplicate, and delete folders and files in the Workspace browser window. You can even add comments about these audio files that will be visible in this window, within this or other Pro Tools sessions.

From the Workspace browser window, you can drag the audio files (seen in their original disk locations) directly to the Regions List or onto an audio track with a matching number of channels (for example, mono or stereo). You can import audio files into Pro Tools from audio CDs by dragging tracks directly from the Workspace browser window to the Regions List or onto a stereo audio track in the Edit window. The Preview button enables you to listen to audio and MIDI files before deciding to import them into your session. A pop-up selector, which you access by right-clicking the Preview button, enables you to use two additional preview mode options: Loop Preview, which loops playback of the selected file while the button is active, and Auto-Play, which initiates preview playback as soon as you select each source audio or MIDI file while in this browser. The preview volume can be adjusted by a pop-up fader when the volume display next to the Preview button is clicked and held. The audio output path will be determined by your Audition Path settings in the I/O Setup dialog box (while preview playback of MIDI files is determined by the Default Thru Instrument setting in the MIDI tab of the Preferences dialog box). In Pro Tools versions 7.4 and higher, clicking a Metronome button at the top of this browser window enables the Audio Files Conform to Session Tempo button. In this mode, audio preview of all REX files, ACID files, and tick-based audio files with Elastic Audio analysis will be conformed to the current session tempo (per the mode currently appearing in the Elastic Audio plug-in selector, immediately to the right of this button in the browser window). This is obviously very useful for loop selection, for example. If you want to automatically create a new track, either drag the file from the Workspace browser window into the Tracks List at the left edge of the Edit window or hold down the Shift key as you drag it directly into the Edit window's track display area.

You can also preview standard MIDI files in the Workspace browser window and import them by dragging them into the Regions List. If you instead drag the MIDI file into the Tracks List (when visible at the left edge of the Edit window), an appropriate number of new MIDI tracks is created. An Import MIDI Settings dialog box enables you to choose whether to import the existing tempo map in that file and whether to delete existing MIDI/Instrument tracks and/or MIDI regions. There's a Search button (the one with the magnifying glass) in the Workspace and Project browser windows; you can click it to search for files by name on multiple volumes (including searches with wildcard characters and the Boolean operators OR/AND), by kind (folder, audio, video, session, OMF, AAF, MIDI, or region group), and by modification date. You can constrain searches to certain volumes and folders, or you can scan the entire system simultaneously. With DigiBase Pro, you can additionally search by attributes in the other columns of these windows, such as file format, sample rate, bit depth, creation date, and comments. This is powerful stuff!

Don't Use Your System Volume for Audio Recording In the Workspace browser window, you can designate each of the disk volumes on your system (whether entire disks or logical partitions on a single physical disk) for audio playback and/or recording (P or R), or transfer only (T). Be sure that your system volume (the disk or partition containing the operating system used to boot up the computer, and usually most of the program files as well) is set to Transfer to prevent session audio files from getting stored there as the result of recording or editing operations.

Project Browser Window

This window (shown in Figure 8.28) provides powerful features for organizing complex projects and for working in collaboration with other people on large Pro Tools sessions. It also helps you keep track of which files are used in the current session, including their disk locations and other attributes. For example, for each source audio file, columns in the Project browser window can display its name, a waveform graphic with an Audition button, its absolute duration, a user-editable file and database comments, creation and modification dates, the number of channels, file size, format, sample rate, bit depth, and the original and user timestamp information. Very

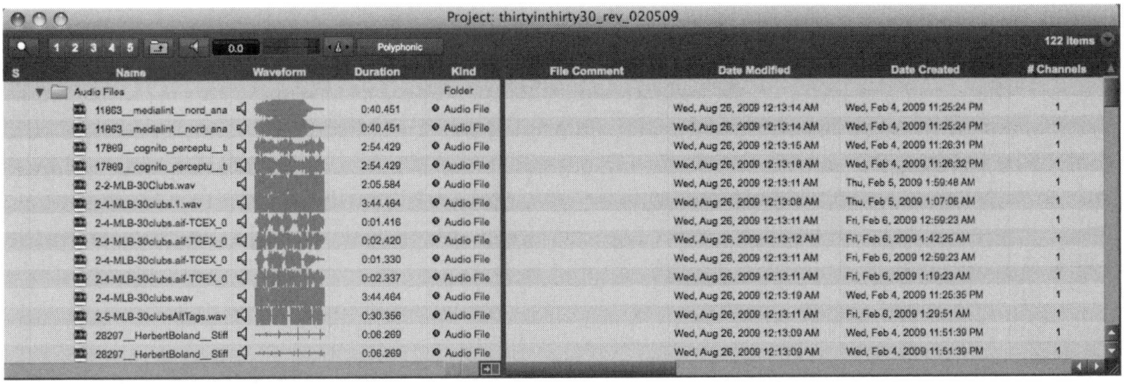

Figure 8.28   The Project browser window.

importantly, the full disk/folder path to this file's location on your computer system is shown in the Project browser window, with a unique file ID assigned by Pro Tools. When you find audio files missing upon reopening a Pro Tools session (perhaps because you changed their disk or folder locations or moved this project from one Pro Tools system to another), the Project browser window provides tools for relinking references from regions used in that session to the correct source files in the form of the Relink Missing Media browser. The unique file IDs that Pro Tools assigns to each audio file you import make it much easier to locate them afterward in the Project browser window, even if there are other files on the same disks with similar or identical names.

Find and Import Files Directly from Workspace, Project Browser Windows After you locate an audio or MIDI file you want to use, you can drag it from either one of these DigiBase browser windows directly into the Regions List or a Pro Tools track with a matching number of channels to import it into your current session. To create a brand-new audio track at the same time, either drag the audio files into the Tracks List or hold down the Shift key as you drag the region to a specific timeline location in the track display area. You can also preview and import source tracks on audio CDs from these windows in the same manner.

Catalog Browser Window

Catalogs are a feature of DigiBase Pro, included in HD versions of Pro Tools. This feature is also available via the separately purchased DV Toolkit 2 and Complete Production Toolkit options for LE versions and the Music Production Toolkit option for LE and M-Powered versions. Like a list of favorite shortcuts or aliases, items in a catalog represent references to files that reside in many different disk/folder locations. You can store and recall many different catalogs when locating files in your Pro Tools sessions. To add files or entire folders to the currently displayed catalog, drag them directly into the Catalog browser window from either of the other two Dig-iBase browser windows. Alternatively, you can create a new catalog by selecting a group of files in one of these other browser windows and using the Create Catalog from Selection command in the browser window's pop-up local menu. To copy all the files referenced in a catalog to a new disk location, drag the catalog in the Workspace browser window onto another disk volume. And as with the other two DigiBase browser windows, you can drag and drop catalog items directly into the Regions List or Tracks List or onto audio, MIDI, or Instrument tracks in the Edit window.

Big Counter

This menu item opens a large display of the current playback location, visible from across the room as you perform. Time units in the Big Counter window reflect those of the main time scale (the active ruler, whose time units are also reflected in the Main location indicator). You can type new values into the Big Counter window's fields to change the play location or click and drag to scroll numerical values in any of its columns up or down. For some reason, a lot of users seem to overlook the Big Counter; this is a shame, because it's *very* convenient!

Automation Enable

The buttons in this window (the LE/M-Powered version of which is shown in Figure 8.29) enable you to suspend *all* automation in a Pro Tools session or to individually enable or disable recording for each type of automation data (volume, pan, mute, and plug-in parameters; level, pan, and mute for sends). In Pro Tools HD, the Automation Enable window includes additional controls. For instance, the AutoMatch button enables you to return controls to their previously existing levels while writing a new automation pass at a rate determined by the AutoMatch Time setting in the Mixing tab of the Preferences dialog box. (When using the D-Control or D-Command control surface, you can AutoMatch individual controls, such as sends, inserts, and plug-ins, without affecting other types of controls.) Another useful automation feature in HD systems is AutoJoin, which enables you to automatically pick up automation recording at the point in time where a previous automation pass in Latch mode ended. (And when using one of the Digidesign-supported control surfaces, you can *manually* select the point to resume auto-mation recording.)

Figure 8.29   Here, we've used the Automation Enable window to completely disable automation in this Pro Tools LE/M-Powered session. You can also separately enable or disable each type of automation data for recording.

Disabling Automation on Individual Tracks You can set the Automation Mode selector for any individual track to Auto Off, disabling *all* automation on that track. You can also suspend any *specific* automation parameter on an individual track. Use its Track View selector to display that type of automation (for example, the level of send "a," which you may have routed through a bus to an Aux Input where a delay effect was inserted). Next, Command-click (Ctrl-click in Windows) on this track's Track View selector (containing the name of the currently displayed automation parameter—send "a" in this case). The name will be dimmed, indicating that this type of automation data no longer plays back. Command-click (Ctrl-click in Windows) the Track View selector again to re-enable playback of that automation type. Reminder: In the Output window for any track, a Safe button for automation helps prevent accidental writing of automation into that track.

Memory Locations

Take some time to improve your use of memory locations, even if you're already a Pro Tools user! Memory locations are timeline positions; they can be *marker* memory locations (a single point) or *selection* memory locations (a range). Both types of memory locations can store any of the following properties: current zoom settings, pre-/post-roll times, track show/hide state, track heights, window configurations, and active groups. (You can even create general properties memory locations with their time properties set to None that won't alter the current timeline selection.) Both markers and selections can refer to absolute time locations or Bars:Beats values (whose location in absolute time varies according to the current tempo). Memory locations support adding comments up to 255 characters long, which you can optionally display in the Memory Locations window.

Markers

Markers are memory locations that identify single points in time. They appear on the Markers ruler (in the timeline at the top of the Edit window)—yellow diamonds for absolute time references and yellow chevrons for relative time references to Bars:Beats. You might use markers to flag the verses and choruses of a song or a scene transition in a video or film project. Click the button at the left end of the Markers ruler to create a new marker (or selection) at the current position or simply press the Enter key on the numeric keypad. This can even be done during recording and playback. Clicking any marker symbol in the Markers ruler moves the playback cursor to that position and recalls view properties stored with that marker, if any. You can click one marker and then Shift-click another to select the entire range between them on all tracks. You can also drag markers to new positions within the Markers ruler (their movement is affected by Grid mode). To reposition markers numerically, click them while in Spot edit mode. You can change the properties of a marker by double-clicking it either in the Markers ruler itself or in the Memory Locations window (look ahead to Figure 8.30).

Creating Markers on the Fly In either Play or Record mode, you can create memory locations by pressing Enter on the numeric keypad. This is handy, for example, to mark sections of a song or narration even as it's being recorded. (Remember, you can always drag markers around in the Markers ruler to fine-tune their locations afterward or use Spot edit mode to change marker locations numerically.) While recording a performer, you may notice mistakes, noises, or other items that you'll need to fix afterward. When this happens, create markers on the fly so that you can easily find those locations later. If you don't want to deal with the New Memory Location dialog box as you do this, enable the Auto-Name Memory Locations When Playing option in the Editing tab of the Preferences dialog box.

Selections

A selection memory location stores the currently highlighted range in the Edit window's timeline as either an absolute time reference or as Bars:Beats relative to the current Tempo setting. They can include multiple tracks. For example, if you need to bounce a section of the timeline to disk more than once (perhaps an entire song, with enough extra time at the end to allow for reverbs and delays to decay completely to silence), create a Selection memory location for it and call it Bounce. Or if you find yourself repeatedly highlighting a section of music for editing, perhaps the bridge of a song, and like to view it at a specific zoom level (for detailed vocal editing perhaps, or so that eight bars fits into the Edit window), create a selection memory location that also recalls the current zoom setting. While recording punch-ins by selecting the range within the track where recording should occur, it is also a good idea to create a selection memory location for the punch-in range. If you accidentally deselect the punch-in range while listening back to takes, you can simply recall the memory location. Unlike markers, selection memory locations do not appear in the Markers ruler. The Memory Locations window (shown in Figure 8.30) lets

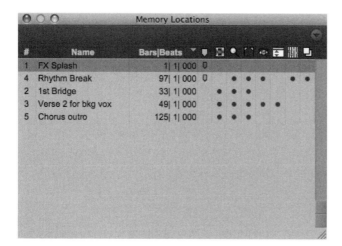

Figure 8.30 You can use memory locations to create markers or to recall selections (along with their zoom settings, track heights, and other attributes, if desired).

you view all markers and selections in your session, change their properties, rename them, or double-click to move the Pro Tools playback cursor directly to that location.

Video Universe

The Video Universe window displays the center frame of each video region in the main Video track and gives the user options to select and zoom in to/out of active video regions in the session. The zoom function can be activated by moving the cursor over the top half of the video frames within the Video Universe window. Actions the user can perform with the zoom function include filling the Edit window with a video region by double-clicking on the region's frame with the zoom cursor and selecting a range of video regions to fill the Edit window by dragging on the desired video frames. Moving the cursor along the bottom of the video frames causes the cursor to act like the Selector tool; users can then perform actions such as double-clicking a region's frame to select an entire video region and dragging the cursor over regions' frames to select a number of video regions.

Color Palette

You open the Color Palette window (shown in Figure 8.31) via this command in the Windows menu. You can also open this floating window by double-clicking a color strip (assuming they are visible in the Mix and/or Edit windows). You can assign colors to currently selected tracks and to regions and region groups either within tracks or in the Regions List. You can also assign colors to Mix and Edit groups; these color assignments will appear in the pop-up group indicator for each track in the Mix window.

Figure 8.31 Use the Color Palette window to assign colors to tracks, individual regions, groups, or markers.

Color-coding options in the Display tab of the Preferences dialog box enable you to automatically assign colors to tracks according to track type, group assignments, MIDI device, and channel assignments. For regions, you can also automatically assign colors per all of the above plus track color, Regions List color, and marker locations.

If you assign colors to markers, these colors are shown in the Markers ruler of the Edit window. (Always Show Marker Colors must be enabled in the Display tab of the Preferences dialog box in order for marker colors to be displayed.) The range from one marker until the next (or until the end of the session timeline, if it's the last marker) is highlighted in the preceding marker's color, and Pro Tools automatically assigns different colors (which you can change afterward using the Color Palette window) as adjacent markers are created in the timeline. This is especially useful when editing large sessions; even when you're at a high zoom level for editing events, you'll know you're within a specific scene or song section because you can see the color you assigned to that marker in the Markers ruler.

Most useful, perhaps, is that in the Edit window, you can use the Color Palette to manually assign colors to selected *regions* within tracks. This is a huge productivity booster, as anyone who has managed sessions with scores of individual loops, sound effects, vocal segments, or guitar segments within a single track can tell you. For example, by assigning colors before copying and pasting regions around, it's much easier to identify at a glance all the occurrences of a repeated item or the smaller regions created by cutting up a much longer one. Color-coding your source regions is also very helpful when *comping* (compositing) a vocal track from multiple source takes.

New to Pro Tools 8 is the ability to assign colors to channel strips in the Mix and Edit windows, making desired groupings of tracks considerably easier to quickly identify. Look for the Apply to Channel Strip button next to the Apply to Selected pull-down menu and click to toggle the function on and off.

Undo History

Another very welcome feature, the Undo History window, enables you to step back through various operations (edits, menu commands, and so on—anything that is immediately reversible via the Edit > Undo command). Pro Tools supports 32 levels of undo. In this columnar display, you can also choose to display the hours and minutes for each editing and recording action you've carried out (the Creation Time), as shown in Figure 8.32. Backing up to a previous state can be as easy as clicking the appropriate position in the Undo History window's list of actions. Note that the Options selector enables you to manually clear the Undo Queue; however,

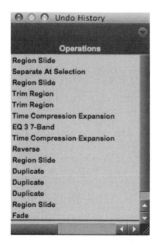

Figure 8.32 The Undo History window lets you step back through multiple editing operations rather than only one step backward, as with the Edit menu's Undo command.

certain editing actions also clear it automatically, such as deleting or importing tracks or using one of the Select Unused Regions commands in the local menu of the Regions List.

Disk Space and System Usage

The System Usage window shows approximately how much of your system's processing capacity the current session is using: the CPU, disk usage, and the computer's PCI bus (which is relevant if your system includes Pro Tools audio cards). On HD systems, the System Usage window (shown in Figure 8.33) can also show how DSP resources on any HD audio cards are currently allocated to mixing and plug-in processing tasks.

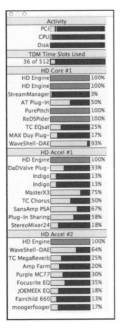

Figure 8.33   The System Usage window. Shown here, a Pro Tools|HD 2 system with two HD Accel cards.

Summary

As stated at the beginning of this lengthy chapter, only the more essential menu selections are highlighted here. Further information about these menu selections (and others we've omitted) is available in PDF documents provided with Pro Tools, including the *Pro Tools Reference Guide*, *Keyboard Shortcuts*, *DigiBase Guide*, and especially the *Menus Guide*. It is well worth your time to explore these.

The next chapter explores plug-ins, inserts, and sends in more detail; digital signal processing (DSP); RTAS and TDM audio plug-in architectures and ReWire; plus some tips for getting the most power out of the audio resources that your Pro Tools system provides. Read on!

9 Plug-ins, Inserts, and Sends

T his chapter looks a little more closely at how audio can be processed and routed within Pro Tools' software-based mixing environment. Plug-ins, inserts, and sends are discussed in Chapter 2, "Pro Tools Terms and Concepts," and especially in Chapter 7, "The Mix Window," but this chapter will help deepen your understanding of how audio moves around in Pro Tools' virtual signal-routing environment. If you are completely new to Pro Tools, be sure to read Chapter 7 first, which introduces you to the elements in the Mix window; this chapter expands on the concepts presented there.

Signal Routing in Pro Tools

Appendix E, "Signal Flow in Pro Tools," provides basic diagrams of audio signal flow within Pro Tools. While you record audio onto a track in Pro Tools, the signal flow is often as simple as this: An input source is connected to one of the analog or digital input channels on your audio hardware, and is then recorded straight to hard disk by a record-enabled audio track that was assigned to that channel.

Note that unless your Pro Tools audio hardware has physical controls for input gain, you must adjust your levels *at the source*. Audio interfaces in the Mbox 2 family (like its predecessor, the Mbox) have two front-panel gain knobs for two of their analog inputs, because these audio interfaces incorporate microphone pre-amps prior to the ADC (analog-to-digital converter). For similar reasons, the Digi 003 and Digi 002 have individual gain adjustment on their four mic/line inputs, while their line inputs 5–8 can be switched as a group between fixed +4dBu and −10dBV levels. Among the M-Audio audio interfaces for Pro Tools M-Powered, all the current FireWire models (and others that have microphone-level inputs) provide front-panel knobs for pre-amp gain adjustment on at least some of their channels. Make sure to consult the documentation for your particular interface.

As far as what you *hear* on an audio track, the signal path is pretty much the same whether its signal source is the track's input in record-enable or input-only monitoring mode, an audio file from disk, or one of the internal audio busses in the Pro Tools mixing environment. It goes like this: Input audio (which goes directly to hard disk from the selected input path, if a recording is in progress) goes through the Inserts section (after which it can optionally be directed to *pre-fader send destinations), then through the track's main volume fader (a *gain stage*), and then optionally to any *post*-fader send destinations, through the pan control, and finally to the track's current output assignment (either physical outputs or a mixing bus within Pro Tools).

Figure 9.1 shows typical signal flow for an audio track in Record versus Playback mode. (As you will see later in this chapter, the signal path for Aux Inputs is similar, while Master Faders differ because they have no sends and their inserts are always post-fader.) There are also several ways audio tracks can be set to monitor their selected input even when *not* in Record mode. For example, enabling Track > Input Only Monitor affects all audio tracks, and on HD systems, a Track Input Enable button on each audio track switches it to Input Monitor mode during normal playback, even if it already contains audio regions.

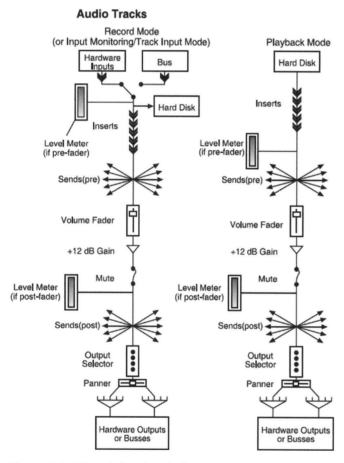

Figure 9.1 Virtual signal path for an audio track, in Record mode versus Playback mode.

Track Volume Faders Do Not Affect Record Level While you record on an audio track, its volume fader and mute button have *no effect* on the input level to the audio hardware.

This gives you the freedom to adjust monitoring levels while recording, either for your control-room mix or for the comfort of the performer(s). Unless Preferences > Operation > Link Record and Play Faders is enabled, when the track is no longer record-enabled, its volume fader returns to its previous playback level. The volume fader on audio tracks (as well as Aux Input, Instrument, and Master Fader tracks) can either decrease the track's level or apply as much as +12dB of gain boost.

About the Level Meters in Pro Tools   When Options > Pre Fader Metering is enabled, during *playback*, level meters on audio tracks, Aux Inputs, Instrument tracks, and Master Faders always reflect *post*-insert, *pre*-fader levels. In Pre-Fader Metering mode, the displayed levels on tracks *do* reflect any gain changes resulting from their inserts or plug-in effects, but are unaffected by current volume-fader settings (or the track's mute button).

When the Pre-Fader Metering setting is *not* enabled (the default), meters are post-fader. If you reduce a track's main volume fader, this is reflected in its level meter.

Whenever tracks are record enabled (or when Track > Input Only Monitor is enabled), the track level meters display *pre*-insert levels at the track's input. In contrast, on MIDI tracks the level meters display MIDI note-on velocities.

Input Channels

As explained in Chapter 2, to avoid confusion, this book distinguishes between *channels* for input/output of audio on the audio interface and *tracks* within the software itself—even though in the Mix window, tracks look like channel strips on a conventional mixing board. (Although the Pro Tools documentation often refers to "channel strips" in the Mix window, when describing Pro Tools and other digital audio workstation software, we make an effort to call these "mixer strips" so that it's clear that we're talking about a view of a track's virtual signal path and not necessarily an input/output path to or from the outside world.) Every Pro Tools system has some finite number of actual audio input channels on the hardware (either digital or analog). Some systems, such as the Mbox 2 Mini and original Mbox (like the Mbox 2 and M-Audio FireWire Solo, if you aren't prepared to use their S/PDIF digital I/O simultaneously with the analog I/O), offer only two input/output channels. Others, like the Digi 003, Digi 002, and some M-Audio hardware, provide a larger but still pre-determined (non-expandable) maximum number of inputs. Finally, greatly expandable hardware configurations are possible with Pro Tools|HD systems. Whatever system configuration you're using, the number of independent channels on your audio hardware determines the maximum number of discrete audio sources you can record simultaneously. For example, even though the original Mbox model has two analog audio inputs plus digital input and output in S/PDIF format, it is still a 2 × 2 interface. The digital output always mirrors channels 1–2, and either the analog *or* digital inputs can be selected in the Hardware Setup dialog box; unlike with the Mbox 2 or FireWire Solo, you can't use both at the same time. In contrast, the 96i I/O for Pro Tools|HD systems is a 16×2 interface; it offers 16 input channels and only two output channels (while digital S/PDIF input can be selected instead of the analog inputs for channels 1–2, the S/DIF is always actively mirroring analog outputs 1–2). Of course, Pro Tools|HD supports multiple audio interfaces. These expandable systems can reach large numbers of I/O channels by adding more audio interfaces.

Some audio interfaces—such as Digidesign's Digi 003 and Digi 002 families, 96 I/O, 192 I/O, and 192 Digital I/O, as well as M-Audio's FireWire 1814—offer ADAT Lightpipe connectors for input/output of digital audio. Each Lightpipe connector supports up to eight channels of audio via a Toslink optical cable. These input channels can be used *simultaneously* with any analog inputs on the interface. For example, on a (Digidesign) Digi 003, Digi 002, or (M-Audio) Fire-Wire 1814 interface, you could record up to 18 separate source channels by using all eight ana-log inputs, the eight Lightpipe channels, plus the stereo S/PDIF digital input. But of course, digital inputs require a digital source. Unless the external source you're recording or monitoring is already equipped with a Lightpipe digital output (like some keyboards, effects, and multi-channel mic preamps), an additional device is required to convert its signal to Lightpipe prior to your Pro Tools interface if you need to take advantage of all these simultaneous optical and analog/digital inputs.

Remember that the input of each audio track or Aux Input can be assigned to any available audio input path on your Pro Tools system, and that the I/O Setup dialog box allows you to define these input paths (mono, stereo, or multichannel, according to which system you're using) and assign them convenient names.

Audio and Aux Input Tracks

Tracks are discrete audio pathways in the Pro Tools virtual signal-routing environment. Obvi-ously, in ordinary Play mode, an audio track's source signal derives from the playback of audio data (within files on one of your system's disks) that is referenced by the audio regions within the track. With Track > Auto Input Monitor enabled, whenever an audio track's Record Enable button is lit (or during punch-in recording), the selected input source is monitored through it.

For audio and Aux Input tracks, the input source can be either a physical audio input path on your hardware or one of Pro Tools' internal busses. (A *bus* is a utility pathway for routing audio signals around within Pro Tools; for more information, see the "Busses" section later in this chapter, and also Chapter 2 for a basic definition.) Figure 9.2 shows the signal path for an Aux Input.

Input Sources for Audio Tracks In addition to hardware inputs (or audio regions from hard disk during normal playback, of course), a Pro Tools mixing bus can also be the selected input for any audio track or Aux Input track. On audio tracks, a bus could be used as a front end during recording, combining a larger number of inputs from external sources (if you have a multichannel audio interface, as opposed to a stereo-only alternative like the Mbox Mini, original Mbox, Audiophile, MobilePre, Ozone, or Black Box). Here's an example: You might create a stereo Aux Input for each pair of physical audio inputs on your audio inter-face where audio signals from external MIDI modules are connected. If you like, compres-sion, EQ, or any other insert effect could be instantiated on each Aux Input. Assign the main outputs from all these Aux Inputs to bus pair 15–16, for instance. Select that bus pair as the input source for a stereo audio track, and record to disk. Creating this stereo audio submix from your MIDI instruments could have several advantages. First, this session will be usable on other Pro Tools systems without the MIDI gear attached. Second, you don't have to worry about reestablishing audio connections, gain structure, and so on if you ever reopen this session in the distant future. Lastly, using this submix instead of monitoring the outputs from these external MIDI devices (either temporarily or permanently) frees up all those inputs on your audio interface for recording other sources.

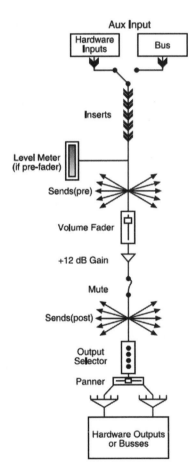

Figure 9.2 Virtual signal path for an Aux Input track. If any enabled auxiliary outputs are available from software instrument plug-ins in the session, they are also available as an input source.

Whatever the source of the audio, the controls on audio and Aux Input tracks are otherwise very similar. This might be audio data being read from disk, an audio input or bus being recorded and/or monitored on an audio track, the selected audio input or bus being monitored on an Aux Input, or a software instrument operating via an RTAS or DigiReWire plug-in in either track type's track's Inserts section. An Aux Input track has no Record button, of course, because it cannot contain audio regions. Both track types can be mono (one audio channel), stereo, or multichannel. If you insert a mono-to-stereo plug-in at any point on a mono audio track or Aux Input, however, the remainder of its audio path becomes stereo, including both the subsequent insert slots and its main output stage. The main output from each audio track or Aux Input can be assigned to one or more physical output paths or, again, to any of Pro Tools' internal mixing busses. As a matter of fact, if you hold down the Control key (Start key in Windows) as you reopen the pop-up selector, you can assign *additional* output destinations from the same track.

Instrument Tracks

Instrument tracks combine aspects of an Aux Input and a MIDI track. As seen in the Mix window, Instrument tracks look fairly similar to Aux Inputs—with a keyboard icon that indicates their track type. However, like MIDI tracks, they have a Patch Select button and a Record Enable button for MIDI instead of audio. Instrument tracks also have an audio input selector. Many instrument plug-ins don't actually use this input audio signal, in which case this audio input path is simply cut off at the point where that instrument plug-in is instantiated in the track's signal chain. In the Edit window, however, Instrument tracks are treated much like MIDI tracks. (However, they offer audio-related view options in the Edit window, like inserts, sends, and so on, that aren't available on a MIDI track. Also, in addition to MIDI controllers, audio parameters such as pan and volume can be graphically edited on an Instrument track, just as on an Aux Input.) One of the main reasons the Instrument track feature was created was so that, for single-timbre instrument plug-ins, a single track can provide a MIDI event display in the Edit window and a channel-strip view of its audio signal path in the Mix window. For multi-timbral plug-ins, however, you will typically route the MIDI outputs from various conventional MIDI tracks to that plug-in—whether it resides on an Instrument, Aux Input, or audio track. (Even if you *do* instantiate an instrument plug-in on an audio track, if you ever decided to render its output to audio form—for instance, so that its resultant signal would be available even on another Pro Tools system that didn't have that particular plug-in available—it would still have to be recorded to yet another audio track.)

Display of the Instrument section can be enabled at the top of the Mix window for this track type. It can also be displayed as a column at the left of the track display area in the Edit window. Controls in the Instrument section affect the active software instrument plug-in on an individual Instrument track. There are selectors for the track's MIDI input and output (allowing the Instrument track's MIDI data to be additionally routed to another destination), volume, pan, and mute, plus a small LED and velocity meter for MIDI data on that track. On an Instrument track, inserts and sends (which are covered in the next two sections) work identically to Aux Inputs and audio tracks. (However, aside from the occasional instrument plug-in that actually uses the audio signal at the track's input somehow, it doesn't make any sense to place any insert effects prior to the software instrument in the track's signal chain.)

Enable Audio Inputs on Your Instrument Tracks Some instrument plug-ins, such as the MOTU MX4 version 2, actually use the selected audio input for the Instrument track as part of their processing (although most won't). Nevertheless, you may often find that even if you know the selected instrument plug-in doesn't use that source audio in any way, if you *don't* select some physical input on your interface—instead of None—the instrument plug-in won't sound.

Inserts

After each track's selected input (or disk-playback source, in the case of audio tracks), the signal pathway passes through 10 insert points. Effects can be placed on these inserts in the form of software modules called *plug-ins*. Alternatively, hardware I/O inserts can be spliced into these access points in the track's signal path, using physical inputs and outputs on the audio hardware to route the track's audio to and from external devices. (This is obviously a more practical alternative on a multichannel audio interface than one of the 2×2 configurations!) In either case, for audio tracks, Aux Inputs, and Instrument tracks, inserts are always *pre*-fader. This means that the level of the signal passing through the Inserts section is entirely unaffected by the track's main volume fader or volume automation. In contrast (as mentioned in Chapter 7), inserts on Master Faders are always *post*-fader.

A track's entire signal passes through each of the inserts, and each insert on the track affects the signal level entering the next one; they're in a series labeled "a" through "e" and "f" through "j." It is entirely possible to overload any one of them and produce clipping if you are careless about the levels on the previous insert!

Sends

As explained in Chapter 2, a *send* is an access point from which a track's audio can be routed to a secondary audio pathway, independently of the main output assignment for the track. In Pro Tools, 10 sends are available for each audio, Aux Input, and Instrument track. They're organized into two groups of five: "a" through "e" and "f" through "j." Separate sections in the Mix and Edit windows allow you to enable display of these two sends sections separately. Mono or stereo sends are supported in all versions of Pro Tools (even from a mono source track); stereo sends incorporate a pan slider. On HD systems, sends can also be created to multichannel paths. If the Follow Main Panner (FMP) button is enabled in Pro Tools versions 7.3 or higher, the pan position of this send will follow that of the track's main pan control. The destination of each send might be a single physical audio output on your hardware (or a multiple output, if the send is to a stereo or multichannel path). Even more typical is to select a mono or stereo (or multichannel) bus within Pro Tools as the destination for a send. If the send is set to *pre*-fader (that is, its Pre button is enabled), the source of its signal is directly after the output of the Inserts section in the track's audio pathway. The level of a pre-fader send is therefore not affected by the main volume setting or mute button on its track. In contrast, the level of a post-fader send (the default send type) is also reduced whenever the track's main volume fader is lowered, because it follows the fader in the track's signal path.

Typically, when you enable a new send in Pro Tools, its level is automatically set to the absolute minimum, $-\infty$; no level is sent at all (although you can change this setting in Preferences). In the Output window that automatically opens for each new send, drag the level slider upward to increase the audio volume being sent to its destination. At any time, you can Option-click (Alt-click in Windows) a send's level fader to set it directly to 0dB. You can also Option-drag (or Alt-drag in Windows) to copy sends from one track to another. The FMP button in the Output window for sends was introduced in version 7.3 of Pro Tools. It links the pan setting of the send to the track's main panner. This is useful for setting up panning in cue mixes that reflects that of your main mix, for example. It's also handy when you want the send's position in the stereo bus that feeds a delay or reverb effect to match its position in the main stereo mix. Also, for HD users, there is the Copy to Send function, which copies either the current settings of the selected automation controls or their entire automation playlists to the sends that you specify. You can select from volume, pan, mute, and LFE automation to copy, which is especially useful when a send is used for a cue headphone mix. You can access the Copy to Send dialog box via the Edit > Automation menu command.

Again, a send's audio source can be either directly after the Inserts section of the source track on pre-fader sends (and therefore after any software instrument or ReWire channels in that track's signal path) or after the main track volume fader (and mute button) on post-fader sends. Each option has its uses, as you will see elsewhere in this book. When you click any send to edit its parameters, its Output window opens (see Figure 9.3 for mono and stereo versions).

Busses

In Pro Tools, a *bus* is an audio pathway for moving audio around within the program's mixing environment. Among other things, you can use it as a sort of pipeline for routing audio signals from multiple inputs, track outputs, or sends to a common destination. Pro Tools LE and M-Powered versions provide 32 busses (versus 16 in versions prior to Pro Tools 7), while Pro Tools HD software has 128 (versus 64 versions prior to Pro Tools TDM 6.9). You can use busses individually in mono or as stereo pairs: 1–2, 3–4, 5–6, and so on. On HD systems, you can also create multichannel bus paths—for surround mixing, among other things. Common uses of busses are reviewed in Chapter 7.

Some people use busses to create subgroups or submasters on a physical mixing console. For example, you might reassign the outputs from multiple drum tracks to bus pair 3–4, and then

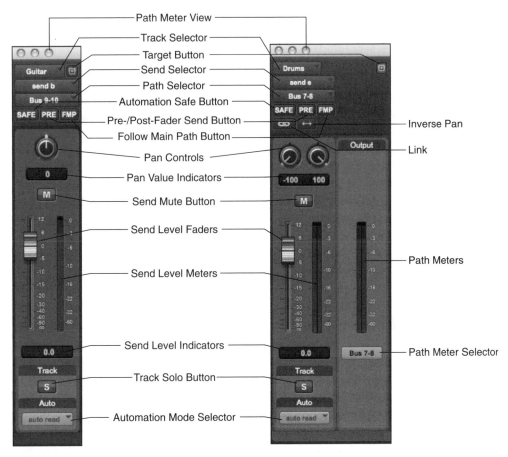

Figure 9.3 Output windows for sends: Track selector (switches to other tracks, without leaving this window), Send selector (switches among 10 sends on the current track), and Path selector (the send's destination—busses or physical outputs). Solo and Automation Mode selector buttons for the source tracks are duplicated here. Because the target icon is dimmed in this mono send's Output window, it remains open even as you open others. The Path Meter view has been enabled in the stereo send's Output window.

select that bus as the input for a stereo Aux Input. This lets you use a single fader to control the overall volume of the drums, and stereo insert points where a single EQ or compressor plug-in could be applied across the entire stereo drum mix. This construct would be equally useful for stacks of backing vocals, walls of backing guitars, or, in audio for video, an entire foundation of sound effects and ambience.

Other people use busses like aux sends on a hardware mixing console: Sends from multiple tracks route a portion of their signals to a common audio pathway that in turn feeds either some effect like a delay or reverb or perhaps a cue mix. To accomplish something similar in Pro Tools, you could select an internal bus path (previously defined in the I/O Setup dialog box) as the input for an Aux Input track where the delay or reverb effect has been inserted (or that has an external effect patched into it as a hardware I/O insert). Alternatively, the main audio output path of the Aux Input monitoring that bus could be the source of a performer's headphone mix out in the studio.

You can also use busses to route the output from an Aux Input to the input of an audio track while recording. A sidebar earlier in this chapter entitled "Input Sources for Audio Tracks" alludes to this possibility—using multiple Aux Input tracks to combine audio from several external MIDI modules before recording them to a stereo audio track. (You might also do this with a single audio source, however, if you want to print it to disk with effects already incorporated.) Here's how:

1.   Create one or more Aux Input tracks with the appropriate input sources selected.

2.   Instantiate whatever plug-in effects are required.

3.   Assign the main output from the Aux Input track(s) to a bus (either mono or a stereo pair, as appropriate).

4.   Create a new mono/stereo audio track, select this mono/stereo bus as its input, and click its Record Enable button.

5.   To adjust the input recording level to the audio track—perhaps because some of the plug-in effects you're using are altering the gain of the original input signal—simply use the main level fader on the Aux Input track(s) that are that audio track's signal source.

The possibilities are immense, but keep in mind that essentially, a bus is nothing more than a convenient pathway for you to move audio around inside Pro Tools. You can assign the output from any audio, Aux Input, or Instrument track, or the destination of any send to any bus, bus *pair* (if it's a stereo track output or send), or multichannel bus path (in Pro Tools HD) that was previously defined in the I/O Setup dialog box. But if no Aux Input is listening to that bus (because the bus hasn't yet been selected as the *input* to be monitored by anything), you won't hear it!

Clipping, Overload, and Distortion *Clipping* is a form of distortion caused when the top of the audio waveform is cut off (clipped) because it reaches amplitude levels that exceed the capacity of the channel or device it is passing through. On some gear, like tube guitar amplifiers and magnetic tape recorders, a controlled amount of this kind of distortion can be desirable and warm sounding. But digital clipping is nasty, rude, and butt-ugly—it should be avoided.

Audio tracks, Aux Input tracks, Instrument tracks, and Master Faders have clipping indicators—the top-most red segment on their level meters. As a general rule, if you see any of these red indicators light up as you play back your mix, you should adjust your gain structure so that they don't. (Remember, if necessary you can use the Trimmer tool to scale any existing volume automation up or down.) Click a level meter to reset its clip indicator; Option-click (Alt-click in Windows) to reset the clip indicators on *all* tracks simultaneously. (Note: The behavior of the clip indicator can be changed in Preferences—for example, if you only want it to stay lit for three seconds after a peak is detected.)

Obviously, clipping is a critical issue while recording audio tracks (many people advise keeping peak levels during recording to Pro Tools audio tracks down as much as −6dB), but also be careful when using plug-in effects during mixdown that can increase gain—such as EQ and compression—and especially when routing multiple sends or track outputs to the same destination. Many of the DigiRack plug-ins (for dynamics and reverb, for example) include Volume meters with clipping indicators within the Plug-in window itself. Keep an eye on these!

So what do you do when you import an audio file that was recorded right below maximum level, and you need to use an EQ to brighten it—which will raise the audio file's level enough to clip? Here's a quick solution: In the channel, insert the Trim plug-in (found in the "Other" section of a channel's Insert pull-down menu) before you insert the EQ plug-in. Lower the fader of the Trim plug-in a proper amount, like 6dB, and then adjust the EQ and keep your eyes on the EQ plug-in's output meter. Another possibility is to use an EQ plug-in that has an input level control, which in effect provides the same function as the Trim plug-in, and lower the input gain enough that raising the level of the high frequencies with the EQ won't clip the plug-in's output.

Lastly, you might have to import an audio file that was recorded too hot and has clipping distortion inherent in the sound. There is rarely if ever a way to completely remove the effects of clipping distortion, but there are many plug-in offerings that have functions to lessen the sonic effect of clipping. One very effective plug-in is part of the NoNOISE Audio Restoration suite by Sonic, but currently it is available only for Pro Tools HD systems.

Master Faders

A Master Fader track either controls the signal passing through either an output bus for a physical output path (a mono output, an output *pair* if it's a stereo master, and multiple channels if it's for a multichannel output path), or one of the mono, stereo, or multichannel busses within the Pro Tools mixing environment. Master Faders have no sends and no pan controls. Like audio and Aux Input tracks, Master Fader tracks have 10 inserts, in two groups of five each. However, Master Fader inserts are *post-fader only*; the input level to these inserts will always be affected by the Master Fader's main volume fader. Master Faders are also convenient for placing post-fader plug-in effects or hardware inserts on the entire mix output, such as limiting, compression, EQ, and others, or *especially* dithering plug-ins (discussed in Chapter 16, "Bouncing to Disk, Other File Formats").

Because you can use a Master Fader as a final gain stage for the audio output path used for your mix output, it is a very convenient place to manage your final levels. For example, you will often create a stereo master fader for outputs 1–2 on your audio interface, if that's the source for the stereo mix you're hearing through your studio monitors (and perhaps the selected output path when you bounce a mixdown file to disk). If you see that your levels are clipping on this Master Fader—or conversely, if they're way too low—your solution might be as simple as adjusting the volume fader on that Master Fader track. Of course, another possible approach to taming the dynamics in your mix is placing a compressor, limiter, or some more sophisticated gain optimization plug-in on the Master Fader to affect the entire mix (such as Digidesign's Maxim, the multiband compressor in IK Multimedia's T-Racks, or one of the well-known maximizer plug-ins from Waves). As always, the best choice depends on the sound you're after. However, when you do use a dithering plug-in on the Master Fader for your mix output (because you're bouncing or recording digitally to a lesser bit depth), always make sure it's the *last* plug-in on the Master Fader.

About Master Faders on Bus or Output Paths The stage in the signal path of any bus or output path represented by Master Fader tracks always exists, whether these are currently visible as a track (or mixer strip) in Pro Tools or not. This is why creating additional Master Fader tracks has no effect on the DSP usage and almost no effect on the performance of your system. For audio routed to external destinations (for example, cue mixes and broadcast feeds), Master Faders can sometimes be more useful than Aux Inputs. Their exclusively post-fader inserts are also handy. More importantly, although the Path Metering view in the Output window for any send that has been routed to the internal mixing busses in Pro Tools is handy, you will find that a good metering plug-in such as the Phase-Scope plug-in included in versions 7.3 and higher is much more informative about the levels going through the bus that the Master Fader controls.

Output Channels

As with inputs, the potential number and type of output channels available to you (selectable as send destinations or track or mix outputs) depends on the audio interface used in your Pro Tools configuration. For many users, a stereo output pair is the source for mixes they bounce to disk or record to DAT. Even if your final mix is going to be bounced to disk as a stereo file, in the Bounce dialog box, you still choose the stereo output (either a pair of physical outputs or a stereo bus pair) that will be the source for this bounced mix. For stereo mixing, you would generally use the same pair of physical audio outputs you've been monitoring during the edit process (that is, a stereo output *path*, configured in the I/O Setup dialog box). Some users record their mix in real time to another device instead of bouncing mix files to disk. For example, they might record their Pro Tools output digitally to a DAT (be sure to read about dithering plug-ins, in Chapter 16). In typical video postproduction scenarios, real-time output from Pro Tools is used when performing a layback of mixed audio to master video tape—although with computer-based video-editing systems like Avid, Media 100, and FinalCut Pro, it's more common to bounce out a mixdown file or use the OMF interchange format for audio data).

For some situations, *direct-out routing* from individual tracks to output channels can also be handy. Each output channel on a multichannel audio interface can be assigned as the mono output path from individual tracks instead of all of them being routed to some common stereo output pair as in more typical mixing scenarios. A sidebar in Chapter 7 describes how to set these track assignments quickly. This can be useful when transferring an entire session to a multitrack tape recorder, for instance, or when you use an external mixing board for mixing and processing while Pro Tools essentially acts as a multitrack playback machine. Some post-production operators will assign many individual outputs from the Pro Tools audio interface to physical inputs on hardware-based digital surround mixers with dedicated joystick controllers. However, with the availability of surround encoding/decoding plug-ins for HD and other TDM-compatible systems, like the Digidesign Surround Mixer, Dolby's Surround Tools, and SRS's Circle Tools (not to mention the joystick controllers on several of Digidesign's external control surfaces), many Pro Tools users create their surround mixes completely within Pro Tools (in LCR, Quad, LCRS, 5.1, 6.1, and 7.1; for Dolby Surround/Pro Logic, Dolby Digital, DTS, and SDDS formats).

You use the Pro Tools I/O Setup dialog box to configure multichannel routing in Pro Tools. Multichannel tracks (for example, six channels for Dolby Digital 5.1) allow you to edit regions in their native multichannel format. Multichannel sends, Aux Input tracks, Instrument tracks, and Master Faders can also be created for any multichannel bus or output path. In the I/O Setup dialog box, you define main *paths*—logical groupings of input or output channels, inserts, or busses. This may be as simple as the main stereo output pair you use to monitor a mix, or six physical outputs on your audio interface that are your 5.1 path (the five surround speakers plus the LFE subwoofer channel). Each mono signal path that comprises a stereo or multichannel main path is known as a *subpath*. For example, even in stereo, the main output used for your mix consists of two mono subpaths—perhaps outputs 1 and 2—on your audio interface. After creating a new stereo or multichannel path, if you also want the option of individually addressing the subpaths within it, you would use the I/O Setup dialog box's New Subpath button to enable these. This might be handy, for instance, if you wanted the low-frequency effects (LFE) channel in a surround path to also be available as a send destination.

Plug-in Architectures

So what's a plug-in, again? As explained in Chapter 2, a *plug-in* is a software component that acts as an add-in module for processing audio within Pro Tools or other digital audio work-stations. Many Digidesign plug-ins are included with Pro Tools, such as the AudioSuite and DigiRack (RTAS) plug-ins provided with all systems and a similar DigiRack collection of

TDM plug-ins provided with HD systems. There are also many plug-ins available from Digidesign and numerous other manufacturers for the TDM and RTAS plug-in architectures directly supported by Pro Tools version 8.

Unlike AudioSuite plug-ins (which are *offline*, or processed-based effects in the AudioSuite menu, and save the results of their processing to an audio file), real-time plug-ins (RTAS and TDM) can be placed into the virtual signal path of Pro Tools at any one of the 10 inserts provided for audio tracks, Aux Inputs, Instrument tracks, and Master Faders. A track's audio signal passes through each insert in turn (from "a" through "j"), and therefore through any real-time plug-in effect placed at any of these insert locations.

Virtual Instrument Plug-ins Because this chapter is mainly concerned with signal flow and effects processing in Pro Tools, we discuss plug-ins specifically in that context. However, most software-based instruments are also used within Pro Tools as plug-ins (although some standalone applications that also contain software instruments communicate with Pro Tools via ReWire, like Reason, Live, and Gigastudio3). Instrument plug-ins are discussed in Chapter 10, "MIDI."

AudioSuite

AudioSuite effects are not real-time processes; they are file-based. After adjusting the effects parameters of an AudioSuite effect and using the Preview button in its window (if available for that effect type) to hear a short sample of how its current settings will affect the final audio, you click the Process button. Generally, a new file is then created, wherein the effect is applied to whatever audio was selected. (If you wish, the results of the processing can instead be destructively written over the data in the original file.) Some of Digidesign's own DigiRack plug-ins are available both as offline AudioSuite processes and RTAS real-time effects. This can be useful if you need to conserve your real-time DSP resources by printing effect treatments to new disk files. Figure 9.4 shows the AudioSuite window and the parameters for the Normalize process (which includes an RMS mode, in addition to the traditional Peak mode for calculating target gain levels).

Figure 9.4 The AudioSuite window for the Normalize function.

RTAS (Real-Time AudioSuite)

The Real-Time AudioSuite (RTAS) plug-in architecture was developed by Digidesign for Pro Tools. RTAS plug-ins operate in real time as insert effects on audio tracks, Aux Input tracks, Instrument tracks, or Master Faders. DigiRack plug-ins in RTAS format are provided with Pro Tools LE and Pro Tools M-Powered. (Some of these are also available as non–real-time effects that process audio files, under the AudioSuite menu.) These same DigiRack RTAS plug-ins are also included with HD systems (as well as TDM equivalents for most of them—and other plug-ins that are TDM-only).

RTAS plug-ins are *host based*; that is, they rely on the computer's CPU for their effects-processing power rather than relying on specialized DSP chips on a Digidesign card within the computer (as is the case with TDM plug-ins used in Pro Tools|HD systems). In addition to the DigiRack plug-ins for RTAS included with all Pro Tools versions, many more are available from Digidesign and other manufacturers. Like TDM plug-ins, you can enable many parameters of an RTAS plug-in for automation by clicking the Auto button within its plug-in window, allowing you to build up some very complex and interesting mixes. For example, you might automate the feedback parameter on a delay plug-in to change the number of repeats at different locations in a song. Lastly, many virtual instrument plug-ins are also offered in RTAS format. These can be used as the sound sources for data in MIDI and Instrument tracks in Pro Tools. The Click plug-in that provides a metronome sound (typically inserted on an Aux Input track) is also a sort of rudimentary RTAS instrument plug-in. Figure 9.5 shows a typical plug-in window.

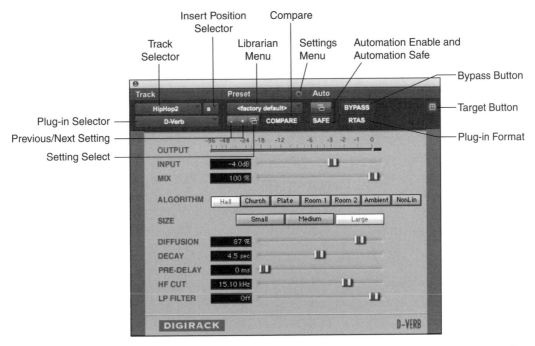

Figure 9.5 Plug-in windows have these common controls. Seen here: D-Verb, which Pro Tools provides in RTAS, TDM, and AudioSuite formats.

Maximizing RTAS Plug-in Capacity Obviously, you want to prevent any other system tasks (background processes, energy savers or "sleep" functions, other open programs, and so on) from competing with Pro Tools for access to the computer's CPU. Here are a few more tips for doing so:

- The capacity of your system to handle larger numbers of simultaneous RTAS plug-ins (especially more intensive types such as reverbs and software instruments) is proportional to the size of the hardware buffer (which you set via Setup > Playback Engine). Because LE and M-Powered systems exclusively support the RTAS plug-in format, this is an important system-performance issue. It also affects HD users who, for example, rely heavily on RTAS software instruments because, like some reverbs, software instruments tend to be relatively processing-intensive. If you start hearing choppy playback or get a "CPU is too busy" message, try increasing this setting. (On USB-based interfaces such as those in the Mbox 2 family, the original Mbox, and some M-Audio interfaces, the "CPU usage is holding off USB audio" message may also occasion an increase in this buffer size.) On LE/M-Powered systems, however, larger buffer sizes increase monitoring latency during recording and the response time of software instruments to real-time MIDI input, which can negatively affect timing of performances. Among the ways to circumvent this issue are the mix knob on the Mbox 2 family and original Mbox, similar features in the control panel software for your M-Audio interface, and the Options > Low-Latency Monitoring command when using a Digi 002 interface.

- For host computers with two or more processors, the RTAS Processors selection in the Playback Engine dialog box allows you to assign more than one CPU to RTAS processing.

- The CPU Usage Limit selector in the Playback Engine dialog box can be set up to 99% on single-processor systems. However, on slower systems, this highest setting may affect video playback or screen response. Otherwise, the maximum setting is usually desirable when you're using a lot of RTAS plug-ins—especially software instruments—and want to dedicate more of your CPU's processing power to RTAS.

Using RTAS Plug-ins in Pro Tools HD RTAS plug-ins are compatible with LE, M-Powered, and HD versions of Pro Tools. The basic set of DigiRack RTAS plug-ins is also included with Pro Tools HD software (in addition to their TDM versions).

On HD systems, for most DigiRack plug-ins, the Plug-in window will have a Convert Plug-in button that switches the current TDM plug-in to its RTAS counterpart (if available) or vice versa. Look for a small inverted triangle to the right of the TDM or RTAS text and the Target icon (as shown in Figure 9.5). For DigiRack plug-ins, switching from TDM processing on your DSP cards to host-based RTAS processing is a possible strategy if you ever max out the available DSP resources on your HD cards. As a general rule, to avoid excessive use of playback voices, you should avoid placing TDM plug-ins between two RTAS plug-ins in the same track. Also, be aware that side chaining on an RTAS plug-in uses an extra voice.

TDM (Time-Division Multiplexing), TDM II

TDM is a high-performance effects-processing and signal-routing architecture, introduced by Digidesign for Pro Tools in the early 1990s. (A redesigned version, with much more robust capabilities, was introduced in 2002 with the high-resolution Pro Tools|HD hardware family. Although this technically is known as "TDM II," for the sake of simplicity we simply refer to TDM plug-ins and architecture.) Unlike AudioSuite and RTAS architectures (which can be used concurrently with the TDM option), TDM enables the use of specialized Digidesign hardware, providing a more stable platform that is less dependent on the host CPU and better support for demanding signal-routing and processing capabilities in expanded, high-resolution systems. Specifically, the HD Core and Accel (or HD Process) cards in Pro Tools|HD systems all contain DSP (digital signal processing) chips, which are required to support TDM processing.

By using these hardware resources to support its audio-processing needs, TDM doesn't exclusively depend on the processing power of the computer's CPU (which also supports the operating system and other tasks, including the Pro Tools program itself) in order to process audio in real time. Plug-in developers can count on this hardware-based DSP capacity when creating more calculation-intensive effects-processing algorithms, often achieving sonically superior results. Also, the monitoring latency during recording (the delay between the selected source and when it is heard back out through the mixer) is less significant on TDM systems than on host-based LE and M-Powered systems. Most importantly, the processing latency induced by each TDM plug-in can be compensated for automatically by the Pro Tools software. (For the standard DigiRack TDM plug-ins, this is usually about 3–4 samples at the session's sample rate, but some other plug-ins have much greater amounts of latency.) Some plug-ins are available exclusively in TDM format—both effects plug-ins and software instruments such as Access Virus Indigo and others. TDM-based Pro Tools systems support a larger number of voices and I/O channels than non-TDM configurations, as well as audio hardware expansion through the addition of multiple audio interfaces. Figure 9.6 shows an example of a reverb TDM plug-in for HD systems, while Figure 9.7 shows a dynamics processing plug-in available in both TDM and RTAS formats.

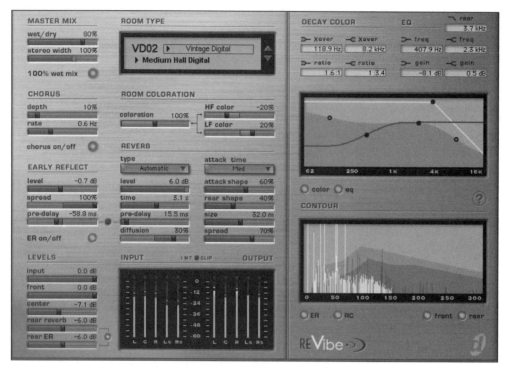

Figure 9.6   ReVibe, a TDM reverb plug-in for Pro Tools|HD systems only.

Figure 9.7   Smack!, a TDM/RTAS compressor/limiter plug-in, supports multichannel tracks and can emulate tube and analog tape saturation with second- and third-order harmonic distortion.

About HTDM Plug-ins (Discontinued) HTDM plug-ins were used on 24 MIX and HD systems with software versions prior to Pro Tools 7. They are *not* supported in any current versions. Like RTAS plug-ins, HTDM plug-ins relied on the processing power of the host computer's CPU to carry out their tasks, although they were instantiated and routed within the TDM environment. When you open an older session containing HTDM plug-ins, where possible these are automatically converted to their RTAS equivalents.

Duplicating Plug-ins   You can Option-drag (Alt-drag in Windows) plug-ins (and inserts) to copy them from one track to another, along with their current settings, *if* the source and destination tracks have the same number of channels. Also, if you hold down the Option key (Alt key in Windows) as you enable a plug-in on an audio track, it will simultaneously be created in the same insert slot on all other audio tracks that again have the same number of channels. (You can also use this shortcut to simultaneously create the same plug-in on multiple Aux Inputs.) Bear in mind, though, that the digital signal-processing resources of even more powerful Pro Tools systems have some practical limit. You will often *instantiate* (that is, create instances of) equalization or compression plug-ins, which typically make relatively small demands on your system's processing power, on numerous audio tracks. However, it is usually more DSP-efficient (and simpler to manage) if you place delays and reverbs on Aux Inputs, using these as a common send destination from multiple source tracks.

Wrapped Plug-ins

Wrapper programs allow for the use of plug-ins that were originally created for one architecture—for example, VST—within a different architecture, like RTAS for Pro Tools (or Apple's Audio Units plug-in format). One excellent example is the VST-to-RTAS Adapter for Mac/Windows by FXpansion. It supports a great number of VST effects plug-ins, plus various VST virtual instrument plug-ins. When available, wrapped plug-ins appear as a separate category when you open the pop-up plug-in menu for Pro Tools inserts (and the AudioSuite menu, if applicable for that particular plug-in). Although most users agree that there are stability issues with wrapped plug-ins used as real-time effects in channels, just the ability to tap into the vast network of VST plug-ins being created by the worldwide music and programming community is worth the price alone. One way to deal with the instability issue is to insert a wrapped plug-in on the desired channel, tweak its settings to your liking, and then permanently apply the effect to the chosen audio files by using the Bounce function (File > Bounce To > Disk). You will have to then import the newly created files into the session. (Yes, it involves some work, but it's worth it if the wrapped plug-in's effect is unique.)

Multiple Outputs from Software Instrument Plug-ins In addition to the main output from a software instrument plug-in that continues on through the other insert slots in its host track, plug-ins with multiple output capabilities allow you to enable mono or stereo auxiliary outputs. Whenever any of these are active in a session, they appear as options in the track input selector for audio and Aux Input tracks (mono or stereo, as appropriate). For example, you could route the drum parts from a software instrument plug-in through a separate Aux Input track, where distinct reverb or compression treatments can be applied without affecting the other instrumental parts played by this plug-in through its main track output.

Plug-in Effects

In addition to the DigiRack plug-ins included with all versions of Pro Tools (and others frequently provided with your system as part of a promotional bundle), many more are available from third parties. Digidesign's Web site always includes updated information about the plug-ins available for the various Pro Tools versions—from Digidesign and many other companies. These range from familiar effects such as reverb, delay, dynamics, processing, EQ, and so on, to much more exotic processes. In order to provide a little context, this section briefly reviews what digital signal processing is and groups audio-processing effects into a few very broad categories.

About Digital Signal Processing (DSP)

For the purposes of Pro Tools users, *digital signal processing* means the use of special computational algorithms to alter the data that represents audio waveforms. These algorithms can simulate classic analog audio-processing devices such as equalizers (which change the frequency content of the original material); dynamics processors such as compressors, expanders, and limiters (which alter the level of the audio over time in response to loudness changes in the original signal or some secondary source assigned as the key input); delay and modulated delay effects (which reproduce some or all of the original signal at some later point in time); and so on. Other plug-ins simulate actual devices, such as tube amplifiers and analog tape. Many other special effects plug-ins are hard to categorize!

Categories of Audio Effects

Many effect types can be grouped into several simple categories. Plug-ins appear within hierarchical submenus according to their category (as assigned by the plug-in's manufacturer) or subgrouped by manufacturer if you enable that option in Preferences. The grouping used in this chapter is much more general, however, and does not correspond to the categories used in the Pro Tools menu. Although there are many variants within each effect category (and plug-ins that combine aspects of various categories), this overview simply provides a conceptual framework. We are primarily concerned with effects plug-ins here, so we don't discuss noise-reduction, software instruments, tuners, metering, and other tools that are also implemented via plug-ins in Pro Tools. For experienced audio professionals, most of this will be review. However, some of the Pro Tools–specific aspects mentioned here are worth keeping in mind for all users.

Frequency-Based Effects

These affect the frequency content of the audio input, usually by increasing or decreasing the gain (level) in various frequency ranges. Equalization, or EQ, is the most common frequency-based effect; Figure 9.8 shows an example of an EQ plug-in. There are two main types of equalizers:

■ **Parametric EQ.** These are so named because the characteristics of one or several bands of boost/cut are adjusted per various *parameters*, such as the amount of boost/cut (gain setting), the center frequency of the affected frequency band, and the curve at which the amount of boost/cut decreases at frequencies progressively farther from the band's center frequency. (Known as the slope, or Q, this describes the shape of the curve of boost/cut around that band's center frequency.)

■ **Graphic EQ.** This divides the frequency spectrum into a fixed number of bands and allows you to boost or cut each frequency band. When the individual bands correspond to octaves or subdivisions of an octave, as is common, the absolute frequency range of each band gets progressively larger because each higher octave is double the frequency of the previous one. Traditional graphic equalizers were essentially banks of band-pass filters at set frequencies and a fixed Q. The volume sliders for each frequency band provide a graphical view of how the frequency spectrum is being altered.

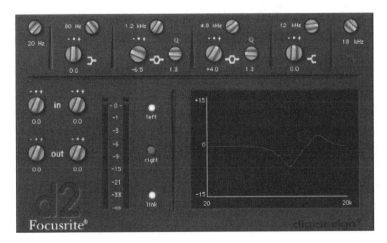

Figure 9.8 D2 by Focusrite, a 4- or 6-band EQ plug-in for TDM.

Gain-Based Effects

Dynamics processors apply gain changes (affecting the amplitude of the audio waveform) to the original audio signal over time. Examples include compressors, limiters, expanders, gates, and

Figure 9.9 Two compressor plug-ins from Digidesign: the included DigiRack Dynamics III compressor included with all versions and the optional Impact mix-bus compressor for Pro Tools|HD.

de-essers. You can use them in many ways to decrease or increase the dynamic range of the input audio. Figure 9.9 provides two examples of compression plug-ins:

- **Compressors.** Compressors (and limiters) are often used, for instance, to reduce peak levels in an audio track so that the entire track's level can be increased after compression for a louder, in-your-face sound throughout the track (usually essential in contemporary music mixes for bass, guitars, and vocals, for example). A compressor reduces the signal level by a specified ratio whenever it exceeds the threshold setting. (A limiter completely prevents the audio from exceeding a specified threshold, like a compressor with an extremely high ratio— or banging your head against the bottom of a table!)

- **Expanders.** Expanders do the opposite: Audio levels *beneath* a specified threshold are even further reduced, again by a specified ratio. For example, they can be useful for decreasing noise from the pickups or amplifier between phrases on an electric guitar or room noise between sentences during a voice-over. A *gate* is like an expander at an extremely high ratio—any audio levels under the threshold are completely closed off by the gate (which might be very handy when other drums can be heard leaking into your kick drum microphone, for example).

A *de-esser* is technically a specialized type of compressor. Instead of reacting to the entire frequency range of the input signal to determine how much gain reduction to apply, only a narrow frequency band—adjustable within a range roughly corresponding to "s" sounds in the human voice—is used as the key input for the compression effect, which then acts upon the full frequency range of the input signal. By using a de-esser to clamp down on the track's level where prominent "s" and "ch" sounds occur in a voice, for example, you can apply more high-frequency boost to the track in general without this sibilance becoming too noticeable. Like any other effect, however, de-essers also have other creative uses—for example, controlling sibilance on vocal sends before they enter a reverb or reducing finger squeaks on an acoustic guitar.

The amount of gain change applied by a dynamics processor is typically based on the level changes within the input audio itself. Alternatively, gain changes on the current track can be keyed by level variations within a completely different audio source. This technique is called *side chaining*. To side chain (or *key*) a dynamics plug-in in Pro Tools, activate its External Key mode (if it offers this feature) and designate some other Pro Tools bus (to which you have routed a send from another track) or input path as the key source. This could be handy with a compressor for slightly *ducking* (reducing) the level of background music (or rhythm guitars, in a rock mix) whenever the voice is present. You could also use a kick drum track to key an expander, using a slight amount of expansion to make the bass guitar bump a little harder with each beat of the kick drum.

Time-Based Effects

Delays store and then reproduce all or some of the input signal at a later time. Sometimes, a portion of the delayed signal is re-routed back to the input to be delayed again. (This is called *regeneration* or *feedback*, and can be used to create multiple repeats, or echoes.) For plug-ins, as a general rule, longer delays require more processing power than short ones to store and process a potentially longer amount of delayed audio in digital memory.

Modulated delays additionally apply a varying amount of change to the delay time, usually controlled by the values of a low-frequency oscillator, or *LFO* (or its software equivalent). You can adjust the frequency of the LFO as well as the degree of effect it has on the amount of delay. When such an oscillation is applied to very short delays, as the delayed signal is then mixed with the original audio, a characteristic sweeping, comb-filtered sound is produced, especially when the Feedback (regeneration) value is increased. This is the basis of so-called *chorus* and *flange* effects, whose base delay times may be 20–30 or 2–10 milliseconds, respectively, and may also incorporate multiple simultaneous delays and/or polarity inversion. Figure 9.10 shows one example of such an effect. The effect can be even more dramatic if differing delay times and/or modulation speeds are applied in the left and right channels. Pro Tools includes RTAS Chorus and Flanger plug-ins among its AudioSuite (non–real-time) effects, under the Modulation category of the hierarchical AudioSuite plug-in selection menu. Novice Pro Tools users should be wary of overusing chorus and flanging on rock and pop rhythm tracks, however. As many a rock guitarist or bassist will attest, these tend to soften or diffuse the visceral impact of the track to which they're applied—which may or may not be desirable, according to the musical style.

Figure 9.10   Instant Flanger, by Eventide, is part of the Anthology II bundle for TDM.

In current versions of Pro Tools, the DigiRack medium, long, and extra long delay plug-ins can be synced to the current Pro Tools tempo. This lets you easily set delay times to specific rhythmic intervals (musical note values) without making any calculations—sometimes a good idea for music projects, especially with multiple delay repeats. This tempo-syncing feature is enabled or disabled by a button in the plug-in window that looks like a metronome.

Reverb Effects

Reverberation is technically another type of time-based effect. In practice, though, it's complex enough to merit its own heading because it involves aspects of all the preceding categories. In technical terms, *reverb* is the persistence of a sound within an acoustical space—that is, multiple reflected sound waves that continue after the original sound has ceased.

Reverb processors simulate the reverberant characteristics of an acoustic space—the myriad reflections/delays and persistence of ambient sound following the original sound, early reflections, resonances, and other acoustical aspects of the environment. Various spaces can be modeled (halls, rooms, cathedrals, and so on), as well as classic electronic reverb units (plate, spring) and special-effect reverb types (nonlinear, gated, reverse, and others). Most sophisticated reverb processors include elements similar to delays (for introducing pre-delay prior to the reverberation, or early reflections) and EQ (for high-frequency damping and tailoring the resonances of the modeled reverberant space). In fact, for many mixes, the reverb can often have more influence over the mix's overall character than any other single effect processor, especially as it is applied to the snare or lead vocal track in rock or dance mixes.

Compared to most compressor, EQ, and delay plug-ins, though, reverb is a much more intensive form of digital signal processing. It consequently makes greater demands on the processing power of your CPU (or the DSP chips on the cards of your Pro Tools|HD system). D-Verb is included with all Pro Tools systems, but other more sophisticated or specialized reverbs are available from third parties (the ReVibe room-modeling reverb for Pro Tools|HD and Venue systems, and Reverb One for TDM). One of these is shown in Figure 9.11.

Figure 9.11   Altiverb, by Audio Ease, is a convolution reverb plug-in for TDM, RTAS, and other plug-in formats.

More Information About Effects on the Web If you want to explore more technical details, Scott Lehman has published an excellent series of articles about common effect types on Harmony Central, including circuit diagrams, waveforms, graphs, and audio examples. To find them, go to http://www.harmony-central.com, click the Effects link, and then click Effects Explained.

Pitch-Based Effects

Pitch plug-in processors apply real-time pitch changes to the input audio. This may be a fixed amount (for example, an octave up or down, or just a few cents—1/100 of a semitone—in order to achieve more subtle doubling effects through detuning). Other more sophisticated pitch-based processors offer more intelligent correction to a specific musical scale, such as Antares Auto-Tune as shown in Figure 9.12.

Modeling Effects

Some effects emulate an existing physical device (or, sometimes, one that could never exist). Although these processes certainly involve frequency, dynamics, and time-based elements, the overall result is much more complex. Examples of physical modeling among digital plug-ins and processors include simulators for guitar effects and amplifiers (such as the one shown in Figure 9.13), speaker cabinets, rotary speakers, microphones, tube preamplifiers, tape saturation, classic mixing board channels, previously existing hardware effects, and so on.

Other: Special FX

Many special effects defy categorization. For example, phase shifters, vocoders, and exciters (such as the one that appears in Figure 9.14) incorporate aspects of several of the preceding categories, making them hard to pin down. Other effects are just too odd to classify (and that's why we love 'em!). For example, the D-Fi plug-in bundle from Digidesign includes Sci-Fi (various combinations

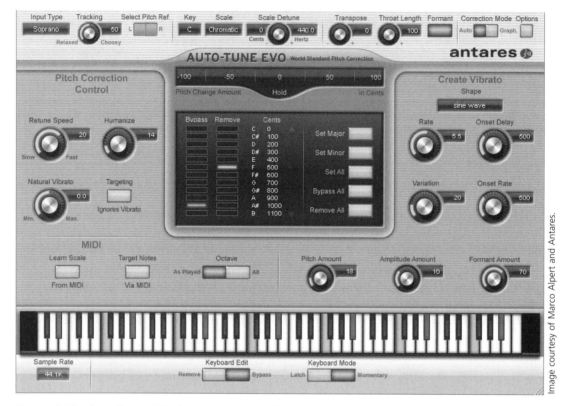

Figure 9.12 Auto-Tune EVO, by Antares: a pitch-processing plug-in for TDM or RTAS.

of effects related to ring modulation and resonance), Lo-Fi (a sort of digital bit crusher and distorter), Recti-Fi (harmonic processing, additive synthesis effects, and rectification), and Vari-Fi (vari-speed effects, including changes over time). Vocoders are another type of effect that combine characteristics from many categories. Digidesign's Bruno and Reso bundle for TDM offers cross-synthesis, with time-slicing and resonance effects. Various stereo imaging plug-ins are available, including S1 and the PS22 Stereomaker plug-ins from Waves.

Plug-ins Included with Pro Tools 8

With the introduction of Pro Tools 8, Digidesign has considerably increased the number of plug-ins included with the core software, very likely as a reaction to the offerings of other platforms on the market such as Apple's Logic. There are three developer groupings within the Digidesign plug-ins: DigiRack, Advanced Instrument Research, and third-party developers acquired by Digi such as Bombfactory and Trillium Lane Labs. Although the following list of plug-ins comes with the base Pro Tools HD, LE, and M-Powered software, it should be stressed that Digi regularly changes bundled plug-in packages. Plug-ins may vary with upgrades to the base Pro Tools software versus newly purchased Pro Tools software package, and there are frequently specific

Figure 9.13 AmpliTube 2, by IK Multimedia: an amp-simulation plug-in available in RTAS format.

Figure 9.14 MaxxBass, by Waves: a psycho-acoustic bass extension plug-in.

plug-in packages involved when hardware is included with the Pro Tools purchase. It is always best to consult the Digidesign Web site for details or talk to a pre-sale agent at Digidesign's offices.

- **Frequency-based effects:** AIR Kill EQ, EQ 3 1-Band, EQ 3 4-Band, EQ 3 7-Band

- **Gain-based effects:** Bombfactory BF76, Compressor/Limiter Dyn 3, De-Esser Dyn 3, Expander/Gate Dyn 3, Maxim, Gain (AudioSuite only), Normalize (AudioSuite only), Trim

- **Time-based effects:** AIR Dynamic Delay, AIR Multi-Delay, Extra Long Delay 2, Long Delay 2, Medium Delay 2, Short Delay 2, Slap Delay 2, Mod Delay 2 (AudioSuite only), Multi-Tap Delay (AudioSuite only), Ping-Pong Delay (AudioSuite only)

- **Reverb effects:** IR Non-Linear Reverb, AIR Reverb, AIR Spring Reverb, D-Verb

- **Pitch-shift effects:** AIR Frequency Shifter, Pitch-Shift (AudioSuite only), Time-Shift (AudioSuite only), Vari_Fi (AudioSuite only)

- **Modulation effects:** AIR Chorus, AIR Ensemble, AIR Filter Gate, AIR Flanger, AIR Fuzz-Wah, AIR Multi-Chorus, AIR Phaser, AIR Talkbox, AIR Vintage Filter, Sci-Fi, Chorus (AudioSuite only), Flanger (AudioSuite only)

- **Harmonic effects:** AIR Distortion, AIR Enhancer, AIR Fuzz-Wah, AIR Lo-Fi, Lo-FI, Recti_Fi, SansAmp PSA-1, Eleven Free

- **Instrument effects:** BFD Lite, Boom, D8-33, MelodyneEssential, Mini Grand, Structure Free, Vacuum, Xpand2

- **Sound field effects:** AIR Stereo Width, PhaseScope (stereo only), TL AutoPan, BF Essential Meter Bridge, BF Essential Noise Meter, BF Essential Correlation (stereo only), TL MasterMeter

- **Additional effects:** Click, TL Metro, TimeAdjuster Long, TimeAdjuster Medium, TimeAdjuster Short, Dither, POWr Dither, Signal Generator, TL InTune, BNR (DINR Broadband Noise Reduction), BF Essential Clip Remover (AudioSuite only), DC Offset Removal (AudioSuite only), Duplicate (AudioSuite only), Invert (AudioSuite only), Reverse (AudioSuite only), Time Compression/Expansion

It should be mentioned that the Advanced Instrument Research (AIR) plug-ins currently bundled with Pro Tools are not available as AudioSuite plug-ins. For guidance in using the plug-ins, Digidesign offers various manuals, such as the *DigiRack Plug-ins Guide*, in the Support section of its Web site. Those looking for info on the AIR plug-ins will have to search out individual manuals for each specific plug-in.

Making a Plug-in Inactive Every plug-in window has a Bypass button, which allows input audio to pass through without any processing applied. (Hardware I/O inserts cannot be bypassed.) To bypass any plug-in directly from the Mix window, Command-click (Ctrl-click in Windows) its plug-in button in the Inserts section. However, even in Bypass mode, the plug-in is still in the signal chain and utilizes the same proportion of your system's DSP resources. (On HD systems, the Show System Usage window provides an overview of how the DSP resources on your PCI cards are currently allocated to plug-ins, mixing, and other Pro Tools tasks.)

To make a plug-in *completely* inactive, thereby freeing up its demands on your system's resources, right-click its insert button and use the Make Inactive command in the pop-up menu. Alternatively, you can hold down the Command and Control keys (Ctrl and Start keys in Windows) as you click the plug-in's button. As opposed to simply removing the plug-in from the track, making it inactive retains its current settings for whenever you choose to re-activate it. Use the same key combination to make a plug-in active again.

Third-Party Plug-in Developers

Digidesign offers various additional plug-ins for purchase, including the Focusrite plug-ins that Digidesign distributes. Another Acrobat Reader (PDF) document, the *Digidesign Plug-ins Guide*, explains how to use all these Digidesign-distributed plug-ins. This document comes with some versions of Pro Tools, and the current version can always be downloaded from the Support area of http://www.digidesign.com.

In addition to Digidesign, many other companies offer plug-ins that are compatible with TDM or RTAS architecture—for example, DUY, URS, Waves, Antares, TC|Works, Sonic Solutions, Native Instruments, Aphex, Serato, Arturia, Line 6, Trillium, Audio Ease, IK Multimedia, Synchro Arts, Sound Toys, Sonnox (formerly Sony), Serato, iZotope, Roger Nichols Digital, Massenburg Design Works, Drawmer, and McDSP, to name a few. The Products > Plug-ins section of the Digidesign Web site will help you seek them out.

Tips for Using Sends (to External I/O, PT Busses, and Aux Inputs)

When it comes to effects processing and building a creative mix, you should of course feel free to break all the rules! However, to avoid some of the common pitfalls and to get a good start on designing a coherent soundscape, keep these basic observations in mind when using sends to additionally route part of the audio from a Pro Tools track to a secondary destination:

- As a general rule, unless they're unique to a single track, delays and reverbs are usually better placed on Aux Inputs, because it's typical to create sends from more than one audio track to common delay or reverb destinations. This also simplifies controlling the mix of wet (processed output from the effects) to dry audio. Obviously, it's also a more efficient use of your system's DSP resources to send a little bit of five vocal tracks to one reverb versus using five separate reverbs, one on each vocal track! Even if you aren't terribly concerned about running out of DSP power, using one or several common reverb destinations for multiple tracks can be the glue that helps a mix hang together. It contributes to the impression that the sounds all share a common space. This all depends on what you're trying to achieve, of course, and personal taste. But when you're overdubbing multiple parts and need some help making them sound cohesive, keep this in mind—you'll see what we mean!

■ Remember that when you send audio from multiple tracks to a common bus, you can exceed its maximum level and create some nasty digital clipping. If you find that the clipping indicators on the Aux Inputs with your effects plug-ins are lighting up, reduce the send levels from each track (and remember that you can use the Trimmer to scale down any existing automation for each track's send level). Pro Tools offers two tools that are especially useful for monitoring the busses you're using for sends. First, by clicking the Path Meter View button in any send's Output window, that simple level meter will give you an idea how the levels are in that send's destination bus. Second, you can also create a Master Fader for any bus path in Pro Tools. This gives you a full-size track level meter in the Mix window and also allows you to instantiate PhaseScope or some other sophisticated metering plug-in on the Master Fader in order to determine exactly what your levels are.

■ Sometimes sends are routed to physical outputs (for external effects processors, cue mixes for performers, and other uses). Be careful to watch your gain structure here as well. Creating a Master Fader for that physical output path is a good way to monitor its levels.

■ If required, signals can pass through more than one bus path within Pro Tools. Here's one example: Say you create a send from a track that should eventually pass through some reverb or delay plug-in placed on an Aux Input (with a bus selected as its input). For the effect you want, however, you'd like one track's audio to be filtered before it hits the delay, while audio sent from other tracks to the same delay should *not* be filtered. Just set that source track's send destination to another bus, create a second Aux Input track that monitors that bus as its input, and place the EQ on that Aux Input. Then assign the output of that second Aux Input to the bus already selected as the input source for the Aux Input where the delay or reverb is inserted.

■ Lastly, don't overlook the Follow Main Pan (FMP) button in the Output window for each send in Pro Tools versions 7.3 and higher. This links the send's panner to the main panner of the track itself.

ReWire

ReWire is a standard for real-time routing of digital audio between separate programs that was developed by Propellerhead Software (the manufacturers of Reason, which is shown in Figure 9.15). Compatible ReWire programs can be slaved to Pro Tools so that they follow the Pro Tools tempo and Transport functions. After instantiating the DigiReWire plug-in in Pro Tools (on an Aux Input, Instrument track, *or* audio track), you can select which of the virtual audio channels coming from the separate ReWire application you want to be streamed into the Pro Tools mixing environment. From that point, those channels are subject to the same options for plug-in processing, mix automation, and send routing as any other input signal passing through this track. Many users will find it convenient to instantiate ReWire plug-ins on Instrument tracks (even though no instrument plug-in is enabled on this same track). That way, not only is it immediately clear from the track's Mix window icon that this mixer strip

Figure 9.15   You can integrate Reason's audio outputs into the Pro Tools environment by instantiating the DigiReWire plug-in.

represents an instrumental sound source, but you can also use that Instrument track's MIDI track functionality in the Edit window to record and edit a MIDI performance for that ReWire destination.

Rewired Programs and Voice Allocation in Pro Tools   On TDM systems, each ReWire channel you enable on an audio track occupies one voice out of your system's total pool of voices for audio playback. This is *not* the case when the ReWire plug-in is enabled on Aux

Input or Instrument tracks of LE and M-Powered systems, however. Depending on how the slaved ReWire application is used—especially considering that several of them support not only virtual instruments but long samples and audio tracks—this may present some interesting possibilities for overcoming the 32-voice limitation in the basic version of Pro Tools LE and M-Powered (which can be expanded to 64 voices with the Music Production Toolkit or DV Toolkit 2).

Additionally, many ReWire applications include their own virtual instruments (for example, the synthesizers, samplers, and programmable drum machines in Reason, or in Gigastudio3—a sampler instrument with many other features). When a slaved ReWire application is detected, you can choose any of these as output destinations from your MIDI tracks within Pro Tools.

Any ReWire setup requires one program to act as the master and another as the slave—being controlled via the other program's transport and tempo and also relying on the other program for access to the audio hardware and mixing environment. Some programs—including the current version of Apple's GarageBand, many MIDI sequencers, and Pro Tools itself—must be the ReWire "master" (or "host") program and therefore can't be slaved to Pro Tools via ReWire. Examples of ReWire applications that *can* work in slave mode with Pro Tools include the following:

- **Reason.** Virtual instruments, effects, mixing, and sequencing, from Propellerhead Software. A limited-feature version, Reason Adapted, has been bundled with certain Pro Tools configurations. Unlike some other ReWire applications, Reason supports only one stereo pair; the remainder of its channels must enter Pro Tools via mono instances of the DigiReWire plug-in. (Refer to Figure 9.15.)

- **Live.** Sophisticated looping tools, recording, mixing, and effects, from Ableton; available for both Mac and Windows.

- **Soundminer.** Catalog-management and auditioning tool for audio files, from Soundminer.

- **Gigastudio3.** A sampler program for Windows from Tascam that includes sample streaming from disk, sequencing, mixing, convolution effects, custom sample recording, and mapping. Versions 3 and higher support ReWire.

Getting the Most Out of Available DSP

Especially if you don't have an unlimited budget, in complex Pro Tools sessions, you may eventually get one of those dreaded messages from Pro Tools, such as "CPU is too busy" or "CPU Usage is holding off USB Audio" on one of the USB-based Mbox 2 or original Mbox interfaces, meaning that you've reached the limit of your system's resources. At that point, you have several choices (besides hustling out to buy another HD Accel card, if you have a Pro Tools|HD system!). Obviously, the first thing is to look at is whether you're really using the routing and plug-in processing of Pro Tools in the most efficient manner. It's typical to add effects and sends on an ad-hoc basis during the edit process. Once a session becomes sufficiently large and complex, it can definitely be worth taking a moment to re-examine how you have your signal routing and processing set up. It might even make the final mix much easier!

Here are some strategies to try if you ever slam into this limit on your projects:

■ Check your CPU Usage Limit setting (under Setup > Playback Engine). This can be set as high as 99% on single-processor systems, or 90% on dual-processor systems. Even though you might notice that the highest setting slows down screen redraws on slower computers, it might just be enough to get your project finished and bounced to disk!

■ If your computer has two or more processors and you're a Pro Tools LE or M-Powered user, or for Pro Tools HD sessions that use a lot of RTAS plug-ins, open the Playback Engine dialog box from the Setup menu and confirm that the RTAS Processors parameter is set to two or more processors.

■ Try increasing the value for the Hardware Buffer setting, under Setup > Playback Engine. Higher settings allow more intensive use of RTAS plug-ins. However, especially on LE and M-Powered systems, the amount of latency is also directly proportional to the size of the hardware buffer. (This affects monitoring delay between the track's input and output while recording, and real-time response of software instruments to MIDI performances from your external controller.) You will therefore usually want to use a smaller buffer setting while still recording tracks, perhaps increasing it during mixdown as you activate a lot of RTAS plug-ins (especially reverbs and software instruments).

■ Pro Tools|HD and previous TDM systems have a Number of Voices pop-up selector in the Setup > Playback Engine dialog box. Setting this to a lower number (although still high enough to support the voices required by your mono, stereo, and multichannel audio tracks, as well as your RTAS plug-ins, of course) also frees up some processing power for plug-ins.

■ Where appropriate, try placing a single instance of a plug-in on Aux Inputs where multiple tracks are routed instead of placing similar plug-ins on each individual track. For example, if you have four or five backing vocal tracks, instead of putting a compressor on each one, route all their outputs to a single stereo bus and then place a compressor on the stereo Aux Input monitoring that bus. You might even find that this makes the parts sound tighter once a single dynamic shape is uniformly affecting them all.

■ Bear in mind that every active bus, send, and hardware insert also uses some of the available DSP resources on your system. For this reason, try not to create an excessive number of these in any template (stationery) documents, and be sure to eliminate them after they are no longer needed. For example, if you only required a send, a bus, and an Aux Input for a headphone mix during the recording process, consider eliminating these if your DSP resources are running short during the final mix.

■ Take a look at how you're using your plug-ins and DSP resources. On Pro Tools|HD (as well as previous systems using the TDM architecture), the first instance of a given plug-in type requires more of your DSP resources than subsequent instances of the same plug-in. Therefore, from an efficiency standpoint, it makes fewer demands on your available DSP to use the same compressor type in two different places (with different settings, of course) rather than using, say, a Digidesign compressor on one track and a Focusrite compressor on another—as long as the sound you want can still be achieved.

■ With Digidesign's EQ, it's the *total* number of bands of EQ used that determines usage of your DSP resources on TDM systems. If you're only boosting or cutting one band in any of your 7-band EQ plug-ins, try making them 1-band EQs instead. Likewise, on all Pro Tools systems, the longer the delay, the larger the demand on available DSP resources. It's inefficient to use the Long Delay plug-in if its current delay time setting is short enough for the Medium or Slap Delay instead. Fortunately, with DigiRack delays, as you change from one type to another, their settings are maintained—including the delay time, as long as it fits into the maximum duration of the new, shorter delay type.

■ You could bounce out some of your tracks to disk with effects and then re-import them into the session (via the Import After Bounce check box in the Bounce to Disk dialog box). Afterward, use the Track > Make Inactive command (also available by right-clicking the track name in all versions 7.3 and higher) to completely disable the original tracks containing the plug-in effects so that they no longer make any demands on your system's DSP resources. For some projects, you could also bounce out the entire mix and import it into a brand-new session with no plug-ins at all.

■ If you're reasonably sure you can live with the current settings of a DigiRack plug-in for a while, use the plug-in window's pop-up Settings menu to copy its settings, and then paste them into the AudioSuite version of the same effect. First, make a duplicate of the track's current playlist (using its pop-up Playlist selector in the Edit window), and then select the entire contents of the audio track and process it with the AudioSuite plug-in. Don't worry—when you click the Process button to apply the effect parameters, new regions can be created, leaving your original audio regions still available should you have second thoughts at some later point (assuming you *don't* enable the Overwrite Files option in the AudioSuite window). If the Use in Playlist button is enabled, the new, processed regions will take the place of the original regions in the track (which will still be available in the Regions List). If you ever need to revert to the original state of the track to readjust the processing, just use the track's Playlist selector to restore its original form (containing the original, unprocessed versions of all those regions).

Where to Place Plug-ins

Plug-ins can be placed on any track type except MIDI tracks. The best option depends on what you're trying to achieve, but here are a few basic thoughts:

■ As mentioned already, it's often more efficient to assign the main outputs of multiple tracks to a single bus and place a single plug-in on the Aux Input that monitors that bus rather than inserting redundant plug-ins into each individual audio track. If you're layering up a dozen harmony tracks with the same vocalist, it's an inefficient use of DSP capacity to instantiate identical EQ plug-ins on each of them, and also makes adjusting your settings more laborious later. As an added bonus, in many cases—such as multiple backing vocals or rhythm guitars, for example—having a single compressor apply its dynamic shaping to that entire submix can also contribute to a tighter, more coherent sound.

- As a general rule, except when they are an integral part of a single track's sound, get into the habit of putting delays and reverbs on Aux Inputs rather than in any single audio track's signal chain. It gives you more control and flexibility later if you decide it might be handy to send some additional track's signal to that same delay.

- EQ affects gain! Therefore, the amount of gain or boost you apply in an EQ plug-in affects not only audio levels on the track's main output (and any post-fader sends) but also the level entering any plug-ins that follow the track's signal chain. If EQ is followed by a compressor or limiter, for example, a dramatic boost in some frequency range would cause that dynamics-processing effect to clamp down harder—because the increased gain coming out of the EQ plug-in causes the track's peak audio levels to exceed the specified threshold more often. With high-frequency boosts, the net result may be to darken the sound somewhat. There are no set rules for effects processing, of course, but as a general guideline for a more transparent sound, we usually start by placing the EQ *after* any dynamics-processing plug-ins on the track.

- Speaking of EQ, remember that if you can't quite achieve the sound you're looking for with a delay or reverb plug-in, you always have the option of placing an EQ plug-in before and/or after it in the Aux Input track where it resides. For example, reducing the amount of high frequencies entering the effect can solve problems with vocal sibilance or other bright transients from the source tracks that might otherwise clutter up your mix after they hit the effect. (To avoid confusion, note that generally in reverb and delay plug-ins, Low-Pass Filter or High-Frequency Cut controls apply to the effect's output or delay regeneration, *not* its input signal.) Compressors or even de-essers can also be effective for taming the dynamics of a signal entering a delay or reverb. This would allow you to increase the effect's overall level without worrying about whether occasional peaks in the source tracks will create splashes of reverb that are too prominent in the mix.

- Reverb plug-ins don't usually have gated reverb presets (although "nonlinear" reverb algorithms sound somewhat similar), and novice users often seem to consider this an omission. If you're overcome by 1980s nostalgia (and long to see monster snares again stalk the land, terrifying peaceful villagers everywhere!), here's a quick pointer: In Pro Tools 8, you can instantiate up to 10 plug-ins on any track, right? Among the plug-ins included with any Pro Tools configuration, you have a reverb, and also a gate that could follow it in the same track's signal chain. You can figure out the rest!

- Remember that inserts on Master Fader tracks are always *post*-fader, while on audio tracks, Aux Inputs, and Instrument tracks, inserts are *pre*-fader. On a Master Fader, the input level to its plug-ins is therefore affected by that track's main volume fader. If you're using a limiter or compressor plug-in on the Master Fader for your main mix output, you could use the track's main volume fader to adjust how hard you're driving the input of that plug-in, as with many traditional hardware compressors. When you use dithering plug-ins for bouncing to disk or recording digitally to another device at a lower bit depth, the dithering step should always be the *last* plug-in on the Master Fader (or other track controlling a selected bus) that is the source for your mix output.

Copying/Moving Plug-ins Option-drag (Alt-drag in Windows) any plug-in to copy it to a different track, along with all its current settings. (The source and destination track must have the same number of inputs and outputs.) You can also drag plug-ins among the different "a" through "e" insert locations within the same track, which changes their signal-processing order and the resultant sound. In versions 7.3 and higher of Pro Tools, this can even be done during playback! (Remember that on HD systems, RTAS plug-ins should generally be placed *before* any TDM plug-ins in the same audio track.)

In addition to saving and recalling plug-in settings from disk (as shown in Figure 9.16), you can also copy and paste them directly. For example, to copy current settings from the 7-band EQ plug-in on one track to another, use the Copy Settings and Paste Settings commands in the pop-up plug-in settings menu within the plug-in window.

Figure 9.16 Settings for each plug-in type can be saved, recalled, cut, pasted, or imported from other Pro Tools sessions and systems.

AudioSuite Effects Versus Real-Time Plug-ins

AudioSuite processing is discussed in Chapter 8, "Menu Selections: Highlights." As stated there, two basic classes of software effects are available in Pro Tools. First there are plug-ins that function in real time as inserts on audio, Aux Input, Instrument, or Master Fader tracks. Depending on your system configuration, these may be in RTAS or TDM format. In contrast, the effects in the AudioSuite menu are file based—they must either destructively alter the data in the original file or, more typically, create a new file to store the result of the processing. As mentioned in the section "Getting the Most Out of Available DSP" earlier in this chapter, if your system's DSP resources are extremely limited (for example, if you're using a Pro Tools LE or M-Powered version on an older Macintosh G4 model), there may be times when you start off using one of the DigiRack RTAS (Real-Time AudioSuite) plug-ins and eventually copy and paste its parameters into the corresponding AudioSuite plug-in. This is one way to free up that DSP power for subsequent mixing tasks. Even on the more current LE/M-Powered versions of Pro Tools and contemporary computers, there will be cases where you hit the limit for processing capacity on your system; it will be good to know you still have some options for getting your project completed!

Bouncing Effects into Tracks and Submixes

We've already mentioned bouncing out mixes in order to free up DSP resources. Here are a few more observations that may be helpful during this process.

Managing Multiple Session Documents

Remember that the Select > Unused Regions command in the Regions List menu only looks at the *current* session document! If you have bounced out a submix and created a new session (perhaps through the File > Save As command) in order to keep adding more tracks, be cognizant that this new session knows nothing about how any of the audio files and regions referenced by its Regions List may be used in *other* sessions. Also, remember that when Save Session As creates a new session document, that new copy still uses the same Audio Files and Fade Files folders as the previous session (not to mention the Session File Backups, Region Groups, and Rendered Files folders, plus the cache file for waveform overviews), as shown in Figure 9.17.

Session copies created by the File > Save Copy In command also continue to use the original audio files in the current session's folder—*unless* you specify in the Save Session Copy dialog box that source audio files should be copied to a new folder along with the session file itself. However, any session created by the Save Copy In command will subsequently use its own subfolders for any new audio or fade files created by recording or editing.

Keep in mind that audio regions and bounced files are automatically timestamped by Pro Tools with their original location information. This allows you to use the Spot dialog box to make sure that the bounced files you import into other session copies are placed exactly in their original location.

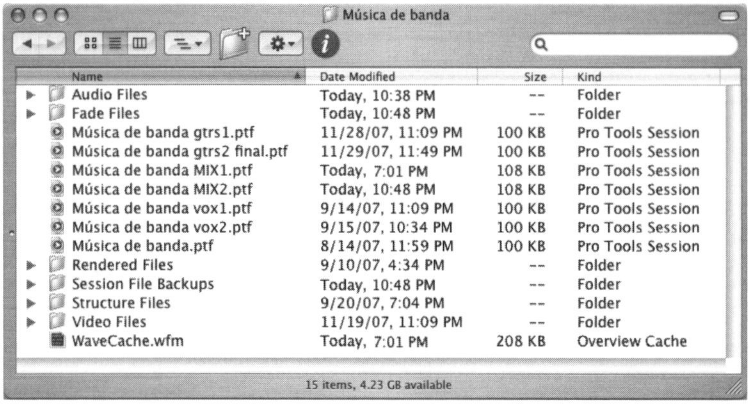

Figure 9.17   Multiple versions of this session (created with the Save As command) share the same Audio Files and Fade Files folders.

Turning Voice Assignment Off

If you turn a track's voice assignment to Off as opposed to Dynamic (or, in certain cases, a manually assigned voice number on HD systems), it is made inactive. It no longer competes with other tracks for voices and, of course, won't be heard. It's usually more effective to use the Track > Make Inactive command. You might do this on multiple source tracks after they have been bounced to disk as part of a submix and re-imported into another track.

Track Muting, Voice Allocation Within a Session (HD Only)

Generally, you will want the Options > Mute Frees Assigned Voice option enabled, especially if you are going through this process of bouncing out tracks to which effects have been applied and then re-importing them into the session to free up DSP resources. That way, when you mute the original track, that voice is now available to play other tracks.

Summary

The possibilities for signal routing in Pro Tools are as varied as the working styles of each operator. You will see another example in Chapter 13, "A Multitrack Music Session," which includes setting up cue mixes for performers. Multichannel tracks and surround mixing are discussed in Chapter 14, "Postproduction and Soundtracks." Also, if you skipped Chapter 7, you may want to flip back to it now for more insight into the virtual mixing, signal-routing, and processing environment that Pro Tools provides for your virtual studio.

10 MIDI

As explained in Chapter 2, "Pro Tools Terms and Concepts," *MIDI* stands for *Musical Instrument Digital Interface*. MIDI devices transmit and receive data about a performance—how you struck a key, pressed a pedal, applied pressure to the keyboard, turned a knob, pushed a slider, and so on. MIDI is a communications language; it transmits instructions rather than audio signals. To put it another way, although sound does not travel though MIDI cables, the data that MIDI cables carry can be used to *control* things that can make sound.

A Technical Overview of MIDI

The MIDI standard is maintained and expanded on an ongoing basis by the MIDI Manufacturer's Association, a consortium of hardware and software companies (http://www.midi.org). In technical terms, MIDI is a 31.25 kilobaud serial communications protocol that uses 5-pin DIN connectors to cable together MIDI-compatible devices. MIDI event messages and timing references are transmitted as binary code.

MIDI was introduced in 1983 to address incompatibility issues between electronic musical instruments from different manufacturers (synthesizers, samplers, and so on). The MIDI specification defines data events and timing references to be commonly recognized by all devices that support the standard. For example, a Note On event includes two additional parameters: the note number (from 0–127) and the velocity with which the key was struck (from 1–127). For common performance controllers such as the damper (sustain) pedal on a keyboard, the modulation wheel or lever, the pitch bend wheel or lever, or the main volume control and panner, standard controller numbers and their range of possible values were also agreed upon. The result was that you could connect the MIDI Out of one keyboard to the MIDI In of another, and it would more or less respond with the same notes. This was quite an improvement over the voltage-controlled synthesizers and early digital-connection protocols from different manufacturers, all of which were mutually incompatible!

Fortunately, the developers of the MIDI specification were much more ambitious than this. MIDI sequencers (data recorders that capture MIDI performance events in real time) needed a common timing reference, called MIDI Clock, so that events could be timestamped in order to play back in proper order and timing, as well as to synchronize one MIDI sequencer to another. Naturally, as personal computers became commonplace in the early 1980s, MIDI interfaces were developed so that MIDI cabling could be connected to personal computers, and software sequencers could receive and retransmit MIDI performance data. Later enhancements to the MIDI specification included the following:

- **MIDI time code (MTC).** This encodes the same time-location information as SMPTE time code (more about this in Chapter 11, "Synchronization").

- **MIDI Show Control.** These are event and controller message types relating to lighting, special effects, hydraulics, audio level controls, and so on.

- **MIDI Machine Control (MMC).** This protocol is used for remote control and interlocking of audio or video tape deck transport functions with other devices (including Pro Tools) via MIDI. This is the MIDI counterpart of an even more prevalent machine control method, based on serial connections between hardware devices. As discussed in Chapter 14, "Post-production and Soundtracks," with the Digidesign MachineControl option, you can use DigiSerial ports on HD cards or 9-pin serial ports on the Sync HD to slave external devices such as video decks and DAT recorders together with Pro Tools if these don't support MIDI Machine Control.

For Pro Tools users, MIDI time code and MIDI Machine Control are especially relevant. Additionally, it's worth mentioning that all parameters of PRE, Digidesign's microphone preamplifier, are controllable via MIDI (and therefore can be restored when a session is reopened), as are many external effects processors.

MIDI Data

Chapter 1, "About Pro Tools," touched on some basic MIDI concepts. We're not going to go into all the technical details here—that is, the communications protocol, interfacing, and the low-level structure (status bytes, data bytes, most- and least-significant bits, and so on) that actually comprise the messages transmitted from one MIDI device to another. There are many excellent relevant resources on that topic in both book and online form, including *MIDI Power* by Robert Guerin, published by Course Technology. Some MIDI messages represent actual performance events—a key or pedal was pressed, a lever or slider was moved, and so on. Other message types are more system level, perhaps telling the receiving device to switch to a different sound or operating mode, controlling its internal sequencer or even loading sound-parameter data that is specific to that device alone. At any rate, however MIDI tracks may appear onscreen (for example, horizontal bars for note events or data curves for modulation, aftertouch, and other types of continuous controllers within Pro Tools), what is actually recorded and played from your MIDI tracks is a series of numerical MIDI messages. Figure 10.1 shows the MIDI Event List window in Pro Tools, which gives you a simplified view of what's actually going on.

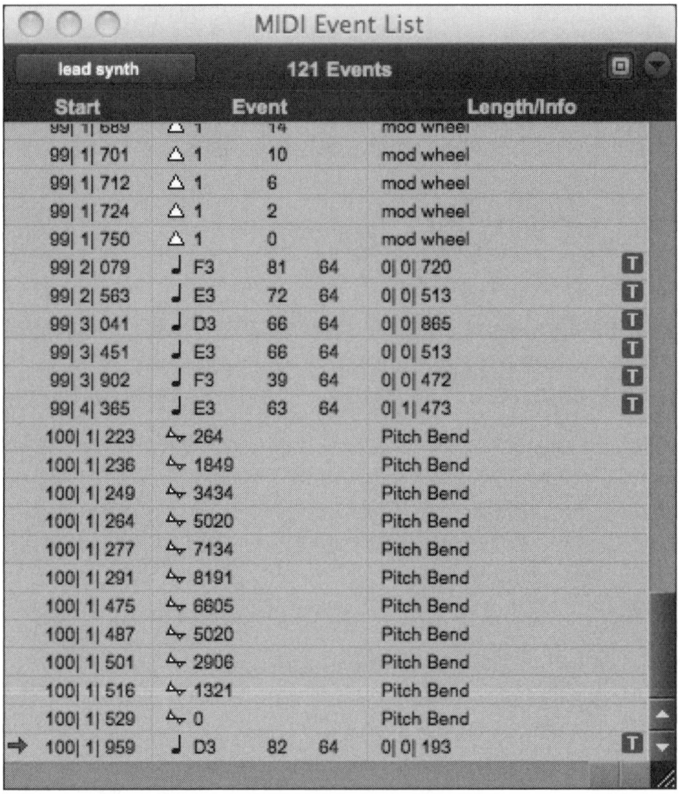

MIDI Event List

lead synth		121 Events			
Start		**Event**		**Length/Info**	
99| 1| 689	△ 1	14		mod wheel	
99| 1| 701	△ 1	10		mod wheel	
99| 1| 712	△ 1	6		mod wheel	
99| 1| 724	△ 1	2		mod wheel	
99| 1| 750	△ 1	0		mod wheel	
99| 2| 079	♩ F3	81	64	0| 0| 720	T
99| 2| 563	♩ E3	72	64	0| 0| 513	T
99| 3| 041	♩ D3	66	64	0| 0| 865	T
99| 3| 451	♩ E3	66	64	0| 0| 513	T
99| 3| 902	♩ F3	39	64	0| 0| 472	T
99| 4| 365	♩ E3	63	64	0| 1| 473	T
100| 1| 223	↲ 264			Pitch Bend	
100| 1| 236	↲ 1849			Pitch Bend	
100| 1| 249	↲ 3434			Pitch Bend	
100| 1| 264	↲ 5020			Pitch Bend	
100| 1| 277	↲ 7134			Pitch Bend	
100| 1| 291	↲ 8191			Pitch Bend	
100| 1| 475	↲ 6605			Pitch Bend	
100| 1| 487	↲ 5020			Pitch Bend	
100| 1| 501	↲ 2906			Pitch Bend	
100| 1| 516	↲ 1321			Pitch Bend	
100| 1| 529	↲ 0			Pitch Bend	
⇒ 100| 1| 959	♩ D3	82	64	0| 0| 193	T

Figure 10.1 The MIDI Event List window displays MIDI events as numerical data. For the most part, you will deal with Channel Voice messages in Pro Tools (although other types of MIDI messages, such as System Exclusive messages, are also supported).

Although there are many types of MIDI messages, they can all be classified into five basic categories:

- **Channel Voice messages.** These represent performance events such as Note On/Off, volume, pan, modulation, pitch bend, aftertouch, pedals or breath controllers, and so on. Each Channel Voice message is transmitted specifically on one of the 16 MIDI channels (a Note On message on channel 5, for example). Program Change messages are also in this category—usually causing whichever part or patch that is listening to that MIDI channel to switch to a different sound for responding to the MIDI note events it receives.

- **Channel Mode messages.** These include messages for switching between operating modes on the receiving devices, which determine how the device will respond to incoming notes and other MIDI events. In Omni mode, the device responds to incoming note events on any channel; in Poly mode, it responds to incoming MIDI events on multiple channels, each with an independently selectable timbre; and Mono mode responds to a single channel only. All Notes Off is also a Channel Mode message, used for stuck notes (there's a command for this in the Pro Tools MIDI menu).

- **System Common messages.** These include Song Position Pointer, Song Select, and Tune Request messages.

- **System Real Time messages.** These are used for messages such as MIDI Clock, Start/Stop, Active Sensing, and so on.

- **System Exclusive messages.** These messages contain manufacturers' proprietary control data. They are ignored by all units that don't respond to the unique manufacturer ID at the beginning of each message. They're used for editing, loading, or archiving sound parameters that are specific to that instrument.

For the most part, when you're editing data in Pro Tools MIDI tracks, you will be dealing with Channel Voice events, although each of the other types can come into play in given situations.

Aftertouch: Can Pro Tools Handle the Pressure? In addition to registering attack and release velocity (how rapidly you strike and release each key on your MIDI controller), the MIDI specification includes two types of aftertouch controller data: channel pressure and polyphonic pressure.

Channel pressure, often simply referred to as aftertouch data, generates a series of values as you change the amount of pressure applied to the entire keyboard. On many synthesizer patches, for example, pressing harder on the controller keyboard as you hold a note or chord may increase the filter cutoff frequency, amount or speed of low-frequency modulation, volume, and so on.

Polyphonic pressure data (sometimes called polyphonic key pressure or polyphonic aftertouch) reflects the pressure applied to each individual key. Only some MIDI controllers are capable of generating this type of data, and many sampler programs and synth patches may not respond to it at all. Polyphonic pressure events can also dramatically increase the density of your recorded MIDI data, since a continuous stream of pressure events is generated for each key instead of a single value for the entire keyboard as in the case of channel pressure data. If none of the MIDI modules or software synths you're using respond to this type of controller data, consider using the MIDI menu's Input Filter selection to disable recording of polyphonic pressure into Pro Tools.

Although channel pressure (mono aftertouch) is one of the standard Data Display options for MIDI tracks in the Edit window, the MIDI Event List window is the *only* place you can view/edit polyphonic pressure events in Pro Tools.

MIDI Interface Options

As mentioned in Chapter 3, "Your System Configuration," a MIDI interface is a sort of adapter that translates the MIDI data communications protocol to a format that your computer can understand. MIDI interfaces can be external devices—typically connected to the computer via USB in current models (especially when interfaces with numerous MIDI connections are required). Many generic Windows sound cards have built-in connectors for MIDI, where for simple applications you could attach a simple break-out cable with one DIN-5 connector for MIDI In and another for MIDI Out (although some consumer-level cards may present conflicts with professional audio programs).

Digi 003, Digi 002, Mbox 2, and Mbox 2 Pro systems have MIDI input/output connectors integrated into the external Digidesign audio interface itself (although in some cases, you may not be able to use them from programs other than Pro Tools). Digidesign's Command|8 control surface communicates directly with Pro Tools via USB (unlike some other external control surfaces that communicate via MIDI or Ethernet); it also includes a one-in, two-out MIDI interface. Several M-Audio audio interfaces that are compatible with Pro Tools M-Powered also incorporate MIDI inputs/outputs, which you can use with Pro Tools as well as with other programs.

Whichever MIDI interface you're using in your Pro Tools configuration, the number of independently addressable MIDI inputs or outputs (ports) it provides will determine the total number of MIDI channels available for communicating with external MIDI devices—16 MIDI channels per port. For example, if you have a one-in, two-out MIDI interface (as on the Digi 003 and Digi 002 interfaces), that's 16 MIDI input channels and 32 output channels available for external MIDI communication to or from each Pro Tools MIDI (or Instrument) track. Of course, many different types of MIDI interfaces are available, with varying numbers of ports. More sophisticated units might include routing or filtering capabilities for the MIDI data passing through them, stored presets and operation in standalone mode without a computer, SMPTE time code synchronization, word clock features for slaving your audio hardware's sample rate to external sources, and the ability to slave multiple MIDI interfaces together to expand the number of independently addressable MIDI ports. Pro Tools supports most external MIDI interfaces currently available, including units from MOTU, M-Audio (another division of Avid, the parent company of Digidesign), Yamaha, E-MU Systems, and others.

MIDI via USB and FireWire Various MIDI controllers and sound modules can connect directly to the host computer via USB—from M-Audio, Fatar, Alesis, Roland/Edirol, E-mu, Korg, and others. M-Audio offers keyboard controllers that also act as audio interfaces, such as the KeyStudio 49i and the ProKeys Sono 61 and 88.

Digidesign MIDI I/O

The MIDI I/O (shown in Figure 10.2), no longer produced but still prevalent in the audio industry, is the first external MIDI interface under the Digidesign name. It features 10 MIDI inputs (with two of these on the front panel) and 10 outputs, and connects to the host computer via the USB port (which also powers the device). In addition to working with the Pro Tools program, the MIDI I/O also features a standalone hardware thru mode. You can daisy-chain up to four MIDI I/Os together, for up to 640 MIDI channels (16 channels per MIDI port).

Figure 10.2   Digidesign's MIDI I/O, a multiport MIDI interface, connects to the host computer via USB. Two of its 10 MIDI inputs/outputs are available on the front panel.

Although there are many options for multiport MIDI interfaces, a unique feature offered by the MIDI I/O is support for Digidesign's MIDI Time Stamping feature for MIDI data in Pro Tools. This addresses an inherent timing problem when you transmit many channels of dense MIDI data in real time over a single connection. Imagine you're sending or receiving 30–40 separate channels of MIDI data, each containing constant pitch bend and polyphonic pressure events or fader and knob movements recorded from an external control surface for Pro Tools that communicates with the computer via MIDI. The sheer volume of MIDI events could exceed the real-time capacity of a single USB connection. Even more likely, a conventional MIDI interface may not be able to receive, convert, and reroute all this information between multiple ports and the data connection to the computer itself without some kind of processing delay, or latency. The result will be random timing discrepancies that become an audible problem in your project. Via the MIDI Time Stamping feature, each incoming MIDI event is automatically timestamped during recording. During MIDI playback, data sent from Pro Tools is *preloaded* into a buffer in the MIDI I/O in real time to ensure more timely playback.

MIDI Setup

Pro Tools handles MIDI setup slightly differently in Macintosh than in Windows. In Mac OS X (operating system versions 10 and above), you use the Audio MIDI Setup utility to configure the MIDI interface and external MIDI devices (for example, keyboards, guitar, wind, and percussion controllers, drum machines, and sound modules). The available selections for MIDI input/output (I/O) on Pro Tools tracks reflect the currently active configuration in that utility. Once you've run the installer program for whatever drivers an external MIDI interface requires (if any), this interface automatically appears in Audio MIDI Setup.

In Windows versions of Pro Tools, the MIDI Studio Setup window automatically finds MIDI interface drivers and translates that information into XML-based documents. You can assign custom names for the MIDI ports on the interface and use XML-based patchname documents (which can be customized, as in Mac OS X) for selecting sounds on your external MIDI devices. You must always first run the installer program provided with the MIDI interface itself. Note that the proper procedures in Windows can be highly variable from one model to another—read the instructions before installing *anything*!

Again, Digi 003 and Digi 002 interfaces include one MIDI input and two MIDI outputs. Some of the current M-Audio interfaces for Pro Tools M-Powered also offer a single MIDI input and output, as does Digidesign's Mbox 2 family (which includes the LE version of Pro Tools) and the Command|8 control surface. For any other Pro Tools hardware configuration, the MIDI interface is a separate hardware peripheral (or possibly a port commonly found on generic Windows sound cards, if the modest performance offered by this option is sufficient for your needs).

Macintosh (Audio MIDI Setup)

The Audio MIDI Setup utility (shown in Figure 10.3) is part of Mac OS X. It can be launched directly from within Pro Tools using the Setup > MIDI Studio Setup command. You use it to configure what type of MIDI interface (if any) is connected to your computer and how your external MIDI controllers and sound modules are connected to it. Many devices are already preconfigured so that you can select by manufacturer/model, but you can manually configure any other device. The most important issues are how many MIDI ports the device has, which MIDI channels it transmits/receives, whether it receives or transmits MIDI Beat Clock and MIDI time code, and whether it's General MIDI compatible. You then simply drag onscreen cables between the MIDI inputs/outputs on each MIDI device and the corresponding ports on the MIDI interface to mirror their actual physical connections.

Windows

Most MIDI interfaces come with their own driver installer disks. MIDI drivers are installed via INF files for Windows Device Manager (WDM), which instructs the operating system about how and when to use those driver files. For common (SoundBlaster-compatible) PC sound cards, an optional cable converts a DB-15 data connector on the card into MIDI In/Out 5-pin DIN connectors. However, for professional applications, USB is currently the most common connection for attaching external MIDI interfaces to Windows computers. Installation procedures can vary widely by manufacturer and model. Be sure to carefully read the manufacturer's instructions before installing software for a new MIDI interface on your system; doing so takes much less time than trying to undo an improper installation!

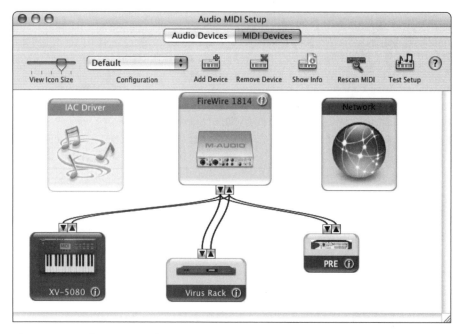

Figure 10.3 The Macintosh OS X Audio MIDI Setup program provides a uniform method for configuring the communication between all MIDI-capable programs and any MIDI interfaces, external keyboards/controllers, and modules attached to your system.

The Pro Tools for Windows MIDI Studio Setup window (shown in Figure 10.4) makes it simple to manage a complex MIDI configuration, including the external MIDI devices and the sounds within them. Here you define *instruments* for each of your external MIDI devices by clicking the Create button. Properties appear in the right panel of this window for each selected instrument. A list of predefined instruments is provided in your Pro Tools installation; these MIDI device files are written in a language known as *XML* (Extensible Markup Language). If the MIDI device you're defining as a new instrument is included in that default list, you can select it in the Manufacturer and Model pop-up lists. Otherwise, you can leave these fields set to None and simply enter your own name for the instrument. You can also define where this instrument is connected for input and output to and from Pro Tools by indicating the port on your MIDI interface. Lastly, you indicate which MIDI channels the device is sending on and the specific output MIDI channels from Pro Tools to which this device responds. For example, your keyboard may be configured to transmit only on MIDI channel 1, while it can respond to all 16 MIDI channels. A MIDI module may not transmit on any channels at all, but respond to all of them. A MIDI guitar controller may transmit on six MIDI channels simultaneously, while some MIDI percussion controllers transmit on an even larger number of simultaneous channels.

The active instruments in your current MIDI Studio Setup configuration then appear in the MIDI Input and MIDI Output selectors on MIDI tracks. (To make an instrument not appear,

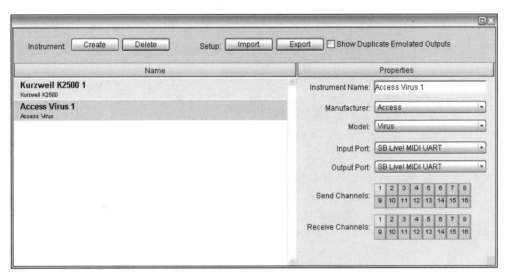

Figure 10.4   The MIDI Studio Setup window is used in Pro Tools versions for Windows.

without having to delete its definition from MIDI Studio Setup, change its input and output port assignments to None.)

Patchname files, which are also written in XML and use the .midnam file extension, also enhance management of multiple external MIDI devices. As with MIDI device files, a collection of predefined patchname files is included with the Pro Tools installation (and resides in the Program Files > Common Files > Digidesign > MIDI Patch Names > Digidesign subdirectory). MIDI tracks have a Program button in both the Mix and Edit windows that opens the Patch Select dialog box. (This functionality has been available in Mac versions for quite a while, but wasn't implemented in Windows until version 6.7.) In this dialog box, you can select a patchname file for the current track (using the Change button) from among the MIDNAM files residing in that directory. If you choose a Korg Triton, for example, all the factory internal programs and banks for that device will appear *by name* rather than simply by program number each time you open the Patch Select dialog box. This is a huge boost to productivity, making it much quicker to select and experiment with different sounds for your MIDI parts. These patchname files are ordinary text files, however—as are the patchname files used with the Macintosh Audio MIDI Setup utility. If you've edited program names or customized the contents of the user bank on your external synthesizer, you can edit the program names inside the corresponding patchname file on your computer using any text-editor program. Be sure to make a backup copy of the original first, however! Some third-party librarian or patch-editor programs also provide tools for creating your own patchname files from scratch. You can find many of these patchname files on the Web if your particular device isn't included in the predefined list provided with Pro Tools.

External MIDI Devices

There are many types of external MIDI devices, including standard synthesizers or samplers with keyboards, MIDI sound modules with no keyboards, and MIDI controllers that feature no internal sound-generation capabilities at all (keyboard controllers, guitar controllers, wind controllers, electronic percussion, and so on). Of course, many other devices also support MIDI. For example, you can control parameters of many effects processors via MIDI, as well as control automated mixers or, for that matter, some lighting gear and amplifiers.

Besides using a MIDI controller for performance (keyboard, guitar controller, wind controller, electronic drums, and so on), there are also MIDI peripherals that you can use as control surfaces for Pro Tools itself. The Mackie Control Series, the J.L. Cooper Media Command Station 3000 Series, the CM Labs MotorMix2, and the Euphonix MC Control and Mix are some examples of external devices that you can use to externally control Pro Tools faders, sliders, and/or the Pro Tools Transport via a MIDI connection.

Lastly, there are other alternatives for connecting musical peripherals to your computer: USB controller keyboards and/or USB modules are available from M-Audio, Roland/Edirol, Alesis, E-mu, Fatar, Korg, and others that don't require a MIDI interface at all. These alternatives are especially attractive for laptop users; some of the smaller keyboard controllers can even run off batteries! For users who rely exclusively on software instruments as MIDI sound sources—and as time passes and computers become more powerful, this is an increasingly common option—a full-featured keyboard controller with a direct USB connection and no internal sounds may be all that is required. In fact, two units from M-Audio, the Ozone (connected via USB) and Ozonic (connected via FireWire), also double as audio interfaces for Pro Tools M-Powered.

The following sections discuss software-based virtual instruments. You can use them in conjunction with or instead of any external sound modules for MIDI. You also have the option of using third-party programs via the DigiReWire plug-in, which routes the external program's audio output into an Aux channel in Pro Tools. In Figure 10.5, you see the Digidesign AIR Xpand! plug-in on an Instrument track controlled by an M-Audio Oxygen8. The audio output of this Instrument track is sent out the bus labeled MIDI Audio Bus, which is also chosen as the audio input of the audio track Xpand! Record. This enables the user to record the output of the Instrument track, creating an audio file within the session.

Virtual Instruments

Software-based MIDI instruments are among the most exciting tools to have emerged for computer-based music production in the last 15 years. Virtual instrument plug-ins have been around for a while in RTAS and TDM formats (as well as VST, AU, DirectX, and additional formats used by other audio programs). ReWire technology enables many more options for integrating software-based synthesizers and samplers into the Pro Tools

Figure 10.5 A Pro Tools LE session with the virtual instrument Xpand! on an Instrument track controlled by an M-Audio Oxygen8 keyboard. Note that via the MIDI Audio Bus routing, the audio track xpand_rcrd can be used to capture the output of the Instrument track as an audio file.

environment. Virtual instruments for current Pro Tools versions can be broken down into four general classes:

- RTAS synthesizer/sampler plug-ins (for Pro Tools HD, LE, and M-Powered).

- TDM synthesizer/sampler plug-ins (for Pro Tools HD).

■ Separate synthesizer/sampler programs such as Reason, Gigastudio4, or Ableton Live, whose virtual audio outputs can be routed into Pro Tools via the DigiReWire plug-in (Pro Tools HD, LE, and M-Powered).

■ Plug-ins in other formats that are not native to Pro Tools, used via so-called "wrapper" programs. One very useful example is the VST to RTAS Adapter program, by FXpansion, which allows you to use VST effects and instrument plug-ins within the Pro Tools RTAS plug-in environment on either Mac or Windows.

You might instantiate a virtual instrument plug-in in one of the insert slots of an Instrument or Aux Input track—although you could also place them on an audio track. Alternatively, if the virtual instrument is within a separate program communicating with Pro Tools via ReWire (like Reason, Gigastudio4, or Ableton Live), you would select that program as an insert via the Digi-ReWire plug-in. You can then use its ReWire plug-in window to select which of that program's output channels you want to stream into Pro Tools at this insert point on the track. From that point in the signal chain, treatment of the audio output from any virtual instrument on a track is identical to other signal sources in Pro Tools, including mix automation and plug-in processing and creating sends and other routing assignments. Not only do software-based instruments greatly simplify your life when working with multiple projects and MIDI sound sources, but the virtual signal path from these synths and samplers into the Pro Tools mixing environment is as clean as it gets!

Why Use Virtual Instruments Instead of External MIDI Gear?

Software-based instruments have numerous benefits over physical MIDI devices. First, they can be less noisy because there are no physical inputs/outputs, cabling, digital converters, and so on, all of which are subject to whatever compromise in quality the manufacturer had to make to sell the instrument at a given price. Second, virtual instruments can be more cost effective because you aren't buying RAM, disk storage, and so on for, say, an external sampler, which frequently may not be of a type that is as readily available and inexpensive as its counterpart for standard desktop computers. The whole routing and reconnection scenario becomes immensely simple as well: There are no cables to reconnect (or induce noise).

In the case of ReWire, you can launch the separate virtual instrument application, reloading its patch and entire routing configuration, the next time you open that Pro Tools session—without touching any cables or adjusting levels. For sampler virtual instruments, the fact that these use standard PC or Mac disk and file formats (as opposed to the proprietary formats used by many standalone samplers) means that you can much more easily create or acquire new audio files for them. (The sound-generation method in samplers relies on playing back digital audio recordings from RAM, varying their playback speed or resynthesizing as required to produce different pitches and sometimes looping shorter audio segments to produce sustained tones.) You may even decide midway through a Pro Tools session that you'd like to use a particular audio region sampler style, triggering its playback at different speeds/pitches via MIDI note events. No problem; you bounce out the region as a file (in the same standard AIF or WAV formats you're already using with Pro Tools) and load it up into a Structure, SampleTank2, Kontakt4, Mach-Five 2, or Gigastudio4 instrument so that it can be played from the keyboard, for example. Need to apply some editing to that sample so that it works better in the software sampler? Open it again in Pro Tools, make your changes, save again to disk, and reload.

To be fair, though, there are some advantages to using external synthesizers and samplers (not to mention more traditional instruments whose physical characteristics are an essential aspect of their sound and the playing experience itself). For one thing, virtual instruments make intensive processing demands on your system's processing resources, which can limit how much is left over for high audio-track counts and DSP-intensive plug-ins. Also, especially on LE and M-Powered systems and relatively underpowered host computers, audio and plug-in demands may make it impractical to reduce the size of the hardware buffer enough so that latency during the actual MIDI performance doesn't create perceptual or timing problems.

Virtual Instrument Programs (ReWire)

Most ReWire programs support both audio and MIDI processing, and many offer robust sequencing and composing tools of their own. In addition to streaming their audio output into Pro Tools tracks via the DigiReWire plug-in, you can use MIDI-capable software instruments within client ReWire programs as sound sources by assigning them as the output from your MIDI or Instrument tracks in Pro Tools. Several of these ReWire-capable applications offer VST plug-in support, chord, scale matrix, and arpeggio generators, and other powerful real-time MIDI processing tools (for example, the Follow Actions and Racks functions in Ableton Live). These can be a very interesting adjunct to Pro Tools' basic MIDI functionality. Third-party programs that are compatible with ReWire and can work in client mode (under the control of Pro Tools, which is always the ReWire master in this setup) include the following:

- Reason (Propellerhead Software).

- Live (Ableton).

- Gigastudio4 (Tascam; Windows only).

- ACID by Sony Creative (originally developed by Sonic Foundry; Windows only).

- Bidule (Plogue).

- VST to ReWire Adapter (FXpansion). This hosts VST instruments in Mac or Windows so that they can be controlled by Pro Tools MIDI tracks and multiple outputs from them routed back into Pro Tools via ReWire.

Virtual Instrument Plug-ins for Pro Tools

Software-based synthesis and sampling plug-ins have proliferated over recent years. These software-based samplers, synths, and drum modules must be in RTAS format to be used as plug-ins directly within Pro Tools LE and M-Powered systems, while HD systems support software instrument plug-ins in TDM format in addition to RTAS. The parameters (and reference to any external sample files on disk, if applicable) of any software instrument plug-ins are stored and recalled along with the session document. This is a huge productivity advantage, as any veteran user of multiple external modules can attest. The sound-generation parameters of these software instrument plug-ins can also be enabled for Pro Tools automation (like most other plug-ins), even from an external control surface.

Other virtual instruments can be used via separate ReWire programs that communicate with Pro Tools. The audio output from the virtual instrument is incorporated into the Pro Tools mixing environment at whatever insert point you place the DigiReWire plug-in. Audio plug-in or hardware I/O effects can be used on the insert slots following the instrument or ReWire plug-in in a track to further process its output. You can also create sends from any track containing an instrument plug-in.

Because Pro Tools LE and M-Powered use RTAS virtual instrument plug-ins (including wrapped VST plug-ins and any separate software-based instruments that stream into Pro Tools via DigiReWire, an RTAS plug-in), the performance of these virtual instruments depends on your system's resources—the CPU type and speed, available RAM, and so on. This is also true of the Pro Tools LE or M-Powered program in general. If your computer is already having a hard time with the number of tracks and plug-ins you're using in Pro Tools, this may set a practical limit on how many voices, channels, and effects you can use within any software instruments. Pro Tools HD users will also experience this when using RTAS instrument plug-ins; however, they also have access to some TDM-only instrument plug-ins that rely on the DSP capacity of the HD cards themselves for their processing needs. Shown in Figure 10.6 is the Digidesign AIR Xpand! virtual instrument and synth and sample workstation currently bundled with the HD, LE, and M-Powered versions of Pro Tools.

Recording into MIDI and Instrument Tracks

Pro Tools MIDI and Instrument tracks can record from any active port on your MIDI interface, on whatever channel(s) your controller is transmitting. Ordinarily, you will have the MIDI Thru function enabled (via a selection in the Options menu). That way, regardless of which MIDI input you record *from*, the MIDI output (either within the software, a physical port on your external MIDI interface, or a direct USB connection), MIDI channel, and program number you've chosen for the currently record-enabled track will be echoed through to the correct instrument, channel, and program.

If, however, the selected output for the current track happens to be the same MIDI keyboard controller you're currently playing, the MIDI Thru function can present some issues. In this situation, the sound generation within your synth can end up not only responding directly to its own local keyboard, but also to the same note and controller events echoed back around through Pro Tools via the current track assignment. You will hear doubled notes and the

Figure 10.6 The Digidesign AIR Xpand! virtual instrument plug-in in RTAS format. Currently included with all versions of Pro Tools, Xpand! features more than 1,000 preset sounds along with volume envelope, portamento, and low-pass filter cutoff controls (among others).

external keyboard might lock up due to the infinite loop you've set up between the output assignment on your MIDI/Instrument track and the global MIDI Thru feature in Pro Tools. As with other MIDI-capable programs, when using MIDI Thru, you can avoid this problem by simply turning Local mode off on your external keyboard. When a MIDI controller's Local mode is off, its internal sound-generation capability no longer responds to its own keyboard; instead, it responds only to incoming MIDI events at its MIDI input. (If you need to use this MIDI keyboard later in standalone mode, don't forget to turn Local mode back on!)

MIDI Recording Modes

In addition to the four standard recording modes in Pro Tools, a button in the Transport window enables MIDI Merge mode (more about this in a moment). Let's take a look at how these modes affect MIDI recording, because there are some differences compared to audio:

- **Normal mode.** Non-destructive. If you record anywhere into a MIDI or Instrument track where MIDI regions/data already exist, a new region is created for the newly recorded MIDI data. The region(s) replaced by the new MIDI recording in the track are still available and unchanged in the Regions List.

- **Destructive mode.** In MIDI and Instrument tracks, there is no difference between Normal and Destructive modes; they work in exactly the same way. In contrast, in audio tracks, Destructive recording mode actually overwrites any existing audio data at that track location.

- **QuickPunch mode.** Not required for MIDI and Instrument tracks, because for all record-enabled MIDI tracks, you can *always* use the Transport's Record button to drop in and out of recording mode.

- **Loop Record mode.** Works similarly to loop recording on audio tracks. A new MIDI region is created and auto-numbered for every pass through the looped selection (although in MIDI tracks, if you don't play anything on a pass, Pro Tools waits until the next time you play something before creating and auto-numbering additional regions). As with multiple audio takes recorded in Loop Record mode, you can Command+click with the Selector tool (Ctrl+click in Windows) within the region currently in the track to view the Takes List pop-up menu. MIDI Merge mode (see the next bullet) cannot be used in Loop Record mode; its button in the Transport is dimmed whenever Loop Record mode is active.

- **MIDI Merge mode.** When this button in the Pro Tools Transport window is enabled, as you record over existing MIDI regions, the new MIDI data is *added* to the MIDI data already in the track instead of replacing it. However, if you enable Loop Playback mode before recording MIDI, each subsequent pass that you record through the looping section of the timeline will be merged into the previous one (drum-machine style) instead of replacing it,

---

Loop Recording You can record MIDI and/or audio in Loop Record mode! Simply set pre- and post-roll parameters, make a timeline selection, and enable Loop Record mode (in the Options menu or by right-clicking the Record button). As you record, the portion of the session's timeline between the Transport window's Start and End indicators (the time-line selection) is looped until you press the spacebar to stop. A new region is created for each pass. To discard all takes recorded so far without exiting Loop Record mode, press Command+Period (Ctrl+Period in Windows).

Afterward, if you Command-click (Ctrl-click in Windows) with the Selector tool within the loop-recorded region, the pop-up Takes List appears, allowing you to switch between multiple takes. In versions 7.3 and higher of Pro Tools, you can also right-click the region to select among alternate matching regions via a pop-up menu.

Editing MIDI and Instrument Tracks in the Edit Window

When MIDI and Instrument tracks are in Regions or Blocks view, you can drag MIDI regions with the Grabber. Use the Selector to highlight areas within them for cut/copy/paste operations, more or less like audio regions. But there's one important difference here: When the initial Note On message for any MIDI note event begins inside the region's current boundaries, even after trimming the end of this MIDI region those notes extend beyond the region's right edge (and sound for their full lengths). Conversely, if you trim a MIDI region's left edge so that it no longer includes a note's beginning, that note is no longer part of the region (and won't play).

In addition to using the standard Trimmer mode to shorten/lengthen the boundaries of MIDI regions, you can also use the Time Trimmer (the TCE mode of the Trimmer tool) to compress or expand not only the region's length, but the spacing of all the MIDI events within it as well. As always with the editing tools, the currently active Edit mode affects this time trimming. Spot mode opens the Spot dialog box, Slip mode allows free adjustment of the duration, Grid mode snaps the region boundary from one grid increment to another as you drag, and Shuffle mode always leaves the beginning of the new compressed/expanded MIDI region at the same start point as the original region whether you trimmed its beginning or end. In particular, using the TC/E Trimmer in Grid mode may be handy for composers; compressing a four-bar region to two bars creates a double-time version of the events it contains, while expanding it to eight bars creates a half-time version.

Things get more interesting in Notes and Velocity data-display formats. Here are some specific tricks you should know when using the different Edit window tools on MIDI tracks while in Notes view:

- **Grabber.** You can drag individual notes, or multiple selected notes, around. Use the Shift key to select/deselect additional notes and Option-drag to copy notes instead of moving them (Alt-drag in Windows). When you click between notes in the track, the Grabber cursor turns into a selection rectangle so that you can select ranges of notes.

- **Trimmer.** This trims note lengths (end or beginning). Hold down the Option key (Alt key in Windows) to force the Trimmer to change direction (that is, to trim the note at its beginning or its end), regardless of which half of the note graphic you're in.

- **Pencil.** This inserts new note events. Hold down the Option key (Alt key in Windows) to change the Pencil to the Eraser so you can delete notes. The velocity of newly created notes is set in either the Edit, MIDI Editor, or Score Editor windows. When the Pencil is in Freehand mode, click and drag as you create new MIDI notes to stretch them out to a desired length. In the other Pencil drawing modes, if you click and drag, a series of notes is created at a single pitch whose spacing corresponds to the current grid value. If you use the Line drawing mode, all these notes will have the default Note On Velocity value. In the Triangle, Square, and Random drawing modes, you still can only create notes of a single pitch. (Parabolic and S-curve shapes can be used for adjusting velocities and editing controllers, but *not* for creating new notes.) However, the *velocities* of these new notes created by dragging will vary: every eight notes for a full cycle of the triangle shape, alternate notes for the square shape, and, well, *random* for the random shape! The pop-up selector for Pencil drawing modes has a Custom Note Duration option. When enabled, an additional pop-up selector for note durations (it looks like a musical note, as shown in Figure 10.7) appears below the Pencil tool itself. This allows you to create various combinations of note spacing and durations as you draw with the Pencil tool. For example, a series of ⅛ notes (the Grid value), each with a duration of a ¹⁄₃₂ note (the Custom Note Duration value), would produce a more staccato effect.

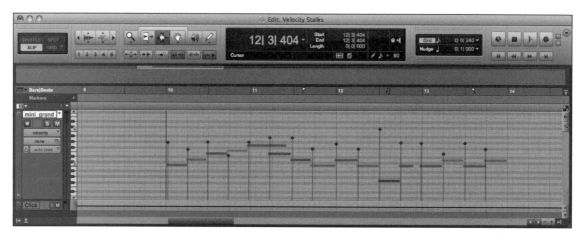

Figure 10.7 You can edit these stalks, which represent the attack velocity for MIDI notes, with the Grabber, Trimmer, and Pencil tools.

Zooming Shortcuts for MIDI Tracks You can use the Edit window's MIDI vertical zoom buttons to change how much of a MIDI track's pitch range fits into the track at its current height. You can also use the Command+Shift (Ctrl+Shift in Windows) keyboard shortcut and the left and right square bracket keys ([and]) to zoom in/out vertically on MIDI and Instrument tracks.

- **Selector.** No mystery here, although you will notice that a MIDI note isn't selected unless the highlighted range includes its beginning (the Note On event). And no, you cannot select the tail end of a MIDI note and press the Delete key to shorten it; use the Trimmer tool instead.

- **Scrubber.** You can use the Scrubber tool to play through a MIDI or Instrument track's notes either backward or forward, but keep in mind that the Scrubber cannot act the same way it does when applied to audio files!

Edit with Your Ears As a general rule, Pro Tools operators who use MIDI should enable the Play MIDI Notes When Editing option found in the Edit, MIDI Editor, and Score Editor windows. That way, as you drag or create notes, you will hear the notes echoed out to that track's MIDI destination.

Selecting MIDI Note Ranges with the Mini-Keyboard Each MIDI/Instrument track in the Edit window has a mini-keyboard at the left edge of the display area. In Pro Tools versions 7.3 and higher, when Notes view is selected, you can click the appropriate key to select all instances of a given pitch on the track or click and drag (or simply Shift-click on an additional key) to select a range of pitches. To hear a pitch on this keyboard without selecting all those note events in the track, hold down the Option key (Alt key in Windows) as you click the key. Command-click (Ctrl-click in Windows) to remove or add keys from a previous selection or to select non-contiguous keys on this mini-keyboard.

In Velocity view (shown in Figure 10.7, and also discussed in Chapter 6, "The Edit Window"), velocity stalks appear for each MIDI note. You can drag these stalks up and down with the Grabber, draw contours with the Pencil tool (especially in its Line drawing mode), and trim the attack velocities of selected note ranges. Bear in mind, of course, that each program (or *patch*) on a MIDI instrument may respond differently to variations in attack velocity. Whether the sound actually gets louder (or softer) at higher attack velocities, adds another sound layer, or switches to a completely different sound depends entirely on how that program is designed within the currently selected destination instrument. If you switch a MIDI track's output assignment to a different MIDI instrument or program number, you may have to occasionally adjust the velocities of MIDI notes.

Editing MIDI Note Velocities Here's another easy way to edit individual note velocities that's especially handy when several notes coincide: Hold down the Command key (Ctrl key in Windows) as you click and hold directly on a note in the track (or several previously selected notes); dragging up and down changes its velocity value.

Editing MIDI Note Names, Attack/Release Velocities As shown in Figure 10.8, when a single MIDI note is selected in Notes view, the Start, End, and Length indicators reflect these values for that note. Three additional fields display the pitch (Note Name), attack velocity, and release velocity. Click any of these fields to enter a new value. (A fairly large proportion of MIDI controllers do not transmit release velocities, in which case all note events recorded into Pro Tools appear with the default Note On velocity you set in the MIDI tab of the Preferences dialog box. Likewise, many sampler and synthesizer patches do not respond to variations in the Release Velocity values that are received.)

Any time you press the forward slash (/) key on the numeric keypad while in the Edit window, the Start field is selected. Repeatedly pressing this key toggles through the End and Length fields.

You can also enter values in most MIDI note and velocity fields throughout Pro Tools from your MIDI controller. For example, you could select the MIDI Note field and play the correct note, again pressing Return (or Enter in Windows) to confirm your entry.

If multiple notes are selected, the amount of change (or *delta*) is displayed in these fields. For example, if you type 15 into the Attack Velocity field and press Return (or Enter in Windows) on the alphanumeric keyboard, the velocity values of all currently selected notes are increased by that amount.

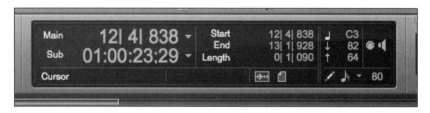

Figure 10.8 When MIDI notes are selected, Note Name, Attack Velocity, and Release Velocity fields appear to the right of the Start, End, and Length indicators.

The MIDI Editor Window

New to Pro Tools 8 is the MIDI Editor window, a separate window from the normal MIDI and Instrument track display in the Edit window that offers several new features to speed the MIDI editing process and provide options for how editing is performed. As shown in Figure 10.9, many of the displays included in the MIDI Editor window are the same as those featured in the Edit window. In fact, most of the tools and function selection options, like the Grid selector and the edit modes, function exactly how they do in the Edit window. There are major features unique to the MIDI Editor window, however, which offer new ways of tweaking one's MIDI, Instrument, and Auxiliary tracks.

The quickest way to open the MIDI Editor window is to right-click a MIDI region in a track and choose Open In MIDI Editor from the menu that appears. Unlike a MIDI or Instrument track display in the Edit window, which can show only that particular track's note and controller information, the MIDI Editor window can superimpose note and velocity information from several tracks into one display, even color-coding each track's information for quick recognition if desired.

Note that one track listed in the Tracks pane (found on the left side of the MIDI Editor window) is displayed in the MIDI Editor window. You can include additional tracks' note and velocity information in the MIDI Editor window by toggling their Show/Hide buttons in the Tracks

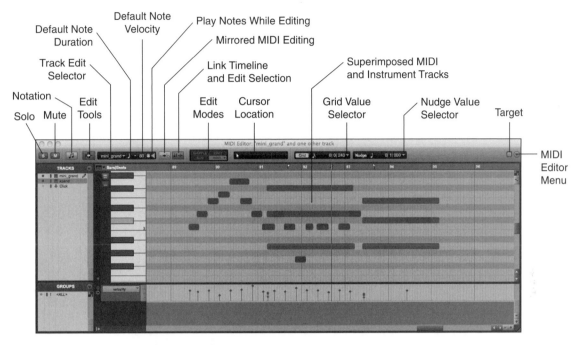

Figure 10.9   The MIDI Editor window.

pane. What you see is the familiar notes display with the velocity display in a lane below it, both representing all the tracks selected in the Tracks pane.

You can color-code items in the MIDI Editor window by track or by velocity (see Figure 10.10). When you select the Color Coding by Track option (located below the Ruler Menu selector in the MIDI Editor window), each source MIDI or Instrument track's note and velocity information will reflect the color of that track's color strip. When you select the Color Coding by

Figure 10.10   The Color Coding by Track option and, below it, the Color Coding by Velocity option.

Velocity option, located below the Color Coding by Track option, all the notes will turn red but will have varying degrees of saturation depending on the note's velocity. The darker the note's red, the higher the note's velocity.

Similar to the optional lanes introduced in Pro Tools 8 for audio tracks, which display automation information like track volume below the primary track display, the MIDI Editor window gives you the option to display controller and automation lanes for the selected tracks, as shown in Figure 10.11. Click the Add Lane button at the far left of the velocity lane, and a new lane appears. Notice that when multiple tracks' note and velocity data is displayed, when you create a new controller or automation lane, each track is represented by its own sub-lane. This is because unlike with velocity, all other automation or controller data is *not* merged in the display. Using the Controller/Automation pull-down selector, choose the type of data you want to view in the newly created lane/sub-lanes. Use the Remove Lane button, represented by the minus sign, on lanes you no longer need to display.

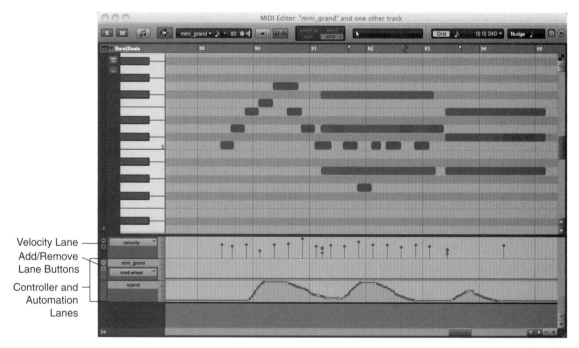

Figure 10.11   The velocity lane with controller/automation lanes for the Mini Grand and Xpand! tracks immediately below.

The editing of notes in the MIDI Editor window is the same as in the Edit window in terms of tool function, the basic Edit menu functions like Cut and Copy, and the insertion of items like key and meter changes. Right-clicking in the main Notes pane displays a convenient menu of functions like the ones just discussed. That said, the fact that the MIDI Editor window can display multiple tracks' note data might cause some consternation if you want to use the Pencil tool to manually insert notes in only one track. To address this, the MIDI Editor window includes the option to pencil-enable a track. Simply click in the track's Pencil column in the Tracks pane to display a small pencil icon. This enables you to use the Pencil tool to insert new notes the same way you would in a MIDI or Instrument track in the Edit window. You also have the option to insert notes in multiple tracks at the same time; to enable this, click in the Pencil column for the first track, hold down the Shift key, and click in the Pencil column for all other desired tracks. Any notes you create using the Pencil tool will be reflected in all the previously selected tracks. To deselect the tracks, simply click in the Pencil column again to remove the pencil icon for the chosen tracks.

Also available in the MIDI Editor window is the option to view a track or tracks' note information in a standard music notation display. When you select the Notation View button to the right of the Mute button at the top of the MIDI Editor window, music notation is displayed in Grand Staff, Treble, Bass, Alto, and Tenor staves in a linear fashion similar to the Note pane. The velocity lane and any automation or controller lanes are found below this Notation pane. On the left side of the Notation pane is a column with tracks' names showing what staves belong to the individual track note information. Editing in this Notation view is covered in Chapter 17, "The Score Editor Window," which delves into the brand-new notation options in Pro Tools 8.

The Event Menu

Chapter 8, "Menu Selections: Highlights," reviews the selections in the Event menu. If you are a composer, arranger, or performer who uses MIDI in Pro Tools, however, you will want to explore all these options in much more detail. We will start with a discussion of the Time Operations, Tempo Operations, and Event Operations submenus (see Figure 10.12).

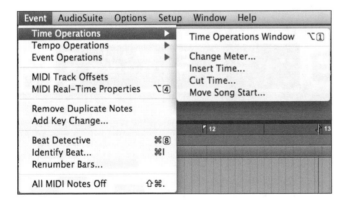

Figure 10.12 The Time Operations submenu.

Time Operations

All the functions listed in the Event > Time Operations submenu are also accessible as pages within the Time Operations window, which you can open by pressing Option+1 on the numeric keypad (Alt+1 in Windows).

Change Meter

Selecting the Change Meter command opens a window for inserting a meter change event into the Meter ruler. A pop-up selector lets you choose whether this new time signature should remain in effect through the end of the session, the current bar only, or only for the selected range of bars. This Change Meter page of the Time Operations window also provides the option to change the meter of the click.

To better understand how this function works, imagine that the bridge of your song needs to change from 4/4 to 3/4 time signature for four bars beginning at bar 33, followed by 32 more bars of 4/4, and then another 3/4 section at bar 69 when the bridge is repeated. Before you start recording your audio and MIDI parts, take a moment to set up the song structure using the following steps:

1. Switch to Grid edit mode. If you haven't already done so, switch your main ruler to Bars:Beats format (via the Display menu). Using the pop-up selector in the Edit menu, change the Grid Value setting to 1 bar.

2. Using the Selector tool, highlight bars 33–37 either within an existing track or in the ruler itself if you haven't yet created any tracks in this session.

3. Select Event > Time Operations > Change Meter. The Time Operations window opens with its Change Meter page displayed, as shown in Figure 10.13.

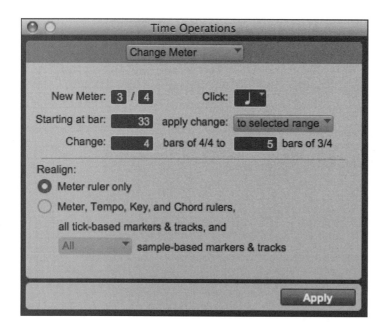

Figure 10.13 The Change Meter page of the Time Operations window. Here, we're changing a four-bar selection to 3/4 time signature.

4. Change the new meter to 3/4. For this example, leave the pop-up click selector at ¼ notes. However, if this section was in 3/8—not to mention 5/8, 7/8, or 11/8—you would usually have the click change to ⅛ notes during this section only and then revert back to ¼ notes when the song returns to 4/4.

5. Bar 33 is already selected as the starting bar for the meter change. Use the pop-up selector to the right of this field to choose To Selected Range (rather than To Session End or Until Next Bar).

6. Be sure to specify that you want these four bars of 4/4 changed to *four* bars of 3/4 (and not some other number) because in this case, you want the tempo to remain constant— that is, the ¼ notes should be equivalent between the two sections.

7. In this case, the Realign option will be fine if left set to its default, Meter Ruler Only.

8. Click the Apply button.

9. If the Meter ruler is currently visible (enabled either using the Ruler Options pop-up selector in the Edit window or via the View > Ruler submenu), two new Meter Change events now appear: one for the beginning of the 3/4 section and another where it returns to 4/4.

10. Highlight bars 69–72 (the next occurrence of the 3/4 section) and repeat these steps.

Insert Time

The time units displayed in the Insert Time page of the Time Operations window always reflect those of the currently active main ruler. Even if you're not a MIDI user and don't edit music at all, the Insert Time and Cut Time functions will occasionally be useful. For example, when creating soundtracks for video or multimedia, somewhere along the line, you may need to add more time at the beginning of the session because the segment needs a longer intro. When creating music with MIDI, of course, this command is essential, allowing you to work in Bars:Beats time units, adding bars at the beginning of the song or at any point within its timeline as shown in Figure 10.14. Usually, you will choose to have this command affect locations of all the subsequent markers and tempo and meter events; they are then pushed later in the timeline by a corresponding amount. (One exception might be when working on a video or film soundtrack, where you add bars to the music but don't want the positions of sample-based markers—absolute time locations—that reference dialog or sound effects to be affected by the time insertion.)

Cut Time

Options in the Cut Time page in the Time Operations window are similar to those for Insert Time. Time units here also reflect the currently active main ruler. If desired, you can adjust all subsequent markers, tempo events, and meter events to an earlier position in the session's time-line after the specified range is cut.

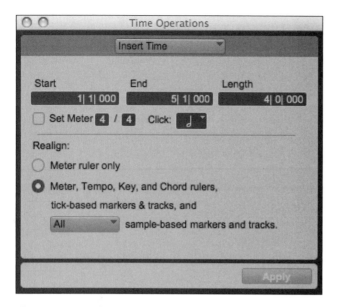

Figure 10.14 The Insert Time page of the Time Operations window. Here, we're inserting four bars at the beginning of the song.

Move Song Start

In the Move Song Start page of the Time Operations window, choosing musical bars as the time units (time base) for this function allows you to move the beginning of the session's timeline to a specified bar location and at the same time assign a new bar number to that new location (if desired). Whether you choose to have this operation apply to marker locations and audio tracks that are sample-based (that is, their positional references are based on absolute time rather than being relative to musical bars and beats) depends on the situation. As with the Insert Time function, when scoring a soundtrack, you might use Move Song Start to move a music cue to a later position. Using the Minutes:Seconds time units here, for example, allows you to specify that bar one should now start at exactly five seconds into the timeline while leaving sample-based markers and tracks unaffected. This is shown in Figure 10.15.

In the Tempo ruler of the Edit window, a Song Start marker appears (a small red diamond-shaped icon, which appears at the beginning of the session's timeline by default). The Song Start marker's position changes as a result of applying the Move Song Start function. However, you can also accomplish more or less the same thing by dragging this marker directly in the Tempo ruler if you prefer. As with most events in the Edit window, if Grid edit mode is active, the current grid value governs the movement of the markers you drag in the rulers; they will snap from one grid increment to another (for example, seconds might be convenient in Minutes:Seconds format, or frames on system configurations supporting SMPTE time code format for Grid mode). When moving the song start in this manner, it's important to note that, by default, the position of regions and other events in all tick-based tracks will also be affected. If instead

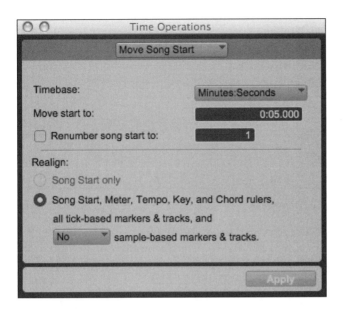

Figure 10.15 The Move Song Start page of the Time Operations window. Here, we're inserting five seconds at the beginning of the song without affecting bar numbering or the position of any markers or regions within tracks whose timebase is set to samples (absolute).

you want only tick-based events to be affected (including all MIDI track events and regions, or automation event locations in audio tracks, Aux Input tracks, and Master Fader tracks whose timebase is set to Ticks), hold down Shift+Control (Shift+Start in Windows) as you drag the Song Start marker.

Tempo Operations

All selections in this submenu open the Tempo Operations window, and the result of all these functions is to insert one or more tempo events into your session's timeline. Tempo events can be viewed in the Tempo ruler and graphically edited in the Tempo Editor window that can be opened beneath the Tempo ruler. You can also drag existing tempo events around in the Tempo ruler itself (even when the Tempo Editor window is not visible). If Grid edit mode is enabled, this will affect their movement.

When you adjust tempos in Pro Tools, the positions of all events in tracks set to the Ticks timebase are displaced by a corresponding amount. In contrast to the absolute time references in tracks set to Samples timebase, event positions in tick-based tracks are defined by musical time references—bars, beats, and ticks (subdivisions of a ¼ note). Consequently, they are always *relative* to the current tempo. If you're using audio regions for cymbal crashes, individual drum hits, or sound effects in conjunction with MIDI or Instrument tracks, for example, using the Ticks timebase in those audio tracks will keep those audio region locations in sync with the MIDI tracks even after a tempo change is applied. Likewise, events on tick-based tracks with active Elastic Audio plug-ins (in versions 7.4 and higher of Pro Tools) will be adjusted for the tempo-change operations you make in this window. In this case, Tempo Event–Generated Warp Markers (thick black vertical lines, similar to Warp markers but without the triangle at their base) will appear within the affected audio regions to indicate where elastic audio processing has been applied to conform their audio to the changed tempos.

Following are brief descriptions of each tempo operation. Incidentally, when you are concerned about where the selection will end in real time (minutes, seconds, and milliseconds, for example), you will almost always want to enable the Advanced checkbox in the Tempo Operations window. Lastly, although we cannot dedicate space to the subject here, several of these options can be useful for building tempo maps should you ever need to build a MIDI orchestration based on a recorded performance with constantly changing tempos.

- **Constant.** Applies a single tempo setting to the currently selected range. A single tempo event is created at the beginning of the range and any previously existing tempo events within it are deleted. If the Preserve Tempo After Selection option is enabled, a second tempo event returns the tempo to its previous setting at the end of the selection.

- **Linear.** Creates a series of tempo events to establish a ramp-shaped progression from one tempo setting to another. As with some of these other tempo operations, if you enable the Advanced option, you can specify the density and resolution of the resulting series of tempo events. A pop-up selector among the Advanced options (also available for the other shapes here for tempo change) allows for the automatic calculation of the new real-time end point that will result from your tempo-change settings (in minutes and seconds, for example).

- **Parabolic.** Instead of a straight ramp up or down between the two tempo settings, you can adjust the curvature of this parabola shape with a slider or numerical field. A zero curvature is a straight ramp identical to the Linear tempo operation. Larger positive values push most of the tempo acceleration toward the end of the current selection, while negative values push it toward the beginning.

- **S-curve.** With this shape, you can specify the exact time location for the midpoint (in time units corresponding to the currently active main Time ruler, as with all these other tempo operations). You also specify exactly what tempo (somewhere between the starting and ending tempo values for the range) should be in effect at that midpoint. The Curvature value determines how steeply the tempo increases or decreases between the midpoint and the start/end points of the range. Larger positive values push most of the tempo acceleration from the midpoint value toward the start/end points of the current selection, while negative values bunch most of the acceleration to/from the midpoint tempo around the midpoint itself.

- **Scale.** Unlike the other tempo operations here, scaling tempos doesn't overwrite existing tempo events. Instead, scaling is used to relatively increase or decrease the value of all tempos within the currently selected range. You can specify this either as a percentage or by altering the average tempo within the current selection (which is automatically calculated for you).

- **Stretch.** Figure 10.16 shows an example of using the Stretch function to automatically adjust the tempo of the current selection to match a specific duration.

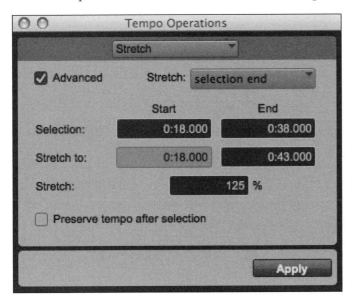

Figure 10.16 The Tempo Operations dialog box. Here, we're automatically adjusting the tempo so that the selected musical segment will match a given length of time.

Using the Tempo Ruler's Tempo Change Dialog Box

Bear in mind that the tempo operations described here must be used on a currently selected range in your session's timeline (either within any track or in a ruler). You could also insert a single tempo event, either at the beginning of the timeline or at some specific point in the timeline. (Tempo events remain in effect until the end of the session or until another tempo event is reached.) After setting the Start value to the desired location—either by clicking a region with the Grabber tool or by clicking somewhere with the Selector tool—click the + (plus) sign at the left end of the Tempo ruler. The Tempo Change dialog box (shown in Figure 10.17) opens.

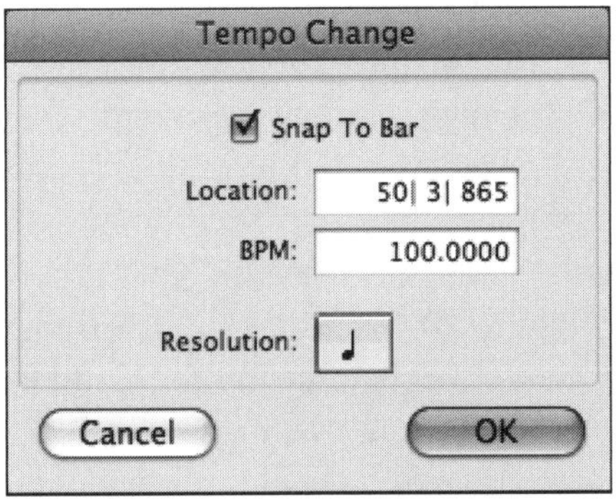

Figure 10.17 The Tempo Change dialog box.

Event Operations

All selections in the Event Operations submenu (shown in Figure 10.18) open the Event Operations window: Quantize, Change Velocity, Change Duration, Transpose, Select/Split Notes, Input Quantize, Step Input, Restore Performance, and Flatten Performance. A pop-up selector in this window switches between pages for these options that alter currently selected MIDI data (or quantize audio data, when using the Elastic Audio features in Pro Tools versions 7.4 and higher). You can click the Apply button repeatedly to apply the current settings for each function without leaving this window. You can find brief descriptions of each of these operations in Chapter 8, but the next section explores the Pro Tools quantization features for MIDI note events and Elastic Audio events in more detail, along with the use of Flatten/Restore Performance and the Step Input feature.

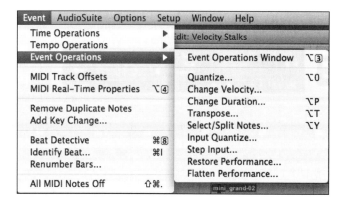

Figure 10.18   The Event Operations submenu.

Using the Event Operations Window on MIDI Events After clicking the Apply button in the Event Operations window to hear the effect of your change on selected data, you can undo the operation by pressing Command+Z (Ctrl+Z in Windows). If you want this window to stay open after applying each function, click the Apply button or press Enter on the numeric keypad. If instead you want the window to close after applying a function, press Return (Enter in Windows) on the alphanumeric keyboard instead.

All the functions in the Event Operations window (shown in Figure 10.19) are for transforming currently selected MIDI data. As with many other windows in Pro Tools, pressing the Tab key cycles through the fields (press Shift+Tab to move backward), and you can use the up and down arrows to increase/decrease selected field values. When any pitch or velocity field is selected, you can also enter new values by playing a note on your MIDI controller.

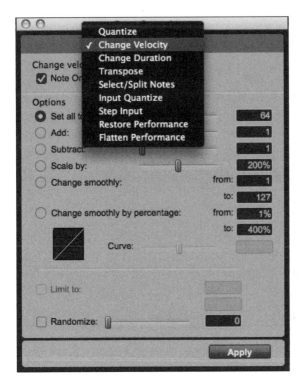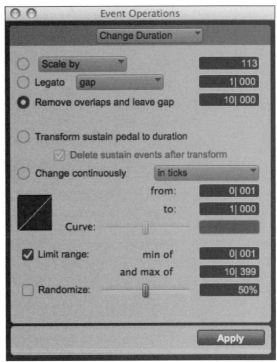

Figure 10.19 Without leaving the Event Operations window, you can use a pop-up selector to switch between Change Velocity/Duration, Quantize, Transpose, Flatten/Restore Performance, and other functions.

Quantize

As explained in Chapter 8, quantization snaps all MIDI notes (and audio events in Pro Tools versions 7.4 and higher) within the current selection to a specified rhythmic value. The attacks and/or releases of MIDI notes (their beginnings or ends, as defined by Note On and Note Off events) are moved to the nearest increment on a horizontal time grid. The spacing of this quantization grid is determined by the selected note value in this window. Quantization doesn't affect the beginning and end positions of MIDI *regions*, however. Many of the options in this window (see Figure 10.20) are self-explanatory, so this section mentions just a few items of special interest. Note that the Option+0 (zero) keyboard shortcut (Alt+0 in Windows) opens the Quantize window directly.

Quantize Grid. In this pop-up selector, you can choose among note values that will serve as the increments for the quantization grid (the basis for adjusting audio or MIDI note event positions, in conjunction with the other parameters in the Quantize window). Along with standard note values (whole and ½ notes, ¼ notes, ⅛ notes, and so on), you can choose dotted values and triplets.

You can also choose from among various DigiGroove templates that are provided with the program or others that you created with Beat Detective. Groove templates are irregular grids that you can use to quantize MIDI events. Sometimes, these can produce more human-sounding

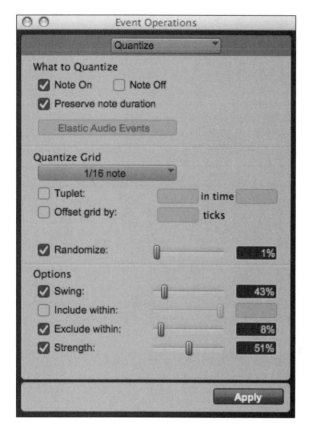

Figure 10.20 Use the Quantize window for adjusting time locations of MIDI notes. It can be useful for cleaning up rhythmic timing or conforming multiple recordings by some percentage toward a common feel.

results than simply adding a swing factor to a straight (symmetrical) time grid for quantization. For example, try manually creating a straight MIDI drum part with a constant ¹/₁₆-note hi-hat pattern and applying various grooves to get a feel for the effects they produce. For recorded MIDI parts, one trick is to use the percentage sliders to reduce somewhat the effect of quantization on note position, relying more on velocity patterns from the groove template to produce a more subtle transformation.

As discussed in Chapter 12, "The Pro Tools Groove," you can create your own DigiGroove templates based on audio or MIDI selections and use these as the template for quantizing MIDI events and audio regions. If you combine live MIDI performances (especially MIDI parts created with the Step Input feature), this is an essential technique for obtaining a tighter groove between multiple overdubbed parts.

Tuplet. A *tuplet* is a rhythmic grouping where some irregular number of notes fits into the normal duration of two (or four, and so on) notes (see Figure 10.21). For example, ¹/₈-note triplets

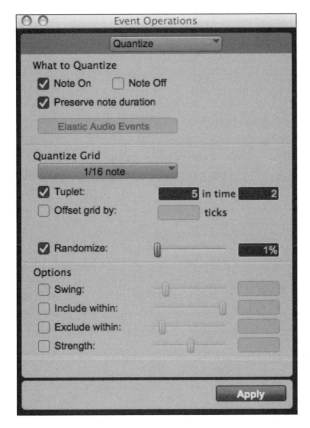

Figure 10.21 Tuplets allow you to create rhythmic groupings of the main beat that aren't multiples of two or three. For example, here we've selected ¹/₁₆-note quintuplets as our basis for quantization (with a small degree of randomization).

are a 3:2 tuplet because three ¹/₈ notes fit into the duration of two normal ¹/₈ notes (three notes at 1|000, 1|320, and 1|640 instead of only two at 1|000 and 1|480). So all you folks creating dance music, just quantize everything to some funky ¹/₈-note quintuplets and septuplets; we promise to be the first ones on the dance floor!

Randomize. Marketing types like to claim that *randomizing* is the way to humanize MIDI parts that have been overenthusiastically quantized. Pardon us for getting on the soapbox for a moment here, but generally speaking, while the timing of good musicians is indeed irregular, we contend that it's actually more complex than that—not simply random. Nevertheless, if your completely quantized parts really do sound stiff, some *small* amount of randomization (less than 10%) can sometimes help. However, on a drum part, for example, you may get better results applying the randomness to only one element (say, the hi-hat or small percussion parts) rather than the entire groove. And even in these cases, try a very small amount of randomization on the *velocities* first (using the Change Velocity command) rather than the actual position of the events in time. Here's another recommendation: In our experience, the stiffness of overquantized parts usually has more to do with the upbeats, rather than the downbeats, being too rigid. For this reason, try using very small amounts of swing—10% or less—to loosen up a drum groove rather than randomizing the timing in general. To our ears, it usually sounds better.

Swing. Any swing factor greater than 0% delays every upbeat of the specified musical value. In other words, if you're swinging ⅛ notes, the ones that coincide with ¼-note divisions are unaffected by the swing factor but the ones between ¼ notes are moved somewhat later than exactly halfway between the ¼ notes. This can go from a very subtle groove factor (<10%) through various degrees of shuffle to a full triplet feel (100%) or even more. Very small amounts of swing (for example, 2–5% on ⅛ notes or ¹⁄₁₆ notes in drum and/or bass parts) can make a huge difference in feel on quantized MIDI parts that sound a little stiff compared to the audio tracks you've laid down.

Swing quantization is very musically useful, but many users find its parameters a bit confusing in Pro Tools. Here's how it works:

- **0% swing.** Applies no swing at all. If we're quantizing a series of ⅛ notes, each ¼-note downbeat in a measure is obviously 1|000, 2|000, and so on, and each ⅛-note upbeat is 1|480, 2|480, and so on. (Because there are 960 ticks, or subdivisions, for every ¼ note in Pro Tools, each ⅛ note corresponds to exactly half that: 480 ticks.)

- **100% swing.** A full triplet (or 12/8) feel. Each ⅛-note upbeat is quantized to the third note of an ⅛-note triplet: 1|640, 2|640, and so on. 960 ticks per ¼ note divided by 3 equals 320, so the three notes in an ⅛-note triplet are at 1|000, 1|320, and 1|640. The effect of 100% swing is the same as quantizing to a 3:2 tuplet (see Table 10.1). As always, the ¼-note downbeats (the first note in each triplet group) stay at 1|000, 2|000, and so on, and are unaffected by any ⅛-note swing percentage.

- **150% swing.** Quantizes each ⅛-note upbeat to the fourth ¹⁄₁₆ note: 1|720, 2|720, and so on. (960 ticks divided by 4 equals 240, so the four ¹⁄₆ notes are at 1|000, 1|240, 1|480, and 1|720. It's the same thing as quantizing to dotted ⅛ notes, in this example.)

- **300% swing.** If 100% swing moves each ⅛-note upbeat one-third of the way (160 ticks) toward the following downbeat, 300% swing moves it *all* the way there. It's as if you quantized to ¼ notes, except that notes are always moved to the *following* ¼ note.

In Table 10.1, you can see how progressively greater amounts of swing gradually move the timing of offbeat notes toward a full triplet value (or even beyond it at swing factors greater than 100%). There are no hard and fast rules here; you will have to experiment with all the values to achieve the feel you want. However, you will find that this is one of your most important tools for achieving a more natural feel in heavily quantized MIDI parts.

Include Within. This quantization parameter is worth exploring; it only quantizes notes within a certain distance of the specified note value. For example, you might use this if you want to make

Table 10.1 It Don't Mean a Thing... Quantizing with Swing*

Note Value	0% Swing	25% Swing	50% Swing	75% Swing	100% Swing	150% Swing
⅛ note	1|480	1|520	1|560	1|600	1|640	1|720
¹⁄₁₆ note	1|240	1|260	1|280	1|300	1|320	1|360

*(¼ note = 960 ticks)

sure the downbeats of the hi-hat part coincide exactly with kick and snare ¼ notes (which are strictly quantized) without changing any of the looser upbeats between them. Select the hi-hat notes only and then set the Quantize grid to ¼ notes, changing the Include Within parameter to 50% or less (which leaves anything further than a ¹⁄₁₆ note in either direction from the nearest ¼ note unaffected). Your hi-hat downbeats are moved to exactly 1|000, 2|000, and so on (unless you set the Strength parameter to less than 100%, of course), while the upbeats remain at their original locations.

Strength. When this parameter is set to anything less than 100%, notes are moved only that percentage of the distance between their current location and the nearest quantization grid increment. This improves timing while preserving some of the natural feel of your performance.

Quantizing Regions The Region > Quantize to Grid command does *not* apply quantization to individual MIDI notes, even when MIDI regions are selected. A more accurate description of this function would be "snap regions to grid." It moves selected audio or MIDI regions and all their contents by snapping their left boundaries—or the sync point within them, if they contain one—to the nearest grid increment per the current grid value. The Quantize to Grid command predates the relatively sophisticated MIDI editing and Elastic Audio features in current versions of Pro Tools. However, because the underlying idea of quantization is that a phenomenon (in this case, possible start time positions of MIDI notes or regions) doesn't permit a continuous range of possible values, but can only jump from one discrete increment (quantum) to another, the Region > Quantize to Grid command *is* correctly named. We mention it here because many novice Pro Tools users (including veterans of other MIDI programs) might otherwise think this command is the obvious way to quantize their MIDI drum part to ⅛ notes, for instance. Not so!

---

394   Pro Tools 8 Power!: The Comprehensive Guide

Restore Performance

Pro Tools "remembers" the original recorded MIDI performance in MIDI regions, even after you've made multiple edits, saving and reopening the session many times. The Restore Performance command opens that page of the Event Operations window (shown in Figure 10.22), where you restore selected MIDI regions to their original recorded form (or to the most recent flattened version; see the next section), choosing one or all of the following attributes for restoration: Timing, Duration, Velocity, and Pitch.

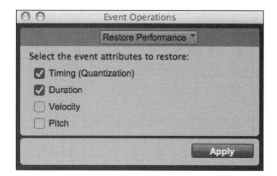

Figure 10.22 Restore Performance let you return parameters of a MIDI recording to their original, "as recorded" state.

Flatten Performance

The Flatten Performance page of the Event Operations window, shown in Figure 10.23, enables you to freeze the current state of the selected MIDI region. This flattened version will thenceforth be the state to which this region returns the next time you execute the Restore Performance command. As before, you can choose Timing, Duration, Velocity, or Pitch as the parameters for flattening.

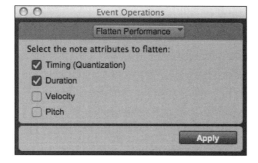

Figure 10.23 Flatten Performance establishes the current state of a MIDI recording as the condition to which it will revert if you later apply the Restore Performance command.

Here's a typical scenario for using the Flatten Performance command: Imagine you've applied some basic note corrections, global velocity changes, or other edits to a drum part you've previously recorded on a MIDI or Instrument track. Now you will apply some quantization before recording additional parts because the timing seems a little too loose. A common pitfall of quantization, however, is that you can "correct" all the humanity right out of a piece by applying too much of it. Once you've added a few more instrumental parts, you may discover that the original timing in the drums really wasn't as bad as it once seemed when heard all by itself or with only one or two other parts. The Restore Performance function is great because it lets you go all the way back the original performance. But what if you'd really rather not lose all those changes you made *before* starting to quantize? No problem: At any point in the process when you know that all changes made so far to the selected MIDI region are keepers, apply the Flatten Performance command. This now becomes your new go-back state for that region should you ever decide to retrace your steps and apply a different set of edits to it from that point forward.

Step Input

Even if you're not severely keyboard challenged, non–real-time entry of a sequence of MIDI notes or chords can sometimes be a useful technique. The important thing to understand about Step Input mode is that you can enter one or several notes simultaneously. Some people use step entry when creating specific drum patterns, for example. Of course, you can also use this feature to create "impossible" *ostinatos* (rhythmic, persistently repeating musical figures) and arpeggios.

Following are some basic rules and techniques for using Step Input to create sequences of MIDI notes in Pro Tools:

■ Step input begins at the Edit window's current Start position, so you should set this to the correct time location before you begin entering notes.

■ As you can see in Figure 10.24, options in the Step Input window allow you to either fix the note velocities at a specific value or use the velocity data created as you strike notes on the keyboard (or other MIDI controller).

■ A destination MIDI or Instrument track must be selected as the target for step entry. If you want to hear these notes as you're entering them, you will also usually want to record-enable that MIDI track. That said, Pro Tools allows you to change the destination MIDI track for the note events you're creating in Step Input mode on the fly, which opens up some interesting possibilities for *hocketing* (rapid alternation of notes or very short phrases between distinct instrumental timbres) or call-and-answer effects between two different tracks, for example.

■ Set the Note Length percentage to less than 100% if you want a more *staccato* style (that is, each note ends before the next one begins, as opposed to *legato*, where the end of each note joins with the beginning of the following note). You can also use length percentages greater than 100% if you instead want each note to overlap the beginning of the one following it.

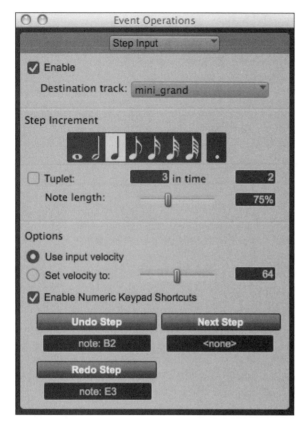

Figure 10.24   The Step Input window allows non–real-time entry of MIDI notes. In this example, keys on the MIDI controller have been mapped to the Undo Step, Next Step, and Redo Step functions.

- When the Step Input window's Numeric Keypad Shortcuts option is enabled, the Transport commands for these keys are temporarily suspended and you can use them for Step Input functions. The shortcuts are as follows:

  - The numeric keypad's Enter key is the same as the Next Step button; it skips the insertion point for new notes forward to the next step. Therefore, you can use it to create rests, for example.

  - The 0 key on the numeric keypad is the same as the Undo Step button; it undoes the previously entered step and moves the insertion point for step-entering a new note back to its previous position.

  - While still holding down the key(s) on the MIDI controller during step input, you can also use the Next Step and Undo Step buttons—or their keyboard shortcuts—to lengthen or shorten these notes by the current step increment value.

  - The 1 key on the numeric keypad selects whole-note step increments.

- The 2 key on the numeric keypad selects ½ notes.

- The 3 key on the numeric keypad enables tuplets in relation to the selected step increment (for example, 3:2 tuplets with an ⅛-note step increment creates ⅛-note triplets; 5:2 creates quintuplets; 7:2 creates septuplets; and so on).

- The 4 key on the numeric keypad selects ¼ notes.

- The 5 key on the numeric keypad selects ⅛ notes.

- The 6 key on the numeric keypad selects ¹⁄₁₆ notes.

- The 7 key on the numeric keypad selects ¹⁄₃₂ notes.

- The 8 key on the numeric keypad selects ¹⁄₆₄ notes.

- The decimal point key on the numeric keypad enables dotted-note values (half again as long as the ordinary note value—so a dotted ⅛-note increment is 720 ticks instead of 480, for example).

MIDI Real-Time Properties

The MIDI Real-Time Properties window enables you to apply real-time, non-destructive changes to the events in MIDI tracks and regions. These include quantization of note positions, changes to the duration and velocity of MIDI notes, transposition of their pitches (in octaves and/or semitones), and delay (which supports making the MIDI events in the affected track or region play back either sooner or later than their original position).

In Figure 10.25, you can see the Real-Time Properties window for a selected MIDI region. Note that unless you click the Write to Region button, these changes are applied in real time and don't affect the actual contents of the affected region. In fact, unless you specifically enable that option in the MIDI tab of the Preferences dialog box, Pro Tools always displays the original "source" location of MIDI events, not their position as modified by MIDI real-time properties applied to the region or track where they reside.

There is also a Real-Time Properties column in the Edit window that affects entire tracks. As you can see in Figure 10.26, many of the options here are similar to region-level properties. It's important to understand that region-level properties always override track properties. Region-level properties can be a powerful compositional tool, especially when combined with Mirrored MIDI editing mode (which you can enable via a button in the Edit window or via a selection in the Options menu). For example, if you want to double a part at the octave, one method is to copy the MIDI region to another track (by Option-dragging, or Alt-dragging in Windows while in Grid editing mode) and then apply a transposition value of +12. If you enable Mirrored MIDI editing, any note changes you make in the original copy of the region are immediately reflected in all other identically named copies. You might apply additional real-time property changes to the transposed part, such as velocity or duration changes, according to the characteristics of the sound used on the MIDI destination for each track. Within a single track, you might use Mirrored MIDI editing to apply region-level properties

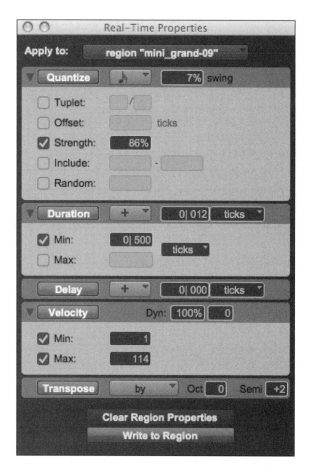

Figure 10.25 From the Event menu, you can open the Real-Time Properties window for a selected MIDI region.

to various copies of a single MIDI region—perhaps repeating a bass line or melody shifted by an interval of a fifth or octave higher, for example.

Figure 10.1 at the beginning of this chapter shows the MIDI Event List (which is also briefly described in Chapter 8). You will note that where MIDI events are affected by real-time properties, a T or R appears to indicate whether these are track or region level.

Remove Duplicate Notes

Especially when you are layering up parts in Loop Record mode (drum-machine style), it is all too easy to end up with duplicate notes. Especially after quantizing, these duplicate notes may not be easy to see, but they can cause phase-cancelled, flanger-like effects as notes are double triggered. While the MIDI Event List might also be handy for these instances, this command makes the process much easier.

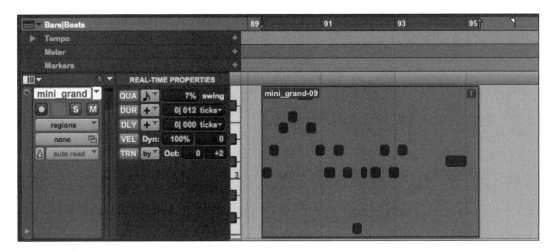

Figure 10.26 Parameters in the Real-Time Properties column of the Edit window affect the entire MIDI or Instrument track (which in turn may contain regions with their own real-time properties).

Beat Detective

Beat Detective is discussed in more detail in Chapter 12. You can extract DigiGroove templates from either audio or MIDI selections (to be used by the Grid/Groove Quantize command in the MIDI Operations window).

Identify Beat

This command is one of the ways you can tell Pro Tools what the starting and ending bar/beat positions should be for the current selection. One thing you can do with this command is use a precise audio selection (four or eight bars that you've precisely selected using Looped Playback mode, for example) to establish a Pro Tools tempo so you can effectively edit in Grid mode. (Steps for this technique are also described in Chapter 12.)

Renumber Bars

The Renumber Bars command is very straightforward; selecting it simply renumbers the bars in your song. A typical scenario for renumbering bars is when your song begins with a drum fill of some kind, but it's much easier to keep track of its structure (with four- and eight-bar sections, and so on) if bar 1 corresponds to the point where the band enters. Similarly, for songs with a slow or *rubato* introduction (freely played, without a strict tempo), you may prefer to have the point where the groove kicks in numbered as bar 1. In either of these cases, all the bars before bar 1 will have negative numbers after renumbering.

All MIDI Notes Off

This command silences any stuck MIDI notes (caused by system malfunction or interruption of MIDI data transmission—a Note On message is transmitted, but a Note Off message is never received). The keyboard shortcut for this command is Command+Shift+period (Ctrl+Shift+period in Windows). If you are a MIDI user, memorize it now!

Other Commands Relating to MIDI

These are also discussed in Chapters 5, "The Transport Window," and 8, "Menu Selections: Highlights." Briefly, however, a few are defined here:

- Options > Click turns transmission of the MIDI metronome click on and off. This command is also accessible from the Transport.

- Setup > Click/Countoff opens the Click/Countoff Options dialog box. This command is also accessible by clicking the metronome click button in the Transport.

- Options > MIDI Thru enables what you play into a record-enabled MIDI track in Pro Tools to be echoed back out of Pro Tools, according to that track's settings (MIDI port and channel, program number, volume, pan, and so on).

Summary

Pro Tools has some very powerful tools for editing MIDI events and for creating musical arrangements based on MIDI performances mixed with digital audio. Be sure to check out Chapter 12, "The Pro Tools Groove," and Chapter 13, "A Multitrack Music Session," for more musical applications of Pro Tools. Obviously, there are some other audio-savvy programs whose emphasis is more strongly on MIDI and composition—Digital Performer, Logic Pro, Cubase, and SONAR, to name just a few. Whenever required, Pro Tools can import and export Standard MIDI Files (for which using the .smf file name extension will facilitate recognition of the file type on Windows systems). Nevertheless, we know many people who use nothing *but* Pro Tools for their projects, regardless of whether their emphasis is more on MIDI or audio. Pro Tools is certainly up to the job!

11 Synchronization

If you need to synchronize playback and recording in Pro Tools to some external device (such as a video deck or a multitrack tape recorder), this chapter will be of special interest to you. It includes both basic concepts and some fairly technical information. You may not absorb it all at first reading, but it will provide some context for dealing with synchronization issues when they arise.

As you will see, there are various levels of synchronization possible with Pro Tools. Your synchronization requirements may be no more complicated than simply triggering playback at the correct position in the session's timeline, when the corresponding time code location is received from the master device (trigger sync). More sophisticated techniques lock the internal audio clock of Pro Tools to a very stable external reference (for example, video sync, a digital reference known as word clock or word sync, or a timing reference generated by an external synchronization peripheral such as Digidesign's Sync I/O). When Pro Tools and the master device share a common *reference sync*, they can stay perfectly locked together over longer periods of time. Sample-accurate sync is also extremely important when Pro Tools audio channels are combined with other audio playing simultaneously from another source, especially where there might be some shared information in these signals (like microphone leakage!). Otherwise, phase cancellation can occur due to slight differences in playback speed on the two devices (for example, between Pro Tools and a multitrack tape recorder).

Synchronization Defined

By *synchronization*, we mean the technology and procedures required to ensure that two (or more) devices record and play back information together in a consistent fashion over time. One device always has to start at the same position relative to the other—and, ideally, *stay* in the same relative position as both devices continue to operate so that the two devices don't drift apart.

Synchronization Theory: The Basics We don't digress into pure theory in this book; our focus is always on practical applications of the concepts in Pro Tools. But in the interest of being clear, here's just a bit of theoretical perspective, drawn from Vol. 3 (Desktop

Audio) of this publisher's CSi (*Cool School Interactus*) and Course Clips CD-ROM series, which includes interactive examples to further explain synchronization concepts.

For synchronizing (audio and video) devices, three fundamental time attributes come into play:

- A defined unit of measurement for the information storage method (for example, time units such as hours, minutes, seconds, frames, samples—or inches on a moving tape)

- A nominal rate at which these measurements are taken (how many measurements per unit of time—for example, how many frames, samples, or inches per second)

- A stable timing reference that ensures measurements are recorded and reproduced at a precise rate, maintaining their correct time relationship (for example, video sync, sample clock or word sync, capstan tachometer)

In short, we require a *measurement*, a *speed*, and a *reference* that keeps that speed consistent.

Lastly, for time-code work, we add a fourth element: timestamp, or location information. Like the address of your house, a *timestamp* is a precise, numerical reference. It's used for positioning devices for playback from specific time locations, or to indicate exactly where an event (a video edit, a sound effect, the beginning of a musical cue, and so on) should occur.

SMPTE time code (and its equivalent in the MIDI protocol, MIDI time code) is the standard timestamping (addressing) method, used to get playback from two devices to start from the correct point in time. For digital audio, some sort of digital clock sync should also be used as a timing reference if these devices need to stay precisely locked together over longer durations. (Both continuous resync and reference sync methods use an external timing reference to control the playback sample rate of Pro Tools; these are discussed later in this chapter.)

In any synchronization setup, one device is designated as the *master*. The other devices in the setup, the *slaves*, get their location information from this master and start (trigger) playback at the appropriate location. Figure 11.1 shows a simple configuration, where Pro Tools is slaved to another device via an external SMPTE interface on the host computer. Pro Tools can instantly begin playback after analyzing the received timestamp information, unlike analog or digital tape machines that first have to rewind or fast-forward the tape to reach the appropriate location. In certain situations, a master also provides a speed reference for the slaved devices (for example, two synced analog tape machines, or a digital audio device whose sample rate is continuously adjusted to that of an external source).

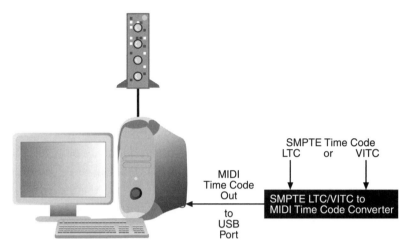

Figure 11.1 A typical SMPTE synchronization setup. An external SMPTE interface translates incoming SMPTE data from its audio- or video-encoded format to MIDI time code (MTC), which is then routed to Pro Tools via the computer's USB port.

In audio-for-video production, the video transport is typically the master (although Machine-Control users often reverse this relationship; see Chapter 14, "Postproduction and Soundtracks"). The master provides a location reference (in the form of SMPTE time code) that triggers where audio playback begins so that audio events can be correctly placed in relation to the picture. In most professional facilities, a speed reference is also provided in the form of a stable video signal called *black burst* or *house sync*. With the appropriate synchronization peripheral (like the Sync I/O or Digital Timepiece), this external timing reference can be converted to control the audio sample rate of the external Pro Tools hardware interface itself.

SMPTE Time Code

Named for the Society of Motion Picture and Television Engineers, the organization that standardized the format, SMPTE time code is used throughout the video and film industries for cameras, switchers, editing systems, and audio postproduction. Time-location data is encoded into a data "word" that consists of 80 bits, representing hours, minutes, seconds, frames, and subframes. The number of frames per minute depends on the application or geographical location (see the "Frame Rates" section later in this chapter). SMPTE time code provides a standard language for identifying time locations among various operators and devices in an audio, video, or film project. *Edit Decision Lists* (*EDLs*) are text documents that contain time-code locations for edits made from multiple source tapes; they can be automatically generated by some video-editing systems (and are comparable to *playlists* in Pro Tools tracks). Hit points for audio events (events in the video to which specific sounds or music cues are synchronized) are also sometimes listed in a similar format.

SMPTE time code allows events to be properly placed during edit, and permits multiple devices to maintain a correct time relationship during recording and playback. When Pro Tools is in Online mode (that is, playback location is controlled by incoming time code), it looks at the incoming SMPTE timestamp information (from a separate SMPTE peripheral attached to your computer) and then calculates the proper position to start playback within the session's timeline. (This offset for the timeline of your Pro Tools session, known as the Session Start time, appears in an editable field of the Session Startup window, which is opened via Setup > Session.)

If the incoming SMPTE location is *prior* to the start of the session, Pro Tools waits until the Session Start time is reached before starting playback. If the first time-code location received is *later* than the Session Start time (for example, if you press the Play button on the video deck that's serving as the master device when it's somewhere in the middle of the tape), Pro Tools will jump to the appropriate position in its timeline and start playing back—regardless of whether the session actually contains any regions, and so on, at that point. (So make sure you get your SMPTE references right!)

Synchronization Example with an External Video Deck

Let's say a video editor provides you a BetaCam SP master tape containing a 30-second spot. She tells you that the time-code location for the beginning of the program is one hour, zero minutes, zero seconds, zero frames (01:00:00:00), and most importantly, that the time code format is 29.97 frames per second, non-drop. You pop the tape into your BetaCam deck and notice that prior to the actual beginning of the spot, there are color bars, audio tones, and so on. (The LTC time-code output of the BetaCam deck—a BNC connector for audio—is connected to the time-code audio input of your computer's SMPTE/MIDI interface, which you indicate as the synchronization source for Pro Tools.)

1. Create a new Pro Tools session. Set the sample rate of this session to 48kHz (standard for professional video).

2. Open Setup > Session. Set the Session Start time to 01:00:00:00. Use the pop-up Time Code Rate selector to choose 29.97 fps.

3. Create a stereo audio track. You want to record the original sound from the video master into Pro Tools—not only because it will inevitably require your audio engineer's magic touch to correct inconsistent levels, background noise, and so on, but because the finished stereo mix you lay back onto the video tape must contain your music and sound effects as well as the original spoken dialog and ambient sound!

4. Arm your track(s) for recording and check your levels. If your video editors have been doing their jobs, you can trust that the reference tones prior to the spot truly represent 0dB (but you'd better check, just in case). If you get no level at all, check to see if the audio outputs of the Beta deck are really connected to your audio hardware inputs. (Hey, it happens!)

5. Open Setup > Peripherals and select the Synchronization tab. Confirm that the configuration is correct for the synchronization hardware you're using, as shown in Figure 11.2.

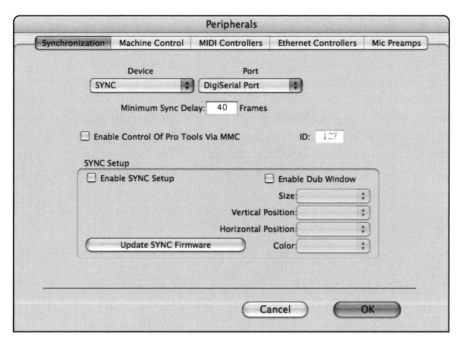

Figure 11.2 The Synchronization tab of the Peripherals dialog box, accessed from the Setup menu, enables you to specify what type of external synchronization device(s) you're using.

6. Still in the Preferences dialog box, under the Operation tab, confirm in the Record > Online Options section that the Record Online at Time Code (or ADAT) Lock setting is enabled.

7. Now enable the Online button in the Pro Tools Transport window so that recording of Pro Tools will be engaged when time code is received, at the corresponding location in the session's timeline, according to the session start time you've specified in the Session Setup window.

8. Click the Record button in the Pro Tools Transport window.

9. Roll the video master back perhaps 9–10 seconds prior to the top of the hour and press the Play button on the video deck. After a few seconds, you should see Pro Tools kick into Record mode at the beginning of the session's timeline, 01:00:00:00.

10. Once the spot has finished playing, press Stop on the video deck.

11. Click the Record button again in Pro Tools to disable recording mode. However, keep Pro Tools in Online mode so that time code arriving from the video continues to

determine where Pro Tools starts playback as you're placing sound effects and music in your session.

12.   At the end of the edit process, you can record the stereo mix from Pro Tools back onto the video deck, while still locked to time code (that is, with the Online button enabled), a procedure known as *layback*.

One final note: In many video facilities, when you lay your audio back to the master, you might actually be locking playback of Pro Tools to SMPTE time code arriving from a video deck in a completely separate room. In that case, you would route your audio through either analog or digital tie lines, to be recorded directly onto the first-generation master tape in the video-editing suite rather than the tape copy you've been using while editing. This layback procedure is typical in "online" video editing suites (that is, real-time and tape-based suites). However, when collaborating with Avid or other computer-based video editing systems, it's much more common to either bounce out an audio mixdown file they can use directly or export a file in either the OMF or AAF interchange format. See Chapter 14 for more details.

Spotting Sound Effects and Music to Time-Code Locations Remember to use Spot mode when Pro Tools is slaved to a master video transport! Use the video transport itself, rocking its jog/shuttle wheel to locate the precise frame location where an audio effect should be placed. Then, in Spot mode, click regions with the Grabber (or drag regions out into the Edit window from the Regions List) and type their target time position directly into the Spot dialog box's Start time field. Or, once the Spot dialog box is open, roll the video tape and press the = key at the desired location or click the Current Time Code field in the dialog box. That time-code position will be automatically entered into the Start field of the Spot dialog box, and the beginning (or sync point) of the selected region will be moved there when you click the OK button. If you're using VITC (SMPTE time code that is encoded into each video frame), you can capture the current time code even when the master video transport is stopped!

SMPTE Time Code Formats: LTC, VITC, and MTC

There are three ways to encode and transmit SMPTE time-code information. Pro Tools can work with any of these time-code formats, depending on the optional synchronization hardware you add to your Pro Tools rig.

- **LTC (longitudinal time code).** The most common type. An audio signal encodes the time data through biphase modulation (encoding that rapidly alternates a carrier signal between two tones). The audio signal containing the time-code information might be recorded onto an audio track of a video deck, or onto one track of a multitrack audio recorder. LTC may also be directly generated by either of these (possibly via some additional device) in real time, based on the device's own internal timing reference. Because an audio signal is conveying the SMPTE data, the master device's transport has to be in Play (or Record) mode for SMPTE information to be sent to Pro Tools as the slave device.

■ **VITC (vertical interval time code).** Incorporates time-code data into a video signal within the *overscan* area (that is, the first few lines at the top of each video frame, which are not usually visible on consumer televisions). Figure 11.3 shows a video frame where the VITC information is visible in line 22 of the video image. VITC is used in video post applications; it offers a great advantage in that time-code values are sent even when you are paused in a frame or jogging from one frame to another with the video transport paused. Obviously, a synchronization peripheral that supports VITC will have a video input.

■ **MTC (MIDI time code).** Conveys SMPTE information as MIDI data. MTC is in fact the SMPTE format that Pro Tools eventually receives, no matter what type of external SMPTE synchronization peripheral you're using (audio, video, or MIDI). Some digital multitracks and computer programs can transmit MTC directly through their MIDI outs. In this scenario, the MTC could be received by Pro Tools even with a standard (that is, non-SMPTE) MIDI interface. MTC should not be confused with MIDI Clock, whose 24 pulse per quarter note (ppqn) subdivisions represent longer or shorter absolute time values depending on the current musical tempo, and which is sometimes transmitted by the onboard MIDI sequencers in MIDI keyboards. MTC is exactly the same absolute-time reference as SMPTE; it has no relation to the current musical tempo.

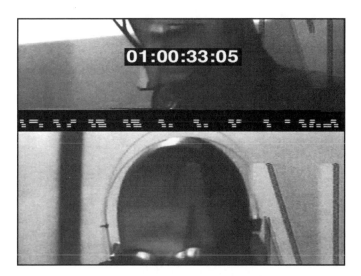

Figure 11.3   Here, we've pulled down the top fields of a video frame so that the VITC in video field 22 is visible.

Frame Rates (30/29.97 Drop/Non-Drop, 25, 24 Frames per Second)

As we've said, various SMPTE frame rates are employed depending on the application or television standard in use at your geographical location. In the Pro Tools Session Setup window, you select the SMPTE time-code format. Obviously, if your selection doesn't match the actual time code being received, Pro Tools will start playback at the wrong place or drift out of correct synchronization!

- **30 frames per second (fps).** The original SMPTE format developed for monochrome (black and white) television in North America. 30 fps is still the standard for audio-only applications in North America. It's also sometimes (though rarely) used for short-duration, industrial video, although 29.97 non-drop is much more common and recommended even for these applications.

- **30 fps drop frame.** Used only for film sync pull-up applications—and even then, only infrequently—for correcting transfer errors between film and video.

- **29.97 fps drop frame.** Used in NTSC color video broadcast applications. (*NTSC* refers to the National Television Standards Committee standard, used in North America, most of Latin America and most of the Caribbean, South Korea, Japan, Taiwan, and so on.) The 29.97 drop frame format is especially indicated for longer-duration projects, where SMPTE time-code values need to exactly match absolute time. Also, as a general rule, 29.97 drop is mandatory for any video submitted to broadcast stations in countries using the NTSC standard. (As stated before, many industrial video production houses in North America use 29.97 fps *non-drop* SMPTE for short durations—corporate and marketing videos and the like—in spite of the gradual discrepancies, simply because it makes calculating event timings less complicated than when using drop frame format.)

How Drop-Frame Format Works Because the 29.97 frame rate used in NTSC color television doesn't evenly divide into minutes and seconds, certain frames are dropped in order for SMPTE to keep pace with actual time as measured by the clock. By skipping two frames at the beginning of every minute—specifically, skipping from frame 29 to frame 02 (except with minutes that are multiples of 10—00, 10, 20, 30, 40, 50, and so on)—a total of 108 frames are dropped per hour. This compensates for the accumulated discrepancy between 30 fps and 29.97 fps, which amounts to 3.6 seconds per hour. (Two frames skipped times 60 minutes, less a total of 12 extra frames for the six minutes per hour that don't skip two frames, equals 108 skipped frames per hour.)

- **29.97 fps non-drop.** Used in NTSC color video applications, especially for broadcast and shorter-duration pieces. This format makes no drop-frame adjustments in its frame-numbering scheme, and for each hour that passes, accumulates an approximate 3.6-second timing discrepancy (108 frames, the equivalent of three seconds plus 18 frames) compared to actual time. For this reason, use of 29.97 fps non-drop is common in NTSC video projects of shorter duration, such as consumer and industrial videos, where precise durations with respect to the wall clock don't have to match exactly. In contrast, 29.97 drop frame is required when producing a 30-minute video program for broadcast.

- **25 fps.** Used with the European PAL and SECAM video standards, which run at 25 frames per second. The PAL television format is also known as EBU (European Broadcast Union). The 25 fps rate is used for video throughout Europe, Africa, Brazil, Paraguay, Uruguay, Argentina, the Middle East, Australia, and most of Asia. 25 fps is commonly used in Europe for many audio-only applications. Converting between video frames and real time is elegantly simple in this environment: One frame equals 40 milliseconds, end of story!

- **24 fps.** Used for film applications. At 24 frames per second, each frame of time code corresponds exactly to one frame of film. There is also a 24 fps frame rate used for 24P high-definition video.

- **23.976 fps.** Another frame rate used for high-definition video. DV Toolkit 2 is required to support this frame rate in Pro Tools LE—and since DV Toolkit 2 doesn't support Pro Tools M-Powered, this frame rate is not available in that version.

MIDI Time Code (MTC)

MIDI time code (MTC) is the MIDI equivalent of SMPTE time code. The MTC addendum to the MIDI specification became official in 1987. The timing formats are identical, but the time-stamp information is conveyed as MIDI data rather than carried in an audio or video signal. Like SMPTE, MTC is an absolute timing reference, and is independent of musical tempo. Generally, in order to synchronize to an external time-code master, Pro Tools requires an external interface (translator) that converts SMPTE (LTC or VITC) to MIDI time code, which is the format that Pro Tools directly understands. Often, a single device performs both of these functions; for example, some MIDI interfaces feature an audio or video input for receiving SMPTE time code from a master audio or video master device, which is then translated to MTC for the Pro Tools software. This information then enters the computer via the port where that peripheral is attached (typically USB in current configurations).

Digital Clock Sources for Pro Tools This chapter focuses on synchronization as a means of sharing location information between devices in a studio configuration. On a more basic level, however, it's also common to sync devices together on more of a hardware level. For example, video sync is used to ensure that the boundaries between frames in the video signals generated by two separate devices correspond exactly (even if their current locations within the material are unrelated). For digital audio devices, word clock (a.k.a. word sync) serves a similar function, ensuring that the devices' audio sample clocks, which control the *rate* of audio playback, are exactly in sync. (Again, because word clock alone transmits no *location* information, this doesn't ensure that the multiple devices will start playback at the appropriate point. That's what SMPTE time code is for!) Simply put, you might think of word clock as a way to keep digital audio playback from multiple devices in phase.

The Hardware Setup dialog box in Pro Tools allows you to select the AES/EBU, S/PDIF, or ADAT Lightpipe digital inputs on your audio hardware (if available) as the clock source for your Pro Tools session (or word clock, if your audio interface supports this connection, usually via a BNC connector on the rear panel). The clock source defaults to internal, where the audio-playback rate is determined by the audio interface's own internal sample clock. When you are digitally transferring audio tracks from a DAT or ADAT into Pro Tools, it's often desirable to also designate that source audio device as the clock source. Just make sure that, in addition to slaving their clocks together, you specifically set the source and destination to the same nominal sample rate. Also, after completing a digital transfer into Pro Tools, if you later disconnect or power off the external device, be sure to set the Clock Source setting in Pro Tools back to Internal; otherwise, you may hear some strange playback! Conversely, when you are transferring audio *from* Pro Tools to another device, you would typically set the Clock Source setting in Pro Tools to Internal and configure the destination device to slave its sample clock to the incoming digital audio signal from Pro Tools. Again, after the transfer is completed, set that device back to its internal clock source—unless you are using a separate, external clock source for all these devices (such as the Sync I/O, Big Ben, Aardsync, SSG192, Nanosyncs, TL-Sync, and so on). As discussed later in this chapter, a central clock source is highly recommended when using multiple sources and destinations and frequent two-way transfers in your studio configuration.

SMPTE Peripherals

Of course, the Pro Tools program understands these time-code values, which are received by Pro Tools via whatever SMPTE synchronization device you're using. The Pro Tools hardware doesn't feature any inputs for SMPTE sources, whether encoded in an audio or video signal; you purchase an SMPTE peripheral separately, according to your requirements. Most synchronization peripherals include other features; for example, many MIDI interfaces for computers also offer SMPTE-synchronization capabilities, especially LTC (SMPTE information encoded within an audio signal). Various degrees of precision are possible, according to your requirements and budget. To help you get a handle on the capabilities of the units out there, here's a theoretical breakdown of the three basic methods for synchronizing Pro Tools with external devices:

- SMPTE/MIDI interface (trigger sync)

- SMPTE/MIDI interface plus separate hardware clock

- Synchronizers that include reference sync

SMPTE/MIDI Interface (Trigger Sync)

This category includes many common MIDI interfaces that offer an audio input only for LTC (SMPTE information encoded into an audio signal). Along with the MIDI data that they transmit/receive from their MIDI ports, they also translate the audio time code into MIDI time code (MTC) and communicate this to Pro Tools via whatever connection this external device has with the computer. However, once playback starts from Pro Tools (after it figures out the appropriate location based on the time code received), the program no longer attempts to keep strict pace with the SMPTE location data being received (other than eventually stopping once the SMPTE *stops* arriving). Therefore, a certain amount of drift could result. This sync relationship is represented in Figure 11.4. For MIDI-only projects, for example, this degree of precision may be sufficient. But for audio, especially where the audio from Pro Tools must maintain a sample-accurate level of precision with audio or video from some other device over a more extended period of time, a more sophisticated synchronization method is called for. Trigger sync simply starts playback when the correct timestamp (location) value is received. Once playback starts, the slaved device doesn't again calibrate its position to the incoming time code (other than to stop when time code stops being received) and the playback speed of the slave device is not governed by the incoming time-code information.

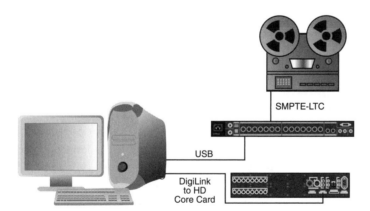

SMPTE-LTC

USB

DigiLink
to HD
Core Card

Figure 11.4   LTC (encoded as an audio signal) from a multitrack audio recorder is "translated" for Pro Tools by a MIDI interface that also has SMPTE synchronization capabilities.

SMPTE/MIDI Interface Plus Separate Hardware Clock

In these configurations, in addition to the timestamp information received as MTC from the SMPTE/MIDI interface, a separate connection links the internal clock that controls the sample rate for audio playback in the Pro Tools hardware (that is, its speed) to an external source. In some situations, both the timestamp and the clock information may come from the same master device, but often they do not. For example, in video-production houses, it is common to use a single, stable video signal known as *black burst* or *house sync* as the timing reference for all devices in the facility, providing speed information for all video decks, switchers, and Pro

Tools systems equipped with the appropriate hardware. (Otherwise, it wouldn't be practical to use a video switcher to combine video signals from various sources, because their scan rates would be out of sync.) This signal contains no timestamp information, although it does help Pro Tools lock on to incoming time code somewhat more quickly. Because both the video master and the sample clock of your Pro Tools hardware are slaved to the same speed reference, they remain in frame-accurate synchronization over long durations. This is shown in Figure 11.5.

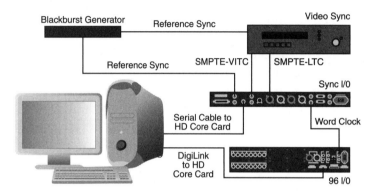

Figure 11.5 Often, as shown here, a single unit can perform both functions—SMPTE for location reference, plus various methods for resolving the sample clock of the audio hardware to an external source.

Certain devices, including Digidesign's Sync HD and the now-discontinued Sync I/O and the Video Slave Driver, can translate this video-sync reference to various digital word clock input formats, including the higher-frequency Loop Sync and SuperClock used by Digidesign audio interfaces, so that the audio clock of the hardware itself is locked to the master video sync (the speed reference). Digital clocks in common use for audio hardware are called *word sync* or *word clock*. The advantage of using a common speed reference for both the video and audio hardware is that the beginning of each received SMPTE time-code frame, and the beginning of each actual frame in the reference video signal, correspond *exactly* (that is, they're *edge-aligned*). This helps Pro Tools determine the correct location and lock on to SMPTE time code more quickly and reliably and also maintains more precise sync with the video master over extended periods of time. In fact, many synchronization units combine both SMPTE synchronization (location) and hardware clock sync in the same unit (see the following section in this chapter).

That said, there are situations in which the sample clock of your Pro Tools hardware (which governs audio-playback speed) may be slaved to an external source. (Keep in mind that this doesn't necessarily have anything to do with whether the start location for audio playback and MIDI inside Pro Tools is coordinated to the location reference provided by SMPTE time code.) In the Hardware Setup dialog box, you can switch the Sync Mode setting from Internal (the internal sample clock of your audio hardware) to Digital (where your audio hardware's sample rate is slaved to that of a digital audio signal arriving on the specified input). For example, you would usually switch to digital sync mode while transferring audio from a DAT machine via S/PDIF or AES/EBU digital inputs, or transferring from an ADAT via the Lightpipe input (or from one of Tascam's digital multitrack tape recorders via TDIF) on some audio interfaces. In fact, if you forget that you left digital sync mode on, it can make for some, er, *interesting* listening; if the DAT is missing or powered off the next time you open Pro Tools, it will still try to sync playback speed to a nonexistent clock source!

More About Digital Audio Clock Sources A single digital clock reference for multiple devices can be a very useful tool for audio-production facilities. Just as house sync provides a single reference for video gear, using a single device as the digital clock reference for all your audio devices can make it much easier to route audio among digital mixers, multitrack recorders, Pro Tools, DAT recorders, digital patch bays, digital effects, and so on. One example is Apogee's Big Ben Master Clock. It supports a variety of sample rates (including pull-up and pull-down; see Chapter 14) and generates a very stable, low-jitter clock reference usable by all these devices. Lucid, Aardvark, HHB/Rosendahl, Apogee, and Session Control also make some excellent master clock generators; see Appendix B, "Add-ons, Extensions, and Cool Stuff for Your PT Rig," for more details.

Synchronizers That Include Reference Sync

These devices combine SMPTE and sample clock–synchronization duties into a single unit. Examples from Digidesign include the Sync HD (shown in Figure 11.6), a high-end synchronization peripheral, and its predecessors, Sync I/O, Universal Slave Driver, and SMPTE Slave Driver. With these units, not only can you control Pro Tools playback according to the location

Figure 11.6 Digidesign's Sync HD features SMPTE synchronization in LTC (audio), VITC (video), and MTC (MIDI) format; hardware-level synchronization through video sync (black burst); word clock (audio hardware sync); and two 9-pin serial ports (for interlocking transport functions with video decks via the MachineControl option for Pro Tools). It can also add time-code window burns to passed-through video signals.

references arriving via SMPTE time code, you can simultaneously synchronize the speed of the sample clock in your audio hardware to various external sources. These devices also feature *continuous resync* mode, where the audio hardware's playback rate is resolved to the incoming time code (rather than to some hardware-based speed reference), making continuous and minute adjustments to the playback rate so that it stays phase-locked to the incoming timestamp information. In other words, in continuous resync mode, these units generate a speed reference that is derived from (and continually adjusted to) the location references being received as SMPTE time code.

Types of Synchronization

Now that you've taken a brief look at the physical methods for synchronizing Pro Tools to external sources, let's review some general synchronization concepts from a more theoretical perspective. Remember, our objective in synchronization is simply to ensure that events on multiple devices happen consistently over time at the appropriate places! Relationships between the master and slave device(s) for dealing with location and speed references roughly break down into the following categories: trigger sync, continuous resync (also referred to as jam sync), and reference sync.

Trigger Sync

Trigger sync has a master/slave relationship for start, or trigger, information, but no resolving capabilities. Instead, trigger sync relies on each device's internal speed reference and stability for them to play in sync. Figure 11.7 is a simplified representation of this synchronization relationship. Once the slaved device receives time code, it calculates the correct place for playback to commence; then, after playback starts (possibly following some rewind/fast-forward action on a tape transport), the slave's playback speed is not affected by time code that continues to be received.

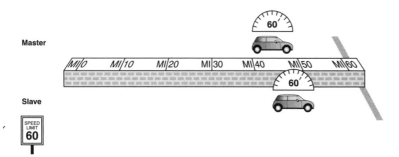

Figure 11.7 Trigger sync. Both devices start out at an agreed-upon speed of 60 miles an hour after the master provides the start command, or trigger, but the slave device can't monitor the master's speed in order to keep pace with it. Instead, it relies on its own speedometer—its internal speed reference. Therefore, some drift may occur over time.

Continuous Resync

Continuous resync also has a master/slave relationship for start, or trigger, information, plus resolving capabilities through the use of a device known as a *synchronizer*. The synchronizer compares the time-code location of the devices and adjusts the speed of the slave so that event playback continuously matches the location of the master. After the master machine provides a start command (trigger) and location information, the synchronizer compares the master and slave locations and tells the slave where to go to match the master. Once *lock* (matched locations) is reached, the synchronizer continues to compare the two locations. If the two drift apart, the synchronizer tells the slave(s) to speed up or slow down to match the master's location (hopefully rather smoothly). Figure 11.8 illustrates the basic idea of continuous resync. In this situation, the SMPTE location information received from the master provides a constant speed reference for the slave.

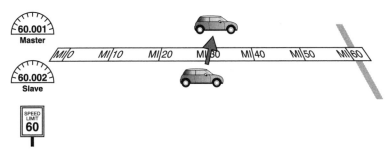

Figure 11.8 Continuous resync. After receiving the trigger to start, the slaved device continually adjusts its speed to keep pace with the master, matching the location information that the master continues to send to the slave. The slave can watch and compare its speed with the master and resolve its own speed to it so that they stay synchronized over extended periods.

Reference Sync

Reference sync (see Figure 11.9) has a master/slave relationship for start, or trigger, information, and additionally utilizes a common clock or reference signal to resolve the speed of the two devices (sometimes from the master itself, or from an external source, as in the case with house sync). In larger studio configurations, it is often best to sync all digital audio devices to

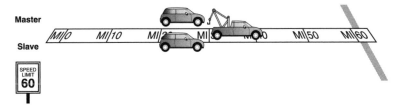

Figure 11.9 Reference sync. Trigger (location) information received from the master starts the slave into motion, while an external device controls the speed of both vehicles. They resolve to it instead of to each other.

a single, highly stable clock source that will be the common timing reference for their sample rates. In Appendix B, under "Word Clock and Sync Generators," we mention a few of the current options.

Using QuickTime, Other Digital Video File Formats

For Pro Tools users who collaborate with nonlinear video editors, importing digital video files into a session can be very attractive. Using a digital video file as your "master" allows you to do audio postproduction for video projects without having a video deck in your studio at all. (Working with video files in Pro Tools is discussed in more detail in Chapter 14. Pro Tools HD supports multiple video files in the same session, as does Pro Tools LE when equipped with the DV Toolkit 2 option.) Video-editing systems such as Avid Xpress, Avid Media Composer, and other Avid video-editing systems; Media 100; Apple FinalCut Pro; and Adobe Premiere can export a video project for you as a QuickTime file (an industry-standard format for video files). The original video frame rate and audio sample rate (48kHz in professional video) should be retained in the file provided for your use in Pro Tools. But to minimize file size (thereby avoiding having Pro Tools slow down during record and playback, especially if you're not using a video accelerator card and/or have an underpowered system), you will typically ask the video editor to reduce the image size of the video frame—perhaps to 320×240 pixels or smaller.

You import the video file(s) into your Pro Tools session via the File > Import > Video command. This creates a Video track in the Edit window. (You can also import video files by dragging from the Finder/Desktop, a DigiBase browser window, or Regions List.) You will usually also import the audio soundtrack inside that video file to your session. As when using VITC on an external video deck, using a digital video file inside Pro Tools as your video master allows frame-accurate positioning of audio events with respect to video frames (which you can zoom in to view individually as "picon" thumbnails in the Video track) even while video playback is stopped. Nonlinear access is another advantage; you can jump immediately from any point in the video program (that is, the session timeline) to another. Using digital video files eliminates the hassle and expense of shuttling a video transport back and forth as you edit your audio.

The Video window, where the video plays in real time, is also enabled after you import a video file into your session. Keep in mind that playing back video files makes additional demands on your computer's processing power. For large-scale postproduction work, a video accelerator card with a separate monitor and/or a separate hard disk dedicated to video playback is highly recommended for optimum performance. However, on any Pro Tools system, you will find that changing the Video track to Blocks view (or even closing the Video window) greatly reduces the overhead from video playback and improves the speed of operation. In Pro Tools versions 7.3 and higher, the Edit Window offers a Video Online button for the Video track, and the Video window can be resized within Pro Tools by dragging one of its sides or corners.

Some audio facilities also have their own video-capture hardware—perhaps the same card that will accelerate video playback in the Pro Tools computer—so that outside clients can simply submit video tapes, even on VHS! For example, AVoption|V10 video hardware for Pro Tools| HD systems on Windows, now a "legacy" peripheral, consists of a rackmountable unit connected to the computer via FireWire cable. It can capture video and send out a standard video signal for your NTSC monitor or video projection system. For serious professional work, viewing the video master on large-format monitors makes the postproduction process more comfortable. In addition to a dedicated hardware option, you can also enable Options > Video Out FireWire. This routes video playback through your computer's FireWire port to any video peripheral with an IEEE 1394 port, including many common video cameras and digital video decks.

When you've finished assembling all the audio for the project, you have several options:

- Bounce out a stereo file (or multiple mono files for surround mixing), which the video editor then imports and places in the video-editing software.

- Use the File > Bounce to > QuickTime Movie command to bounce your mix directly into a QuickTime movie. You might do this, for example, when the final destination is a CD-ROM or the Internet, and your audio work is the last stage in the process (because the video data in the QuickTime file has already been compressed to the final size for playback). However, it is sometimes a good idea to use this option even when your audio is going to be used on a video-editing system. Most video-editing software can import just the audio tracks from the QuickTime file you've provided. (Note that although they can be imported, AVI, MPG, and other digital video file formats cannot be bounced back out from Pro Tools.) That way, if there's ever any question about how you thought things were supposed to sync up between the audio and video, the video editor has the file you provided as a reference.

- Export the session as an Open Media Framework Interchange (OMFI) file (sequence), supported by video-editing systems such as Avid, FinalCut Pro, Media 100, and others (not to mention other digital-audio programs such as Digital Performer, Nuendo, Cubase, Logic Studio, and SONAR), using the optional DigiTranslator program from Digidesign (which is not compatible with the M-Powered version of Pro Tools). Please note that exporting your session as an OMFI file will *not* keep the effects of the real-time plug-ins used as inserts on your tracks.

- Use the optional DigiTranslator program to export your session as an Advanced Authoring Format (AAF) sequence to be used by Avid and other video-editing systems. AAF sequences always refer to external media files (unlike OMFI files, which can optionally have media files embedded within them), and may in turn refer to OMF media files. While AAF is a newer and more versatile format than OMFI, for most situations you will simply provide whichever exchange format the video editor requests.

Summary

Hopefully this gives you a bit of grounding for synchronizing Pro Tools with other devices. We revisit some of these concepts in Chapter 14 and discuss MIDI MachineControl technology and the Pro Tools MachineControl option. In Appendix B, "Add-ons, Extensions, and Cool Stuff for Your Rig," you'll find further information about synchronization peripherals. Sync or swim!

12 The Pro Tools Groove

This chapter looks at a few specific techniques for basic beat mixing: combining samples from various sources with MIDI performances and additional audio recording to build up a groove in, for example, the dance, trance, or pop style. It also provides some details about the Elastic Audio features introduced in Pro Tools version 7.4.

If you talk with seasoned dance mixers who use Pro Tools, you will discover that they usually supplement the program with numerous synthesizers and samplers (either the software or external hardware variety) and/or dedicated programs for manipulating beats and loops such as ACID by Sony/Sonic Foundry (Windows), Live by Ableton, and so on—some of which can work in tandem on the same computer with Pro Tools via ReWire. If you're involved in this genre, we urge you to investigate the sampling/synthesis plug-ins for Pro Tools mentioned later in this chapter. Having your entire complex synthesis and signal-routing setup tightly integrated into a single Pro Tools session is an enormous benefit and allows you to experiment, continually perfecting previous mixes. As you can imagine, every Pro Tools user has his or her own methods, and you can make things as simple or as complicated as you like. This is definitely a subject that, by itself, could fill an entire book! This chapter focuses on the basics, limiting its discussion to techniques available to *all* Pro Tools users, and lets you build from there.

Combining MIDI and Audio

We promise this is the last time we'll remind you: MIDI is *not* audio! MIDI is a communications protocol. That is, it's a way to represent performance events (such as pressing a key or pedal on your MIDI controller, striking a drum pad, and so on) so that these can be transmitted from one device (or program) to another. With a MIDI interface connected to your computer, you attach MIDI cables (In to Out, Out to In) between the interface's ports and those of any external MIDI controllers and/or sound modules (or a MIDI-controllable effects processor, recorder, and so on). Alternatively, many current MIDI modules can be connected directly to the computer via its USB port. MIDI and Instrument tracks in Pro Tools record incoming MIDI data and provide you with editing tools to alter or create MIDI information. As mentioned in Chapter 10, "MIDI," software-based synthesizers and samplers are a very powerful alternative. These can be RTAS plug-ins (all systems), TDM plug-ins (HD systems), or separate programs whose audio output is streamed into the Pro Tools mixing environment via ReWire technology (all systems).

Let's assume for a moment that your setup consists of a single MIDI keyboard sitting beside your Pro Tools rig, and you're using that keyboard's internal sounds for some of your MIDI tracks. What are your options for combining the audio output of this external MIDI device with audio tracks playing back from hard disk within Pro Tools?

■ You could connect the audio outputs from the external MIDI keyboard to available inputs on your audio interface, and configure Aux Input or Instrument tracks to monitor those inputs within Pro Tools. If your audio interface has numerous inputs available—as opposed to just two or four, as is the case with some interfaces for LE and M-Powered—the audio outputs from *several* MIDI modules can stay more or less permanently connected, leaving the remaining inputs free for audio recordings (guitar or vocal tracks, for example). This is simple to set up. For example, you might create a stereo Aux Input track, selecting input pair 7–8 on your multichannel audio interface as its source (where you've connected the audio outputs from your MIDI keyboard). The signal from this Aux Input (with whatever plug-ins or additional audio routing you have created) will be included when you bounce a mixdown to disk in real time.

Instrument Tracks Can Also Be Used for External MIDI Devices Many people immediately associate Instrument tracks with software instrument plug-ins. In this case, a single track serves as the audio channel (similar to an Aux Input) whose sound source is an instrument plug-in in its insert slot, and also as the track where you record and edit MIDI performances. This saves screen space and makes your session easier to manage. You can also use Instrument tracks for external MIDI modules, however. As the audio input for your Instrument track, select the ports on your audio interface where the external MIDI device is connected. Then, with the Instrument controls section visible at the top of the Mix window (or the corresponding column in the Edit window, if that option is enabled), select the appropriate MIDI port and channel to configure that external device as the MIDI destination for this track. Even if you end up using additional MIDI tracks for a multitimbral external module, having separate Mute and Solo buttons for the Instrument controls section (MIDI) and the audio portion of Instrument track itself makes it easy to manage this "hybrid" track.

■ If you're using a small mixer to monitor your Pro Tools outputs, you could also monitor the audio output from your MIDI keyboard(s) directly through the mixer. In this scenario, you'd have to record the mixer's stereo output to some other device in real time—for example, a DAT. Mixing to an external recorder has some operational disadvantages (not to mention the additional expense), however. For one thing, once you've bounced out a series of mixes, you may have to record them right back onto hard disk if you're going to use Pro Tools or another program to sequence them and apply any other mastering processes. Some users may find themselves in this situation anyway—for instance, if the number of external, real-time audio sources entering their mix exceeds the available inputs on their Pro Tools audio hardware. This would be the case if, for example, you have stereo outputs coming from five different MIDI modules plus several external effects processors used as send destinations from Pro Tools outputs and only eight analog inputs available on your audio interface. Even so, a more practical alternative might be to use a small external mixer to *submix* audio from these devices, perhaps entering the Pro Tools mixing environment via a single stereo Aux Input. In this scenario, however, it's usually preferable to separately record the stereo audio output from each of your MIDI modules to its own audio track before mixdown and definitely before disconnecting those modules and archiving the Pro Tools project. That way, you have mixable tracks and reproducible levels if those modules are no longer connected in the future.

■ If a single external keyboard is your sound source for multiple MIDI tracks, you may opt to record each instrumental part onto a separate audio track before mixdown. This enables you to apply separate plug-in processing to each part in Pro Tools, usually producing superior quality for the shared, built-in effects on the MIDI keyboard or module itself. For example, you might use compression or a small-room reverb on the recorded audio track for the MIDI drum part and a completely different effects treatment on the other instrumental parts recorded from this MIDI sound source. Again, having an audio version of your MIDI parts saved with the final mixdown session also guarantees that the project will sound the same in the future if that original MIDI sound source is no longer available.

Using "Assembled" Percussion Parts and Region Groups

Multitrack percussion constructions can be a creative way to put together a groove. Besides the simplistic technique of assembling a pattern out of individual drum-hit samples, you could also use more exotic industrial and ambient sounds to put together interesting rhythmic patterns. Working in Grid edit mode is an essential part of this process. Another handy command is Region > Quantize to Grid, which moves the beginning of audio regions to the nearest grid increment as specified in the Grid Value field. If a sync point exists within the region (see Chapter 8, "Menu Selections: Highlights" for a description of the Region > Identify Sync Point command), the sync point itself is snapped to the nearest grid increment instead of to the region's beginning. This is handy for a snare sample with backward reverb on the front end or turntable scratch and vocal effects, for example.

When using individual samples to build a percussive groove on a series of audio tracks in Grid mode, be sure to set the Timebase selector for all these tracks to Ticks. That way, if you subsequently alter the tempo, the regions in these tracks (set to the Ticks timebase) are automatically repositioned to maintain their same relative Bar:Beat locations in relation to the new tempo. Later, you could either group all these "percussion" tracks together or assign all their outputs to the same bus pair that's being monitored by a stereo Aux Input track and then hide them to save screen space.

This is also a case where region grouping can facilitate the editing and composing process. To create a region group, simply select all the regions you want to include—in this case, perhaps your entire eight-bar groove that spans multiple audio tracks. Then choose the Region > Group command. That entire selection now appears as a single region group graphic, with a region group icon in the lower-left corner. Region groups can be looped, duplicated, trimmed, and so on. Since the composite beat you constructed is on tick-based tracks, if the Pro Tools tempo changes, the start point for each instance of the region group *and all the source regions within it* will adjust accordingly to maintain their previous Bar:Beat locations. (This capability is also essential to working with REX and ACID files, by the way.) Later in this chapter, Figure 12.3 shows a composite percussion track that was combined into a single region group and then looped.

You can use the Region > Ungroup command to re-edit the regions in a selected region group. If a region group (such as the "assembled" percussion grooves we're discussing here) is being used elsewhere in the current session, you can use the Region > Regroup command after making your edits to its ungrouped components. In this case, a dialog box will present you with two choices: to modify the original region group (affecting all other instances) or to create a new copy (leaving other existing instances of this region group unchanged). Alternatively, if you use the Region > Group command again, Pro Tools will simply create a new region group definition from the current selection.

Looping Audio Regions

Certain styles of music involve repetition of rhythm loops, drum beats, and other sounds. For that matter, in postproduction, it is not uncommon to loop certain background sounds—especially the source audio from an effects library, which may not be long enough to fill the required duration. The Edit menu's Duplicate and Repeat commands (for creating multiple duplicates of selected regions in a single operation) will be useful for this, as will the Loop mode of the Trimmer tool that is available in versions 7.3 and higher. Here we take a look at some other aspects of looping audio in Pro Tools, starting with how you set your Pro Tools tempo based on the current selection.

The Event > Identify Beat Command

As you know from reading previous chapters, you can loop any selection via the Options > Loop Playback menu command. Pro Tools will keep cycling between the start and end locations until you stop playback.

Let's say that, instead of importing an existing loop, you've imported a full-length stereo rhythm groove from CD (at a single, steady tempo), and you want to use bits and pieces to create a completely new rhythm track. You can use the Event > Identify Beat command to generate a

Pro Tools tempo event based on any audio selection. Here's the traditional method (make sure Insertion Follows Playback is not selected):

1. Drag the original rhythm groove region onto a stereo audio track. Click the Selector tool anywhere in that track prior to the beginning of the section you want to loop and then press the spacebar to start playback in Pro Tools.

2. Press the down-arrow key on your computer keyboard at the beginning of the four-bar phrase you want to loop. Then press the up-arrow key on the next downbeat *after* the end of the phrase.

3. Stop playback. A portion of that track's audio waveform is selected, exactly where you pressed the down- and up-arrow keys.

4. Make sure the Options > Loop Playback option is enabled (it can also be enabled via the right-click pop-up menu for the Play button itself) and then press the Play button (or the spacebar) again. No matter how nimble your fingers and how rock-solid your sense of rhythm is, chances are your loop is not exactly smooth yet. Let's refine our selection to create a sample-accurate loop.

5. Use the Zoomer to click and drag immediately around the beginning of your current selection. Then switch to the Selector tool and, while holding down the Shift key, adjust the beginning of your selection until it exactly matches the downbeat of the phrase, with no excess audio selected before the attack but without omitting any of the attack. You may need to zoom in and out several levels to zero in on the proper position. (Remember: You can hold down the Command key, or Ctrl key in Windows, and use the left/right bracket keys to zoom in or out.) After each adjustment, click Play to confirm that your phrase starts *exactly* at the beginning of the selection. Next, we will adjust the end point of the selection.

6. Once you've precisely defined the beginning, press the right-arrow key on your computer keyboard once. This moves the waveform display to the end of the current selection. Now, while holding down the Shift key, adjust the end of your selection so that it ends immediately *before* the downbeat of the following phrase. Press the spacebar to play your selection after making each adjustment; you'll know you have the end point exactly right when the selected phrase loops around smoothly.

7. Choose Edit > Separate Region > At Selection. Name this new region 4 Bars and click OK to close the dialog box.

8. Eliminate the audio preceding the 4 Bars region in this track by selecting it with the Grabber and pressing the Delete or Backspace key on your computer keyboard. Then drag the 4 Bars region all the way to the beginning of the track.

9. With this region still selected, enable the Tempo Ruler Enable button (conductor icon) in the Transport window; then select Event > Identify Beat. Indicate to Pro Tools that

the beginning of the current selection is bar 1, beat 1 in 4/4 time, and that the end of the selection is bar 5, beat 1.

10.   Switch to Bars:Beats as your main time ruler units (View > Main Counter > Bars: Beats). Enable Grid mode, and set Grid value to ¼ notes.

11.   If you've made an accurate phrase selection for the Identify Beat command, you can highlight anywhere within the rest of the drum groove that remains on the track, and your selection will automatically snap to the nearest ¼-note increment. You're ready to start carving up some phrases out of the groove and put them back together into a different arrangement.

Other Ways to Adjust Selections In Chapter 6, "The Edit Window," in the discussion of the Selector tool, we describe another method for making precise phrase selections: using the Scrubber tool and then *nudging* the selection with the plus and minus (+/−) keys. You can also hold down the Option or Command modifier keys—Alt or Ctrl in Windows—to nudge only the end or beginning of a selection without affecting its other boundary. For drum loops, however, the Tab to Transients button is usually the quickest way to define a loop selection. Click with the Selector tool somewhere very close to the beginning of the audio you want to define as a region to be looped and press the Tab key. The cursor jumps forward to the next detected transient peak in the audio material. Hold down the Shift key and click somewhere prior to the end of the selection you want to define. Then press Shift+Tab; the selection will extend to the next transient detected.

The Region > Loop/Unloop Commands

You can loop both individual regions and region groups (whether on single or multiple tracks). Figure 12.1 shows the dialog box that appears when you select the Region > Loop command.

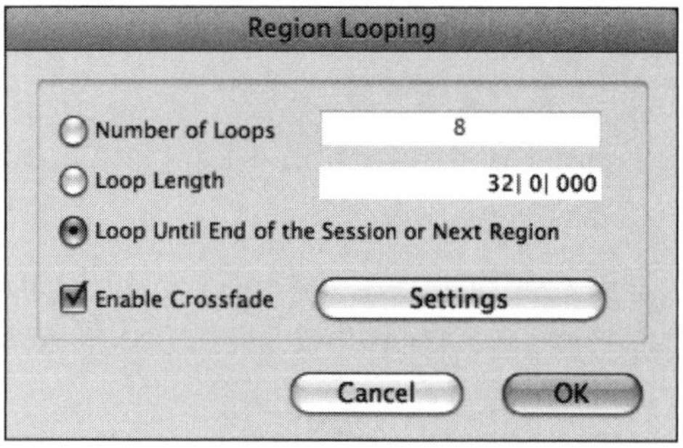

Figure 12.1 Options for looping a selected region (or region group). The crossfade option doesn't apply to looped MIDI regions.

You can choose a specific number of repetitions, a total duration (in which case the last loop "alias" may be truncated if the target duration for the entire set of loops isn't an exact multiple), or that the region should continue looping until it reaches either the end of the session's timeline or the next region boundary within that track. You can also specify a crossfade time between adjacent loop repetitions. However, as always with crossfades, there must be enough additional material before and/or after the boundaries of the region proper within its parent file to fill the desired crossfade duration. This can often produce smoother transitions, especially when cymbal decays or reverb at the end of the loop might otherwise be abruptly cut off at the splice point.

Loop *aliases* are created, following the original source region. This entire series of loop repetitions can be dragged, copied, and so on, much like a single region or region group. If you drop some other region somewhere within an existing looped region (as seen in Figure 12.2), that topmost region sounds, and then the remainder of the underlying loop repetitions continues. This is obviously very useful when you're building up an arrangement from a simple repeating beat, for example.

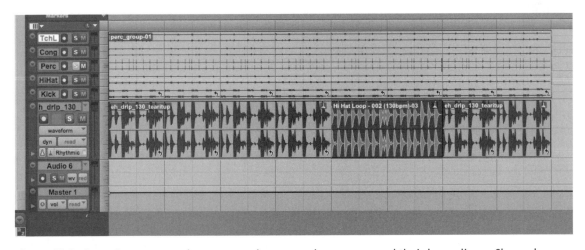

Figure 12.2 Loop icons appear in source regions or region groups and their loop aliases. Shown here: a multitrack percussion assemblage that has been made into a region group and looped, plus a looped audio region with another region dropped amongst its loop repetitions.

Using the Trimmer tool on looped regions allows you to increase or decrease the number of repetitions. The last repetition may be truncated by this operation, for example, if you want to shorten it to a lesser number of bars or beats to make room for a fill or transition. If you hold down the Control key (Start key in Windows) while trimming looped regions (but not necessarily region groups), the total duration changes by even multiples of the source region's length. This is one of the quickest ways to create additional repetitions of the entire loop.

The dialog box that appears when you execute the Region > Unloop command (shown in Figure 12.3) lets you either revert back to a single instance of the source region or region group or

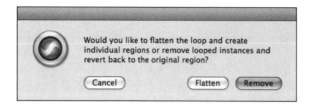

Figure 12.3 Options for unlooping a selected region (or region group).

flatten the current looped set into separate regions. Unless you've used the Loop Trimmer—see the next section—the result is similar to having used the Edit > Repeat command in the first place; however, if the last loop repetition was truncated to match the desired duration, a separate region definition is created for it.

We should add that the usefulness of region looping isn't limited to musical applications. In audio post, background ambience, or walla, wind, water, or traffic sounds pulled from sound-effect libraries, are often not long enough to fill the required duration. Using region looping (instead of the Edit menu's Duplicate and Repeat commands) provides a more convenient method for building a base over which you can layer other background sounds.

Loop Trimmer

In Pro Tools versions 7.3 and higher, the Trimmer tool's Loop mode can be selected in addition to its standard and TC/E modes. This enables you to directly create loop aliases as you trim the left or right boundary of a single existing region within a track without having to use the Region Looping dialog box. In contrast to how the Trimmer tool's standard mode behaves on looped regions, the function of the Loop Trimmer changes according to whether you are over the top or bottom corner of the region graphic, as indicated by the cursor shape. When in the upper corner, it behaves like the standard Trimmer mode, including the Control-key combination (Start key in Windows) that constricts the trimmed length to even multiples of the original loop's duration. When in the lower corner of the looped region graphic (where the loop icon appears), the length of the looped region itself can be trimmed. For example, you might use this in Grid editing mode to trim a two-bar looped region down to a single bar. The number of loop aliases is adjusted accordingly (exactly double, in this case) to maintain the same total duration of looped repetitions. Note that this resizing with the Loop Trimmer does *not* apply time compression/expansion; it merely redefines the boundaries for the looped region. If you *do* use the Time Trimmer on looped audio regions or audio region groups, a single, consolidated region is created that contains the results of that time compression/expansion operation, including the effects of any fades on the source region(s).

Duplicating Automation in Your Loop Aliases

If there is any automation data associated with your source region or region group, this is *not* copied into the loop aliases. The idea in Pro Tools is to provide flexibility for creating automation that may extend across multiple loop repetitions. Copying and pasting automation (once you have changed the track view to display the desired automation parameter) has always been possible in Pro Tools. Submenus for Cut Special, Copy Special, and Clear Special provide options for applying these operations to all automation types, pan data only, or plug-in automation only. After you copy automation data to the Clipboard with the Cut Special or Copy Special commands, you can paste it elsewhere with the normal Paste command without affecting any overlapping regions at the track destination, even if no automation parameters are currently visible in that track.

There is also a Paste Special submenu. These Paste Special modes are especially relevant for our region-looping examples. Merge combines the pasted data with any existing automation data. The To Current Automation Type command allows you to paste an automation shape from one type of automation to another; for example, you could paste pan automation into a reverb send. You can use Repeat to Fill Selection to paste enough copies of a shorter segment of automation data to fill a larger duration. Because loop aliases initially don't include any automation accompanying the source region or region group that is being looped, you could use Edit > Copy Special > All Automation, highlight all the loop aliases (spanning multiple tracks, in the case of the multitrack percussion grooves discussed earlier in this chapter), and then use Edit > Paste Special > Repeat to Fill Selection. Now the automation shapes from the source region are repeated with all the loop aliases.

Using the Time Trimmer for Adjusting Durations

When you change the Trimmer tool to TC/E (Time Compression/Expansion) mode, its cursor changes to the Time Trimmer. In this mode, as you trim any audio or MIDI region, its contents are adjusted to fit into the new duration. For instance, using this mode to reduce a MIDI region from a duration of four bars to two bars produces a double-time version. Using the Time Trimmer on audio regions applies the time compression/expansion plug-in—for example, Time Shift, the older Digidesign TC/E plug-in, or some other optional time-stretching plug-in that may be on your system—and the default settings specified in the Processing tab of the Preferences dialog box.

Suppose you import some four- or eight-bar drum loops that don't match the current session tempo. Before the introduction of the Elastic Audio features in Pro Tools 7.4, the Time Trimmer was one of the quickest ways to conform their durations to the equivalent number of beats. You would switch to Grid editing mode and then drag the four-bar loop to exactly four bars at the current session tempo. Easy! Naturally, the more extreme the ratio of time compression/expansion, the more artifacts will be heard in the results.

Working with REX and ACID Files

Both of these formats are optimized for time-sliced loops—that is, audio files that have been analyzed and broken down into their rhythmic components. The REX/REX2 format (which uses a .rex or .rx2 file name extension) was developed for the ReCycle program, by Propellerhead Software. The ACID format (.wav files containing additional metadata about tempo, time slices, and other parameters) comes from a program of the same name, originally developed by

Sonic Foundry and now owned by Sony Creative. Many loop-savvy programs—including Reason, ACID, Ableton Live, Fruity Loops, Logic, and Cubase—support REX and/or ACID files and can play these loops at any tempo without pitch changes. Pro Tools can also use these time-sliced audio file formats. As with files analyzed by Beat Detective in Pro Tools, having individual rhythmic components automatically sliced up within the file makes it much easier to rearrange them into new rhythmic patterns.

Importing REX/ACID Files into Pro Tools

You can import REX and ACID files into Pro Tools by dragging them directly from the Workspace browser window (or from the Macintosh Finder, Windows Explorer, or the desktop) into the Regions List or onto an existing track, which should usually be tick-based for this purpose. If you want a new track automatically created to contain them, drag these files directly into the Tracks List or into an empty area of the Edit window itself. As you preview each of these files in the Workspace window using the speaker icon, its tempo is automatically adjusted to match that of the current start time in the Pro Tools timeline. In Pro Tools versions 7.4 and higher, what happens when you create a new tick-based track by dragging REX and ACID files into the Tracks List (or to an empty space in the Edit window) depends on your settings in the Preferences dialog box's Processing tab (see Figure 12.4). Using the default preference in Pro Tools

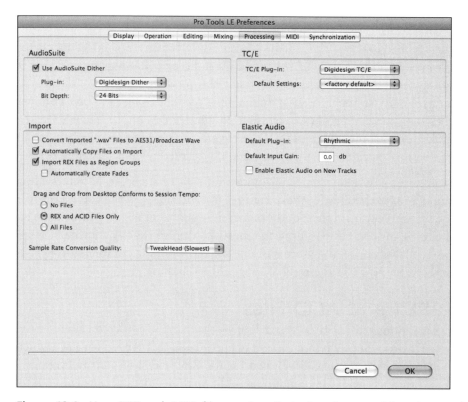

Figure 12.4 How REX and ACID files are handled when imported into Pro Tools depends on these settings in the Processing tab of the Preferences dialog box.

versions 7.4 and higher, time slices in imported REX/ACID files are consolidated for use by Elastic Audio and any newly created tick-based audio track will have Elastic Audio enabled (with the default Elastic Audio plug-in).

Using REX/ACID Region Groups in Your Tracks (Versions 7.3 and Lower)

In previous Pro Tools versions (and if the Import Sliced Audio Files as Region Groups setting is enabled in version 7.4, as in Figure 12.4), a new region group is created in the Regions List, reflecting the name of the original audio file. In this case, you have the option of subsequently ungrouping those time-slice regions and reordering them. (For these time-slice regions to appear in the Regions List, the option to view auto-created regions must be enabled in its local menu.) A checkbox in the Preferences dialog box's Processing tab enables you to choose whether fades are automatically created if REX and ACID files are imported as region groups, and of what type.

If you ever drag a region group created from a REX or ACID file from the Regions List, Workspace browser, or desktop onto an *existing* audio track, make sure the timebase for that track is set to Ticks. That way, if you create any tempo changes, the locations of the time slices within these region groups (derived from the original REX/ACID files) are automatically adjusted to maintain the same relative Bar:Beat locations. (Nothing *prevents* you from dragging them onto an audio track with a Samples timebase, but Ticks timebase is more convenient and flexible for most musical applications.) For consistency and flexibility when working in this manner, we also recommend enabling the Transport window's Conductor button rather than using manual tempo settings.

You can cut, copy, paste, trim, or loop these region groups, just as you would any other region in Pro Tools. In fact, if you want access to the individual slices within them in order to rework the beat itself, just use the Region > Ungroup command. (If during import the ACID/REX loop's tempo speed was increased to match the current tempo in your Pro Tools, you will notice that some of these time-slice regions will overlap.) Among other things, you could use the Region > Quantize to Grid command to pull the time slices into a more rigid rhythmic alignment and then regroup.

Using REX/ACID Files with Elastic Audio (Versions 7.4 and Higher)

By default, in versions 7.4 and higher, dragging REX or ACID files into the Tracks List or an empty area of the Edit window creates a new tick-based track with the default Elastic Audio plug-in enabled (unless the aforementioned Import Sliced Audio Files as Region Groups setting is active). When sliced REX and ACID files are imported onto Elastic Audio tracks, the slices they contain are interpreted with 100% confidence, so the Event Sensitivity setting in the Elastic Properties dialog box for those regions has no effect afterward.

Building a Better Groove

Okay, you've chopped out enough good phrases to build a basic arrangement and you've even overdubbed a few additional MIDI and audio parts (perhaps some vocals and an instrumental part or two). Now you want to add some nuances to the rhythmic arrangement. Until now, you've left it fairly repetitive, stringing the same few phrases together many times, almost like a click track or drum loop. What are your options for making it sound less mechanical? Here are just a few ideas:

- Use some of the drum sounds in your MIDI modules, especially small percussion such as shakers, maracas, cabasa, and so on, to layer more variation into your drum groove. Unless you're deliberately seeking a full-blown Latin or world-music groove, try mixing this down underneath the drum track's level—too loud, and it will sound cheesy. The idea is to add some varying patterns, changing up velocities and swing factors, to create some longer phrases overlaid on the repetitive four-bar base. Even better, if you have a microphone and some hand percussion (and enough rudimentary technique to not just make matters worse), you can perform some of these subtle texture parts yourself for a guaranteed human feel. As a general note, you may be surprised to see how much difference just *one* human-played part, even mixed at a very low level, can make toward a good groove feel—*especially* with quantized MIDI arrangements!

- Use AudioSuite functions to process some of the existing phrases in your groove (using the Create Individual Files option so that your original file is unaffected). For example, you might use the EQ to perform some radical adjustments to the frequency content of some phrases or extreme compression/gate settings. You can then drop fragments of these processed regions into an additional audio track, trimming their beginnings and ends to create effect fills in fiendishly clever locations.

- Use the AudioSuite menu's Expander-Gate function on a rhythm phrase selection, activate the External Key function, and choose one of your other audio tracks (or busses) as the side-chain input. The signal that controls the opening/closing of the gate during your selected phrase is whatever occurs simultaneously in that other track/bus. (In other words, you're imposing the gain/envelope changes of the side chain's source audio on your selection.) Depending on where you do this, what source you select, and of course how extreme your Expander-Gate settings are, you can create some interesting rhythmic effects. Again, a new audio region is created for your results, and you can trim out bits and pieces to use as rhythm accents over your basic groove.

- Take advantage of Pro Tools' ability to automate sends (and plug-in parameters, of course). Create a send (at send position C, for example) from your drum tracks; route its output to an internal Pro Tools bus (#3, for example). Then create an Aux Input, with bus 3 set as its input and drop a reverb plug-in on one of that Aux Input's inserts. Choose a nonlinear or gated reverb setting (or small room, snare room, and so on). Now, change the Track View selector on the audio track where your drum track resides to Send C > Level. In Grid mode, set at perhaps $1/8$-note increments, use the Grabber to create breakpoints that outline $1/8$-note-long spikes in the send level right on the snare backbeats—for example, 2 and 4 of each bar (or wherever amuses you). Remember, when viewing breakpoint automation in Pro Tools, you can hold down the Option key (Alt key in Windows) and click a breakpoint with the Grabber tool to delete it. Don't bother drawing your shapes in every single bar; get it right in a couple of bars and then copy and paste this automation data into the rest! Also remember that you can trim automation data to scale it up or down. Yes, we know: You're sending an entire drum mix to the reverb, which would sound pretty rude if it were enabled all the time. But by keeping the volume of your Aux Input fairly low (and by occasionally using an EQ plug-in on the insert prior to the reverb to reduce high and low frequencies so that the hi-hat and kick drum aren't overly prominent), these rhythmic shots to the reverb can blend into the track, creating subtle dynamic pushes on certain beats. Of course, if subtlety is not your intention, the technique is equally applicable for changing dramatic, dub-style shots into a delay or reverb.

■ Try routing some of your percussion grooves (drum loops or entire drum set mixes, for example) through a second channel with extremely aggressive dynamics processing applied. For example, create a send from your drum loop track and choose one of the bus pairs in Pro Tools as a secondary destination. Create a new Aux Input track with that bus pair selected as its input source. Use plug-in inserts to apply very large amounts of compression or limiting to that Aux Input track (plus some EQ, if you choose). You can now blend this with the main, unprocessed version of that percussion groove, having it drop out or enter at key points in your arrangement. An even larger number of these *mults* or alternate submixes could be used for creative effect. Also consider applying this "iron fist in a velvet glove" approach with lead vocals when you want them to sound more powerful or aggressive than your singer may be capable of delivering naturally. A solid, dynamics-processed backbone may be just the thing you're looking for.

Thinking Outside the Bar Lines A common problem when stringing together rhythm phrases is that they contain events that should hang over the bar lines at the beginning or end of the phrase. For example, if the drummer hits the crash cymbal on the fourth beat of the last bar, it sounds unnatural for this cymbal sound to cut off abruptly when the following phrase begins. The Fades dialog box is your best ally for dealing with these situations. A post-splice crossfade after the boundary between the two adjacent regions allows you to smoothly extend the cymbal's decay across the beginning of the next phrase (as long as it's similar to the preceding one—remember that the two regions will overlap during the crossfade). To do this, select the two adjacent regions with the Grabber; then select Edit > Fades > Create (Command+F in Mac, Ctrl+F in Windows). In the Batch Fades dialog box (see Figure 12.5), set the Link option to None so that you can select the Fade In and Fade Out shapes independently. Then select the Post-Splice option under Position, Preset Curve 1 for the *in* shape of the second region (so that it starts immediately, with no fade-up), and one of the more gradual curves for the first region's *out* shape. Select about 200–300 milliseconds for the fade's initial length; you can always adjust this fade duration later with the Trimmer tool.

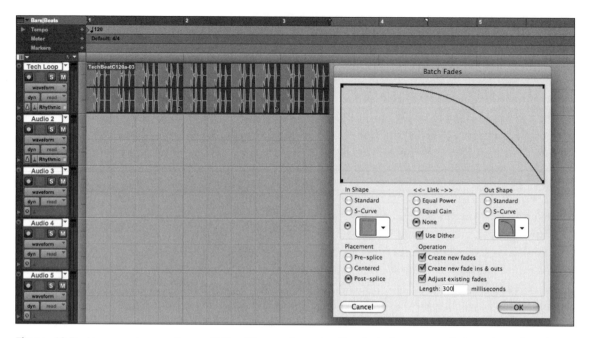

Figure 12.5 Here, we're creating a 300-millisecond, post-splice fade between all the selected regions. At each boundary between them, the second region begins immediately at full volume, while additional material *after* the end of the first region fades out over it.

Elastic Audio

Elastic Audio was the most notable feature introduced in Pro Tools version 7.4. Essentially, Elastic Audio is a set of software tools that enables *warping* of events within audio regions, conforming them to the tempo and rhythmic feel of your Pro Tools session and to each other. As shown in Figure 12.6, various Elastic Audio analysis modes can be selected via the pop-up Elastic-Audio plug-in selector in the controls for each audio track: Polyphonic, Rhythmic, Monophonic, Varispeed, and X-form (available for rendered audio regions only). (You can also select None.) This is a unique plug-in selector; it has nothing to do with the track insert plug-ins you use elsewhere in Pro Tools.

The Elastic Audio analysis modes look at the transients (momentary attacks) within the source audio file to determine where the most significant audio events are located. When an audio region gets stretched or squeezed to match the current session tempo, the Elastic Audio processing applies time compression or expansion and very short-duration fades between these significant transient events. Not only is the total duration adjusted to the desired tempo on tick-based tracks, but the important transients within the audio region are intelligently adjusted to the appropriate subdivisions of the beat.

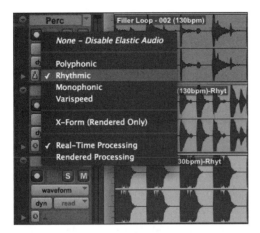

Figure 12.6   The Elastic Plug-in selector on audio tracks (available in all versions 7.4 and higher).

Event Markers and Warp Markers

The analysis carried out by Elastic Audio plug-ins creates Event markers for the significant transients in the source audio. When you switch the track display format to Warp or Analysis view, these Event markers are visible as gray vertical lines over the audio waveform (see Figure 12.7). In contrast, Warp markers anchor a given event within an audio waveform to a specific location in the Pro Tools timeline (usually a Bar:Beat location on a tempo-based track); they appear as thicker vertical black lines with a triangle at the base. For instance, you may have identified a snare backbeat in an imported drum loop and want to make sure that, no matter how other audio events in this region are moved around to match the rhythmic subdivisions or swing factor of the session, this backbeat stays firmly on the second quarter note of the bar. To quote the *Pro Tools Reference Guide* (your best source for details about Elastic Audio), you can think of the audio region as a rubber band, the timeline as a ruler, and Warp markers as pins stuck into that rubber band. If you change the tempo of the Pro Tools session, the absolute positions of Warp markers will automatically shift to retain their current Bar:Beat locations. Time compression or

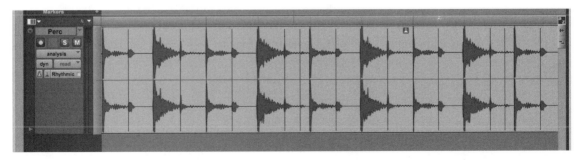

Figure 12.7   An audio track in Analysis display format, showing the Event markers detected by Elastic Audio.

expansion will be applied to the audio between these warp markers to maintain a continuous audio file according to the method of the Elastic Audio plug-in you currently have activated on that audio track.

Editing Event and Warp Markers

Two track display formats are specifically related to Elastic Audio: Analysis and Warp. In Warp view, you can create and move Warp markers, which pin the start of an individual audio event within the region to a specific time location (a relative Bar:Beat location if the region is on a tick-based track, or an absolute time position on sample-based tracks). In Analysis view, you can edit Event markers. Sometimes you will do this to ensure that Event markers correspond exactly to the transients you want to be adjusted to beat subdivisions. (Sometimes adjustments are necessary, especially if a sound has a relatively long attack or other background sounds may be causing the Elastic Audio algorithm to trigger an attack transient slightly too early.) In other cases, you might add or delete Event markers to avoid false triggers. One of the most typical applications of Warp markers is to adjust the time of individual audio events, perhaps to make specific drum hits or notes on an instrument align more precisely to the nearest $1/8$ note, for example.

1. Switch the display format of this audio track (tick-based, with one of the Elastic Audio plug-ins enabled) to Warp.

2. Enable Grid editing mode and select whatever Grid value is appropriate.

3. Locate the event that is too early or late.

4. Select the Grabber tool.

5. Drag that Event marker to the desired grid subdivision

Creative Sound Manipulation with Event Markers If you're mangling drum and rhythm loops with Elastic Audio while the track is in Analysis display format, one trick you will want to explore is squeezing or stretching a single event (that is, the area between one Event marker and the next in the audio waveform) to a different duration as a special effect. For instance, if you isolate a single kick or snare hit (that doesn't include any intervening hits on the hi-hat) and stretch it to twice or four times its original duration, you might find this to be an interesting accent or variation to work into your groove.

Elastic Audio Plug-in Window

Click the Elastic Audio Plug-in button to open this window, shown in Figure 12.8. The parameters available in the Elastic Audio plug-in depend on which analysis mode is active on the track. Here we provide some general guidelines, based on Digidesign's own documentation. You will

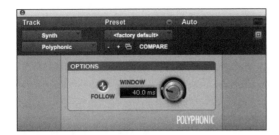

Figure 12.8 The Elastic Audio plug-in window for the Polyphonic mode. Shorter analysis window lengths generally work better for drums and percussion. The Follow button enables an envelope follower to retain more of the original acoustics, especially when more extreme amounts of time stretch are applied.

quickly discover, however, that with a given audio loop (and depending on how aggressively you are stretching and squeezing things), you may need to experiment with more than one mode and adjust parameters according to your own ears.

- **Polyphonic.** This Elastic Audio mode is useful for loops with harmonic or melodic elements (although it's sometimes useful for more complex rhythm loops). A single parameter, Window, is available for Polyphonic mode. As a general rule, Digidesign recommends starting from the default range of 30–40ms, increasing to as much as 60ms for pads and other legato material or decreasing toward 20ms for more percussive material.

- **Rhythmic.** As you might imagine, this works best on drums, percussion, and similar material with distinct transients. Decay Rate is the only parameter for Rhythmic mode. It controls how much of the audio following each detected event will be audible. In particular, this can be useful when processing has slowed the original region down and you don't want unnaturally long decays on a tambourine, clap, or cowbell sound, for example. At the 100% setting, audio between detected transient events is stretched to fill the gaps completely (with microfades at the boundaries, as with all Elastic Audio processing).

- **Monophonic.** Monophonic Elastic Audio processing would be suitable for bass lines, single horn lines, and so on. There are no adjustable parameters for Monophonic mode.

- **Varispeed.** In this mode, the playback pitch of the affected regions changes in proportion to how much Elastic Audio processing alters them from their original duration, as with tape-speed manipulation and traditional samplers. There are no adjustable parameters for Varispeed mode.

- **X-Form.** This plug-in mode is available only for rendered processing (which creates new audio files). It is the highest quality of the Elastic Audio plug-ins, however. There are two adjustable parameters. Quality is self-explanatory, but keep in mind that the maximum setting increases processing time as the new file is generated, which might be an issue on longer files. When the Formant button is enabled, the processing algorithm attempts to maintain the characteristic resonances of the original sound after Elastic Audio processing. As you can imagine, this is more likely to be a concern with vocal, brass, and woodwind samples, for example.

Elastic Audio and Tempo Events If you have tempo events in your session (which can be seen in the Tempo ruler and its graphic Tempo Editor), Elastic Audio will take them into consideration. For instance, if you have used a tempo curve to create a *ritardando* (gradual slowing of the tempo) at the end of a song or phrase, the timing of Elastic Audio–processed events will follow this. In the process, tempo event–generated Warp markers are created within the affected audio regions, which cannot be edited manually.

Elastic Properties Window

The real-time elastic properties of each audio region in an Elastic Audio–enabled track can be adjusted in the Elastic Properties window (shown in Figure 12.9), which can be opened for a selected region from the Regions menu. Even easier, just right-click on an audio region and choose Elastic Properties from the pop-up menu or press Option+5 (Alt+5 in Windows) on the numeric keypad. In this window, on tick-based tracks, you can change the settings for the source length in bars and beats, source tempo, and source meter (time signature). The Event Sensitivity setting is important because it enables you to adjust the threshold at which transients within the audio will be analyzed as events for Elastic Audio processing (because too many false triggers would be counterproductive). The Source Length and the Source Tempo fields can be edited. The Meter field enables you to make corrections if the analysis misses the fact that the loop is actually in 3/4 or 7/8, for example (because the Elastic Audio analyses *always* assume that source regions are in 4/4 time).

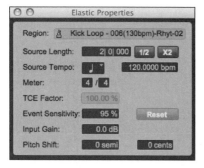
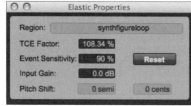

Figure 12.9 The Elastic Properties window for an audio region with tracks set to Ticks timebase (left) and sample timebase (right). Note that Elastic Audio analysis always assumes that source audio is 4/4 time; when that is not the case, change the Meter setting.

Backward Compatibility of Elastic Audio with Pro Tools Session Formats Prior to 7.4 If you disable Elastic Audio processing on an audio track, a dialog box appears where you can optionally revert audio regions on that track to their original durations and internal timings. However, the Commit option here generates a new audio file (in the session's Audio Files folder) and whole-file region definition for every audio region currently residing in that track that will incorporate the effects of Elastic Audio processing and any fades currently applied to those regions. For subsequent flexibility, each of these newly created files will also include an additional five seconds of audio from their original source files, if available. You can then use the File > Save Session Copy In command to save this session back to an older Pro Tools format.

Using the DigiBase Browsers with Elastic Audio

Assuming that the tempo of your Pro Tools session has already been established (perhaps from an existing drum loop or various tracks already recorded by live musicians), when you preview rhythm loops and other audio files in the Pro Tools Workspace (or Project) browser window, they can automatically be auditioned at the correct tempo for your session. Here is a typical workflow.

1. In the Pro Tools Workspace browser window, locate the audio file(s) for the drum loops you might like to import (perhaps from a sampling CD that you have purchased).

2. Enable the Conform to Session Tempo button (shown in Figure 12.10, it looks like a metronome, and is located in the upper toolbar portion of the browser window).

3. Select the Elastic Audio plug-in you want to use for previewing files in this browser. For this example, since we're mainly interested in drum loops, choose Rhythmic.

4. Click to highlight an audio file. Then use the browser's pop-up menu or the pop-up right-click menu to select the Calculate Elastic Analysis command. Once the analysis is complete, a checkmark will appear in the column to the left of the file name. Also, if the analysis detects a regular tempo (hopefully the case with our drum beats), a metronome icon will indicate that it is tick-based and its native tempo will appear in the Tempo column.

5. Click the audition button (the speaker icon) to preview the file with its tempo automatically adjusted to that of your Pro Tools session.

6. If you want to use this drum, you can simply drag it into the Tracks List area at the left edge of the Edit window. Pro Tools automatically creates a new tick-based audio track and makes any necessary conversions to your session's audio file format, sample rate, and bit depth, as well as splitting stereo source files to mono.

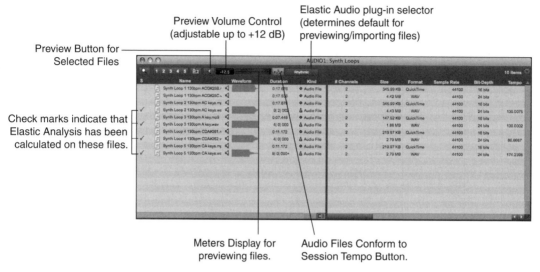

Figure 12.10 Shown here, several Elastic Audio tools in the Workspace browser window.

7. In the new track, the new audio region for your drum loop is automatically adjusted to the session tempo. You will also note a Warp indicator icon on that region waveform, indicating that this is a tick-based region that has been processed by Elastic Audio.

8. If you are using any swing factor in this session (or if you would like to apply it to the drum loop you have just placed into the track), open the Quantize page of the Event Operations window via the Event > Event Operations > Quantize command. (Even better, learn to use the keyboard shortcut: Option+0, or Alt+0 in Windows.) As you will note, you have most of the same options for quantizing Elastic Audio events as are available for MIDI events, including quantization to an existing groove template. As with the overall tempo-conforming capabilities of Elastic Audio, as the positions of detected events *within* the source waveform are moved around, a multitude of small-time compression and expansion adjustments are made in the background to ensure smooth playback of the processed audio.

9. You may want to optimize how this audio is processed and played back. For one thing, the Elastic Audio plug-in selector for this track in the Edit window lets you experiment with other real-time algorithms on this drum loop—for example, Polyphonic (sometimes useful even for rhythm loops without melodic or harmonic elements) or Varispeed (which changes the pitch in proportion to the duration, as on tape and traditional samplers).

10. Additionally, you can open the Elastic Audio Properties window via the pop-up menu that appears by right-clicking on this region. The options here depend on whether the timebase of the track is set to Ticks (as in this drum-loop example) or samples. In particular, you may want to adjust the Event Sensitivity value so that only transient events detected with a relatively high degree of confidence are displayed (since extraneous, falsely detected transient events can degrade the playback quality). Lowering the Input Gain value should be necessary only if you see clipping in the Elastic Audio plug-in window.

Dumb Tricks with Pro Tools Automation The Pencil tool in Pro Tools has several interesting drawing shapes (in addition to Free Hand, the default, and the Parabolic and S-curve shapes), as shown in Figure 12.11. In particular, Triangle, Square, and Random modes can provide some interesting results when drawing automation. Each shape creates steps (individual automation breakpoints) whose spacing is determined by the current Grid value and whose amplitude is determined by the vertical mouse position. For example, say your Grid mode is set to ½ notes, you're viewing a track in Pan Data Display mode, and you've selected the Triangle mode for the Pencil tool. As you click and drag rightward in the track, repeating triangle shapes occur every two beats; the distance between their upper and lower apexes (the *amplitude* of the triangle shape) is determined by how far you drag the mouse up and down as you draw. This is one way to create panning (or send levels, volume, and so on) that is synchronized to the beat. The spacing between the resultant breakpoints is determined by the current Grid value. The Square mode works the same way, as does Random (the *range* of random values also depends on the vertical movement of the Pencil tool as you draw). And remember: You can always scale automation up or down later with the Trimmer. This technique might be a little radical for a classical piano recording, but can be just the ticket when you're trying to create an unusual mix!

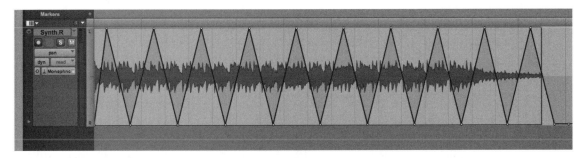

Figure 12.11 You can use the Pencil tool's drawing shapes for creating automation (and audio waveforms, at the appropriate zoom level). In this example, we've set the Grid value to ¼ notes and are drawing pan automation within our audio track using the Pencil tool's Triangle shape.

Beat Detective

You open Beat Detective (shown in Figure 12.12) via the Pro Tools Event menu. The standard Beat Detective LE version included with LE and M-Powered versions lacks the Collection mode shown in this figure, but is otherwise identical to the full version in Pro Tools HD. Collection mode *can* be added to the LE version via the Complete Production Toolkit, the Music Production Toolkit 2, and the DV Toolkit 2 bundles, however. Beat Detective automatically identifies the transients in the current selection to generate tempo information (bars and beats) and largely eliminates the need to use the Identify Beat command described earlier in this chapter.

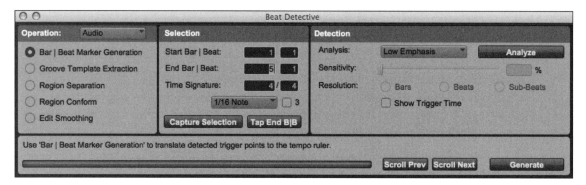

Figure 12.12 Beat Detective includes Collection mode in HD versions (and LE versions equipped with the optional Complete Production Toolkit, the Music Production Toolkit 2, and the DV Toolkit 2), while the Beat Detective LE version in Pro Tools LE and M-Powered does not.

You provide the starting and ending Bar:Beat locations and the time signature and then adjust the Sensitivity parameter and other parameters. The four mode buttons enable you to choose whether Beat Detective simply generates Bar:Beat markers in the Tempo ruler; separates the selection into multiple regions based on the detected beats (beat triggers); *conforms* (moves) the separated regions to the session's tempo; or, when conforming separated regions to the tempo, eliminates gaps or clicks between separated regions with crossfades and so on. Obviously, you will get best results with rhythmic material, at steady tempos, and with well-defined attacks on the beats (drum loops and mixes with rhythm sections, for example).

It's extremely important that your initial selection be *exact*! Before applying Beat Detective to a four-bar phrase selection, for example, use the Zoom features while using the Selector to precisely adjust the beginning and end of your selection to the correct downbeats.

One of the areas where the operational advantages of Beat Detective have *not* been overshadowed by Elastic Audio is in the generation and manipulation of time slices in audio files with the Region Separation mode. This makes it very easy to break a beat down into its rhythmic components, reordering them as you wish.

Beat Detective Modes

There are various Beat Detective modes, as follows:

- **Bar:Beat Marker Generation.** Generates these tempo events and beat triggers based on transients in the audio waveform. You tell Beat Detective how many bars long this selection is (by specifying start and end bars), the time signature, and what note values generally make up the smaller subdivisions of this beat (because generating too many or too few Bar:Beat markers is inconvenient). You can fine-tune the detection mode. As shown in Figure 12.13, the Sensitivity slider adjusts how it reacts to dynamics (although setting this to 0% allows you to generate only a single tempo event in the Tempo ruler, thus enabling you to avoid using the Identify Beat command described earlier in this chapter). You can adjust whether Beat Detective looks more toward low frequencies (Low Emphasis, useful when kick drum is the main defining element of the beat, for example) or high frequencies (when hi-hats, acoustic guitar arpeggios, and so on should be the elements that key the generation of beat subdivisions). You then click the Analyze button so that Beat Detective examines the selected audio data. If you see that the bar or beat lines in the display are improperly located, adjust the Sensitivity slider—it's possible, for example, that a softer snare or tom accent on beat four-and-a-half is falsely triggering Beat Detective, causing it to think the downbeat should be there. If you want even more control, especially when working with higher sub-beat resolutions like $1/16$ or $1/32$ notes, you can also manually drag the beat marker to a precise location in the waveform. (Option-click, or Alt-click in Windows, to delete any of these beat triggers. Command-click, or Ctrl-click in Windows, to promote a beat trigger from a subdivision to a main beat or bar trigger.)

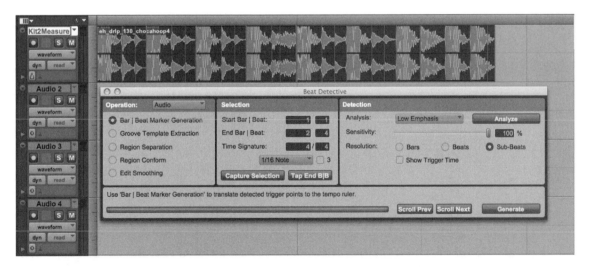

Figure 12.13 In Bar:Beat Marker Generation mode, greater sensitivity increases the number of beat triggers that will be detected in this drum loop.

- **Region Separation.** Based on the beat triggers you've defined using this analysis and detection, this function splits the audio selection into multiple regions.

- **Groove Template Extraction.** This function creates a DigiGroove template, based on the current beat trigger analysis of your selection. This can be either stored temporarily in the Groove Clipboard or saved to disk (as shown in Figure 12.14), where you could use it with the Grid/Groove Quantize function for MIDI data—a great way to impart the feel of one audio or MIDI part to other MIDI parts.

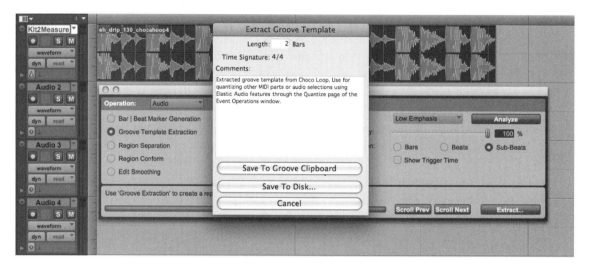

Figure 12.14   Here, we're saving a DigiGroove that was extracted from an audio selection to disk.

- **Region Conform.** In Standard mode, Region Conform adjusts the location of the multiple regions created by the Region Separation command ("quantizes" them) according to the session's current tempo settings. Further options include Strength (less than 100% retains some of the region's original feel by not moving the separated regions all the way to the nearest grid increment in the session's timeline), Exclude Within (if already within a certain distance of the nearest grid increment, the event won't be moved), and Swing. Once an audio selection is converted to multiple regions, you can also conform region locations either to one of the predefined DigiGrooves in Pro Tools or to the current contents of the Groove Clipboard. Prior to the introduction of Elastic Audio, this was the most practical method for matching the feel of the current selection to existing MIDI parts or to DigiGroove information you've extracted from another audio selection (so that two drum loops sound tighter when played simultaneously, for example).

- **Edit Smoothing.** This mode applies trimming and crossfades so that there are no gaps left between the regions at their new locations after they've been conformed. Otherwise, after the separated regions are repositioned, you may hear some clicks or choppiness wherever there's silence between two regions or where their boundaries overlap. You can specify the length of any required crossfades.

■ **Collection (HD version only).** With Bar:Beat Marker Generation and Region Separation modes, Collection mode allows you to apply Beat Detective to multiple tracks—with individual detection settings—to build up a composite *beat trigger* map. This is useful for multiple drum set tracks, for example. Collection mode can be added to LE or M-Powered versions via the Complete Production Toolkit, the Music Production Toolkit 2, and the DV Toolkit 2.

You can also use Beat Detective with MIDI tracks. You can generate groove and tempo information from MIDI tracks and apply it to audio tracks or vice versa (although Elastic Audio also provides the capability to apply groove templates to quantize the events with audio regions). For example, you could extract a groove template from a drum loop and then apply this to a MIDI part you created through step input. MIDI chord recognition parameters included among the options in the Analysis pop-up menu (shown in Figure 12.15) enable you to control how Beat Detective interprets the location of beats in relation to the varied timeline positions of the various notes that make up a chord (since in a real-time performance, these are rarely identical). You can establish the beat trigger according to the first, last, lowest, highest, loudest, or average note position in the chord.

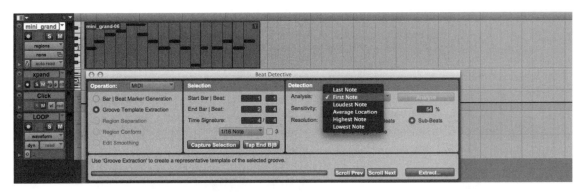

Figure 12.15 When analyzing MIDI with Beat Detective (or extracting a DigiGroove as shown here), options in this pop-up menu allow control over how notes within chords are interpreted.

If you're a beat mixer using loops and other "found" audio to build grooves, it will be well worth your while to explore Beat Detective. Although we've provided only a superficial overview here, the *Pro Tools Reference Guide* PDF document dedicates an entire chapter to Beat Detective.

Set Your Delay Times in Relation to the Current Tempo Sometimes, you might want the delay time to correspond to a specific note value (say, an ⅛ note or a ¼-note triplet) in relation to the current tempo of the music. Although you can automatically sync the DigiRack delays included with Pro Tools (and some other third-party delay plug-ins) to the session's tempo, it's also fairly easy to accomplish this manually. Some people also like to use tempo-related time settings for pre-delays on reverbs—LFO (low-frequency oscillator) speeds on flangers and chorus effects, for example. Setting these additional time factors in a mix to some logical relationship with the tempo can sometimes help avoid clutter, *especially* with delay repeats.

The DigiRack delays include short, slap, medium, long, and extra-long variations (with maximum delay times of 43, 171, 341, 683, or 2726ms, respectively; longer delay types utilize a larger fraction of your system's processing capacity, even if their current delay time value is short). Except for the short and slap versions, you can sync these DigiRack delays to the current Pro Tools tempo, as you can see in Figure 12.16. This makes it easy to set repeat times to some rhythmic value without needing to make any calculations. The tempo-syncing feature is enabled or disabled by a button that looks like a metronome in the Delay Plug-in window (shown in Figure 12.16). The Meter and Tempo fields are disabled when Tempo Sync is active; otherwise, you could use these to manually specify your delay times in terms of a musical tempo and time signature. The Groove slider is useful for adding some swing factor to delay repeats; that is, each offbeat is progressively later or earlier as you increase/decrease the amount of swing. When using the medium and long versions, you can set delay times in musical values for a specific meter and tempo setting using the Meter, Tempo, and Groove controls.

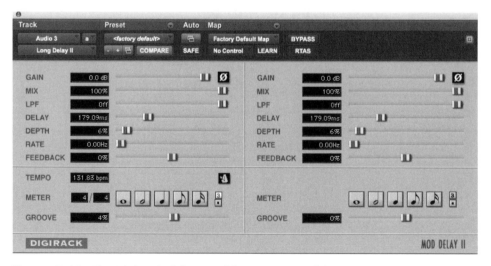

Figure 12.16 The DigiRack delays enable you to set delay times in relation to musical tempos—often a good idea!

Unfortunately, some older delays (especially the external, hardware variety and some third-party plug-ins) only allow you to specify delay times in milliseconds, not note value/bpm, and so on. Here's a method to calculate delay in milliseconds within Pro Tools:

1. Change the Main counter (either in the Transport window or at the top of the Edit window) from Bars:Beats to Min:Secs.

2. Switch to Grid mode and use the Grid Value selector to choose Bars:Beats as the grid time units and the desired note value as the grid increment. The increments of the grid (at your specified Grid value) now appear as blue vertical lines in the Edit window.

3. Use the Selector tool to highlight a duration of only one increment anywhere within a track. The Length field now displays the duration of your selection in milliseconds.

4. Open up the Plug-In window and type that number into the Delay plug-in's Delay field. If you were in 4/4 time, for example, with the tempo cranked up to 180bpm (beats per minute), an ⅛ note would be 166ms and a ¼ note triplet would be 222ms. (Although Min:Secs timings are only accurate to the nearest millisecond, note that the delay times can actually be adjusted as fine as hundredths of a millisecond. If you need greater precision—perhaps because you're going to use high Feedback values in the delay so that a large number of repeats will stay in time to the tempo without drifting—you may have to break out the calculator!)

Aside from helping your mix sound less cluttered when multiple delays are used, synchronizing your delays to a subdivision of the musical beat has another advantage: When bouncing out loops from selections that contain delays (for example, for an interactive CD-ROM background, sampler, or loop-based audio program), you'll get smoother loops when your selection doesn't end randomly between two delay repeats.

bpm: The Not-So-Secret Formula 60 divided by the bpm equals the duration of each beat in seconds (but you knew that). If you prefer to calculate the duration of each beat in milliseconds, it's 60,000 divided by the bpm, of course. If your tempo is 120 beats per minute (bpm) in 4/4 time, each ¼ note is 500ms (and each ½ note is a full second, and each ⅛ note is 250ms). If your tempo is 150bpm in 6/8 time, each ⅛ note is 400ms. What about ticks, you say? Pro Tools divides every ¼ note into 960 ticks ... or every ⅛ note into 480 ticks if you're in 6/8 time, for example. The actual duration of each tick depends on the tempo setting. If the tempo is 120bpm, each tick actually represents 500ms/960, or about .520833333ms. Aren't you glad you asked?

Summary

Obviously, the suggestions in this chapter barely scratch the surface and don't approach the subject of how sampler instruments (including Digidesign's own Structure, which is also available in a free downloadable version) can be extremely useful for creating grooves and manipulating audio samples. The power is there to create remarkable mixes, and as you surely know, thousands of hit records have been created in Pro Tools. Get in there and start working!

13 A Multitrack Music Session

This chapter takes a look at using Pro Tools with multiple live musicians in the studio as opposed to working alone in your project studio. This presents some particular challenges—for example, providing multiple cue mixes for performers (because they won't all want to hear the same headphone mix), dealing with monitoring latency issues on Pro Tools LE and M-Powered hardware configurations, and configuring the Pro Tools mixer to easily switch modes from tracking to editing to mixing. (Unlike the analog recording process, in Pro Tools, you're often doing all three things at once.) This chapter also provides a brief overview of strategies for live recording with a basic Pro Tools system (that is, without a Venue configuration). Note, though, that it doesn't exhaustively explore all the aspects of music production with Pro Tools...that's a topic to fill an entire book!

Your own studio projects will be different, but for the sake of our hypothetical session, let's assume that the input source requirements for our studio recording mirror those shown in Table 13.1.

This band wants to record all at once rather than layering tracks one by one, although they will later overdub a replacement vocal and perhaps some backing vocals or a solo. We're obviously assuming here that you have a MIDI interface on your Pro Tools configuration and that your audio hardware allows recording 16 simultaneous analog audio inputs—for example, the 96i I/O. Other interfaces with only eight analog inputs, like the Digi 003 and Digi 002 families, 96 I/O, and 192 I/O, could also have an eight-channel mic preamp plugged into their ADAT Lightpipe digital input. (The 192 I/O alternatively supports eight-channel TDIF digital input and could be expanded up to 16 channels of analog input via a 192 AD card.)

We're also assuming that you have sufficient microphone preamps for recording all these microphone sources. As a general rule, analog audio inputs on most Digidesign audio interfaces for Pro Tools|HD systems accept only line-level signals. There are only two mic-level inputs on Digidesign's Mbox 2 family (and none at all on the Mbox 2 Micro!), four on the Digi 003 and Digi 002, one on M-Audio's FireWire Solo, eight on the ProFire 2626, five on the NRV10...and you're going to need 12 for this session! You could use a good analog mixer with direct channel outputs or, even better, a couple of dedicated multichannel microphone preamplifiers, like Digidesign's PRE high-end mic preamp (see Figure 13.1); Focusrite's OctoPre eight-channel mic preamp with optional digital outputs; PreSonus' DigiMAX, an eight-channel

Table 13.1 Sample Input Source Requirements

Input	Instrument	Description	Location
Audio inputs 1–8	Drums	Eight microphones: kick, snare, hi-hat, two rack toms, floor tom, plus left/right overheads	In drum booth
Audio input 9	Bass	Direct mono signal from bass preamp	In main room
Audio input 10	Electric guitar	Microphone on amplifier	In main room
Audio inputs 11–12	Acoustic guitar	One on the bridge of the guitar, another over the fingerboard where it meets the body (angled slightly back toward the sound hole)	In isolation booth #1
Audio inputs 13–14	MIDI keyboard	Two direct audio outs for monitoring only (because you're recording this MIDI performance data on a Pro Tools Instrument track, to facilitate subsequent sound selection and editing)	In main room
Audio input 15	Saxophone	Microphone	In isolation booth #2
Audio input 16	Lead vocal (reference track while recording)	Microphone	In isolation booth #3
MIDI input	MIDI In from keyboard		

mic preamp with ADAT Lightpipe output; or any larger combination of single and dual-channel mic preamps—whatever your budget permits!

Track Setup and Click Track for Recording

First of all, you need to create a new session with audio tracks for all the sources you are going to record! You'll also create a click track via the Track > New > Create Click Track menu command (unless you have already configured your Preferences to create a click track automatically), plus a stereo Instrument track that will not only record the MIDI performance from the keyboard but also monitor its audio while recording. You will create additional Aux Inputs to use as send destinations for effects (even during recording, to provide a less sterile-sounding

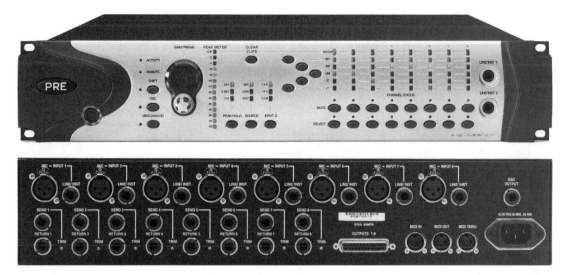

Figure 13.1 You can configure Digidesign's PRE, an eight-channel high-end microphone preamp, from within the Pro Tools software (via MIDI). Its settings are recalled when you reopen the session.

headphone mix for the performers). In fact, you will create several Aux Inputs strictly for use during the recording phase of this project to provide different cue mixes for different groups of performers. Note that this requires multiple headphone amplifiers, since you want to feed a different mix to each of them from one of the output pairs on your Pro Tools audio interface.

Track Setup for Recording

This is one of the remarkable things about working with a digital audio workstation: Within the limitations of your system configuration and the design of the software itself, you configure your mixer with exactly the number of tracks and effect sends that the project requires—no more, no less. You can even reconfigure the mixer during different phases of a single project—for example, recording, editing, and mixdown.

Create Audio Tracks and Aux Inputs

For the recording phase of this project, you need to create audio tracks to record input signals and an Instrument track for the external keyboard. Aux Inputs will also be used to provide effects in the performers' headphone mix. The initial positions of new tracks reflect their order in the New Tracks dialog box. You can change track order at any time, but using the creation order described here will help you avoid having to drag tracks around afterward.

1. Create a new Pro Tools session. Then choose Track > New (Shift+Command+N in Mac, Shift+Ctrl+N in Windows) to open the New Tracks dialog box (see Figure 13.2). Use the pop-up selectors to specify five mono audio tracks (in Samples timebase, for now—this can be changed later) for the kick, snare, hi-hat, plus the rack and floor toms.

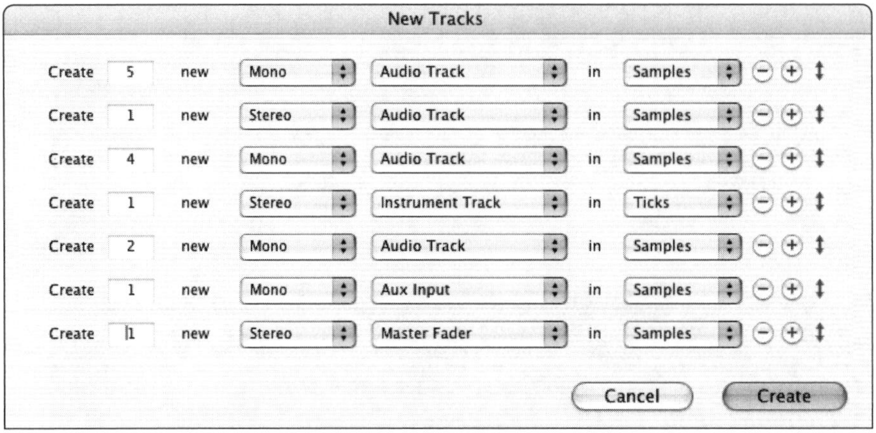

Figure 13.2 You can create multiple track types simultaneously in the New Tracks dialog box.

Then click the plus sign (+) button to create another row in the New Tracks dialog box. (As you create the following tracks, you will repeat this process for adding each new row while still within the dialog box.)

2. Create a single stereo audio track for the drum overheads.

3. Create four mono audio tracks—one for the bass, one for the electric guitar, and two for the acoustic guitar microphones. (Even though the two acoustic guitar micro-phones will be panned hard left and right, they will be recorded to two separate mono tracks so that you can apply different EQ, compression, and so on to each.)

4. Create one stereo Instrument track to record your keyboard player's performance. (It will default to Ticks timebase.) The Instrument track will serve a similar function to an Aux Input, allowing you to monitor the keyboard as an external audio source. At the same time, you will use the Instrument track to record the MIDI output from the keyboard, giving you flexibility to edit or expand this part later—but don't forget to record the result to an audio track if the performer is going to walk out of the studio with this particular keyboard before you finish mixing!

5. Create two more mono audio tracks, for the saxophone and lead vocal.

6. If Pro Tools has not already created one for you by default in this new session (accord-ing to your user preferences in versions 7.3 and higher), select the Track > New > Create Click Track menu command to generate the metronome sound.

7. Create one stereo Master Fader (we're assuming output pair 1–2 will be the source for your stereo mix).

8. Click the Create button to close this dialog box and create the new tracks.

9.   Open the Options menu and choose Pre-Fader Metering. This enables you to look at the level of the signal as it enters the inputs of your audio interface. If the level in the meter hits red, lower the audio level output from the source as you risk creating a clipped, distorted recording of the signal.

10.   Save your session! If you don't save often, don't complain later if you lose your work!

Learn These Keyboard Shortcuts in the New Tracks Dialog Box! As you start to get comfortable in Pro Tools, you can really speed up the setup for new Pro Tools sessions by learning the following shortcuts for each row in the New Tracks dialog box:

■   To toggle the number of channels between mono and stereo (and multitrack, on HD systems), hold down the Command key (Ctrl key in Windows) and press the left/right arrow keys.

■   To toggle between audio, Aux Input, Master Fader, VCA Master (HD only), MIDI, and Instrument track types, hold down the Command key (Ctrl key in Windows) and press the up/down arrow keys.

■   To toggle the track timebase between ticks and samples, hold down the Command+Option keys (Ctrl+Alt in Windows) and press the up/down arrow keys.

■   To add a new row for creating more tracks of a different type without leaving this dialog box, hold down the Command+Shift keys (Ctrl+Shift in Windows) and press the down arrow key. (If you press the up arrow key instead, the current row will be deleted.)

■   As in other Pro Tools dialog boxes, you can use the Tab key (or Shift+Tab) to toggle between the Number of Tracks fields in successive rows.

Name Your Tracks; Select Their Input Sources

Next, you should edit all your track names. Not only does this make it easier to see what's going on in your mix, it also affects how region names are created when you start recording.

1.   If necessary, switch to the Mix window. Rename tracks Audio 1 through Audio 6 Kick, Snare, Hi-hat, Rack Tom, Mid Tom, and Floor Tom, respectively. As you do, notice the Next and Previous buttons in the Track Name/Comments dialog box. Holding down the Command key (Ctrl key in Windows) as you press the right or left arrow key is the keyboard shortcut for these buttons. Get in the habit of naming all your tracks and Aux Inputs before closing this dialog box!

2.   Change the stereo audio track's name (currently Audio 7) to Overheads. Click the OK button to close this dialog box for now.

3. Use the input selectors of the mono drum tracks to select inputs 1–6. The following order is fairly typical for mic inputs in drum tracks: kick, snare, hi-hat, toms from higher to lower pitch, and then overheads, left-right. At any point in the recording and mixing process, you can drag the drum tracks into any order that's convenient, regardless of their input assignments.

4. Using the input selector for the stereo Overheads track, choose input pair 7–8 as its input source for recording.

5. Rename the next track (currently called Audio 9) Bass, selecting input 9 as its source.

6. Rename the remainder of your audio tracks, selecting the appropriate inputs for their recording sources. While you're at it, pan the two acoustic guitar tracks hard left and right. (Again, the reason you're using two mono tracks for the stereo-mic'ed acoustic guitar instead of a single stereo track is so that you can place different EQs and such on the signal from each microphone.)

7. Rename the stereo Instrument track Kybd. Select input pair 13–14 as its source (where you've connected audio outputs from the MIDI keyboard out in the studio); see Figure 13.3. If necessary, enable display of the Instrument section of the Mix window via the View > Mix Window > Instruments command and select the MIDI input and channel where the keyboard is connected to your MIDI interface.

Name Your Tracks at the Beginning! Naming tracks before you begin recording is *important*. In Pro Tools, all the audio regions created by recording inherit the name of their source tracks. In a session this large, if all the original audio files and auto-created regions in the Regions List (and within the tracks, for that matter) have cryptic names like Audio 6_01, you *will* get confused!

---

8. Save your session! You're now ready to start record-enabling audio tracks so that you can check input levels. Remember that input levels have to be adjusted *at the source* (the line output, the mic preamp, and so on) if you see any clipping indicators. (Don't stress about recording the absolutely hottest possible levels, either—especially when you're recording at 24-bit resolution. You're not fighting to overcome hiss and other limitations of analog tape, and digital clipping *always* sounds very nasty—not at all like the warm tape saturation that's sometimes a desirable effect.) It's also worth mentioning here that performers tend to hold back a little while checking levels. Inevitably, when the record light is on, they sing a little harder and play a little louder. Leave yourself some headroom. Also remember that volume faders on audio tracks have no effect on the audio signal level being recorded to disk!

Figure 13.3 At this point in the session, you're using an Instrument track to monitor the keyboard instead of recording its audio to disk, since you expect to use its recorded MIDI data with a software instrument plug-in later. Overhead microphones for the drum set are on a single stereo track. You're using two microphones on the acoustic guitar, but recording them to separate mono tracks.

9.   As you are checking input levels, adjust your tracks' main volume faders to obtain an approximate mix for the song. You will use this later as the basis for your cue mixes; see the section "Setting Up a Cue Mix with Effects" later in this chapter.

Click Track

The band wants to record this song with a click track (which, incidentally, is going to make it very easy to edit in Grid mode afterward), so you need to set this up before recording. Some people opt for using an external MIDI source for click sounds. Others who want to conserve DSP resources and/or extremely precise metronome timing—a legitimate concern in complex sessions with many tracks—will either record the output of the Click plug-in to an audio

Figure 13.4 The Click plug-in lets you choose from a variety of metronome sounds. In versions 7.3 and higher, multiple Click plug-ins can be active simultaneously in separate tracks, each with its own metronome sound, and you can set your MIDI preferences so that a click track is created automatically in each new session.

track or use repeated audio regions on a track as their click sound. For this example, you're going to use the Click plug-in on an Aux Input track as the source for your metronome sound. The options in the Click plug-in window are shown in Figure 13.4.

If you prefer, the metronome click from Pro Tools (based on the current tempo and meter settings) could also be transmitted as a MIDI note event so that some external MIDI drum machine or synthesizer produces the click sound (which would then need to be monitored and possibly recorded into the Pro Tools session). Most users will opt to use the Click plug-in, however. For the sake of simplicity, let's assume your entire song is in 4/4 time (Pro Tools' default time signature) and the musicians want ¼-note clicks.

1.   In the Transport window, double-click the Metronome button to open the Click/Countoff Options dialog box, shown in Figure 13.5.

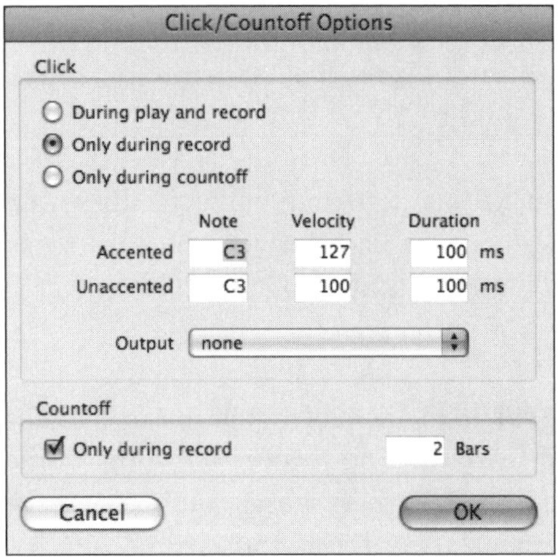

Figure 13.5 The Click/Countoff Options dialog box. Here, the Click plug-in's audio output is selected.

2.   Because you're going to use the Click plug-in's own metronome click sound in this session, leave the MIDI output selector in this dialog box set to None (instead of selecting any other MIDI destination).

3.   If necessary, click the Transport window's Metronome button to enable the metronome click sound.

4.   Press the spacebar to start playback in Pro Tools. You should now hear the click sound (from the plug-in) in the Click Aux Input at your session's current tempo. In the pop-up Presets selector within the Click plug-in window, notice that you can choose from various metronome sounds.

5.   Now you need to adjust the tempo, with the assistance of your performers. Be aware that musicians' perceptions of appropriate click tempos are notoriously unreliable while they are not actually playing. You can always set the tempo manually in the Transport window's Tempo field, but you'll probably find that tapping in a manual tempo setting is usually much more reliable. Have the band run through the song until they get their groove on. First, make sure that the Tempo Ruler Enable button is disabled (it has a "conductor" icon in the MIDI Controls section of the Transport window). Click the Current Tempo field and use the T key on your computer keyboard to tap in the tempo as the musicians play. Alternatively, you could enable Use MIDI to Tap Tempo in the MIDI tab of the Preferences dialog box, then use a MIDI keyboard controller—such as a key on a keyboard or pad on a drum module—to tap in a manual tempo.

Grooves on Tap When you set click-track tempos for musical groups, tapping in a manual tempo is *always* the most reliable method! As described previously, have your musicians simply play through the song a couple times while you set an appropriate tempo—before you even let them hear a click track. Be aware, however, that bands with less studio experience often lose the sense of appropriate song tempos when they're in cold and unfamiliar studio conditions, typically ending up slower when the adrenaline rush of live performance isn't there. In that case, ask the band to bring a tape of any good live performance or rehearsal version and use *that* for tapping in your manual tempo setting. (Sound quality doesn't matter for this purpose; a cassette is fine.) Even if you *do* end up backing the tempo off slightly from there (because live tempos are sometimes too fast for studio recordings), everyone will be happier in the long run!

In the Beginning, There Was a Drum Fill... You might think that once you calculate the proper tempo, you enable the Count Off button in the Transport window, and you're all set to record; all the musicians will jump in at the beginning of the session timeline, at bar 1, beat 1. Wrong! It turns out that the drummer plays a couple of pick-up notes to lead into the first bar. When recording bands to a click track in Pro Tools, you should learn how to use the Event > Renumber Bars command (see Figure 13.6) to establish some point farther into the Bars:Beats timeline (bar 5, for example) as bar 1. That way, you're sure to capture any pick-up notes (or studio chatter that you may later decide to leave in the final mix) at the beginning of the session timeline. More importantly, the bar numbers you see in Pro Tools will make sense in terms of the song structure you discuss with the musicians. You can also use the Move Song Start command in the Time Operations window for this purpose. If the Tempo ruler is visible in the Edit window, another method is to enable Grid edit mode and simply drag the Song Start Marker to the desired position.

Figure 13.6   The Renumber Bars dialog box enables you to establish some point farther into the timeline as bar 1 to allow for pick-up bars, anticipated notes, intro fills, and so on.

Creating Effects and a Drum Submix

As we've laid out in previous chapters, the typical location for reverb and delay effects is on an Aux Input track whose input is set to one of the internal mixing busses in Pro Tools. You then use sends from individual tracks to add their audio to the input bus for the Reverb Aux Input, for example. The other typical use of Aux Input tracks is to create mix subgroups that combine the outputs from multiple source audio tracks. In this example, you're also going to bus the outputs of all the drum tracks to a single, stereo Aux Input. This simplifies the adjustment of the overall level of the drum mix and also allows for the placement of effects on the entire drum submix rather than on each individual drum track.

1.   In the Mix window, create two stereo Aux Input tracks. Name them Reverb and Drums. Option-click (or Alt-click in Windows) on their volume faders to set them to 0dB.

2.   Set the input of Reverb to bus pair 1–2 and the input of Drums to bus pair 3–4.

3.   Place the D-Verb plug-in on the Reverb Aux Input track so that sends from any track to bus pair 1–2 pass through its Reverb plug-in.

4.   Use the output selectors of your six drum tracks to change all their current output assignments to bus 3–4, which is the selected input source for the Drums Aux Input track you just created. Now you can control the overall volume of the drums in the mix with a single volume fader, as shown in Figure 13.7. While you're at it, you could also choose

Figure 13.7 The outputs of all these drum tracks are assigned to stereo bus pair 3–4, the selected input source for the Drums Aux Input. Compressor and EQ plug-ins on this Aux Input track affect the entire the drum submix.

Setup > I/O and rename stereo bus pairs 1–2 and 3–4; call them RevSend and DrumSub, for example. For that matter, if you're using version 7.3 or higher, busses, input paths, and output paths can be renamed in a pop-up menu that appears when you right-click any send button or input/output selector assigned to them in the Mix window.

5. Create a stereo send to bus pair 1–2 (the Reverb Aux Input's input) on send A of the vocal track. You'll probably end up creating additional sends to the Reverb Aux Input from other tracks as the musicians request it.

Don't Smoosh Your Crashes! In the current example, you've assigned all drum tracks to a single stereo Aux Input track, mainly for the convenience of having a single volume fader (and Mute/Solo buttons) to control the entire drum submix. The other advantage of doing this is that you can apply a single stereo effect to the entire drum submix—for example, a Compressor plug-in on this Drums Aux Input track. Be careful, though; you may not like what a large degree of compression does to the sound of your cymbal crashes. We generally prefer to submix everything *except* the stereo overhead microphones (presumably your primary source for cymbals) to a stereo Aux Input when heavy stereo compression is to be applied. You could always assign the output of this Aux Input (and that of the stereo overheads) to yet *another* stereo bus/Aux Input if you still want a single volume fader to control the entire drum submix. A different approach to drum compression would be to use sends from individual drum tracks (but not the cymbals, perhaps) to a stereo Aux Input where heavier compression is being applied and then blend that together with the main stereo drum mix.

Recording Modes Pro Tools' destructive recording mode is discussed in Chapter 8, "Menu Selections: Highlights." You can toggle it on and off by choosing Options > Destructive Record. Unlike the default non-destructive recording mode—which creates new regions for each additional take, leaving previous ones intact—destructive recording mode erases any previously recorded audio data in the area of the track being recorded. When recording rhythm sections, for example, you may occasionally work in destructive recording mode to conserve disk space; if you know that you have barely enough available disk space for a multitrack project, it doesn't always make sense to retain numerous false starts, especially at higher resolutions and 16 or 24 tracks each! (Of course, you can always use the Select Unused and Clear Selected commands in the Regions List submenu at any point to eliminate unwanted audio files and recover disk space.) Especially when recording vocal and instrumental overdubs, however, non-destructive recording mode offers more flexibility and the very useful possibility of compositing an ideal version from several takes at some later point in the process. Always using non-destructive recording also allows for the possibility of rediscovering some brilliant earlier take that no one recognized as a "keeper" at the time. Loop recording mode (also described in Chapter 8) and the Takes List pop-up menu are other invaluable tools during the overdubbing process; be sure to learn about these.

Setting Up a Cue Mix with Effects

At this point, you've created audio tracks for every input and created Aux Input tracks to monitor the Click plug-in and external MIDI keyboard (whose audio output is not currently being recorded, although that certainly would be an option). You can hear all the tracks, even adjusting the volumes and pans for each (without affecting the levels recorded to disk) to get an idea of how the mix will start to take shape. You're almost ready to record—but you still need to provide a cue mix so that the musicians can hear each other in their headphones as they play. Not only does the cue mix need to be unaffected by your volume changes, mutes, solos, and so on as they're recording, but different musicians are going to require different mixes to be comfortable during the recording process.

Let's assume you have three stereo headphone amps out in the studio, so you can provide up to three distinct cue mixes (from three different stereo output pairs on your Pro Tools audio interface). Here's a typical scenario:

- The guitars, keyboards, sax, and trumpet want more or less the entire, balanced mix in their headphones. In our case, the source for this mix will be outputs 5–6 on the audio interface, but it could be any output pair other than the one you're using for your main stereo mix output.

- The vocalist wants to hear the vocals a little louder than in the band's mix and would like plenty of reverb. The source for this cue mix will be outputs 7–8 on the audio interface.

- The bass player and drummer want lots of their own instruments so they can lock up a groove; they also want the click track extra loud in their headphones. The source for this cue mix will be outputs 9–10 on the audio interface.

We're going to create Aux Input tracks for each of the three cue mixes and then use sends from source audio tracks so that you can create distinct mixes for each group of instrumentalists. As with many things in Pro Tools, there are many ways to accomplish this; the options presented here may or may not be appropriate for your working style.

One of the simplest methods would be to use multiple output assignments for each audio track and Aux Input. For example, while using physical outputs 1 and 2 on your audio hardware for monitoring in the control room, you can create an additional output assignment from all individual audio tracks and Aux Inputs to outputs 3 and 4 (where you've connected the headphone distribution amplifier, providing an identical mix for all the performers).

Creating Multiple Output Assignments on Audio and Aux Input Tracks As you know, the Output selector for each audio, Aux Input, and Instrument track determines the main destination for its audio. To create an *additional* routing assignment for a track's main output, hold down the Control key (Start key in Windows) as you reopen its Output selector. Afterward, a plus sign (+) in the Output selector indicates any tracks that have more than one output assignment. If you also hold down the Option key (Alt key in Windows) as you select an extra output assignment for a track, it is simultaneously added to all tracks. Incidentally, you can also assign each send on a track to multiple destinations using the same Control key (or Start key in Windows) technique.

This method (multiple output assignments from tracks) isn't very practical for control room/ studio situations; you can't solo/mute tracks or change their levels during recording because doing so would affect what the performers hear in their headphone mix. In most recording situations, therefore, it's usually preferable to create a separate cue mix for the performers' headphones that won't be affected by changes you make to the control-room mix while recording (for example, soloing a bass track during recording because you think you're hearing a buzz from the instrument's pickups).

Creating Multiple Cue Mix Sends

This is the classic approach, most similar to the method used on traditional mixing boards. It can be very effective and offers maximum flexibility for adjusting the level and pan position of individual instruments in each separate cue mix.

1. Create three stereo Aux Input tracks. Name them CueMix, CueVox, and CueRhyth.

2. Set the input of CueMix to busses 5–6, the input of CueVox to busses 7–8, and the input of CueRhyth to busses 9–10.

3. Create a stereo send C on each audio track *except* the drum tracks to bus pair 5–6. Click the Pre button in the Output window for each send as it is created to make them all *pre*-fader sends; that way, they will not be affected by the source track's main volume fader or Mute button. In other words, you're routing all these pre-fader sends to the input of the CueMix Aux Input via bus 5–6. (If you like, choose Setup > I/O Setup and change the names of busses 5 and 6 to Cue-L and Cue-R, respectively. Just a thought....)

4. Create a similar stereo send C (to bus 5–6, or Cue-L/Cue-R) on the Kybd stereo Aux Input that you're using to monitor the keyboards, on the Click mono Aux Input, on the Drums stereo Aux Input (your submix for all the drum tracks), and on the Reverb stereo Aux Input so that these can also be heard in the cue mix.

Creating Sends on All Tracks, Copying Sends and Plug-ins If you hold down the Option key (Alt key in Windows) while creating a send on any track, the same send is created in that position for all audio tracks as well as all Aux Input (and Instrument) tracks. This can be a real timesaver, but in our example, you would then have to *un-assign* some of these send copies because you don't want both the original drum tracks and their drum submix to go to the same send, nor would you want to create sends from one Aux Input to the other two (or to itself, in this case). While it's slightly advanced, one way around this is to previously create a Mix group for all the tracks that will need sends created for the cue mix. Then use the Mix Groups list to display only this "needs cue send" group of tracks before using the aforementioned Option (Alt) key technique. Alternatively, you can Option-drag (Alt-drag in Windows) to copy sends from one track or position to another.

---

5.   To quickly adjust the pans/levels of your stereo sends to bus 5–6, change the view in the Mix window. Ordinarily, all sends appear as buttons, and you click any one of them to open the Sends Editor window. Choose View > Sends A–E and select Send C. Send C's Pan, Level, Mute, and Pre/Post buttons are now simultaneously visible on all tracks. (Figure 13.8 shows the two different views available for sends in the Pro Tools Mix window.)

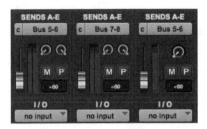
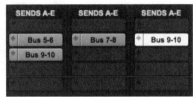

Figure 13.8   By default, the Sends section of the Mix (or Edit) window displays up to 10 possible send assignments—sections A–E and F–J for each audio Aux Input or Instrument track—with a bus or physical output assignment for each. Under View > Sends, you can also choose to show individual controls for one send position (globally, on all tracks), including Level, Pan, Mute, and Pre/Post.

6.   In order to manually adjust your send levels from each track to the cue mix, you also need to mute all audio tracks, but not the CueMix Aux Input. Because all your sends are pre-fader, they're unaffected by track Mute buttons. Also, if you Command-click (Ctrl-click in Windows) the Solo buttons for all your Aux Inputs, they will be "solo-safe"—that is, they won't be muted even if you solo an audio track.

7.   Repeat steps 1–6, creating a send D from all these tracks to bus 7–8 and a send E to bus 9–10.

Copying Track Volume and Pan Settings to Sends in Pro Tools HD   If you're working on an HD system, you could select all the audio tracks for which you've created a send and choose Edit > Copy to Send. (This command isn't available in LE or M-Powered versions of Pro Tools.) Specify send C as the destination for copying each track's current main volume and pan values (then D, then E). Of course, you will able to fine-tune these levels and pan positions afterward. Otherwise, on LE and M-Powered systems, you must adjust the volume and pan settings manually in each send's Output window.

---

8.   Now let's get your three cue mixes routed out into the studio so you can start to record! Set the output of the CueMix Aux Input to outputs 5–6 on the audio interface, CueVox to outputs 7–8, and CueRhyth to outputs 9–10. (You can use any output

pairs you like; we chose these because they might be easier to remember since they match the bus pair assignments for each separate cue mix.) See Figure 13.9 for how your Mix window looks when you use this method for individual sends to three different cue mixes.

Figure 13.9 Three cue mixes: Each audio track (plus the Drums, Kybd, and Click Aux Input tracks) has a separate pre-fader send for each cue mix destination. (Notice that we have also created a post-fader send A from the vocal track to the 1–2 bus pair selected as the input for our reverb Aux Input.) You can store a basic track, send, and Aux Input setup for cue mixes as a session template for your studio.

9.   Unmute all your audio tracks; you're ready to record! First, though, have the band do another run-through not only to confirm your input levels but to accommodate their requests for changes in the cue mixes.

10. One last issue remains to be addressed: The output assignments from each of your cue mix Aux Input tracks are now set directly to the output path where the headphone distribution boxes for the performers are attached, so how do *you* hear a cue mix in the control room if you ever need to make adjustments? Assuming the cue mix outputs from your audio interface are not passing through any mixing board in the control room on their way out to the studio—in which case you could just as easily have used Master Faders for each cue mix bus instead of Aux Input tracks—one method would be to create a stereo send from each cue mix Aux Input to the main stereo output. You normally keep that send muted, except when you need to hear that cue mix; just Option-mute (Alt-mute in Windows) all the other tracks as before, and unmute the send from that cue mix's Aux Input.

Markers and Selections As mentioned in Chapter 8, Pro Tools allows you to create two types of memory locations: *markers* and *selections*. Markers identify *single points* in time and can appear in the Edit window's Markers ruler. Selections identify a *range* within the timeline, such as the bridge of a song, the points where a guitar solo will be punched in/out, and so on.

Both markers and selections can be either *absolute* (a specific Minutes:Seconds reference) or *relative* (a location in Bar:Beat, whose absolute position depends on the current Pro Tools Tempo setting). For this hypothetical session, with a click track governed by the Pro Tools tempo, relative memory locations are most useful because your discussions with the musicians will generally refer to bars and beats rather than minutes and seconds.

You can drop markers on the fly any time, even while recording; just press the Enter key on the numeric keypad. If you find it cumbersome or distracting to negotiate the New Memory Location dialog box while doing so, choose the Editing tab of the Preferences dialog box and enable the Auto-Name Memory Locations When Playing option. Marker 1, Marker 2, and so on will automatically be created without requiring you to open the dialog box. You can always double-click a marker to change its name or properties, or drag it within the Markers ruler to change its position. If you're in Grid mode, marker movements are snapped to the nearest grid increment.

You can also use markers to reset where Pro Tools will start playback. To reset the Transport window's current Start position, just click a marker in the Memory Locations window or the Markers ruler (choose View > Rulers > Markers to make the Markers ruler visible in the Edit window). If you click one marker and then Shift-click another, the

Transport window's Start and End values are set to those positions. (This can be very useful for overdubs or to perfect mix parameters while looping a specific section of the song.) For example, to select the entire second verse for playback or punch-in recording, you might click the marker Verse2 and then Shift-click Chorus2. If Link Edit and Timeline Selection is enabled (either via the Operations menu selection or by enabling the Edit window's Link Selections button), not only are both the edit and timeline (play) selections set, but the contents of the current track are also selected between these markers. This will make it quick and easy to copy entire sections later (holding down the Option key—Alt key in Windows—as you drag with the Separation Grabber) in order to create your slammin' extended-play remix!

Making the Most of Available Tracks

On large sessions with many source audio tracks, you may reach the limit of available playback voices in your Pro Tools system. In music projects, this can happen sooner than you think on 48-voice Pro Tools LE systems such as the Mbox 2, Digi 003 and Digi 002 families, or M-Powered systems using M-Audio hardware. (LE and M-Powered versions can be expanded to 64 mono/stereo tracks via the Music Production Toolkit option, and LE can be expanded to a maximum of 128 mono tracks with the Complete Production Toolkit.) If you are an HD user, this will be the time to review how Pro Tools voice allocation operates (as explained in Chapter 2, "Pro Tools Terms and Concepts") and see whether you can make this work to your advantage. On HD systems, if audio regions on two tracks never coincide (for example, a saxophone solo in the middle of a song and a backing vocal track at the end), they can share the same voice assignment; the effects, sends, and output assignments of one track are still completely independent of the other.

In Pro Tools LE, when your tracks exceed the number of available voices you have left, the lowest tracks without a voice allotted to them will appear grayed out, as shown in Figure 13.10. Remove any voiced tracks (or make voiced tracks inactive via the Track > Make Inactive command), and the corresponding number of grayed-out unvoiced tracks will become fully voiced and active.

Thinking Ahead: Arm Yourself for Editing When recording drums, once you have your basic levels set up, ask the drummer to give you one clean, solid hit on each drum and cymbal. Record these, and be sure to rename and keep these regions in your session. You don't have to make a big deal to the performers about possibly needing these to fix something in the mix—but you never know!

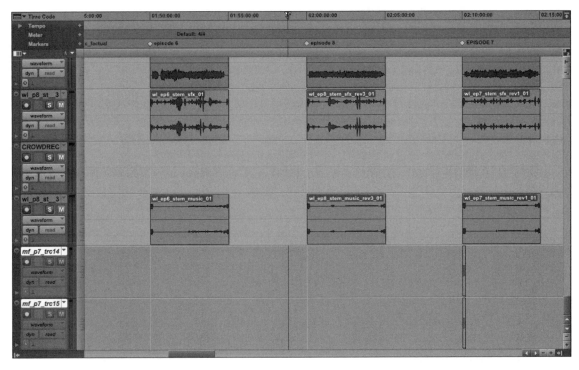

Figure 13.10 The bottom two tracks on this Pro Tools LE system have no free voices available to them. They are grayed out to show that they are either awaiting a free voice or made inactive via a menu command.

Tips for Remote Recording with Pro Tools

Recording live ensemble performances with Pro Tools is indeed a practical possibility. Naturally, you will want to have as compact a setup as possible, possibly rackmounting most of your gear for quick load in/out. Here are a few tricks we've picked up along the way:

- **Mixing board.** It can be very cost effective to use a conventional mixing board with multiple microphone inputs and individual line outs on the input channels. Obviously, the mixer's microphone preamps need to be high quality to get acceptable results. Fortunately, a number of economical small mixers fit the bill and might also be an ideal mixer for your Pro Tools project studio—not only providing additional microphone inputs, but also useful for monitoring multiple sources in your studio configuration. If your mixer is rackmountable, that's also a benefit, because you can cable its channel outputs to your audio interface inputs (and cable the main output pair of your audio interface to a mixer channel to monitor the Pro Tools mix output) before you even wheel your rig into the venue.

- **Microphone preamplifier.** Another way to go is a dedicated, multichannel microphone preamplifier. Options range from the high end (for example, Digidesign's PRE or Focusrite's

OctoPre) to more economical mid-range units for professional applications from PreSonus and others. Again, the fact that these are generally rackmountable can be very attractive because you can arrive at the performance with all the cable connections between the microphone preamplifier and your rackmounted audio interface already in place.

■ **Compression/limiting.** Levels can be very unpredictable in live performance! When you're recording a live performance (or conference), you can't risk an unexpected peak in level ruining the historical recording that you're being paid to capture. Be conservative with your input levels. Although you might try to maximize input levels to improve signal/error ratio as incoming audio is digitized in a relatively controlled studio situation, it would be foolhardy to be overly aggressive about this in a live performance situation! That said, good compression/limiting on your microphone inputs can also give you peace of mind—and maybe even save your skin on occasion. Because you have compression in Pro Tools, the idea isn't to use compression to shape the sound, consistently clamping down on the signal; instead, you want to avoid the occasional "rogue" peak from producing a horrific digital distortion sound that would mar an overall good-sounding recording. You can always correct low levels in the mix afterwards, but the clipping distortion produced during recording will be there to stay.

Recording Live Theater If you record live theater, you may find that performer levels onstage are even more unpredictable than a rock band's club performance (which is saying a lot!). At any point, an actor is likely to step right up to your PZM microphone and scream at the top of her voice, even if her mark during rehearsal was several yards away; it's just part of the natural performance flexibility they require. But unlike a rock band, where the vocalists are close to the microphone and therefore the dynamic range has reasonable limits, in theater, each microphone is required to capture sounds anywhere from several yards to as close as a couple of feet away. It's a great idea to have compression or limiting in place for microphones that might be subject to unexpectedly extreme levels (front-of-stage microphones in theater productions, lead singers, lead guitar amplifiers, and so on).

■ **Snake.** A snake gives you a lot of XLR connectors (and usually some ¼-inch connectors) at one end of a single long cable. These connectors reappear at the other end as either a fan of separate cables/connectors or a stagebox with jacks. That's how you get all those microphone and line inputs from the stage back to your mixer and recording rig. (These should be balanced, by the way, to avoid transmission loss in longer cables; use a direct box and so on if required.) If you're sharing microphones and other input sources with another person mixing sound for the house system, you should use a splitter snake; double outputs at your end allow both you and the house mixer to get your input directly from the snake's channels. Figure 13.11 shows a typical live-recording configuration with Pro Tools.

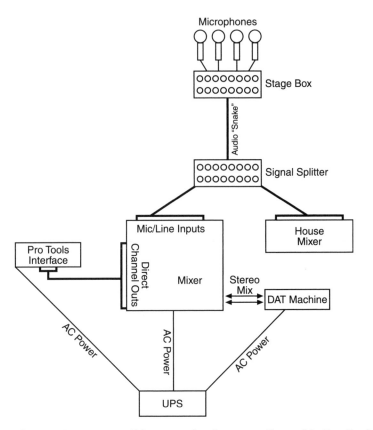

Figure 13.11 A possible setup for live recording with Pro Tools. A splitter snake provides both the recording rig and the house sound mixer with direct microphone (or line/direct box) feeds from the stage. We're using a clean portable mixer with multiple mic-level inputs and direct outputs from each channel to our multichannel Pro Tools audio interface. We're simultaneously feeding a rough stereo mix directly from the mixer to a DAT recorder as a precaution. Everything is on a UPS (uninterruptible power supply).

- **Paranoia.** Many people simultaneously record performances in stereo to a DAT recorder directly from the mixing board (rather than from the Pro Tools main L–R output). If someone kicks out your power cable or your computer hangs (it *is* a computer, after all!), at least the performance will be intact as a live stereo mix on the DAT tape. A UPS (uninterruptible power supply) may also save your reputation, kicking over to battery power until you have restored the AC (and thrashed the responsible parties, if possible). Recording a DAT mix directly from the mixing board also guarantees that you'll have documented whatever portion of the performance transpires if you have no alternative but to restart your computer.

- **Headphones and ear plugs.** As the recordist, you obviously know the usefulness of headphones. You will usually want a design that covers the ear fairly well to isolate outside sounds (often called *circumaural*, *closed-back*, or something similar, as opposed to open or semi-open). This is not only so that you can hear what's coming through the headphones in a noisy environment, but also to protect your ears when recording extremely loud performances—that is, if you're planning to *use* your ears in the future! Along the same lines, a set of musician's ear plugs is highly advisable (or at the very least some cheap foam ones that you can buy in a drugstore). If the opening bands or even the house music system blows out your ears beforehand, you may miss defects or make errors while recording—not to mention incurring lasting ear damage. Don't forget to bring along an extra set for any assistants, especially if you will be sending them onstage to make adjustments during a loud performance.

Monitoring Latency with Pro Tools LE and M-Powered Any digital audio system has some small degree of delay, or *latency*, between when an analog audio signal actually enters the system, is digitized (and/or routed within the system's internal mixing environment), and then converted back to an analog audio signal on an output of your audio hardware. Even on HD systems, whose dedicated DSP cards provide mix/routing latency times so low that for practical purposes, they're usually not an issue while recording, there is still a small amount of delay required for the A/D/A (analog > digital, digital > analog) converters themselves to do their work.

But for all native or host-based digital audio workstations that rely on the computer's processing power for their mixing/routing tasks, as is the case with all LE and M-Powered versions of Pro Tools, the large input buffer they require produces monitoring latency that is typically several milliseconds at the very least and sometimes considerably more, depending on audio resolution and other factors—enough to produce a noticeable delay. You will discover that this latency can be enough to disconcert or affect the timing of your performance if you don't deal with it properly. Using a mixing board as the front end for recording microphone sources into Pro Tools and monitoring input audio directly from the board (and not via Pro Tools) is one way to bypass this problem.

Within Pro Tools LE and M-Powered software, you can also reduce latency by using the Playback Engine dialog box to lower the Hardware Buffer Size setting to 128 (or 256) samples while recording tracks. If you have an extremely fast host computer, you can probably use this buffer setting all the time. If you're using one of the slower supported CPUs, however, beware: Lower buffer sizes can reduce how many simultaneous audio tracks can be recorded without system-performance problems such as slow screen re-draws or recording errors or affect playback of sessions with complex plug-in processing and routing setups in many tracks. If that's your case, set the buffer back to 512 or 1,024 samples when editing and mixing, especially when using processing-intensive plug-ins such as certain reverbs and software instruments.

The Low Latency Monitoring option in the Options menu of Pro Tools LE versions with the 002 interfaces, 003 interfaces, and Mbox 2 Pro provides the lowest-possible latency on outputs 1–2 of this audio hardware only. (In this case, you might have to use outputs 1–2 not only as the single cue mix send for your performers out in the studio but also for monitoring in the control room, because Pro Tools automatically bypasses all plug-ins and sends on any tracks assigned to outputs 1–2 while Low Latency Monitoring mode is active. Also, remember to disable Low Latency Monitoring mode once you start mixing; otherwise, when you bounce to disk, none of the audio from any Aux Input tracks will be included in the bounced audio file!)

The Mbox 2 and Mbox family of hardware (except for the Mbox 2 Pro, and of course the Mbox 2 Micro, which has no audio inputs) offers another interesting alternative for overcoming the latency issue. A mix knob on the front of the interface itself allows you to fade what will be heard on its analog outputs between its analog inputs and playback from Pro Tools. While recording, you could simply mute the track to which you're recording (so that its delayed signal doesn't interfere with the timing of your performance). The mix knob adjusts how much of your (dry) signal at the input(s) goes directly into the stereo mix output from the interface (or its dedicated headphone output) for zero-latency monitoring. However, when recording from a mono source—for example, one microphone on a guitar, voice, or wind instrument—be sure to also press the Mono button on the front panel so that this source will be heard in both left and right channels of your control-room monitors or headphones.

Several of the M-Audio interfaces compatible with the M-Powered version of Pro Tools also offer a similar feature via internal routing options in which selected inputs can pass directly to other outputs on the interface itself (including headphone outputs, if available) without first being routed through the Pro Tools mixing environment. This is configured via the control panel software provided with these interfaces, which can also be opened from the Pro Tools Hardware Setup dialog box.

Summary

Every musical project is different. Some classical musicians record together as an ensemble, and don't require individual cue mixes or headphones—let alone a click track. Many bands don't (or won't) record with a click track. You can still edit later in musical bars and beats; that's what the Identify Beat command in Pro Tools is for! Many bands don't record all at once, of course. Instead, they layer up tracks, perhaps starting from only the most basic rhythm section in the initial recording session.

In many cases, a single cue mix is acceptable for all the simultaneous performers. If so, you could dispense with the more complex setup described here and instead use a single pre-fader send from each track to a single output pair that feeds your performers' headphone mix. Even in this case, though, it's usually convenient to route these sends through a stereo bus to an Aux Input or Master Fader track, where you can apply a compressor or limiter to keep headphone levels under control.

Be sure to enable the Auto Backup feature (known as AutoSave in Pro Tools versions prior to 7.3) in the Operation tab of the Preferences dialog box. And one last reminder, especially important with paying clients and any group of performers out in the studio: *Save your session often as you work!* Good performances are ephemeral moments. If you lose one due to a system (or human-operator) problem or power outage because you hadn't saved for many minutes, musicians may find it difficult to forgive you! Indeed, make the File > Save shortcut Command+S (Ctrl+S in Windows) a second-nature reflex at least once a minute.

14 Postproduction and Soundtracks

This chapter explores some of Pro Tools' capabilities for film and video soundtracks. Chapter 11, "Synchronization," provides a general background on the technical aspects of SMPTE time code and an overview of synchronization methods and peripherals for a Pro Tools configuration. We focus here on basic production strategies, tips for collaborating with users of nonlinear video-editing systems (Avid, Media 100, Apple's Final Cut Pro, Adobe's Premiere, and others), and basic postproduction methods, and include a cursory overview of how you can use Pro Tools for surround mixing. This chapter (along with Chapter 11) is merely a primer for using Pro Tools in postproduction; the particulars vary immensely according to each production facility and the immediate task at hand. Indeed, there are entire books dedicated to the subject of postproduction alone!

Synchronization Setup

As discussed in Chapter 11, there are many options for synchronizing Pro Tools to SMPTE time code. These range from simple trigger sync setups (after playback starts at the correct point, Pro Tools no longer references the time-code information to maintain speed) to external reference sync (for example, house sync or black burst, providing a common reference for both Pro Tools and the video gear), and continuous resyncing/resolving Pro Tools to the time-code master (via a Sync HD or a similar device). If you principally deal with short-duration projects such as 30-second spots, your requirements may not be as stringent as for creating, say, 30-minute programs or feature films, where even a small amount of drift creates real timing problems.

Figure 14.1 shows Sync HD, a high-end synchronization peripheral from Digidesign with continuous resync/resolving capabilities for locking Pro Tools hardware with external time code or video sync. It also translates SMPTE to and from VITC (video) or LTC (audio) format. More importantly, it can continuously adjust the sample clock of your audio hardware to keep Pro Tools in sync with incoming time code over extended periods. This external, rackmounted synchronization peripheral can slave to an external video reference (for example, black burst), an industry-standard word clock, or Digidesign's 256x SuperClock. Its dual Sony 9-pin serial ports can link Transport functions of Pro Tools with external video/audio devices via the MachineControl option.

Figure 14.1 Digidesign's Sync HD is a high-end synchronization peripheral for Mac or Windows computers.

If your synchronization peripheral is a standard SMPTE interface (which translates incoming time-code location information from its audio or video format to MTC, then routes it into your computer, perhaps via the USB port), the Synchronization tab of the Setup > Peripherals dialog box tells Pro Tools the device type—for example, a generic MTC reader versus a Sync HD—and the port to which it is connected. (See Figures 14.2 and 14.3.)

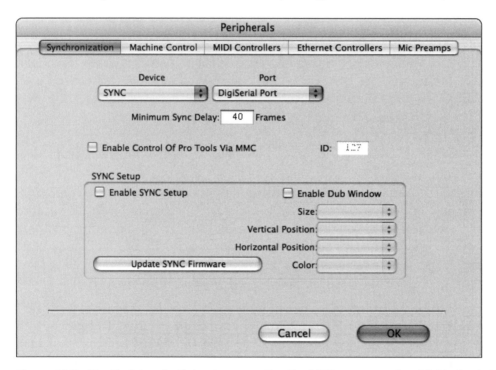

Figure 14.2 The Peripherals dialog box on a Pro Tools|HD system, using Digidesign's Sync HD, which can add a time-code window to video signals passing through it.

MachineControl

MachineControl is an option for Pro Tools|HD systems (and some of their TDM predecessors) that enables you to link the Pro Tools transport functions with professional video decks or other compatible devices via their Sony 9-pin serial ports or V-LAN, either as a master or a slave. You

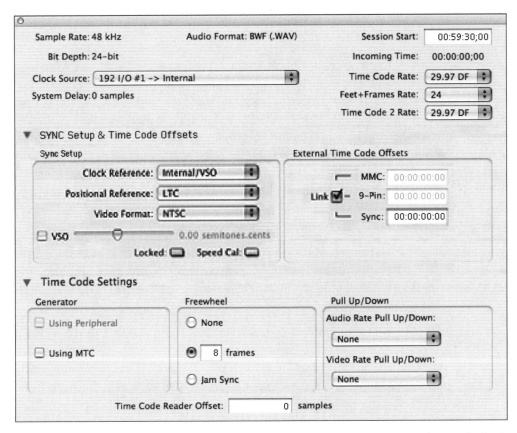

Figure 14.3 Settings in the Sync Setup section of the Session Setup window include the positional reference (the time-code source) for your synchronization peripheral.

can also remotely arm tracks on the device for recording from within Pro Tools (using the Machine Track Arming window).

MachineControl uses a serial connection to the external devices. Digidesign's Sync HD features Sony 9-pin serial ports. Because the HD Accel cards include the DigiSerial port, users who *don't* have a Sync HD can also use that DigiSerial port for the MachineControl option; otherwise, they would use the 9-pin serial port(s) on the synchronization peripheral itself. Both positional (SMPTE) and clock references are required for MachineControl to synchronize Pro Tools with other devices. A third option for MachineControl is to use MOTU's MIDI Timepiece AV (connected to the USB port) for position and clock reference and the DigiSerial Port on the HD Accel card for serial MachineControl communication with other devices.

A pop-up Transport selector in the Pro Tools Transport window lets you specify the master device (Pro Tools, the MachineControl device, an ADAT with an optional interface, or a MIDI MachineControl device). When Pro Tools and an external video or audio deck are linked by MachineControl, they can be scrubbed together, meaning you can review picture and audio in tandem.

When you select Pro Tools as the master, in Online mode, all devices connected via Machine-Control respond to transport and playback functions from Pro Tools (in Offline mode, they don't). Naturally, if these are tape-based devices such as video or audio decks, some time may be required for them to rewind or fast-forward to the appropriate location (with the amount of pre-roll specified in Preferences) before playback actually commences. Using Pro Tools as the master with an analog tape machine, ADAT, DA-88, or some other digital multi-track causes more wear and tear on these transports (and slows you down) as they chase the Pro Tools Transport. For this reason, it is more typical to designate these machines as the master; because access to audio material is nonlinear in Pro Tools, it will instantly jump to the correct playback position once the external tape transport is ready.

When you select Machine as the master, Pro Tools follows and locks to the Machine master when in Online mode. In Offline mode, the Pro Tools Transport still controls the machine, and as you move the video master to different locations, the playback cursor in Pro Tools reflects its position.

Note that in addition to many professional video decks, several audio DATs and the Tascam DA-88 and DA-98 digital multitrack audio recorders are also compatible with the MachineControl option. The first time you enable MachineControl, it polls the serial ports to automatically detect what device types are connected. You can also configure devices manually, from a pop-up menu.

AVoption|V10

Digidesign's AVoption|V10 for Windows systems—still common in the audio industry but currently out of production—consists of a single rackmountable interface, connected to the host computer via FireWire. This video subsystem supports the playback of Avid video media (including 24p/25p resolutions) within Pro Tools and provides video output for an external PAL or NTSC monitor. It includes BNC connectors for analog and digital video I/O, plus FireWire connectors for DV decks and cameras. Component, composite, S-video, and SDI (Serial Digital Interface) connections are supported for input/output, as well as a Video Ref input for external black-burst or house-sync sources.

AVoption|V10 allows you to see Avid edits and various simultaneous clip resolutions within the enhanced Video track in Pro Tools, use a unique Scrub Movie window, and even spot video clips to new locations within the Avid Movie track. Unlike the standard Video track in Pro Tools, there is a record-enable button and an I/O View for selecting among the available video-input sources, outputs, and disk volumes for video recording. The optional Media Station|PT software also allows you to capture NTSC/PAL video from external sources directly into the Avid Movie track. This can be as simple as highlighting the range to capture, arming the movie track for recording, enabling the Transport window's Online button, and then pressing Record. The included software also allows you to convert source files into Avid video format as well as import, digitize, and render Avid sequences directly for AAF import into Pro Tools. DigiTranslator software is included as part of the AVoption|V10 package and offers pre-configured Send to Pro Tools templates.

Note that when using AVoption|V10 with HD systems, the 96i I/O cannot be the primary audio interface. It *can* be a secondary interface, however, linked to a 192 I/O or 96 I/O. Digidesign's Sync I/O synchronization peripheral, a predecessor of the aforementioned Sync HD, is required in order to use either AVoption|V10 or Avid Mojo (collectively known as Avid DNA video peripherals) on Pro Tools|HD systems).

Avid Mojo SDI

The desktop Avid Mojo video interface connects to the host computer via FireWire. It offers DV video I/O plus analog I/O for video conversion to/from DV format, and supports many of the same software features as the AVoption|V10 system. It allows HD systems to play back video via an external monitor, open video sequences created with Avid Xpress Pro and Avid Media Composer Adrenaline systems in Pro Tools, tabbing from cut to cut and then exporting finished audio for re-integration into an original Avid sequence. Mojo supports uncompressed MXF or JFIF, DV25 and DV50, OMF, AAF, plus several 24P/25P progressive-scan resolutions. The Component Video I/O option for Avid Mojo allows you to connect component video sources to its built-in S-video and composite BNC video jacks. (DigiTranslator software must be purchased separately for Mojo systems.) Pro Tools versions 7.3 and higher are required for Avid Mojo SDI, and all HD and most LE systems can integrate the MOJO SDI.

DV Toolkit 2 (Pro Tools LE Only)

This software bundle includes DigiTranslator, which allows you to import/export projects either as OMF (Open Media Framework) or AAF files between Pro Tools and Avid Xpress DV, Final-Cut Pro, and other compliant video-editing programs. The DINR LE noise-reduction plug-in is also included (broadband noise reduction only; no hum removal), as well as the TL Space Native convolution reverb plug-in and VocALign AudioSuite plug-in for time alignment. With DV Toolkit installed, the SMPTE time code (including subframes) and Feet+Frames ruler formats (which are ordinarily available only on current HD systems) are available for Pro Tools LE systems, as well as other time code–related features for importing files. Pull-up and pull-down rates for audio and video are supported, as well as absolute/relative or user-defined time-code mapping when importing tracks. The more sophisticated Import Session Data options available in Pro Tools HD software are also available with this option. DV Toolkit 2 also increases the maximum track count in Pro Tools LE from 48 to 64 mono or stereo tracks. Up to 32 tracks can be armed for QuickPunch recording mode at 44.1and 48kHz, and several automation functions are provided that would otherwise be available only in the Pro Tools HD software. Lastly, the MP3 Export Option and DigiBase Pro features are included in the DV Toolkit 2 bundle.

DV Toolkit Is for Pro Tools LE Systems Only The optional DV Toolkit 2 software bundle is compatible only with the LE version of Pro Tools (for Digi 003, Digi 002, and Mbox 2 families, for example). It *cannot* be used with Pro Tools M-Powered.

Using Video Files in Post

As mentioned in Chapter 11, a QuickTime movie, an AVI video file, or an MPEG video file can be used as the video reference for postproduction work (as well as VC-1 video on Pro Tools 7.4 systems running on Windows Vista and, presumably, Windows 7) without requiring a video deck in your audio studio at all. If you are collaborating with video editors who use nonlinear systems, they can export a QuickTime movie for use as your master while posting the project in Pro Tools. (By *nonlinear* systems, we mean computer and hard disk–based editing systems—not only high-end systems using specific manufacturers' hardware such as Avid and Media 100, but also software-only solutions such as Apple's Final Cut Pro and Adobe Premiere. These may require only a FireWire input from a DV camera and perhaps a video accelerator card—and probably even more hard disk space than *you* require for Pro Tools!)

In either case, if you are using a dedicated video subsystem with Pro Tools (such as the AVoption|V10 or Mojo), you will generally ask for a video file sized down to 320×240 pixels or smaller. This minimizes the load on your system, especially if you don't dedicate a separate hard disk for video playback and/or have a video accelerator card to view the video on a separate computer monitor. (Both are highly recommended, especially for long durations, sessions with many tracks, complex signal processing, or high-resolution audio.) Remember that even though the frame *size* of the video should be reduced, the original frame *rate* must be maintained. Likewise, if you are going to import 48kHz stereo audio tracks from the video original, their audio bit depth and sample rate should be maintained. Sometimes you *won't* want to import audio from the video—for example, if an Avid editor is separately providing an OMFI file (and/or audio files) for the project, discussed later in this chapter.

The video plays in real time within the Video window (which in all versions 7.3 and higher can be resized by dragging), and individual frames are displayed in the Video track right alongside your audio waveforms, MIDI, and automation, as shown in Figure 14.4. As you jump around in the session (using the Transport buttons, memory locations, the Selector tool, and so on), the Video window immediately reflects the new position; no waiting for rewinds, time-code lockup, and all the other encumbrances. In short, using a digital video file as your master provides most of the advantages of VITC, without requiring you to drag around a video-tape transport while you work in Pro Tools.

Resizing the Video Window in Versions Prior to 7.3 In current Pro Tools versions, you simply drag an edge or corner of the Video window to resize it, regardless of the actual size (in pixels) of the source video file. You can also right-click to choose from a selection of sizes for the

Video window. If you've upgraded to QuickTime Pro (at $30, an essential tool for anyone who regularly deals with digital video), resizing is also easy in previous Pro Tools versions. Close your Pro Tools session and open the video file in the QuickTime (Pro) Player. Drag the corner of the video playback window to the desired size, and save. The next time you open your Pro Tools session, the video file will play back at whatever size you last saved it.

Figure 14.4 The Video track can display thumbnails of individual frames, allowing precise placement of audio in relation to video. Use the plus (+) and minus (−) keys on the numeric keypad to jog forward and backward through the Video track (per the current Nudge value). Hold them down to simulate shuttle mode.

Tips for Recording Voice-Overs

First, whether you apply some compression in real time prior to the Pro Tools input or you apply it 100% afterward via Pro Tools plug-ins, a healthy amount of compression and/or limiting (dynamics processing, to limit the range of variation in the signal level) is essential to producing quality voice-over (VO) recordings. Especially if the narration is for a book on tape, a radio spot, or a live event, the amount of compression will be a lot higher than what is conventional for vocal recordings in a music project, for example. Appendix E, "Power Tips and Loopy Ideas," provides some additional tips, but here are a several technical pointers:

- Be aware that large amounts of compression can sometimes darken a voice's timbre because many of the momentary peaks may be mid/high-frequency sibilance—"s," "t," and "ch" sounds, for example. As a general rule, try putting the EQ insert after the compressor in the

VO channel first, but don't be afraid to reverse the order if the voice strikes you as sounding somewhat weak.

- Destructive Recording mode in Pro Tools is handy for recording very long narrations—for example, a 30-minute infomercial or industrial video, and *especially* books on tape that may be many hours long. Aside from using less disk space, it can make file and Regions List management much simpler on these extremely long projects. Just be careful to check where the current insertion point is before you resume recording. It's called "destructive" for a good reason! Even if you don't use Destructive Recording mode, it's often useful to enable Timeline Insertion/Play Start Marker Follows Playback, in Preferences > Operation (which can be toggled on and off with the N key while Command Focus mode is enabled). Each time you stop, the next playback/recording will resume from the point you left off instead of from the same place you started previously, which is the normal mode in Pro Tools.

- When punching in new takes into existing voice-over recordings, provide a few seconds of pre-roll for the voice talent so he or she can match the timbre of the immediately preceding audio. For example, if you're going to pick up recording at 1:30, place the playback cursor there and enable perhaps four seconds of pre-roll before pressing Record and Play. Remember these keyboard shortcuts: To start recording, hold down the Command key (Ctrl key in Windows) and press the spacebar (also keep in mind the handy F12 shortcut). Press the spacebar again to stop recording or playback. To stop the recording currently in progress *and* discard the take, press Command+period (Ctrl+period in Windows).

- If you have a third-party multiband compressor (or limiting) plug-in, experiment with it on your voice-over tracks (in addition to its more conventional use on the overall mix or sub-mix). Aside from the obvious advantages for gain optimization, this offers a completely different approach for shaping vocal timbre as you alter the crossover points and dynamics settings for each frequency band.

- Pardon us for being so rudimentary, but let's just note that along with a pop filter, a professional-quality microphone is required (not a $100 rock 'n' roll model) to record great-sounding voice-overs! Likewise, provide a good copy stand for your voice talent (even if it's just a music stand); some pens, pencils, and highlighters; a great-sounding room (not too dead, not too noisy); some decent lighting; a comfy but quiet chair if desired; and a glass of water!

Shuffle Lock Mode In Pro Tools versions 7.3 and higher, you can Command-click (Ctrl-click in Windows) the Shuffle mode button to disable this function. Not only will the button itself not activate Shuffle mode while locked, but all keyboard shortcuts and control-surface switches for this mode are also disabled. Because deleting, cutting, or trimming events in this mode can cause the positions of ensuing events in the track to shift, there are times when disabling Shuffle mode can prevent editing mishaps.

Spotting Techniques, Sound Effects

Options for spotting sound effects and other audio events to video obviously depend on your synchronization method. If you are using an imported video file or VITC as your timing reference (time code embedded into each frame of the video signal), then you can spot sound effects to precise locations, even when the video is stopped on a single frame. In contrast, if you're using LTC (time code location information conveyed within an audio signal) to receive SMPTE position data, the master video deck (or other device) must be in Play mode to send the audio signal containing this encoded SMPTE location information.

Spot Edit Mode

As explained in Chapter 6, "The Edit Window," whenever you click a region with the Grabber tool (or Trimmer) in Spot edit mode, the Spot dialog box opens (see Figure 14.5). Time values entered here determine where that region's start, end, or sync point will be moved when you click OK. (See Chapter 8, "Menu Selections: Highlights," for a description of how sync points can be used to spot sound effects.) You can type the desired start time for currently selected region(s) or click the Current Time Code field to automatically capture that value. If you're using a VITC synchronization peripheral such as Digidesign's Sync HD or MOTU's Digital Timepiece with an external video source or MachineControl, you can simply move the master to the correct frame while stopped (using the jog/shuttle wheel on the video deck, for instance). Then, click Current Time Code (or press the =, or equals, key) to automatically enter that location into the currently selected field.

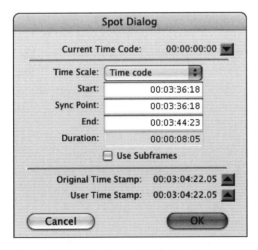

Figure 14.5 The Spot dialog box is essential for postproduction in Pro Tools. Clicking the Current Time Code field or pressing the = key captures the time code value if SMPTE time code is being sent to Pro Tools, entering it into any currently selected field in this dialog box. Using the Trimmer tool in Spot mode also opens the Spot dialog box for adjusting a region's start or end point.

Even if you are using LTC to synchronize to your time-code master (where an audio signal contains the encoded SMPTE timestamping information), you can still use this capture feature on the fly as the video master plays. Of course, if the video editor provides you with a window dub video copy with a numerical time-code window, you could crawl the tape to locate precise frame locations and enter time-code values manually. In either case, do your back a favor: Move your video deck close enough to the mouse and keyboard of your Pro Tools rig so that you don't have to stretch yourself into some grotesque posture to reach both at once! Also, note that although the Spot dialog box supports subframe precision ($^1/_{100}$ of a frame), time-code values can only be *captured* to the nearest whole frame.

Here, Spot! Whether or not you are in Spot edit mode, you can also snap regions to the current playback cursor position (if nothing is selected within the Edit window) or to the same timeline position as the beginning of your current edit selection. With the playback stopped, just Control-click (Start-click in Windows) that region with the Grabber tool. This is handy, for example, for forcing the beginning of an additional region to coincide with that of the currently selected region.

Here's a related trick: Make a selection in the Edit window and then hold down the Control key (Start key in Windows) as you click and drag other regions out from the Regions List into tracks. The beginnings of these regions will be snapped to the same timeline position as the beginning of your current edit selection. You can use this technique to replace the selected sound on the same track or align the new sound with it on another track.

Auto-Spotting Regions

The Auto-Spot Regions feature is especially useful when you're using an imported video file, VITC, or the MachineControl option. In these cases, the time-code information is available even when the master is stopped. To use it, enable Options > Auto-Spot Regions. Then, when you enable Spot edit mode, click any region with the Grabber (or drag it out anywhere onto a track from the Regions List) to automatically move that region's beginning (or sync point, if it contains one) to the current movie, time-code, or machine location.

Replacing All Occurrences of a Region (HD Only) Pro Tools HD makes it easy to swap all instances of a certain sound effect (or perhaps a drum sound, in musical applications) through the session. Just select the audio region you want to replace within a track, then Shift-Command-drag (Shift-Ctrl-drag in Windows) its substitute out from the Regions List. The Replace Region dialog box appears, where you can choose to replace just this occurrence with the new region, replace all occurrences in this track, or replace all occurrences in *all* tracks. As you can see in Figure 14.6, other options in the Replace Region dialog box let you restrict matches even further to occurrences of the region that start and/or end at exactly the same positions in the Pro Tools timeline. For postproduction, the Fit To options are of special interest. Original Region Length is the most commonly used. As the new region is swapped in to replace the previous one, its length is trimmed to match if it is longer, and any excess from the old region is removed if it's shorter. Original Selection Length also trims the replacement if it is longer but doesn't remove any excess from the old region if it's shorter. The last option, Replacement Region Length, is the simplest: If shorter, the new region replaces the old one without retaining any excess length from it; if longer, the replacement region doesn't get trimmed to match the old one's length.

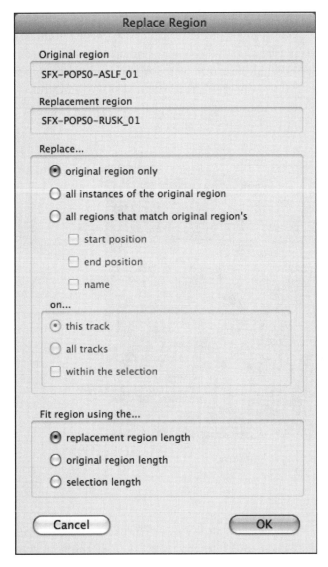

Figure 14.6   The Replace Region dialog box (Pro Tools HD software only).

VocALign

VocALign is available as an AudioSuite plug-in from Synchro Arts. It is useful for ADR (automatic dialog replacement), among other things. VocALign Project for Pro Tools (shown in Figure 14.7) is included in the DV Toolkit 2 bundle for LE systems or can be purchased separately for any Pro Tools system. VocALign Pro is also an AudioSuite plug-in compatible with all current Pro Tools versions, but adds support for multichannel alignment (versus stereo/mono only), longer alignment length, transfer of alignment path between different signals, and iLok copy protection instead of the challenge/response method. VocALign is available for several digital workstations (including Digital Performer, Fairlight, and Soundscape) or as a stand-alone program. You can use this product to automatically align the timing of one audio signal (the *dub*) to another (the *guide*). Not only are the leading edges of each detected segment within the source audio file aligned to the guide, but time compression and/or expansion are also applied. As you can imagine, this is extremely useful for doing dialog replacement while maintaining proper lip sync as well as for quickly aligning Foley and other sound effects to original sync sound from a video shoot. Music mixers also appreciate this automated time alignment for achieving extremely tight tracking of doubled lead vocals and stacked-up backing vocal parts.

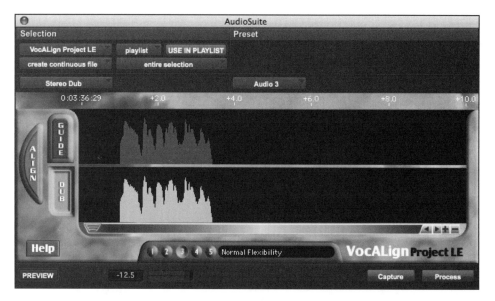

Figure 14.7 VocALign Project (in its AudioSuite plug-in window).

Surround Mixing

After a multichannel audio track, Aux Input track, Instrument track, or Master Fader has been created, its level meters in the Mix window display multiple channels, as does the metering within any of its plug-in windows—for example, six channels in 5.1 format. For a 5.1 mix, for example, the output path might typically be the first six outputs on your audio interface (leaving outputs 7 and 8 free for an alternate stereo mix, if you wish).

Point One Surround format names with a .1 indicate that there is one separate LFE (Low Frequency Effects) channel dedicated to the subwoofer. If any surround format with two LFE channels were to become an industry standard (such as 10.2), it would consequently have a .2 suffix.

The multichannel paths that you create in the I/O Setup dialog box are essential to surround mixing. A 5.1 main path would consist of six mono subpaths: the five surround speakers and the LFE subwoofer feed. You can also use multichannel paths for purposes other than surround mixing, however. For example, you might create a multichannel path consisting of simultaneous stereo cue mix, monitoring, and master recorder feeds to three distinct pairs of physical outputs on your audio hardware. The I/O Setup dialog box (shown in Figure 14.8) also enables you to

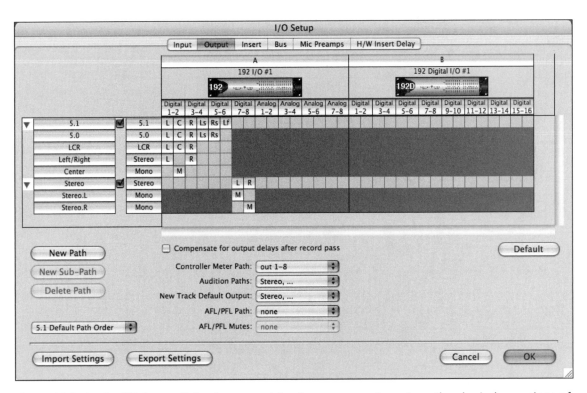

Figure 14.8 In the I/O Setup dialog box, a matrix allows you create main paths—logical groupings of inputs, outputs, inserts, or busses that consist of individual mono signal paths. The paths created in your configuration (mono or multichannel-stereo or multichannel surround) determine input and output options for audio tracks, sends, Aux Input tracks, Instrument tracks, and Master Faders.

create multichannel paths incorporating multiple stem mixes—for example, spoken dialog, effects, or music that is fed to separate outputs (subpaths).

For multichannel tracks, an X/Y panner (as seen in Figure 14.9) facilitates positioning of sources within the surround field. Unlike with the standard pan sliders for stereo tracks, you move a point within a grid. An additional Divergence parameter for the X/Y panners determines how much the sound source will spread from its designated position into adjacent speakers (the lower the Divergence percentage, the wider the sound will spread into other speakers). Naturally, the Surround Mixer plug-in must be installed in your Plug-ins folder for these features to be available (and is installed by default with Pro Tools HD, along with the Stereo Mixer plug-in). The Surround panner modes are X/Y, Divergence Editing, Three-Knob (handy for discrete, straight-line panning between two specific speakers), and AutoGlide. The Output window for each multichannel track offers choices for alternative panning methods: X/Y panning, plus knobs

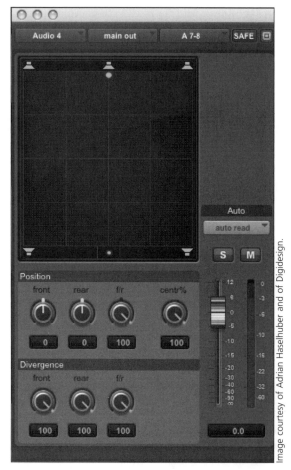

Figure 14.9 X/Y panners facilitate positioning of sources within the surround field.

for front/rear percentage, center percentage, divergence, LFE feed for the subwoofer, and other surround controls. These also appear separately when you view the panning automation data on multichannel tracks in a surround format.

Surround Formats Overview

There are several surround formats in common use:

- **Dolby Digital.** Currently the most common format for home-surround systems. It was formerly known as Dolby AC-3. Dolby Digital is used for surround encoding most DVDs, high-definition television broadcasts, and theatrical film presentations. It's a 5.1 format (full-range channels for left, center, right, left/right surround, plus a dedicated channel, known as LFE, for sending low frequencies to the subwoofer from 3 to 120Hz). Not all DVDs actually incorporate the five discrete channels (plus subwoofer channel). They may have only the Dolby Digital 2.0 soundtrack (stereo or Pro Logic compatible; this audio track is mandatory), and can additionally have Dolby Digital 1.0 (you guessed it: a mono audio track) and/ or the full Dolby Digital 5.0 soundtrack, of course.

- **DTS (a.k.a. DTS Digital Surround).** A competing 5.1 format to Dolby Digital. It's also used for theatrical film presentations and sometimes as an alternate surround-track option on consumer DVDs. DTS uses higher data rates for its audio stream than Dolby Digital (either 1.5Mbps or 754Kbps versus 448Kbps or 384Kbps in Dolby Digital); in other words, a lesser degree of "lossy" audio data compression is applied to the original audio. On consumer DVDs supporting both surround formats, the lower DTS data rates are generally used due to space considerations. Like Dolby Digital, while the majority of titles are 5.1, other channel configurations are also supported by the DTS format, including 4.1 and 4.0.

- **Dolby Surround Pro Logic.** The precursor to Dolby Digital and still the surround format used in hi-fi tracks of VHS videocassettes, LaserDiscs, and most analog television broadcasts. It's a four-channel format—left, center, right, plus a single channel for both rear surround speakers—and is backward compatible with stereo-playback systems. All four channels are matrix-encoded into a stereo audio track (and then decoded back into their individual components during playback). Therefore, Dolby Pro Logic is also known as LCRS. Dolby Pro Logic II is similar but incorporates two separate full-range audio channels for the surround speakers. In contrast, the classic Pro Logic specification uses a single band-limited channel (containing only frequencies from 100Hz to 7kHz) for both surround speakers.

- **THX Surround EX (a.k.a. Dolby EX).** This is an extension of Dolby Digital 5.1 and was jointly developed by Lucasfilm THX and Dolby Laboratories. In theatrical settings, the two surround speakers for Dolby Digital 5.1 are actually placed at the sides of the cinema. THX Surround EX (Dolby EX) adds two additional surround-back channels for speakers located behind the audience. For that reason, this is sometimes called a 7.1 format (because there are seven speakers plus a subwoofer). Technically, though, in the implementation of this format for home theater, the two surround-back channels are matrix-encoded into the left and right surround channels of a 5.1 setup, so these EX formats might more correctly be called extended 5.1. Thanks to the use of this matrix-encoding method, EX formats are backward compatible with Dolby Digital just as Dolby Surround Pro Logic is backward compatible with stereo systems.

- **DTS-ES Discrete 6.1.** Another extended format. Unlike THX Surround EX (see the preceding bullet), it truly adds a discrete channel to the DTS 5.1 format for the surround-back speakers. This format is backward compatible with standard DTS decoding systems.

- **SDDS.** A 7.1 format, using seven full-range speakers plus a low frequency effects channel: left, left-center, center, right-center, right, left surround, right surround, and LFE (subwoofer) channel.

Software and Hardware Accessories for Surround

A Surround Panner option is available for Digidesign's D-Control work surface that includes a touchscreen interface (which can be used for both parameter control and panning moves), dual joysticks, rotary encoders, and dedicated buttons for surround parameters. J.L. Cooper also offers a standalone surround panner peripheral that can be attached to Pro Tools|HD systems via MIDI. It is specifically designed to complement the D-Command work surface, but could be used with any HD configuration. In addition to the joystick, it includes various rotary knobs and switches for real-time parameter adjustment on surround channels. Digidesign's Edit Pack add-on for the discontinued ProControl control surface added two DigiPanner motorized joystick pan controls for surround mixing, an alphanumeric keyboard, a trackball, and multichannel metering.

Dolby Surround Tools 3 for TDM (shown in Figure 14.10) not only includes a surround-panning interface and supports the Pro Tools surround panner but also complete surround encoder and decoder plug-ins matching the industry-standard SEU4/DP563 and SDU4/DP564 hardware equivalents that support sample rates up to 96kHz. Mono/stereo and surround switching is provided, as well as a delay parameter for the surround channel. Surround Tools supports the Dolby Pro Logic Surround format (LCRS), where information for four channels (left, center, right, plus a single channel for the two rear surround speakers) is matrix-encoded into a single stereo-compatible file. While it does not support Dolby Digital 5.1 surround mixing, template and detailed instructions are provided for performing downmixes of 5.1 sessions to LCRS for Dolby Surround encoding.

If you're serious about mixing in surround, another item to consider is the use of surround reverb plug-ins. After all, if the purpose of reverb effects is to simulate characteristics of an acoustic space and you're mixing in 5.1 surround, how much sense can it make to use a reverb that operates in only two channels (left/right)? Digidesign's ReVibe reverb plug-in for HD systems is very impressive for this purpose, as is the TDM version of TL Space by TL Audio (whose software assets are now owned by Digidesign). Waves also offers the 360° Surround Tools plug-in bundle,

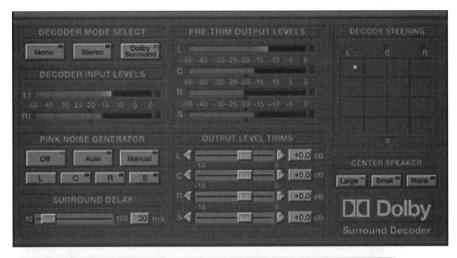

Figure 14.10 Dolby Surround Tools is an LCRS surround encoder/decoder for Pro Tools TDM systems.

including a reverb, a compressor, a limiter, a panner, a low-pass filter for the LFE channel, an encoder plug-in for quad and LCR mixes, plus other tools.

Apple's DVD Studio Pro program for Macintosh users not only supplies tools for creating DVD-Rs that can be played in any standard video DVD player (and includes MPEG-2 encoding) but also allows multiple mono WAV, AIF, or SDII file *stems* bounced out from Pro Tools to be dropped into the appropriate channel slots for encoding into a single AC-3 (Dolby Digital) surround file.

Monitoring in Surround on a Budget

Here's a very economical alternative: Many current surround receivers used for home DVD viewing and Dolby Digital surround offer component audio inputs for each 5.1 surround channel. This enables you to configure six outputs from your Pro Tools audio interface as the surround output bus and connect these to your receiver to monitor your surround mixes in realistic conditions. Be aware, though, that audio inputs on consumer gear are generally referenced to −10dBV, so if your audio interface is pumping out +4dBm (the more common professional standard), you will be slamming the inputs! (Some Digidesign audio interfaces support switching analog output levels to −10dBV reference levels.)

Various manufacturers (including Mackie, Genelec, Blue Sky, Alesis, ADAM, and JBL) offer 5.1 powered monitor packages that can be connected directly to your audio interface's outputs (or patchbay). Naturally, when you are using multiple outputs from your Pro Tools audio interface for the surround mix, many more professional options are available for dedicated surround-sound monitoring.

Stereo Compatibility

Dolby Pro Logic matrix-encodes all four channels of its surround mix into a single stereo-compatible signal. You may be using the Dolby Surround plug-in (and a Pro Logic decoder or even a common surround-compatible receiver) to properly route the four channels of audio out to your speakers (LCRS: left, center, right, plus one channel to both rear surround speakers). Before committing to a mix for Dolby Pro Logic, be sure to switch into ordinary stereo mode to make sure there are no drastically inappropriate shifts in levels or imaging when playing back the mix through only left and right speakers. Phase problems are the most common thing to watch out for here, and the Leq(A) meter of the PhaseScope plug-in included with all versions 7.3 and higher can be a useful tool.

Similarly, playing a 5.1 mix back as stereo (commonly known as *downmixing*) can be an important compatibility check. The Waves M360° Surround Mixdown plug-in (part of their 360° Surround Tools bundle) permits the derivation of mixes in stereo, mono LCR, and other formats when placed on your multichannel surround (5.1) Master Fader output path. A variety of external hardware options are also available for this purpose.

SurroundScope for Pro Tools|HD Systems SurroundScope is included in both TDM and RTAS formats as part of the Signal Tools bundle for Pro Tools|HD systems. Because this plug-in can be instantiated only on multichannel tracks, it is not available for M-Powered systems, or LE systems without the use of the Complete Production Toolkit. (That said, PhaseScope can be used in stereo on *any* current system.) SurroundScope provides monitoring and analysis tools for the multichannel surround mixing process through visualizations of level, phase, and surround positions of multiple channels in the surround field. Supported surround formats include LCR (left-center-right), quad, LCRS (left-center-right-surround; Dolby Surround/Dolby Pro Logic), 5.0, 5.1 (used on video DVDs), 6.0, 6.1, 7.0, and 7.1.

The plug-in's Surround display shows the position of the current track's signal in the surround field. Input level meters show levels for each surround channel. The Lissajous meter reflects amplitude and phase of stereo signals to help you optimize stereo imaging. The Phase meter monitors phase coherency of the left and right channels (only) in the surround mix. As with the stereo PhaseScope plug-in, various metering behaviors can be selected for displaying levels in your surround channels, such as Peak, RMS, Peak + RMS, VU, BBC, Nordic, DIN, and Venue.

Audio Editing for Avid-Based Video Projects

In 1995, Digidesign merged with Avid Technology, one of the world's most important manufacturers of nonlinear (computer- and hard disk–based) video workstations. Even before that, by participating in the development of the OMFI format, Digidesign positioned itself as an important audio-editing platform for video projects and for Avid in particular. Avid offers several lines of video-editing systems and software, including Avid Media Composer 4, Avid DS, Avid Mojo SDI, Avid Media Composer Mojo DX, Avid Media Composer Nitris DX, and Avid Symphony Nitris DX, as well as NewsCutter system for the news industry, Deko systems for broadcast graphics, and Pinnacle Studio packages for the consumer market. New products are regularly introduced, so the best up-to-date resource is always www.avid.com.

High-Speed Networking for Production Facilities If you will routinely transfer projects between multiple Pro Tools suites and nonlinear video-editing systems in your facility, trust us: standard Ethernet-based local area networking is *not* fast enough! You may want to check out some of the Fibre Channel–based networking alternatives. All these require a separately purchased networking card in your computer. Some solutions even include a high-speed file server or disk array (perhaps in a centralized machine room), which facilitates sharing files with other workstations as you collaborate on projects. We list some of these in Appendix B, "Add-ons, Extensions, and Cool Stuff for Your Rig."

File Formats

Most commonly, nonlinear video editors can import or export AIF and WAV audio files (and SDII on some older Mac-based Avid systems) for their soundtracks. An audio-only QuickTime is essentially an AIF file as well, but offers additional resources for playback by Apple's QuickTime Player. Remember that you can also bounce the mix directly into a copy of the current QuickTime movie in your Pro Tools session. In any case, a 48kHz sample rate is standard for most current industrial and broadcast-video applications (as opposed to the 44.1kHz sample rate used for audio CDs), and 16-bit audio files are still more common than 24-bit. Be sure to ask the video editor, however; more recent systems are moving toward 24-bit files.

Specifically, all Avid video-editing systems understand audio files in AIF formats (AIFF-C, to be precise, even though Avid systems do *not* compress audio data within these files). In years past, Macintosh-based Avid systems supported SDII files (especially because they used Digidesign audio interfaces, which was once the exclusive audio file format used by early Mac versions of Pro Tools). Windows-based Avid editing systems and all Mac versions of Media Composer 8.0 and higher support WAV audio files, in most cases using them directly. The trend toward Broadcast WAV files as a digital audio standard (particularly for higher sample rates) continues, especially given that the AES/EBU are recommending this as a standard delivery and interchange format.

OMF, AAF, and the DigiTranslator Program

OMF and AAF are file-format standards developed in collaboration by various manufacturers (especially Avid) to promote a common format for interchange of data between different computer-assisted, nonlinear editing systems for video and audio. OMFI (or simply OMF—the terms are more or less synonymous even though OMF more properly refers to the entire enabling technology and a body of standards) allows all the original audio tracks from an Avid Media Composer project, for example, to be translated for a Pro Tools system. The Advanced Authoring Format (AAF) standard was introduced in 2001 and is supported by all DigiTranslator versions 2.0 and higher; it encompasses both OMF and many other source formats. Note that OMF exports are limited to 2GB total size, which can be an issue if you export a project as a single OMF file with the source audio files embedded within it.

DigiTranslator is optional software that must be purchased from Digidesign. It is also included in the DV Toolkit 2 for Pro Tools LE. (DV Toolkit 2 is *not* compatible with M-Powered versions of Pro Tools.) DigiTranslator is used to export or import OMFI/AAF files between Pro Tools and other programs. These consist of video editors as well as numerous digital-audio workstations, including current versions of Digital Performer, Logic Pro, and Cubase. With DigiTranslator, you can import OMFI/AAF files from other video and audio workstations directly into Pro Tools via the same File > Open Session command used to open an existing Pro Tools session. Most importantly, if necessary, DigiTranslator enables you to convert Pro Tools sessions to OMFI format for use with these other programs.

DigiTranslator (shown in Figure 14.11) converts between cuts and dissolves in the Avid environment and their counterparts in Pro Tools: regions and fades. Avid's audio clips are translated to Pro Tools regions. Also, volume or pan levels and automation created in Avid can be translated to Pro Tools automation on the appropriate track. Here's the basic procedure: The Avid editor exports the current project in OMFI format. (Generally, you would not export video into the OMFI file, only audio data.) The OMFI Audio Only option incorporates duplicate copies of all audio files in the Avid project into the OMFI file in AIF format; it therefore requires much more disk space. The OMFI Compositions Only option incorporates only the audio playlist into the OMFI file, and it would therefore be necessary to provide the source audio files separately for the Pro Tools system—perhaps on a shared network drive. (The Avid editor should first run the Consolidate Audio Files command. It's similar to Compact Audio in the Pro Tools Regions List, except it creates an entirely new folder to store compacted files, containing only audio clips actually used in the Avid project rather than their entire source audio files. The editor exports the sequence with the OMFI Compositions Only option and gives you the OMFI file plus this folder of compacted audio files created with the Consolidate command.) After that, with DigiTranslator installed on your Pro Tools rig, you can import this OMFI file directly into Pro Tools using the File > Open Session command.

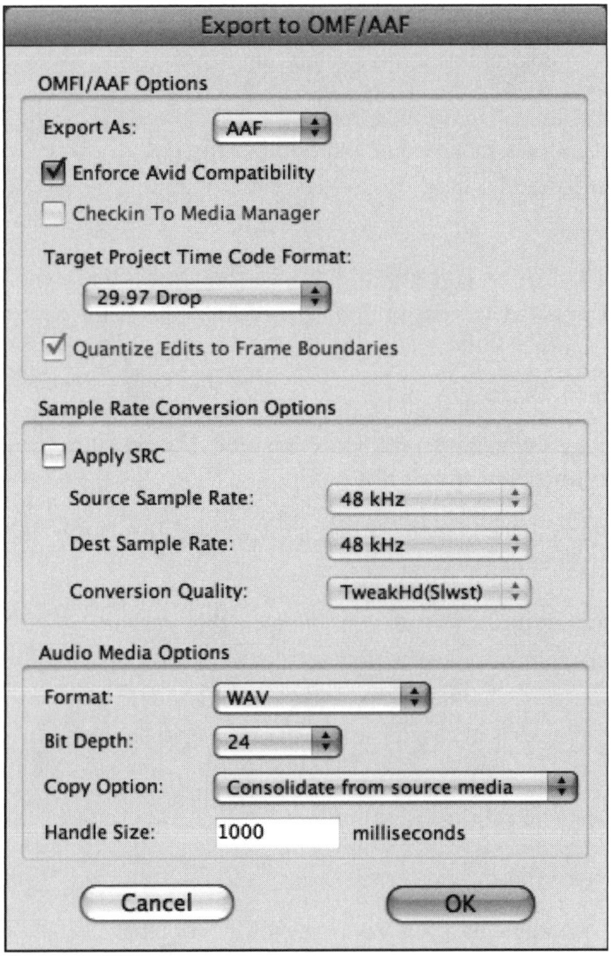

Figure 14.11 With DigiTranslator, you can transfer projects between Pro Tools and video or other audio workstations via OMF or AAF interchange formats.

Avid/Digi Terms Good communication with video editors starts with learning a few words in each other's language!

- **Automation gain (clip-based or keyframe-based).** The Avid equivalent of track automation in Pro Tools. For example, the Avid equivalent to volume automation in a Pro Tools track is called Avid keyframe volume.

- **Bin.** A database where master clips, subclips, effects, and sequences are organized for a project. Somewhat comparable to the Regions List in a Pro Tools project. Avid projects can have *multiple* bins, however, and the feature set is larger because video editors deal with more varied source media types: audio, video, animation sequences, still images, and so on.

- **Dissolve.** Strictly, a video fade to black or a mix through to another image, but video editors often use the term for audio fades to silence and crossfades between two audio segments.

- **Gang**. The approximate Avid equivalent of an Edit group. Edits performed on one track are mirrored in the others, like tracks that are grouped together in the Edit window of Pro Tools.

- **Master clip.** The Avid equivalent of a whole-file audio region. (In Pro Tools, audio regions that correspond to entire files usually appear in boldface within the Regions List but won't when the project was imported from OMF/AAF.)

- **Media data.** The actual audio or video data contained in the source files. This is the largest portion within most OMF or AAF interchange files.

- **Metadata.** Information within the source project or session file itself that can be included in the OMFI or AAF format. This includes pointers to files and information about their sample rate, bit depth, source reel, timestamp, and so on. Metadata also includes all the information about where parts of these files are placed in the timeline and about automation.

- **Real-time audio effects.** The Avid equivalent of plug-ins.

- **Segue.** Occasionally used as a synonym for an audio crossfade.

- **Sequence.** The Avid video-project equivalent of a Pro Tools session document.

- **Stem.** In the film/video production industry, stems can be compared to the signal paths you define in the Pro Tools I/O Setup dialog box—a logical grouping of inputs, outputs, or busses treated under a single name. In a film mix, source tracks might be grouped into a smaller number of stems according to type—for example, dialog, sound effects, Foley, music, and so on. Just as you might use an Aux Input or Master Fader as the overall volume control for a group of tracks or output channels, having a large number of source tracks grouped into stems simplifies the adjustment of overall levels in complex film mixdowns.

- **Subclip.** The Avid equivalent of an audio region within a large source audio file. A subclip represents a smaller section within a master clip, just as many audio regions represent smaller sections within whole-file audio regions.

When you use OMFI or AAF files to move audio from Avid to your Pro Tools system, all the original tracks and names, fades, and various other parameters are retained. (Video editors frequently use multiple tracks—for example, slugging in music cues and sound effects under the camera soundtracks, which you might refine later. They also create fades or edits on audio to correct dialog, remove extraneous noise, match video fades to/from black, and other audio operations. You get all these when the project is imported into Pro Tools.) Of course, the editor on *any* nonlinear video-editing system could also mix audio tracks to stereo and export an audio file for you or simply incorporate the full-resolution 48kHz audio into a QuickTime movie provided as your editing reference (instead of a tape). In fact, if the editor hasn't added audio tracks to the original sync sound from the video shoot, either of these methods can frequently be just as practical as exchanging OMFI or AAF files. (One drawback is that you won't have any additional audio available at region boundaries to correct clicks or artifacts at their edit points using crossfades, and so on.)

The Import Session Data dialog box provides options for how metadata from the original project will be interpreted upon import into Pro Tools. For instance, you could choose to ignore rendered audio effects (this doesn't import the results of real-time EQ, etc., that have been applied in the source video project), ignore clip-based gain, or convert it to breakpoint automation. You can also choose to copy the source media files, convert them to your session's audio format, and/or consolidate (compact) the source files during the import. The Consolidate Handle Length value is similar to the Padding parameter when compacting files in the Regions List; it leaves a few extra milliseconds around each region boundary so that you have the option of lengthening these for fades and so on. When deciding on the length of the handles, it is always better to err on the side of caution and account for more handle than you might end up needing.

Avid Export Templates for Pro Tools Current versions of Avid's Media Composer, Film Composer, Symphony, and Avid Xpress include *export templates* for many programs, including Pro Tools, which appear in a pop-up list in their Export dialog box. This can save you a lot of discussion (and/or confusion) when collaborating with Avid video editors. The External options leave audio files in a separate folder, while the Embedded option incorporates the Avid composition and all the audio into a single large file, most practical for short-duration spots and when transferring OMFI files over a local network.

Render Unto Pro Tools... Remind your collaborators on Avid video-editing systems to *render* all their AudioSuite effects before exporting OMFI/AAF files of the project for use in Pro Tools! Otherwise, all these effects will be skipped when the files are imported—or worse, will cause the OMF to not import at all.

Gain Optimization for Video

When delivering a mix for a video project, ask the video producer for the level specs with which he or she will need the audio to comply. For resolution and fidelity purposes, logic would tell you to deliver the mix as close to maximum level as possible, but rarely if ever is that allowed for professional video projects. Obviously, the best thing is to watch levels on the Master Fader for the output path used for your main mix; the PhaseScope plug-in included with all Pro Tools versions 7.3 and higher will be very useful here. Gain-optimization plug-ins, such as Digidesign's Maxim and several others from Waves, Ltd., are extremely useful in audio for video because they enable you to transparently limit peaks within your audio program.

Normalization

Normalization changes the audio level of a sound file or a selected region within it. Typically, this process finds the peak signal level and either automatically increases it to 100% (0dB, or *full code*) or adjusts it to a specified number of decibels down from 0 (in which case, contrary to a common misconception, the peak audio level may actually *decrease*). The amplitude of the rest of the audio changes proportionally. Most Avid systems (but not Avid Xpress) have the same AudioSuite normalization function as Pro Tools; you will discover that many video editors don't bother to use it, however.

Normalization is rarely used in professional video for adjusting the level of final mixes, but is frequently used for individual sound files with low levels included in the mix program. Often, an audio mixer working with an OMF or AAF file exported from a video editor will find that a portion of field-recorded files have levels so insufficient that adjusting the track volume can't compensate for the weak level. This is where normalization comes in handy. With the Audio-Suite Normalization plug-in, you can select all the sound files that need the level adjustment and batch-process them all at once. You can even normalize the audio file directly in the Regions List with the AudioSuite plug-in (see Figure 14.12).

Figure 14.12 Normalization adjusts the loudest peak in a selection to a specified level, which increases or decreases the sound's volume (depending on the settings in this dialog box).

The RMS mode (as opposed to the traditional Peak mode) for the normalization process is also useful because it generally gives a better idea about *apparent* loudness of multiple sound sources. Instead of the traditional normalization approach, where a single peak determines the maximum amount a selection's gain can be increased, the RMS (root-mean-square) method enables you to specify an average target level. Be conservative, however; depending on the dynamic range within the selected material, clipping can result.

The Gain plug-in (another AudioSuite plug-in) also features an RMS mode. Unlike the Normalization plug-in, it provides the useful ability to detect the current RMS (or peak) level in the current selection. This makes it much more practical to make RMS gain adjustments (more like an average level, enabling you to more accurately adjust apparent the loudness of a selection).

Compression

The general practice is to compress video mixes pretty hard. This is especially true for industrial videos, be they training videos, marketing and product videos, or video modules for live events. Single-band compression (like the DigiRack compressor provided with Pro Tools and the Focusrite D3) is very effective on single audio sources—for example, the voice-over or and/or background music in a video program. There are also many excellent single-band options for compressing entire mixes, including Digidesign's Impact and Smack! plug-ins. Multiband compressors (such as Waves' C4, Drawmer Dynamics, PSP's Vintage Warmer, and McDSP's MC2000 plug-ins) can often be more transparent when compressing entire mixes; they simultaneously apply differing amounts of compression in three or more frequency bands. With multiband compression, the entire mix doesn't necessarily get clamped down if there is some momentary peak exclusively in the low- or high-frequency end of the spectrum. This often produces more natural-sounding results at higher compression ratios.

Don't Forget to Duck (A Side Order of Compression, Please) *Side chaining* is a classic dynamics-processing technique in which a different audio source determines the amount of gain change to apply to a track. For example, when applying ordinary compression to a music underscore for a video project, level changes in the music itself determine the amount of gain reduction applied (per the compressor's current ratio and threshold settings). Sometimes, though, you'd like the music's level to drop whenever the voice-over is present, rising back up between phrases (a technique called *ducking*).

To duck your music underscore, create a stereo send from the VO track routed to any unused Pro Tools bus pair. Option-click (Alt-click in Windows) the send's level slider to set it to 0dB. Insert a compressor plug-in on your music track (preferably before any subsequent EQ inserts in the track) and use its Key Input pop-up (called Sidechain Input in the Focusrite D3 compressor) to select the bus pair where you've sent the voice-over track's signal as the key audio source for the compression process. When you enable the external key, the voice-over's level changes control the amount of gain reduction applied to the music track. Adjust the compressor's Level and Ratio parameters for the desired amount of ducking on the music. Also, bear in mind that the Release parameter affects how quickly the music comes back up after each voice-over phrase.

Rock 'n' rollers: Small amounts of compression applied on rhythm guitars and other backing instrumental parts, which are keyed (side chained) by your lead vocal, can also be very effective. Both will seem to be in your face at the appropriate times and can give the impression that the vocal has a little more power to cut through an aggressive mix. Conversely, using the kick drum as the side-chain input for an expander plug-in on a loosely played bass track can help tighten up a groove.

Digidesign's Maxim peak-limiting and gain-optimization plug-in (see Figure 14.13) is very effective when applied to entire mixes. Try placing Maxim on the Master Fader for your stereo mix. By flattening out isolated amplitude peaks (keeping in mind that extreme settings distort the sound), you will obtain greater overall levels afterward when you normalize the bounced mix

Figure 14.13 Digidesign's Maxim is a gain-optimization and peak-limiting plug-in for both RTAS and TDM architectures.

to −.5dB, for example. Unlike conventional hardware limiters, Maxim can read ahead so that limiting is applied with no *latency*, or reaction time, which yields more transparent results.

The T-Racks mastering plug-in suite from IK Multimedia also includes a three-band limiter that is very effective on stereo mixes. You can adjust the input drive as well as the crossover points, threshold, and output levels for each of the three frequency bands. PSP's Vintage Warmer is a compressor plug-in that can operate in either single or multiband mode.

Several limiting plug-ins are available from Waves, including L1, L2, and L3. These are even more sophisticated tools for optimizing gain and bit-depth conversions in your Pro Tools projects. They offer single-band peak limiting and other functions including Waves' proprietary IDR dithering algorithms for high-quality gain optimization and conversion to lower bit depths. As with Maxim, you might typically insert these plug-ins on a Master Fader, although you could also use them on a vocal track, for instance. The L3 Multimaximizer (shown in Figure 14.14) provides peak limiting in five separate frequency bands, with adjustable crossover points and a linear phase crossover to avoid phase distortion between bands. The brick-wall limiting in individual bands can be completely independent or progressively more linked up to the point where, at 100%, L3 functions like a single-band limiter. A variety of dithering options are also included, and up to 12dB of post-limiting boost or cut in each frequency band. The Waves Suite of limiters has become a standard in national broadcast audio production.

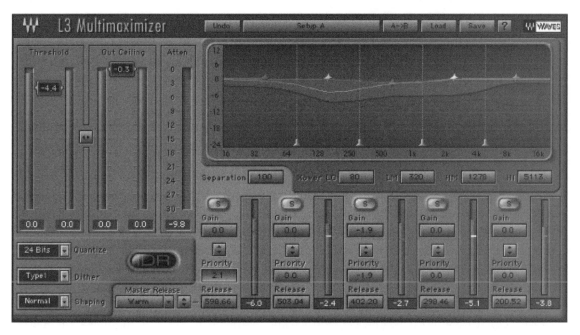

Figure 14.14   L3 Multimaximizer is a powerful gain-management and dithering plug-in for TDM.

One last reminder about these gain-optimization processors: The harder you slam your mix against a limiter to constantly maintain maximum loudness, the less dynamic range is retained in the original material. For some applications, this may be just what you want—for example, multimedia, on-hold or background music, live events such as awards banquets, or aggressive-sounding television commercials. Keep in mind, though, that this can quickly become overbearing and fatigue listeners (especially at louder playback levels). It's as if someone is speaking loudly all the time, shouting out each and every syllable at maximum volume—how long would you put up with *that*? As brilliant as these tools are, their excessive application—to the point of squashing all vestiges of dynamic range—is a legitimate complaint about many current movie soundtracks and *especially* CD music releases that aim to sound really "loud." Try not to lose your ear for subtlety!

Audio Editing for Linear (Tape-Based) Video Suites

In this situation, you typically play back your audio with the Pro Tools Transport in Online mode, recording from the selected outputs of your Pro Tools hardware to a master video deck. Sometimes you will perform this layback directly to the video master tape you've been using in your audio suite. In other situations, you may use tie lines to send audio directly to the video-editing suite (slaving Pro Tools to the video master as the SMPTE synchronization source), where your audio is recorded directly to the video edit master. This is preferable especially when using professional video decks with analog-only audio inputs (for example, Beta-Cam) because it eliminates a tape generation.

Digital Video Decks Professional digital video decks (like D2, D4, D1, the Digital BetaCam family, and the HDCam family) generally also have digital audio inputs and outputs. (The audio tracks of a BetaCam SP deck are digitally *recorded*, but the audio I/O is strictly analog.) If your Pro Tools audio interface has AES/EBU digital I/O, this is definitely preferable for audio layoff and layback. Digital audio I/O on professional video gear is almost always in AES/EBU format, with XLR connectors. Manufacturers generally recommend that digital cable lengths not exceed 30 feet, although many people successfully run greater lengths. You should use 110-Ohm digital-type cable and *not* ordinary mic/line cable for all AES/EBU connections—especially for longer lengths!

Audio Transfer from Tape Master

When dealing with linear (tape-based) video-editing suites, the first step in the audio postproduction process is to record existing audio from the original video into Pro Tools while synchronized to SMPTE time code. Ideally, this comes directly from the video master itself, even if afterward you use a second-generation tape in your local deck as the time-code master while editing. Audio could also be transferred directly from that work tape copy; but if it's an analog copy (onto BetaCam, for instance), you're already one analog generation removed from the master's audio quality.

Here's a typical sequence for pulling the audio from a supplied video master tape into your Pro Tools session:

1. Connect the video master's stereo outputs (analog or digital, as mentioned in the note preceding this section) to one of the input pairs on your Pro Tools audio hardware.

2. Connect the video deck's time-code output (audio if you're using LTC, video if you're using VITC) to your synchronization peripheral.

3. Create a Pro Tools session (typically at a 48kHz sample rate). Set the appropriate frame rate and session start time in the Session Setup window. Typically, the video program itself will be preceded by color bars and tones. Recording these tones is handy to confirm that consistent levels are maintained when you eventually lay your audio back up to the video master. In this case, if the video program starts at 1:00:00, your actual session start time might be 0:59:00 (if your facility follows the fairly standard practice of laying down 30 seconds of tone followed by an additional 30 seconds before program start).

4. Create audio track(s) for recording from the video. Set their input selector to the appropriate input path for the incoming audio from the video deck. Next, either record-enable the track(s) or temporarily switch to Input Only Monitoring, under the Track menu.

5. Put Pro Tools in Online mode; then press Play on the video master. Confirm that Pro Tools locks to time code, starting playback at the appropriate location.

6. Meanwhile, if you're recording via an analog input, adjust input levels to the Pro Tools hardware.

7. Press Record in the Pro Tools Transport and then press Play *on the video master's transport*. Because Pro Tools is in Online mode, it should drop into Record/Play mode automatically. Press Stop on the video transport after the layoff is completed.

Specifications: Audio Tracks on VTRs

Digital (a.k.a. *PCM*) audio tracks on professional video-tape recorders most frequently use a 48kHz sample rate. BetaCam SP is an extremely common videotape format for industrial video (local television spots; training, product, marketing, and corporate videos; and video modules for playback during live events). BetaCam SP offers two PCM audio tracks (digital audio tracks, also known as *hi-fi* on these machines) plus two analog/longitudinal tracks that are not generally used for professional audio applications. As mentioned elsewhere in this chapter, D2, D5, D1, and Digital BetaCam offer multiple digital audio tracks and feature digital I/O for audio.

DVCAM (Sony), DVCPRO (Panasonic), DV (known as DVC when launched in 1995), and mini-DV also feature digital audio tracks (usually only two, at a 48kHz sample rate and 16-bit resolution). If IEEE 1394 digital connections are used (more commonly known as FireWire, the original name for this specification developed by Apple, or i.LINK, a proprietary Sony name for its implementation of this industry-standard 1394 connector) to transfer video from cameras or decks to your hard disk–based video-editing application, the audio is also transferred digitally as part of the DV codec QuickTime file that these programs create from the DV source.

Pull-Up and Pull-Down Sample Rates

These specialty sample rates are sometimes employed when film and NTSC video are used in the same project. For video- or audio-only projects, they are not an issue (unless you select one of these sample rates by accident).

Film is shot and projected at 24 frames per second (fps), while NTSC color video (the American broadcast standard) uses 29.97fps. When using Pro Tools to post audio for a film, it is convenient and cost-effective to use a video copy as the image source during the editing process. Transferring each frame of a film at 24fps to videotape at 29.97fps presents a problem, however; the math becomes difficult. To make life easier, transfers from film to NTSC videotape use a frame rate of 30fps (the original frame rate for black-and-white television).

To do a little math, 24 is divisible by 6, and so is 30. Thus, the ratio 4:5 is associated with this transfer because there are four frames of film for each five frames of video. To get around this problem, when the film is transferred to video (referred to as the Telecine process), the video records at the 30fps standard so that 24 frames of the video can be evenly divided over the video frames. Telecine devices convert each four frames of film into five frames of video. (Each frame of video consists of two interlaced fields, while each film frame contains a complete image. The second and fourth film frames are repeated over three video fields, rather than two, producing one additional video frame for each four original film frames.)

To make the production tracks match the slower video played at 29.97fps, the audio is recorded at standard sample rates, which is then *pulled down* during playback (perhaps using Sync I/O, Nanosyncs, or TL Sync) while synchronizing to the video. During the transfer process back to film, the audio gets pulled back up. Therefore, the 44,100Hz sample rate can be pulled down to 44,056Hz, and 48,000Hz can be pulled down to 47,952Hz. Again, unless you're working on projects involving film transfers to video for editing, you probably won't deal with these sample rates (and will generally use 48,000Hz for most industrial and broadcast video projects).

Synchronized Layback

After you've edited the audio for a video project, you must transfer it back to the video master—in perfect synchronization, of course. Just as Pro Tools has to stay tightly in sync during the initial layoff and throughout the edit process, it naturally must maintain the correct time relationship with the image as you record your audio back to the video master. You will therefore keep Pro Tools in Online mode while the video operator enables the master video deck for audio recording (unless you're laying the audio directly back to the videotape in your own audio suite).

Sync Issues: House Sync

As explained in Chapter 11, house sync (a.k.a. black burst) is a stable video signal that provides a common timing reference for an entire production facility. With appropriate peripheral hardware, the audio clock of a Pro Tools hardware interface can also be resolved to this external timing reference. This eliminates drift between Pro Tools and the video master, especially important for long-duration projects, and improves Pro Tools' lock-up time to SMPTE. Devices that can accommodate house sync for Pro Tools include the Sync HD by Digidesign, the Digital Timepiece by Mark of the Unicorn (MOTU), Lucid, Aardvark, Apogee, and others. (See Appendix B for descriptions of some of these units.)

Analog Versus Digital

As mentioned, professional digital video decks generally use AES/EBU digital I/O for audio. If your Pro Tools hardware supports it, this is a preferable way to transfer your audio back to the video master for all the obvious reasons. But digital audio inputs on professional video gear are notoriously finicky about syncing to external digital audio sources, including Pro Tools. If you experience difficulties, by all means troubleshoot the situation—but it may not turn out that you're doing anything wrong.

When a video deck is recording audio via *analog* input, you must provide reference levels for the video operator (and have the courtesy to confirm beforehand that your mix's peak levels are actually reaching maximum).

Reference Levels and Tones from Pro Tools For years, many Pro Tools operators have kept audio files of *tones* (100Hz, 1kHz, and 10kHz) handy on their system so they could drop them into a Pro Tools session as a level reference for external devices with analog inputs. The Signal Generator plug-in provided with Pro Tools makes this largely unnecessary, especially if you simply need a momentary reference for a video deck's analog input. Create a new, empty audio track; then place the Signal Generator on it as an insert. In the Plug-In Settings window for Signal Generator, specify a frequency and waveform (sine waves are preferable for this purpose); be sure to set this plug-in's level slider to 0dB. If the main volume fader for your Master Fader is also set to 0dB, all the video operator has to do is adjust his or her input level until your tone registers at 0dB, and everybody will be in agreement. Easy! On the other hand, if the video editor provides tones in the video master (brought into Pro Tools via either analog or digital input), you should also return these same tones when you lay your audio tracks back onto the video master so that level consistency can be easily confirmed.

Summary

Postproduction professionals will note that we've only scratched the surface here. It's a huge field, and synchronization, tape formats, mix formats, and work processes vary tremendously from one facility to another. For the most part, we hope to have provided a little perspective on the process for more audio-oriented Pro Tools users. If you want to be involved in soundtrack work, probably the most important thing we can say is—go out and do it! You don't have to wait for the plum assignment at a top-flight video or film house to start getting your act together. There are tons of independent film and video producers out there—and the advent of high-quality DV cameras with 24p resolution, plus programs like Adobe Premiere, Sony Creative's Vegas, and Apple's FinalCut Pro, have immensely increased their numbers—who would be delighted to have you collaborate on their project. Also, interactive media developers often seek out Pro Tools collaborators for voice-over recording and postproduction of video files used in their applications (see the next chapter for more information about these opportunities). If the developer or editor provides a small QuickTime or other video file type for you to use, you can post video projects on any reasonably capable computer. It's a credit, it's a learning process, and it just might hit the jackpot—you never know!

15 Sound Design for Interactive Media

Pro Tools is an excellent platform for creating music and voice-over narrations for use in interactive applications on CD-ROMs, Web pages, DVD-ROMs, kiosks, and so on. It's also quite useful for creating sound effects associated with buttons and other hyperlinks—for example, while the cursor hovers over an object or when the user clicks the button or link. You can use many different programs to create media-rich interactive content that prominently includes audio and video files at a decent resolution. The file formats and constraints for audio usage vary for each program and situation; you will need to ask the authors/programmers many questions up front before starting to design sounds for an interactive project.

The unfortunate truth is that, for educational and business-oriented interactive presentations (such as CD-ROMs and broadband Web pages with Flash content on the Internet or intranets within organizations), the budget for professional-quality, original audio is often dismayingly small. Among other things, this reflects the fact that many interactive authors come from graphic-design backgrounds rather than from video or audio. They may be less cognizant than you might expect of just how much good audio enriches the texture and quality of the interactive experience. That's why so many pieces are in circulation with noisy, poorly compressed narrations, generic button sound effects that were included with the authoring program or harvested from enthusiast Web sites, and other unfortunate audio. Indeed, you may have to *sell* these people on the benefits of using your services for professional sound design and recording. As always, the best approach is to lead by example. Bring your examples of killer button sounds, background loops, clean and present-sounding voice-overs with small file sizes, and so on.

In contrast, sound design for the gaming industry has grown, becoming a vital part of the audio industry with its own protocols and workflows. The same can be said for music programming and composing for games, which involves specific use of MIDI and loop-oriented production that is very different from conventional music production.

At any rate, it's not enough to simply be the hottest Pro Tools jockey in town or an all-around studio professional (although this certainly will help). You need at least a rudimentary idea of what interactive authors actually *do* when incorporating sound files into their programs—the restrictions, the bottlenecks, and so on. If you're new to all this, one of the best things you can do is get together with a friend who works in Flash, Director, Visual Basic, ToolBook, AuthorWare, Adobe Presenter (formerly known as Breeze Presenter), Icon Author, PowerPoint, Keynote, and so on. Have that person show you the exact steps required to place a looping sound file as a background for a page, assign button-click sounds, play a sound while the cursor is over a button, trigger graphic events or advance to the next frame based on audio playback location, and other operations for handling audio. Get a good look at the file import dialog boxes in that program so that you know exactly which audio file formats are supported.

As a general rule, with Flash being a notable exception, *you* will need to perform the conversions to lower sample rates or compressed audio file formats. That way, all the audio files you deliver are ready to be plugged directly into the authoring environment. One of the third-party options for Macintosh is shown in Figure 15.1. If you instead deliver everything at uncompressed 44.1kHz stereo, leaving it up to the interactive folks to perform audio file format conversions according to their needs, we can practically guarantee you will not be pleased with the results! Also, be sure to ask about the desired durations for sound effects (and be prepared to have to adjust these later in the process). As we mention later in this chapter, it's also extremely important to be organized and consistent about file-naming conventions for the audio files you deliver. If possible, try to establish these with the authors in the earliest phases of the project, as you're defining the list of required audio.

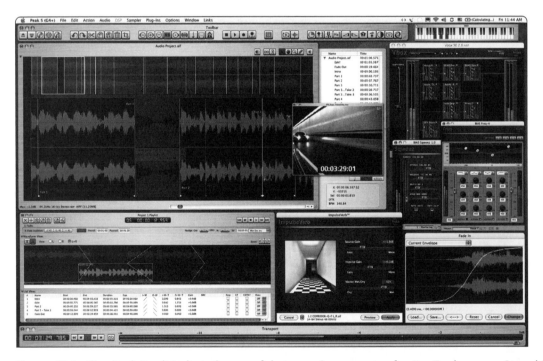

Figure 15.1 Bias Peak Pro (Mac) can be a useful companion program for Pro Tools, as can Sound Forge or WaveLab (Windows). These programs assist with supplemental file conversions and allow for the creation of cue points/markers within audio files for use by interactive programs, as well as loops.

Sound-Effects Libraries, Synths/Samplers, Sound Creation

General video-oriented sound-effects libraries on CD can provide some useful source material for interactive sound creation. Bear in mind, though, that licensing agreements and intellectual-property rights apply as much to an interactive CD/DVD or Web page as to any book or video program. If the sound-effects library is not a *buy-out*, where the purchase price of the CD includes the right to use its contents as part of any other program without paying any additional royalties, you could get yourself into trouble. Read the fine print!

Obviously, when creating button sounds and so on, you only use a small portion of generally longer sound effects provided in these libraries. Unless you're creating a specific stereo effect (and the constraints of the project allow you to do so), button sounds are typically mono. The sound designer's craft makes use of all the tools that Pro Tools provides for sound manipulation: pitch shifting, time compression/expansion, and dynamic and filtering effects. We suggest that your mindset always be that source sound effects are just one layer in a more complex sound that you will build up on multiple tracks (yes, even for a single button) rather than a solution in and of themselves.

We're also very fond of using synthesizers and samplers (*especially* the software-based variety) to create interactive sound effects. Aside from the obvious benefits of a more flexible sound palette, you can shape sounds with filtering and layer sounds on multiple MIDI channels in order to build a texture. Using software instruments also makes it very easy to produce groups of related sounds with consistent durations and dynamic levels. For example, this can be useful when creating a series of ascending tones for five or six similar buttons on a page. On audio regions, you can also apply one of the pitch-shifting functions in the Pro Tools AudioSuite menu to achieve a similar purpose.

Encourage your interactive collaborators—who wouldn't dream of using clip art in professional projects—not to use "clip sounds" either! Original sound is more creative, giving their programs a much more distinctive feel—there's an obvious analogy to cinema here. Plus, it may also provide you more work, right?

The Envelope, Please The *envelope* of a sound describes the contour of its changes in amplitude, pitch, or timbral characteristics over time. When creating interactive button sounds from existing audio files (for example, sound effects from a CD library or from other sources you've recorded), one of the common problems is that the initial *attack* of the sound may not be pronounced enough to make a satisfying impact when the user clicks the button. One solution is to add another layer (an additional sound in another Pro Tools track) with a heavier attack on the front end that quickly fades out. First, however, try switching the track's data display format to Volume and simply *drawing* the loudness contour you'd like for this button sound: a full-volume spike at the beginning, ramping down to a more general level after a couple hundred milliseconds (see Figure 15.2). For simple button sounds, a similar effect might also be achieved by using a compressor plug-in set to a high ratio but with a very long (>100 millisecond) attack.

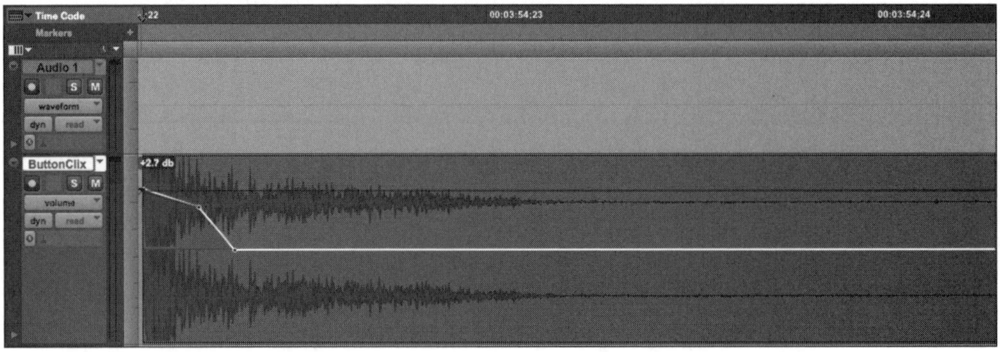

Figure 15.2   When creating button sounds for interactive media, you can use automation to create the desired volume envelope. Here, we're increasing the level of the sound's initial attack.

Common Multimedia File Formats

We discuss common audio file formats in Chapter 1, "About Pro Tools." Here's some additional information, specific to providing audio for interactive developers:

- **WAV and AIF.** WAV was originally developed jointly by Microsoft and IBM, while AIF (sometimes known as *AIFF*) was originally developed by Apple Computer. This probably explains the relative abundance of these audio file formats on each platform. Their characteristics are fairly similar. Both WAV and AIF files are supported audio-recording formats for Pro Tools sessions (Mac versions can also use SDII, discussed in a moment), but WAV format is *required* for recording at sample rates higher than 48kHz on *any* Pro Tools system. (Even though technically Pro Tools uses Broadcast WAV format for recording, this is backward compatible with WAV and uses the same extension.) Bouncing or exporting audio from Pro Tools to WAV format is standard for many Windows audio programs (some of which do not accept AIF or especially the obsolete SDII file format), and AIF files are supported by almost every audio-capable Mac program. However, current versions of most interactive applications on both platforms can accept *either* WAV or AIF.

- **Sound Designer II.** Also known as SDII or SD2, this format was originally developed by Digidesign for its Sound Tools stereo audio workstations. It was also the native file format for early Mac versions of Pro Tools, but is not directly supported by Windows versions of Pro Tools—or for any sample rates over 48kHz on *either* platform. The header data in the SDII format includes information about region definitions (which, as with AIF and WAV, can be exported into the parent SDII files from a Pro Tools session when required), loops, and so on. SDII isn't supported by any current interactive program. Even on Mac versions of Pro Tools, it should *not* be used as the audio file format for sessions unless compatibility with older versions (such as Pro Tools Free 5.01 for Macintosh OS 9) is a specific concern.

■ **MP3.** MP3, short for MPEG Audio Layer-3, is part of the MPEG compressed audio/video data standards. It uses a perceptual encoding technique to reduce the size of audio data. When you encode an MP3 file (MP3 encoding is an inexpensive add-on purchase for Pro Tools; a 30-day trial version is included with all versions), you choose *a bit rate* for the resulting file. The smaller the bit rate, measured in Kbps (kilobits per second, also abbreviated Kbit/s), the more digital *artifacts* may be noticeable in the result. You can also embed title, author, and copyright information into MP3 files. This format became popular for exchanging music over the Internet because of the small file sizes it can produce (although, being a lossy compression method, there is always some proportional compromise of audio quality). It is also very attractive for interactive developers because it produces better-sounding audio in smaller files (compared to knocking files down to a 22,050Hz sampling rate, a common strategy a decade ago). Be aware, though, that MP3 is not universally supported, especially in older versions of interactive authoring software. For example, some game-authoring programs still don't support MP3 at all. Apple's Keynote presentation software supports MP3 (and AAC) files, as do current versions of Microsoft's PowerPoint. Current versions of the Director and AuthorWare programs support MP3 files, as does the Adobe Presenter and Adobe Connect Training (formerly known as Breeze) software for online course development. Flash (by Adobe, originally developed by Macromedia) also frequently uses MP3 files given its common use in low-bandwidth Internet environments. Longer MP3 files can even be streamed as part of a Flash piece. Note that for looping sounds such as musical phrases and button rollOver sound effects, you will sometimes find that MP3 conversion introduces a very small amount of silence at the beginning and end of the waveform. This will cause your loop to hiccup in Flash. In these cases, you may be obliged to deliver WAV or AIF instead, and allow audio compression to be applied when the final Flash project is saved out (which usually will not cause these audio looping problems). As with all audio for computer playback, you will generally apply generous amounts of audio gain compression and maximize the level of your original audio in Pro Tools. Be aware that even at low levels, low-frequency noise—especially pops and breath noises—can cause problems for encoding algorithms that compress audio data (and incidentally, is *especially* problematic for time-expansion and pitch-shifting processes). Be sure to monitor your material with good speakers and listen to it at a reasonably loud volume. If necessary, try dropping a high-pass filter (using one of the DigiRack EQ plug-ins included with Pro Tools, for example) on the offending track. Prior to delivery, however, be sure to actually *listen* to your MP3 files on inexpensive computer speakers! Unexpected differences in the apparent dynamic range or the prominence of various background and instrumental elements in your mix can often require bouncing out a new file.

- **AAC.** Short for *Advanced Audio Coding*, AAC, like MP3, was developed by the MPEG Group. It is used by Apple in its iTunes Music Store. Version 7 of Apple's QuickTime Pro can also save AAC audio files. AAC is actually part of the MPEG-4 audio spec and uses signal-processing technology from Dolby Laboratories to apply more complex compression algorithms to audio data. These not only reduce the data size more efficiently than MP3 but also produce better-sounding results at any comparable data rate—*especially* for music. To put it another way, AAC encoding can obtain the same quality as an MP3 file that would be 30–35 percent bigger.

- **WMA.** Short for *Windows Media Audio* and introduced by Microsoft in 1999, this compressed audio format is common on the Windows platform and can be played on Mac systems with appropriate add-in software such as the Flip4Mac component for QuickTime. It is also the default destination format when ripping files from CD in Windows Media Player (although this preference can be changed to MP3). The WMA specification also includes alternate codecs: WMA Pro (supports higher resolutions and multichannel audio), WMA Lossless, and WMA Voice (optimizes voice content at lower bit rates).

- **RealAudio.** This streaming, compressed audio file format, often used on the Internet, was developed by Real Networks. The RealPlayer free download also supports streaming video files—and is notorious for invasively altering playback defaults for various media file types to make itself the default player as well as being very difficult to completely remove from a Windows system. You can reduce audio to various throughputs according to the requirements, with audible compression artifacts resulting from more extreme compression levels. Real Networks' SureStream technology incorporates several different versions of the audio into a single file link. The appropriate density is selected for playback according to the available bandwidth when a user starts playing that file over the Internet. Again, not all interactive authoring programs support RealAudio, and some require the purchase and/or licensing of a separate plug-in. RealAudio is mostly effective for spoken-word projects because the level of audio artifacts is rather high at typical Internet bandwidths.

- **AU.** Also known as mu-law or Sun/NeXT, this is the audio file equivalent of an audio data-compression standard developed for telephony. 16-bit source audio is reduced to 13 bits (thereby discarding the three least significant bits and increasing quantization error), and then encoded into an 8-bit format. AU is an older standard (prior to MP3, for example), and frequently used with an 8kHz (8,000Hz) sample rate. As you might imagine, from an audio engineer's perspective, this represents a pretty drastic reduction in sound quality compared to current alternatives for audio data compression. However, AU sound files will still occasionally be requested by Internet developers when the methodology or programs specifically require this format. A separate program is required to convert bounced mixes from Pro Tools to AU format.

- **QuickTime.** This is principally a video format, although audio-only QuickTime files can be created. On Windows computers, QuickTime file names must end in the .mov extension to be automatically recognized by QuickTime Player. One reason for using audio-only QuickTime files, for example, would be when using the movieTime property in the Director program. This allows other events to be triggered at certain positions while the QuickTime file plays. Playback can be initiated from specific positions within the QuickTime file—for example, when the user clicks a button to hear a specific section.

Great-Sounding Compressed Audio Within QuickTime Movies If you have any influence on how the audio tracks you contribute for QuickTime movies will be processed later, encourage the interactive authors to consider choosing the MPEG-4 codec for the soundtrack. (Figure 15.3 shows some of the export options from Apple's QuickTime Pro, a $30 upgrade from the free downloadable player for Windows or Mac.) Other traditional and extreme methods (stereo to mono, reducing sample rate, and other compression codecs) exist for drastically reducing the data rate and overall file size for audio tracks in QuickTime movies. However, we think you'll agree that among the current alternatives, MPEG-4 does the least damage to your audio!

How Audio Is Used in Interactive Media

Terminology varies greatly from one interactive authoring program to another, but there are some common concepts for typical uses of audio. Things that can be clicked on (which may actually look like a button or may simply be a linked text or graphic) should make noise when they're clicked so the user knows that the program has responded. Often, screens within a presentation or game will play longer audio pieces or loop a smaller audio segment to conserve disk space and reduce competition for disk access between the graphics and audio. Of course, graphic events are frequently scripted to specific locations within a narration (that is, an audio file you've provided). Loading of graphics, animations, and other data competes with whatever audio files are playing for access to whatever disk the presentation is playing from (for example, a hard disk or CD), and for the computer's resources in general. So you need to be adept at getting good-sounding results at low file sizes. It does you no good to create luxurious, high-bandwidth audio if in actual use it's going to take forever to start playing—or skip during playback!

Voice-Overs

Voice-overs are narrations or phrases other than those spoken by an onscreen character. This is one of the most frequently requested services you will be asked to provide for interactive media projects. The general technique is similar to voice-over recording for worst-case video scenarios; you should use compression and other dynamics processing to ensure solid, consistent audio levels that overcome all the intrinsic obstacles to intelligibility during computer playback (cheap speakers, extremely tiny speakers on laptops and LCD displays, noisy computers, low playback levels, and so on).

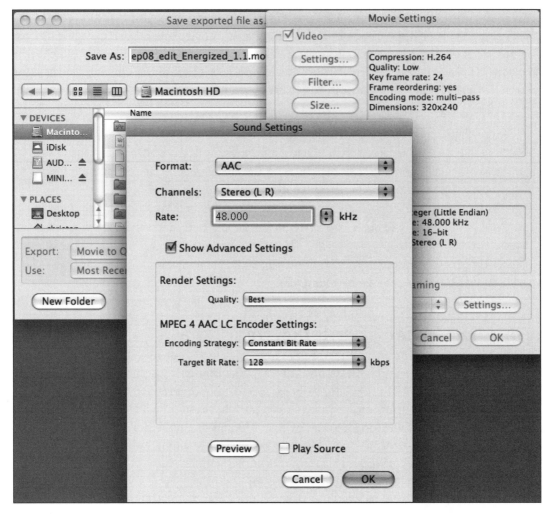

Figure 15.3 Options when using QuickTime's File > Export command and the selection of Movie To QuickTime Movie as the format of the exported video file include compression of the soundtrack using MPEG-4 (AAC).

Remember: Good audio does make a difference in any interactive project. Voices should be recorded in a relatively noise-free environment, using a quality microphone with a pop filter. In typical interactive development scenarios, the two worst noise offenders are computers with their hard disks and fans, and air-conditioning/heating systems in the building. Noisy voice recordings—even for projects that will never be played on anything but computer speakers— will come back to haunt you later. For this reason, even though it's critical to reality-check your audio files on cheap computer speakers before releasing to the client, make *sure* you monitor your audio work on good-quality speakers and headphones. Some users may have better audio-monitoring systems on their computers than you!

Audio for PowerPoint Audio file formats supported by Microsoft's PowerPoint presentation software include WAV, AIF, and MP3. Although a single audio file can play through a sequence of slides or an entire presentation, for voice-overs that sync to graphic events on each slide (for example, revealing bullet-text points as they are mentioned in the voice-over), it's more common to provide your PowerPoint collaborator with a series of sequentially numbered audio files—for example, Slide01, Slide 02, and so on. Apply plenty of compression/limiting to these voice-over files, and make sure they are very close to maximum levels; the audio playback conditions for this kind of presentation are usually far from ideal!

Buttons/Links

There are two basic techniques for using sounds with buttons or links. First, when the user rolls the mouse cursor over the "hot" area, a sound file can be triggered (either a single pass or a looping sound that you have created for this purpose). These are called *rollOvers* in the Director and Flash programs, *mouseovers* in JavaScript, and *focus states* in some other programs. The idea is to attract the user's attention to the fact that something will happen once the screen object is clicked. Often, rollOvers also incorporate a graphic effect—for example, a glow around the button, a color change, or an animation effect. When creating looping sounds to bounce from Pro Tools, be sure to check them afterward in another program that can seamlessly loop audio selections. (The QuickTime Player does *not* loop audio seamlessly.) In some situations (occasionally with LE/M-Powered versions, and especially when creating MP3 files), some excess data may appear at the beginning of a bounced audio file—just enough to mess up the seamless loop you were hearing in Pro Tools.

Second, when the user clicks the button, some sort of positive, auditory feedback should occur. This could be a click sound, a whoosh, or whatever cool audio effect you come up with. This is called a *mouseDown* event in Director and Flash and an *onClick* event in JavaScript. It might also involve some graphic effect along with your sound effect. In practice, it is more customary for actions, sounds, and graphic effects on a button to occur on mouseUp—that is, when the user *releases* the mouse button. This allows users to roll back off the button before releasing the mouse if they really didn't intend to click there.

Generally, we find that audio levels for background and button sounds (both mouse click or mouseDown sounds and the rollOver sounds) should be lower than first-order content, like voice-over narrations, the contents of video files, and so on. Start by setting their peaks to about 10–12dB (a little over 30 percent of full code—remember that decibels are logarithmic, not linear). Whatever the level you set for background and button sounds, be consistent unless there's a specific reason for making an exception. (Sometimes a particular sound still *sounds* louder even after it has been normalized down to the same peak level as all the others. Compression via the Dynamics3 plug-in within Pro Tools, or more sophisticated gain optimization plug-ins such as Digidesign's Maxim or Waves' L1, L2, and L3, can help even out levels by eliminating transients in the pre-normalization level.) It's difficult for developers to deal with dozens of button sounds with no consistent levels. In short, when creating sound effects for interactive projects, you can't just normalize everything to full code (100 percent maximum volume) and figure you've done your job.

Creating Cue Points In interactive applications, one very common technique is to create cue points (also known as *markers*) within audio files. A simple handler script (on exitFrame in Director, for example) tells the interactive program to wait until a specific cue point is reached in the audio file before advancing to the next frame in the sequence. By using cue points or simple time references, graphic events can be triggered when specific locations within the audio are reached during playback. This makes it possible to do things like bring up titles, bullet points or graphics as certain words are spoken in the voice-over. Cue points must be created in separate programs—such as Bias Peak Pro, Steinberg WaveLab, or Sony Sound Forge—usually by the authors themselves, although you may occasionally be asked to assist in this process. Contrary to what you might imagine, the Marker memory locations you create in Pro Tools are *not* reflected as cue points within bounced audio files.

Music/Effects Backgrounds

When you create music or ambience backgrounds for scenes in an interactive CD-ROM, DVD-ROM, or Web site, be aware of what *else* will be going on while your audio is playing. If a great deal of animation and graphics interaction is occurring simultaneously, this can severely affect the throughput available for playing your audio. In this situation, if you don't reduce the size of your audio background file (for example, by reducing from stereo to mono, reducing sample rate, or ideally by using data compression), it may skip on playback—especially on slower computers, on slower CD drives, or when insufficient RAM is available (which affects the program's ability to preload graphics and other content for timely playback).

Interactive applications often loop playback of audio effects or music as a background for scenes. There are pros and cons to this technique. For one thing, it is an art to create musical loops that are both interesting enough and adequately nondescript so as not to become annoying after a couple of repetitions. There are also technical considerations. Obviously, one of the main reasons for using audio loops is to save disk space (or download time). Instead of a full four to five minutes of audio for the time a user may spend in each screen, 20 seconds worth of well-looped audio might be equally effective. However, in the Director program, looped audio files must be entirely loaded to RAM. (Normally, longer audio files stream directly from disk.) Depending on the RAM and CPU requirements your interactive authors can demand of their potential audience, looped audio can sometimes impose more strict limitations on duration, number of channels, and resolution than would apply for simply playing back a longer file directly from disk.

Some programs, like the current versions of 3D GameStudio and Flash, can only loop the entire audio file. In contrast, Director will recognize any loop definitions found *within* an AIF file. You must create the loop definition with some program other than Pro Tools, such as Peak, Sound Forge, or WaveLab. As a music and sound designer for Director projects, you can include a header or intro that precedes the looping portion of the file. This is useful not only for music (an eight-bar intro that eventually settles down to a four-bar loop, for example) but also for looping rollOver sounds on buttons and other objects.

In Flash, interactive authors can specify how many times an audio file should loop. They can also create fade-in and fade-out envelopes for that sequence of loop repetitions. If the Flash piece will be playing from a Web site, however, bear in mind that audio-file sizes are usually reduced drastically to avoid inconveniently long download times. Another pitfall to be aware of is that Flash developers often create loops over a certain range of frames in the timeline itself, and then simply stretch your loop audio across that duration. In these cases, find out what frame rate they're using! If it's 15 frames per second, make sure your loop's duration corresponds exactly to $1/_{15}$ of a second subdivision—even if this means applying time compression/expansion afterward in Pro Tools or some other program. Do the math! Otherwise, there will be a distinct hiccup each time this looping portion of the Flash timeline repeats.

Squash Your Loops It can take a while to get the knack of creating smoothly looping musical/ambient backgrounds for interactive applications. When the loop needs to repeat seamlessly (for example, a humming, glowing sound, or a funky groove), here's one trick we sometimes find useful: Apply relatively extreme amounts of compression (basically, limiting) on the looping selection. This increases the possibility that the end of the loop and the beginning will have similar levels, which is at least one step toward a smoother loop.

As you can guess, in Pro Tools, you would use the Options > Loop Playback option as you perfect selections that will be bounced out as looping audio for interactive applications. If the sound sources for a loop include MIDI instruments (either external devices or software synths), it is often preferable to record these to an audio track before defining your looped selection and bouncing it out. Otherwise, their delay or reverb effects from the end of the looping selection may sustain across the beginning, giving a false impression of how smooth the loop really is. Don't forget to save your bounced selection as a Selection memory location before closing the Pro Tools session in case you have to bounce it out again! In Chapter 6, "The Edit Window," you will find some specific hints and shortcuts for fine-tuning your selection by nudging.

Don't Assume! Audio selections that loop smoothly at 44kHz within Pro Tools may not do so after they've been converted to 22KHz (more precisely, 22,050Hz) or especially when converted to a compressed data format, such as MP3! Also, if subsequent normalization on the bounced loop files increases their gain, some clicks at the loop point may become audible. (Beginning and ending your loops at zero crossings can help avoid this.) Be sure to check your loop files (for example, in Peak, WaveLab, or Sound Forge) before turning them over to your interactive clients and collaborators! By the way, looped playback in Apple's QuickTime Player and Windows Media Player always *pauses* slightly between repetitions of the audio file, so they are not useful for this purpose. Be aware, too, that even with non-looping audio files you bounce out from Pro Tools that don't begin or end at zero amplitude crossings, a large gain increase resulting from normalization can occasionally raise these non-zero values enough to produce an audible click as they are triggered in the interactive program. Be sure to check your normalized files!

For the Sake of Good Order... Think through the naming conventions you will use *before* starting to bounce out files for interactive projects! For the most part, multimedia authors will import your files via a standard File Open dialog box (see Figure 15.4). If the audio files you provide naturally appear in proper order, you will greatly reduce the potential for confusion. For example, when you have more than 10 similarly numbered files, use leading zeroes so that file10.AIF doesn't appear between file1.AIF and file2.AIF!

When providing both rollOver sound and a mouseUp sounds for the same button (also known as focus state and click sounds, or MouseOver and OnClick in some programs), make the first part of their file names similar so they are automatically sorted together in the file list: QuitRoll.AIF, QuitClik.AIF, and so on.

Note for Mac users: Without a file-name extension, Windows programs generally don't know anything about a file's type. Unless you actually put the appropriate extension on the files you submit to Windows developers (.wav, .aif, .mov, and so on), they may not even be recognized as audio files!

Sharing Well with Others: About Bandwidth

At higher bit depths and sample rates, file sizes are much larger. This creates important issues for interactive media. High-resolution audio files obviously occupy more disk space or cause longer download times from the Internet. Most importantly, as an interactive application runs, audio playback shares the computer's (and disk's) throughput capacity with the other graphic files and animation. You may get killer sound quality by maintaining your audio files at higher resolutions, but if they're going to skip during playback because animation and graphic files are loading from the same disk, it defeats the purpose, right? So you need to be aware of how and when

Figure 15.4   The Flash program can import various audio file formats. Audio waveforms can be viewed within its timeline in relation to graphics and animation events.

your audio files are going to be used (and especially what else is happening while they're played) and what the target system requirements are for the application. For example, if the authors still have to support 12*x* CD-ROM playback on older 333MHz computers (or slower) with 16MB of RAM, this imposes much more drastic limitations on audio file sizes than if they require 18× SuperDrives or the Intel Xeon CPU, or equally powerful current computer configurations.

Obviously, if your source material isn't stereo, you shouldn't create stereo files for the interactive application. Believe it or not, we see people doing this all the time—for example, using stereo files for simple voice-overs! Even if your source *is* stereo—for example, music—when you find yourself obliged to make drastic reductions in audio file sizes, consider whether it's a greater loss to lose the stereo image or to lose all frequencies above approximately 10kHz if the sample rate is reduced to 22,050Hz (or everything above 5kHz or so at the even more drastic 11,025Hz sample rate). Either option reduces the file to half of its former size. Listen to each; trust your ears! Again, if the interactive application supports compressed audio file formats such as MP3, this is usually the preferable method for reducing file size and throughput requirements.

Sample Rate

Audio file size is directly proportional to sample rate (doubling the number of samples per second also doubles the file size), and to the number of channels (stereo files are twice the size of mono). As discussed in Chapter 1, under the "Digital Audio Basics" heading, higher sample rates allow the recording/playback of higher audio frequencies. For interactive applications, the two most commonly used sample rates for linear (uncompressed) audio are 22,050 samples per second and 44,100 samples per second (often shortened to 22K or 44.1K in digital audio parlance), although 11,025 (11K) is sometimes used when bandwidth available for audio is extremely limited—for instance, when an application needs to run smoothly on much older computers or on the Internet.

Converting audio down to 22K/16-bit can actually sound okay on typical computer speakers, especially for voice-overs and button sounds (some of which can even be knocked down to 11K if high-frequency components aren't crucial). Remember that, unlike reducing bit depth (which is discussed in the following section), reducing the sample rate to 22,050Hz does not make your audio files any noisier; it simply eliminates high-frequency information (above about 10kHz). One of the tricks employed by standalone file-conversion applications such as Autodesk's Cleaner (Mac) or Cleaner XL (Windows) is to augment the apparent brightness of lower sample rate files by adding a slight equalization peak just below the cutoff frequency. Even if you don't have these tools at your disposal, you can approach the same effect. For example, place an EQ plug-in on the Master Fader/output pair that is the source for your bounce. Then use the high-shelf filter to add several decibels of boost from about 9kHz upward.

Bit Depth

Bit depth describes the size of the digital word representing each audio sample. The number of bits (binary digits) in the number used to capture the input audio signal's voltage for each sample period determines how many discrete amplitude levels can potentially be represented. Like the vertical spacing on graph paper, the fewer increments that are available (the fewer bits per sample), the less accurate the representation, compared to the continuous variations in the original waveform. Early computer multimedia and computer games often used 8-bit audio files (256 possible amplitude levels); the noticeable *quantization error* in 8-bit files gives them their characteristic fizzy sound quality. Incidentally, if the project really does require you to bounce out 8-bit files from Pro Tools, be sure to enable the Use Squeezer check box in the Bounce dialog box. This slightly increases the quality of the resultant 8-bit audio, especially for voice-overs, by applying some proprietary gain processing prior to the conversion.

16-bit audio files are currently the norm for CD-ROM interactive applications. This is the same bit depth used on standard audio CDs (which are stereo, of course, and use a 44.1kHz sample rate). 24-bit audio (often with higher sample rates) is the current norm for the most demanding professional audio recordings, but is rarely used in interactive applications.

Managing Audio Levels

Generally, you want to ensure that the dynamic range in audio files intended for computer playback consistently remains near the specified maximum level. For example, you will almost always use a compressor plug-in (and/or limiting) on voice-over narrations to smooth out any variations in volume. As an added benefit, this generally makes voice-overs more intelligible (punching through the general noise of a computer's fan and disk drives, for instance). That way, if you normalize an audio file you've bounced from Pro Tools, the peak level used by the normalization process as the benchmark for adjusting its gain will be closer to the overall levels in the rest of the file (see Figure 15.5). Another more sophisticated technique is to use gain optimization plug-ins, which apply other techniques to produce good-sounding audio at very consistent, in-your-face levels (that is, with very little variation in their dynamic range).

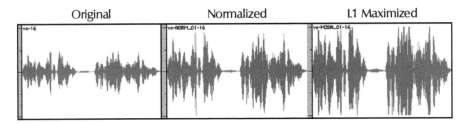

Original	Normalized	L1 Maximized

Figure 15.5 The effects of gain optimization: The first waveform was compressed during recording, prior to the Pro Tools input. The second was normalized to 100 percent (its peak level corresponds to full code). The third was processed with L1, by Waves. Note that its amplitude is more consistently near the maximum level.

As mentioned in the "Buttons/Links" section earlier in this chapter, normalization is a key tool for preparing audio for use in multimedia. Even though any experienced Pro Tools operator keeps a careful eye on Master Fader levels in all original Pro Tools sessions (always the primary method for managing levels), in the interactive-development scenario you frequently have to maintain extremely consistent levels throughout dozens or even hundreds of similar audio files because the final user may switch rapidly between them while navigating from section to section. Despite the common misconception that normalizing always increases peak audio levels to 100 percent (and to be sure, in some very rudimentary audio programs, this *is* the only option), Pro Tools and most professional batch-conversion programs support normalization to any level. For example, if the main voice-over files are at nearly 100 percent, your entire collection of backing music loops and button effects might be normalized to peak levels of −6dB or −10dB (50.1 or 31.6 percent of full code, respectively). That way, the various categories of audio files you deliver come into the authoring program pre-mixed instead of depending on the interactive author's skill level with handling audio levels—or occasionally confronting severe practical limitations for such adjustments in the authoring program itself.

For music and ambient backgrounds especially, the RMS mode of the Gain plug-in (under the AudioSuite menu) will be very useful. Adjusting the RMS gain of diverse sounds to an identical level can be a more reliable way to make them *seem* to be of similar loudness. In contrast, when using the ordinary Peak mode of Normalization (or Gain) processing, isolated transients and other variations in the dynamic range of the source audio can still leave you with files that appear to be of unequal loudness, even if their peaks are all carefully adjusted to, say, −10dB.

Audio Data Compression

Data compression reduces the size of the data representing the original audio waveforms. It is always a lossy process—some of the original information is lost. Among the various methods for reducing the size of audio data, some are more effective with certain types of sounds than others (for example, for spoken word versus a music file). Of course, it's important not to confuse data compression with audio *gain* compression (which reduces the dynamic range, or volume variations, within an audio signal).

MP3 encoding (discussed earlier in this chapter) is a compression method for audio data that takes advantage of the characteristics of human hearing. We tend to hear mainly the loudest sound in each of a series of critical bands of frequency, so other sounds within the same band are converted to lower bit depths with little noticeable deterioration of sound quality. MP3 encoding also compresses redundant data that is present in both channels. (This is, of course, a gross oversimplification of the MP3-encoding method, designed to give you a general idea.) MP3 really does provide spectacular reductions of file size before obvious digital artifacts appear. If an interactive application supports MP3 files for longer audio files (and doesn't require cue points to trigger events), this is a *much* more attractive option than reducing sample rate (let alone reducing bit depth), preserving as much as possible of your original sound quality at a smaller file size. MP3 audio is especially prevalent in Flash-based Internet applications. SWA, the Shockwave audio format associated with Director, also generally uses MP3 compression. By all means, offer to do the MP3 audio encoding yourself rather than leaving it in the hands (and ears) of the interactive designers. They will, however, need to provide you with guidelines for the target bit rate (audio data density, measured in kilobits per second, or Kbps) according to their design requirements. Otherwise, it's all too likely that they will use some general compression preset from their host program (see Figure 15.6 for an example) that compresses audio relatively drastically in favor of retaining graphic quality.

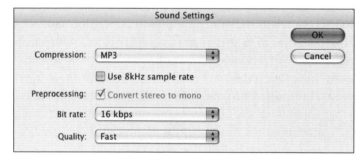

Figure 15.6 The program's default settings for audio quality (unless changed by the user) when publishing a Flash presentation from Adobe Flash CS3 Professional. Ouch!

Make Some Noise about Audio Quality! As you can see in Figure 15.6, the default settings for handling audio in Flash are drastic, to say the least. Most Flash developers will request that you submit uncompressed WAV (or AIF) files. So far so good. But when they publish the completed presentation to create a Flash SWF file that can be run within a browser program, the default sound settings will severely degrade the quality of your audio if you don't intervene. Ask them to open the Flash tab of the Publish Settings dialog box and change the Audio Stream and Audio Event properties to a 128Kbps bit rate and, if necessary, to disable the Convert Stereo to Mono checkbox.

AAC and MPEG-4 audio (in some ways, two aspects of the same thing) are newer, more efficient methods of compressing audio data. By all means, *if* the target application supports this codec for audio (many, including Flash and Director, do not), it is one of your best choices. For example, for a comparable quality level, MPEG-4 audio files can be as much as 30 percent smaller than MP3 (which is already far smaller than uncompressed, or linear, audio). QuickTime video files now also support MPEG-4 encoding in their audio tracks (not to be confused with MPEG-4 encoding in their video track, a different matter). In fact, if you own QuickTime Pro, you can convert the audio tracks within QT movies you've bounced from Pro Tools (see the next section) into MPEG-4 and/or AAC when using QuickTime Pro 7. We think you'll be impressed with the sonic results, considering the huge reduction in file size.

You Need Some Crappy PC Speakers! If you create music and sound effects for the average computer, a cheap set of computer speakers is a *necessity*! Your tiny near-field studio monitors are *too* good, as are the speakers on an Apple iMac, for that matter. Always reality-check everything on the mediocre sort of mini-speakers included with the average PC (price limit $20, if you're buying them separately). Those way-low bass and percussion sounds you spent so much time on might disappear entirely or come back in some exaggerated and unpleasant form when played on PC speaker setups with a subwoofer. The general prominence of parts within musical arrangements can change radically—occasionally an issue when files are heavily compressed to MP3 and similar formats. Even more importantly, the apparent levels of voice-overs and dialog versus background music or sound effects can change drastically on these setups compared to even modest studio monitors. Speaking from personal experience, I can say it is not amusing when a bumpin' rave bass line becomes completely inaudible or when an apparently innocuous timbre, after suffering the indignity of data compression and playback through Cheezo-Tech computer speakers, turns into some sort of flatulent buzz.

Creating Audio for Digital Video Files

Sometimes, animations created in other programs will be converted to QuickTime, MPEG, or AVI files to facilitate playback within an interactive application. You can add audio from Pro Tools into new copies of existing video files via the File > Bounce to > QuickTime Movie command. Here's how:

1. Select File > Import > Video. In the File Open dialog box that appears, locate and double-click the digital video file. If there is any audio in that video file that you want to bring into your Pro Tools session, be sure to enable the Import Audio from File checkbox in the Video Import Options dialog box. The video image will appear in the Video window of Pro Tools, and a Video track will be created that shows thumbnails of the individual frames in the QuickTime movie.

2. Using the Video window (which plays the file in real time within Pro Tools) and the Video track as a guide, create your soundtrack. If you find that redrawing of the video thumbnails within the Video track slows down the editing operation, switch it to Blocks track view.

3. Now you are ready to bounce your audio mixdown directly back into the QuickTime movie using the File > Bounce to > QuickTime Movie command. This will not affect the video tracks within the source video file; they're simply cloned into the new copy.

4. In the Bounce dialog box (shown in Figure 15.7), choose mono or stereo for the bounced audio, keeping in mind that stereo requires twice as much throughput for playback in the target program. Consult your interactive authors about data-rate guidelines for this QuickTime file. The Squeezer option appears in this dialog box if you're forced to convert down to 8-bit audio within the QuickTime file. (You should be prepared to compress audio data, sacrifice stereo, and/or reduce sample rate before ever

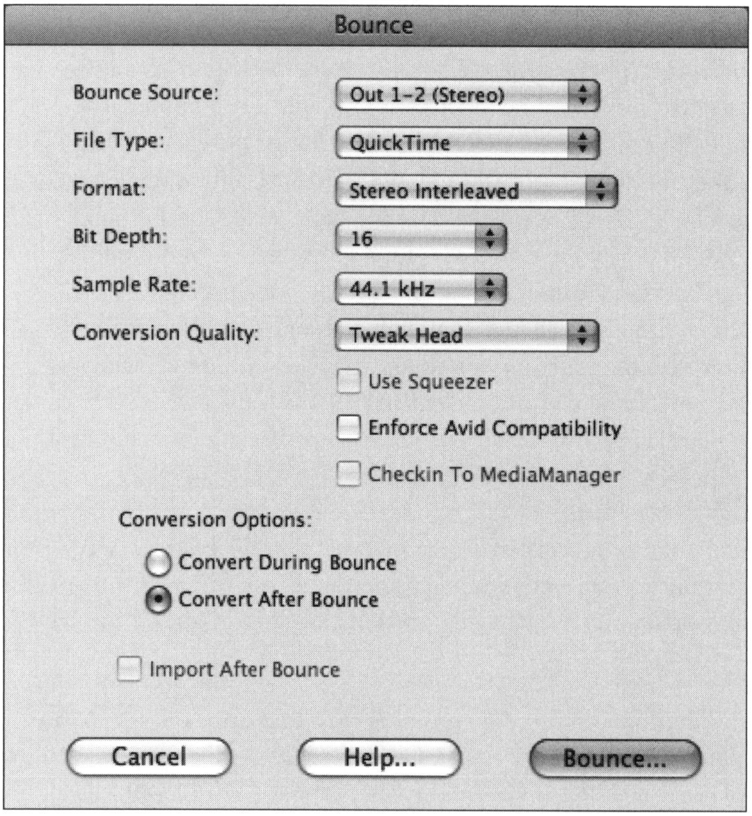

Figure 15.7 The dialog box for bouncing to a QuickTime movie. This is similar to bouncing audio files to disk, but incorporates the audio output from Pro Tools as the soundtrack within a cloned QuickTime copy of the video file currently being used in the session.

resorting to 8-bit audio!) If your source Pro Tools session is 48kHz or higher, you may also want to convert the audio to a 44.1kHz sample rate for playback within interactive applications. If required, you can perform data compression on the soundtrack of the resultant video file afterward, using QuickTime Pro (via its File > Export command), Peak Pro, WaveLab, Sound Forge, or another audio-editing program that supports QuickTime video files. As a matter of fact, QuickTime Pro supports a good selection of audio-compression codecs (including MPEG-4/AAC) that can produce smaller video files that are still excellent sounding and compatible with most interactive authoring environments.

Summary

How the audio you provide is used within an interactive piece varies widely between programs, as well as from one author to the next. It's crucial to plan things out with the developers before starting to create sounds and bounce out files. Among other things, you must know what file formats and resolutions they require, the bandwidth limitations on the target computer platform (because this determines your options for sample rate or audio data compression, for example), what file-naming conventions are preferred, whether voice-overs and music underscores can be long durations or must be broken up scene by scene, whether the host program can loop audio smoothly, and whether Standard MIDI Files (also known as SMF; they have the .mid file-name extension) are one of the preferred media types.

Pay special attention to maintaining consistent levels among all the voice-overs, button and background sound effects, videos, and music that you create for an interactive project. It is not especially convenient for interactive authors to make individual volume adjustments as they play back your sound files; in fact, it's usually a pain in the neck. So it's up to you ensure that all the sounds you create in a given category have consistent levels (normalization is an invaluable tool for this), usually with distinct levels for each category of sounds—for example, buttons, background audio, and voice-overs.

The basic concepts explored in this chapter should give you a start, at least for asking the right questions when you are approached to produce audio for interactive projects. Although almost any current Pro Tools system is well equipped for this kind of work, the more first-hand knowledge you have about how the authors will actually use the audio you provide, the better your chances of getting the assignment.

16 Bouncing to Disk, Other File Formats

As you know, a Pro Tools project consists of a session document plus many additional audio files that are referenced by it. If you're mixing a stereo project, for example, you would listen to your audio via two outputs on your audio hardware. In fact, for those who record their mixes in real time to a video master or some external two-track recorder, this may be all that is required. On the other hand, you may need to create *reduction* mixes from your Pro Tools project as a submixing strategy, or especially *mixdown* files in order to create audio files that can be used by other programs. To cite a common example, you will frequently create stereo mixdown files from Pro Tools so that you can write an audio CD (using another program) or so that a video editor or multimedia programmer can use that finished mixdown in a project. Pro Tools provides many powerful options for exporting audio files to standard formats. This chapter provides some guidelines for producing files to be used by other programs.

Bounce to Disk

The File > Bounce to > Disk command creates a new audio file containing the result of all the audio regions, automation, processing, and other MIDI/audio or mix data contained in your session (or the current timeline selection). Exactly what you're hearing through the selected Pro Tools output pair (unmuted tracks, real-time sources on Aux In or audio tracks, plus all the inserts, plug-in processing, automation, and signal routing) will be incorporated into the bounced file. Pro Tools always bounces files to disk in real time, so external sends/returns and inserts can be incorporated, plus any software-based instruments and effects or external sound sources connected to the audio interface (monitored through Aux In tracks).

The Bounce dialog box (shown in Figure 16.1) also allows you to apply file conversion, either during the bounce or afterwards. For highest accuracy in the rendering of plug-in automation, Digidesign recommends converting *after* the bounce. Regardless of the audio file type used for the original Pro Tools session, you can always choose among other supported formats for the bounced mixdown file. The Import After Bounce option brings the bounced audio file back into the Regions List. It's only available, however, if the file format, bit depth, and sample rate for the bounced file match that of the current session.

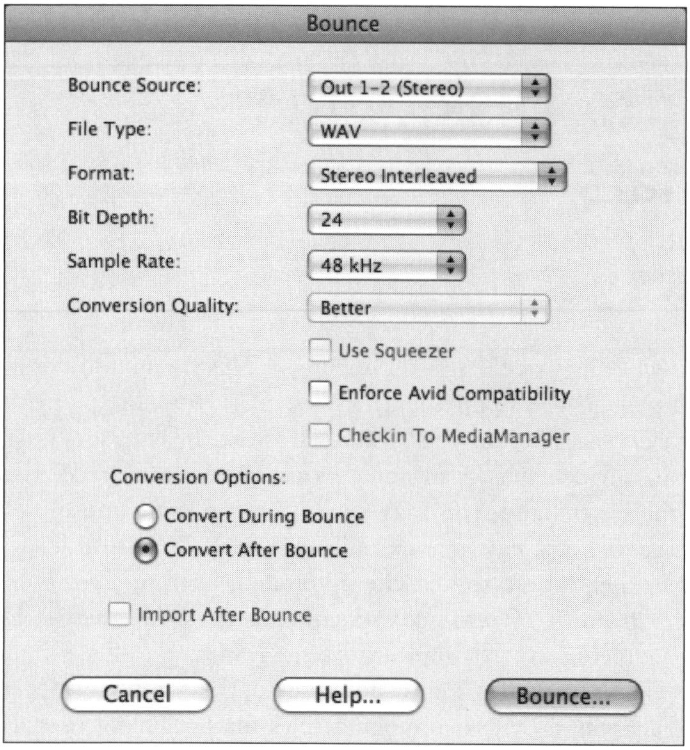

Figure 16.1 The Bounce dialog box for exporting a mix of either the entire session timeline or the current timeline selection to a new file.

Don't Get Your (Reverb) Tail Caught in the Door! When selecting events to bounce a file from Pro Tools, be aware that delay repeats, reverb decay, and amplitude envelope decay from a virtual instrument may extend beyond the end of the current timeline selection. If this selection (as shown in Start and End fields of the Transport window) extends only to the right end of the last region, the final delay repeats or reverb decay may get abruptly cut off. Be sure to add enough space at the end of your selection for these to fade out naturally.

Likewise, when bouncing out audio files to be looped (for example, backgrounds for a CD-ROM or Web page), remember that as you're listening to looped playback of a selection within Pro Tools, the decay of any reverb and delay effects from the selection's end overlaps the beginning of the next repetition. You may be surprised later to hear a significant drop at the beginning of your bounced loop because it won't include overlapping delay repeats from the previous repetition. To work around this problem, *duplicate* the selection to be looped and bounce out two full repetitions. Then re-import into Pro Tools (or open them in another stereo audio-editing program) and trim the new region down to only the smoothly looping second half (whose beginning *will* include the delay repeats from the previous repetition). From Pro Tools, you could then use the Export Regions as Files command in the local menu of the Regions List to save the trimmed audio region out from Pro Tools as a new file for looping.

When bouncing out a mix file that uses reverb or delay at the end, again remember that the reverb tail or delay repetitions may last longer than the actual program. The quickest way to deal with this is to create a fade-down using the volume automation on the audio or Aux Input tracks that host the reverb or delay plug-ins. Create it to coincide with the end of the program, and use your ear to judge how long the fade-down should be. Another possibility is to create a volume-automation fade-down on the Master Fader track. Remember, though, that all plug-ins are post-fader on the Master Fader track; listen carefully to the effect of the fade-down after its creation.

Converting to Common Audio File Formats

The Bounce dialog box allows you to select AIF, WAV, audio-only QuickTime, and MP3 files (with the separately purchased MP3 Export Option—a 30-day trial version is included with Pro Tools). Mac versions can additionally bounce to Macintosh sound resource (SND) files, while Windows versions can additionally bounce to Windows Media Audio (WMA) files. Lastly, you can bounce out MXF files if the DigiTranslator option is installed on your system. Chapter 1, "About Pro Tools," provides brief descriptions of the characteristics of each of these audio file types. Each may offer additional parameters (especially in the case of MP3 and WMA) during the process of bouncing to disk from Pro Tools. You could also choose the bounced file's sample rate—for example, reducing to 44.1kHz from your session's higher sample rate to burn a standard audio CD.

You can choose from among various bit depths for the resultant file. Even if your source session is 24 bit, for example, you may frequently reduce bounced files to 16 bits to burn audio CDs with more consumer-oriented programs. If you are ever forced to convert audio to 8 bit (for telephony or older interactive programs), a Squeezer checkbox will appear, which allows better quality during that conversion. Make sure you've considered all other options first, however, including audio data compression and lower sample rates.

For *surround* mixing, you will often need to deliver files in DTS or AC3 multichannel formats (for DTS and Dolby Digital 5.1 formats, respectively). You'll find additional information about surround mix formats in Chapter 14, "Postproduction and Soundtracks."

About MXF Files DigiTranslator is optional software, available separately for Pro Tools HD or LE, or as part of the DV Toolkit 2 bundle for LE systems. It is not compatible with M-Powered. Among other things, it enables bouncing directly to the MXF file format from Pro Tools. The Material eXchange Format has been described as a wrapper format that facilitates interchange of audio and video material in the content-creation process. The MXF file structure is built upon the AAF data model and contains clips of *essence* (audio and MPEG/DV video, for example) plus MXF metadata informing applications about duration, required codecs, and other information that can include shot location, production company, crew or talent information, and so on. The MXF standard is becoming more prevalent not only in exchange of postproduction content but also for real-time streaming of content in broadcast networks. MXF is principally described by SMPTE standard 377M. It was promoted by the Pro-MPEG forum with a coalition of manufacturers and professional organizations including SMPTE, the EBU (European Broadcasting Union), and the AAF Association.

Foreign Travel Tips for Mac Users   Macintosh files generally include a *resource fork*. This section of data within the file header indicates the file type so that the operating system launches the appropriate program when you double-click a file in the Finder. When you burn a data CD-ROM for Windows users using Toast, choose the Mac OS and PC (Hybrid) CD option. This ensures that, as seen from the ISO partition (for Windows, Linux, and Unix), the aliases of your audio files will have the Mac resource fork stripped out. (This is also what people mean by *flattening* a QuickTime file or saving it as "self-contained." A data header that is specific to the Mac operating system is stripped out.) Mac-only (HFS) data CDs are problematic for most Windows users—except for the more cosmopolitan ones who have purchased a utility to read directly from HFS volumes.

Also, Windows generally depends on a three-letter file name *extension* to distinguish, say, a WAV audio file (with the .wav extension) from a QuickTime file (with the .mov extension). When you supply files for Windows users (whether on CD or over the Internet), you should *always* append the appropriate file extension (for example, .wav, .aif, .mov, .mp3, or .sd2). Indeed, this is not a bad idea even for your own purposes. We also recommend taking advantage of the full 31 characters in file names (this is the maximum supported by Mac operating systems prior to 10.4) to add 22K, stereo, mono, or the bounced-on date into file names.

Lastly, if you exchange Pro Tools session files with Windows users, remember that on Windows systems, the Pro Tools 8 session document itself must have the .ptf extension. (Pro Tools versions 6.*xx* and earlier used the .pts extension, which is added automatically if you ever use the File > Save As command to save a Pro Tools session back to an older format.)

Bounce to QuickTime Movie

The File menu's Bounce to > QuickTime Movie command bounces the session's audio mix (or currently selected range) in real time into a new, cloned copy of the digital video file currently being used in this session. This will be in QuickTime format regardless of whether the original video file was MPEG, AVI, or some other format. As shown in Figure 16.2, most options in the Bounce dialog box opened by this command are identical to the ones you see after selecting the File > Bounce to > Disk command. Within the new copy of the video file, your mono or stereo audio mix is combined with the video track. Although you can import MPEG movies into Pro Tools, you *cannot* bounce audio directly back into that format. Windows users can use the Windows Movie Maker program to add audio tracks bounced out from Pro Tools into videos that are in the WMV (Windows Media Video) format. Interactive authors will often request a lower sample rate for the audio in their QuickTime movies (like 22,050Hz or even 11,025Hz) to keep file size and throughput requirements to a minimum. When audio throughput is a concern, however, be sure to ask about using one of the current audio codecs for data compression instead, like MP3 or MPEG-4. These will sound a *lot* better than reducing the sample rate! 48kHz is the most common sample rate for professional video applications; use this if the Quick-Time movie itself is your method for returning a soundtrack to the video editor.

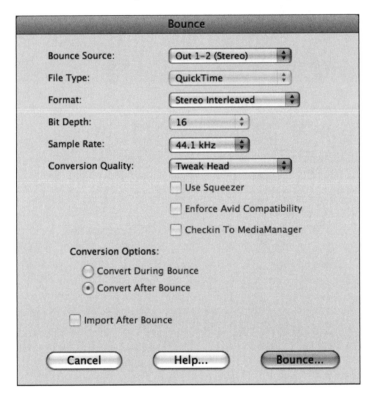

Figure 16.2 The File > Bounce to > QuickTime command opens the dialog box shown here. Your audio mix will be the soundtrack within a new copy of the digital video file being used in the current session.

Another Way Out There is another method for exporting audio regions from Pro Tools to other file formats: the Export Regions as Files command, in the pop-up local menu of the

Regions List. As shown in Figure 16.3, the options here for the output file format are similar to the Bounce dialog box, with the additional option of combining split stereo regions with .L and .R suffixes into a single interleaved stereo file. This command exports selected regions as is; in contrast, the bounced audio files created by the Bounce to > Disk command incorporate real-time plug-in processing or automation applied to any active, unmuted tracks within the current timeline selection. On the other hand, because the Export Regions as Files command can be used on *multiple* selected regions, it can be useful for batch exporting them out to disk.

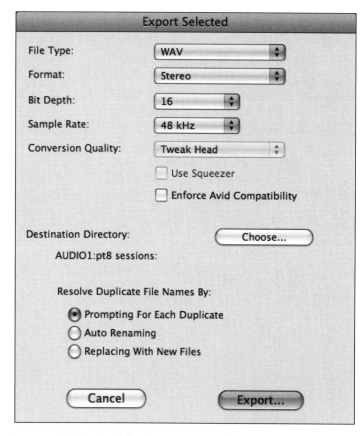

Figure 16.3 This dialog box appears when you select the Export Regions as Files command from the Regions List's pop-up menu.

Normalization and Gain Optimization

As explained elsewhere in this book (including Chapter 8, "Menu Selections: Highlights"), the normalization process locates the peak level within an audio file and, if required, increases the entire file's level to bring that peak to the level you specify using the Level slider in the

Normalize AudioSuite plug-in dialog box. If your original peak levels are lower than this setting, levels throughout the rest of the audio file will increase proportionately as the peak levels are increased to the specified value (including background noise, if any). This ensures that a bounced mix file (and any one-off audio CD that you burn from this file) will peak at exactly the level you want. (We recommend normalizing to −1dB or as much as −3dB compared to full code, which is 0dB, to leave some headroom and reduce the potential for digital "overs" occurring as this digital audio is transferred from one digital device or program to another.) Even more importantly, if you're recording a bounced file from a Pro Tools analog output to another device such as a video deck, normalization helps you ensure that the reference level you provide actually represents the peak level within your audio program. On the other hand, for commercial CD and DVD mastering, unless you have knowledge and experience of the mastering process, have very high-quality mastering and metering plug-ins, and so on, you would be well-advised to leave this final step to the experts at a good-quality mastering house (who always prefer that you do *not* apply normalization or any other dynamics processing to your bounced mixes). It also bears repeating here that your first area of attention for ensuring optimal levels in your bounced mixes should always be the Master Fader levels for the selected output path, assisted by the PhaseScope plug-in provided with Pro Tools or some other third-party alternative.

Peak/RMS Mode Selectors in Plug-ins The choice between RMS and Peak calibration modes for the Normalization function (also available for the Gain and Signal Generator plug-ins) was introduced with Pro Tools version 7. Normalization in all previous versions worked in Peak mode only. The RMS (Root-Mean-Square) mode normalizes based on the effective *average* level of the current audio selection and is therefore most useful when normalizing to levels significantly less than 100% and especially when trying to match apparent loudness levels between multiple mixes or selections.

Contrary to what you might think, it's also very common to normalize to some value *other* than 0dB (100% full code). In some cases, the normalization process might actually *reduce* the audio levels within files if the peaks in the original audio exceed the specified level for the normalization function. For example, when creating a collection of sound effects for use in multimedia, you might establish −10dB (about 31.6% of full code; remember that decibels are a logarithmic scale) as the maximum level for normalizing all button sounds so that these automatically come into the interactive authoring program at relatively softer levels. Figure 16.4 shows the dialog box for the Normalize function, located under the AudioSuite menu.

Most importantly, when you create mix files for professional audio CDs and video projects, it can be *undesirable* to normalize to 0dB (100%). There's also a great deal of discrepancy between devices from different manufacturers as to what levels appear on their meters as 0dB. Most have some built-in fudge factor so that occasional peaks won't immediately produce digital distortion, but this varies from one unit to another. The exact level where the clipping indicator will light up

Figure 16.4 The AudioSuite dialog box for the Normalize function in Pro Tools. You can overwrite the original regions/files or create one/several files for the result. If multiple regions are selected, their *over-all* peak can be the basis, or each can be individually normalized according to its *own* peak level.

on these units also varies—some of them exactly at 0dB input level, others only when this level is exceeded or even just *before* 0dB is reached! When you bounce out mix files to be used directly for burning one-off audio CDs, this will generally not be an issue, even when normalizing to 0dB. If, however, you're recording a normalized mix output digitally to another device (for example, to a DAT or real-time CD recorder) or especially when creating your own CD duplication master, it's prudent to hedge a little on your definition of "full code." For this reason, most professionals always normalize their mixes to some lower value (−1dB or even −3dB) just to be on the safe side. Otherwise, in certain situations, a digital audio signal that you know perfectly well does not exceed 0dB at any point will actually produce audible clipping when played back or recorded to a target digital audio device with this kind of discrepancy as well as to many consumer CD players.

The important thing is that you should always *listen* to any audio files you bounce out or normalize! Likewise, if you record in real time to another device, listen to what was recorded, *especially* at the points within the material where you know peak levels occur. The few extra minutes spent on quality control of your output are nothing compared to the years it may take to regain a client's confidence if a problem occurs!

Normalizing Within Pro Tools

You can apply the AudioSuite > Normalize command to any audio track selection in the Edit window or directly to audio regions/files within the Regions List; its dialog box is shown in Figure 16.4. Like other AudioSuite functions, you have the choice either to destructively (permanently) overwrite the contents of the currently selected file(s) or to create a new file containing the result of the processing (or several individual files, if more than one region is selected within a track). Bear in mind, of course, that many plug-ins increase the *level* of the audio passing through them—for example, when you boost one of the frequency bands in an EQ or increase the Gain parameter in a compressor. If normalizing regions in a track results in such a gain increase, be sure to check that any subsequent plug-ins processing in the track's signal chain don't push their level into clipping.

Normalizing Bounced Mixes

When you re-import a bounced mix into Pro Tools, the audio file appears in the Regions List. If you wish, you can directly normalize any file or region there using the AudioSuite > Normalize command. If you imported a disparate collection of stereo mixes into Pro Tools to assemble a one-off audio CD, for instance, one strategy might be to normalize them all in the Regions List (always to a peak value *less* than 100% in order to leave yourself a little headroom for gain increases as a result of EQ, for instance) before dragging them out onto audio tracks to apply EQ, limiting, or whatever other processing is required.

Aside from applying normalization to files within Pro Tools, you can use a variety of other programs to apply normalization and gain optimization, including all the additional audio-editing programs mentioned later in this chapter. Some standalone programs can apply normalization as part of batch file format conversions.

PhaseScope and Signal Tools All Pro Tools versions 7.3 and higher include an RTAS stereo metering plug-in called PhaseScope. This can be used on the stereo Master Fader for the output pair that is the source for your bounced mixes. The behavior of its level meters can be toggled between Peak, RMS, Peak + RMS, VU, BBC, Nordic, DIN, and VENUE. A Phase Meter display is available, which can also be switched to Leg(A) mode to display the weighted average of the power level passing through the channel. A Lissajous display reflects the amplitude and phase relationship of the affected audio. As has been mentioned at various times in other parts of this book, optimizing the gain structure in your Pro Tools sessions and maintaining consistent levels in bounced mixes should primarily be accomplished by keeping a close eye on the levels in your Master Faders for the selected audio output path. You will retain more audio quality by adjusting levels here in the Pro Tools mixing environment (32-bit floating-point in LE and M-Powered versions, 48-bit fixed in Pro Tools HD) than normalizing a mixdown file that has already been truncated or dithered down to 16-bit resolution.

Digidesign Dither Plug-ins

Especially for music applications, you should generally place dithering plug-ins, including the Digidesign Dither plug-in (all versions) or the more sophisticated POW-r Dither plug-in (not available in Pro Tools M-Powered), on the Master Fader for the output pair used to bounce 16-bit stereo mixes (or to record to a lower-resolution device from the digital output of your

Pro Tools hardware). Dithering reduces the prominence of quantization error (distortion) at low signal levels when audio files are reduced to a lower bit depth. (Bit depth is also known as *word length* because it's the length of the binary number used to represent the amplitude value of each audio sample in the file.) Dithering should always be the *last* plug-in on the Master Fader for your mix output; get in the habit of placing the dithering plug-in in its last insert slot right from the start. As shown in Figure 16.5, these dithering plug-ins have only two parameters:

- **Bit Resolution selector.** When you bounce a file, this should be set to the bit depth of the target bounced file. When recording from digital outputs of Pro Tools, set this to the resolution of the target device—for example, 20 bits if you're recording into the digital input of an older digital multitrack such as the ADAT XT 20. When recording out from the analog outputs of your Pro Tools audio hardware, set it to the maximum resolution of those analog outputs—for example, 18 bits for older audio interfaces such as the 888 or 882 I/O or 20 bits for an 882|20 I/O or 1622 I/O. Dithering should not be used when an analog recorder is attached to the analog outputs of any audio interface whose digital-to-analog converters already offer full 24-bit resolution. This would be the case with the 96 I/O or 192 I/O interfaces for Pro Tools|HD, Mbox 2 family or Mbox, Digi 003, Digi 002, Digi 001, 888|24 I/O, or any of the M-Audio interfaces for M-Powered. (When you bounce to an 8- or 16-bit file from these hardware configurations or when you record to the digital input of a 16-bit DAT recorder, it would still be appropriate to insert a dithering plug-in on the Master Fader for that output pair.)

Figure 16.5 The POW-r Dither plug-in and the older Digidesign Dither plug-in optimize results when audio is transferred digitally to a lower-resolution device or recorded in analog from an audio interface with a lower maximum bit depth than the source session. 16-bit dithering is appropriate when bouncing out a 16-bit file to disk for burning an audio CD.

- **Noise shaping.** This setting applies specialized filtering to further reduce the prominence of quantization distortion in the critical 4kHz frequency band, where it is most apparent to human hearing. We generally suggest that you enable this setting. Although the older Digidesign Dither (the only dithering plug-in supplied with M-Powered systems) offers only on/off for noise shaping, POW-r Dither supports three different types: Type 1, Type 2, and Type 3. Which works better for each project depends on the nature of the material and your personal taste. The *DigiRack Plug-ins Guide* (a PDF included with the program) makes some general observations about this—for example, that Type 1 is flattest and perhaps best suited for solo instrument recordings or voice-overs, while Type 3 has the most pronounced noise shaping and is most suitable for material with a wide stereo image and extended frequency range. But trust your own ears on this, and experiment.

Other Dithering Options

Various plug-ins for mastering and dynamics processing also include dithering. Master X^3 by t.c. electronic (shown in Figure 16.6) is a mastering plug-in for HD and Venue systems that includes 3-band dynamics processing, soft-clipping, fine gain adjustments, and dithering. The iZotope Ozone is another mastering plug-in in RTAS format; it includes multiband dynamics and a harmonic exciter, parametric EQ, mastering reverb, stereo image control, a loudness maximizer, and dithering. The L3 Ultramaximizer from Waves (included in its Diamond and Platinum bundles) also includes dithering and noise shaping, along with its sophisticated multiband limiting.

Although this chapter is mainly concerned with dithering as an aspect of bouncing out audio files to disk, it is worth mentioning that there are also many excellent professional *hardware* devices available for real-time conversion of digital audio signals from one bit depth or sample rate to another. These can be handy, especially when exchanging digital audio signals between multiple units in your studio (digital mixers, keyboards, effects, Pro Tools, digital multitracks, and others). The Z-3src, from Z-Systems Audio Engineering, is an external digital audio device that provides real-time conversions for bit depth and sample rate in a variety of formats. The t.c. electronic Finalizer (available in Express and 96K versions) provides these functions plus other useful mastering features including limiting, gain optimization, and multiband compression. The aforementioned Master X^3 plug-in is based on that justly famous piece of studio hardware.

Sample Rate and Bit Depth

Regardless of whether your current Pro Tools session document is 16 or 24 bit, the Bounce dialog box allows you to choose 24-, 16-, or 8-bit bit depths for the bounced file. If you're going to burn a standard audio CD, for example, the source files for many CD-burning programs should be dithered down to 16 bits (although some, like WaveLab, Jam, and WaveBurner, offer their own dithering options for reducing from 24 to 16 bits during the CD-writing process). Audio files at 8-bit resolution have a characteristic fizzy or crunchy quality, much associated with older computer applications, inexpensive video games, and toys. This is due to the high degree of quantization error—a kind of angular, digital distortion of the original waveform due

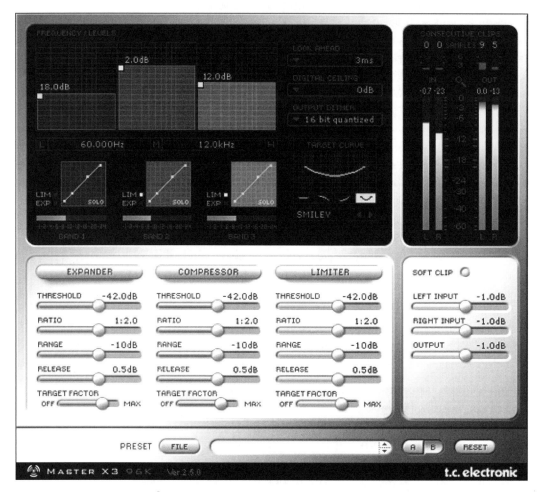

Figure 16.6 The Master X³ plug-in, from t.c. electronic, is a plug-in for HD/Venue systems derived from this company's Finalizer hardware unit. It combines several types of processing often used on vocals or stereo mixes: 3-band compression, EQ, limiting/expansion/soft clipping, gain adjustment, and dithering.

to its true amplitude variations being rounded off to only 256 possible values. If you are ever required to create 8-bit files, by all means make sure that you maximize your gain first by using compression or some other dynamics processing. You should also select the Squeezer option in the Bounce dialog box to optimize conversions to 8-bit resolution, especially if your source is a voice-over file.

Compressed File Formats (MP3, AAC, MPEG-4, RealAudio, and So On)

Audio data compression (which should not be confused with *gain* compression of audio signals) is supported for audio tracks within QuickTime movies and is an essential part of how the afore-mentioned audio file formats and MPEG (.mpg) video files are structured. QuickTime, WAV, and AIF audio files support the older Adaptive Delta Pulse Code Modulation (ADPCM) method for compressing audio data. ADPCM exists in two mutually incompatible variants:

- **IMA-ADPCM.** Standardized by the International Multimedia Association, it typically appears as IMA 2:1 or IMA 4:1 in file-conversion dialog boxes. Now largely outmoded, it was the most prevalent audio data compression format for AIF files for some years.

- **MS-ADPCM.** This is Microsoft's take on the format.

ADPCM used *companding* as well as frequency-selective bit-depth reduction to reduce the size of audio data. Like the more advanced MP3 and RealAudio compression methods, discussed in a moment, this is a *lossy* process; some of the original audio information is lost. For spoken-word recordings in particular, ADPCM-compressed files can be relatively acceptable for computer playback. Some music files and loops adapt better to this type of compression than others; it is definitely worth a few minutes of experimentation if the project requires large reductions in audio file size (bearing in mind that you must do this in a program other than Pro Tools). But unless the authoring or telephony application for which you're bouncing out audio files doesn't support any of the more-contemporary methods for audio data compression, you'll find that the sonic results of IMA and MS versions of the older ADPCM codec are decidedly inferior to MP3, MPEG-4/AAC, and other current-generation audio-compression techniques.

Although Pro Tools does support bouncing out MP3-compressed audio format (with the separately purchased MP3 option), it can only create full-linear (uncompressed) audio when you choose QuickTime, (Broadcast) WAV, SDII, or AIF formats for bouncing out audio files. However, other audio-editing and conversion programs (including Autodesk's Cleaner XL program, whose main purpose is data compression for digital video files) *can* create files incorporating ADPCM data compression for audio—a format that may still sometimes be requested for interactive media applications (and is discussed in more detail in Chapter 15, "Sound Design for Interactive Media").

Better-Sounding Results with Compressed Audio Data Formats As a general rule, the compression algorithms used for audio data don't react well to low-frequency noise. Rumble from traffic, air conditioning, and vocal pops, for example, will occasionally produce audible artifacts in compressed audio (just as they do with time-stretching and pitch-shifting processes), especially when file sizes are more drastically reduced. To avoid ugly surprises, be sure to listen to your material on a good monitoring system at reasonably high volumes before committing. Naturally, a pop-filter is a must for recording voice-overs. To eliminate some of this low-end garbage from recorded audio, try using the Hi-Pass filter provided by the EQ plug-ins in Pro Tools; adjust its cutoff frequency as high as possible without compromising vocal timbre. Also, Apple's iTunes incorporates an option for eliminating frequencies below 10Hz while encoding audio to MP3 format (look ahead to Figure 16.7).

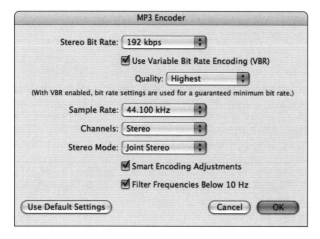

Figure 16.7   iTunes provides conversions from AIF/WAV to MP3 or AAC (a variant of MPEG-4). Shown here: the custom settings dialog box for MP3 conversion.

MP3

MP3 is yet another file-format selection in the Bounce dialog box. (To bounce to MP3 directly from Pro Tools, you need to purchase the MP3 Export Option after the 30-day trial version included with Pro Tools expires, but it's only about $20.) Short for MPEG Audio, Layer 3, MP3 is a compressed audio file format that can dramatically decrease file size before severely impairing sound quality. It is, of course, "lossy"—that is, something is lost in the compression process. The selected bit rate for the resultant file (measured in kilobits per second, or kbps) determines the amount of compression to be applied. (Lower bit rates create smaller files, but with consequently greater deterioration of the sound quality.) A second dialog box allows you to enter title, author, genre, and copyright information. For sending approval mixes via the Internet (as well as finished audio, such as voice-over recordings for corporate clients, radio spots, and so on), MP3 can be an excellent choice, as it often reduces file size such that you can send the file as an e-mail attachment (perhaps choosing a bit rate of 128Kbps or less). If you are producing audio files for interactive developers, whose throughput requirements are more restricted to ensure smooth playback alongside the interactive graphic content, be sure to ask if MP3 audio files are supported. MP3 is the most common audio file format for Macromedia's Flash, for instance, although usually this compression will be applied by the developer when the Flash project is published. For high-quality background effects and especially music, you will be much happier with MP3 compression compared to reducing the sample rate to 22kHz or converting audio files from stereo to mono.

If you *don't* opt for the MP3 option for Pro Tools, you could bounce out in any linear (non-compressed) audio file format and then perform the MP3 conversion afterward in another program. For example, Apple's iTunes program (included with Mac computers and downloadable for Windows systems; upgrades are available at http://www.apple.com) provides excellent MP3 conversions. Figure 16.7 shows some of the options in the advanced Preferences for MP3 conversion in iTunes. Remember that lower bit rates reduce audio quality. You will generally find it advisable to specify the sample rate and force the number of channels to stereo if appropriate, and always enable the 10Hz high-pass filter for MP3 conversions. Joint Stereo mode is highly recommended for all data rates under 128Kbps. Other professional stereo audio-editing programs, such as BIAS' Peak Pro (Mac), Sony's Sound Forge (Windows), and Steinberg's WaveLab (Windows), also provide MP3 conversion, as does Audacity, a freeware program for Mac, Windows, and Linux.

MPEG-4 and AAC

MPEG-4 is not among the audio file formats you can bounce directly from Pro Tools, but it is well worth knowing about. This is also true of AAC (Advanced Audio Coding), a specific application of the MPEG-4 specification. These formats were developed by the MPEG Group. They are used by Apple in its online service for downloading music, the iTunes Store, and are supported by QuickTime Player, iTunes, and many interactive applications. In these formats, signal-processing technology from Dolby Laboratories applies more complex compression algorithms that not only reduce data size much more efficiently than MP3 but also produce better-sounding results at comparable data rates—*especially* for music. To put it another way, AAC encoding can obtain the same quality as an MP3 file that would be 30–35% bigger.

About QuickTime Pro 7 QuickTime Pro 7, in addition to the MPEG-4 export capability already supported in version 6, can save audio files in AAC format. It also supports multi-channel audio, real-time video capture from digital video cameras via FireWire, and the very efficient H.264 video codec (part of the MPEG-4 standard) that is also used in Blu-ray and HD-DVD video.

Additional Audio-Editing Programs

Although Pro Tools is a hugely powerful audio program, there will almost certainly be occasions when you will also use other audio-editing programs, especially for manipulating mono and stereo audio files. We've already alluded to using additional programs for certain types of audio data compression. For multimedia sound design, batch-conversion programs for changing file formats or sample rates, applying normalization, and other transformations can obviously be useful—for example, when you're saving out 39 button-click sounds and 39 associated rollOver sounds, and you want to normalize all their peaks to 10dB down! Likewise, when you create audio files that should loop smoothly in an interactive application, these programs will be useful for double-checking every file—in case you have to adjust loop points after conversion to 22kHz, for instance.

A program that can edit stereo audio files directly is also very convenient for trimming start and end points of the mix files you've bounced out from Pro Tools, adding cue point markers for interactive authoring, applying effects in plug-in formats not available in Pro Tools, editing audio directly within video files, and so on. This section mentions only a few of the most common programs used for professional applications. And just to keep the record straight, Digidesign's venerable Sound Designer program (now discontinued) was the godfather of all modern audio-editing programs!

Peak Pro (Mac)

This comprehensive audio-editing program for Macintosh from BIAS supports many mono, dual mono, and stereo audio file formats (up to 192kHz, 32-bit floating-point resolution in the full version). It also offers many file conversions (including import from audio CD, and MP4/AAC and MP3 encoding from source audio files in other formats), DSP functions, looping tools, direct file transfers with various samplers, batch-file processing, and online playback of audio files while locked to external time code (MTC). Peak also supports several real-time plug-in formats, including VST and Audio Units simultaneously, in five insert slots that can be configured in series or parallel signal-routing configurations. You can also use it to insert markers (called *cue points* in some programs) into audio files, used by interactive authoring programs to cue graphic events to locations within an audio file. Peak supports video files in QuickTime, DV, and other formats so that audio tracks within them can be edited and processed directly without bouncing out a new copy. Peak includes creation of Red Book–compliant audio CDs (including CD-TEXT, PQ editing, ISRC codes, and DDP export), as well as POW-r Dither for reductions down to 16 bit from higher–bit-depth source files. Playlists support using regions from many different source files, either for CD assembly or bouncing out a new audio file, with gain adjustments, crossfades, real-time effects, and other features. In version 6, podcasts can be authored and uploaded as RSS feeds directly from Peak.

Sound Forge (Windows)

Sound Forge—originally developed by Sonic Foundry (also the developers of ACID Pro) and now owned by Sony Creative—is another full-featured audio-editing program. It supports a variety of mono and stereo file formats at sample rates up to 192kHz and 32-bit resolution and offers MP3, Windows Media, and RealAudio conversions; import from audio CD; DSP functions, including sample-rate conversion; plus support for Direct X audio plug-ins with automation. You can burn audio CDs directly from Sound Forge in track-at-once mode; it also supports file transfer with samplers, editing of audio soundtracks within video files, and non-destructive playlists of audio regions within a file. Sound Forge also supports video files so that you can process or edit the soundtracks within them, including DV, 24p, QuickTime, AVI, MPEG, RealMedia, and WMV. Like Peak, Sound Forge supports the placement of markers/cue points into files for use by interactive authoring programs. There are also tools for creating ACIDized loops. A more economical, feature-limited version, Sound Forge Audio Studio, is available. Sound Forge is by far the most widespread program for professional editing of stereo and mono files on the Windows platform. *Sound Forge 8 Power!* by Scott Garrigus (published by Course Technology) provides power tips and loads of useful theory that will help you get the most out of Sound Forge. There is also an interactive CD-ROM, *Sound Forge CSi Starter*, by Robert Guérin. Visit the Music Technology section at http://www.courseptr.com for more information.

WaveLab (Windows)

Yet another professional audio-editing program by Steinberg (developers of Cubase VST), WaveLab supports many audio file formats, including MP3, AIF, WAV, SDII, multichannel surround, and WMA Pro 5.1 and 7.1. It also supports numerous DSP effects and file/sample-rate conversions, looping and sampler tools, plus data CD-ROM and audio CD burning (including non-destructive real-time effects processing and a fully compatible implementation of the Red Book audio CD standard for duplication masters, even directly from 24-bit source files with built-in Apogee UV22 dithering) and authoring and extraction tools for DVD-Audio. Audio playback can be synchronized to external MTC time-code sources, and the Audio-Montage feature offers non-destructive playlist editing with volume/pan automation. WaveLab also supports batch processing of multiple files, including plug-in effects.

Audacity (Mac, Windows, Linux)

This is a free, open-source program for Mac OS X, Windows XP, and GNU/Linux. While it doesn't offer many of the advanced features in the aforementioned professional programs, Pro Tools users will find it surprisingly useful. It can be just the thing for trimming the start and end of bounced mix files, normalizing and making other gain adjustments, inverting polarity, changing sample rates for interactive projects, exporting MP3 or Ogg Vorbis audio files, adding end fades, or even trimming file lengths so that they loop smoothly. Audacity can also record directly to hard disk. Not too bad, considering it's free! You can download Audacity at http://audacity.sourceforge.net.

Autodesk Cleaner, Cleaner XL

These batch file-conversion programs are immensely useful when you have to apply similar audio conversions to many files. Sound designers who must convert the resolution and file format of dozens of button sounds prior to delivery (while at the same time normalizing them all to a single level) will also appreciate the ease and uniformity that is possible when using these programs. Typically, batch-conversion programs also allow you to save presets so that successive batches are converted with the same parameters. Because Pro Tools doesn't directly support ADPCM compression (a relatively older data-compression method also known as IMA) in the audio it bounces into QuickTime, WAV, or AIF files, these programs can be useful when those compressed audio formats are required (for CD-ROM playback and certain interactive applications, for instance).

The focus of Autodesk Cleaner (Mac) and Cleaner XL (Win) is batch-processing of video files (compression, cropping, frame-rate conversion, audio track conversion, and many other video-specific features). However, it also supports a variety of batch audio file–conversion processes, including normalization and file-format conversion that can be performed simultaneously.

Supported audio and video file formats include QuickTime (including MPEG-4 and AAC), DV, AIF, WAV, AU, Real, Windows Media video and audio (WMV/WMA) in stereo and multichannel formats, Kinoma (for Palm OS PDAs), plus MPEG 1, 2, 3, and 4. For sound designers who manage large collections of files or need to import and export a variety of audio and video file formats, Cleaner can be an invaluable tool.

DVD Studio Pro (Mac)

This program from Apple allows Macintosh users to author and record DVDs. It incorporates more professional features than Apple's iDVD program, which is bundled with Macintosh models featuring Apple's SuperDrive (which can record both CD-Rs and DVD-Rs). It is also part of the iLife software bundle. DVD Studio Pro encodes video into MPEG-2 for playback in any common video DVD drive, and supports subtitling, multiple languages, PAL/NTSC, 4:3 or 16:9 aspect ratios, and other advanced features. As an interesting added bonus for Pro Tools users, it also includes an AC3 (Dolby Digital 5.1) encoder that allows up to eight mono AIF, SDII, WAV, or QuickTime audio file stems to be encoded into a single surround soundtrack, compatible with standard DVD players and surround receivers.

Using Pro Tools Region Definitions in Other Digital Audio Programs Region Synch is a Windows program developed by Rail Jon Rogut that converts in both directions between the region definitions exported to source audio files from your Pro Tools session and the region definition format used by Sony/Sonic Foundry's Sound Forge program. (In Pro Tools, region definitions are actually contained in the session document, not the source audio files it uses. Use the Export Region Definitions command in the Regions List's local menu to embed pointers for regions into the source audio files themselves.) Because Sound Forge regions are also supported by Adobe Audition, n-Track Studio, Samplitude, and Steinberg's WaveLab—not to mention Sony Creative's own Vegas and CD Architect programs—this can be immensely useful. For example, imagine you're bouncing out a long continuous file that will need CD track markers embedded into it (perhaps a live concert or an audiobook CD). Enable the Import After Bounce option, drag the bounce file onto a track, and then use the markers and events already in your session as a guide as you make selections and create a series of contiguous region definitions corresponding to each CD track. Once you export these region definitions back out into the source file and convert them to Sound Forge regions, you can use Sound Forge, CD Architect, or WaveLab to create audio CD tracks based on the region definitions within this single continuous file. You can download a demo version of this very economical Windows program at http://www.railjonrogut.com. From this same site, you can also download the immensely useful (and free) sdTwoWav program for Windows. sdTwoWav performs batch conversion of Sound Designer II files—that you have retrieved from older Mac versions of Pro Tools, for example—to Broadcast WAV format.

Audio CD Creation

The requirements for creating one-off audio CDs for clients and promotional use are considerably more informal than when submitting a CD as the master to a commercial CD-duplication house. If you're burning your own CDs for evaluation, for playback in standard audio and computer CD drives, or for your band to sell at local gigs, you'll generally have pretty good compatibility using almost any of the current CD-writing programs. Obviously, given the current fashion, you might want to take the time in Pro Tools to normalize your mixes and possibly apply some peak limiting and other gain optimization so that your CD slams as hard as the other discs in everyone's changer. (But don't overdo this; 100% full-code levels can create digital overs that produce audible distortion on some systems. Relentlessly smashing every mix up against the ceiling of the dynamic range creates a fatiguing listening experience!) On the other hand, if you plan to submit a CD-R that will directly serve as the duplication master for a commercial release, its format must conform to a set of standards called the Red Book, which includes ISRC information and other data in the P and Q subcode channels.

The Red Book Specification for Audio CDs Developed jointly by various manufacturers, particularly Sony and Philips, this specification was originally published in a book with a red cover—hence the name "Red Book." CD-DA (audio) discs permit up to 99 stereo tracks of 16-bit digital audio at a sample rate of 44.1kHz (only!). The internal timing reference on audio CDs is grouped in hours, minutes, seconds, and frames—at 75 CD frames per second (not to be confused with SMPTE frames). To be acceptable Red Book masters for commercial duplication, CDs must include all the appropriate subcode data for the P and Q channels, which only certain CD-writing programs provide, in order to create a glass master (used for stamping CD copies) directly from your CD-R. Recently Disc Description Protocol (DDP) filesets have been adopted as a common method for optical disc replication. The advantage of DDP filesets is that they deliver both audio data and metadata in an error-protected format. (CD masters can also be submitted on 1630 or DDP tape, which some CD-mastering programs, including Digidesign's long-discontinued MasterList CD for Mac OS9 only, can create.) If your CD-writing program cannot create the additional subcode information, you can still submit your audio on a CD-R, but expect to pay an additional setup fee.

Commercial CDs incorporate eight channels of subcode data (P, Q, R, S, T, U, V, and W), interleaved with audio data at one complete subcode frame for every 588 audio samples. However, audio CD players read only the P and Q channels. The P channel simply indicates when selections are playing. The Q channel incorporates disk and track running times, copy-prohibit and emphasis flags, a TOC (table of contents), error detection, and a UPC catalog code for the entire disk. The Q channel also includes ISRC information (International Standard Recording Code) for each track, identifying the composition's owner, country of origin, serial number, and year of production.

Programs for One-Off Copies

The following are general-purpose CD-writing programs you can use to create audio CDs as well as data CD-ROMs. Some, like Toast, allow you to adjust spacing between CD tracks. Audio CDs created by these programs will generally play just fine in most CD drives. By the way, just to clear up a common misunderstanding: These programs *do* create Red Book–compatible CDs. They just don't implement *all* the features of the Red Book specification (UPC, ISRC, PQ codes, and so on) that would be required for creating a master directly usable for commercial CD duplication. You might say that CDs created by these programs conform to a *subset* of the features in the Red Book specification.

Toast (Mac)

Manufactured by Roxio (formerly part of Adaptec, but now a division of Sonic Solutions), Toast is by far the most prevalent CD-burning program on the Macintosh platform, not least because versions of it are bundled with so many brands of CD-R drives. Audio CDs, enhanced audio CDs (which might include photos or videos in addition to the audio), and MP3 audio CDs can be created from most source audio file formats, and you can adjust the spacing between CD tracks (including zero spacing in disk-at-once mode). CD-Text information can be included on audio CDs created with Toast. This information (stored in the R and W subcode channels of the lead-in area on the audio CD) allows compatible players to display data such as disk title, artist name, and track titles while playing your CD. Toast supports creation of data CD-ROMs (including Mac/Win hybrid format), data DVDs, and data on Blu-ray discs, as well as MP3 CDs, video CDs, Super Video CDs, and video DVDs. Toast versions 8 and higher also support plug-ins in Audio Unit (AU) format and various types of crossfades between tracks.

iTunes

Apple bundles this user-friendly audio CD–writing program with all Macintosh models featuring a recordable CD drive (or recordable DVD/CD drive). There is also a Windows version. iTunes accommodates a variety of source file formats, including AIF, WAV, and MP3. It can rip tracks from audio CDs to MP3 or AAC format (that is, it simultaneously extracts the CD audio data and applies a specified level of compression while creating one of these file types on your disk) or to AIF and WAV files with no data compression. Like Toast, iTunes also supports burning MP3 CDs. It includes a 10-band equalizer that can be non-destructively applied during the CD-burning process, a feature to create crossfades between CD tracks, and rudimentary tools for fine-tuning individual track levels. iTunes also provides excellent options for MP3 or AAC conversion from your source AIF and WAV mixes bounced out from Pro Tools if you opt not to purchase the MP3 option from Digidesign, which enables direct creation of MP3-encoded files while bouncing to disk.

Easy Media Creator (Windows)

Also manufactured by Roxio, Easy Media Creator (and its predecessor, Easy CD Creator) is a prevalent CD-burning program for Windows and is included with many CD-R drives. It supports both recordable CDs and DVDs. Like Toast, it supports burning data CD-ROMs and audio CDs from a variety of different source audio file formats (including MP3), and a Sound-Stream normalizer feature to ensure consistent levels on audio tracks from multiple sources. It supports creating Red Book–compliant ISRC codes, UPC codes, and PQ subcode channel information on audio CDs.

Sound Forge (Windows)

This robust, industry-standard audio-editing program from Sony (originally developed by Sonic Foundry) also includes features for *track-at-once* writing of audio CDs; support of MP3, WMA, and many other audio/video file formats; and support of source sample rates up to 192kHz and 64-point floating point resolution. Sound Forge offers loop tuning and ACIDized loop-creation tools, automatable real-time effects including multiband compression, noise reduction, VST, and DirectX plug-in support, as well as support for Flash SWF files, multichannel Dolby AC-3, and Windows Media Audio.

Programs for Creating Duplication Masters for Commercial CDs

As we've said, additional information must be incorporated into a CD master for commercial duplication. Not surprisingly, a CD-writing program included with your CD-R drive isn't necessarily going to support the extra features required to create a Red Book–compliant CD master. However, it *will* produce audio CDs that perform acceptably in most CD players or that a commercial CD-duplication house can use as the basis for creating a CD-duplication master after adding the appropriate data in the Q subcode channel (for a fee). The programs discussed here, however, incorporate the necessary features for professional CD duplication (from a CD-R or in some cases from a tape). As with mastering and gain optimization of your stereo mixes for release (discussed in a moment), if you aren't extremely familiar with all the requirements for assembling a duplication-ready CD master and the particular requirements of your duplication house, it is a good investment to pay an expert to do this properly. In any case, you'll need one of these programs if you intend to create indexes within CD tracks or to create CD track numbers *within* a single audio file (in the middle of a crossfade or applause in a live performance, for example).

Sony CD Architect (Windows)

This professional CD-creation program from Sony accepts source audio files at sample rates up to 192kHz and 32-bit resolution, with high-quality resampling and dithering to standard CD audio. Tools for placement of CD track markers and indexes are provided, along with the requisite information for the P and Q subcode channels, UPC/EAN codes, and many other features required when creating master CDs for commercial duplication. Normalization and non-destructive gain envelopes can be applied to any audio event. More than 20 DirectX plug-ins are also included with the program and can be applied non-destructively during the CD-burning process. A variety of crossfade shapes can be created between adjacent audio regions, and across CD track markers between them, and you can create hidden tracks. CD Architect supports

Sound Forge regions directly, and you can open audio events from CD Architect into Sound Forge for other types of editing.

WaveLab (Windows)

This audio-editing program from Steinberg (manufacturers of the Cubase audio/MIDI sequencer, Nuendo, and other MIDI-related software and interfaces) includes features for creating audio CDs and data CD-ROMs. Like the CD-writing programs already discussed, WaveLab can also create all the ISRC and other information in the Q subcode channel, create track numbers and indexes within a single audio file, and so on, to produce a CD-R master for direct commercial duplication. Non-destructive, real-time VST plug-ins, multiband compression, parametric EQ, stereo expansion, and other audio processing can be applied during the CD-creation process, as well as UV22 HR dithering (the current "high-resolution" form of Apogee's popular UV22 dithering algorithm used in many audio programs and hardware units). WaveLab also supports source audio at sample rates as high as 384kHz(!) and 32-bit floating point resolution in many different file formats. Audio-Montage playlist features include crossfades between separate files and up to 10 simultaneous effects, all of which can be applied non-destructively in real time.

Nero (Windows)

This suite of software from Ahead Systems (http://www.nero.com) includes powerful tools for creating audio CDs, DVDs, CD video, and data CDs. Features for audio CD creation include crossfades, CD-Text, copyright information and UPC/EAN codes, copy-prohibit flags, index creation within CD tracks, CD track IDs within a continuous audio file, MP3 CD creation, mixed-mode and CD Extra formats, non-destructive normalization while burning CDs, and disk-at-once or track-at-once writing modes.

Leaving Mastering to the "Masters" When we talk here about creating a CD master for duplication, we mean the physical process of organizing the data—all the IRSC and UPC/EAN codes, indexes, pre-gaps, copy-protection flags, and other data required for a commercial release. This is complicated enough; if you're not completely familiar with all this stuff, do *not* try this at home! Nowadays, most CD-duplication houses can handle this for a reasonable fee—but be sure to thoroughly check the test CD they provide, programming various track orders in your player, skipping between tracks, and so on.

On the other hand, *mastering* is an entirely different process, where dynamics processing, EQ, and other adjustments are applied to finished stereo mixes to make them sound better, with more uniform quality. Experienced mastering engineers know how to optimize for CD, vinyl, radio, and other playback scenarios. They also occasionally work miracles, applying corrective measures for any deficiencies in your original mixes or simply making a disparate collection of tracks sound more uniform.

When submitting audio files of a mix to a mastering engineer, provide these at the maximum resolution possible without any intrusive processing, sample rate, or bit-depth conversions on your part. Bounce the mix out at your original session's sample rate with no dithering plug-ins and at 24-bit resolution. Don't alter the stereo mix with dynamics processors or normalize it, either. It's better to leave this to the experts, not least because they should have much more sophisticated tools (and expertise) at their disposal. Supplying a 16-bit audio CD, 100% normalized or with its dynamic range already stomped on in some other way, severely curtails a mastering engineer's flexibility. Providing a second CD with your squashed mixes as a reference only may be useful for indicating the approximate sound you're after, but be sure to provide your raw, high-resolution mixes as audio files within folders on a separate data CD-R or DVD-R.

Broadcast WAV files (with either the .wav or .bwv extension) are becoming the preferred submission format, in part because of AES/EBU recommendations that record companies stipulate this as the delivery format for audio projects (not only mixes, but source audio tracks in the project). Nevertheless, be sure to check with your mastering engineer first so that you bounce your Pro Tools project to the format he or she prefers.

Summary

Hopefully we've provided some context for sending your audio from Pro Tools out into the world. As always, when you're converting audio to a lower bit depth (with an inferior signal/error ratio) or to a compressed audio data format, be sure to manage your gain structure and mix output levels to get the best-possible dynamic range and as few artifacts as possible. When collaborating with others, always ask what file format they prefer and determine all the file formats that their system or program supports; you might be able to make a useful suggestion!

17 The Score Editor Window

In 2006, Digidesign acquired Sibelius Software, Inc., a manufacturer of one of the dominant music-notation software programs on the market, so it's not a big surprise that Digi would eventually modify Pro Tools to include a notation function. And while it should be stressed that the actual Sibelius notation software is not bundled into Pro Tools 8, the Score Editor window that debuts with this version is an extremely useful new feature that not only can generate scores for printing but also offers a musically sensible way of editing MIDI and Instrument tracks. And the Score Editor window enables those who also have the full Sibelius software to export files that can then be opened and modified in Sibelius!

As shown in Figure 17.1, which contains a simple example of "London Bridge" in C major, the Score Editor window has many familiar features. Not only does the staff configuration reflect traditional score appearance, but almost all of the Pro Tools–specific controls are what you will find in both the Edit window and the MIDI Editor window. If your MIDI sequence begins right at the beginning of your session's timeline, the Score Editor window will reflect that by having the notation start right at the head of the staves. If, however, your project starts the MIDI

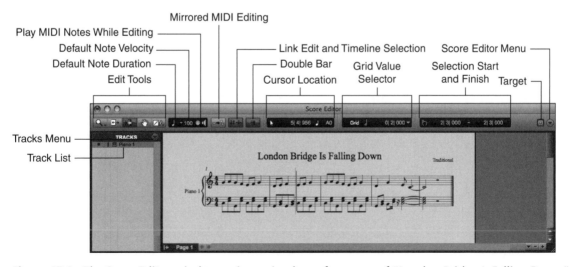

Figure 17.1 The Score Editor window, using a simple performance of "London Bridge Is Falling Down" as an example. Note the expanded toolbar display at the top.

sequence a number of bars after the start of the timeline (perhaps you used the Move Song Start function from Event > Time Operations to move the song start 10 measures ahead), then a corresponding number of empty bars will appear in the Score Editor window. Also, the number of empty bars after the last MIDI region of your sequence is affected by the Double Bar option selector, the one new features in the Score Editor window's Edit tools. With this option selected, the traditional double-bar notation will appear at the end of the last measure of your score. If you do not select the Double Bar option, a number of empty measures will appear after the last measure containing any note information. The number of empty measures is entered in the MIDI tab of the Preferences dialog box, accessible from the Setup menu. Just look for the "MIDI/Score Editor Display" section.

Using the Edit Tools

To bring up the Score Editor window, simply right-click on a MIDI region and choose Open in Score Editor toward the bottom of the menu. If you find yourself using the Score Editor window on a regular basis, consider choosing it under the Double-Clicking a MIDI Region Opens menu in the MIDI tab of the Preferences dialog box. If you are familiar with how the Edit window tools work with the Notes display in MIDI and Instrument tracks (covered in Chapter 10, "MIDI"), then you are pretty much ready to start editing the notation in the Score Editor window. To recap, the Selector tool, referred to as the Note Selector tool in the Score Editor window, can be dragged over notes in a single staff or several staves, allowing various menu functions as well as actions by the Grabber tool to then be applied to the selected notes. Speaking of the Grabber tool, you can also select multiple notes by clicking the first note with the Grabber and, with the Shift key held down, clicking on additional notes. Then drag the notes to a different pitch or time on the staff or staves. You can use the Trimmer tool to lengthen notes by positioning the Trimmer on a note and dragging to the right. Similarly, positioning the Trimmer tool on a note and dragging to the left will shorten the length of the note. Before trimming notes, make sure you know whether Allow Note Overlap in the Notation Display Track Settings dialog box is selected. (This is explained later in this chapter in the sidebar "Display Quantization and Note Overlap.")

Editing with the Pencil Tool

The Pencil tool acts the same way in the Score Editor window as it does on the Note display in MIDI and Instrument tracks. The power of the combination of the Pencil tool in Freehand mode (selected via the Score Editor toolbar's Pencil tool menu) and the ability to work with musical notation becomes apparent when step editing or programming. For those of us who cut our teeth step programming using event lists with columns of dry data, the ability to perform note placement using a graphic representation of music notation is a dream.

First, let's take a look at what is selected for the Default Note Duration and Default Note Velocity settings, to the right of the Edit tools at the top of the Score Editor window. As in the MIDI Editor window, you have a range of a $1/64$ note to a full bar to choose for step-entering notes with the Pencil tool, as well as a velocity range of 0 to 127. Also take note as to what is selected as the

Score Editor window's Grid value, as that will affect lengthening or shortening notes with the Pencil tool, not to mention the Trimmer tool. In addition, the Display Quantization setting in the Notation Display Track Settings dialog box will affect the resolution of notes inserted by step programming as well as how much one can lengthen or shorten new notes using the Pencil tool or existing notes using the Trimmer tool.

For this example we'll use a default note duration of a ¼ note and a Grid value of a $^1/_{16}$ note. We'll also make sure the meter is 4/4. Click the Pencil tool in Freehand mode anywhere in a staff, and a ¼ note will be inserted. Note that with the appearance of the ¼ note, any rest notation is adjusted to reflect the newly added note. Click the Pencil tool again anywhere in a staff and drag to the right, and the duration of the note will increase by $^1/_{16}$-note increments as selected in the Grid value, again appropriately changing any rest notation present in that measure. Similarly, click anywhere in a staff and drag to the left, and the note duration will decrease down to one $^1/_{16}$ note. You can also use the Pencil tool to transpose a note by dragging up or down either while you are creating it or after the fact, when the Pencil icon changes to a Grabber-like finger icon when hovering over an existing note.

Other modes of the Pencil tool let you create multiple notes of the same pitch, with variations between the tool modes in note length and velocity. The Pencil tool's Line mode enables you to create a string of notes the same pitch and the velocity amount specified by the Default Note-on Velocity selector. The length of the notes is determined by the Grid value and the Display Quantization of the Notation Display Track settings. Simply click at the desired starting beat on a staff and drag to the right. The Pencil tool's Triangle mode will do the same, except with the velocity of the subsequent notes changing from the default value to 127 and back in a triangle pattern. Click and drag with the Pencil tool in Square mode and the resulting notes—their lengths again decided by the Grid and Display Quantization values—will alternate velocities between the default value and 127. And Random mode sets the velocity at its whim anywhere between the default value and 127 for the created notes when click and drag with the Pencil tool on a staff.

Keys, Meters, and Chords in the Score Editor Window

As in the MIDI Editor and Edit windows, you can work with key changes, meter changes, and chord symbols in the Score Editor window. Unique to the Score Editor window is the ability to display chord diagrams used for guitar tabs. Look at measure 5 in Figure 17.2. The meter changes from 4/4 to 3/4, and at measure 9, the key modulates up a half step to D♭ major, complete with triad chords accompanying the melody with added chord diagrams and symbols for guitar accompaniment. Except for the chord diagrams, all these changes will appear in the corresponding Meter, Chord, and Key rulers in both the Edit and MIDI Editor windows.

Meter Change

To insert a meter change, right-click with the Pencil, Note Selector, or Grabber tool and choose Insert > Meter Change or open the Event menu and choose Time Operations > Meter Change. In the Meter Change dialog box that opens (see Figure 17.3), you can choose the location of the

Figure 17.2 Examples of meter and key changes as well as chord diagrams and symbols used in the Score Editor window.

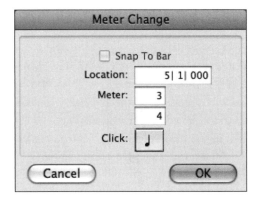

Figure 17.3 The Meter Change dialog box. Insertion of a new meter in the Score Editor window will be reflected in the Meter ruler found in the Edit and MIDI Editor windows.

change, whether that location corresponds to the exact start of a bar (with the Snap to Bar selection), and the new meter you desire. You can also choose the note duration of the click, which is handy when choosing meters like 6/8, where a dotted ¼-note click would be much easier on the ears than straight ⅛ notes. If ever you want to edit the meter or its location, simply double-click the meter event with the Grabber tool and make your changes. If you decide against keeping a meter change, choose the Grabber tool and Option-click (Alt-click in Windows) the meter event to delete it.

Key-Signature Change

With key-signature changes, you can apply the methods described for meter changes to create, edit, and delete key events. The Key Change dialog box that opens (see Figure 17.4) presents a choice of keys; you determine their mode by choosing either the Major Keys or Minor Keys selector in the upper-left corner. You then choose a starting location of the key event as well as specify how long the newly chosen key will be in effect: until the next key signature, a location

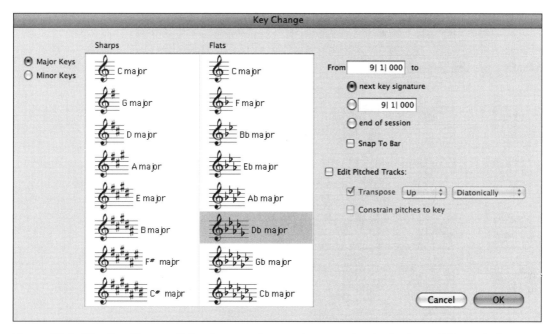

Figure 17.4   The Key Change dialog box, used to put key notation in the Score Editor window as well as in the Key ruler. Also use this to transpose the notes affected by the key-signature change.

decided by the user, or the end of the session. As with the Meter Change dialog, you can make sure the event lines up with a bar start via the Snap To Bar selection. You also have the option of having Pro Tools intelligently transpose the notes included in the start and end location with the Edit Pitched Tracks checkbox. With this selected, you can transpose note pitch up or down either diatonically or chromatically. Most of the time, you will want to use the Constrain Pitches to Key selection.

Chord Change

New to Pro Tools 8 is the ability to use chord symbols in the Edit and MIDI Editor windows' Chord ruler and chord symbols and diagrams in the Score Editor window. Creating, editing, and deleting chord changes follows the same methods used for meter and key changes. As shown in Figure 17.5, the Chord Change dialog box asks you to choose the chord's tonic with the Chord selector, the chord mode with the Chord Quality selector, and the chord inversion with the Bass selector. It then displays in guitar notation the resulting options from your selection; choose one by double-clicking its chord diagram or single-clicking the desired diagram and then clicking OK. If you choose an inversion of the chord, the chord symbol in the Score Editor window will list the root and mode of the chord, and then the bass note to the right above the chord diagram. A corresponding symbol is placed on the Chord ruler to be viewed in either the Edit window or the MIDI Editor window.

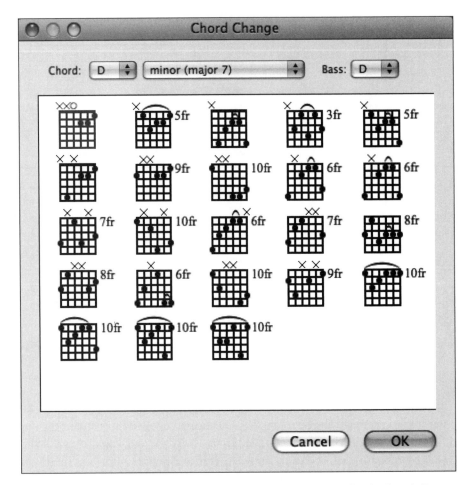

Figure 17.5 The Chord Change dialog box, used to create both chord diagrams and symbols in the Score Editor window and chord symbols in the Chord ruler found in the Edit and MIDI Editor windows.

Settings and Setups

The appearance of all elements in the Score Editor window is determined by two groups of settings: the Notation Display Track settings and the Score Setup settings. Both can be accessed via the Tracks menu in the Score Editor window or by right-clicking anywhere in the notation portion of the window. Consult these two dialog boxes to establish general settings for spacing and what information is actually shown within the notation as well as specific settings concerning transposition for band and orchestral instruments.

The Notation Display Track Settings

Upon opening the Notation Display Track Settings dialog box, shown in Figure 17.6, make sure the correct track is chosen with the pull-down menu at the top of the track. Directly below that is a pull-

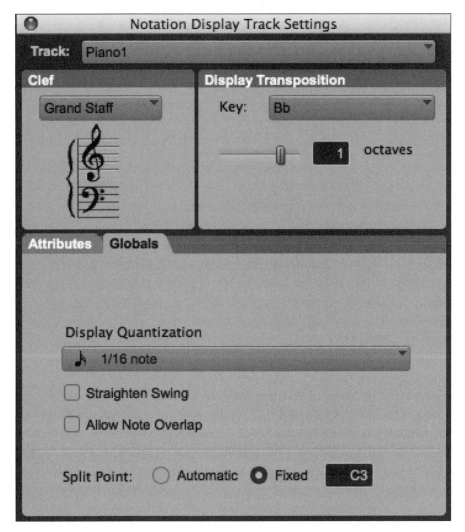

Figure 17.6 The Notation Display Track Settings dialog box, with a transposition setting appropriate for a concert B♭ instrument like clarinet or trumpet.

down menu that lets you choose the appropriate clef for the instrument that the MIDI or Instrument track represents. Choices are Grand Staff, Treble, Bass, Alto, and Tenor. To the right of the Clef selection is the Display Transposition setting, which enables you to alter the notation to represent instruments that transpose from concert pitch. For instance, if you want a MIDI or Instrument track to represent a part for a trumpet, which would need to play a C to represent concert pitch B♭, simply choose B♭ from the Key pull-down menu and choose +1 with the Octaves slider.

The lower-half of the Notation Display Track Settings dialog box deals with the note-duration resolution of the notation and gives you two tabs with the same selections: Globals and

Attributes. Think of the settings in the Globals tab as your default settings that you can choose initially or revert back to if desired. In the Attributes tab, you will notice the Follow Globals selection; that chooses the settings currently found under the Globals tab. Deselect the Follow Globals selector and the settings you make in the Attributes tab will apply. Also note that your Attributes tab settings will not change if you choose the Follow Globals selector; they will merely not apply to the notation. Also present are selectors for Straighten Swing as well as Allow Note Overlap. In addition, when Grand Staff is selected as the clef, you can choose what note separates the treble and bass staves or let Pro Tools do the job. The Fixed button applies the note specified in the field to the right of it, and the Automatic button lets Pro Tools analyze the MIDI or Instrument track for note groupings and logically divide them between the two staves.

Display Quantization and Note Overlap There are a couple things worth highlighting about the Notation Display Track Settings dialog box. First, if you ever play a nice pastoral melody of ¼ and ⅛ notes in a MIDI or Instrument track and notice that notation peppered with $1/_{32}$ grace notes appears in the corresponding Score Editor window for that track, you will want to check out what's selected in Display Quantization. A good rule of thumb is to start by setting the duration one shorter than the shortest note length in the performance. In the case of the pastoral melody, try a $1/_{16}$-note duration and take a look at how the notation in the Score Editor window has changed. If you're not satisfied, try selecting an ⅛-note duration. Remember that this only affects how the performance is displayed in the Score Editor window, not the performance itself. Also, if you are planning to step-program in the Score Editor window, set the Display Quantization amount before starting as its setting will override what is selected as the MIDI Note Duration setting at the top of the Score Editor window.

If you find yourself hitting a wall when using the Trimmer tool to extend certain notes' durations in the Score Editor window, most likely the Allow Note Overlap function in the Notation Display Track Settings dialog box needs to be selected. This enables you to create slurred or tied notes to signify their overlap of the next performed notes. Again, settings for Display Quantization will affect how small a duration you can extend a note to with the Trimmer tool.

The Score Setup

The Score Setup dialog box, shown in Figure 17.7, lets you choose the settings for the general appearance of the page. Like the Notation Display Track Settings dialog box, you can access the Score Setup box by right-clicking in the notation-portion of the Score Editor or through the Tracks pull-down menu. Starting with the Information Section, you can attach a name to the score, which appears top center, and note the composer of the score, which appears top right.

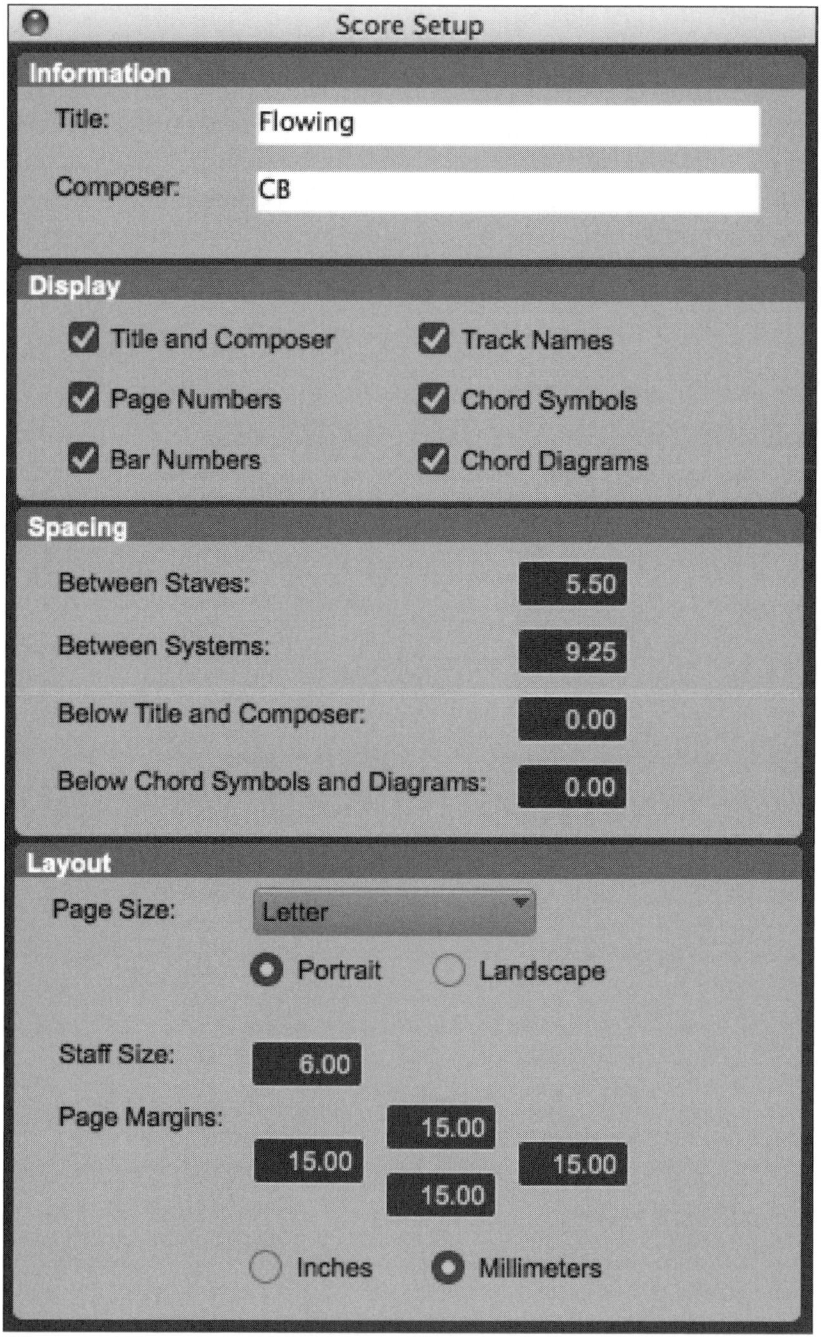

Figure 17.7 The Score Setup dialog box, which allows you to insert both Title and Composer information, as well as choose the general appearance and orientation settings.

Immediately below the Information section is the Display section, which lets you toggle on or off elements in the Score Editor window, including the title and composer, track names, page numbers, chord symbols, bar numbers, and chord diagrams. The Spacing section lets you set the length of space between staves, stave systems, below the title and composer text, and between the chord diagrams and symbols and the staff underneath. Lastly, the page and staff size as well as the page margins and orientation are set in the Layout section of the Score Setup dialog box. You can choose between Letter, Legal, Tabloid, and A4, in either Portrait or Landscape mode, for the Page Size setting. The staff size and margins can be set in inches or millimeters.

Summary

With the addition of the Score Editor window in Pro Tools 8, the functionality of the music-making aspects of the Pro Tools platform has greatly increased, especially for composers and arrangers. One could perform a piece of music in Pro Tools using MIDI and Instrument tracks, edit and arrange the resulting performance, play the sequence for the intended musicians, and then print out the score for a live performance, all within Pro Tools. Even if the original performance is intended to be kept within Pro Tools, the ability to edit and step program in the Score Editor window—especially combined with the editing choices in the MIDI Editor window—offers time-saving flexibility to the user in how he or she ultimately creates music. Clearly, Digidesign intends for Pro Tools to be the ultimate one-stop shop for electronic music making.

18 Pro Tools Power: The Next Step

The learning process never stops. Not only is Pro Tools constantly evolving with new software features, new audio hardware, and so on, but your own ambitions will no doubt increase as you gain more experience with audio production (and Pro Tools features), which means you'll need to learn how to accomplish these more advanced goals!

This chapter briefly reviews typical upgrade paths for the current generation of Pro Tools hardware. (Appendix B, "Add-ons, Extensions, and Cool Stuff for Your Rig," discusses other peripheral equipment and accessories for Pro Tools systems.) In addition, we make some basic suggestions here for deepening your knowledge and enhancing your career possibilities.

Upgrade Path: For Your System

One of the things that makes a digital audio workstation like Pro Tools so attractive is that you can upgrade it as your requirements and budget dictate. You can incrementally increase the power of your production system: bigger and faster hard disks, more plug-ins, more RAM, additional or higher-resolution audio hardware, more sophisticated synchronization and MIDI connections, a faster computer.

Naturally, because Pro Tools is largely software based, the creative environment itself evolves over time. In contrast, your options for expanding and updating the system configuration are more limited with most hardware-based alternatives for editing audio and MIDI.

Inevitably, as your use of Pro Tools becomes more sophisticated and you tackle more ambitious projects, more demands are placed on your system. The options for expanding the Pro Tools hardware itself depend on which system you're using. Pro Tools|HD (like the older Pro Tools|24 MIX hardware and its predecessor Pro Tools III, none of which support Pro Tools 8) is modular by nature. The Mbox 2 family, original Mbox, the Digi 003, and the now-discontinued Digi 002 families, on the other hand, offer more fixed I/O configurations, as do the M-Audio interfaces and the now-discontinued Digi 001 and ToolBox systems (although you can still enhance most of these systems via external preamps equipped with Lightpipe or S/PDIF digital outputs, as discussed in this chapter). In addition to the audio hardware itself, with the rapid advance of technology, there will always be more powerful computer platforms available for Pro Tools—but be sure to do your homework before making any upgrade. The program will *not* necessarily be compatible with brand-new motherboard chipsets, computer models, and other hardware without an upgrade. Be sure to check the compatibility documents in the Support area of Digidesign's Web site before proceeding. Also, the Digidesign User Conference (DUC) is an excellent place to learn about other users' real-world experiences; you may even find parts lists and suppliers for putting together your own custom rig. In particular, with more sophisticated plug-ins, higher track counts and audio resolutions, and especially software instruments, you may constantly crave more memory, storage, and processing power from your host CPU. Let's review some of the typical options (and a few potential pitfalls) for expanding your rig here.

Pro Tools Hardware Upgrades

Several of the audio interfaces for Pro Tools|HD systems include vacant bays where you can install an expansion card for more analog or digital I/O plus a Legacy Peripheral port for connecting older Digidesign audio interfaces from the now-discontinued 24 MIX family (which never supported Pro Tools 7, let alone 8), such as the 888|24 I/O, 882|20 I/O, 1622 I/O, or 24-bit ADAT Bridge I/O. You can further increase the number of audio inputs and outputs by adding a second interface to your configuration.

You can increase the DSP capacity of these Pro Tools systems by adding extra PCI (or PCIe) cards from Digidesign (one or more HD Accel cards on Pro Tools|HD, either within the computer itself or in a PCI expansion chassis available from Digidesign and others). Among other things, this allows you to use more simultaneous plug-ins. A larger number of simultaneous tracks, sends, inserts, and so on may also be supported, if DSP capacity was the factor previously limiting this in larger sessions. Having more HD Accel cards on your system also enables you to increase the number of hardware I/O channels in your system by connecting additional audio interfaces to each of them.

Pro Tools|HD systems support daisy-chaining two 96 I/O, 96i I/O, 192 Digital I/O, or 192 I/O interfaces on the HD Core or Accel Core card. Each HD Accel card you add supports 32 more potential channels of I/O (the Pro Tools HD|2 configuration has one HD Accel card; the HD|3 has two). Therefore, even on the entry-level Pro Tools HD|1 system, adding a second audio interface to increase your physical I/O for audio from 16 to 32 channels wouldn't require any additional cards.

Current Mac Pro models from Apple have only four PCIe card slots, and one of these will already be occupied by the graphics card. (The G5, G4, and G3 have only three or four PCI card slots.) For expanded configurations with many audio cards, you can add an external PCI expansion chassis to the computer, connected via a single PCIe card in one of its internal slots. With Pro Tools|HD and a powerful computer, however, the greater processing power of each Pro Tools card means that large track counts and higher audio resolutions are supported, even when only the available PCI slots within the computer are used.

Caution: PCI Versus PCI Express (PCIe) Current Mac Pro (and all Macintosh G5 computers since the end of 2005) use an expansion slot specification known as PCI Express, or PCIe. Because cards in the older PCI format are incompatible with PCIe, Digidesign now offers its Pro Tools|HD cards in both PCI and PCIe formats. (The conventional PCI/PCI-X cards continue to be offered for users of other computers because the PCIe cards are not backward compatible with PCI slots.) For example, the Magma PE6R4 is a six-slot external PCI expansion chassis that allows you to use existing PCI cards for Pro Tools|HD with a host computer that offers only PCIe slots. It is connected via a PCIe card installed in the computer.

Computer Hardware and Operating System Upgrades

The biggest item here is a second monitor. If you're working long hours, especially with larger Pro Tools sessions, this makes a huge difference in your productivity. Viewing the Mix and Edit windows on separate monitors and keeping more plug-in and Output windows anchored and visible really speeds up work. Many currently available graphics cards supporting dual monitors provide excellent results with Pro Tools. On older G5 and G4 Macintosh models, only an Apple DVI-to-ADC adapter is generally required to connect a second monitor. Another option is a single mega-monitor, such as Apple's 24- and 30-inch cinema displays. These give enough room to spread out both the Edit and Mix windows side by side or have one conveniently long Edit window.

Adding more RAM to your computer can also improve the operation of Pro Tools. For most current systems, 1GB should be considered the rock-bottom minimum for most practical purposes, with more strongly recommended in many cases. Any aggressive user will need 4GB of memory to avoid reaching high levels of computer-performance frustration.

Certainly, the faster your disks, the more channels of audio can play back reliably. (7,200 RPM is recommended for all but the smallest configurations; 10,000 RPM is also worth a look.) If you ever approach 90% disk capacity, you're asking for trouble! Mbox 2, Mbox, Digi 003, and Digi 002 users will eventually want to expand beyond the internal drive supplied with their computer, especially to support higher track counts and/or higher sample rates or bit depths. Aside from installing an additional SATA drive internally (or the slower ATA drives on older Mac CPUs), faster FireWire and SATA drives are a better option for these users because of their superior performance with Pro Tools in particular—as long as you confirm that any drive you buy meets the requirements posted on Digidesign's Web site. Many don't, and aside from general performance issues, can actually cause error messages in the program!

Before laying out your hard-earned cash to upgrade to any new operating-system release for your computer, make absolutely *sure* it is compatible with your current version of the Pro Tools software. The same applies for new motherboard chipsets and computer models. Digidesign maintains current compatibility documents in the Support area of its Web site (http://www.digidesign.com).

Audio production is a demanding real-time application, and you will find that Digidesign is fairly conservative about certifying new operating systems and hardware. If the contacts at your Digidesign dealer are technically qualified regarding computer hardware and operating-system issues, seek their advice. Otherwise, contact Digidesign Sales and Support via e-mail. You can also find the latest in the Digidesign User Conference (http://duc.digidesign.com). Keep in mind that, as with all online forums, posts here can range from helpful and technically impeccable to pugnacious and histrionic. In short, if your Pro Tools system is currently working, don't be stampeded into the latest operating-system upgrade until you've done adequate research. And if you must experiment, don't beat up on Digidesign if you experience unpleasant side effects!

Pro Tools Software Upgrades

Digidesign regularly releases new versions of the Pro Tools software. As a registered user, you are entitled to these upgrades at a reduced fee for major version upgrades, and usually free for downloadable minor customer-service updates. Be sure to verify that each software upgrade is appropriate for your hardware, though. Sometimes, an incremental version exists simply to support new hardware and may not be required by—or even compatible with—your current configuration!

As is common with other software manufacturers, Digidesign offers a series of maintenance updates between major upgrades of the Pro Tools software. Again, some of these exist merely to support new hardware options. Be sure to check out all the Read Me information on Digidesign's site (and the compatibility documents, of course) before downloading and installing any upgrade. And *be sure to register your Pro Tools system* so that you are informed of important upgrades and new products; likewise, let Digidesign know if you change your address (you can do this on the Digidesign Web site). In our experience, Digidesign is very good about not selling user lists to junk mailers. At most, you'll occasionally receive announcements directly from Digi along with the sporadic invitation to a road show or product presentation in your area.

Second-Hand Pro Tools Systems If you've purchased a second-hand Pro Tools system, you can still register with Digidesign, which entitles you to service and future upgrades. (You can download the PDF version of the Transfer of Ownership form from the Support section of Digidesign's Web site; it must include serial numbers, be printed, and be signed by both you and the seller!) Make sure you understand exactly which computer models and operating systems are supported by the used Pro Tools hardware you intend to buy, however. Also, for your own records, make sure to get the original sales receipt for any used Pro Tools system that you purchase if possible.

Pro Tools Peripherals

Upgrading from a simple MIDI interface to a multiport model is a typical upgrade path for many users, as is adding sophisticated SMPTE synchronization (with reference sync, if your hardware supports it). An external control surface is another (see Appendix B for information about these). Rackmountable, high-performance hard drives from Avid, Glyph, and others are also attractive options; unlike most hard drives, their performance level specifically with Pro Tools is guaranteed, and they're also designed to be relatively *quiet*. This brings up another common Pro Tools peripheral: an acoustical housing of some sort to isolate the fan noise from the computer and hard drives from your critical control-room listening environment. (USB and DVI/VGA extenders are an attractive option, allowing you to move the computer and drives out of the control room altogether; see Appendix B.) If working in a home studio, a well-ventilated closet with some soundproofing may be a good solution.

Audio Hardware

Certainly, there are a lot of great microphones and microphone preamps that you can add to your system; the sky's the limit! As mentioned various times in this book, Digidesign's PRE, an eight-channel mic preamp, is attractive not only because its microphone preamps sound good but also because you can control its settings directly from the Pro Tools session via MIDI and the I/O Setup dialog box on HD systems. Each time you reopen a session document, the previous settings on the PRE are restored. This is a huge help for maintaining consistency in your levels and overall sound throughout multiple songs, recording dates, and overdub sessions. Many other high-quality microphone preamps are available; each has a unique sound (and often additional options for processing or otherwise coloring the sound prior to the Pro Tools input), and many even offer digital outputs that can be connected to your audio interface.

Combining a multichannel Pro Tools system with external reverbs, compressors, and other effects is simple using sends or hardware I/O inserts (routed through the inputs/outputs of your audio interface). As a Pro Tools user, though, you're more likely to build up the majority of your arsenal for effects processing via plug-ins rather than stacking up boxes in your studio racks. As you can guess by this point in the book, that's exactly what *we* would suggest!

If there are multiple digital audio devices in your studio, you might also investigate the master audio clock generators that are available (this is also known as *word clock* or *word sync*). Slaving all your Pro Tools audio hardware, multitrack digital recorders, DAT recorders, digital effects and patchbays, and so on to a single sample clock source can make life much simpler, facilitating digital transfers and phase-accurate playback. As when using a synchronization peripheral to slave your audio hardware to a house sync (black burst) video signal, having the playback speed of all your playback and recording devices precisely slaved together at the hardware level reduces lock-up times and facilitates the maintenance of sync over extended periods of time. Extremely high-quality clock sources can also audibly improve sonic quality, especially on older 24 MIX or Digi 001 hardware (not compatible with Pro Tools 7 and 8) as well as most of the current hardware options for Pro Tools LE and M-Powered versions.

Digidesign periodically offers hardware upgrades at a reduced price for existing users, especially when introducing new hardware. The Hardware Exchanges sections on the Digidesign Web site list any offers currently in effect. Your decision will depend on many factors, usually including money, money, and money! Other issues include whether you mostly require more inputs and outputs, a superior recording resolution, or a different *type* of I/O (multitrack digital formats such as Lightpipe or TDIF, for example). Also, be sure to consider what *other* equipment upgrades may be required by your Pro Tools upgrade. For example, your existing hard disk setup for an older Pro Tools 24 MIX configuration with a single eight-channel interface may be entirely inadequate for 16 simultaneous channels of 24-bit, 96kHz audio with an HD or Digi 003 system.

If a greater number of simultaneous audio inputs and outputs in Pro Tools is your most pressing need, you might consider acquiring an additional audio interface. Doubling your number of simultaneous audio sources for recording proportionately increases the load on your system and disk space/performance requirements. Hardware expansion options depend on which base configuration of Pro Tools you're using. Figure 18.1 shows some options for an expanded Pro Tools|HD configuration.

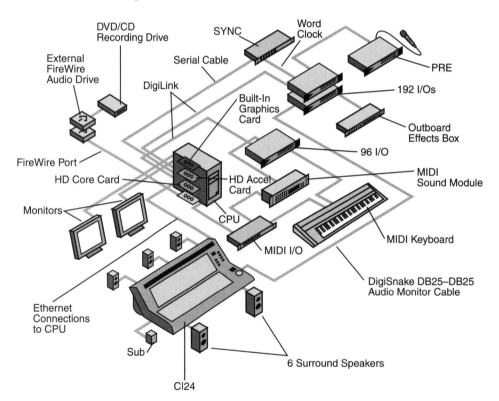

Figure 18.1 An expanded Pro Tools|HD configuration.

Pro Tools|HD Systems

The 192 I/O, 192 Digital I/O, 96 I/O, and 96i I/O audio interfaces have an Expansion port, where you can directly connect a second HD audio interface via DigiLink cable. The HD

Core card, included with all Pro Tools|HD systems, supports up to 32 channels of simultaneous I/O (for example, two of these audio interfaces). Additional audio interfaces can be connected to each HD Accel card (or to the older HD Process card) in your system. Among current preconfigured HD Accel configurations, one HD Accel card is included with Pro Tools|HD 2 Accel, and two are included with Pro Tools|HD 3 Accel.

These HD audio interfaces (except the 96i I/O) also include a Legacy Peripheral port, where you can attach some older audio interfaces from the Pro Tools 24 MIX hardware family (888|24, 882|20, 1622, or 24-bit ADAT Bridge I/O). The Legacy Peripheral port supports either a single 16-channel interface or two eight-channel interfaces (using Digidesign's 16-channel cable adapter). These interfaces are limited to their original sample rate of 44.1 or 48kHz. The Expansion port and Legacy Peripheral port cannot be used simultaneously, however, because they both use Group B, input/output channels 17–32 on the host HD card.

The 96 I/O provides 16 simultaneous channels of I/O (from the 20 available I/O connections). For each channel pair, you can select among eight analog ins/outs, ADAT Lightpipe I/O, AES/EBU digital I/O (XLR connectors), and S/PDIF digital I/O (coaxial or optical). This audio interface supports sample rates of 96, 88.2, 48, and 44.1kHz.

The 96i I/O provides 16 analog inputs and two analog outputs (all with ¼-inch TRS jacks) and S/PDIF digital I/O with RCA jacks only (no AES/EBU or ADAT Lightpipe). Unlike the 96 I/O, this interface has no Legacy Peripheral or Expansion ports. The gain on inputs 1–4 can be continuously varied via software (Hardware Setup) between −12.0dBV and +4dBu, while inputs 5–16 can be switched via software between −8dBV and +4dBu.

The 192 I/O also supports a maximum of 16 channels of simultaneous I/O and all the sample rates supported by the 96 I/O plus 176.4 and 192kHz. It features an I/O card bay, where you can install eight additional analog inputs, analog outputs, or digital I/O (via the 192 AD, 192 DA, or 192 Digital cards). This would allow you to use up to 16 analog, ADAT, or TDIF inputs or outputs simultaneously. The basic interface includes eight channels of analog I/O via DB-25 connectors; these require separately ordered DigiSnake breakout cables with conventional XLR or TRS audio connectors (although you can also wire your own compatible cables or order them from other sources). There are up to 16 channels of 48kHz ADAT Lightpipe digital I/O (two sets of eight, the second of which can alternatively be configured for optical S/PDIF at even higher sample rates), eight channels of Tascam TDIF I/O, eight channels of AES/EBU digital I/O (accessed via a second 25-pin D connector, identical to that used for TDIF), plus two additional channels of standard S/PDIF or AES/EBU digital I/O. The 192 I/O is also the only Digidesign interface to offer real-time sample-rate conversion on incoming digital signals and includes a soft-clip limiting feature. Again, any 16 of the ports on this interface can be active simultaneously. If you have both the 192 1/O and a 96 I/O on your system, the 192 1/O should always be the first interface connected to the Pro Tools|HD card. A DigiLink cable is connected from the Expansion port on the first interface to the Primary port of the second interface.

The 192 Digital I/O is similar to the 192 I/O, without the eight-channel analog input and output sections and with a second digital section. The base unit has two sets of ADAT Lightpipe inputs/outputs (16 channels), plus two TDIF connectors (another 16 channels), plus two additional channels of standard S/PDIF or AES/EBU digital I/O. It additionally provides 16 channels of single-wire AES/EBU I/O (or up to eight channels of dual-wire AES/EBU I/O at a 192kHz sample rate) via two 25-pin D connectors. Digidesign sells a 12-foot snake cable that breaks out each set of AES/EBU channels from the DB25 connector on these interfaces (that is, a D-shaped 25-pin connector) to the standard XLR connectors (four male and four female) commonly used for AES/EBU digital connections to and from other gear.

Slave Clock Connections on Your Audio Interfaces When Pro Tools|HD configurations have multiple interfaces, they are cabled together via their Loop Sync ports. This slaves their audio sample clocks together to maintain sample-accurate synchronization between them at the hardware level. The Loop Sync output of the primary interface is connected to the Loop Sync input of the secondary interface, and so on through the others. (Like most word-clock ports, these have BNC connectors.) Finally, if *all* the interfaces are HD hardware (192 I/O or 96 I/O families, as well as the SYNC synchronization peripheral), the Loop Sync output of the last HD audio interface is connected back to the first one's Loop Sync *input*. (On the other hand, if your last interface is a legacy peripheral such as the 888I 24 I/O, its Slave Clock Out should *not* be connected back to the primary interface's Loop Sync input!)

Alternatively, as mentioned previously, you could also slave the Pro Tools audio interfaces—and all the other digital audio gear in your studio—to a centralized clock source in a star configuration. Ideally, this would be a standalone unit, such as the highly accurate clock generators available from Lucid Audio and others, although an extra-stable sample clock output from certain high-end devices or an add-in card on several digital mixers might also serve this purpose.

One last note about Pro Tools|HD hardware: In addition to the 12-foot DigiLink cable supplied with the HD Core card and the 18-inch DigiLink cable supplied with each HD audio interface, you can also order these cables in 25-, 50-, or even 100-foot lengths. This would enable you to move one or all of your audio interfaces into the studio or soundstage, eliminating many meters of analog cabling (and its associated potential for noise, hum, and RF interference) from the input path to the analog-digital converters on your HD audio interface. The maximum length for 192kHz operation is 50 feet, while at 96kHz operation, 100-foot DigiLink cable lengths are supported.

HD-Only Plug-ins One of the most attractive features of Pro Tools is that it offers you the ability to expand its functionality though additional plug-ins and other auxiliary software. This chapter and Appendix B focus mainly on hardware-expansion possibilities, however.

Scores of developers are constantly introducing new software, plug-ins, and upgrades for their Pro Tools–compatible products, and any comprehensive listing here of the latest cool stuff and its capabilities would become outdated very quickly. Your best starting point for the latest information about plug-ins is always the Plug-in Finder on Digidesign's Web site.

Nevertheless, since the introduction of Pro Tools|HD, an entire generation of plug-ins has emerged that specifically require the processing architecture and more powerful 321 DSP chips on the HD cards. Not surprisingly, the sonic results of these more processing-intensive plug-ins can be quite impressive. Here are some notable effects-processing examples:

- **ReVibe (Digidesign).** A room-modeling reverb. It can process audio at sample rates up to 96kHz. Supports 5.x surround formats, with independent reverb, early reflection, and level controls for the rear channels.

- **Impact (Digidesign).** This compressor plug-in supports sample rates up to 192kHz and surround formats up to 7.1. It's mainly designed for applying console-style compression on the mix bus (that is, on the Master Fader track for your mix output path that is the source for bouncing your mixdown to disk), although it also supports side chaining and has many other applications. Impact's sound and the simulated ballistic characteristics of its onscreen gain-reduction meters emulate classic compressors used on mixing consoles.

- **Smack! (Digidesign).** Although also available in an RTAS version for all Pro Tools systems, the TDM version of this compressor/limiter plug-in requires HD hardware. It supports sample rates up to 192kHz and multichannel formats, offering controllable harmonic distortion and side chaining, with many tonal coloration possibilities that are especially useful for music applications.

- **Massenburg Design Works Hi-Res Parametric EQ.** Five fully adjustable bands of EQ, each of which can function as a boost/dip, low-pass/high-pass, or low-shelf/high-shelf filter. All bands offer 6dB/octave slopes for the low- and high-pass filter mode; band 5 also supports 18 or 24dB/octave slopes. Frequency selections are available from 10Hz to 41kHz. This EQ plug-in operates at 48-bit resolution and high sample rates (at 88.2 or 96kHz, for example, even in sessions that are 44.1 or 48kHz), and can be used on mono, stereo, or multichannel tracks. It emulates the constant-shape reciprocal filter curves of Massenburg's own GML 8200 parametric filter, a high-end stereo hardware unit. Many parametric EQ plug-ins are available for Pro Tools, but when the *inventor* of the parametric EQ (not to mention award-winning producer, engineer, and sound designer) puts one out, it's worth a listen!

- **Forte Suite (Focusrite).** Also available in an RTAS version, the TDM version of this plug-in requires HD hardware. It emulates a channel strip on Focusrite's high-end Forte recording console from the mid-80s, using physical modeling to simulate the vintage ISA 110 EQ, plus the expander, gate, de-esser, and surround compressor from the 130 series (with side-chaining capability) for multiple effects in a single plug-in instance.

- **TL Space TDM (Trillium Lane Labs).** Among other things, this convolution reverb simulates reverberant spaces as well as well-known digital, spring, and plate reverbs. It can use up to eight DSP chips to accomplish its extremely processing-intensive tasks without latency, including multichannel surround configurations. Based on an impulse response (derived from a recording of the ambient space or similar device), TL Space convolves the incoming signal, imposing that space's characteristics upon it. Of particular interest is its online library of impulse responses to simulate new spaces.

- **Phoenix (Crane Song).** This suite of TDM plug-ins emulates analog tape compression as one more mastering tool for increasing apparent loudness without increasing gain. Five separate plug-in components are included: Luminescent, Iridescent, Radiant, Dark Essence, and Luster. Each provides diverse characters and degrees of coloration and is based on Crane Song's proprietary Harmonically Enhanced Digital Device (HEDD) technology.

- **Eventide Anthology II bundle (Eventide).** A plug-in suite of 15 classic Eventide effects, including two channel-strip modules, EQ45 parametric EQ, EQ65 filters, H3000 Band delays, Quadravox, H949 and H910 harmonizer pitch shifters, phaser, flanger, and dynamics. Also included are reverb algorithms from Eventide's DSP4000, Eclipse, and Orville hardware units, with 3-band parametric EQ provided both before and after the reverb.

- **Sonic NoNOISE (Sonic Solutions).** This extremely powerful tool for audio restoration (removal of broadband noise, peak distortion, clicks, crackling, hum, and buzz) can also be used as an AudioSuite process, but requires Pro Tools|HD hardware for non-destructive, real-time operation.

Digi 003 and Digi 002 Systems

Both of these audio interfaces offer enough inputs for recording up to 18 channels simultaneously: eight mic or D/I line analog, eight ADAT Lightpipe, and two S/PDIF digital. (Note that the Digi 002 is now discontinued, although it continues to be supported for current versions of Pro Tools LE.) For musical applications, however, having only eight analog inputs can be a little tight (see Figure 18.2).

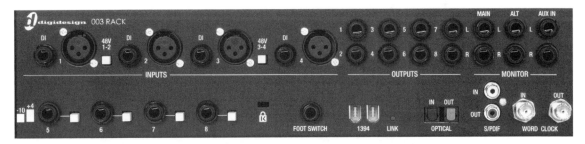

Figure 18.2 Analog and digital audio connectors on the Digi 003 Rack.

Standalone mic preamps with digital outputs can be a good way to expand your analog input capacity (budget permitting), through either the S/PDIF or Lightpipe input sections on your Digi 003 or Digi 002 interface. Mono, stereo, and eight-channel models are available, according to your requirements and budget. Here are just a few examples:

■ **ART Digital MPA.** Dual channels with hardware inserts, S/PDIF, AES/EBU, and Lightpipe digital output, sample rates up to 192kHz.

■ **dbx 386.** Part of the "silver" series. Dual pre channels with a tube preamp section. Includes S/PDIF and AES/EBU digital outputs and supports sample rates up to 96kHz.

■ **Joemeek TwinQ/OneQ.** Dual or single channel, with 4-band EQ, enhancer, de-esser, compression, analog inserts, and digital output in AES/EBU or coaxial/optical S/PDIF format, supporting sample rates up to 96kHz. A word clock input is also provided.

■ **Aphex 1788A.** High end. Eight-channel microphone preamp with optional digital output card for ADAT Lightpipe, TDIF, and AES/EBU supporting sample rates up to 96kHz (although 48kHz is the highest sample rate supported for Lightpipe). A word clock input is also provided. Includes a built-in limiter for the microphone inputs. Can be remote-controlled via MIDI from Mac/Windows software or from Aphex's optional 1788RC hardware controller to keep analog cable runs from microphones as short as possible. (Also controllable from D-Control and D-Command.)

■ **PreSonus DigiMax D8 and DigiMax FS.** Mid to high end. Both models feature eight class A XMAX mic preamps and 24-bit ADAT digital output. While the D8 supports 44.1 and 48kHz sample rates, the FS can support up to 96kHz. The FS model also offers word-clock input and output as well as direct outputs and inserts on every channel, while the D8 offers the choice of using external sync via a BNC word-clock input and direct outputs on every channel but no inserts.

■ **Focusrite ISA 220 (mono) or ISA 430mkII (dual) with optional digital output board.** High end, with parametric/shelving EQ, compressor, de-esser, and optional 430mkII ADC digital output card supporting S/PDIF (optical or coaxial), AES/EBU, word-clock and Digidesign SuperClock output, and sample rates up to 192kHz.

- **Focusrite OctoPre/OctoPre LE.** The OctoPre is another high-end unit. Eight channels with compression/limiting and word-clock input/output, plus S/PDIF and AES/EBU, via an optional digital output card (plus Lightpipe digital outputs with another more-sophisticated version of the digital output card) that can be installed in the back panel, supporting sample rates up to 96kHz. The OctoPre LE is a more economical version that also supports the digital output option for Lightpipe.

- **Focusrite LIQUID4PRE.** Four-channel physical modeling unit for more than 40 mic preamps (with more downloadable online), with Lightpipe and AES/EBU digital I/O and BNC connection for word-clock sync, controllable from within the Pro Tools software (and/or with the D-Command, D-Control, and VENUE control surfaces) via an included RTAS or TDM plug-in, which also allows storing up to 99 presets and locking the front panel against unwanted alterations to this preamp's settings. Supports sample rates up to 192kHz.

On Digi 003 Rack or (now-discontinued) Digi 002 Rack systems, you can use Digidesign's Command|8 control surface to have physical faders and transport controls plus knobs/sliders for controlling the volume and pan controls, send levels, plug-in parameters, and so on within the Pro Tools software. Focusrite developed this control surface for Digidesign, which also provides a monitoring section for external sources and dedicated outputs for the control-room and headphones.

Some users will also add an extremely stable, high-quality digital word-clock source to their 003 or 002 systems (options from Apogee, Lucid, and other companies are listed in Appendix B).

Mbox 2 Systems

The Mbox 2 (shown in Figure 18.3) offers up to four simultaneous channels if you use both the stereo analog and digital inputs simultaneously. (However, its S/PDIF digital *output* always mirrors analog outputs 1–2.) The Mbox 2 Pro can record six separate inputs: Channels 1–2 can be switched between two combo XLR/TRS microphone inputs on the rear panel or two DI instrument-level inputs with TS jacks on the front panel. The Aux In inputs on the rear panel can be switched between line-level TRS jacks or a phono preamp with RCA jacks, and appear as channels 3–4 in Pro Tools. It also has stereo S/PDIF I/O that is independent of the other inputs. In contrast, the Mbox 2 Mini offers only stereo analog I/O (TRS connectors for both channels 1–2,

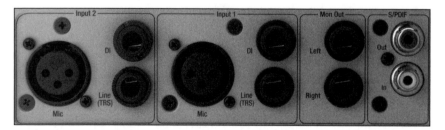

Figure 18.3 You can use the analog and digital connections on the Mbox 2 independently for 4 × 4 operation.

which can be switched between line and instrument, plus an XLR mic input that can alternatively be selected for channel 1).

Obviously, for any economical audio interface with a digital input, one attractive option might be a mega-dollar, high-end mic preamp with digital output (perhaps including some internal effects, if you prefer to apply some moderate amount of compression or limiting prior to the record input). While recording or monitoring a digital input, the internal sample clock of the audio interface can be slaved to that source. (On the Mbox 2 and Mbox 2 Pro, when you switch to the S/PDIF input source in the Hardware Setup dialog box, the Clock Source selector automatically preselects S/PDIF instead of internal sync.) Some MIDI modules and guitar/bass preamps also offer S/PDIF digital outputs. Using digital audio connections wherever possible can reduce accumulated background noise in your projects—especially after you layer up many tracks—and makes managing input levels much simpler.

The Original Mbox

The original Mbox (now discontinued, and unsupported on Mac OS X 10.6 Snow Leopard) is always limited to two simultaneous inputs and two simultaneous outputs—either the combo connectors for input that are switchable between mic, line, and instrument levels, *or* the S/PDIF connectors (RCA) for stereo digital I/O, as shown in Figure 18.4. (Digital outputs 1–2 always mirror analog outputs 1–2 on this interface.) The Mbox's microphone preamps offer acceptable quality for a unit at this price If you're a lone wolf and don't require more than two simultaneous inputs (for example, you're a composer with a project studio or you're a voice-over artist), you can add a high-quality mic preamp with digital output and a stable sample clock. These, along with good microphones and a quiet room, can result in surprisingly good-quality recordings.

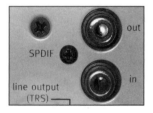

Figure 18.4   As on most audio interfaces for Pro Tools, coaxial S/PDIF digital I/O on the original Mbox uses RCA jacks. On some other interfaces, a Toslink connector is available for optical S/PDIF I/O.

Analog inserts in the input signal path are another unique feature of the original Mbox. A special insert cable (the same kind used for inserts on small Mackie and Soundcraft boards, for example) can be inserted into the insert jack for each of the Mbox's analog inputs to break this ¼-inch TRS (tip/ring/sleeve) connection out into two ¼-inch TS (tip/sleeve) plugs. While recording or monitoring an external source, these would be connected to the input and output on any external device you want to patch in prior to the input of the Mbox's A/D (analog-to-digital) conversion stage. For instance, you might use these points in the input signal chain to insert a killer-sounding analog compressor or limiter, permanently coloring the sound before it enters Pro Tools. (Interfaces in the Mbox 2 family do not include analog inserts.)

M-Powered Systems

An external control surface such as the Command|8 might be desirable for those M-Powered users who prefer physical controls, as most of the audio interface options from M-Audio don't offer this functionality. Additionally, many of the M-Audio interfaces that are compatible with Pro Tools M-Powered include S/PDIF digital inputs (with the exception of the Delta 44, Mobile Pre USB, and Fast Track USB, for example). For these, the comments already made in this chapter about the advantages of high-quality mic preamps with digital outputs also apply. The ProjectMix I/O (which, like the NRV10, does incorporate a control surface) and FireWire 1814 also offer ADAT Lightpipe I/O, so the previously listed multichannel mic preamps with Lightpipe digital output would also be an excellent complement to these units. (In fact, using the ADAT Lightpipe input is necessary to fully exploit their potential number of I/O channels.) In addition to the capability to slave the interface's sample clock to a selected digital input (shared by all M-Audio interfaces that have an S/PDIF and/or ADAT Lightpipe input), the ProjectMix I/O also includes BNC connectors exclusively dedicated to word-clock input and output. Figure 18.5 shows the analog and optical inputs on the rear of the FireWire 1814 interface.

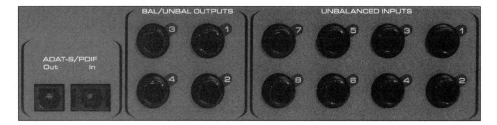

Figure 18.5 Analog and optical I/O (usable as either ADAT Lightpipe or optical S/PDIF) on the rear of the FireWire 1814 interface, by M-Audio. A separate breakout cable provides RCA connections for coaxial S/PDIF.

Upgrade Path: For Your Mind

In Appendix A, "Further Study, and Resources on the Web," you'll find a few suggestions for further study, including Web sites, CD-ROM training (see the next section), magazines, and books. Regardless of what further study you undertake, the most important thing is to try to make some time in your schedule to get crazy with Pro Tools. Experiment with dopey mixing effects and other offbeat ideas to build up your arsenal of techniques. (Yes, it *is* hard to find time for this in a working production facility!) Also, take advantage of opportunities to work on projects with your Pro Tools system that are completely outside your daily routine. If your audio-engineering work with Pro Tools mainly involves video post, take on a CD-mastering project for a local band. If you're mainly a music mixer, record a spoken-word piece—perhaps a narration for a training piece, a local poet reciting her work, a family history, a radio spot, or what have you. The left-field requests from these clients can take you into areas of Pro Tools—not to mention into effects applications and signal-routing techniques—that you may not have explored before. You're guaranteed to learn something along the way that will prove useful in your regular work.

Cool School Interactus Special note of these top-of-the-line educational CD-ROMs must be made, as many are the creation of two of the co-authors of this book, messieurs Colin MacQueen and Steve Albanese (who founded Cool Breeze Systems and created the Course Clips platform). These interactive CD-ROMs for Mac and Windows walk you through basic digital audio concepts and specific Pro Tools examples. Several volumes deal with Pro Tools specifically; one is an overview of digital audio workstations and digital audio in general, with modules about synchronization and MIDI. Others cover Logic Audio, Digital Performer, Nuendo, and a variety of other audio programs. In the *Starter* series, you will find volumes about Pro Tools, Reason, GarageBand, ACID, Logic, Digital Performer, Sound Forge, and SONAR. *Course Clips Master* volumes cover Nuendo, Ableton Live, Cubase 4, Digital Performer, older versions of Pro Tools, and audio plug-ins in general, as well as one about Waves plug-ins specifically. In comparison to, say, reading this book, the CD-ROM learning experience is less linear, using movie tutorials to show real-world applications of the Pro Tools software. (Pardon the self-promotion here, but honestly, these contain huge amounts of information and loads of movie tutorials to walk you through program operations step by step.)

Career Options

Pro Tools is used in music-production studios, video-production houses, film studios, radio- and television-broadcast stations, film and historical archives, record companies, multimedia development houses, and in audiobook publishing houses. If you are trying to establish yourself as a Pro Tools operator, don't wait around for your perfect vision of a job to materialize. Get out there and visit the production houses in your community—even if there is not a position currently available. Ask to see their installations and how they operate. Remember that *any* job that keeps you working in Pro Tools on a daily basis will help you hone your skills with the program. Even if your ambition is music production, many of the Pro Tools techniques you master while posting industrial videos or recording the spoken-word bits for Web and CD-ROM projects will carry over into subsequent phases of your career.

If you are a musician using Pro Tools in your own home-project studio, consider working for some other local clients. Take out an ad out in the local paper, and offer to record singer/songwriter demos at a fixed rate for a fixed number of hours, including a CD copy at the end of the session. Of course, you will have to fix the parameters of the services you offer according to your system's capabilities; if you have only one or two microphones, you can't have a whole steel-drum band trooping into the basement or spare bedroom! Be aggressive in your initial pricing. If you do a good job, a fair percentage of these people will book additional hours and subsequent sessions. Even with a single microphone, any Pro Tools system is perfectly equipped to record oral histories or any other spoken-word piece, such as an author or poet reading her work or corporate-training and motivational presentations.

With many of the more portable systems (for instance, an Mbox 2/Mbox, Digi 003/002, or several of the M-Audio interfaces with a recent iMac or appropriately powerful Mac/Windows laptop), you can go on site to record, making your service even more attractive. You might prepare an offer of x dollars for x hours, including two CD copies, or something along these lines. Again, you're guaranteed to learn something along the way, improving your Pro Tools chops. For that matter, if you have a high-quality matched pair of microphones, you can even record local music and theater performances on location with your luggable Pro Tools rig. (Just make sure nobody pours a drink on your computer!) If you have a high-quality handheld digital recorder or DAT, you could instead take that out on location and then transfer the recording to Pro Tools for editing and for mastering of the CD. And of course, you can write off your audio-equipment purchases, mileage, and so on against any declared income!

If you have a friend who needs a voice-over demo, offer to record it for him or her—for *free*, if necessary! Interactive media developers are increasingly contracting voice talent directly. If your collaboration with this friend can deliver finished voice-over files in immediately usable formats (see Chapter 15, "Sound Design for Interactive Media," for more information), you can both make some money!

Maintaining a Learning Attitude and Finding Additional Resources

This book has pursued two objectives: first, to provide a quick start for novice Pro Tools users, condensing the most essential features and techniques (and crucial technical concepts) in order to be productive with Pro Tools in the shortest time possible. Second, we've tried to make some specific useful suggestions for people already using the program, including insights that will be helpful even for experienced operators.

This is just a start, however. If you've spent some time with the excellent manuals and PDF documentation Digidesign provides with Pro Tools, you've probably noticed many additional keyboard shortcuts, tool modes, parameters, dialog-box selections, and other application-specific information that we don't discuss. This is not only for space considerations (and the obvious fact that this book isn't intended as a substitute for the manual), but also because we've deliberately sought to narrow our focus somewhat. Building on the essential facts, this book aims to walk you through typical situations for applying Pro Tools features rather than taking the one-size-fits-all, purely descriptive approach that a technical manual necessarily follows.

In short, then, we urge you to read the Digidesign documentation! Take a printout of the *Pro Tools Reference Guide* home or out to lunch with you (after you've finished *this* book, of course). Print out the *Keyboard Shortcuts* document, make notes to yourself about shortcuts and features you want to remember, and post them around your keyboard and monitor.

Give Your (or Your Employer's) Printer a Break In the DigiStore section of Digidesign's Web site, you can purchase printed manual sets that include the *Pro Tools Reference Guide*, the *DigiRack Plug-ins Guide*, and the *DigiBase Guide*, containing the same text as the PDF versions included with the program, but in a spiral-bound book. Other products available in the DigiStore include reference cards and keyboard stickers for the Mac or Windows versions, padded carrying cases and backpacks for interfaces and compact control surfaces, Digidesign cables, plug-ins, and software upgrades—plus the usual shirts, water bottles, and pens with the manufacturer's logo, of course!

Make time to experiment with features and techniques; try something excessive! Seek out other Pro Tools users and spend time with them as they work. You can always pick up something—even from users who, in theory, are less technically grounded in Pro Tools than you are. Especially if your Pro Tools work is routinely in a single field (like audio for video, for example), pick up some great ideas by collaborating with other Pro Tools operators who use it for something completely different, like music production or multimedia.

There are many learning resources out there. A few suggestions are collected in Appendix A. Digidesign's Web site includes the Digidesign User Conference online forum, plus an excellent technical-document library with downloadable reference guides for its software and hardware add-ons for Pro Tools. The Digidesign site also sells books, DVDs (including the *Method One* DVD, which is included in the Ignition Pack bundles for HD and LE systems) and Berklee-developed online training about Pro Tools, and the free online *DigiZine*. Other learning options for Pro Tools users include the *Course Clips* series of instructional CD-ROMs (see the Music Technology section of http://www.courseptr.com and the CD in the back of this book for movie tutorial examples from this series). In Appendix A, you will also find suggestions for further study.

Summary

As a Pro Tools user, you're involved with one of the most popular and powerful audio tools available. If you're just breaking into the business, make some calls to local production facilities—not only to network, but also to learn how they work with Pro Tools. We can tell you, after collaborating with so many Pro Tools users over the years, that there's rarely a single best way to do things. Every time you sit by while another Pro Tools user works (at any level), you have a chance to learn something. Don't stop there, though; find an opportunity to teach someone *else* how to use Pro Tools. Not only is this a swell thing to do, but as anyone who has ever taught will tell you, in the process of clarifying your ideas for someone else's benefit, you will attain a higher level of knowledge yourself.

The following appendixes provide additional technical information, tips (be sure to check out Appendix D, "Power Tips and Loopy Ideas," if you're already an experienced Pro Tools user!), and resources for further study, plus information about archive and backup.

Thanks for reading. Enjoy!

Appendix A: Further Study, and Resources on the Web

You may wish to dig deeper into digital audio, sound recording in general, or MIDI, depending on your interests and immediate requirements. We've been at this for years and certainly never run out of interesting things to study! What follows here is very brief—a few pointers for learning more about subjects related to Pro Tools.

Books About Audio

When you're ready to read more about digital audio in general and Pro Tools in particular, use this list as a starting point:

- *Digital Audio Explained: For the Audio Engineer* by Nika Aldrich. Published in 2004 by Sweetwater Press. One of the best sources for practical information about digital audio. The author provides in-depth, clearly written explanations about sample rate, bit depth, digital filters, ADC/DAC design, sample clocking, dithering, and other key concepts. If the rudimentary digital audio concepts in Chapters 1, "About Pro Tools," and 2, "Pro Tools Terms and Concepts," of this book were all news to you, this is a great place to start. Our favorite chapter—and required reading for all you experienced digital audio workstation cosmonauts—is "The Myths of Digital Audio."

- *Pro Tools 6 Power!* by Colin MacQueen and Steve Albanese. Published in 2004 by Thomson Course Technology. A predecessor to this book, covering 6.*xx* versions of Pro Tools. If you are using a Digi 001 or 24 MIX system (which are limited to versions 6.4.1 and lower of the Pro Tools software), this book is for you.

- *Pro Tools Power!* by Colin MacQueen and Steve Albanese. Published in 2001 by Muska & Lipman Publishing, a division of Course Technology. Another predecessor to this book, covering 5.*xx* versions of Pro Tools.

- *Digital Audio Dictionary* by Colin MacQueen and Steve Albanese. Published in 1999 by Howard W. Sams & Co. Yes, us again—a large glossary in book form.

- *Principles of Digital Audio, Fifth Edition* by Ken C. Pohlmann. Published in 2005 by McGraw-Hill. First published in the 1980s and still a respected source for a technical, theoretical grounding in digital audio.

- *Sound Recording Handbook* by John Woram. Published in 1989 by Financial Times Prentiss Hall. Provides in-depth information about recording in general—analog *and* digital audio—at a rewardingly technical level.

- *Audio Production Techniques for Video* by David Miles Huber. Published in 1987 and again in 1992 by Butterworth-Heinemann. In-depth postproduction information, including all the "old school" techniques.

- *Modern Recording Techniques, Seventh Edition* by David Miles Huber and Robert E. Runstein. Published in 2009 by Focal Press. Excellent reference for audio recording in general, and for digital audio. This book is used in many schools and universities.

- *Handbook of Recording Engineering, Fourth Edition* by John Eargle. Published in 2002 by Springer. Comprehensive reference work about general audio recording.

- *Handbook for Sound Engineers, Fourth Edition* edited by Glen Ballou. Published in 2008 by Elsevier. Current version of the series descended from the Audio Cyclopedia. Massive and authoritative reference resource; deep, detailed technical information on a wide range of general audio topics, circuit diagrams, formulas, graphs—the works!

- *The Art of Mixing, Second Edition* by David Gibson and George Petersen. Published in 2005 by Thomson Course Technology. A thought-provoking book about mixing from a visual perspective; a little offbeat, but applicable to any analog/digital mixing environment.

- *Mastering Audio: The Art and the Science, Second Edition* by Bob Katz. Published in 2007 by Focal Press. Excellent discussion of both analog and digital audio principles, dithering, jitter, bit-depth and sample-rate issues, noise reduction, equalization, metering, and other good stuff.

- *Pro Tools for Video, Film and Multimedia, Second Edition* by Ashley Shepherd. Published in 2008 by Course Technology PTR. Coverage of mixing/sync and delivery formats, plus description of Pro Tools editing and mixing techniques in general.

Magazines

- *Electronic Musician*
- *Keyboard*
- *Mix Magazine*
- *Recording*
- *EQ*

- *Sound on Sound*

- *Tape Op*

- *Computer Music*

- *Future Music*

- *Music Tech*

CD-ROM/DVD Training

Okay, modesty aside (since two of the authors of this book have been involved in their development), among other CD- and DVD-based options, the *Course Clips* CD-ROM series is one of the best interactive learning tools out there for digital audio workstation training. Several volumes in the *Course Clips* series focus specifically on Pro Tools, from basic digital audio concepts to MIDI, synchronization concepts, signal routing, and plug-in architecture and automation. Narrated movie tutorials walk you through techniques in Pro Tools as you watch and hear program operations, with specific recommendations for common tasks. See this publisher's Web site, http://www.courseptr.com, for further information. Additional titles in either the *Master* or *Starter* lines in the *Course Clips* series cover Waves plug-ins, plug-ins in general, Reason, Ableton Live, Logic, Cubase, Digital Performer, SONAR, ACID, Sound Forge, and GarageBand.

www.digidesign.com

Be sure to thoroughly investigate the Support section on Digidesign's Web site, where you will find a FAQ section, detailed compatibility information for all current or legacy software and hardware, as well software downloads. Digi also posts a majority of the manuals and Read Me files for their hardware and software products in the Technical Documents Library. This is an extremely useful resource when you're trying to figure out if an expansion option or upgrade is suitable for your own needs. Information is also provided about technical support and customer service, as well as hardware exchange offerings for users upgrading to more powerful or recent systems. The interactive Answerbase is another a great resource, especially for newbie questions. Digidesign's monthly online magazine, *DigiZine*, is of interest for Pro Tools users at *all* levels.

If you click International Sites at the top of the page, you can choose among various languages for the Digidesign Web site (with a significant quantity of translated technical documents and product information), including Spanish, French, Italian, German, Dutch, Swedish, Danish, Norwegian, Japanese, Chinese, and Korean.

DAE Errors If you ever get an error message from Pro Tools citing a DAE error number, you can research this problem on Digidesign's Web site. Go to the first page of the Support area and type the error number into the Support Search field to see possible causes and remedies for your problem.

Other Useful Web Sites

In addition to the Digidesign Web site, you'll find scores of other useful Web sites for the audio engineer:

- **duc.digidesign.com.** The Digidesign User Conference is a free forum hosted by Digidesign, with sections for Pro Tools TDM, LE, and M-Powered versions on Windows or Macintosh; DigiDelivery; Pro Tools Free 5.01; Digidesign's external control surfaces and other products; as well as forums specific to Post and Surround users. Especially if you are a new user, you should lurk here for a while—it's unquestionably the best forum for Pro Tools users at any level. Aside from the occasional user rants and squabbles found on any online forum, there are some pretty smart folks here offering productive advice and opinions to the brave souls who post dumb questions you may be too embarrassed to ask! It's also very active on nights and weekends; the advice you obtain from other users might get you out of a jam sometime. Just be sure to include your actual question or topic in the subject line of your post (as opposed to, say, "Help!") and specify exactly which version of the Pro Tools software and hardware you're using so that people can help you. Even veteran Pro Tools users will find some fairly high-fiber content here. *Highly* recommended!

- **www.whatis.com.** This site is oriented toward information technology (IT) in general, but over the years has been an invaluable resource for sorting out acronym clutter and manufacturer jargon. When the alphabet soup and cryptic computer talk has you stymied, this may be a good place to start!

- **www.harmony-central.com.** Topics here range from gear, tech, and the music business to just plain silly (not that there's anything wrong with that!). Of particular interest to Pro Tools users: the Recording forum, Phil O'Keefe's In the Studio Trenches forum, Craig Anderton's Sound, Studio & Stage forum, and Nuestro Foro (en español).

- **www.musicplayer.com.** Explore this site's forums related to music and audio. Of particular interest to Pro Tools users: Ethan Winer's Acoustics forum, the Project Studio forum, and the Keyboard Corner.

- **www.synthzone.com.** This exhaustive, well-organized site has a little bit of everything: links to manufacturers, to sites dedicated to MIDI instruments, to dealers, to MIDI software, to alternate tunings, to information about sound cards and audio hardware, and to digital audio workstation software (including Pro Tools, of course). It's really a useful resource. Kudos to Nigel Spencer, who maintains, designs, and owns it!

- **digitalprosound.digitalmedianet.com.** As advertised, this site features a collection of information about products and techniques related to professional digital audio. The Tutorials section is of the most interest, with articles about podcasting, noise reduction, voice-over techniques, various audio and video programs, ADR looping, soldering, and building portable sound booths, to name just a few topics we have browsed.

- **www.recording.org.** A general audio Web site that includes a section of forums about digital audio workstations and other topics. Within the DAW area, you may find occasional posts about Pro Tools, Digidesign hardware, and related topics, but again, experienced users and reliable information about Pro Tools–specific issues are more frequently found on the Digidesign User Conference. Nevertheless, because even Pro Tools–based studios contain audio devices from many other manufacturers, some of the forums here can be a valuable resource. As with all online forums, though, bear in mind that the experience and maturity level of members here run the full gamut. If you decide to register in any of the forums we mention here and participate in a thread yourself, please be respectful and tolerant—and *helpful*!

- **www.gearslutz.com.** In these online forums, you will find both project studio folks and industry heavy-hitters, with threads about studio gear, digital audio, mastering, and post-production, as well as discussions about many computer-based audio/MIDI programs, including Pro Tools.

- **www.tapeop.com.** This is the companion Web site for a bi-monthly magazine (available by free online subscription) about music recording, with tips and gear reviews plus excellent interviews with engineers, producers, and artists. *Tape Op* maintains a refreshingly practical focus, placing more emphasis on how-to's and how-they-did-it than on glamour profiles of the latest electronic gizmos. Online forums can also be found on this site.

- **www.apple.com/pro.** Mac users of Pro Tools should explore this part of Apple's Web site for an excellent section regarding music and audio solutions using their products. This is a great place to get heads-up information about new Apple models and operating systems, product releases from numerous audio and MIDI manufacturers supporting the Mac platform, plus some very good articles about specific artists and solutions. Also, if you're using a qualified Mac, be sure to check out Apple's music toolkit program, GarageBand. This program is a blast even for experienced pros, and of course individual tracks or sub-mixes can be exported from GarageBand as AIF files for further mayhem in Pro Tools.

- **www.aes.org.** This is the Audio Engineering Society's Web site. Although you must be a member to access the online journal and some other areas, the technical articles in PDF format are available to anyone visiting the site, as are most of the standards documents (including the society's *Recommended Practices* documents). For digging deeper into technical aspects of audio production, this is one of the most reliable sources available. Pro Tools audio professionals especially should read the 2003 document AESTD1002.1.03-10, "Recommendation for Delivery of Recorded Music Projects," found in the Technical Documents section. Among other things, this document suggests Broadcast WAV Format (BWF) as the standard delivery format for digital audio files; lists recommended sample rates; provides printable forms for recording, mixing, and duplication notes; and provides track sheets, delivery labels for analog and digital media, and an excellent (albeit brief) technical glossary.

- **www.midi.org.** This official Web site of the MIDI Manufacturers Association provides technical dope on the *MIDI Specification* itself, plus proposed and forthcoming standards, much of which are available in downloadable form. A comprehensive About MIDI section includes educational articles about the MIDI basics, General MIDI, Standard MIDI Files, and XMF (eXtensible Music Format) files, at both beginning and more-advanced technical depths. If you're new to MIDI and want to explore beyond the very basic MIDI concepts laid out in Chapters 2, "Pro Tools Terms and Concepts," and 10, "MIDI," this should be your first online stop.

- **www.kvraudio.com.** This Web site is devoted to news about audio plug-ins, various plug-in hosts, and displaying press releases and announcements of newly released or updated plug-in products. This site is invaluable to those Pro Tools users who have wisely invested in the VST to RTAS Wrapper from FXpansion, which opens up the world of VST plug-ins to Pro Tools users otherwise limited to TDM or RTAS-format software. Having a loyal and vast user base, KVR also features fantastic forums, from a music tracker to a "music café" forum where users can post links to their original work, as well as cooperation from manufacturers for a database of online support for many products. This is one of those sites you end up checking every day.

- **www.macosxaudio.com.** An absolutely massive resource for all things audio for the Macintosh. Pro Tools is duly represented here in the forums, as are many other platforms. In addition to the forums on effects, instruments, and hardware, there are also forums delving into the topics of the business of music and audio, music theory, and the development of software. Plenty of material to sink your teeth into for both novice and experienced users.

Schools

Pro Schools (facilities offering standalone, intensive training by Digidesign-certified instructors), certified training locations, and sponsored colleges offer Pro Tools certification courses. These three-day courses include Pro Tools 101 (Intro), Pro Tools 110 (Essentials) and 201 (Production Essentials), 210M and 310M (music production techniques, basic and advanced), 210P and 310P (postproduction, basic and advanced), and 310I (mixing techniques with one of the ICON control surfaces). Certificate titles issued based on this training and final exams include Certified Pro Tools Operator, Certified Pro Tools Expert, and Certified ICON Mixer. Go to the Training area of Digidesign's Web site for more information about certification courses and training centers. There, you'll also find some online courses offered by the Berklee College of Music (including several designed by Digidesign), the official *Pro Tools 101 Official Courseware* textbook for the training programs, the *Method One* instructional DVD, and other options.

Appendix B: Add-ons, Extensions, and Cool Stuff for Your Rig

There are tons of options—both hardware and software based—for expanding a Pro Tools configuration. Given the huge number of software plug-ins available for Pro Tools and how quickly they are updated, you should always start by referring to Digidesign's Web site for information about them and then confirm the absolute-latest versions on each plug-in developer's own Web site. Accordingly, this appendix concentrates on *hardware* enhancements for the various Pro Tools system configurations. Digidesign offers multiple audio interfaces, additional cards and I/O, the MachineControl option, rackmounted high-performance hard drives, and so on. This was discussed in Chapters 3, "Your System Configuration," and 18, "Pro Tools Power: The Next Step." Here are a few other ideas you may find useful.

External Control Surfaces

Using nothing more than a mouse or trackball to control all the functions in Pro Tools is a perfectly practical method. Indeed, this is how the vast majority of Pro Tools users operate. (Note that we *strongly* recommend that all Mac users still using a no-button factory model mouse immediately switch to a two-button wheeled mouse, a trackball, or Apple's Mighty Mouse for use with Pro Tools. Aside from the ability to scroll vertically and horizontally in the Edit window without moving the cursor from the track display area, these types of mice enable you to right-click various spots in the Mix and Edit windows in all Pro Tools versions 7.3 and higher to access local menus that offer quick access to many common operations.) Nevertheless, it can sometimes be convenient to use a more sophisticated physical peripheral in a fast-paced professional studio environment, with dedicated buttons, faders, and so on, that you can operate with two hands—and without looking down. For one thing, multiple physical faders allow you to automate mixes on the fly, moving several faders simultaneously and independently. (With a mouse or trackball, of course, you can only drag one slider at a time. Despite the advantages of grouping tracks in the Mix or Edit windows to gang their faders together, you could never, say, move one fader up while moving a second one down.) External control surfaces (also known as *virtual control surfaces*) are nice, too, because they can be larger and placed in the control room for access from various positions by various people if necessary. Having large, tactile transport buttons and illuminated buttons for record-enabling and muting tracks facilitates a more heads-up relationship between the Pro Tools operator and performers or other collaborators. The more upscale virtual controllers for Pro Tools have large, illuminated level meters and illuminated parameter displays for track names, levels, pan, and many other features similar to standalone digital mixers, plus dedicated controls for functions that are specific to Pro Tools. In short, they facilitate rapid, two-fisted operation of Pro Tools, which can really increase productivity—especially when you have a roomful of clients or performers.

ICON-Integrated Console Environments

The ICON family of integrated console solutions currently centers around two console/control surfaces that can be used with Pro Tools: the large-format D-Control (see Figure B.1) and the medium-format D-Command. Both of these offer motorized faders, buttons, rotary encoders, transport control, and signal-routing options. They also both use the rackmounted XMON monitoring/cue mix module, and are purchased as part of various bundled configurations for surround, music, or postproduction that include Pro Tools|HD hardware and various Digidesign peripherals. (These include all the current Surround, Music, or Post bundles include a Pro Tools|HD 3 Accel Core system, one or more 192 I/Os, a Sync HD, and Digitranslator. Other peripherals and plug-ins vary according to the configuration.)

Photo courtesy of Digidesign.

Figure B.1   The basic D-Control tactile work surface consists of a master module plus a 16-channel fader module. It can be expanded to up to 80 channels/faders.

D-Control and D-Control ES

The core D-Control *tactile work surface* consists of a main unit, plus a single 16-channel fader module that can be mounted on either side of it. The D-Control ES variation, introduced in Fall of 2007, features a darker color scheme, updated higher-contrast text and graphics for improved legibility in low light, and a new switch LED color layout. (Digidesign offers a kit to update an existing D-Control unit to the ES design scheme; the two units are similar in functional and mechanical aspects. The original D-Control is no longer produced.) You can add up to four more optional fader modules to these basic configurations for a maximum of 80 channel strips/faders. There are dedicated LED displays for the Main/Sub time indicators, and for the Start, End, and Length fields of the Pro Tools software on the main unit. Dedicated buttons are provided for switching between windows in the Pro Tools software, such as Mix, Edit, Transport, Memory Locations, MIDI Operations, Beat Detective, and others. Additional dedicated buttons for Pro Tools functions include the four edit modes, track height up/down, and Edit menu commands such as Undo, Redo, Cut, Copy, Paste, and Repeat. You can use a Focus channel strip in the center master module for editing any selected channel's parameters without leaving the center of the console. In addition, the D-Control has dedicated EQ and Dynamics panels on the master module that you can switch to control any channel on the fly. The D-Control has a built-in alphanumeric keyboard, a two-button trackball, and a shelf for an optional computer monitor or swinging arm for mounting a flat-panel display. A built-in talkback microphone and switch are also included, with a dedicated monitoring section for internal/external talkback, listenback, input source selectors for the control room, separate level controls for main and near field monitors, dim and mute buttons, input selection, and separate controls for three cue mixes, as well as level controls for headphone outputs and a feed to loudspeakers out in the studio room. The D-Control connects to the Pro Tools|HD Accel system's host computer via Ethernet (10BaseT, with RJ45 connectors).

In addition to touch-sensitive motorized Penny & Giles faders, each channel strip on the fader module has six multifunction rotary encoders with LED rings around them to indicate current parameter values or metering. LED meters are provided for each channel strip, plus eight channels of metering for the master section. Each channel strip provides 29 illuminated pushbuttons for switching channel modes, attributes, and so on. LED displays indicate channel names or the currently selected editing parameter for each channel strip.

There is an optional surround panner module available for D-Control that includes a color LCD touchscreen, two touch-sensitive joysticks with punch buttons, two touch-sensitive rotary encoders with LED rings, and six mode buttons for each panner. Among other methods, you can move sources in the surround field by dragging onscreen icons within the LCD display. An AutoGlide function allows programming smooth transitions from one setting to the next. Other interesting creative options are available when various plug-in parameters are custom-assigned to the XY axes of the surround panner module—for example, filter frequencies, feedback amounts on delays, modulation depths for LFOs, and so on.

In addition to supporting surround mixing, the rackmounted XMON Monitor System, included in D-Control configurations (as well as the D-Command), provides dedicated outputs used for three separate stereo cue mixes, talkback, listenback, studio monitors, and headphones. It is connected to the D-Control via a single 15-pin cable.

D-Command and D-Command ES

The D-Command and D-Command ES have been described by Digidesign as "mid-format" consoles. Like the D-Control, the non-ES version is no longer produced. The main unit features a central control section with monitoring and communications controls and eight touch-sensitive, motorized 100mm channel faders. The D-Command communicates with the host Pro Tools computer system via Ethernet using RJ-45 connections and a separate Ethernet hub (not included) to which both are connected. Each channel strip has two rotary encoders with LED rings to show either the current parameter setting or metering. It is expandable up to 40 faders via a two 16-channel fader module, which would be connected to an additional port on the same Ethernet hub as the computer and the main unit of the D-Command. On each channel strip, one six-channel LCD beneath the rotary encoder displays information about the current parameter while another serves as a scribble strip (displaying channel name, or plug-in parameters if the channel mode is flipped). Each of these channels can function independently, in a separate mode from the others. There are illuminated pushbuttons and bar-graph meters on each channel, plus eight more bar-graph meters in the master section. The center section has dedicated control panels for editing EQ (with 12 rotary controls) and dynamics plug-ins (with six rotary controls and dedicated output, gain reduction meters). The transport panel includes a jog/shuttle wheel (which you can also use to scrub and then trim region boundaries to that point), and dedicated buttons for Loop Playback, TrackPunch, QuickPunch, MachineControl, and other functions. The D-Command includes the same XMON remote, rackmounted analog I/O audio monitoring and communications system as the D-Control. The monitoring section on the D-Command itself provides control for up to two 5.1 surround inputs, three stereo inputs, and two cue sends. Like the D-Control, the D-Command (shown in Figure B.2) is for HD systems only and does not support M-Powered or any LE version of Pro Tools.

Control|24

The Control|24, no longer produced but still in use in many studios, combines a virtual control surface for either HD or LE versions of Pro Tools (but *not* M-Powered), with 16 phantom-powered Class A mic/line preamps engineered by Focusrite (see Figure B.3). The first two channels also include an instrument-level direct box setting. The Control|24 features a surround monitoring section and a built-in talkback microphone for communicating with performers out in the studio or onstage. It also includes a dedicated 8×2 analog line mixer, which can be useful for submixing multiple keyboards, live feeds from a mixing board, or other outboard devices. Also provided are 24 touch-sensitive 100mm moving faders as well as dedicated EQ and dynamics switches on each channel; illuminated switching for mute, solo, record enable, channel select, and automation buttons for each channel; plus dedicated transport keys with a scrub/shuttle

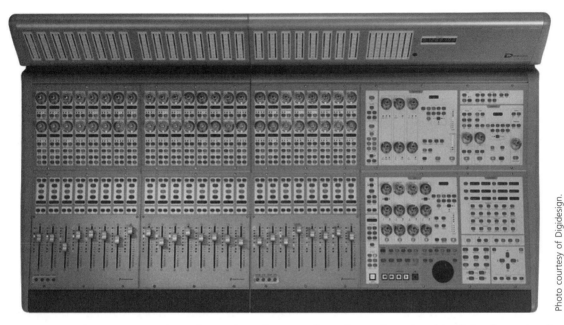

Photo courtesy of Digidesign.

Figure B.2 The D-Command tactile work surface consists of a main unit with eight channel strips, which you can expand via a 16-channel fader module.

Photo courtesy of Digidesign.

Figure B.3 Control|24, by Digidesign.

wheel. There are dedicated buttons for Loop Play, Loop Record, QuickPunch, Online, and Pre-/Post-Roll enable functions in the Pro Tools software. Modifier keys are provided, which you can use while enabling buttons or changing parameters, like the Command, Option, Control (Ctrl, Alt, and Start on Windows), and Shift keys.

The back panel of the Control|24 has numerous analog connectors, including 16 line/microphone inputs with phantom power, slate and dual aux inputs and outputs, and two DB-25 connectors for connection to Pro Tools audio interfaces via DigiSnake cables (eight output channels each). A third DB-25 connector provides eight outputs for speakers (via a DigiSnake breakout cable). The Control|24 communicates with the Pro Tools program via a 10BaseT Ethernet connection (RJ45 connectors).

C|24

The C|24 (shown in Figure B.4) was introduced in Fall of 2007. Like the Command|24, it is compatible with HD and LE versions of Pro Tools, but not M-Powered. It includes features listed for the Command|24 in a redesigned format carried out exclusively by Digidesign. The faders are arranged in three banks of eight each, and the LED scribble strips have two lines of six characters each. The mic input section is a newer design that includes high-pass filters and −20dB pads on each channel. These mic preamps are based on the Digi 003 design. The 8 × 2 mixer section can be routed directly to the monitoring section. The C|24 also includes an

Photo courtesy of Digidesign.

Figure B.4   C|24, by Digidesign.

updated 5.1 analog monitoring section with individually trimmable outputs (in .5dB increments) for convenient calibration. Soft keys are also provided for controlling certain functions, and a Windows Configuration button directly accesses this feature (available in Pro Tools versions 7.3 and higher).

Command|8

The Command|8 connects to the host computer via USB (Universal Serial Bus); see Figure B.5. Transport controls, eight motorized faders, and eight rotary encoders with LED rings around them indicate current parameter values or metering. The unit has a backlit LCD display (two rows of 55 characters) for track information and parameter values. Each channel strip has solo,

Photo courtesy of Digidesign.

Figure B.5 Digidesign's Command|8 control surface communicates with the host computer via USB, incorporates a MIDI interface, and offers control room–monitoring features.

mute, and channel select buttons. Dedicated buttons are provided for transport controls; Mix, Edit, and plug-in windows; loop play/record; undo; and creating memory locations. You can use a zoom button and arrow keys in the navigation section to zoom in or out. Flip buttons on each channel strip allow you to reassign their main faders to send levels or plug-in parameters on that track. The Command|8 incorporates a one-in, two-out MIDI interface and a footswitch jack for hands-free punch in/out of recording.

The monitoring section of the Command|8 was designed by Focusrite; the back panel includes two stereo input pairs for audio sources to be monitored through the Command|8. You could connect outputs 1–2 of your Pro Tools audio interface to the main input and use the external source input for a CD player or video, for example. A speakers output is also provided for monitoring your main stereo output from the Command|8. Like the two audio inputs, you can switch it between −10dBV and +4dBu level. In the Control Room section on the front panel of the unit, you can switch this output between the main and external source inputs, and this output features mute and mono buttons. Finally, there is a headphone jack on the front panel with its own level control.

The Command|8 can be used with HD, LE or M-Powered versions of Pro Tools (as well as Avid Media Composer). You can combine it with certain other tactile control surfaces from Digidesign such as the Pro Control, Control|24, or the Digi 002. You can also use this unit as a control surface for the Digi 003 Rack and 002 Rack (although this combination with the Digi 003 Rack does not provide *all* the features of the Digi 003, with its built-in control surface). Combining the Command|8 as a fader expansion unit with the Digi 002 yields a total of 16 faders. It can also operate in a standalone MIDI controller mode for use with other MIDI applications.

CM Labs MotorMix2

Each MotorMix2 control surface module provides eight 100mm motorized faders (see Figure B.6). You can add more modules to your system as your requirements (and budget) increase. MotorMix2 communicates bidirectionally with Pro Tools via MIDI; fader changes and other parameter adjustments in one are immediately reflected in the other. The Motor-Mix2 also includes an 80-character backlit LCD display and LED illuminated switches. You can use the eight non-motorized rotary pots to alter values of many different controls in Pro Tools (for example, send levels, pan controls, or plug-in parameters). A rotary selector determines which of up to seven different target parameters on target tracks the rotary pots control, while in Plug-In mode, all eight of them control various parameters within the currently active Plug-in window. There are dedicated Pro Tools transport controls, plus dedicated buttons for Pro Tools windows and Mix/Edit group selection. In Locate mode, dedicated controls enable QuickPunch, Loop Record, memory locations, and so on. Once you add MotorMix2 as a controller in your MIDI setup, you select it as your external controller for Pro Tools from a pop-up selector in the MIDI Controllers tab of the Setup > Peripherals dialog box.

Photo Courtesy of CM Labs.

Figure B.6 MotorMix2, by CM Labs.

Mackie Control Universal Pro (MCU Pro)

This is a more recent control surface by Mackie Designs that communicates with Pro Tools via MIDI using the HUI protocol (see Figure B.7). The MCU Pro directly supports a number of other DAW programs, including Logic Pro, Cubase, Nuendo, ACID, SONAR, Digital Performer, and others. Overlays are included for the master section of the unit, showing the program functions for Pro Tools, Cubase, Nuendo, SONAR, Digital Performer, and Cool Edit Pro. You can order other program overlays for a small fee from Mackie's Web site.

The MCU Pro includes nine motorized, touch-sensitive 100mm Penny & Giles faders (eight channel faders plus a master fader), V-pot rotary encoders (multifunction, assignable knobs that you can use for send levels, pan or plug-in parameters, and many other purposes), and dedicated record, solo, mute, and select buttons on every channel. There are also dedicated transport buttons, a jog/shuttle wheel for the transport or for scrubbing audio within tracks, a backlit LCD display showing metering and track names, and a dedicated seven-digit display for time code. When used with Pro Tools (and as printed on that overlay for the unit), the MCU Pro has dedicated zoom controls; buttons that directly open the Mix, Edit, Transport, and Memory Location windows; and other buttons for Enter (OK) and Cancel, Undo, and other functions. A Plug-in button switches the LCD display to that view, and V-pots 1–4 control values of plug-in parameters in the currently active Plug-in window. The pan button assigns V-pot knobs to that function on all channels. You can also select Pro Tools automation writing modes from

Figure B.7   Mackie Control Universal Pro (MCU Pro).

dedicated buttons. You can add additional Mackie Control Extender fader expansion packs (eight channel strips each) to the base unit.

Frontier Designs TranzPort

The TranzPort is a wireless remote control unit for Pro Tools and many other digital audio workstations (see Figure B.8). A small RF receiver (the Tranzceiver, which communicates with the remote at 2.4GHz) is connected to a USB port on your Mac or Windows computer, and the remote itself runs on four AA batteries. You can locate it as far as 30 feet (10 meters) from the receiver without requiring line of sight. It weighs about one pound and is 7×5.5 inches in size, supports mounting on a mic stand, and accommodates a footswitch for punching in/out of recording mode. There are 18 buttons for functions including transport control, rec/solo/mute

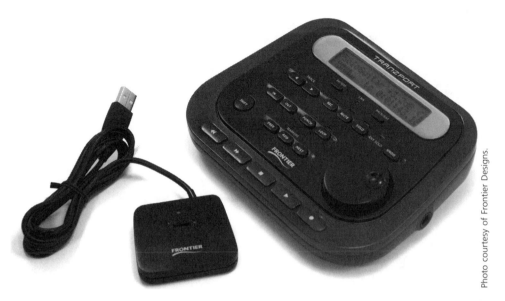

Figure B.8 TranzPort, by Frontier Designs (shown here with the USB receiver that attaches to the host computer).

for the currently selected track, and a dedicated Undo button (as well as others relating to markers and to Loop and QuickPunch modes). You can use its data wheel to scroll or scrub in the Pro Tools timeline. Communication is two-way, so that time code, current track name, volume/pan values, and so on can be displayed on the TranzPort's 2×20 character LCD display. To use this unit with Pro Tools, you use the TranzPort's control panel to put the device in HUI emulation mode, and then open Pro Tools and add an HUI controller in the Peripherals dialog box, choosing Frontier Designs TranzPort as the Receive From and Send To assignment. With this gizmo, you can easily control monitoring levels and basic recording functions from the sound booth or across the studio, away from noisy computers. It's just the thing for project studios and other people who have to perform while running the recording rig.

Frontier Designs AlphaTrack

The AlphaTrack (shown in Figure B.9) is compact desktop control surface that connects to the host computer via USB. It features a single touch-sensitive, motorized 100mm fader; a 32-character backlit display; and three touch-sensitive rotary encoders that also function as pushbuttons. The AlphaTrack Manager software included with the unit is used to select HUI emulation mode for use with Pro Tools. Dedicated transport buttons are provided, as well as record/solo buttons, an automation write button, and function buttons that can be used for zooming, undo, pre-/post-roll, and other Pro Tools features. A touch-sensitive strip at the bottom of the controller can be used to move through the Pro Tools timeline, either jogging (when dragging with one finger) or shuttling (when dragging with two fingers). Alternatively, you can tap at either end of this touch strip to jump to the previous or next marker in Pro Tools. The Flip mode allows the

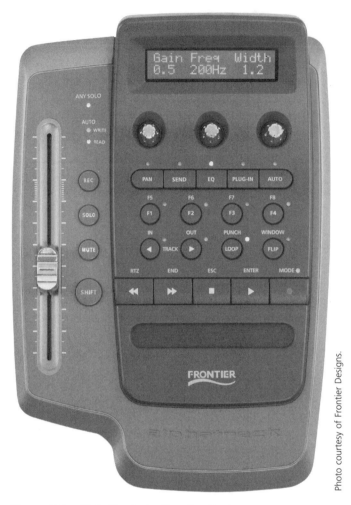

Photo courtesy of Frontier Designs.

Figure B.9   AlphaTrack, by Frontier Designs.

use of the 100mm fader (instead of the right rotary encoder) to control send levels. Pan, Markers, Send, EQ and Plug-in modes can also be selected for the encoder section.

Synchronization Peripherals

As explained in Chapter 11, "Synchronization," if you need to synchronize playback and recording of Pro Tools to an external SMPTE time-code source, you must add an external synchronization peripheral to your core Pro Tools configuration. Digidesign itself offers two devices, with features to resolve audio-playback speed over extended periods of time to either a clock or a video reference, or to the incoming time code itself. There are also many third parties offering excellent synchronization peripherals (often doubling as a MIDI interface) at a variety of performance levels and price points. Just a few are mentioned in this section, and new models continually appear, of course. In addition to starting playback or recording at the appropriate time according to *location* information received from SMPTE (or MIDI) time code, all the options listed here offer the additional ability to *slave* (resolve) the internal sample clock of Pro Tools hardware to an external source.

Digidesign Sync HD

The successor to the Sync I/O, Digidesign's Sync HD is a high-end synchronization peripheral that connects to Mac or Windows computers via USB (see Figure B.10). It translates SMPTE time code to and from VITC (video) or LTC (audio) format and can resolve (continuously adjust) the sample clock of your audio hardware to keep Pro Tools in sync with incoming time code over extended periods. Alternatively, the Sync HD can resolve the sample clock of the Pro Tools hardware to an external video reference (black burst/house sync), industry-standard word clock (1× the audio sample rate), or Digidesign's SuperClock (a timing reference for audio hardware operating at 256× the sample rate). The Sync HD can *burn* a time-code window into video signals passing through it. Dual Sony 9-pin serial ports can be used to link Pro Tools transport functions with external video/audio devices, if the optional Machine-Control software is installed in Pro Tools. The word clock supports up to 192kHz, as well as standard video and film pull-up or pull-down rates.

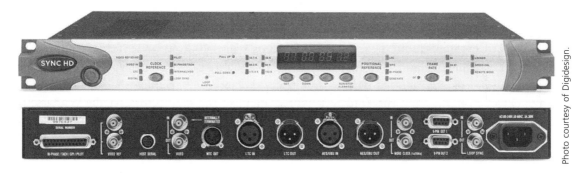

Figure B.10   Sync HD.

MOTU MIDI Timepiece AV (USB)

The MIDI Timepiece AV connects to the host computer via its USB port (see Figure B.11). This rackmountable interface features eight independent MIDI ins/outs for 128 total MIDI channels, all of which are individually accessible from within Pro Tools (via the Audio MIDI Setup on Mac or via the supplied MOTU drivers for Windows). This unit includes hardware synchronization outputs (9-pin ADAT sync and word clock), plus a video-sync input. (The video-sync input and the word-clock output have BNC connectors.) You can switch the word clock output

Photo courtesy of Mark Of The Unicorn.

Figure B.11 MIDI Timepiece AV, a multiport MIDI interface from MOTU, which also offers LTC synchronization.

between 1× and 256× the sample rate used to slave your Pro Tools hardware to the MTP AV, which in turn you can *genlock* (slave to match frame rates) to the black burst/house sync video signal at its video-sync input. The MTP AV also supports LTC (audio, via a ¼-inch phone input) time code at any SMPTE frame rate, and can convert this to hardware sync (ADAT or Pro Tools SuperClock) for resolving your audio hardware's sample rate to this time-code reference. The MTP AV is also a full-featured MIDI patchbay, merger, and processor. You can access all its features from the front panel during live performance or, more importantly for Pro Tools users, via the included software. The MIDI Express XT and the Micro Express are simpler MIDI/ SMPTE interfaces in MOTU's product line.

Digital Patchbays and Routers

Users with many digital audio devices in their studios will definitely want to look into *digital patchbays*. Reaching around to the rear panels of rackmounted devices every time you want to switch digital inputs and outputs between multiple devices is inconvenient and will inevitably damage cables over the long run (or, even worse, damage the connectors on the gear itself). Digital patchbays and routers provide a convenient way to move digital audio signals around between Pro Tools, multitrack digital recorders, effects, DAT recorders, and so on, without having to bend over and show your rear end to clients as you swap digital cables on the back of these devices. Many of these units also translate between different digital formats, so you could route ADAT channels into Pro Tools via S/PDIF, quickly switch the S/PDIF or AES/EBU inputs/ outputs on your Pro Tools audio interface between several other devices in the studio, and so on.

Z Systems OptiPatch and z-8.8a Digital Detanglers

The OptiPatch is an ADAT Lightpipe patchbay (eight-in, eight-out) and distribution amplifier with real-time sample-rate conversion. Stereo optical S/PDIF signals are also supported on the same Toslink connectors used for Lightpipe. It also supplies bidirectional conversions between Lightpipe and S/PDIF optical stereo formats (with sample-rate conversions, if required, between the 96kHz maximum on S/PDIF and the 48kHz maximum supported by Lightpipe). You can order the z8.8 Digital Detangler in various eight-way configurations—for example, four AES/ EBU, two S/PDIF coaxial plus two S/PDIF optical, or all AES/EBU. Of particular interest is the x8.8a unit, another automated ADAT Lightpipe patchbay and distribution amplifier that can perform real-time, bidirectional conversions between Lightpipe, AES/EBU, and S/PDIF. Z Systems offers many other Detangler units for routing multiple AES/EBU and Lightpipe connections, some of which you can order in custom configurations.

Z Systems z-128.128r Digital Detangler Pro

The z-128.128r is an automated patchbay, router, and distribution amplifier for digital audio signals in AES/EBU or S/PDIF formats at sample rates up to 192kHz, housed in a five-unit-high rackmountable chassis (see Figure B.12). Router-control software (via an RS-422 serial connection) is provided for both Mac and Windows. From the basic 16×16 configuration, you can add 16-channel expansions for up to 128 input/input channels. (There is also a z-256.256r model, with—you guessed it!—*double* the maximum number of inputs/outputs.) Breakout cables are required to break its DB-25 connectors out to eight standard XLR or RCA connectors (for AES/EBU or S/PDIF, respectively). Z systems also offers an adapter cable for interfacing this unit with the DB-25 connectors used for AES/EBU digital audio on Digidesign's 192 I/O and 96 I/O audio interfaces for Pro Tools|HD.

Photo courtesy of Z Systems.

Figure B.12   Back panel of the z-128.128r Digital Detangler Pro, by Z Systems.

Word Clock and Sync Generators

As mentioned elsewhere in this book, in studios with multiple digital audio devices, it can be very useful to synchronize the audio sample clocks of all these devices to a single, central source (similar to the way house sync is used in video studios to synchronize frame rates). Obviously, this source's clock must be extremely stable. For some situations—such as recording from a digital source or playing Pro Tools back in sync with a digital multitrack—it may be sufficient to simply lock them together via word-clock connections on the audio interfaces or use the Clock Source option in the Hardware Setup dialog box to synchronize Pro Tools to the digital input. Some devices generate a stable clock reference as part of their standard features (like the

Finalizer, from tc electronic, not to mention Digidesign's own Sync HD). Some digital mixers offer an optional card (such the Apogee Electronics Clock I/O card for the Mackie Digital 8-bus) that can provide a stable clock reference to Pro Tools and other digital audio devices. Nevertheless, for larger configurations and especially for demanding, high-resolution audio, professional users will opt for a higher-quality standalone word clock/sync generator to effectively eliminate jitter (sonic artifacts caused by minute variations in the sample clock) that can degrade the sonic image. Here are just a few examples.

Lucid Audio GENx-192

This device from Lucid Audio (see Figure B.13) acts as an extremely stable master clock source for digital audio configurations, at sample rates up to 192kHz. In addition to 1× word clock, it also directly supports Digidesign's 256× SuperClock format (used for the 888, 882, and 1622 audio interfaces on older 24 MIX systems). An amazingly accurate master clock for the price.

Figure B.13   The GENx-192, by Lucid Audio.

Rosendahl Nanosyncs HD

The Nanosyncs HD supports 1× word clock, Digidesign 256× SuperClock, AES/EBU sync, and video black burst/house sync, at sample rates up to 96kHz (see Figure B.14). It incorporates USB connection to a host computer that can generate MIDI time code or provide it to the DAW software by converting it from incoming LTC time code. The Nanosyncs HD has six video outputs (supporting both NTSC and PAL, including high-definition frame rates and Tri-Level Sync), AES/EBU and S/PDIF sync outputs, and eight separately configurable word-clock outputs with BNC connectors.

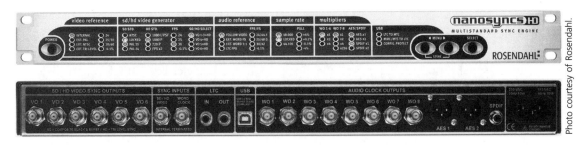

Figure B.14   Front and back panels of the Nanosyncs HD, by Rosendahl.

Session Control TL-Sync

The TL-Sync supports 1× word clock, Digidesign 256× SuperClock, AES/EBU sync, and video black burst/house sync at sample rates up to 96kHz, and four video outputs, including PAL video format (see Figure B.15). It includes two low-jitter, isochronous digital clock rate generators. It also supports the Pro Tools MachineControl option in virtual 9-pin mode *or* via MIDI MachineControl. It converts incoming LTC (SMPTE time code) or video sync to word clock or SuperClock format for Pro Tools. Originally developed by Timeline Vista, the TL-Sync is now manufactured by Session Control, which also offers the RC-Sync remote control for this unit.

Photo courtesy of Session Control.

Figure B.15   The TL-Sync, by Session Control.

Apogee Big Ben

This high-end, extremely low-jitter digital clock source from Apogee Electronics supports sample rates up to 192kHz (see Figure B.16). Inputs/outputs include two AES/EBU digital with XLR connectors, S/PDIF on both coaxial and optical connectors, ADAT Lightpipe, S/MUX II or IV, and six BNC connectors for word clock (1× only for highest sample rates, up to 2× at 96kHz or 88.1kHz, or up to 256× at 48kHz and 44.1kHz). The SureLock feature maintains steady clock adjustment if there is any interruption (and subsequent re-establishment) of an incoming clock source. With the optional X-Video card, incoming video sync (black burst) or video-sync generation is also supported in PAL or NTSC, with pull-up and pull-down sample rates. The Big Ben also includes a front-panel LCD display for the exact sample rate. When using the Big Ben on HD systems with multiple audio interfaces, attach each directly to the Big Ben via its Ext In word-clock input (with BNC connector) rather than connecting these interfaces together via

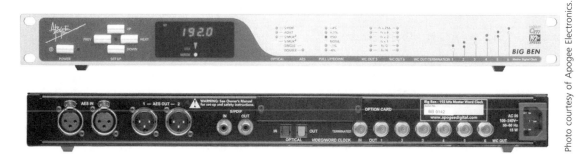

Photo courtesy of Apogee Electronics.

Figure B.16   Front and rear panels of the Big Ben, by Apogee Electronics.

their LoopSync ports in the usual fashion. Then open the Pro Tools Session Setup window and select Word Clock as the clock source for each of your HD interfaces.

Ergonomics, Rackmounting, Extenders

Let's face it: You spend long hours working at your Pro Tools rig. Whatever helps you to hunch, stretch, strain, hunt, or squint a little less will improve your quality of life! Standard office furniture—and for that matter, typical computer workstation furniture—doesn't always provide the most ergonomic setup for the way you work in Pro Tools. Just how many times a day are you willing to stand up, bend over, take 2.5 steps across the room to adjust a mic preamp or effect, arm a DAT for recording, and so on, before it's worth investing a little time and money in improving the *efficiency* of your working style? After all, the less wear and tear the work itself inflicts upon your patience and sustained concentration, the more creative you can be. Besides, it just looks and feels better to have all your gear neatly racked, your system components readily accessible at convenient angles, and your cables organized!

Digidesign Pro Tools Custom USB Keyboard

This USB keyboard, available for Macintosh or Windows computers, has color-coded sections (see Figure B.17). Text for standard Pro Tools key commands is printed on each key, as well as the standard QWERTY characters. Because this represents an additional expense (and costs more than conventional replacement keyboards), many, including yours truly, have been skeptical about the value of this option. But after watching several new users adapt to Pro Tools on systems equipped with this keyboard, it's clear that it really does shorten the learning curve in many cases. An added benefit is that these users more quickly become accustomed to using keyboard shortcuts instead of onscreen controls and menu commands.

Photo courtesy of Digidesign.

Figure B.17 Digidesign's Pro Tools Custom USB keyboard for Macintosh.

Rackmounting, Workstation Furniture

You can certainly build your own studio furniture (in some rooms this is a necessity), or perhaps adapt some existing computer workstation furniture for your project studio. Alternatively, various manufacturers provide work surfaces and rackmounting systems that are specifically tailored to the needs of digital audio workstation users.

Omnirax

Omnirax offers various lines of furniture, including the Force line of workstation desks for Pro Tools (with rackmounting systems to accommodate from 12 to 40 rack spaces of gear, depending on the model). Omnirax was the first company to address the special needs of digital audio workstation users, especially with the ProStation line. The Synergy S6C24 XL (see Figure B.18) was designed to house Digidesign's Control|24. The Coda workstation has a space for a small virtual control surface like the Mackie HUI, the Coda D8 holds a Mackie Digital 8-bus, and Coda EX was designed for Digidesign's ProControl. This is a solid company that has supported Pro Tools since the earliest days, and it really stands behind its products. Features specifically aimed toward digital audio workstation users include bridges for mounting computer monitors and near-field audio monitors, various configurations of rackmounting both above and below the work surface, cable channels, heavy-duty casters, and a sliding shelf for easy access to the computer.

Photo courtesy of Synergy.

Figure B.18 The Synergy S6C24 XL is designed to house the Control|24; it's flanked by 12-space rack bays.

Argosy Console

Argosy's studio furniture includes slanted bays for computer monitors, plus rackmounting and work surfaces for computer keyboards, trackballs, or mouse pads, and so on. The company's

Photo courtesy of Argosy.

Figure B.19 Argosy's Mirage DC-24 is designed for Digidesign's D-Command.

90 and 70 series consoles include a variety of models that are custom-fitted for Digidesign's ProControl or Control|24, as well as models for many other popular mixers. Also of interest is their Mirage DC-24, specifically designed for the D-Command (see Figure B.19). It includes a padded armrest, a pull-out tray for a computer keyboard and mouse, and two 19-inch rack spaces, each six units high.

Noren Products

This company's AcoustiLock acoustic isolation enclosures for your computer, hard drives, and rackmounted gear (various sizes are available) enable you to place your Pro Tools system in the control room without creating a noise problem. Of particular interest to Pro Tools users is the ACL16TD model, with up to 16 units of rackmounting, plus three more units on top that slide to the rear for access to cabling patchbays and other frequently accessed devices. Their sealed enclosures provide cooling while requiring no fans, as well as providing equipment noise reduction factors of 99% (from 71dBA down to 33dBA).

Sound Construction and Supply

This company manufactures Isobox Studio and Isobox Post acoustic isolation enclosures for your computer, hard drives, and rackmounted gear (various sizes are available) so that your Pro Tools system can remain in the control room. The Isobox line includes thermostatically controlled fans with digital intake/exhaust temperature displays, thermal alarms, efficient sound traps, and intake HEPA filters for the fans. Sound Construction and Supply also offers custom workstation furniture, including consoles specifically for the D-Command, ProControl, and Control|24.

Extenders

When things don't quite reach in your studio configuration, you may be able to solve the problem with a simple trip to your local audio or computer store. Slightly longer cables for balanced audio connections, MIDI, monitors, FireWire devices, and so on are readily available. Digidesign's DigiLink cabling system supports very long runs of cable—up to 100 feet, or 50 feet at 192kHz sample rates—which conceivably allows you to put your audio interfaces and Digidesign PRE microphone preamps out in the studio or even on stage, minimizing the length of analog cabling in your setup. Sometimes, however, you need to separate things in a different way—for instance, when your CPU and peripherals need to be in an equipment room or closet, far from your monitor and keyboard. Without the proper equipment, this separation can be impractical or degrade the display quality, which certainly won't make it any easier to work for extended periods of time.

Note: If you're using an original Mbox, do not replace *or* extend the USB cable that comes with this unit! Otherwise, no matter how much you spend on premium USB extender cables or ferrite chokes, you'll hear a very annoying high-pitched modulating noise on the Mbox's analog outputs.

Gefen

This company offers some interesting products for removing noisy computers from the control room entirely. Gefen's CAT5•1000 system (one sender, one receiver) permits the separation of a standard VGA monitor (analog video at resolutions up to 1920 × 1200) and USB keyboard/mouse from a Mac/Windows computer by up to 330 feet, using a single Category-5 (CAT-5) cable (a four twisted-pair cable type, also used for 100Mbps and gigabit Ethernet networks). The CAT5•1000 also features a mini 1/8-inch stereo audio connection so that the computer's built-in sound I/O can be brought out to the remote location as well. The CAT5-1500 version offers design refinements for video quality at longer cable lengths, while the CAT5•1000HD version (now discontinued) supports DVI or HDMI computer video sources. The CAT5•5000 system (depicted in Figure B.20) offers similar features, but uses two CAT-5 cables to support two monitors connected to independent video outputs from the computer, and is ideal for dual-screen Pro Tools users. The remote monitors, keyboard, and mouse can be separated by up to 330 feet of cable from the computer's CPU (while simultaneously maintaining a local set at the CPU's location). Gefen also offers a variety of USB-only extenders, FireWire repeaters and extenders (including one that supports fiber-optic cable runs for FireWire of up to 1640 feet),

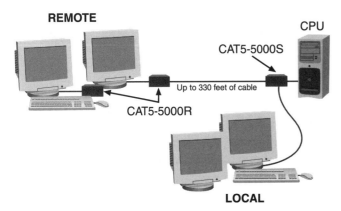

Figure B.20   The CAT5•5000 system, by Gefen.

audio distribution amps using CAT-5 cable to support cable lengths up to 1,000 feet, monitor converters, and other extremely clever accessories for physically extending a computer or video configuration.

Monitoring Control

With enough mic preamp channels, and with one of these sophisticated units for input/output selection in the control room and communication with performers out in the studio, conventional mixing boards could be eliminated entirely from many control rooms! Look for additional alternatives to arrive in the marketplace from upscale manufacturers.

Mackie Big Knob

This tabletop unit combines talkback functions (with an internal microphone for communicating with performers out in the studio), selection between up to three sets of studio monitors, selection between up to four stereo input sources (for example, line inputs for the Pro Tools mix and playback from DATs, CDs, or videos in your studio; the fourth input is phono level for turntables), and a line-level selector and trim knobs on the rear panel. It includes two headphone outputs and a studio output (to the performers' room) with level controls, plus dedicated mono, mute, and dim (attenuate) buttons and a footswitch input for the talkback function. Oh, and of course, there's a big knob for controlling playback volume! (See Figure B.21.)

Presonus Central Station

A rackmountable unit (with optional remote control), the Central Station offers talkback functions with an internal or external microphone, selection between up to three outputs (TRS balanced stereo pairs—speakers, main, and cue), and two stereo headphone outputs with individual level controls (see Figure B.22). You can select up to five inputs (two TRS balanced stereo pairs, Aux Input with RCA connectors, and S/PDIF digital switchable between coaxial and optical Toslink inputs). The front panel has dedicated mono, mute, and dim (attenuate) buttons, and a large 30-segment input LED with peak/hold. The optional CSR-1 remote control is cabled to

Figure B.21   The Big Knob, by Mackie.

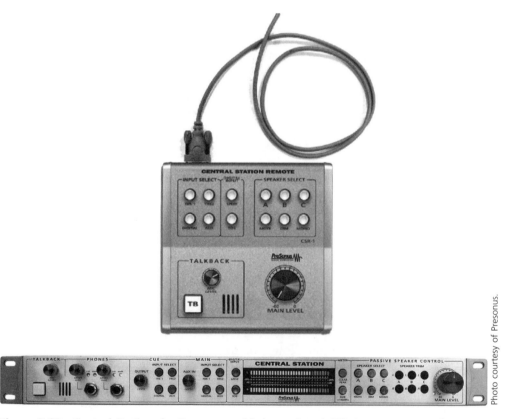

Figure B.22   Central Station, by Presonus, with its optional CSR-1 remote control.

the rackmounted unit via a DB-9 connector, allowing tabletop control of the talkback, master monitoring volume, input/output switching, and mono, dim (attenuation), and mute functions. It features its own internal talkback microphone.

Samson C-control

Samson calls this unit, shown in Figure B.23, a "control room matrix"; it certainly offers a lot of flexibility for a very economical price (about $100). The C-control allows switching between four pairs of stereo line outputs, three sets of line outputs for studio monitors, and three sets of stereo line outputs for output to other devices (a DAT or a CD burner, for example). There's a main volume knob for the control room. There is also a second volume control for matching the volume of speaker sets one and two when switched. A headphone amplifier with level control is provided, as well as a talkback section with a built-in condenser microphone that you can route to either the stereo outputs or the cue output for headphones. The C-control also has mono, dim, and mute switches.

Figure B.23   C-control, by Samson.

Cranesong Avocet

This is a stereo controller for selecting between three digital stereo inputs (supporting sample rates up to 192kHz) and three analog stereo inputs (with XLR jacks) whose input gain can be trimmed within a range of 8dB each. As shown in Figure B.24, it consists of a remote control plus a rackmounted studio box incorporating the audio connections. Balanced line-level outputs are provided for up to three sets of speakers, while the headphone output can be fed either from the selected program source or from the third analog input. The Avocet includes mono, mute, and dim buttons. Another dedicated button allows you to truncate a 24-bit digital audio input to a 16-bit monitoring mode. You can connect an external talkback microphone (no phantom power is provided) with an adjustable amount of dimming on the program audio while talkback is in use. There is also a surround version, which requires three two-channel studio boxes for 5.1 operation and four of them for 7.1 surround monitoring.

Digidesign RM1 and RM2 Reference Monitors

These bi-amplified studio monitors are the first such product offered by Digidesign (designed in collaboration with PMC Ltd.). Class D amplifiers are used for the both the high- and

Figure B.24   Front panel of the remote control for the Avocet, by Cranesong.

low-frequency drivers (80/50 watts on the RM1, 100/50 watts on the RM2). On-board digital signal processing (48-bit, fixed point) provides not only the digital crossover but also bass port emulation (which can be defeated via a switch on the back panel). There are also small knobs for shelving controls to adjust high- and low-frequency levels, plus an overall gain control. Rated frequency response is from 50Hz to 25kHz on the RM1, and 40Hz to 25kHz on the RM2. As shown in Figure B.25, each speaker has an AES-3 digital input on the rear plus a balanced line input (both with XLR jacks). An RJ-45 cable links the two speakers and each speaker has a rear-panel switch so that it can be assigned to monitor the left or right channel of the digital input being received on the first speaker. (The position of this switch is irrelevant when you are using the analog inputs on each speaker. However, even the analog inputs are sampled at 96kHz, 24 bits, and pass through the DSP engine within the speaker.) Digital input signals are supported at sample rates of 44.1, 48, 88.1, and 96kHz; because the analog input is automatically muted when a valid digital source is detected, both inputs can be left connected simultaneously.

Storage, Digital Audio Networking

There are many alternatives for disk and tape subsystems that you can use with Pro Tools, and everyone's requirements are different. Here we simply mention a few items that may be of special interest to Pro Tools operators working in larger studios or production houses.

Photo courtesy of Digidesign.

Figure B.25   Digidesign RM2 and RM1 reference monitors, with a rear view of the RM1.

Glyph Technologies

Glyph offers a variety of rackmountable disk and tape subsystems for Pro Tools. Glyph's GT series is a line of hot-swappable FireWire drive enclosures for Pro Tools and other digital audio workstations, many accommodating multiple disk cartridges ranging up to 750GB (see Figure B.26). This facilitates moving projects and drives around between rooms in a facility, offsite backup, and knowing that you can always add more free drive space by swapping a new, empty drive into the enclosure. There are cheaper drive options out there, but you get

Photo courtesy of Glyph Technologies.

Figure B.26   This GT205 hot-swappable FireWire drive enclosure, by Glyph, has been loaded with four hot-swappable 750 GB FireWire drives, plus an AIT tape drive for backup/archiving.

what you pay for. Glyph is a company that specifically understands the particular requirements of Pro Tools users (for example, *quiet*), offers an excellent warranty, and is there to back you up if problems ever occur. Also, unlike most drive manufacturers, Glyph doesn't make mechanism and firmware changes to its drives without guaranteeing that they will continue to support current versions of Pro Tools—which is worth a *lot*!

Appendix C: Archive and Backup

Digital audio data occupies *large* amounts of disk space. As shown in Table 3.1 in Chapter 3, "Your System Configuration," even at 16-bit resolution and a 44.1kHz sample rate (used on standard audio CDs), each stereo minute of audio consumes 10MB of disk space. If you're using Pro Tools|HD and recording 24-bit audio at 192kHz, each minute on each stereo track occupies 68.8MB!

The large size of Pro Tools projects means that some of the more common methods for backing up and archiving data can become inconvenient. A graphic designer, for example, might make daily backups to rewritable CDs or DVDs or a USB drive, and copy completed projects to recordable CDs or DVDs for long-term storage. But Pro Tools projects with multiple takes on multiple tracks (let alone higher sample rates) can easily exceed the capacity of these storage formats. An extra level of complexity is introduced when multiple disks are used for audio recording with Pro Tools, both for space considerations and to spread the recording/playback load for better performance—especially when using higher resolutions on Pro Tools|HD systems. To effectively back up or archive your projects, you need to understand exactly how Pro Tools handles the audio files referenced in a session.

Where Pro Tools Stores Session Data

The principal file in Pro Tools is the session document. It contains all track and region names, region definitions that are pointers to the parent audio files (and video files, if applicable), the automation and mixing/signal routing, plus all MIDI data used in the session. Session documents contain no audio data, so they are relatively small (generally well under a megabyte, even including a fair amount of MIDI data). As explained in Chapter 8, "Menu Selections: Highlights," the File > Save As command allows you to create successive iterations of your session document, all of which will continue to reference the same Audio Files and Fade Files folders, also using these for any new audio recordings. If you instead create a copy of the current Pro Tools session using the File > Save Copy In command, that session document will use its *own* Audio Files and Fade Files folders to create any subsequent files. This Save dialog box provides the option to copy all audio files currently being used in the source session to the new session document's Audio Files folder. If you *don't* copy all the audio files, the new session copy looks both to the previous session's Audio Files folder for currently used audio files, and also to its own Audio Files folder for any audio files created subsequently. To make a backup or archive copy of that new session, you would therefore need to copy *both* Audio Files folders to be sure you're including all the source audio files it references.

A session's Audio Files folder contains all new audio recordings made within this session. In addition, audio files created as a result of processing functions in the AudioSuite menu are also stored here (such as Pitch Shift, Time Compression/Expansion, as well as Normalization and other functions unless the Overwrite Files option is selected in that dialog box). When you copy source audio files in the Import Audio dialog box (rather than simply adding them as a reference to their original location), copies are also placed within this session's Audio Files folder. (Stereo source files are also copied to dual mono files when imported, and placed in the Audio Files folder.) Lastly, any audio files on audio tracks whose Elastic Audio mode (in Pro Tools versions 7.4 and higher) is set to Rendered Processing (as opposed to Real-Time Processing, which requires more CPU power) are also placed into a Rendered Files subfolder of the main session folder that is created automatically. If you disable Elastic Audio on an audio track and choose the Commit option in the Commit Elastic Audio dialog box, the temporary rendered file is deleted when the resultant file is written into the Audio Files subfolder.

The DigiBase browser windows help keep track of which files are being used in the current session document and where they reside. The Workspace browser shows all disk volumes on your system, what folders and media files they contain, which drives are designated for audio recording and/or playback, and, most importantly, how much free space is currently available. When preparing for backup or archive, though, you will find the Project Browser window (shown in Figure C.1)

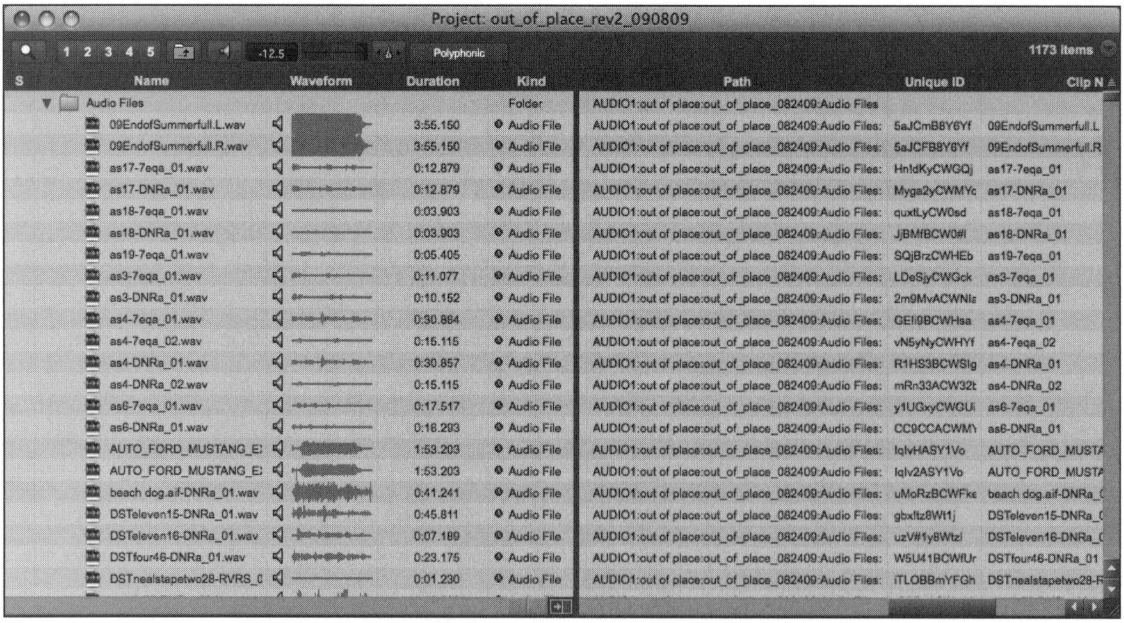

Figure C.1 The Project Browser window helps keep track of the disk locations for audio and video files used in the current session.

especially useful. Among other helpful information about the audio files used in the current session, the Path column allows you to quickly confirm the disk and folder locations where these files reside prior to backup or archival.

Each time you adjust the duration of a fade within a Pro Tools track, a new fade file is created for it (and played back at the appropriate moment within the track). Each of these fade files is an audio file, and not surprisingly, is stored in the Fade Files folder. However, be aware that you don't necessarily have to back up the Fade Files folder. When you open an existing session, if any fade files are not found, a dialog box will appear with a checkbox to re-create any missing fades (which might take a minute or so in very complex sessions). Fade files that are no longer in use will not be re-created.

Using *multiple disks* for audio recording, however, makes the backup and archive scenario a little more complicated. In Setup > Disk Allocation, you can select a specific disk for recording from each audio track. Alternatively, using round-robin allocation, Pro Tools will cycle to the next eligible audio drive for storing audio files with each new audio track you create. (In either case, only disks that have been designated as Record volumes—as opposed to Playback or Transfer only—in the Workspace browser window are eligible.) Whenever multiple disks are used for recording audio (other than the disk where the session file itself resides), a folder with the same name as your session folder is automatically created on the other disk(s), containing Audio Files and Fade Files folders that are used for any tracks allocated to that record drive. So if you're using multiple disks for audio recording and playback—which is extremely likely on Pro Tools| HD systems at higher sample rates—these additional folders on the other disks must also be backed up to ensure you've included all that session's source files.

Lastly, bear in mind that not all audio files used in a Pro Tools session necessarily reside in the Audio Files folder. When an existing audio file being imported into your Pro Tools session *doesn't* require any conversion to the current session's settings, that file remains in its original location—unless you intentionally use the Copy button instead of the Add button in the Import Audio dialog box. For instance, you might keep a folder of standard sound effects for use in multiple projects, or use mixes bounced from other programs or Pro Tools sessions. These could be used in Pro Tools directly from their original location. (In the Import Audio dialog box, Pro Tools would inform you that the file can be added directly to the current session because the file's audio file format and resolution already match the current session, and you would therefore use the Add button instead of the Copy button.) In this case, you may still opt to archive these along with each session where they are used (to ensure a complete, self-contained archive), or to archive these commonly accessed files separately.

Preferences for Importing Audio In the Processing tab of the Preferences dialog box, you can enable the Automatically Copy Files on Import option. When this option is enabled, audio files imported into Pro Tools are *always* copied into the Audio Files folder of the current session, even if their audio format would have permitted them to be used from their original location. Although this increases your usage of disk space, it has several advantages. First, when making nightly backups or archiving the finished project, you know for sure that all its source audio files reside in its Audio Files folder (or several Audio Files folders, if you're using multiple disk allocations for this session). Second, it can be less dangerous! The Regions List's Compact Selected command (like the Clear Selected command if the Delete button is pressed in that dialog box) permanently alters or deletes the original audio files. So does any processing applied with AudioSuite menu options when their Overwrite Files mode is enabled. If you use the same audio files in multiple sessions (and especially if several people use the same Pro Tools system), a careless moment can have catastrophic consequences for other Pro Tools session documents. Having each session make new copies of all imported audio files reduces the risk of this occurring.

In a professional studio setting, it can be a good idea to keep track sheets and project logs for your Pro Tools sessions, indicating what audio files are used and their disk locations. This makes archiving and retrieving multiple sessions easier. The Project Browser window and (on HD systems) the File > Export > Session Info as Text command make this much simpler. You could save these tab-delimited text files, print them, or include them in word-processing documents. Alternatively, you could build a simple database (in FileMaker Pro, for example) with a database record for each archived session and paste this text data exported from Pro Tools into a text field. While you're at it, create additional fields for the project name, client, session sample rate, bit depth, microphones used, account rep, talent phone numbers, or whatever other information about the session you think could be useful.)

Why and When Should You Save Your Data?

Backing up and archiving are performed for different reasons, as explained later in this appendix. In either case, as a Pro Tools user, you are dealing with very large amounts of data. Learn how to use the Select Unused, Clear, and Compact commands in the Regions List's submenu. By eliminating unused takes and compacting longer audio files from which you've used only a few small segments, you can free up considerable disk space and make your backup/archive smaller. Just be sure you take the time to think through what you're doing; don't get ahead of yourself eliminating unused regions if you will be compositing a track from multiple takes afterward, for example!

Backup

Backup is a precaution. You must regularly make safety copies of all your important data (like, say, your client's projects) so that if some disaster (disk malfunction, smoke damage, virus damage, or operator error) causes it to be lost from your computer, you can go back to these copies instead of losing the entire project. It's kind of like what dentists say about your teeth: You don't have to take care of all of them, just the ones you don't want to lose! Ideally, you should make backup copies every work day if you have a fast, convenient means of doing so. A separate hard drive on your computer setup, to which you can drag session folders for mid- and end-of-session copies, is gaining popularity in the industry. Also, you really should store your backup copies in a different room—or, ideally, in a different building. After all, what good will it do you to back up your work if your CD/DVD backup copies are sitting in a box next to the computer if there's ever a fire in the studio? At the very least, you should perform a fairly thorough backup of all your important data once a week—assuming that you don't mind potentially losing an entire week's worth of work and/or feel you can explain to your clients how you've lost several days worth of recordings!

You should also periodically back up your entire computer. The bottom line? The faster and more convenient it is to back up the huge amounts of data you generate in Pro Tools, the more often you will do it! And while we're on the subject of data security, consider investing in a bank's safe deposit box. Keep all your original Pro Tools disks and registration information in this single location. With insurance, new computers and audio hardware can be purchased, but all the installation materials will be a real hassle to get again. (Not as bad as losing the actual *work* you've done in Pro Tools—and possibly your client—if you aren't backing up your project data on a regular basis, but you get the idea!)

Archive

Archiving is more long-term storage, and should be performed on finished projects or seldom-used files that you don't wish to keep on your system for space considerations or other reasons. As with backing up, when archiving, take a moment to carefully eliminate any unused audio regions and compact the remaining audio files in your Pro Tools session (being extra careful to confirm they aren't also being used in other sessions) before archiving the session folder and its related files (for example, bounced mixes). For most Pro Tools users, recordable CDs are simply too small and inconvenient for anything but very small projects; recordable DVDs and/or Blu-ray discs are much more practical, even for mid-sized and project studios, and have a much longer projected lifespan than CDs are estimated to have.

Create and Maintain a Database of Your Archived Work! Once you've been at this for a while, you'll likely have a very large number of archived disks. Locating and retrieving specific sessions or projects becomes unwieldy if you don't get yourself organized. There are many solutions for this, but here is a method that has worked for us: Number each archive disk, of course, and give it a meaningful volume name when it is burned. Then build a simple database (we use FileMaker Pro on both platforms, although Microsoft Access would also serve this purpose). As you archive each disk, enter all the information about the project files it contains into this database, the date of archive, the disk number, who performed the archive, and so on. This makes it easy to find things among the hundreds of archive discs you may accumulate. If you prefer to purchase a solution, have a look at Studio Suite by AlterMedia (http://www.studiosuite.com). This studio-management application for Mac and Windows includes an archive database. It also prints labels (with bar codes) for media; does time tracking for booking and billing your studio rooms, equipment, and people; generates invoices; organizes equipment inventory and barcoding; keeps maintenance logs; and creates patchbay labels. Studio Suite also features a contact manager, to-do lists, a calendar, templates for purchase orders, and a petty-cash tracker!

CD-R, DVD-R

A standard data CD-ROM holds nearly 700MB of data. This seems like a lot to most users, but for backing up or archiving audio (and even worse, video data), 700MB suddenly isn't so spacious after all. Let's say you record 16 channels continuously for four minutes, at a bare-minimum 16-bit, 44.1kHz resolution (higher bit depths and/or sample rates of course creating larger files). Your Audio Files folder will already be over 364MB, and you haven't even started creating fade files, new files/regions with AudioSuite functions, or bouncing out mix files yet—let alone recording multiple takes of the same song or recording overdubs!

If you *have* to archive or back up such a project to CD-R, a program like Retrospect can automatically split it to multiple discs. However, this makes it more difficult to retrieve just one or two files from this session without reloading the entire project to your system. Alternatively, you could take the time to split up your project files into a series of folders that are smaller than 700MB each and then burn each of these to a separate CD—but this is burdensome and takes a surprisingly long time. In short, unless you exclusively do short-duration sessions with a small number of tracks, at today's prices a DVD recording drive on your computer should be considered a must!

A 4.7GB recordable DVD (either DVD+R or the somewhat less popular DVD-R format) actually holds about 4.3GB of data. If your Macintosh computer has a recordable DVD drive (Super-Drive), you could use either Roxio's Toast Titanium program or the Finder to record data to DVDs and CDs, while Nero, Easy Media Creator, and other programs are practical choices for this on Windows systems—as well as the operating system itself, of course. Recordable DVDs are frequently a good choice for archiving Pro Tools projects (especially with smaller numbers of tracks and shorter durations) because many of them *will* fit into 4GB or so—and if not, can perhaps be split between two discs rather than, say, nine or ten CDs!

The capacity per DVD can still be rather small for Pro Tools users with a large number of high-resolution audio tracks in their sessions, however. Splitting large sessions onto multiple DVDs can be unwieldy and time-consuming. More recent double-layer DVD formats offer capacities up to 8.5GB on a single-sided disc (DVD+R9 media). When you use current double-layer (also known as dual-layer) models to write to conventional DVD-R and DVD+R media, 8× and 16× write speeds are supported. For users who record at higher sample rates, longer durations, or higher track counts, a double-layer drive for backing up data to DVD can be a good option.

Blu-ray Disc

Blu-ray is yet another disc format that is quickly gaining support. The name derives from the fact that disc drives for Blu-ray use a blue-violet laser to read and write data at higher densities rather than the longer-wavelength red laser in current DVD drives and recorders. While a 36.5Mbps transfer rate is the current 1.0 specification (useful for recording and playback of HDTV at full quality, among other things), the Blu-ray Disc Association (BDA) has been working on a 2.0 specification that will double this transfer rate. A single-layer Blu-ray disc (also known as BD-25) offers 25GB capacity, while dual-layer versions (BD-50) reach 50GB. In addition to the BD-ROM format used for video and other prerecorded content and the BD-RE format for HDTV recording, of special interest to users of media workstations are the BD-R (recordable) and BD-RW (rewritable) Blu-ray disc formats. Board of Director members of the BDA include Apple Computer, Dell, Hitachi, HP, JVC, LG, Matsushita, Mitsubishi, Panasonic, Pioneer, Philips, Samsung, Sharp, Sony (whose PlayStation 3 gaming unit supports Blu-ray), Sun Microsystems, TDK, Thomson, 20th Century Fox, the Walt Disney Company/Buena Vista, and Warner Bros. The entertainment companies listed here are marketing movies on Blu-ray disc. Obviously, as this format becomes more popular, it will be of great interest to those of us who manage large quantities of media data!

Apple's SuperDrive The SuperDrive included in many Macintosh computers reads audio CDs, CD-ROMs, and data or video DVDs. It can also record data or audio onto write-once CDs (CD-R), rewritable CDs (CD-RW), and data, audio or video onto write-once DVDs (DVD-R), as well as DVD-RW (this last format not supported in some older models).

What About Rewritable Media?

Users often ask about rewritable media (CD-RW, CD+RW, DVD-RW, DVD+RW, and the older DVD-RAM format) for backup and archive. Rewritable media undoubtedly has a place in the backup/archive strategy for any Pro Tools system, but always in conjunction with write-once media. First, some older consumer audio CD players and CD drives on older computers won't play rewritable CDs at all, so these are potentially problematic for burning audio mixes to CD. If the CD players you will be using for this purpose support rewritable CDs, these could be used for burning trial mixes for listening on home stereos, boom boxes, automobile stereos, and so on.

At any rate, given how inexpensive recordable CD media has become, you might as well use write-once CD media for trial audio mixes anyway. Even for backup and archive, there's also a cost issue to consider. You can buy a large number of write-once disks for the price of a single rewritable disc, so for long-term archiving, write-once disks (CD-R, DVD-R) are generally the way to go. Write-once CD-Rs can even be a practical choice for daily/weekly backup of smaller sessions—not to mention all the other non-audio files that are essential to running a studio (billing, archived databases, and correspondence, for example). The price disparity is especially dramatic for recordable CDs (CD-R); bought in spindles of 50–100, they're currently well under 20 cents each, versus up to three or four times more per CD-RW. The price differential for DVD-R versus DVD-RW is similar (again, prices for media and DVD recording drives for computers have dropped so much over the past few years that CD backup isn't really a recommended solution for most Pro Tools users anyway). So you could potentially save various incremental archive/backups onto write-once media as your project progresses for the same price as a single backup on a rewritable disc. (Some of the more rudimentary CD/DVD writing programs don't support creating multisession discs on rewritable media, so each previous backup on the recordable disc must be erased in order to write a new session.) Generally, writing data is also significantly slower on rewritable media than write-once media. Furthermore, if your projects are important (and your clients just might think so), you definitely need more than one generation of backup. Otherwise, what happens if the last session version you backed up was already damaged without your knowing it?

All this being said, many Pro Tools users will still find rewritable discs to be a very practical part of their daily backup routine. For example, at the end of each day you could back up your session onto a rewritable DVD (or several, if necessary), rotating through two or three different daily discs as a safety precaution. When the project is finished, it would then be archived off the system onto conventional write-once DVDs or a tape backup system.

Rewritable DVD Formats

The DVD+RW rewritable DVD format can be read by most standard DVD drives (either in computers or in standard video DVD players). DVD+RW uses 4.7GB media and is currently the most common rewritable DVD format among computer users. The DVD-RW format developed by Pioneer is similar, but lacks the built-in media defect–management features of the DVD+RW format. If you're buying a DVD-recording drive, you can cover your bets by choosing a model that supports both these "plus" and "minus" (sometimes called "dash") rewritable formats. By all means, get the fastest drive you can afford; given their larger capacity, the difference between a 16× DVD burner and a 2× model means a lot less waiting time for the process to be completed.

Now largely obsolete, the original DVD-RAM drives allowed recording up to 2.6GB or 4.7GB (single- or dual-sided media). DVD-RAM Version 2 double-sided discs, introduced in 2000, offered 9.4GB capacity. DVD-RAM drives could also read standard DVDs, CD-ROMs, and audio CDs. DVD-RAM cartridges were encased in a caddy and couldn't be used in standard video DVD players; partially for this reason, most users opted for the DVD+RW and DVD-RW formats instead. On the plus side, a DVD-RAM cartridge could ostensibly be re-written up to 100,000 times (versus 1,000 for DVD+RW, for example). In the past, Apple offered DVD-RAM drive options for certain G4 Macintosh computers (although the CD/DVD-R Super-Drive is more common). This format is mentioned here for the sake of completeness; recorders supporting the DVD+RW and/or DVD-RW formats are usually a more practical choice (drives that support *both* these formats obviously offer more flexibility).

Toast Titanium (Mac) This disc-burning program from Roxio (now a division of Sonic Solutions) supports a variety of disc formats, including CD-R, CD-RW, DVD-R, DVD+RW, DVD-RAM and Blu-ray. For manual backup, it can often be sufficient (as long as *you* know the folder and disk locations where all the files used in your Pro Tools sessions reside). Among the CD formats Toast supports are audio CD (CD-DA); CD-ROM in Mac (HFS), Windows (ISO), or hybrid Mac/Win formats; Video CD; CD-I; MP3 CD; and Enhanced Music CD.

Current versions support writing multiple sessions onto a single DVD+RW disc. (In other words, the previous day's backup doesn't have to be erased from the recordable DVD before you back up today's data.) With the data-spanning feature, large data sets are automatically split across multiple disks while creating archive CDs or DVDs. Restoring from these multi-disk archives (either the entire set or a single file) is equally easy. Versions 8 and higher also support automatic cataloging for the contents of burned discs. Although a basic version of Toast is often bundled with third-party CD- or DVD-recording drives for Macs, the Titanium upgrade is required to take advantage of all these features. Lastly, most of the features of Roxio's Jam program for red-book CD mastering are included in Toast versions 8 and higher.

Removable Disk Options for Data Backup

As the price per gigabyte of hard-disk storage continues to plummet, many Pro Tools users have found external or removable hard drives to be an excellent option for daily backups. Given that compact external FireWire drives are available in capacities of 1TB or more for around $150, for example, this can be your ideal "removable media" for backing up large sessions on a daily basis. And because these are full-performance hard drives, the transfer rates are also faster than DVD, tape, or older removable disk drive systems. Before walking out of your studio at the end of the session, you can just drag your session folders (and supplementary Audio Files/Fade Files folders, if the session's disk allocation spans multiple disks) onto the FireWire drive. After unhooking that drive from the computer, drop it into your briefcase or backpack, and take it home with you for safekeeping. If you spend just a little more for an external FireWire drive that also meets the performance requirements for Pro Tools, you can simply open this session directly from that disk attached to some other Pro Tools system if a disaster ever occurs in your own studio.

Inexpensive FireWire caddies (enclosures into which you can swap a drive mechanism) are also widely available. Not only are these useful for accessing your data on another system, they're also great for swapping various disks into a single enclosure as projects come and go in the same studio.

More sophisticated removable hard drive systems are also available for Pro Tools. For example, Glyph offers the rackmountable GT 103 unit with bays for up to three hot-swappable GT Key

FireWire hard-drive cartridges, with capacities up to 1.5TB each (7,200 RPM mechanisms using the Oxford 911 chipset, which is required for FireWire disks used as audio drives by Pro Tools). Not only does this facilitate using hard drives as a backup medium, it also allows the same Pro Tools system to be used simultaneously for many large sessions because each one could use a completely separate set of removable hard disks, if necessary.

Yet another backup strategy is the use of disk imaging or mirroring systems, such as Norton's Ghost, or backup features included in the Mezzo or Nero Ultra software suites, which are discussed in the "Backup Software" section at the end of this appendix. Having a mirror image of an audio drive is obviously a useful function; these programs, however, can also image the disk where the operating system and all your program files reside. Should these ever become corrupted or lost due to media defects, a virus, operator error, or loss of the computer itself, having this snapshot of the previous system state to go back to will be hugely important, saving downtime and possibly avoiding the loss of a client.

Of course, once the project is complete and you want to permanently *archive* the session, you will want to look at one of the other, more cost-effective data-storage formats discussed here (Blu-ray, DVD or tape archive, for example).

Respect for the Older Generation (Of Backup!) If your projects are mission critical (i.e., it could mean losing a client—or your job—if you were to lose an entire project due to a system malfunction, virus, or human error), then you should take a serious attitude toward backup. Consider this scenario: You faithfully back up your Pro Tools session at the end of the day (or night!), turn out the lights, and go home. In the dead of the night, a fire breaks out, your nitwit partner or intern throws your session in the trash, a virus trashes your entire system in spectacular fashion, your computer blows its cookies due to natural causes, or the Morlocks creep in and drag your computer (not to mention your irreplaceable time machine) off to their underground lair. Okay, possibly after calling the insurance company and making necessary repairs or replacements, you're ready to reload your session and audio files from the backup copy. (You've cleverly stored your backups in a different room or building to prevent them from being damaged by the very same smoke or fire as the computer itself, right? RIGHT?) Much to your dismay, though, you discover that your session file or audio files were already damaged (or "corrupted") when you backed them up. To avoid anguish, embarrassment, and everlasting torment, you should work through two or three different generations of backup. For example, if you *are* using rewritable media (CD-RW, DVD-RW, Blu-ray, tape, and so on), you should rotate through two or three disks (writing backup dates in pencil as you go). That way, if yesterday's file copies were damaged when backed up, you can always go back to the day before yesterday, or the day before that.

Tape Backup Options

A decade ago, when the largest removable disk solutions were 1GB or less, tape drives were the only practical way to back up or archive large media projects. These days, tape drives remain a good option. Common tape formats for data currently include LTO, DLT, AIT, and others. Many of these are supported by the Retrospect and Mezzo backup programs (see the next section), and you will find them in numerous production facilities. Traditional tape backup/restore technology was much slower and not especially more reliable than today's disk-based alternatives. However, current high-capacity tape drives offer excellent data-transfer rates (higher than recordable DVDs, for example), and are a great choice for professional facilities, especially when large projects need to be archived on a regular basis and when the size of the data sets to be archived will necessarily span multiple tapes.

For daily backups (as opposed to long-term archiving of data), here's how the general trend goes in media production: People buy tape subsystems for backup because their capacity requirements exceed that of currently available (or economical) removable disks. Then time marches on, and widely available disk formats overtake the capacity of yesterday's tape drives. (Indeed, the 4GB USB drive you may have hanging from your keychain far exceeds the capacity of the "high-end" tape subsystems available when the first-generation Pro Tools hardware was introduced. Despite its fragility, it might be yet another cheap option for taking home a nightly backup of smaller sessions in progress.) Meanwhile, media applications relentlessly push toward higher resolutions—like you Pro Tools|HD types recording at 24-bit, 192kHz (hey, Flipper says to tweak the high end on the banjo track at about 75kHz!)—and consequently require the latest-generation, higher capacity tape storage systems. Whatever model you choose, it will soon be superseded by another unit with higher transfer rates or larger capacity.

Currently, Linear Tape-Open (LTO) drives are available from various manufacturers in capacities per cartridge of up to 800GB (native capacity of LTO-4 media, some manufacturers list higher cartridge capacities based on data compression). Library or jukebox configurations with up to 16 cartridge slots allow many terabytes of data to be archived in a single operation. Current Advanced Intelligent Tape (AIT) systems offer uncompressed capacities of up to 400GB per tape (using AIT-5 media). SDLT tapes reach capacities of 310GB. Not too long ago, 2GB on a DAT (DDS) tape, or 5GB on an 8-millimeter Exabyte tape was considered impressive! Expensive as these tape cartridges are (especially because you will be rotating through several generations of backup, if you're serious), if your facility archives a very large number of copies during the course of a year (that is, multiple projects, multiple suites, daily incremental backups, and weekly full backups), it will eventually work out to be cheaper to use tape than large-capacity disks for backup and data storage. The economics of your own situation determine the best solution; if you generally work with mid-sized or small Pro Tools sessions at 48kHz sample rates or less, and only 12–32 channels of I/O, then some combination of recordable-rewritable DVDs, large-capacity removable disk systems, or external FireWire drives may be more than sufficient for your backup and archive requirements.

Dedicated backup software used with these tape drives always includes the capability for incremental backups; only files that have actually changed since the previous backup are copied off to tape. This not only greatly decreases the storage capacity required for nightly backups, but also makes the operation much quicker (because unchanged files aren't being copied to tape). For large facilities with multiple users and projects, intelligent, incremental backups are the most reliable solution—even when data is being copied to disk media.

One last observation about removable data storage, either on tape or disk: These systems often have a limited commercial existence. It is entirely possible that, in seven or eight years, a given data-storage format that everybody is using right now may be a) no longer manufactured, b) hard to find media for, or c) incompatible with current computers and operating systems. We encourage you to be conservative; take a good hard look at who manufactures the drive and how widespread it is beyond the media-production industry. Even so, consider what you would do today if someone handed you a 44MB SyQuest cartridge (the *de facto* standard about 15 years ago for transporting "large" quantities of data between computer systems) containing a Sound Designer file to be remastered. Because of this rapid cycle of obsolescence for data-storage media, commercial production facilities often must take the time and expense to periodically transfer their vaults to more current storage formats or otherwise maintain older computer systems and antique storage peripherals for the sole purpose of retrieving these archived projects when necessary.

Ya Gotta Keep 'Em Separated! Storing all your backups and archived projects right next to your computer only increases the chances that both will be simultaneously destroyed by the same smoke, heat, fire, beer party, flood, or Texas twister! Of course, you only need to worry about this for important data; if it will be okay to irretrievably lose your client's archived projects, feel free to put all your eggs in one basket. Otherwise, you should store backups/archives in a second building (even better, *two* copies, in separate locations). Even without such disaster and off-site storage scenarios, given how inexpensive recordable DVD media is, you should consider making *two* archive copies for important projects—just in case one of them turns out to be damaged or have a write error that you didn't detect at the time.

Backup Software

One of the essential techniques for data security is performing daily incremental backups to disk or tape. The backup software looks at modification dates for every file on the disk volumes selected for backup, copying only files that have been modified since the last full or incremental backup. This saves time and avoids wasting tape space by writing redundant copies of files that haven't changed. Many excellent backup programs are available; only a few will be mentioned here—two because they're ubiquitous and also perform admirably, and a third because it understands the project structure of Pro Tools sessions (and many other media programs), making the backup and archival process more efficient.

- Retrospect, by EMC (formerly Dantz), is a widespread and highly reliable backup program for Windows and Macintosh. Retrospect can perform incremental and full backups from multiple disk locations (including other networked computers), which can be stored and repeated later and programmed to occur at specific dates and times. It supports various disk types and tape drives (LTO, AIT, DAT/DDS, DLT, VXA, and Travan, among others). This program can also back up to REV, DVD-R, DVD-RAM, and CD-R discs (and can span several discs for a single data set). Retrospect doesn't have any intrinsic understanding of how Pro Tools projects are structured, however. It is your responsibility to understand that a Pro Tools session may use files and folders on multiple disks, and to make sure these are all included in the selected data for backup.

- Nero 9, by Nero AG, includes the NeroBackItUpandBurn utility for programmed backup operations (either full or incremental). The Nero 9 suite of software also provides excellent tools for creating data CDs and DVDs and labels, an audio editor that supports DirectX plug-ins, a drive-imaging utility, and, among other things, robust capabilities for creating audio CDs.

- Mezzo for Pro Tools, by Grey Matter Response/Mezzo Technologies, is an attractive option for Macintosh systems, especially for users who manage multiple large projects or for facilities where the person responsible for backups may not be the main Pro Tools operator. Like Retrospect, Mezzo supports numerous tape formats (LTO, AIT, DLT, Exabyte, Exabyte Mammoth, and DAT/DDS, to name a few) and disk types including recordable DVDs. Mezzo allows for incremental and full backups to be programmed for repeated use at specific dates and times—even from a central point over a network. However, the great strength of Mezzo is that it understands the data structure of Pro Tools (not to mention other Mezzo versions for Digital Performer, Adobe Premiere, Avid Media Composer, Film Composer and Xpress, Apple FinalCut Pro, and Media 100). When you schedule a Pro Tools session for backup, Mezzo examines your session file to determine which audio files and folders it references, no matter where they reside on your computer's disks. This ensures that the entire project is backed up without depending on the operator to know where audio files used by a Pro Tools project may be stored. When you restore a project later, the files and folders are copied back to their multiple disk locations. Furthermore, Mezzo tracks changes in the audio files and session document as you continue working on a project, enabling you to make nightly, incremental backups of only those files that have been changed. The program can also restore, verify, or back up Pro Tools sessions in the background while you continue working in Pro Tools; it understands idle time, and avoids interfering with audio recording and playback. Also introduced is a disk-mirroring and CD/DVD-R backup suite called Mezzo Mirror, a lower-priced option to Mezzo 4.7. As with any third-party software, those interested in purchasing Mezzo for use with Pro Tools should check both the Mezzo and Digidesign Web site to confirm compatibility with Pro Tools 8.

Appendix D: Power Tips and Loopy Ideas

We've had the privilege of working with Pro Tools since the very first versions, and have also been fortunate to learn from many creative professional Pro Tools users among our friends and clients. What follows is a potpourri of cool tricks and clever workarounds we've picked up along the way. Hopefully, you will find some of these inspiring! Also, for good measure, we threw in a few good keyboard shortcuts that too many users overlook (even though these shortcuts are listed in the great *Keyboard Shortcuts* PDF document provided by Digidesign—which you've already printed out, of course).

Mixing and Processing Tips
The tips in this section concern the Mix window, general mixing techniques, and a few pointers for routing and signal processing.

Pro Tools in Living Color
In versions 7.3 and higher, you can change the fill colors of the mixer strips for all tracks (as well as in the Tracks List in the Edit window) from plain gray to whatever color is assigned to their color strips. First, double-click the track's color strip to open the Color Palette window. Hold down Command+Option+Control (Ctrl+Alt+Start in Windows) as you click anywhere in the Color Palette window. Not only will this brighten up your life (although you can always return them to drab gray by repeating the same operation), but can truly be useful in larger sessions. For example, assigning all drum or backing vocal tracks the same color will facilitate navigating a large number of tracks. Also, don't forget the Color Palette window's Apply to Channel Strip button, new to Pro Tools 8; it makes your color scheme all the more noticeable.

Invert Polarity
Many Pro Tools users seem to miss the fact that many plug-in windows (including the DigiRack EQs, dynamics processors, and delays) have a Phase Invert button, usually to the right of the plug-in's main input, gain, or threshold slider. When this button is enabled, the polarity of any signal passing through the plug-in is inverted. This is useful, for example, if you ever place microphones on both the front and back of a combo guitar amplifier or the top and bottom

of a snare drum. If one of these paired tracks is pulling air while the other one is pushing, you're not going to be happy with the sound.

Waaaah! I Can't Turn the Tape Around to Create Backward Reverb!

Okay, stop your analog sniveling. Creating *preverb* is easy. For the sake of argument, let's say you're creating this effect for the lead vocal track. Here's what to do:

1. In the Edit window, select the entire vocal track, starting from the beginning of the session's timeline and extending a few seconds past the end of the last region in the track (to be sure you can record the entire reverb decay *after* the end of the reversed selection).

2. Duplicate the vocal track's current playlist using the pop-up selector just to the right of the track's name in the Edit window and name this new version Reverse.

3. Apply the AudioSuite menu's Reverse function to the vocal selection, creating one continuous file for the reversed result of the entire selection.

4. Create an Aux Input track with a reverb plug-in and select a Pro Tools bus as this Aux Input's input source.

5. Create a send from the vocal track, routed to the reverb Aux Input's selected input bus. Adjust the send level and reverb parameters to suit your taste.

6. Assign the reverb Aux Input's main output to yet another Pro Tools bus.

7. Create a new audio track and choose that bus as its input source.

8. Record-enable this new audio track.

9. With the reversed vocal region still selected, press Record to record the reverb Aux Input's output into this new audio track.

10. Select the new audio region you just created by recording and reverse it (again using the AudioSuite menu function).

11. Use the vocal track's Playlist selector to switch back to its original, forward version. You should now hear the backward reverb ramping up before each peak in the vocal track. If you also want to hear normal reverb following the forward vocal, assign the output of your reverb Aux Input back to the main stereo mix instead of the bus to which it's currently assigned.

12. If you want to get a little more clever (especially because backward reverb often sounds sloppy within vocal phrases), insert a compressor on the backward reverb track and side chain it with an external key whose source is the bus you're using for the reverb send from the vocal track itself. (Set the ratio of the compressor very high, and its threshold low.) Whenever the vocal track is present, it will duck down the backward reverb.

Squeaky-Clean Acoustic Guitar and Electric Bass

For reducing string squeak on acoustic guitars and especially electric bass (caused by fingers sliding along the strings as they shift positions), you can sometimes get results with a de-esser plug-in. Just lower the de-esser's key frequency way down into the range of 4–5kHz, or lower. Activate the Key Listen feature as you slide around the de-esser's frequency parameter (which defines the center of the narrow frequency band that determines when compression will be applied) to focus on the offending squeaks. Then, adjust the Threshold setting as far down as possible before noticeably altering the instrument's timbre. (There's more latitude on an electric bass; because its fundamental frequencies are lower, harmonics up in the squeak zone are spaced farther apart.)

Adjusting Individual Volume Levels in Grouped Tracks

Ordinarily, after you create a mix group, adjusting the volume level of any of its track faders will move all the faders up or down, maintaining their relative positions. This can be very convenient, for example, for seven or eight drum tracks, several backing vocal tracks, and so on. But what if you want to individually adjust the volume of one track in a group? Obviously, you could use the Mix Groups List (in the lower-left area of the Mix window) to temporarily disable the group, adjust the track's volume fader, and then re-enable the group. (Groups in this list are active only when they're highlighted.) But there's a quicker way: While holding down the Control key (Start key in Windows), you can individually adjust any fader in an active group.

Manual Delay Compensation, with Time Adjuster Plug-in

Generally speaking, each plug-in introduces a small amount of delay in a track's signal path. For example, in Pro Tools HD, this delay is about four samples for a majority of DigiRack plug-ins, while it can be significantly greater for some third-party plug-ins that perform more complex processing. Say you're recording a drum set with multiple microphones and tracks. Without Automatic Delay Compensation (which is not currently available on LE or M-Powered versions), if you insert various plug-ins with significant processing latencies on your snare track and the hi-hat and snare microphones bleed into each other, this could be enough to cause some smearing in the higher frequencies.

The Time Adjuster plug-in provides up to 8,195 samples of delay-compensation adjustment. It also provides positive and negative gain adjustment and a Phase (Polarity) Inversion function. You don't have to get crazy trying to adjust for plug-in delays on every single mono track, but in cases like the one outlined here, where the same signal is present in two different tracks, this is an important issue that can improve the overall sound of your mix—if you're willing to do the math.

On Pro Tools|HD systems, Automatic Delay Compensation automatically takes care of plug-in processing delay adjustments for you. (The maximum delay-compensation limit varies according to the session sample rate and which delay-compensation engine option is currently selected). Manual adjustments with the Time Adjuster plug-in are generally not necessary. Nice!

You can also use one of the Long Delay plug-ins (with its Mix value set to 100%) to compensate when track delays are instead caused by microphone placement. While you can also use the Time

Adjuster plug-in for this purpose, its maximum delay amount may be insufficient for some applications (especially in live situations), and it's frequently more convenient to work in milliseconds than samples. If you already know the distances involved in the microphone placement that cause the time-alignment problems in the first place, you can use the well-known and simple formulas for calculating the corresponding delay times.

Setting Tempo-Related Delays by Ear

Pro Tools enables you to set the timing of delay repeats to note values (in relation to the current session tempo) in all the DigiRack delay plug-ins except for Short and Slap. Chapter 12, "The Pro Tools Groove," discusses a manual method for setting delays to ⅛ note, ¼ note, or other musical values with certain third-party delay plug-ins. Here's yet another way to do it, which doesn't even require calculating a tempo map for the session:

1. Assuming you have a snare backbeat or perhaps a reasonably steady kick figure during some portion of the song that you can loop for moment, create a send from this track to the delay—even if that's not the sound to which you ultimately want to apply the delay.

2. Set your Feedback parameter to several repeats—perhaps about 35% or so.

3. Solo the snare/kick track and the Aux Input track where this delay plug-in is instantiated.

4. While listening to playback, adjust the delay time until the repeats are in time with the ¼ notes. This setting gives you the length of each ¼ note, which then becomes your timing reference for calculating ⅛- and ¹⁄₁₆-note delays (one-half or one-quarter the delay time, respectively), ¼-triplet delays (two-thirds the delay time), and so on.

Groovy Pre-Delays

One typical novice mistake in cluttered-sounding Pro Tools mixes is sloppy timings on multiple delays that clatter around in a nonmusical fashion. We find that setting delay times to specific musical note values, relative to the song's tempo, usually helps create more natural and open-sounding mixes. Hey, it can be hard enough to get the musicians to play in good time in the first place without introducing even more random timing factors into the equation! Most *reverb* plug-ins also feature pre-delay times; adjusting these to ¹⁄₆ notes or some other short, tempo-related value can also help create a better-sounding mix.

EQ: The Zero-Sum Game

Beginning engineers always seem to attack every equalization problem by boosting frequencies. Bass guitar or kick drum doesn't have enough edge? Crank it up! Not enough buzz-saw aggression on the crunch guitar part? Lash on some 2,500Hz! The problem is, maximum level (*full-code*, or 0dB) for the mix never changes. Consequently, because EQ is a *gain* change in the affected frequency range, boosting one instrument's level (or range within that instrument's frequency spectrum) produces more or less the same effect as *reducing* the gain of all others proportionately.

With this idea of a fixed ceiling in mind, experienced mixers often apply the technique of carving out frequency bands for instrumental parts, using gain *reductions* in specific, relatively narrow frequency ranges on other instrumental parts so that they compete less for those ranges of frequencies. On many great mixes, for example, if you were to solo perhaps the bass guitar part, you (or the bass player) might think it could really use a lot more clack in the low mid range. But by slightly notching out these frequencies in the bass part, the engineer has created a space for the corresponding clack of the beater striking the kick drum, which consequently comes forward in the mix—exactly what the song *as a whole* required.

Here's another example: For competing keyboard and guitar parts, instead of radically boosting that frequency range somewhere around 2–2.5kHz, to give edge to crunchy rock guitar parts, try notching this same range downward in the keyboard or bass part. You may find that the guitar really didn't need much more level or EQ at all—once it's no longer getting shouted down in this important frequency band.

Bear in mind that it can be very misleading if you make all your EQ adjustments on individual tracks while they are soloed (especially if a performer is standing at your shoulder, obsessing about his or her sound). Instead, when adjusting EQs, try to think in terms of the entire mix and the key places where each part needs to fit into the overall frequency spectrum to complement vocals and other instrumental parts. As far as overall volume adjustments are concerned, remember that the maximum level for the mix is always the same; so to put it simplistically, *boosting* one instrument's level (or one frequency range) is like turning *down* all the others!

EQ and Stereo/Surround Panning

Where you pan a sound in a stereo or surround mix will also affect your decisions about EQ. Among other factors, two sounds might not conflict as badly in a given frequency range if they are panned to widely separated positions. Furthermore, on a simple perception level, the timbre of a sound can seem to change according to its position in relation to others. However, as with delays, reverb, and other time parameters, relying on the inherent separation in your stereo or multichannel surround mix can come back to bite you later. Even if you aren't using stereo delays, chorus effects, and so on, it's very important to listen to your stereo mix in mono (or your surround mix in stereo, and so on) before making any final decisions about EQ. You may be surprised at the logjam of conflicting frequencies present in your mix that weren't apparent in your controlled monitoring environment. To optimize their mixes for unpredictable real-world playback situations, you will see experienced engineers frequently switching between stereo and mono (and/or surround) as they make decisions about levels and EQ. You should, too!

Path Meter View in Output Windows

A surprising number of experienced Pro Tools users overlook this feature. To the right of the Close button in the upper-left corner of Output windows (either for tracks or sends) is another button for the Path Meter view. Click this button to open an additional right panel in the Output window that displays a level meter for the track or send's assigned path.

One great use for this feature is when many sends are assigned to the same destination (for example, a bus that is the source for an Aux Input track with a reverb or delay plug-in). Just as you can produce clipping and distortion on audio tracks, Aux Input tracks, Instrument tracks, and Master Faders, the summed signals from multiple sends can produce clipping in this bus on their way to the destination effect. After opening the Output window for any of the sends assigned to the bus, clicking the Path Meter View button lets you keep an eye on the levels in that bus. Like other level meters in Pro Tools, the path meter in an Output window has red clipping indicators in its top segment. You can clear these indicators by clicking them or by using the Track > Clear All Clip Indicators command (whose keyboard shortcut is Option+C, or Alt+C on Windows).

Gimme More in the Cans, Man!

This tip reviews yet another way of setting up a cue (headphone) mix in Pro Tools, using a multichannel audio interface. The headphone mix provided to performers is a crucial aspect of any recording session, especially when multiple performers are physically isolated from each other and depend on the headphone mix to hear each other. Here's what to do:

1. In the Mix window, set up your basic mix in Pro Tools (because your main volume and fader settings have no effect on record levels, right?) as the performers run through the song. We're going to base the initial headphone mix on the mix you are monitoring in the control room.

2. Create a stereo send (send A, for example) for the headphone mix so you can adjust its balance separately from the control-room mix. Hold down the Option key (Alt key in Windows) as you create this send on any audio track (using the pop-up selector) so that the same send is simultaneously created from *all* audio tracks.

3. You could simply designate a stereo output pair on the audio interface as the destination for this send, but instead, let's choose an internal bus pair in Pro Tools—for example, bus 3–4—as the destination.

4. Use the Track > New command to create a stereo Aux Input and name it Cue Mix. Select bus 3–4 (which is the destination of all the sends we've created) as its input. This Aux Input provides you with a single volume fader for the headphone mix (which could also have been accomplished with a Master Fader for whatever stereo output is feeding the performers' headphone mix). It also gives you the flexibility to apply compression, reverb, and so on specifically to the musicians' cue mix.

5. Set the output assignment of this Aux Input to the output pair on your audio interface that is connected to the performers' headphone amplifier—for example, outputs 3–4. Also, to prevent this Aux Input from being muted when soloing other tracks in the project, Command-click (Ctrl-click in Windows) the solo button on the Aux Input track to activate Solo Safe mode. Now, when auditioning tracks individually, you are assured that their signal will always be sent through the Cue Mix headphone feed.

6. Open View > Sends A–E, and change the send display option from Assignments to Send A, which you just created from all audio tracks in step 2. You now see mini faders and panners in the send portion of each audio track in the Mixer window; these control send A.

7. Hold down the Option key (Alt key in Windows) as you click on the P button in any of these sends to switch them all to pre-fader. Their level and mute status will be unaffected by that of the track itself, allowing you to make these changes in the control room during recording without affecting the headphone mix.

8. If you are using Pro Tools LE or M-Powered, you must set each send level separately. Remember that as a starting point, you can Option-click (Alt-click in Windows) each send's level slider to set it to 0dB. If you are using Pro Tools HD, however, you can copy the current main mix to all these sends in a single operation. Select all tracks by holding down the Option key (Alt key in Windows) and clicking on any track's name. Select Edit > Copy to Send. In the dialog box, copy the current values of the main Volume and Pan settings to send A as the destination and then click OK.

After you've established this cue mix setup, here's one easy way to switch to monitoring the headphone mix in the control room to make adjustments (we're assuming that outputs 1–2 on the interface are the source of the control-room monitoring mix):

1. Option-click (Alt-click in Windows) any audio track's mute button to mute them all. (Your pre-fader sends to the cue mix are unaffected by their tracks' mute button.)

2. Create a stereo send (send E, for example) from the Cue Mix Aux Input to outputs 1–2. Option-click (Alt-click in Windows) this send's level slider and set it to 0dB.

3. When you're finished making adjustments, mute this send, and then Option-click (Alt-click in Windows) a mute button as before to unmute your source audio tracks.

By setting your cue mix as described here, you could even automate this mix going out to the performers' headphones or use additional sends to route reverb and effect outputs to its bus, providing a near-finished product mix for the talent—which will be especially appreciated during last-minute overdubs. All this takes much less time than manually dialing in a headphone mix on an analog mixing console, leaving you more time for creative aspects of the production.

A Change of Venue

This is really more of a general tip for novice mixers. If you only listen to your mix in one room and always on the same playback system, upon subsequent listening elsewhere you will almost certainly discover that there is much room for improvement. Before you bless any mix, burn a quick CD and play it on a few home stereos, boom boxes, and of course, the infallible gold standard for critical listening: your car! The prominence of vocals, delays, and reverbs—and especially the character of the low end—really does change radically according to the playback situation. We guarantee that performing this reality check early in the mix process will make you happier with the final results.

Editing Tips

In addition to the many editing tips throughout the book, here a few more ideas—both simple reminders and a few more advanced techniques.

Shortcuts in the New Track Dialog Box

Okay, everybody learns the Shift+Command+N shortcut (Shift+Ctrl+N in Windows) for opening the New Track dialog box fairly early in their experience with Pro Tools. However, even though they're clearly indicated in Digidesign's PDF documentation, too many experienced users never memorize the keyboard shortcuts within the New Track dialog box—so let's recap them here:

- Press the left/right arrows while holding down the Command key (Ctrl key in Windows) switch the number of channels on the current row of tracks you are creating between mono, stereo (and multichannel on HD systems). Press the up/down arrows while holding down the Command key (Ctrl key in Windows) to cycle through the possible track types—audio, Aux Input, Instrument, Master Fader, or MIDI.

- While holding down the Command+Option keys (Ctrl+Alt keys in Windows), press the up/down arrows to switch between the track timebase options for the current track entry field—Samples (absolute) or Ticks (relative).

- You can create multiple track types simultaneously without leaving this dialog box by clicking the + sign at the end of each row. Alternatively, pressing Command+plus/minus (+/−) on the numeric keypad (Ctrl+plus/− in Windows) adds or deletes new rows of track entry fields.

Additionally, in Pro Tools versions 7.3 and higher, tracks can be created, duplicated, moved, or deleted during playback, as can sends and inserts. These mixer configuration changes are not permitted during audio recording, but when recording MIDI only.

Yes, I Know! No, Really!

Pro Tools is really good about warning you when an operation will be irrevocable, destructively modifying (or eliminating) audio data. This is a wonderful thing, and it has saved many inexperienced and veteran users from making mistakes. Sometimes, though, you are perfectly sure about what you're doing, and don't want to click through a second alert box to confirm it (like when you're clearing unusable audio tracks and deleting them from disk). In these cases, hold down the Option key (Alt key in Windows) as you click the first OK button; you can bypass the confirmation dialog boxes. But please, think before you click!

Export Region Definitions for Use in Other Sessions

This isn't so much a cool tip as a friendly reminder: Unless you're in Destructive Recording mode, each time you record on a Pro Tools audio track, a new audio file is created. A single region appears in the Regions List that represents the entire audio file for that take. As you edit the audio in your tracks, additional region definitions are created automatically by Pro Tools, and of course the commands in the Edit menu's Separate Region submenu also create new region definitions (pointers to segments within the audio files residing on disk). By default, these region definitions are contained only in the originating Pro Tools session document, not in the audio files themselves. If you try to import regions from one of these audio files into another Pro Tools session, only the whole-file region appears in the Import Audio dialog box—not all the other region definitions within it that you created in the first session.

There are times when you will want to use region definitions from a session in other Pro Tools sessions, other audio programs, or even in a sampler program or plug-in. For example, if you create multiple regions within a drum track to build up new grooves, you might want to use these bits and pieces in other sessions. The Export Region Definitions command in the Regions List's local menu does this for you. Region definitions from the current Pro Tools session are exported into their parent sound files and are subsequently visible in the Import Audio dialog box from any other Pro Tools session.

Cycling Through the Edit Modes (Edit Window)

Pressing the single open quote (') key—the unshifted equivalent to the tilde ~ key on U.S. English keyboard layouts, although it may be elsewhere in other languages—enables you to cycle between the four edit modes (Shuffle, Slip, Spot, and Grid).

Cycling Through the Edit Tools (Edit Window)

Pressing the Esc key (Mac) or the center mouse button, if you have one (in Windows), enables you to cycle between the edit tools (Zoomer, Trimmer, Selector, Grabber, Smart Tool, Scrubber, and Pencil).

Making Selections with the Timebase Ruler (Edit Window)

To make selections with the Timebase ruler in the Edit window, do the following:

- Double-click anywhere in any of the Timebase rulers to select the entire session (from the beginning of the session timeline, including all regions—and/or automation breakpoints—in all tracks).

- Option-click and drag (Alt-click and drag in Windows) within any Timebase ruler to make an edit selection on all tracks simultaneously. Note that selecting the Link Timeline and Edit Selection button in the Edit window will accomplish the same thing when dragging in the Timebase ruler.

You can also use the Markers ruler to make selections. First, position the edit cursor and/or make a track selection either by clicking an existing marker or by using one of the edit tools within a track. Then, Shift-click on the previous or next marker to extend your current selection up to that point.

Extending the Current Selection with the Tab Key (Edit Window)

You can use the Tab key to extend the current selection in the Edit window. Here are your options:

- **Shift+Tab.** This extends the selection to the next region boundary (end of the current region, or to the beginning of the next region).

- **Option+Shift+Tab (Control+Shift+Tab in Windows).** This extends the selection to the previous region boundary (beginning of the current region, or to the end of the previous region).

- **Control+Shift+Tab (Start+Shift+Tab in Windows).** This extends the selection to include the entire next region.

- **Option+Control+Shift+Tab (Control+Start+Shift+Tab in Windows).** This extends the selection to include the entire previous region.

More Tab Key Tricks (Edit Window)

Here are yet more Tab key shortcuts in the Edit window:

- **Tab.** Each time you press the Tab key, the playback/edit cursor jumps forward in the current track to the next region boundary (beginning or end), sync point (if any region contains one), or fade beginning/end.

- **Option+Tab (Ctrl+Tab in Windows).** Same as Tab, except the cursor location moves backward.

- **Control+Tab (Start+Tab in Windows).** Selects the next region or fade in the current track.

- **Option+Control+Tab (Ctrl+Start+Tab in Windows).** Selects the previous region or fade in the current track.

- **Tab to Transient.** When this button in the Edit window is enabled, each time you press the Tab key, the playback/edit cursor jumps forward to a point just before the next transient attack in the top-most selected audio track. To move back to the previous transient, press Option+Tab (Ctrl+Tab in Windows).

Lengthen/Shorten the Current Selection with the Plus/Minus Keys (Edit Window)

To move the end of the current selection by the current Nudge value, hold down the Shift+Command keys (Shift+Ctrl on Windows) as you press the +/− (plus/minus) keys on the numeric keypad. To move the *beginning* of the current selection by the current Nudge value, hold down the Shift+Option keys (Shift+Alt on Windows) as you press the +/− (plus/minus) keys on the numeric keypad.

Power Scrubber (Edit Window)

Many users underestimate the usefulness of the Scrubber tool for editing. Here are a few tricks you should know:

■ While using the Selector tool, you can hold down the Control key (Start key in Windows) to temporarily switch to the Scrubber tool.

■ If you also hold down the Shift key as you scrub, the current edit selection is extended to the point where you stop scrubbing. This makes it really easy to locate audio events by ear! (This Shift key selection technique also works when the Scrubber tool itself is selected.)

■ To drag at extra-slow speed for finer precision, hold down the Command key (Ctrl key in Windows). Try using this in combination with the previous two modifier keys!

■ For extra-*fast* scrubbing (Shuttle mode), hold down the Option key (Alt key in Windows). Shuttle mode is also available when temporarily switched to Scrub mode while using the Selector tool, and you can also use it with the Shift key to make edit selections.

■ Remember that, unlike some other programs, Pro Tools only scrubs *audio*, not MIDI events.

Use Your Scroll Wheel

The wheel on your mouse scrolls vertically in the Mix and Edit windows. Learn these additional modifier-key combinations for scroll-wheel techniques that will boost your productivity (in versions 7.3 and higher).

■ To scroll the Mix or Edit window back and forth horizontally, hold down the Shift key as you scroll the wheel.

■ To zoom in/out horizontally in the Edit window, hold down the Option key (Alt key in Windows) as you scroll the wheel up and down.

■ To zoom the vertical (amplitude) scale of all audio waveforms in the Edit window up/down, hold down the Shift+Option keys (Shift+Alt keys in Windows) as you scroll the wheel up and down.

■ To zoom the vertical (pitch) scale of all MIDI data in the Edit window up/down, hold down the Control+Option+Command keys (Start+Alt+Ctrl keys in Windows) as you scroll the wheel up/down.

The Three-Button Quickstep for Switching Windows

If you are using a mouse or trackball with three buttons, consider assigning a macro to the third button—for example, the Command+= (equal sign) shortcut (Ctrl+= on Windows) that switches between the Mix and Edit windows.

Nudging and Grid Mode

You don't always have to open these pop-up selectors to change between their preset values! Here are a couple of shortcuts that will save you some mouse travel, plus some very useful nudging techniques.

- To toggle through the preset Grid values for the time units currently in use (for example, to select between whole bars and various note values when in Bars:Beats mode), hold down Control+Option (Start+Alt in Windows) as you use the +/− (plus/minus) keys on the numeric keypad.

- To toggle through the preset Nudge values for the time units currently in use, hold down Command+Option (Ctrl+Alt in Windows) as you use the +/− (plus/minus) keys on the numeric keypad.

- To nudge selected regions, MIDI notes, or automation breakpoints left or right, use the +/− (plus/minus) keys on the numeric keypad.

- To extend or shorten the *left* edge of the current selection by the current Nudge value, press Shift+Option (Shift+Alt in Windows) as you nudge. To extend or shorten the selection's *right* edge, hold down Shift+Command (Shift+Ctrl in Windows) instead.

- To nudge the *contents* of a region without affecting the left-right boundaries of the region itself, hold down the Control key (Start key in Windows) as you nudge.

Keyboard Focus Modes

A dismaying number of Pro Tools users never explore the utility of that little AZ button, found in the upper-right corner of the Edit window, that activates Commands Keyboard Focus mode. Shame on you! This book has reminded you many times about printing out the entire *Keyboard Shortcuts* PDF document included with Pro Tools. But if nothing else, definitely print out the pages about Keyboard Focus mode. Many single-keystroke shortcuts here can really speed up your editing in Pro Tools. To name just a few, you can execute commands like Cut, Copy, Paste, and Undo by pressing only a single letter key—no need to hold down a Command modifier key (Ctrl in Windows). The A and S keys trim the start/end of the current region to the insertion point, 1–5 on the alphanumeric keyboard select the five zoom preset buttons, F creates a default fade type without requiring you to open the Fades dialog box. Also, pressing Shift+P moves the edit selection upward one track while Shift+; (semicolon) extends it downward.

Incidentally, Pro Tools provides other keyboard-focus modes for one-keystroke operations—each of them even more underused than Commands Focus! The Regions List and Edit window's

Tracks List both have their own AZ button. When the Regions List's Keyboard Focus is enabled, you can select a region just by typing the first few letters of its name on your computer keyboard. With the Groups List's Keyboard Focus enabled, mix and edit groups can be enabled or disabled simply by typing their group ID letter. Both the MIDI and the Score editors also have their own keyboard-focus modes that mirror the functions of the Edit window keyboard-focus mode.

Using Key-Signature Events on a Looping Ostinato Figure (Pro Tools 7.3 and Higher)

This example is just one creative application of key-signature events in Pro Tools 7.3 and higher. Suppose you want to make a complex ¹/₆-note ostinato figure shift tonalities so that it will match a chord progression playing underneath it—for example C-D7-Ab-G7, two bars each. One approach is to alter the accidentals at each key-signature event in the ruler like so:

1. Create a MIDI or Instrument track. Use that track's playlist selector to ensure that it is set to Pitched so that it will be affected by key-signature events. In Notes view, create the fiendishly intricate ¹/₆-note arpeggio that you want to repeat as a two-bar ostinato figure. To increase your fun quotient, make this arpeggio span at least two or three octaves or perform this whole exercise simultaneously on two or more MIDI tracks that contain intertwining arpeggios.

2. Switch the display format of the track to Regions and switch the edit mode to Grid, with a Grid value of one bar.

3. Using the Loop Trimmer mode of the Trimmer tool, drag this two-bar region rightward until you have four repetitions totaling eight bars. (If you are using a version of Pro Tools prior to 7.3, you would instead use the Region > Loop command and specify four loops in the Region Looping dialog box.)

4. If it is not already visible, use the View > Rulers > Key Signature command to show the Key Signature ruler. You will note that by default, a key signature even in C major already appears at the beginning of the timeline, which works fine for our first chord, C major.

5. Click to position the edit cursor at bar 3, where the chord changes to D7. (Forgive us, a little bit of music theory is going to be required from here on out since we're going to choose relative key signatures to produce scale modes that are most compatible with our chord progression.) Click the plus sign at the end of the Key Signature ruler to create a new key-signature event.

6. The Key Change dialog box appears. In this case, a D Mixolydian scale would sound nice against this second chord, so we choose G major (one sharp) as the key signature.

7. In this same dialog box, enable the Edit Pitched Tracks checkbox. Make sure the Transpose checkbox is disabled, but enable the Constrain Pitches to Key checkbox. Then click OK.

8. Move the edit cursor to bar 5, where the A♭ chord occurs. Create another key-signature event, again enabling the Constrain Pitches to Key checkbox only. This time, we will choose C minor (three flats) to get the equivalent of an A♭ Lydian mode.

9. Finally at bar 7, repeat this process, choosing C major (no flats or sharps) for the equivalent of G Mixolydian mode over that G7 chord.

10. Click the Return to Zero button (in the Transport window or at the top of the Edit window) and then press the spacebar to start playback. You will hear the notes in your looped $\frac{1}{16}$-note ostinato changing as each key signature event is crossed in the track.

General Tips

What follows is an assortment of techniques, advice, options, and other cool stuff that might come in handy as you continue to use Pro Tools.

Digidesign CoreAudio (Mac)

If you choose this option when installing Pro Tools, the Macintosh operating system can redirect all Mac sound input and/or output through your Digidesign hardware. (This is configured under System Preferences > Sound.) The Digidesign CoreAudio Manager application lets you change the buffer size, monitor which client audio applications are using CoreAudio, and even open the Hardware Setup dialog box for your Digidesign hardware.

Calculators for Tempos and Note Values to Milliseconds

Several Web sites offer calculators for tempos and note values:

■ www.macmusic.org/software/. Check out the freeware application called Music Math (for either Mac OSX or OS9), written by Laurent Colson. It converts between beats per minute (BPM) and equivalent millisecond settings for your delay (or LFO modulation rate on a flanger, hmmm?). It also converts between sample durations and tempos, MIDI notes and frequencies, as well as transposition and time-stretching values. Note that you can view this site in French or English (click on the flag icon to select a language).

■ www.analogx.com/contents/download/audio/delay.htm. For Windows users, AnalogX offers the free downloadable Delay Calculator, especially useful for reverb pre-delays, hardware delays, and delay plug-ins that don't allow adjusting delay times per musical values.

That Lock-Step Don't Dance

Quantization and groove templates are incredible tools, especially when used in conjunction with the Elastic Time features for audio warping introduced in version 7.4. They can also be the death of a groove when applied in excess, however. The Restore Performance option for MIDI regions (in the Event Operations window) can undo quantization even after the session has been saved many times or return a MIDI selection to the state it was in the last time you applied the Flatten Performance command. This is great if you realize later in the creative process that an instrumental part that seemed way too loose at the beginning really works fine after additional parts have been added to the session. You should also have a careful listen to many of your favorite tracks; often, the tension between two different rhythmic feels is exactly what makes those grooves sound so great. To cite a famous and extreme example, check out the contrast between the straight $^1/_8$-note feel in the guitar part and the laid-back swing feel in the bass and drum parts, in Chuck Berry's "Johnny B. Goode." Now, imagine how much *worse* this would sound if all those audio events had been quantized to precisely the same $^1/_8$-note swing factor!

Widgets for Mac OS X

Among the myriad utilities you can add to the Mac Dashboard (sticky notes, weather, gas prices, travel, Web cams, voice notes, and so on), there are several that specifically pertain to audio and studio applications. Some of our current favorites available via the Apple Web site include the following:

- **Audio Calculator by Lensco.be.** For conversions between BPM and milliseconds.

- **Oblique by Guy D2.** A widget version of the Oblique Strategies creative unblocking tool made famous by Brian Eno, Peter Schmidt, and Peter Norton.

- **Bean Counter by Seven.** Enter your hourly wage, and this widget calculates your earnings in real time—just the thing to keep your attitude adjusted while clients argue and/or rehearse on the clock!

Things That Make Pro Tools Cranky

Everyone's system has its own set of peccadilloes, but here's a short list of things that can be problematic on almost any Pro Tools system:

- Energy-management, power-saver, and energy-saver features of the operating system (usually enabled via the Control Panel in Windows or System Preferences on Mac)

- Screen savers (also enabled in the Control Panel or System Preferences)

- Background disk optimizers, system-monitoring software, and the like

- Network/Web activities (like serving up MP3 files to the Internet—duh!)

- Fragmented hard drives

- Extremely full hard drives (over 90% is always a problem)

- IDE/ATA hard drives that don't have DMA enabled in Properties (Windows)

- Not repairing disk permissions from time to time with the Disk Utility—especially after installing updates to Pro Tools or its plug-ins (Mac)

- Norton's File Saver

- Some dashboard widgets in the Macintosh dashboard, since it doesn't release these system resources after they are closed

You Don't Have to Archive Your Fade Files Folder!

Pro Tools creates separate audio files for every fade you create inside the Fade Files folder. In large or complex sessions, fades can occupy quite a lot of disk space, which increases storage requirements and time required for archiving projects off your Pro Tools system if you simply copy the entire session folder. If you're struggling to make projects fit onto a DVD-R and you need to free up only a small additional amount of space, remember that it isn't necessary to copy the contents of the Fade Files folder! In this case, go ahead and throw this folder's entire contents into the Trash/Recycle Bin before you archive the session folder and its contents. The next time you open the Pro Tools session, a dialog box will ask you "Where is Fade *x*?" Click the Skip All Fades button and Pro Tools will re-create all fade files required by the session. On sessions with many long fades, this may take a minute—but that's much better than needlessly adding 5, 10, or more megabytes to the size of every archived project!

More Tips for Recording Voice-Overs

Here are a few tidbits we've picked up along the way with regard to recording the spoken word:

- Lip smack and cottonmouth—the bane of your existence, right? And the more you compress that voice-over to squash everything right up to a consistent level, the worse it gets. (There you are, maniacally editing out these extraneous noises for hours on end!) Here's an old trick that might still be new to you: If you're hearing clicks and snaps each time the narrator breathes or opens his or her mouth, offer your talent a few bites of a nice, crispy apple! (We enjoy a nice Fuji or Granny Smith, but anything fairly tart will do the trick.) If you don't have any apples handy (or you're afraid your voice talent will think you're a nut job), bring apple juice instead. This works!

- When editing voice-overs recorded in noisy environments (for example, from on-location interviews, around office or industrial ventilation systems, or anywhere near a computer), after chopping them up into keeper segments, you may find that the background noise popping in and out with each audio region is bothersome. Use the Batch Fades dialog box to create fade-ins and fade-outs on individual regions so that these transitions will at least be a little smoother. This technique can be equally useful for guitar fills played through a noisy amplifier, vocal lines, drum hits that you've split into individual regions using the Split Silence feature with a healthy amount of start and end pad, or just about anything that's intermittent within a track. Select all regions in the track and then press Command+F (Ctrl+F in Windows). In the Batch Fades dialog box, select the fade-in/out shapes you want (Standard is a good place to start). In the Length field underneath the Create New Fade Ins and Outs checkbox, try an initial setting of 50 milliseconds or so. If you've already trimmed the beginning of each VO region too tightly and the attacks on initial words are overly softened by the fade, repeat the operation using a fade-in shape with a steeper slope.

- Professionals who do character voice work may cringe at this heretical suggestion (and to be sure, Mel Blanc and Daws Butler didn't need no stinkin' Pro Tools tricks), but when you're using the same voice talent for many different characters (as in cartoons or simulation scenarios for training videos), a very small amount of pitch shift up or down can be surprisingly effective. The idea is not necessarily to apply some extreme amount as a special effect (not that there's anything wrong with that!), but instead to work in ranges of perhaps a semitone or two at most that listeners won't identify as pitch-shifted. The reason this works so well is that, no matter how adept actors may be at pitching their voices, the characteristic resonances or formants of each individual's vocal tract remain more or less constant. Pitch shifting also shifts these formants, and a very small amount can help sell the idea that it's a different person. Notice that the Pitch Shift dialog box has a Fine slider for adjusting pitch shift in increments of $1/100$ of a semitone, called *cents*. A few tenths of a semitone can make all the difference between the pitch-shifted audio sounding processed or natural. The Transpose field in the Time Shift dialog box can also be adjusted in fine increments if you hold down the Command key (Ctrl key in Windows) as you adjust its value. The monophonic mode of the Time Shift plug-in also allows you to shift formants independently of the pitch shift amount.

Creating Your Own Session Templates

Most users will repeatedly work on certain kinds of projects, creating many sessions with similar configurations. To save time, you should create your own templates. These serve as starting points for new sessions, with a Mix window configuration, including plug-ins, inserts, and sends; track names; Edit window display format; window arrangements; zoom presets; session sample rate and bit depth; SMPTE start time; and so on. Here's a brief how-to, assuming you want to use an existing session already containing audio and/or MIDI regions as the basis for creating your template:

1. Use the File > Save a Copy In command to save this session under a completely new name and in a different location (perhaps onto your Desktop, where it will be handy later). Give it an obvious name, like "30-second spot template." Do *not* enable any of

the other copy options in the Save dialog box (Copy Audio Files and Session Plug-In Settings Folder, Copy Root Plug-In Settings Folder, or Copy Movie/Audio files)! Close your current session, and then open the copy you just created.

2. In the local menus for the Regions List, use the Select All and then Clear Selected commands to remove all existing regions from the new session copy. (Caution: Click the Remove button, not the Delete button, which would permanently eliminate these source audio files from disk, trashing your previous session!) Delete any existing memory locations. If you were using a Video track, delete that from this new session copy as well.

3. If necessary, clean up your track names, display formats, and other settings until they exactly reflect how you want them to initially appear in all newly created sessions based on this template. If you are using Pro Tools version 8, choose Save As Template under the File menu. Choose whether you want to save the template in one of the previously made categories, in a category you will now create, or in a new location on your computer setup (which also prompts you for a new name). Also choose whether you want to include any media in the template (which we do not want to do in this example). Once the save is complete, you are finished. If you are using an earlier version of Pro Tools, see the following steps.

From this point on, the procedure is slightly different on Mac versus Windows systems:

■ **Macintosh (Method A):** In the Finder, highlight the template session document you've created, and then select File > Get Info. In the General tab of the Get Info dialog box, click to enable the Stationery Pad checkbox and then close the dialog box. From now on, whenever you double-click this session document (or open it from within Pro Tools), a dialog box gives you the choice of editing the Stationery Pad file itself or creating a new session based on it. Click the New Session button (and enter a session file name in the subsequent dialog box). A new folder and session file is created based on the Stationery Pad (but as yet containing no audio or MIDI regions). Alternatively, you can use Method B, which is convenient for importing track setups from *any* existing session without requiring that it be saved previously as a Stationery Pad (read-only) file.

■ **Windows or Macintosh (Method B):** From Windows, locate the template session document you just created on your hard disk, right-click the file, and select Properties from the pop-up menu. Click the Read-Only checkbox, and then click OK to close the Properties dialog box. This isn't strictly necessary for the method we're recommending, but it does help prevent accidentally overwriting this template session document if you ever open it again. Create a new, empty Pro Tools session, and then use the File > Import > Session Data command. In the Source Tracks area at the bottom of the Import Session Data dialog box, choose New Track as the destination for whichever source tracks from the template session you want to import. Leave the default settings for the rest of the options in this dialog box and click OK to bring the imported track setup into your existing session. Save your session; you're ready to get to work.

Granted, again concerning Pro Tools versions earlier to 8, using read-only (Stationery Pad) documents via the File > Open Session command is the method you will find discussed in the *Pro Tools Reference Guide*—and this works more or less okay in Mac versions. In Windows versions, however, the newly created session will use the template's Audio Files folder for any new recordings—not at all what you want! After opening a read-only template in the Windows version, you would then have to use the Save Copy In command to make sure that your new session uses its own unique Audio Files folder. To avoid this inconvenience, we recommend that you use Method B. Not only does this avoid the Audio Files folder problem for Windows users, but on either platform *any* existing session could be used as a template—whether previously saved as a read-only (Stationery Pad) file or not. If you *do* import tracks from an existing session containing audio regions, though, choose Link to Source Media in the Audio Media Options selector. You usually don't want to import any audio regions contained in the source session into your new Audio Files folder, and it will be easier this way to simply remove those audio regions from your session afterward (without deleting them, since they are being used in the other Pro Tools session!).

Transferring Sequences from MIDI Workstations into Pro Tools

Suppose you or your clients have songs already recorded into a standalone MIDI sequencer, drum machine, or standalone MIDI workstation (a keyboard synthesizer that includes an internal sequencer for MIDI recording). You'd like to bring this MIDI data into Pro Tools to start adding vocals and other audio tracks. Unfortunately, the device in question can't save a Type 1 Standard MIDI File (SMF) file to diskette; otherwise, you would simply use the File > Import > MIDI to Track command, which creates MIDI tracks as necessary for each MIDI channel within the source file that contains data. An alternative is to record the device's MIDI output in real time. But you have a challenge: The only MIDI source that Pro Tools can synchronize to is MIDI time code (MTC—a variant of SMPTE time code, which is an *absolute* time reference), while the MIDI sequencer can only generate or synchronize to MIDI Beat Clock (also known as MIDI Sync—a *relative*, tempo-derived time reference, based on 24 clocks per ¼ note). Don't despair; it can easily be done!

1.   Use the Setup > MIDI > MIDI Beat Clock command to enable generation of this data on the appropriate MIDI output for your external MIDI sequencer.

2.   Go into the setup of the external MIDI sequencer and change its synchronization mode so that it slaves to an external MIDI Beat Clock rather to than its own internal tempo setting. For example, on a Roland keyboard workstation, change the sequencer's Sync Mode from Internal to Slave. Your external sequencer should now start/stop playback as you click Play/Stop in Pro Tools.

3. Set an appropriate tempo in Pro Tools because its MIDI Beat Clock output now controls the playback tempo of the external MIDI sequencer. (Of course, if the audio output from the external MIDI device is connected to your Pro Tools hardware, you will have to create an Aux Input to monitor it within Pro Tools, right?)

4. Create 16 MIDI tracks in Pro Tools (or fewer, if you already know exactly which of the sequencer's tracks/channels contain MIDI data). Set their input selectors to channels 1–16 on the appropriate MIDI input/device.

5. Arm all these MIDI tracks for recording by holding down the Option key (Alt key in Windows) as you enable the Record button on any one of them.

6. Click Record and Play in the Pro Tools Transport to record the multichannel MIDI output of your external sequencer into Pro Tools.

7. Afterward, remember to assign appropriate device/channel *output* destinations for each of the MIDI tracks, and also to take your external sequencer out of slave sync mode (and/or disable MIDI Beat Clock output from Pro Tools)!

Appendix E: Signal Flow in Pro Tools

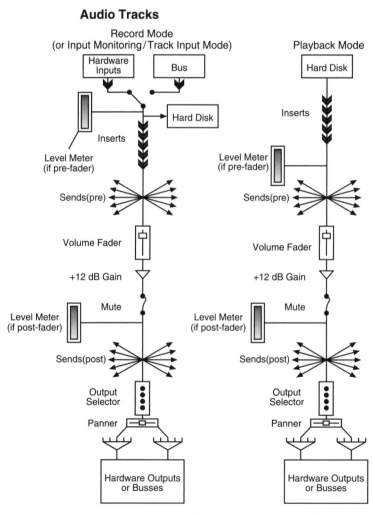

Audio Tracks

Figure E.1 Signal flow for an audio track during recording (as well as when Input Only Monitoring is enabled, or with the TrackInput button enabled on HD systems) and during playback. Notice that the main volume fader is located just before the output stage (and any post-fader sends), and therefore has no effect on input recording levels!

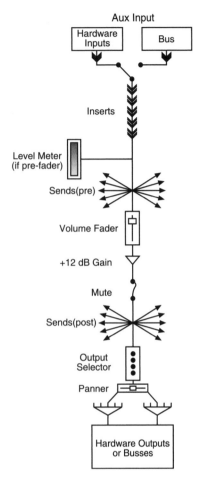

Figure E.2 Signal flow for an Auxiliary Input track. Its input source can be either a physical input on the audio hardware or one of the internal mixing busses in Pro Tools. Notwithstanding their associated MIDI track in the Edit window, from a signal-flow perspective, Instrument tracks are identical to Aux Inputs (and could actually be used as such). In practice, on either type of track, the actual signal source might originate from a plug-in on one of its insert points—a software instrument or the Click and Signal Generator plug-ins, for example.

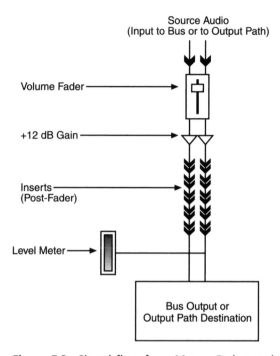

Figure E.3 Signal flow for a Master Fader track. There are no sends on a Master Fader. Unlike audio tracks, Aux Input tracks, and Instrument tracks, the Insert section on a Master Fader is always post-fader.

Index